American Dissidents

American Dissidents

AN ENCYCLOPEDIA OF ACTIVISTS, SUBVERSIVES, AND PRISONERS OF CONSCIENCE

VOLUME 1: A–J

Kathlyn Gay, Editor

ABC-CLIO

Santa Barbara, California • Denver, Colorado • Oxford, England

Copyright 2012 by ABC-CLIO, LLC

All rights reserved. No part of this publication may be reproduced, stored in a retrieval system, or transmitted, in any form or by any means, electronic, mechanical, photocopying, recording, or otherwise, except for the inclusion of brief quotations in a review, without prior permission in writing from the publisher.

Library of Congress Cataloging-in-Publication Data

American dissidents : an encyclopedia of activists, subversives, and prisoners of conscience / Kathlyn Gay, editor.
 p. cm.
 Includes bibliographical references and index.
 ISBN 978–1–59884–764–2 (hardcopy : alk. paper) — ISBN 978–1–59884–765–9 (ebook) 1. Dissenters—United States—Biography—Encyclopedias. 2. Political activists—United States—Biography—Encyclopedias. 3. Social reformers—United States—Biography—Encyclopedias. 4. Civil rights workers—United States—Biography—Encyclopedias. 5. United States—Politics and government—20th century—Encyclopedias. 6. United States—Politics and government—21st century—Encyclopedias. 7. Political culture—United States—History—20th century—Encyclopedias. 8. Political culture—United States—History—21st century—Encyclopedias. I. Gay, Kathlyn.
E747.A678 2012
303.48′4—dc23   2011042833

ISBN: 978–1–59884–764–2
EISBN: 978–1–59884–765–9

16 15 14 13 12   1 2 3 4 5

This book is also available on the World Wide Web as an eBook.
Visit www.abc-clio.com for details.

ABC-CLIO, LLC
130 Cremona Drive, P.O. Box 1911
Santa Barbara, California 93116-1911

This book is printed on acid-free paper ∞

Manufactured in the United States of America

Contents

List of Entries by Broad Topic, ix

Chronological List of Entries, xiii

Introduction, xvii

Abbey, Edward, 1

Abu-Jamal, Mumia, 4

Abzug, Bella, 9

Addams, Jane, 13

Al-Arian, Sami, 17

Ali, Muhammad, 22

Asner, Ed, 26

Ayers, William, 29

Balch, Emily Greene, 35

Baldwin, James, 39

Banks, Dennis, 43

Bari, Judi, 47

Beck, Glenn, 51

Benitez, Lucas, 55

Benjamin, Medea, 59

Berrigan, Daniel, and Berrigan, Philip, 63

Bethune, Mary McLeod, 67

Boggs, Grace Lee, 71

Bowe, Frank G., 75

Brown, Ruth, 78

Brownmiller, Susan, 82

Bullard, Robert, 86

Burroughs, William, 90

Cammermeyer, Grethe, 97

Carlin, George, 100

Carmichael, Stokely/Ture, Kwame, 105

Carson, Rachel, 109

Catt, Carrie Chapman, 113

Chávez, César, 117

Chavis, Benjamin Franklin, 121

Choi, Daniel, 125

Chomsky, Noam, 129

Clark, Ramsey, 134

Coffin, William Sloane, 137

Collier, John, 141

Commoner, Barry, 145

Corbett, Jim, 149

Corrie, Rachel, 152

Coughlin, Charles E., 156

Darrow, Clarence, 161

Dart, Justin, Jr., 165

Davis, Angela, 169
Day, Dorothy, 173
Debs, Eugene V., 177
Dees, Morris, 181
Dellinger, David, 185
Deloria, Vine, Jr., 189
Dennett, Mary Ware, 193
Douglas, Marjory Stoneman, 197
Dowie, John Alexander, 201
Du Bois, W. E. B., 205
Ellsberg, Daniel, 211
Farrakhan, Louis, 215
Flynn, Elizabeth Gurley, 219
Frank, Barney, 223
Franken, Al, 227
Friedan, Betty, 231
Gaskin, Stephen, 237
Gibbs, Lois, 240
Gilman, Charlotte Perkins, 244
Giovanni, Nikki, 248
Goldman, Emma, 253
Goodman, Paul, 256
Gregory, Dick, 260
Hall, Gus, 267
Hamer, Fannie Lou, 271
Hampton, Fred, 275
Hayden, Tom, 278
Height, Dorothy, 282
Herrick, William, 286
Hill, Joe, 290

Hill, Julia "Butterfly," 294
Hoffman, Abbie, 298
Horowitz, David, 302
Horton, Myles, 307
Hubbard, Walter, Jr., 311
Humphry, Derek, 315
Hurston, Zora Neale, 319
Johnson, Harriet McBryde, 325
Jones, Mary Harris, 329
Kelley, Florence, 333
Kelly, Kathy, 337
Kernaghan, Charles, 341
Kevorkian, Jack, 345
King, Martin Luther, Jr., 350
Kochiyama, Yuri, 354
Kovic, Ron, 358
Kuhn, Margaret, 363
Kunstler, William, 366
LaDuke, Winona, 373
LaRouche, Lyndon, 377
Leopold, Aldo, 380
Limbaugh, Rush, 384
Malcolm X, 389
Mankiller, Wilma, 393
Manning, Bradley, 397
McCarthy, Joseph, 401
McCorvey, Norma, 406
Means, Russell, 409
Michelman, Kate, 414
Milk, Harvey, 419

Moore, Harry, 423
Moore, Michael, 427
Murie, Margaret, 431
Nader, Ralph, 437
Norman, Mildred, 441
Ochs, Phil, 447
O'Hair, Madalyn Murray, 451
O'Keefe, James, 455
Oppenheimer, J. Robert, 460
Palin, Sarah, 465
Parks, Rosa, 469
Parsons, Lucy, 473
Paul, Alice, 477
Peltier, Leonard, 481
Perkins, Frances, 485
Rand, Ayn, 491
Randolph, A. Philip, 496
Rankin, Jeannette, 500
Robeson, Paul, 503
Roosevelt, Eleanor, 507
Rosenberg, Ethel and Rosenberg, Julius, 511
Rudd, Mark, 516
Rustin, Bayard, 520
Sacco, Ferdinando Nicola, and Vanzetti, Bartolomeo, 525
Sanger, Margaret, 529
Schlafly, Phyllis, 534

Schneiderman, Rose, 538
Seale, Bobby, 542
Seeger, Pete, 546
Sheehan, Cindy, 550
Sheen, Martin, 555
Silkwood, Karen Gay, 559
Simkins, Modjeska Monteith, 563
Sinclair, Upton, 567
Sontag, Susan, 571
Steinmetz, Charles, 576
Strong, Anna Louise, 581
Tall, JoAnn, 585
Tarbell, Ida, 589
Tiller, George, 593
Vera Cruz, Philip, 599
Vogler, Joe, 602
Walker, Alice, 607
Wallis, Jim, 611
Wiesel, Elie, 615
Wolf, Hazel, 619
Woodhull, Victoria, 623
Wright, Ann, 627
Yasui, Minoru, 633
Yeshitela, Omali, 637
Zappa, Frank, 643
Zinn, Howard, 647

Selected Bibliography, 651
About the Editor and Contributors, 671
Index, 673

List of Entries by Broad Topic

Civil Rights Activists

Abzug, Bella
Ali, Muhammad
Baldwin, James
Benjamin, Medea
Bethune, Mary McLeod
Boggs, Grace Lee
Brown, Ruth
Carmichael, Stokely/Ture, Kwame
Chavis, Benjamin Franklin
Coffin, William Sloane
Collier, John
Corbett, Jim
Darrow, Clarence
Dees, Morris
Du Bois, W. E. B.
Giovanni, Nikki
Hamer, Fannie Lou
Hampton, Fred
Height, Dorothy
Hoffman, Abbie
Horton, Myles
Hubbard, Walter, Jr.
Kelley, Florence
King, Martin Luther, Jr.
Kochiyama, Yuri
Kuhn, Margaret
Kunstler, William
Moore, Harry
Parks, Rosa
Parsons, Lucy

Randolph, A. Philip
Robeson, Paul
Rudd, Mark
Rustin, Bayard
Seale, Bobby
Sheen, Martin
Simkins, Modjeska Monteith
Walker, Alice
Wiesel, Elie
Yasui, Minoru
Zappa, Frank

Disability Rights Activists

Bowe, Frank G.
Dart, Justin, Jr.
Johnson, Harriet McBryde

End-of-Life Issues Activists

Humphry, Derek
Kevorkian, Jack

Environmentalists

Abbey, Edward
Bari, Judi
Bullard, Robert
Carson, Rachel
Commoner, Barry
Douglas, Marjory Stoneman
Gaskin, Stephen
Gibbs, Lois
Hill, Julia "Butterfly"

Leopold, Aldo
Murie, Margaret

Labor Activists

Benitez, Lucas
Chávez, César
Day, Dorothy
Debs, Eugene V.
Flynn, Elizabeth Gurley
Hall, Gus
Herrick, William
Hill, Joe
Jones, Mary Harris
Kernaghan, Charles
Perkins, Frances
Randolph, A. Philip
Schneiderman, Rose
Silkwood, Karen Gay
Tarbell, Ida
Vera Cruz, Philip

LGBT Rights Activists

Cammermeyer, Grethe
Choi, Daniel
Frank, Barney
Milk, Harvey
Rustin, Bayard

Native American Rights Activists

Banks, Dennis
Deloria, Vine, Jr.
LaDuke, Winona
Mankiller, Wilma
Means, Russell
Tall, JoAnn

Peace Activists

Asner, Ed
Balch, Emily Greene
Berrigan, Daniel, and Berrigan, Philip
Corrie, Rachel
Day, Dorothy
Goodman, Paul
Hayden, Tom
Kelly, Kathy
Kovic, Ron
Norman, Mildred
Ochs, Phil
Rankin, Jeannette
Seeger, Pete
Sheehan, Cindy
Strong, Anna Louise
Wright, Ann

Political Activists

Abzug, Bella
Ayers, William
Beck, Glenn
Boggs, Grace Lee
Burroughs, William
Carlin, George
Chomsky, Noam
Coughlin, Charles E.
Davis, Angela
Dellinger, David
Ellsberg, Daniel
Franken, Al
Goldman, Emma
Horowitz, David
LaRouche, Lyndon
Limbaugh, Rush
McCarthy, Joseph
McCorvey, Norma
Moore, Michael
Nader, Ralph
Oppenheimer, J. Robert
Palin, Sarah
Rustin, Bayard
Schlafly, Phyllis
Sinclair, Upton
Sontag, Susan
Steinmetz, Charles
Vogler, Joe
Yeshitela, Omali
Zinn, Howard

Political Prisoners

Abu-Jamal, Mumia
Al-Arian, Sami
Peltier, Leonard
Rosenberg, Ethel, and Rosenberg, Julius
Sacco, Ferdinando Nicola, and Vanzetti, Bartolomeo

Religious Dissidents and Activists

Dowie, John Alexander
Farrakhan, Louis
Malcolm X
O'Hair, Madalyn Murray
Wallis, Jim

Social Justice Activists

Addams, Jane
Asner, Ed
Boggs, Grace Lee
Bullard, Robert
Perkins, Frances
Roosevelt, Eleanor

Women's Rights Activists

Abzug, Bella
Brownmiller, Susan
Catt, Carrie Chapman
Dennett, Mary Ware
Friedan, Betty
Gilman, Charlotte Perkins
Hurston, Zora Neale
Michelman, Kate
Paul, Alice
Perkins, Frances
Sanger, Margaret
Tiller, George
Wolf, Hazel
Woodhull, Victoria

Chronological List of Entries

Below are the people profiled in this book, listed in order by birth date.

Jones, Mary Harris (1830–1930)
Woodhull, Victoria (1838–1927)
Dowie, John Alexander (1847–1907)
Parsons, Lucy (1853–1942)
Debs, Eugene V. (1855–1926)
Darrow, Clarence (1857–1938)
Tarbell, Ida (1857–1944)
Kelley, Florence (1859–1932)
Catt, Carrie Chapman (1859–1947)
Addams, Jane (1860–1935)
Gilman, Charlotte Perkins (1860–1935)
Steinmetz, Charles (1865–1923)
Balch, Emily Greene (1867–1961)
Du Bois, W. E. B. (1868–1963)
Goldman, Emma (1869–1940)
Dennett, Mary Ware (1872–1947)
Bethune, Mary McLeod (1875–1955)
Sinclair, Upton (1878–1968)
Hill, Joe (1879–1915)
Sanger, Margaret (1879–1966)
Perkins, Frances (1880–1965)
Rankin, Jeannette (1880–1973)
Schneiderman, Rose (1882–1972)
Collier, John (1884–1968)
Roosevelt, Eleanor (1884–1962)
Paul, Alice (1885–1977)
Strong, Anna Louise (1885–1970)
Leopold, Aldo (1887–1948)
Randolph, A. Philip (1889–1979)
Douglas, Marjory Stoneman (1890–1998)
Flynn, Elizabeth Gurley (1890–1964)
Brown, Ruth (1891–1975)
Coughlin, Charles E. (1891–1979)
Hurston, Zora Neale (1891–1960)
Sacco, Ferdinando Nicola and Vanzetti, Bartolomeo (1891–1927) and (1888–1927)
Day, Dorothy (1897–1980)
Robeson, Paul (1898–1976)
Wolf, Hazel (1898–2000)
Simkins, Modjeska Monteith (1899–1992)
Murie, Margaret (1902–2003)
Oppenheimer, J. Robert (1904–1967)
Vera Cruz, Philip (1904–1994)
Horton, Myles (1905–1990)
Kuhn, Margaret (1905–1995)
Moore, Harry (1905–1951)
Rand, Ayn (1905–1982)
Carson, Rachel (1907–1964)
McCarthy, Joseph (1908–1957)
Norman, Mildred (1908–1981)
Hall, Gus (1910–2000)
Goodman, Paul (1911–1972)
Height, Dorothy (1912–2010)
Rustin, Bayard (1912–1987)
Parks, Rosa (1913–2005)
Vogler, Joe (1913–1993)
Burroughs, William (1914–1997)
Boggs, Grace Lee (1915–)
Rosenberg, Ethel, and Rosenberg, Julius (1915–1953) and (1918–1953)
Dellinger, David (1915–2004)

Herrick, William (1915–2004)
Yasui, Minoru (1916–1986)
Commoner, Barry (1917–)
Hamer, Fannie Lou (1917–1977)
Seeger, Pete (1919–)
Kunstler, William (1919–1995)
O'Hair, Madalyn Murray (1919–1995)
Abzug, Bella (1920–1998)
Berrigan, Daniel, and Berrigan, Philip (1921–) and (1923–2002)
Kochiyama, Yuri (1921–)
Friedan, Betty (1921–2006)
LaRouche, Lyndon (1922–)
Zinn, Howard (1922–2010)
Schlafly, Phyllis (1924–)
Baldwin, James (1924–1987)
Coffin, William Sloane (1924–2006)
Hubbard, Walter, Jr. (1924–2007)
Malcolm X (1925–1965)
Clark, Ramsey (1927–)
Abbey, Edward (1927–1989)
Chávez, César (1927–1993)
Chomsky, Noam (1928–)
Kevorkian, Jack (1928–2011)
Wiesel, Elie (1928–)
Asner, Ed (1929–)
King, Martin Luther, Jr. (1929–1968)
Humphry, Derek (1930–)
Milk, Harvey (1930–1978)
Dart, Justin, Jr. (1930–2002)
Ellsberg, Daniel (1931–)
Gregory, Dick (1932–)
Sontag, Susan (1933–2004)
Farrakhan, Louis (1933–)
Corbett, Jim (1933–2001)
Deloria, Vine, Jr. (1933–2005)
Nader, Ralph (1934–)
Brownmiller, Susan (1935–)
Gaskin, Stephen (1935–)
Dees, Morris (1936–)
Seale, Bobby (1936–)
Hoffman, Abbie (1936–1989)
Banks, Dennis (1937–)
Carlin, George (1937–2008)
Hayden, Tom (1939–)
Horowitz, David (1939–)
Means, Russell (1939–)
Ochs, Phil (1940–1976)
Frank, Barney (1940–)
Sheen, Martin (1940–)
Yeshitela, Omali (1941–)
Zappa, Frank (1941–1993)
Carmichael, Stokely/Ture, Kwame (1941–1998)
Tiller, George (1941–2009)
Ali, Muhammad (1942–)
Cammermeyer, Grethe (1942–)
Michelman, Kate (1942–)
Giovanni, Nikki (1943–)
Ayers, William (1944–)
Davis, Angela (1944–)
Peltier, Leonard (1944–)
Walker, Alice (1944–)
Mankiller, Wilma (1945–2010)
Bullard, Robert (1946–)
Kovic, Ron (1946–)
Silkwood, Karen Gay (1946–1974)
McCorvey, Norma (1947–)
Rudd, Mark (1947–)
Wright, Ann (1947–)
Bowe, Frank G. (1947–2007)
Chavis, Benjamin Franklin (1948–)
Kernaghan, Charles (1948–)
Wallis, Jim (1948–)
Bari, Judi (1949–1997)
Hampton, Fred (1948–1969)
Franken, Al (1951–)
Gibbs, Lois (1951–)
Limbaugh, Rush (1951–)
Benjamin, Medea (1952–)
Kelly, Kathy (1953–)
Tall, JoAnn (1953–)
Abu-Jamal, Mumia (1954–)
Moore, Michael (1954–)
Sheehan, Cindy (1957–)
Johnson, Harriet McBryde (1957–2008)
Al-Arian, Sami (1958–)
LaDuke, Winona (1959–)

Beck, Glenn (1964–)
Palin, Sarah (1964–)
Hill, Julia "Butterfly" (1974–)
Benitez, Lucas (1976–)

Corrie, Rachel (1979–2003)
Choi, Daniel (1981–)
O'Keefe, James (1984–)
Manning, Bradley (1987–)

Introduction

They march. They rally. They carry banners and handwritten signs. They stand on street corners or in front of government buildings. They sneak into offices to spy on politicians or corporate officials. They leak documents online. They write letters. They lobby and deliver messages of protest to government officials or seek support for numerous causes. They commit acts of civil disobedience—defying laws to bring about social justice or to further their particular cause. *They* are American dissidents and activists.

Scope

The focus of *American Dissidents: An Encyclopedia of Activists, Subversives, and Prisoners of Conscience*, a two-volume biographical encyclopedia, is on twentieth- and twenty-first-century Americans. In a few cases, the individuals profiled lived most of their lives in the late 1800s, but their activities carried over to the 1900s and influenced later generations. Birthdates of people featured in this encyclopedia span from 1830 to 1987, and a great many are active today. The 152 Americans featured are meant to represent diverse ethnic, racial, and religious backgrounds as well as various movements and ideologies. Included are authors, anarchists, civil rights advocates, communists, entertainers, environmentalists, government officials, labor organizers, libertarians, military personnel, muckrakers, pacifists, political activists on the left and right, religious leaders, and women suffragists. Some of them have been labeled subversives, and others have been jailed and are known as political prisoners or prisoners of conscience. Some have been executed for activities considered subversive. Others have been murdered by their opponents. Still others are current activists, deeply committed to the causes they espouse. The entries have been written primarily by longtime reference book author and editor Kathlyn Gay. Those entries are not signed. Seven other contributors have written other entries, and their names appear at the bottom of the entry.

The book is arranged in A–Z order, by individuals' names. At the beginning of the book, there are two helpful lists to help readers learn more about the people featured in this encyclopedia, including the list of entries arranged by broad topic, such as "Civil Rights Activists," "Environmentalists," and "Political Activists"; and a list of the people profiled arranged in chronological order by birth date. Each entry concludes with a list of references, and a selected bibliography provides resources such as books, articles, web sites, and videos for further research and reading on America's dissidents, subversives, and political prisoners. A comprehensive index completes the work.

A Long Tradition of Dissent

The dissidents and radicals of recent times have followed a long tradition. Dissent and challenges to the economy, social order, and government have been part of the American scene since colonial times. Rebels, reformers, and dissenters of the past laid the groundwork for social, economic, and political change in the United States.

Some of the earliest dissenters in American history were Christians such as Anne Marbury Hutchinson (1591–1643). She emigrated from England to the Massachusetts Bay Colony and believed in the right of individuals to determine their own lives. Hutchinson did not recognize civil authority or formal religious laws and doctrines. She and her family were continually harassed and eventually were banished from the colony in 1638. They were forced to move to a small island off of Rhode Island.

Another historic leader banished from the Massachusetts colony was Roger Williams (1603–1683), who disagreed with Puritans and their belief in governing by biblical codes. Puritans persecuted anyone who did not abide by their strict church rules. Williams established a settlement in 1638 that was a refuge for those who believed in religious liberty; the colony became the state of Rhode Island.

William Penn (1644–1718) was another dissident who was adamant about the right of every person to worship as she or he believed. A member of the Religious Society of Friends (or Quakers), Penn founded the Pennsylvania colony that welcomed people of diverse beliefs and those who had no religious affiliation.

The concepts of religious freedom and civil liberty lived on and inspired many rebels who protested British rule of the American colonies. Patrick Henry (1736–1799) was just such a person and loudly proclaimed "give me liberty or give me death." Thomas Paine (1737–1809) was well known for his 1776 pamphlet *Common Sense*, in which he asserts that government at its best is a "necessary evil" and government "in its worst state is intolerable." His words encouraged American rebels to fight for independence from the repressive British government during the Revolutionary War. That radical dissent brought about the United States of America.

Native American Dissent

As colonists from Europe fought for their right to dissent and establish their own form of government, the indigenous people of North America went to war to maintain their "rights of occupancy" of their homelands where they had lived for centuries. From the 1600s to the late 1800s, so-called Indian Wars between tribal groups and white militia and soldiers erupted intermittently. Frequently, tribes lost their battles and their lands. In some instances, tribes signed treaties with the U.S. government, agreeing to exchange their territories for annual payments that would allow Indians to buy food and other necessities. During the 1820s, tribal chiefs agreed to sell their land for as little as 53 cents per acre.

In 1830, the U.S. Congress passed the Indian Removal Act, which was designed to force thousands of Cherokee, Chickasaw, Choctaw, Creek, and Seminole in the Southeast to move to what is present-day Oklahoma. The Cherokees, who believed in nonviolent resistance, fought the removal laws in the U.S. Supreme Court, which ruled in favor of the Cherokee. Chief Justice John Marshall declared that the Cherokee Nation was sovereign and the removal laws invalid. However, President Andrew Jackson, who was elected in 1828, wanted Indian territory and believed that Indians should be sent as far west of the Mississippi River as possible. Jackson defied the High Court's decision. Thousands of Cherokee were forced into concentration camps where contagious diseases killed many, and many others died during the march west with little clothing, food, or shelter from freezing weather. The march became known as the Trail of Tears.

By the middle of twentieth century, Native American groups were rising up to challenge oppression and demand social justice. The American Indian Movement was formed in 1968, and other Indian rights organizations began agitating for their civil rights. Those efforts continue to the present time.

Early Abolitionists and Civil Rights Activists

Important dissenters of the past who risked and sometimes lost their lives in efforts to abolish slavery were individuals such as David Walker (1785–1830), a militant black man who wrote "Walker's Appeal," urging slaves to resort to violence when necessary to win their freedom. Although abolitionist William Lloyd Garrison thought emancipation could be accomplished through persuasion, he ran large portions of Walker's Appeal, together with a review, in his paper, the *Liberator*.

Elijah Lovejoy (1802–1837) was a publisher of an antislavery newspaper, the *Saint Louis Observer*. He was killed by a proslavery mob.

Sojourner Truth (1797–1883) was born a slave named Isabella. She walked to freedom when her owner refused to release her as was required by a New York law. She became a traveling preacher, taking the name Sojourner Truth. Though she could not read or write, she was a powerful orator and was committed to abolition and women's rights. She was often harassed and sometimes brutally attacked when she spoke, but continued her mission until the end of her life.

Sisters Sarah Grimké (1792–1873) and Angelina Grimké Weld (1805–1879), who were from a slaveholding family in South Carolina, became strong abolitionists. They moved to Philadelphia, joined the Quakers, and spoke out loud and clear about their first-hand experiences with the evils of slavery.

Escaped slave Frederick Douglass (1818–1895) was one of the leaders of the abolitionist movement who is still venerated today. He became famous when his autobiography was published in 1845. He was a strong advocate for black voting rights and civil liberties.

Henry David Thoreau (1817–1862) was an activist and dissident who watched over the underground railroad in Concord, Massachusetts, and delivered speeches attacking slavery. He is better known, however, for his essay *On Civil Disobedience*, in which he explained how he refused to pay the Massachusetts poll tax that the U.S. government implemented to fund a war in Mexico and to enforce the Fugitive Slave Law. The essay, in fact, has inspired many Americans to dissent, including Dr. Martin Luther King Jr., who wrote: "During my freshman days in 1944 at Atlanta's Morehouse College I read Henry David Thoreau's essay *On Civil Disobedience* for the first time. Here, in this courageous New Englander's refusal to pay his taxes and his choice of jail rather than support a war that would spread slavery's territory into Mexico, I made my first contact with the theory of nonviolent resistance. Fascinated by Thoreau's idea of refusing to cooperate with an evil system, I was so deeply moved that I reread the work several times" (Katz 1995, 468).

In more recent times, civil disobedience also has been at the core of some antiwar and environmental movement protests and anti-abortion demonstrations.

Separation as Dissent

In their dissent, some Americans separated themselves from established society and founded utopian communities, or communes, in the 1800s. Josiah Warren (1798–1874), for example, founded the colonies Equity and Utopia in Ohio; and Modern Times in New York during the 1830s. None survived for long periods.

One group of German immigrant dissenters began an experiment in southern Indiana. Known as Harmonie, it was founded by George Rapp and his adopted son Frederick, who had emigrated from Wurtemberg (or Wurttemburg), Germany, in 1803. At least 600 people joined Rapp in setting up a colony in Pennsylvania. Members of the community agreed that all their cash and property would be used for the benefit of the community. In turn, they were provided with all the "necessaries of life." In 1824, Rapp sold his utopian experiment to Robert Owen (1771–1858).

Renaming the village New Harmony, Owen formed the Preliminary Society of New Harmony with the stated purpose of promoting worldwide happiness. He hoped to set up an "empire of peace and goodwill." But within two years, New Harmony failed, although Owen's ideas were the basis for other communities, including the Blue Spring Community near Bloomington, Indiana, an experiment called Maxwell in Ontario, Canada, and one in Yellow Springs, Ohio, now the site of Antioch College. But by 1830, all of the Owenite communities had disintegrated.

From about 1885 through the first decade of the 1900s, a number of communal experiments began in the Far West, in northern California, Oregon, and Washington. Some of these experiments were founded by religious groups; others were prompted by socialist and labor movement leaders.

At least six communitarian experiments established in western Washington were based on the ideal of sharing social and economic activities—dissents against the established capitalist system. One of the first was the Puget Sound Co-Operative Colony initiated in 1887, partly as a protest against the Chinese, who had been encouraged by business leaders to immigrate to Seattle and work for low wages. Several white labor organizations in Seattle agitated against the Chinese workers, causing riots and eventually bringing about the deportation of hundreds of Chinese.

Early Protests by Workers and Suffragists

While some of the individuals profiled in this encyclopedia were involved in advocacy for labor during the 1900s, long before that time, working people were fighting for a living wage and shorter workdays, and against deplorable working conditions and oppressive corporations and their wealthy executives. Before the Civil War (1861–1865), labor strikes were common. In 1828, for example, women mill workers struck in Dover, New Hampshire. "They shot off gunpowder, in protest against new factory rules, which charged fines for coming late, forbade talking on the job, and required church attendance," wrote Howard Zinn in his *People's History* (Zinn 2003, 228). In another example, Zinn points out that in 1835, "fifty different trades organized unions in Philadelphia, and there was a successful general strike of laborers, factory workers, bookbinders, jewelers, coal heavers, butchers, cabinet workers—for the ten-hour [work] day. . . . Weavers in Philadelphia in the early 1840s—mostly Irish immigrants working at home for employers—struck for higher wages, attacked the homes of those refusing to strike, and destroyed their work. A sheriff's posse tried to arrest some strikers, but it was broken up by four hundred weavers armed with muskets and sticks" (Zinn 2003, 225–26).

One of the most outspoken advocates for female and male workers in the early 1800s was Sarah Bagley (1806–1847?), one of the "mill girls" (as they referred to themselves) at the textile mills in Lowell, Massachusetts. Bagley became a powerful speaker and writer seeking the 10-hour workday. At the time, workers toiled for 12 to 14 hours per day in the textile mills that 10 corporations had established in Lowell. There, the textile corporations were all powerful. "Most pronounced was the control corporations exerted over the lives of their workers. The men who ran the corporations and managed the mills sought to regulate the moral conduct and social behavior of their workforce. Within the factory, overseers were responsible for maintaining work discipline and meeting production schedules. . . . Male and female workers were expected to observe the Sabbath, and temperance was strongly encouraged. The clanging factory bell summoned operatives to and from the mill, constantly reminding them that their days were structured around work (Lowell National Historic Park).

Bagley with five other women formed the Lowell Female Labor Reform Association in 1847. They petitioned the state legislature to pass a law requiring a 10-hour workday, but the lawmakers refused to act. Nevertheless, Lowell textile corporations gave in to the political pressure and shortened the workday to 11 hours.

In mills and other industries, workers achieved few if any reforms in spite of protests and strikes. Many striking workers were arrested and found guilty of criminal conspiracy, or they were injured or killed in confrontations with local police and state militia. Their sacrifices paved the way for the labor movement of the next century.

Along with workers, suffragists and women's rights advocates were making their presence felt in the 1800s. Individuals like Lucretia Mott (1793–1880), Elizabeth Cady Stanton (1815–1902) and Lucy Stone (1818–1893) were ardent suffragists (as well as abolitionists). Men who publicly supported women's rights included Lucretia Mott's husband James and Lucy Stone's husband Henry Blackwell. Anna Howard Shaw (1847–1919), an ordained Methodist minister and physician, was a forceful orator, and she used her skills to campaign for women's right to vote.

In 1848, suffragists organized the Seneca Falls Convention in upstate New York, which was attended by both women and men. The convention adopted a Declaration of Rights and Sentiments modeled after the Declaration of Independence. It declared "We hold these truths to be self-evident: that all men and women are created equal; that they are endowed by their Creator with certain inalienable rights" and pointed out that "The history of mankind is a history of repeated injuries and usurpations on the part of man toward woman, having in direct object the establishment of an absolute tyranny over her." After listing all the many "injuries and usurpations," the declaration concluded that "because women do feel themselves aggrieved, oppressed, and fraudulently deprived of their most sacred rights, we insist that they have immediate admission to all the rights and privileges which belong to them as citizens of the United States." Sixty-eight women and 32 men signed the declaration, which, when released to the public, generated widespread interest—and controversy—but ultimately paved the way for passage of the Nineteenth Amendment granting women the right to vote.

As American history demonstrates, dissent has been part of the nation's makeup for centuries. It has not stopped. And with all the many forms of communication available currently—from blogs to Facebook to Twitter to YouTube—dissent appears to have accelerated. The challenge often is to determine whether the people dissenting are pursuing social justice or seeking self promotion. Still, the pages following illustrate the ongoing struggles for social and economic justice, religious tolerance, and democratic government, as well as preservation of the natural environment that supports all Americans.

Kathlyn Gay

References

Katz, William Loren. *Eyewitness: A Living Documentary of the African American Contribution to American History.* Revised and updated. New York: Touchstone/Simon and Schuster, 1995.

Zinn, Howard. *A People's History of the United States: 1942–Present.* New York: HarperCollins, 2003.

A

Abbey, Edward (1927–1989)

A prolific author, Edward Abbey penned both novels and essays that "extolled individualism and decried the effects of the destruction of wilderness on human liberty" (Callicott and Frodeman 2008, 1). However, "he often wrote of his penchant for throwing beer cans out of his pickup truck window as he traveled down desert highways" (Duryee 2000). This is not exactly what you would expect to learn about the habits of one of the most preeminent twentieth-century advocates of the environment. Yet such contradictions in his own personal nature served to make Edward Abbey all the more interesting man—albeit a harder one to know, according to fellow author and friend Kent Duryee. In some people, his writings have developed an almost cult-like following. Others feel he was a crackpot—to varying degrees of danger or harm, depending on their personal perspectives on the subject matter about which he wrote and/or their interactions with Abbey himself.

Edward Paul Abbey was born on January 29, 1927, in Indiana, Pennsylvania, and grew up near the town of Home, at the end of what he always described as a "red dog, dirt road." His father, Paul Revere Abbey, was a farmer, and his mother, Mildred Postlewaite Abbey, was a teacher. He was known as Ned to his family (and, later on, as "Cactus Ed" to his friends—perhaps an apt nickname given his reputation for having a prickly personality).

Edward grew up in the Appalachian hills. Coming of age in such a rugged environment did much to dictate Abbey's appreciation of nature. He witnessed firsthand the land sacrificed to the increasing appetites of the logging and mining industries. Public land policies involving these ventures caught his attention early on and were the first of many issues he would come to criticize in the years to follow. His Appalachian upbringing was a strong influence throughout the remainder of his life, one that he addressed throughout the course of his writings, most extensively in two of his books *The Fool's Progress: An Honest Novel* (1988) and *Appalachian Wilderness: The Great Smoky Mountains*, with photographs by Eliot Porter (1970).

In the summer of 1944, Abbey set across the country with the grand sum of $20 in his pocket, courtesy of his father's generosity. Hitchhiking through Illinois, Minnesota, and South Dakota, over the Rockies and into California, he did odd jobs when his meager funds ran low. He went to Yosemite National Park, and then traveled across the desert through northern Arizona, hopping freight trains and experiencing the life of a hobo. In his journal that August, he wrote of his initial impressions: "Across the river, waited a land that filled me with strange excitement; crags and pinnacles of naked rock, the dark cores of ancient volcanoes, a vast, silent emptiness smoldering with heat, color, and indecipherable significance, above which floated a small number of pure, clear, hard-edged clouds. For the first time, I felt I was getting close to the West of my deepest imaginings—the place where the tangible and the mythical become the same" (Bishop 1994, 71).

In Flagstaff, he was arrested for vagrancy and forced to leave town. Hopping on yet another train, this time toward New Mexico, he began what would be his lifetime love affair with the Southwestern desert:

> Proud of my freedom and hobohood I stood in the doorway of the boxcar, rocking with the motion of the train, ears full of the rushing wind and the clattering wheels, and stared and stared and stared, like a starving man, at the burnt, barren, bold, bright landscape passing before my eyes. Telegraph poles flashed by close to the tracks, the shining wires dipped and rose, dipped and rose; but beyond the line and the road and the nearby ridges, the queer foreign shapes of mesa and butte seemed barely to move at all; they revolved slowly at an immense distance, strange right-angled promontories of rose-colored rock that remained in view, from my slowly altering perspective, for an hour, for two hours, at a time. And all of it there, simply there, neither hostile nor friendly, but full of a powerful, mysterious promise. (Duryee 2000)

Both homesickness and reality soon came calling, and Abbey returned home to finish high school. He was editor of the school paper during his senior year and earned a reputation as an excellent debater. But he was equally well known as someone who would pick schoolyard fights with those bigger than himself. He graduated as a top student (although, ironically, he twice failed a journalism course) and then went on to serve in the military.

By the time his training was complete, World War II was over—the Japanese surrendered on the very day Abbey finished basic training. So, Abbey spent his remaining time in the military—his service totaled two years—fairly uneventfully in Naples, Italy. He came out of the military with the same rank as he had gone in: a private. Even though he was awarded two promotions, these were counterbalanced by two demotions in rank, likely for refusing to salute various officers. He said: " 'You're saluting the uniform, not the man,' they taught us in basic training. Really! I'll salute a *man* anytime, but damned if I'll salute an officer" (Bishop 1994, 73–74). His military experiences left Abbey more entrenched than ever in his basic distrust of large institutions and in his belief in the supremacy of self-determination. The military had turned him into an anarchist, cementing the roots already instilled in him via the philosophies of his father, a longtime member of the International Workers of the World.

After his discharge in 1947, Abbey attended the University of New Mexico, where he studied philosophy and literature. Upon graduating in 1951, he accepted a Fulbright Fellowship, allowing him to tour Europe (Peterson 2006, 5). He later returned to earn a master's degree in philosophy from his alma mater.

In 1952, his first marriage ended in divorce and he married Rita Deanin, an art student in New Mexico. They had two children. Abbey divorced and remarried three more times, eventually producing three more children.

Abbey was able to secure a position as a seasonal park ranger with the U.S. National Park Service in the late 1950s. It was at his post at Arches National Monument (now a national park in Utah) that he wrote what started out as simple journal musings and was published under the title of *Desert Solitaire: A Season in the Wilderness* (1968). The book went on to become one of his most famous works, one that has frequently been compared with Thoreau's *Walden*. In fact, writer Larry McMurtry (known for his

Pulitzer Prize–winning novel *Lonesome Dove* and all things literary of the American West) referred to Abbey as the "Thoreau of the American West" (McMurtry 1975).

Abbey wrote prodigiously. He followed up his first book, *Jonathan Troy* (1954), a novel he wanted to disown, two years later with *The Brave Cowboy* (1956), which was later made into the 1962 movie *Lonely Are the Brave*, starring Kirk Douglas. Four years after that, he published *Fire on the Mountain* (1962). In quick succession, *Desert Solitaire* (1968), *Appalachian Wilderness* (1970), *Blacksun* (a novel, 1971), *Slickrock: The Canyon Country of Southeast Utah* (1971), and *Cactus Country* (1973) were published. His most well-known and talked-about book (next to *Desert Solitaire*), *The Monkey Wrench Gang* (1975), is a novel about the exploits of a group of guerrilla environmentalists. In the book, these "eco-warriors" traverse the American West trying to halt out-of-control human expansion via the commission of acts of sabotage against industrial development projects. Abbey always maintained that his book was simply written as a form of entertainment and could, at most, be viewed as symbolic satire. Conventional "mainstream" environmentalists tried to maintain a distance from what they perceived as Abbey's more radical positions. Others saw *The Monkey Wrench Gang* a virtual how-to guide in "ecotage" (sabotage on behalf of the ecology). There was little doubt that the novel served to inspire a certain subset of environmentalists to take matters into their own hands.

One organization, Earth First! formed in 1980 as a direct result of Abbey's writings. Although Abbey never officially joined Earth First! he did associate with many of its members and occasionally wrote articles for the organization. Earth First! advocated eco-sabotage—that is, "monkeywrenching."

One environmentalist who joined Earth First! was Judi Bari, who was attracted to the organization because of members' willingness to risk their lives by blocking bulldozers and chainsaws in order to prevent logging of old-growth trees—redwood trees that were 1,000 to 2,000 years old. However, Bari was against some of the tactics described in Abbey's book if they endangered loggers, and she was dedicated to nonviolent civil disobedience. Bari's activities made headlines nationwide when a pipe bomb in her car exploded, severely injuring her.

Abbey followed up *The Monkey Wrench Gang* with *The Journey Home: Some Words in Defense of the American West* (1977), *The Hidden Canyon: A River Journey* (about his trip through the Grand Canyon on the Colorado River, with photos by John Blaustein, 1977), *Abbey's Road* (1979), *Desert Images: An American Landscape* (with photos by David Muench, 1979), and *Good News* (a novel, 1980). He published excerpts from his journals under the title, *Down the River* (1982) and spent the next two years readying for publication of *In Praise of Mountain Lions* (speeches, 1984) and *Beyond the Wall: Essays from Outside* (1984). *One Life at a Time, Please* (1988), as well as a novel called *The Fool's Progress* (1988). One year later, Abbey's books *A Voice Crying in the Wilderness: Notes from a Secret Journal* (1989) and *Hayduke Lives!* (a novel, 1989) were published; the latter, published after Abbey's death, was a sequel to *The Monkey Wrench Gang*. Abbey used the latter book to put forth the argument that the use of sabotage to protect the environment from destruction by industry is permissible as long as no human injury is incurred in the process.

Edward Abbey died in Oracle, Arizona, on March 14, 1989, from surgical complications. A postscript to *Confession of a Barbarian:*

Selections from the Journals of Edward Abbey, 1951–1989 noted: "In accordance with Ed's instructions, his body was placed in a sleeping bag, and transported ... into the burning heart of a distant and remote desert wilderness ... an exhausting distance to a final campsite offering 'an Abbey kind of view.' There among the rocks, sand and cactus of 'the only Heaven we'll ever know or ever need to know,' with eagles and vultures soaring overhead, doves mourning the midday heat, coyotes crying in the night, Edward Paul Abbey now enjoys the ultimate desert solitaire" (Abbey 1994, 377).

Earth Apples: The Poetry of Edward Abbey and *Confessions of a Barbarian: Selections from the Journals of Edward Abbey, 1951–1989* were published posthumously in 1994.

In *Epitaph, for a Desert Anarchist: The Life and Legacy of Edward Abbey* (1995), James Bishop Jr. explained that Abbey rejected the romanticized view of the West portrayed in movies and novels with "noble cowboys and ecological Indians and sentimental gunfighters and whores." Instead, Abbey "blasted gaping holes in the mythology of the Old West, paving the way for the current generation of revisionist historians.... Early on, he identified clues that presaged a series of momentous societal changes before they were apparent to the rest of the populace. But when he put forth his views in the 1950s and '60s, he was accused of being on the lunatic fringe. After his death, the bulk of those views are now accepted as conventional wisdom" (Bishop 1995, 209–10).

Margaret Gay

See also Bari, Judi

References

Abbey, Edward, and David Peterson, eds. *Confession of a Barbarian: Selections from the Journals of Edward Abbey, 1951–1989.* Boston: Little, Brown & Co., 1994.

Bishop, James, Jr. *Epitaph, for a Desert Anarchist: The Life and Legacy of Edward Abbey.* New York: Touchstone, 1995.

Cahalan, James M. *Edward Abbey: A Life.* Tucson: University of Arizona Press, 2001.

Duryee, Kent. "Edward Abbey: A Man Hard to Talk About." *Desert USA Magazine*, November 2000. http://www.desertusa.com/mag00/nov/papr/abbey.html (accessed March 11, 2011).

Keller, David R. "Edward Abbey, 1927–1989." In *Encyclopedia of Environmental Ethics and Philosophy*, edited by J. Baird Callicott and Robert Frodeman, 2 vols. Detroit, MI: Macmillan Reference USA, 2008.

McMurtry, Larry. "Fertile Fiction for the American Desert." *Washington Post*, September 8, 1975.

Peterson, David. *Postcards from Ed: Dispatches and Salvos from an American Iconoclast.* Minneapolis, MN: Milkweed Editions, 2006.

Abu-Jamal, Mumia (1954–)

He is prisoner #AM8335, whose name is Mumia Abu-Jamal, a former journalist and once president of the Philadelphia chapter of the National Association of Black Journalists (Bisson 2001, 147). Mumia Abu-Jamal has been in state prison since 1981 and on death row since 1983 after he was convicted of killing Philadelphia police officer Daniel Faulkner. To his supporters, who number in the tens of thousands worldwide, Abu-Jamal is an innocent political prisoner sentenced to death for murder, a controversial cultural icon to many who see his trial, conviction, and capital punishment sentence as a reflection of American racism. To law enforcement and many Americans, he is a murderer who should die for his crime.

He was named Wesley Cook when he was born on April 24, 1954, in Philadelphia. Wesley's mother Edith was a Methodist who regularly sent her son to Sunday school. According to author Terry Bisson, Wesley enjoyed learning biblical lessons (Bisson 2001, 11). Little is known about Wesley's father William; he died when Wesley was nine years old.

Wesley was 14 years old when he temporarily took an African name. His high school teacher was a Kenyan who was educating the class about African culture, and he suggested that students adopt African names. Wesley Cook became "Mumia," which means "Prince" in Kikuyu and stands for anticolonial African nationalists who were fighting the British for Kenyan independence. These fighters were called the Mau-Mau by Kenyan whites seeking to prevent African rule.

While he was an adolescent, Wesley attended a George Wallace for President rally in 1968. Wesley wanted to create disorder at the rally (Bisson 2001, 35–36). He was beaten by a group of whites including a policeman, an experience that prompted him to join the Black Panther Party, an organization considered by many Americans to be anti-white and even more anti-law enforcement. Two years earlier, the Black Panther Party issued its Ten-Point Program seeking freedom, full employment, decent housing, education, exemption from military service for all black men, an end to police brutality, and a re-trial for all blacks by black juries (Bisson 2001, 45–49). The following year at the age of 15, he helped form the Philadelphia branch of the Black Panther Party with the title "Lieutenant of Information" (Bisson 2001, 58, 72). He was responsible for publicity and news releases. That same year he dropped out of Benjamin Franklin High School and went to live at the branch's headquarters. In 1969, he traveled to other cities with chapters of the Black Panther Party.

Throughout the next four years, Abu-Jamal was under surveillance by the Federal Bureau of Investigation (FBI). During this time, more than 38 Black Panthers were killed by local police, some involving FBI agents as well (Bisson 2001, 62). Upon leaving the Black Panthers, he returned to his old high school but was suspended for distributing literature for black revolutionary student power. He also led unsuccessful protests to change the school name to Malcolm X High. After attaining his GED, he studied briefly at Goddard College in rural Vermont (Bisson 2001, 88, 106, 159).

He formally took the surname Abu-Jamal ("father of Jamal" in Arabic) in 1971, when he and his wife Biba had a son they named

Convicted police killer Mumia Abu-Jamal is seen in this undated file photo. Abu-Jamal's defense team maintained that he did not receive a fair trial because the jury was both racially biased and misinformed, and the judge was a racist. (AP Photo/Jennifer E. Beach)

Jamal. Abu-Jamal and 19-year-old Biba had a second child, their daughter Lateefa. Their marriage ended soon afterward. Abu-Jamal and his second wife Marilyn had a son, Mazi, in 1978. The couple separated and Abu-Jamal eventually married Wadiya, his third and current wife.

By 1975, Abu-Jamal was a radio journalist, earning the title "the Voice of the Voiceless." He frequently discussed MOVE, an African American commune in Philadelphia. Members lived in an urban compound and advocated a back-to-nature lifestyle that created hostile reactions from neighbors. When police under a court order tried to evict MOVE members from their compound, an officer was killed. After MOVE relocated, the complaints continued and police bombed the compound, killing 11 people. In numerous broadcasts, Abu-Jamal publicly criticized all the police actions, which did not endear him to the police.

Along with being a broadcaster, Abu-Jamal worked part time as a taxi driver. He was on that job when police officer Daniel Faulkner was killed on December 9, 1981. Faulkner stopped a Volkswagen that Abu-Jamal's younger brother William Cook had been driving. Abu-Jamal was at the scene. He had parked his taxi across the street. When he approached the officer and his brother, Faulkner shot and wounded Abu-Jamal; and, according to witnesses' testimony at trial, Abu-Jamal shot and killed Faulkner.

Abu-Jamal collapsed on the sidewalk a short distance from Faulkner. Police took him to a hospital where he received treatment for his bullet wound and other injuries incurred during his arrest. He was then charged with the first-degree murder of Faulkner, who died during surgery at the same hospital (Faulkner 2008, 8–9).

According to the *Philadelphia Daily News* article of December 9, 1981, "One witness told police he saw Wesley Cook fire one shot as he ran across the street toward his brother and Faulkner. The witness reportedly said Faulkner, apparently hit by the shot, crumpled to the sidewalk and that Wesley Cook then stood over him and fired another shot at him point-blank. The witness was not able to say when Faulkner fired his gun . . . Police said five shots had been fired from the gun they believed to be Wesley Cook's. Faulkner had fired his gun once" (Faulkner 2008, 12).

The ballistics evidence showed that the bullets in Faulkner's body matched the gun legally purchased by Abu-Jamal two years earlier. The bullet fired was too deformed to be linked to Abu-Jamal's gun, although it was consistent with such a weapon.

Abu-Jamal was tried in mid-1982, and the judge agreed to allow Abu-Jamal to defend himself with an attorney, Anthony Jackson, advising him. But on the first day of the trial, the judge reversed his decision, declaring that Abu-Jamal was intentionally disruptive, making Jackson his sole advocate.

Four witnesses for the prosecution testified: a cab driver, a prostitute, a motorist, and a pedestrian. All except the pedestrian claimed that Abu-Jamal or someone who looked like him was the shooter. The pedestrian saw the police officer pull over the Volkswagen. Two other prosecution witnesses testified that Abu-Jamal confessed in the hospital.

The prosecution declared that the revolver belonging to Abu-Jamal with five spent cartridges was evidence that his weapon killed Faulkner (Faulkner 2008, 36). However, tests to confirm that Abu-Jamal handled and fired the weapon were not performed, leading his supporters to believe Abu-Jamal was denied evidence of his innocence. The prosecution argued that Abu-Jamal's struggle with the arresting officers at the scene would have compromised the forensic value of such a test (Faulkner 2008, 172–73).

Defense attorney Jackson maintained that Abu-Jamal was innocent of the charges, and that the testimony of the prosecution witnesses was unreliable. Nine character witnesses were put on the stand. One defense witness testified he saw a man running along a street shortly after the shooting, although he did not witness the shooting itself (Faulkner 2008, 41, 45). Other potential witnesses refused to appear in court, as did Abu-Jamal's brother William Cook, who insisted he had nothing to do with the crime. Mumia Abu-Jamal chose not to testify in his own defense, which is his constitutional right.

After three hours of deliberation, the jury delivered a unanimous guilty verdict. In the sentencing phase of his trial, Abu-Jamal read a prepared statement, and was then cross-examined about issues relevant to his assessment of his own character by Joseph McGill, the prosecutor (Faulkner 2008, 47–48). Abu-Jamal criticized his attorney, Anthony Jackson, for failing to follow his recommendations, and criticized Judge Albert Sabo for not allowing him to defend himself pro se. The jury then sentenced Abu-Jamal to death.

Governor Tom Ridge (who later served as U.S. Homeland Security chief) signed Abu-Jamal's death warrant on June 1, 1995, but its execution was suspended until Abu-Jamal pursued his appeals. One of the witnesses called was William "Dales" Singletary, who testified that he saw the shooting and the gunman was a passenger in William Cook's stopped car. Because of inconsistent statements, Singletary's account was considered "not credible" by the court. After hearing other defense witnesses, the Pennsylvania Supreme Court unanimously ruled that all issues raised by Abu-Jamal were without merit. The case then went to the U.S. Supreme Court, but the Court refused to review the decision of the lower court. As a result, Governor Ridge signed a second death warrant on October 13, 1999. Its execution was also stayed as Abu-Jamal commenced his pursuit of a federal habeas corpus, a right granted by the U.S. Constitution. On December 18, 2001, Judge William H. Yohn Jr. of the U.S. District Court for the Eastern District of Pennsylvania upheld Abu-Jamal's conviction but voided the sentence of death, citing irregularities in the original sentencing and jury instructions (Faulkner 2008, 272–76).

Seventeen years after Abu-Jamal's conviction, in 1999, a man named Arnold Beverly claimed that he and an unnamed accomplice, not Abu-Jamal, shot and killed Faulkner as part of a contract killing because Faulkner was interfering with graft and payoffs to corrupt Philadelphia police (Faulkner 2008, 27–28). This affidavit became contentious to Abu-Jamal's defense team, leading to the resignation of two of his attorneys and the firing of two others. A private investigator claimed in 2001 that a prosecution witness was recanting his trial testimony. Another witness was declared dead by the state of New Jersey in 1992—supporters of Abu-Jamal often claim that this person was a police informant who falsified her testimony against Abu-Jamal. Kenneth Pate, a stepbrother of hospital security guard Priscilla Durham who testified that Abu-Jamal confessed at the hospital to the murder of Faulkner, has claimed that Durham admitted to him that she did not hear such a confession, and hospital doctors have stated that the wounded Abu-Jamal was not capable of making such a bedside confession at that time.

Abu-Jamal did not speak publicly of the murder of Faulkner until May 3, 2001, when he stated that he was sitting in his cab across the street when he heard shouting, then saw a police vehicle and his brother's stopped car. Abu-Jamal said he heard the sound of gunshots and saw his brother appearing disoriented across the street. Abu-Jamal said he ran to him from the parking lot and was then shot by a police officer (Abu-Jamal 2001).

Abu-Jamal's statement fails to explain either his gun being found next to him, or the shoulder holster he was wearing at the time. It also fails to explain the five empty bullet casings found in the revolver, and why they were consistent with the fragments retrieved from the police officer's body. Abu-Jamal's first statement came just days after the first statement by his younger brother William, who claimed that he did not see who shot Faulkner though no one else was as close to the shootings as he was.

On May 17, 2007, the Third Circuit Court of Pennsylvania heard oral arguments before three judges. The Commonwealth of Pennsylvania sought to reinstate the death penalty, claiming that a complaint of a biased jury was invalid since Abu-Jamal did not complain of that during the original trial. Abu-Jamal's defense team maintained that he did not receive a fair trial because the jury was both racially biased and misinformed, and because the judge was a racist. The last of these claims was based on a statement from a court stenographer's affidavit that Judge Sabo had vowed to convict Abu-Jamal. Judge Sabo denied making such a comment.

In 2008, a three-judge panel of the U.S. Third Court of Appeals upheld the murder conviction, but ordered a new capital sentencing hearing over concerns that the jury was improperly instructed (Faulkner 2008, 295–301). Since that time, appeals by Abu-Jamal to both the federal appellate court as well as the U.S. Supreme Court have been unsuccessful. Worldwide protests, marches, and 100,000 signatures on a petition in Rome, as well as advertisements in the *New York Times* signed by celebrities, and an op-ed column by E. L. Doctorow have done little to sway the courts.

The widow of Officer Faulkner, Maureen Faulkner, had an entirely different view. She published a book with retired attorney and Philadelphia radio broadcaster Michael Smerconish entitled *Murdered by Mumia: A Life Sentence of Loss, Pain and Injustice* (2008). According to her, Faulkner's partner Garry Bell would later testify that Abu-Jamal admitted he shot Faulkner. A second individual present at the scene confirmed Abu-Jamal's statement under oath.

Mumia Abu-Jamal has received international attention regarding his sentence of death, as well as his conviction for killing a police officer. During his imprisonment, he has published several books and other publications, including *Live from Death Row* (1995). He has written dozens of essays that have appeared on the web site of the International Action Center founded by former U.S. attorney general Ramsey Clark, a political dissident who has provided legal help to numerous controversial figures. Some of his essays call for the release of Leonard Peltier, leader of the American Indian Movement (AIM) imprisoned for the murder of an FBI agent in a case also characterized as a gross miscarriage of justice. Other writings praise civil rights icons and those who work for social justice.

Daniel Callaghan

See also Clark, Ramsey; Malcolm X; Peltier, Leonard

References

Abu-Jamal, Mumia. "Declaration of Mumia Abu-Jamal," *Revolutionary Worker*, May 3, 2001. http://revcom.us/a/v23/1100-99/1103/mumia_declaration.htm (accessed February 2, 2011).

Abu-Jamal, Mumia. *Live from Death Row*. New York: Harper Perennial, 1996 (first published by Addison-Wesley, 1995).

Abu-Jamal, Mumia. "Mumia Abu-Jamal: Essays from Death Row." International Action Center, n.d. http://www.iacenter.org/polprisoners/majessay.htm (accessed September 8, 2010).

Anderson, S. E., and Tony Medina. *In Defense of Mumia*. New York: Writers and Readers, 1996.

Bisson, Terry. *On the Move: The Story of Mumia Abu-Jamal*. Farmington, PA: Litmus Books, 2001.

Faulkner, Maureen, and Michael A. Smerconish. *Murdered by Mumia: A Life Sentence of Loss, Pain and Injustice*. Guilford, CT: The Lyons Press/Globe Pequot, 2008.

Abzug, Bella (1920–1998)

On April 2, 1998, at the Riverside Memorial Chapel in New York City, during a service to commemorate the life and contributions of Bella Abzug, onetime U.S. vice presidential candidate Geraldine Ferraro asserted that Abzug "didn't knock lightly on the door. She didn't even push it open or batter it down. She took it off the hinges forever. So that those of us who came after could walk through" (Braun Levine 2007, ix).

Although perhaps best known for her pursuit and defense of feminist causes, Abzug was both an activist and a full-fledged leader in every major social movement that took place during her lifetime. More often than not, she was typically in the forefront on many of the issues about which she was passionate: representation of labor and civil rights, socialist Zionism, the ban of nuclear testing, the antiwar movement, and both women's and international human rights.

Bella was born in the Bronx borough of New York City to Russian immigrants Emanuel and Ester Stavisky on July 24, 1920—the same year, she liked to point out, in which women in the United States were awarded the right to vote. She grew up in a small apartment that she, her parents, and her older sister Helene shared with her mother's parents. Bella's Uncle Julius also lived with them until he married. After failed attempts at running a laundry and stationer's, Bella's father eventually opened a butcher shop that he named the "Live and Let Live Market." According to Bella's later recollections, "That was his philosophy, and his personal protest against the imperialist World War I" (Braun Levine 2007, 5).

She grew up in a warm and nurturing home. Her grandfather, Wolf, was especially attentive to her, calling Bella his "jewel." Her knowledge of Hebrew was precocious, and her demonstration of those abilities in front of her grandfather's friends made him proud. No matter; eventually she would be dismissed to sit with all of the other women behind the "mechitzah," the curtain that divided the men from the women in the synagogue. The seeds of feminism were planted.

As a young girl, Bella worked at her father's store, and it was not long before her proclivity for activism took root at its very doorstep. She started making speeches about Zionism to passersby. By age 12, she had advanced to soliciting donations from New York City subway riders for the creation of a state of Israel.

Her father died around the time Bella was entering her teenage years. The Staviskys' synagogue held that only male children should perform the 11-month Kaddish mourning ritual for a parent. Bella was undeterred. "I was almost 13, and every morning before school for the following year, I went to our synagogue to say Kaddish for him. In retrospect, I could say that as that to be one of the early blows for the liberation of Jewish women. But in fact, no one could have stopped me from performing the duty traditionally reserved for a son, from honoring the man who had taught me to love peace who had educated me in Jewish values" (Jaffe-Gill 1998, 74).

Bella applied the same resoluteness to her time in school, throwing herself into both sports and academics. She attended the all-girls Walton High School in the Bronx, where she was elected president, and then went on to attend Hunter College of the City University of New York. She was student body president in college, graduating in 1942. After graduating from Hunter, she met Martin Abzug while visiting relatives in Miami, Florida. Martin went on to serve in the military, and after he returned, he contacted Bella at Hunter. The two married in 1944, eventually producing two daughters.

While in school, Bella did not leave her younger activist ideals behind. She marched in protest against the spread of Nazism in Europe and against British and American neutrality during the Spanish Civil War. She also found time to teach Hebrew and Jewish history on weekends, as well as to attend the Jewish Theological Seminary of America.

From an early age, Bella had wanted to become an attorney, and she applied to law school at Columbia, Cornell, and Harvard. The latter turned her down because of her gender. Accepted by the other two, her mother nixed Cornell, saying, "For a nickel on the subway you could go to Columbia and they would probably give you a scholarship too" (Braun Levine 2007, 22). She became editor of the *Columbia Law Review*. Diploma in hand, Abzug joined the firm of Whitt and Cammer and began working in labor law and representing civil rights cases. She was committed to helping those she saw as oppressed to obtain justice from their oppressors. She chaired the Civil Rights Committee of the National Lawyers Guild, a progressive bar association that was founded in 1937 for lawyers and law students.

In the 1950s, during the height of U.S. senator Joseph McCarthy's anticommunist regime, Abzug was not hesitant to take on clients accused of subversive "red" activities. In the next decade, she became a strident supporter of the civil rights movement and took on many cases, one of which even made it to the Supreme Court on appeals. In 1961, she helped to found Women Strike for Peace, as part of a protest calling for the ban of nuclear testing, and she led demonstrations in New York and the nation's capital. After the Nuclear Test Ban Treaty was signed, Abzug helped to broaden the movement to an overall antiwar focus that opposed the Vietnam War.

It was in the 1960s that Abzug became active in the Democratic Party and, by 1970, she ran for and was elected to represent New York City's 19th ward in the U.S. House of Representatives. She had famously campaigned under the slogan, "This woman's place is in the House—the House of Representatives."

Some say that Abzug became known in Washington, D.C., for two things: her big hats and her big mouth. Indeed, Norman Mailer is frequently cited as saying that "her voice could melt the fat off a taxi driver's neck" (Braun Levine 2007, xiii). Her penchant for wearing hats began with her fledging law career, when she was often mistaken for a legal secretary. In those days, professional women wore hats and gloves, so she adopted the habit of dressing accordingly to gain respect. As time passed, the gloves fell by the wayside; but Abzug had become fond of wearing hats, so she continued to do so for the remainder of her life (Braun Levine 2007, 29).

Bella Abzug is seen in this May 17, 1976, photo as she announces her candidacy for the U.S. Senate. (AP Photo)

Those who attempt to dismiss Abzug easily do her and her accomplishments a great disservice. She did garner a great deal of attention upon her arrival at the Capitol. Yet her wardrobe and somewhat abrasive personality were the least of it. Abzug set the U.S. House of Representatives on its heels on her very first day in office when she introduced a bill calling for the withdrawal of U.S. troops from Vietnam by July 4, 1971. She went to Washington, D.C., to promote liberal causes and bring them to national prominence, and that is exactly what she did. And if doing so ruffled a few of her colleague's feathers, then she was more than prepared to deal with the consequences. "There are those who say I'm impatient, impetuous, uppity, rude, profane, brash and overbearing. Whether I'm any of these things or all of them, you can decide for yourself. But whatever I am—and this ought to be made very clear at the outset—I am a very serious woman" (Mansnerus 1998).

As a freshman congresswoman, Abzug boldly sought an appointment to the Armed Services Committee, vowing to take on the military-industrial complex and to seek an end to the draft. Also on her wish list were national health insurance, money for daycare centers and housing, and more money for New York City—all of which she thought could easily be paid for with money wastefully spent on "defense funds" allocated in a largely unquestioned and mushrooming Pentagon budget.

In 1971, Abzug teamed up with Gloria Steinem, Shirley Chisholm, and Betty Friedan, along with other congresswomen and heads of national organizations who all shared a vision of gender equality, to establish the National Women's Political Caucus. This group was and remains dedicated to recruiting, training, and supporting women who seek elected and appointed offices. During her time in the House, Abzug cast one of the first votes for the Equal Rights Amendment.

Other "firsts" followed. She was one of the first members of Congress to support gay rights, introducing the first federal gay rights bill, known as the Equality Act of 1974. She was the first to call for President Nixon's impeachment in the 1970s.

During her tenure, she also coauthored the Freedom of Information and Privacy Acts. Referring to working with Abzug on this legislation, Edward M. Kennedy said:

> She understood the whole penchant for secrecy that is so evident today and the importance of open government... This was a passion that she had. If we got an openness in government, that was truth to power... Even as a freshman congressperson, Bella knew the rules, knew how to try and move a system that doesn't move, and still doesn't move. She stirred the House in such a way to push her view, irritate, antagonize, cajole, persuade, inspire, and lead. (Braun Levine 2007, 164–65)

In 1972, Abzug's ward was eliminated due to redistricting. She instead ran for a seat representing the 20th ward. She lost the primary but her opponent died and she became the Democratic nominee in the general election. She then continued serving in the House of Representatives until 1976, when she gave up her seat in an unsuccessful Senate bid—a race she lost to Daniel Patrick Moynihan by 1 percent. In 1977, she ran an unsuccessful mayoral campaign against Ed Koch. She made two more unsuccessful bids to return to the House. Her husband died during her final campaign.

After leaving office, Abzug continued to practice law and fight for the causes in which she believed. President Gerald Ford appointed her to chair the National Commission on the Observance of International Women's Year and to plan the 1977 National Women's Conference. And President Jimmy Carter named her cochair of the National Advisory Committee for Women. However, Carter soon removed Abzug from her position, an action that caused many of her fellow committee members and her cochair to resign in protest.

Among her accomplishments, Abzug wrote *Gender Gap: Bella Abzug's Guide to Political Power for American Women* (1984). She also started a lobbying group, Women U.S.A. and, in 1990, cofounded the Women's Environment and Development Organization to promote an international agenda of economic equality and environmental sanity.

At the age of 77, after a number of years fighting breast cancer, Abzug developed heart disease and passed away at Columbia-Presbyterian Medical Center in Manhattan on March 31, 1998. She was survived by two daughters, Eve and Liz.

U.S. First Lady Hillary Clinton spoke at Abzug's April 2, 1998, memorial service. Here is some of what she had to say that day:

> As I travel around the world... I am always meeting women who introduce themselves by saying, "I'm the Bella Abzug of Russia," or "I'm the Bella Abzug of Kazakstan," or "I'm the Bella Abzug of

Uganda." Now what these women are really saying, whether or not they wear the hat of an advocate like Bella, is that they, too, are pioneers, that they are willing to take on the establishment and the institutions of their society on behalf of the rights of women but not just that, on behalf of what families need, on behalf of peace, on behalf of civil society, all the many and varied causes that Bella stood for throughout her long and active life . . . She liked to say "First they gave us the year of the woman, then they gave us the decade of the woman. Sooner or later, they'll have to give us the whole thing." She never stopped fighting for the "whole thing." So when women around the world say to me, I am the "Bella Abzug" from somewhere, I know what they really mean is that they'll never give up. (Braun Levine 2007, 284)

In 2004, the Bella Abzug Leadership Institute (BALI) was established. Its purpose is to mentor and train high school and college women to become effective leaders in civic, political, corporate, and community life.

Margaret Gay

See also Friedan, Betty; McCarthy, Joseph

References

Braun Levine, Suzanne, and Mary Thom, eds. *Bella Abzug: How One Tough Broad from the Bronx Fought Jim Crow and Joe McCarthy, Pissed Off Jimmy Carter, Battled for the Rights of Women and Workers, Rallied against War and for the Planet, and Shook Up Politics Along the Way.* New York: Farrar, Straus and Giroux, 2007.

Cook, Blanche Wiesen. "Bella Abzug." *Jewish Virtual Library*, n.d. http://www.jewishvirtuallibrary.org/jsource/biography/abzug.html (accessed March 5, 2011).

Jaffe-Gill, Ellen, ed. *The Jewish Woman's Book of Wisdom: Thoughts from Prominent Jewish Women on Spirituality, Identity, Sisterhood, Family and Faith.* New York: Citadel Press, 1998.

Mansnerus, Laura. "Obituary: Bella Abzug, 77, Congresswoman and a Founding Feminist, Is Dead." *New York Times*, April 1, 1998. http://www.nytimes.com/learning/general/onthisday/bday/0724.html (accessed March 5, 2011).

Addams, Jane (1860–1935)

Many of the hundreds of published accounts about Jane Addams are filled with praise for her pioneering settlement house efforts and social reforms. She helped initiate the settlement house movement, which was to flourish during the late nineteenth and early twentieth centuries. But during World War I, she was highly criticized because of her outspoken pacifist stance and advocacy for women's right to vote. As a writer in the *Rochester Herald* of July 15, 1915, opined, "The time was when Miss Jane Addams of Hull House, Chicago, held a warm place in the hearts of the American people but she is fast losing the esteem, [which] her earlier efforts seem to merit. Her dabbling in politics, her suffrage activity and her ill-advised methods of working for peace have very materially lowered her in the esteem of hundreds of former admirers."

Laura Jane Addams was born on September 6, 1860, in Cedarville, Illinois, near Rockford, Illinois, and the Wisconsin border. She was the youngest child of Sarah (Weber) and John Huy Addams. John Addams was a descendent of Quakers who had lived in Pennsylvania since the 1600s when William Penn founded a colony. He and his wife moved to the Midwest "frontier" where he was one of the founders of Cedarville. Through his business skills and leadership capabilities, John's family became the wealthiest and most prominent in the village.

Jane's mother died when Jane was only two and one-half years old. Sarah Addams, who was pregnant, was helping a neighbor during childbirth—the local midwife was not available. On her way home afterward, Sarah fell and suffered serious injuries. She had a premature birth and died one week later. Although Jane was too young to remember her mother's death, she no doubt heard stories about the tragedy.

In 1867, Jane's father married Anna Haldeman, a widow who brought her two sons to join Jane and her four older siblings. George Haldeman was about Jane's age, and the two became fast companions. As they grew, George was always there to encourage his stepsister to strive for whatever goals she might envision. Because of this, and the quiet support of her father, whom she adored, and her stepmother's encouragement to improve her education through reading, Jane had a nurturing childhood and all the advantages the family's position afforded. John Addams owned a sawmill and a gristmill, founded a railway, established schools and a library, and became a state senator. He was a good friend of Abraham Lincoln and was devastated when the president was assassinated.

The prosperous life of the Addams household did not mean that young Jane had an easy life. She was often ill. Her most serious illness was a form of tuberculosis called Potts disease, which caused curvature of

American sociologist, pacifist and feminist Jane Addams, cofounder of Hull House, the nation's first true settlement house. Addams was active in advocating equal rights for women and African Americans, and consumer protection. She also helped establish organizations to promote world peace. Addams shared the Nobel Peace Prize in 1931. (National Archives)

the spine and back pain that would plague her in later years.

Even though Jane wanted to attend the newly opened Smith College in Northampton, Massachusetts, because it emulated the rigorous instruction common to men's institutions like Yale and Harvard, her father insisted on a school closer to home. Her father was among the few intellectual males who understood education was just as important for girls as it was for boys, and he had sent Jane's older sisters to the Rockford Female Seminary, where John Addams was a member of the board of trustees. Jane early on fancied a vocation in the sciences or even medicine. However, her father insisted on the seminary, and that is where Jane went in 1877.

As a student, Jane joined the science club, read science works, and was attracted to Charles Darwin's *Origin of Species* and his concepts about evolution, even though Darwin's ideas conflicted with the fundamental religious view of the seminary, which accepted the biblical story that the world literally was created in seven days. Jane also studied languages, ancient history, literature, philosophy, and other subjects, and took part in required religious services and prayer meetings daily. She excelled in her studies and as a class leader. Yet, she began to rebel, like many of her classmates, against the strict religious doctrine and conservative control that was at the center of this Protestant seminary. She was criticized by the headmistress, for instance, when she and some other writers for the college magazine began to use that forum as a podium to address societal reform issues.

Her college years were instrumental in developing a new outlook regarding the role of women in society; she believed that a woman's life should be more than domesticity and submission to male dominance. Jane Addams wanted to take her place in the world—perhaps as a doctor or scientist, professions that usually did not welcome women.

During her first year at the seminary, she developed a close friendship with another student, Ellen Gates Starr, who left college after her first year to become a teacher in Chicago and later a cofounder of the famous Hull House settlement project in Chicago. Ellen Starr and another friend, Mary Rozet Smith, were the "two abiding loves of [Addams's] life," but most historical references do not say directly that they were in lesbian relationships—only that Addams "considered herself married" to Mary Smith (Diliberto 1999, 17–18).

Addams intended to go to Smith College after completing the Rockford curricula, but soon after returning home to await the start of the new term, she once again became ill. She complained of backaches and a loss of energy. Each day was filled with depression and despair. The condition persisted for months, forcing her to cancel plans to begin study at Smith. When her father died unexpectedly during this same period, Jane accepted her stepmother's suggestion to travel with her to Philadelphia so that Jane could enroll in the only women's medical school in the country. Before long, however, her back pain and the depression returned, and Jane once more was forced to abandon her dream. She had surgery on her back and recuperated under her sister's care for six months. When she was able, she decided to travel to Europe with a friend, hoping the change would lift her spirits.

While in Europe, Addams was taken on a tour of some English slums; there she saw the exploitation of workers and the most negative results of industrialization. When she returned to her Midwestern home, her family expected her to take on the role of the "kindly aunt" who would tend to the sick nieces and nephews and oversee the family's affairs. But her friend, Ellen Starr, intervened.

Although Starr had gone to Chicago to teach school, the two had stayed in close contact through long letters, and Jane had expressed her concern for the victims of the Industrial Revolution, the poorest residents of the city. The friends developed what they referred to as a "scheme" to aid the poor, to do something about the dreadful conditions in which they were forced to live. Ellen convinced Jane that she should move to Chicago so that they could work on their "scheme." Acting against strong family ties and pressure to remain in a life of privilege, Addams followed Starr's advice and the two moved into a boarding house on Chicago's near West Side.

Within a few months in 1889, using the contacts of her church and her position, Addams raised enough money to establish her "settlement," or sanctuary, in the neighborhood where, as she put it, "representatives of nineteen different nationalities swarmed in the ward... [and] swarmed in foulness. The streets were covered inches deep with packed and dirty refuse over broken pavements; the miry alleys smelled like sewers, and the sewers themselves were in hundreds of instances unconnected with the houses or tenements; the stables, of which there were many, were inexpressibly foul; Greeks slaughtered sheep in basements, Italian women and children sorted rags collected from the city dump, in courtyards thick with babies and vermin; bakers made bread in dirty holes under sidewalks, and distributed it to their immigrant neighbors" (Linn 1968, 168).

Addams and her colleagues purchased a mansion built by Charles J. Hull in what had once been an affluent area, but the wealthy had moved away when tenements and factories surrounded their homes. Hull House took its name from the mansion's builder, and Addams and Starr quickly went to work to provide welfare services for the needy population. Programs were created to help feed, house, and tend the sick and to educate children and adults among the impoverished working class and newly arrived Eastern European immigrants. Hull House also commissioned one of the earliest surveys that resulted in a mapping of the slums of Chicago. As a result, Addams received much publicity for her work, which prompted sorely needed donations for Hull House.

Eventually, Hull House became a complex of 13 buildings, offering services that included nursery care, physical education, recreational activities for children and adults, arts-and-crafts workshops, adult education courses, a music school, theater arts workshops and presentations, and a social service center. Yet for all her positive influence, Jane Addams was frequently branded a radical and was attacked for being a peril to society. She was harshly denounced after Peter Kropotkin, a Russian anarchist and scholar, visited Hull House while on a university and civic lecture tour in the United States in 1901. The nation was in a tremendous angst because a man thought to be an anarchist had shot President William McKinley in the abdomen; the president died days later from the wound. People who had any connection with anarchists were investigated, and Addams was condemned in newspaper articles.

Addams also was criticized for championing labor causes such as better working conditions and pay, work days shorter than 14 hours, and the elimination of child labor. She was a mediator in the 1910 Chicago Garment Workers strike and the earlier strike of Pullman sleeping car porters in

1894. And she was a strong advocate for women's right to vote.

Long before the United States entered World War I, Addams was working for peace. She often lectured at college campuses on the topic of peace, and she helped organize the Woman's Peace Party, becoming its first chairwoman in 1915. She also presided over the first congress of women, which formed the basis for what later became known as the Women's International League for Peace and Freedom. League members gathered from a number of nations at The Hague in the Netherlands to protest war and discuss ways that war would be impossible in the future. When the United States declared war in 1917, Addams was vilified in the press—often being called a traitor—and elsewhere for her outspoken pacifism. Even her social work suffered, as many who had formerly sought her advice refused to contact her.

After the war, during the 1920s, when Addams traveled throughout the United States to solicit funds for German mothers and children who had suffered during the fighting, the attacks against her became increasingly abusive. She was denounced as a communist by those who believed there was a huge communist conspiracy operating in the United States. Nevertheless, she became known as one of the most effective peace advocates in the world, for which she received the Nobel Peace Prize in 1931.

Whether she was attacked or praised, Addams continued to write, lecture, and present her views on pacifism and also on improving economic and social conditions. She wrote books, including the best-known *Twenty Years at Hull House*, and numerous articles published in national magazines. She was a role model for thousands of women during her lifetime, even after she died in a Baltimore, Maryland, hospital of cancer on May 21, 1935. Dozens of places—from museums to parks to streets—bear her name as memorials to social justice activism.

See also Goldman, Emma; Strong, Anna Louise

References

Addams, Jane. *Twenty Years at Hull House*. New York: Macmillan Company, 1912 (reprint of 1910 copy published by the Phillips Publishing Company).

Davis, Allen Freeman. *American Heroine: The Life and Legend of Jane Addams*. New York: Oxford University Press, 1973.

Diliberto, Gioia. *A Useful Woman: The Early Life of Jane Addams*. New York: Scribner, 1999.

Linn, James Weber. *Jane Addams: A Biography*. New York: Greenwood Press, 1968.

Meigs, Cornelia. *Jane Addams: Pioneer for Social Justice*. Boston: Little, Brown and Company, 1970.

Sawaya, Francesca. "Domesticity, Cultivation, and Vocation in Jane Addams and Sarah Orne Jewett." *Nineteenth-Century Literature*, March 1994.

Tims, Margaret. *Jane Addams of Hull House, 1860–1935*. New York: Macmillan, 1961.

Al-Arian, Sami (1958–)

"All they [Americans] hear is that Palestinians bomb civilians, but almost never that Israelis kill our children. You tell me, why will no one in America ever talk about the terrorism we [Palestinians] have lived with since 1948?" (Sugg 2005). This rhetorical question by Dr. Sami Al-Arian, a legal U.S. resident, was posed in a 2005 interview. At the time he had been a political prisoner in the United States since 2003.

Sami Amin Al-Arian was born on January 14, 1958, in Kuwait, the son of Palestinian refugees Amin and Laila Al-Arian. The family left Kuwait and moved to Egypt in 1968, and Sami was raised in Cairo. His wife Nahla, who is three years younger, is an American citizen and the daughter of Palestinian refugees as well. Sami and Nahla Al-Arian have five children: eldest son Abdullah, daughters Laila and Leena, son Ali, and the youngest, daughter Lama, who was sent to live with her grandmother in Egypt out of fear that she was too young to cope with the effects on the family of her father's arrest and imprisonment in 2003.

Sami Al-Arian came to the United States as a student in 1975, becoming a legal resident in 1978. In 1985, he received his PhD at North Carolina State University. By 1986, he had started teaching as a professor of computer engineering at the University of South Florida in Tampa. Outside of his teaching duties, Dr. Al-Arian was deeply committed to the plight of Palestinians and outspoken in his support of a Palestinian state and the rights of Muslims, and was their strongest and best-known advocate in the United States. His activities gained him national and international attention, and photos show him meeting with both President Bill Clinton and President George W. Bush, both of whom supported Al-Arian and his efforts.

In 1988, Al-Arian founded a Palestinian advocacy group called the Islamic Committee for Palestine (ICP). According to Eric Boehlert:

> From Day 1, Al-Arian, while never shying away from his militant support for the Palestinians, has denied supporting terrorism or terrorist activities. . . . He has acknowledged that ICP helped raise funds—$20,000 or $30,000 a year—for Palestinian charity organizations, and suggested in a letter to a friend that anyone looking to help Palestinians should send money to Hamas, the radical Islamic resistance group. Hamas, whose members have staged numerous terrorist attacks against Israel, has a political wing that distributes money to Palestinian widows and orphans of men killed in the conflict with Israel. It can certainly be argued that money raised for Hamas, regardless of its intentions, could end up supporting its terrorist activities. But it was only in 1996, after anti-terrorism legislation was passed, that it became a crime to send money to foreign groups classified by the State Department as terrorist organizations, such as Hamas. (Boehlert 2002)

In 2001, the popular *Newsweek* magazine named Al-Arian as the premier civil rights activist in the United States for his efforts to repeal the use of secret evidence in trials. Two years later, Al-Arian was accused of supporting the use of charitable giving to finance terrorism against Israel. Journalists on television's Fox News began repeatedly showing an old videotape of Sami Al-Arian shouting "Death to Israel" at a rally when he was 30 years old in 1988, a statement he has since regretted saying (Boehlert 2002). Led by Bill O'Reilly, several media, including NBC and radio stations in Tampa, called for Dr. Al-Arian's dismissal from teaching at the University of South Florida (USF) in Tampa, even though he had tenure and an impeccable reputation as a caring and extremely competent professor.

Al-Arian was first placed on forced leave by university president Judy Genschaft, despite protests from fellow professors and their professional organizations both locally and nationwide. Though Al-Arian's home and offices were raided by agents of the Federal Bureau of Investigation (FBI) as early as 1995 and his phones had been bugged by intelligence agencies since at least

1994, the terrorist attacks on September 11, 2001, made Al-Arian a more vulnerable target than ever before. Attorney General John Ashcroft made personal attacks on Al-Arian and used the newly passed powers of the Patriot Act to finally arrest the professor. The 2001 Act gave law enforcement agencies increased authority to search telephone, e-mail communications, and medical, financial, and other records to gather foreign intelligence within the United States. Also arrested were friends of Al-Arian: Sameeh Hammoudeh, a student and instructor at USF; Hatim Naji Fariz, manager at a Tampa medical clinic; and Ghassan Zayed Ballut, who worked at a Chicago mall.

Four others were named in the 50-count indictment, including top Islamic Jihad leader Abdullah Ramadan Shallah. According to Ashcroft, these four are at large in Britain, Syria, Lebanon, and the Gaza Strip. If convicted of the federal charges, these individuals would face life in federal prison. The indictment charged the men with seeking funds for a Muslim charitable organization called Palestinian Islamic Jihad, which provided money to terrorists attacking Israel, resulting in deaths. "Palestinian Islamic Jihad is one of the most violent terrorist organizations in the world," said Attorney General Ashcroft at a press conference in 2003. "We will ensure that

Former University of South Florida professor Sami al-Arian makes his way through the media before entering the United States Courthouse in Tampa, Florida, December 12, 2002. He was tried several times for alleged terrorism activities, but was never convicted. (AP Photo/Chris O'Meara)

both terrorists and their financiers meet the same swift, certain justice of the United States of America." The indictment said that Islamic Jihad had received help from Al-Arian and his friends since 1984, that they had drafted final statements of suicide bombers, that they had provided funds to their families after their suicides, and that they had sent press releases taking responsibility for the attacks.

Many Americans assumed that Al-Arian and his friends constituted a terrorist group that had been hiding in plain sight, plotting to kill innocent Israelis. This blatant lie became a crusade led by Media General's newspaper, the *Tampa Tribune*, which published dozens of news stories by reporter Michael Fechter, who presented evidence that "was mostly circumstantial, with guilt by association being his weapon of choice." Other media joined the *Tribune*'s crusade, including Tampa radio stations owned by the media conglomerate Clear Channel Communications, as well as NBC and Fox News Channel, culminating in a five-minute television interview on the *O'Reilly Factor*. Host Bill O'Reilly loudly and vociferously argued with Al-Arian, not allowing him to respond to O'Reilly's distortions and innuendoes (Boehlert 2002).

David Horowitz, once a liberal activist who became a conservative political writer, referred to Al-Arian as Osama (Sami) al-Arian. He declared in his book *Unholy Alliance: Radical Islam and the American Left* (2004) that Al-Arian "was, in fact, the North American head of Palestinian Islamic Jihad, one of the principal terrorist organizations in the Middle East, responsible for suicide bombings that took the lives of more than a hundred people including two Americans, aged 16 and 20, before he was arrested in February 2003." Horowitz also pointed out that when Steve Emerson, a longtime critic of Al-Arian, "began warning the public about al-Arian's terrorist recruitment efforts and his connections to Palestinian Islamic Jihad, he [Emerson] was ferociously attacked for 'Muslim-bashing' and 'McCarthyism' by prominent figures in the political left" (Horowitz 2004, 188, 190).

In the *Weekly Standard*, one of the most conservative publications in the United States, David Tell wrote that Al-Arian is "the world's favorite victim-symbol of neo-McCarthyite political repression in post-9/11 America." During the 1950s, Senator Joseph McCarthy falsely accused many Americans, including members of the U.S. Army, of being communists or communist sympathizers, victimizing hundreds whose careers were destroyed. As proof of Al-Arian's guilt, which the magazine maintained for over a year, Tell cited the federal indictment, then added "he will have a full and fair trial before it arrives—ours being a sweet land of liberty, the professor's loyalists to the contrary notwithstanding." In that same article, Tell related that in the 121-page indictment, the FBI "has been bugging every telephone and fax machine remotely connected to the man for close to a decade." Tell did not comment on the First Amendment violations involved in 10 years of closely monitoring all communications of this man, or the fact that such spying did not result in charges during that decade. Instead, Tell wrote, "they have him dead to rights, covered in blood. Al-Arian denies everything, of course." Clearly, this publication enjoyed the First Amendment protections that allowed it to convict Al-Arian, who Tell called "an undercover assassin" in the court of public opinion, long before his trial acquitted him (Tell 2003).

For many of the media outlets, including the *Tampa Tribune*'s seven years of news stories, the source ultimately was Steve

Emerson, who made a film, *Jihad in America* (1994), that wildly claimed that Islamic terrorists were already in the United States and were organizing attacks internally, a claim that had no basis at that time.

John Sugg, who has interviewed Al-Arian numerous times, stated in a 2005 article that at Al-Arian's trial, federal prosecutor Terry Zitek claimed that the Palestinian Islamic Jihad (PIJ) "wanted Israelis to give up their land from the river to the sea," and if the Israelis balked," Zitek contended, "the PIJ would kill them." Sugg declared that the federal judge, James Moody, "has allowed only testimony backing Zitek's view of what precipitated the trial, the spin from one side in the tragic events in the Middle East. Even a United Nations resolution mentioned in the government's own exhibits was not allowed to be explained in the closing arguments—because the document might provoke sympathy for the Palestinians" (Sugg 2005).

A jury exonerated Al-Arian on December 6, 2005. Nevertheless, he was imprisoned again for civil contempt because he refused to testify before a grand jury investigating an Islamic think tank. This, according to his lawyers, was Al-Arian's right because of an earlier plea agreement with the federal government that all business between the government and Dr. Al-Arian would end "once and for all."

Al-Arian's treatment in prison could hardly be called humane. As he reported in 2007 to a judge:

> I spent fourteen days in the Atlanta penitentiary under 23-hour lockdown, in a roach and rat infested environment. On two occasions, rats shared my diabetic snack. When I was transported from Atlanta to Petersburg (Virginia) and from Petersburg to Alexandria, they allowed me only to wear a t-shirt in subfreezing weather during long walks. In the early morning, the Atlanta guard took my thermal undershirt which I purchased from the prison and threw it in the garbage and when I complained, he threatened to use a lockbox on my handcuffs which would make them extremely uncomfortable. In Petersburg, the guard asked me to take off my clean t-shirt and boxers and gave me dirty and worn out ones. When I complained, he told me to "shut the f up." And when I asked why he was treating me like that, he said "because you're a terrorist." When I further complained to the lieutenant in charge, he shrugged it off and said if I don't like it, I should write a grievance to the Bureau of Prisons. (Cockburn 2007)

In 2008, Dr. Al-Arian was released on bail to await another trial. In September 2009, the federal government filed a motion requesting that federal judge Leonie Brinkeman of the Eastern District of Virginia deny a defense motion to dismiss the criminal contempt charges against Al-Arian. The motion also called on the judge to reverse her decision allowing Al-Arian to present a defense in the event of a trial. This marked the fourth time that the government attempted to prevent the defense from presenting evidence in a trial. The judge had denied all prior motions by prosecutors. A hearing for Al-Arian was scheduled for October 29, 2010, in Alexandria, Virginia, but Judge Brinkeman cancelled the hearing.

After much negative press and consistent attacks by the federal government, Al-Arian has not been convicted of terrorism. In the view of Alexander Cockburn, editor of the liberal *Counterpunch*, Al-Arian is "just one more object lesson to the world of what can happen to a Muslim—a Palestinian—who tried with some success to combat ignorance and prejudice in the Middle Eastern debate and who established his innocence to a jury on the grave charges the government spent millions to sustain.... Dr. Al-Arian has stayed in the ring with his fearsome and vindictive prosecutors" (Cockburn 2008).

Daniel Callaghan

See also Horowitz, David; McCarthy, Joseph

References

Boehlert, Eric. "The Prime-Time Smearing of Sami Al-Arian." *Salon*, January 19, 2002. http://www.salon.com/technology/feature/2002/01/19/bubba/index.html (accessed November 13, 2010).

Cockburn, Alexander. "The Ongoing Persecution of al-Arian." *Counterpunch*, August 2–3, 2008. http://www.counterpunch.org/cockburn08022008.html (accessed November 13, 2010).

Cockburn, Alexander. "The Persecution of Sami Al-Arian." *Counterpunch*, March 3–4, 2007. http://www.counterpunch.org/cockburn03032007.html (accessed November 12, 2010).

Horowitz, David. *Unholy Alliance: Radical Islam and the American Left*. Washington, DC: Regnery Publishing, 2004.

Kennedy, Helen. "Florida Professor in Terror Bust." *New York Daily News*, February 21, 2003. http://www.nydailynews.com/archives/news/2003/02/21/2003-02-21_fla__prof_in_terror_bust_say.html (accessed November 13, 2010)

"Sami Al-Arian." *Nation*, March 22, 2007.

Sugg, John F. "Sami Al-Arian Speaks." *Counterpunch*, November 16, 2005. http://www.counterpunch.org/sugg11162005.html (accessed September 10, 2011).

Tell, David. "Al-Arian Nation." *Weekly Standard*, February 28, 2003. http://www.weeklystandard.com/Content/Public/Articles/000/000/002/306bdecc.asp (accessed November 13, 2010).

Ali, Muhammad (1942–)

"On perhaps his final morning as heavyweight champion, Muhammad Ali was wondering how history would reflect upon him," wrote reporter Edwin Shrake. Earlier in the interview, Ali had stated:

> I've left the sports pages. I've gone onto the front pages. I want to know what is right... I'm being tested by Allah. I'm giving up my title, my wealth, maybe my future. Many great men have been tested for their religious belief. If I pass this test, I'll come out stronger than ever. I've got no jails, no power, no government, but 600 million Muslims are giving me strength... The people know the only way I can lose my title is in the ring. My title goes where I go. But if they won't let me fight, it could cost me $10 million in earnings. Does that sound like I'm serious about my religion? (quoted in Shrake 1967, 19–20)

Muhammad Ali—originally named Cassius Marcellus Clay Jr.—was born on January 17, 1942, in Louisville, Kentucky. His given name was handed down from his father as a nod to the famed abolitionist of the same name. The latter, a prominent antislavery crusader, had lived from 1810 to 1903 and was the son of one of the wealthiest landowners and slaveholders in Kentucky. He worked toward emancipation, both as a Kentucky state representative and as an early member of the Republican Party. Cassius Clay Jr.'s grandfather grew up on the abolitionist's property.

Cassius Jr., along with his only sibling Rudolph (Rudy), was raised by his middle-class parents, Odessa and Cassius Sr., in a modest home. Although his father was a Methodist, the boys were raised in their mother's Baptist faith. Young Cassius showed little academic aptitude. In hindsight, his parents saw him fated to be a boxer (Hornet 1961, 40). One can only wonder what direction his life might have taken had he not crossed paths with Joe Martin and Fred Stoner as he neared his teens. Cassius Clay caught the eye of Martin, a white policeman with a television show, *Tomorrow's Champions*, featuring novice boxers. Cassius started training at the Louisville Columbus Gym and, tutored by African American trainer Stoner, started to acquire the techniques that would set him apart from other boxers. From the start of his career, he exhibited a sense of over-the-top confidence and boastfulness—traits that would become emblematic of his persona both inside and outside of the ring. Time and experience enhanced his natural aptitude for the sport, and his winning record grew exponentially.

He won consecutive Golden Gloves and Amateur Athletic Union titles for his weight class in 1959 and 1960—both by the age of 18. This qualified him to represent the United States at the 1960 Rome Olympics, where he won a gold medal. Cassius returned home, proudly showing off his prize, wearing it everywhere he went. Several sources recall his tale of being refused service in a downtown Louisville five-and-dime store because he was "colored." At the time, he claimed to have become so irate that he threw the medal in a river. The incident at the drugstore would not be the first time—or the last—that Cassius experienced discrimination, as well as disappointment, after achieving a significant professional accomplishment.

Two other events occurring in 1959 and 1960 were important to Cassius for reasons unrelated to boxing, although they would eventually come to have significant impact upon his professional life. In Chicago in 1959, he first heard about Elijah Muhammad and the Nation of Islam (NOI). In April 1960, he registered for the draft, as required by law (Edmonds 1960, 21). "Following mainstream Islamic practice, the Nation called on its practitioners to lead a moral life, free of alcohol and sexual promiscuity, and to be charitable people. In addition to comforting theology and ethic, the Nation worked hard to provide some social welfare assistance to the black community" (Edmonds 1960, 36). Elijah, himself, had been imprisoned during World War II for encouraging resistance to the draft. Cassius gradually became more involved in NOI, spending time with Malcolm X, known for his controversial advocacy of black separatism, among other militant positions.

Heavyweight challenger Muhammad Ali in Miami Beach training for a title bout with champion Joe Frazier in Madison Square Garden, March 4, 1971. (AP/Wide World Photos)

With regard to his boxing career, Cassius decided to turn professional. An 11-member group of millionaires gave him a 50-50 split contract, incredibly lucrative for a beginning boxer. His talent for self-promotion—things like nicknaming himself "The Greatest" and his famous "float like a butterfly, sting like a bee" catchphrase—had paid off. In fact, at the time, he had fought only eight times professionally; each opponent had been picked believing they would either "keel over or succumb to the blind staggers after a few fast rounds with the boy wonder" (Horn 1961, 40).

Cassius did not tone down his rhetoric as his skill level improved. His boastfulness did more than annoy many in "mainstream" white America. In those days, blacks were supposed to know their "place" in society. That meant staying in the background, being seen and not heard—quite the opposite of how Cassius positioned himself. The stature of African American entertainers and athletes and their accomplishments were irrelevant. They were to show gratitude and smile at their audiences, comprised of the very people who denied them basic civil rights.

When Cassius was 22, he was set to fight Sonny Liston, then U.S. heavyweight champion. The bout was almost cancelled when rumors of Cassius's involvement with the Black Muslims and Malcolm X circulated. Despite the controversy, on February 25, 1964, in Miami, Florida, Cassius took Liston's title in just six rounds. The next day, he announced he would be known from that day forward as "Cassius X, the Islamic heavyweight champion of the world," rather than by his "slave name." A month later, a second and final name change was announced: Muhammad Ali. At first, the sports world refused to accept the change. In fact, one of the very few to offer support was a Georgia senator with devious motivation—he was a rabid segregationist, who vehemently opposed racial integration (Edmonds 2006, 53). Ali defended his title a little more than a year later on May 25, 1965, in Lewiston, Maine, again defeating Liston, this time with a first-round knockout punch.

During the time that Ali was establishing himself as the best U.S. boxer, his nation had been evaluating him in other ways. He was initially given a deferment from military service due to his poor literacy skills. Eventually, standards were lowered across the board and Ali's status was reclassified as "1A," meaning that he was fit to serve. Ali showed up in Houston, Texas, for his scheduled induction into the U.S. armed forces on April 28, 1967. He refused his draft orders, declaring himself to be a conscientious objector, stating that, "It's against the teachings of the *Holy Koran*. I'm not trying to dodge the draft. We are not supposed to take part in no wars unless declared by Allah or The Messenger. We don't take part in Christian wars or wars of any unbelievers" (Shrake 1967, 19–20).

Because NOI's doctrine against making war was not accepted as a valid "conscientious objector" claim (even though the group had been determined to be a religion and not a sect), Ali was arrested. As a result, the New York State Athletic Commission revoked Ali's boxing license. Other commissions, including the World Boxing Association, followed suit. He was stripped of his heavyweight title, as well. In June, a jury found Ali guilty under the U.S. Universal Military Training and Service Act. He later said:

> When I was asked to stand up and be sworn into the service, I thought about all the black people who'd been here for 400 years—all the lynching, raping and

killing they'd suffered—and there was an Army fellow my age acting like God and telling me to go to Viet Nam and fight Asians who'd never called me Nigger, had never lynched me, had never put dogs on me—and outside I had millions of black people waiting to see what I was going to do... I couldn't take that step because I knew the war was wrong, it was against my religious beliefs, and I was willing to go to jail for those beliefs. (McCallum 1975, 73)

After his conviction was upheld by the Court of Appeals of the Fifth Circuit, Ali petitioned the U.S. Supreme Court. By the time his case reached the Court's docket, popular support for the Vietnam War had waned. Additionally, Ali had been touring the country, speaking about his beliefs on college campuses, where antiwar sentiment was especially strong. It was not so surprising, therefore, that the Supreme Court unanimously reversed Ali's conviction on June 28, 1971.

While he had been awaiting his case to come before the Supreme Court, Ali had been permitted to regain his boxing license in Georgia in 1970, due to the fact that it did not have a state boxing commission. Later that fall, the New York State Supreme Court favorably ruled that Ali's denial of a boxing license in its state had been unlawful. Legal woes behind him, Ali met Joe Frazier on March 8, 1971, at Madison Square Garden for what was billed as "The Fight of the Century," in an unsuccessful attempt to regain his title. Bragging rights were his again in 1974 when he beat George Foreman (who had since wrested the title from Frazier). Although he announced his retirement in 1979, Ali fought and lost to Larry Holmes a year later. He fought and lost once more, in 1981, before hanging up his gloves for good. Shortly thereafter, Ali was diagnosed with Parkinson's Disease, with his physicians speculating it to be pugilistic Parkinson's syndrome, brought on by repetitive head trauma and only confirmable by autopsy.

Not letting this diagnosis deter him, Ali chose to step up his involvement in Democratic campaigns. He was involved in a variety of diplomatic activities and took up ongoing causes of children and the impoverished, which he supports to this day. In 1997, he helped to establish the Muhammad Ali Parkinson Center (MAPC), at the Barrow Neurological Institute in Phoenix, Arizona.

Muhammad Ali's awards and achievements are legendary and numerous. In addition to his 1960 Olympic gold medal in boxing, he earned six Kentucky and two National Golden Glove titles and was the first three-time world heavyweight champion; 1983 Olympic Hall of Fame Inductee; *Ring Magazine's* Greatest Heavyweight Champion of All Time in 1987; 1990 International Boxing Hall of Fame Inductee; 1992 Jim Thorpe Pro Sports Award Recipient; 1997 Arthur Ashe Award for Courage; 1998–2008 United Nations Messenger of Peace Appointee; *Sports Illustrated's* 1999 Sportsman of the Century; 1999 BBC's Sports Personality of the Century; International Ambassador of Jubilee 2000; Amnesty International Lifetime Achievement Award Recipient; 2001 Service to America Leadership Award Recipient; 2001 National Association of Broadcasters Foundation Recipient; Germany's 2005 Otto Hahn Peace Medal Recipient; and 2005 Presidential Medal of Freedom Recipient.

Among the accolades often used to describe Muhammad Ali, one is conveyed by the acronym GOAT: Greatest of All Time. For many, this shorthanded reference to his boxing career is all they know about this many-faceted man. And yet, a case can be made that he has achieved more outside of the ring than within its ropes. In the decade of the 1960s, he was a larger-than-life influence on fellow blacks. He put a positive spotlight on the Nation of Islam, especially after leader Malcolm X's assassination. Muhammad Ali became a role model for the African American community—a strong, principled, and unyielding symbol of black manhood and masculinity, both self-made and self-determined.

The Muhammad Ali Center in Louisville, Kentucky, celebrates Ali's life and career while dually functioning as a place where the ideals of respect, hope, and understanding can be "championed."

Margaret Gay

See also Malcolm X

References

Ali, Muhammad. *The Greatest: My Own Story*. New York: Ballantine Books, 1979.

Ali, Muhammad, and Hana Yasmeen Ali. *The Soul of a Butterfly: Reflections on Life's Journey*. New York: Simon & Schuster, 2004.

Celebrity Fight Night web site. http://www.celebrityfightnight.org/Default.aspx (accessed March 25, 2011).

Edmonds, Anthony O. *Muhammad Ali: A Biography*. Westport, CT: Greenwood Press, 2006.

Horn, Huston. "Who Made Me—Is Me!" *Sports Illustrated*, September 25, 1961.

McCallum, J. *The Encyclopedia of World Boxing*. Radnor, PA: Chilton Book Co., 1975.

Muhammad Ali Center web site. http://www.alicenter.org (accessed March 25, 2011).

Muhammad Ali Parkinson Center web site. http://www.thebarrow.org.Neurological_Services/Muhammad_Ali_Parkinson_Center/index.htm (accessed March 25, 2011).

Shrake, Edwin. "Taps for the Champ." *Sports Illustrated*, May 8, 1967.

Asner, Ed (1929–)

Ed Asner has been a political activist for years. In his words: "I've dedicated much of my life to promoting peace and justice issues in America" (Asner 2004). He has been an ardent supporter of animal rights and an advocate for free speech. In addition, he has been outspoken in his support for former Black Panther Mumia Abu-Jamal, who many believe was wrongly convicted of killing a Philadelphia police officer in 1981; Asner has protested the death penalty for Abu-Jamal. Asner also has sought a pardon for imprisoned Native American activist Leonard Peltier, whose imprisonment has been surrounded by controversy and debate. Some doubt that Peltier committed the deeds of which he was accused. Others feel that, regardless of his guilt or innocence, Peltier was convicted by an unfair legal system.

In spite of his activism, Ed Asner is known primarily as an award-winning television, movie, and stage actor, and particularly for his TV role as crusty newspaper editor Lou Grant in the situation comedy *The Mary Tyler Moore Show* (1970–1977). During his long acting career, he has been a familiar figure in dozens of television shows, films, and plays and he has given voice to many animated characters on film. His performances have been honored with seven Emmy Awards and five Golden Globe Awards.

Born in a Kansas City, Missouri, hospital on November 15, 1929, he was named Yitzak Edward Asner by his Orthodox Jewish immigrant parents, Morris David Asner and Lizzie Seliger Asner. Ed was the youngest of five children and the first of his family to be born in a hospital. The family, however, lived in the West Bottoms of Kansas City, Kansas. Morris Asner was a junk dealer, and the family's home was an apartment above the business office. Asner's father "could not read or write English; he spoke Yiddish and he could read Hebrew, and Asner was soon enrolled in a Hebrew school at a local synagogue," according to writer Pete Hamill. At the school, the rabbi encouraged the children to act out biblical stories (Hamill 1982, 28–29).

Asner remembers his early years as pleasant, and not until the family moved to a primarily gentile neighborhood did he experience anti-Semitism. He learned to shrug off some of the bigoted jokes and name-calling.

At Wyandotte High School, Asner played on a championship football team and was a sports announcer for the school's radio station. As an announcer, Asner was taking some of his first steps toward an acting career. He also spent many hours in movie theaters, observing actors and no doubt absorbing some of their skills.

After high school graduation, Asner moved to Chicago and enrolled at the University of Chicago. He joined the campus drama group "Tonight at Eight-Thirty," and he appeared as Thomas Beckett in *Murder in the Cathedral*. In 1951, he joined the military, serving in the U.S. Army Signal Corps for two years. He was stationed in Europe and appeared in plays that toured European army camps. After returning to Chicago, he was a member of the Playwrights Theatre Club, and played the title role in a seventeenth-century satire, *Volpone (The Fox)* by Ben Jonson. From Chicago, Asner went to New York City and appeared on stage in the off-Broadway production of *Threepenny Opera* and acted in Shakespeare festivals.

In 1959, Asner married actress Nancy Lou Sykes, with whom he had three children. The couple divorced in 1988. Asner then married Cindy Gilmore, though they legally separated in 2007 and divorced in 2009.

By the 1960s, Asner and his family were in Hollywood, California, and he was acting in the television series *Slattery's People*. Dozens of acting roles followed, including his long-running performance of Lou Grant in the *Mary Tyler Moore Show*. At the end of that series, Asner's own show, *Lou Grant*, began, with Asner playing the role of a fictional crusading editor of the *Los Angeles Tribune*. The show ran from 1977 to 1982 and dealt with numerous social and political issues, albeit in a fictional format.

Asner's political activism began in earnest in the real world when members of the Screen Actors Guild (SAG) went on strike in 1980. Asner was a vocal supporter of the actors, which helped him win the presidency of the guild in 1981. He served until 1985.

Beyond his SAG involvement, however, Asner was becoming more outspoken about other issues. He was avid in his opposition to the policies of President Ronald Reagan's administration (1981–1989), such as the U.S. military involvement in El Salvador's civil war. The United States backed El Salvador's military government, which was fighting rebel forces. Asner, using his popularity as Lou Grant, was a spokesperson for a fund-raising organization that supported the rebels. That angered some SAG members, who charged that Asner was using his actor role to push his own political agenda. The repercussions that followed were disastrous for Asner and his show. Conservatives attacked. "It was more like a gangland slaying than the work of a lone assassin," wrote Mark Dowie and David Talbot in *Mother Jones*. The writers quoted *Lou Grant* producer Allan Burns, who noted that the attacks on Asner were "swift, continuous, and excessive," and added: "I've never seen anybody transformed so quickly from being everyone's favorite uncle to a communist swine" (Dowie and Talbot 1982, 6).

In 1982, CBS cancelled *Lou Grant*, in spite of the fact that the show had received much acclaim, having won a Peabody Award in 1978 and Emmy Awards in 1979 and 1980. Asner and his supporters maintain that the cancellation was retribution for Asner's liberal political beliefs and actions. Yet that has not stopped the actor, who went on to appear in dozens of other TV productions. These include his role in 1984 as Sam Waltman on the ABC sitcom *Off the Rack*; the leading role of Joe Danzig on the 1987 NBC drama series *The Bronx Zoo*; a role in a revival of *Born Yesterday* in 1989; a role as Guy Bannister in Oliver Stone's *JFK* (1991); and in 1998 Asner costarred with Tom Selleck in the CBS comedy *The Closer*. For the rest of the 1990s and the 2000s, Asner has played roles in other movie and television productions, some of them as "voice-over"—providing the voice for animated characters, including the 2009 critically acclaimed and popular movie *Up*.

Asner's political stance has not changed over the years. He has remained as liberal as ever and is still one of the most controversial actors in Hollywood. He is a member of the Democratic Socialists of America (DSA), which states on its web site "We are activists committed not only to extending political democracy but to demanding democratic empowerment in the economy, in gender relations, and in culture. Democracy is not simply one of our political values but our means of restructuring society. Our vision is of a society in which people have a real voice in the choices and relationships that affect the entirety of our lives." In Asner's view, socialism "means a thing that will curb the excesses of capitalism: the increasing wealth of the rich and decreasing wealth of the poor.... For me, solidarity, civil liberty, and social justice can all be summed up with three simple letters—DSA" (Discoverthenetwork.org). The DSA follows in the footsteps of the socialist leader Eugene Debs (1855–1926) who founded the Socialist Party of America. Asner has received the Eugene Debs Award for his social justice efforts.

To support liberal causes, Asner has contributed to such organizations as Democracy for America, Moveon.org, and Progressive America. He helped provide funds for Michael Moore's first documentary, *Roger and Me* (1989), a film in which Moore chastises General Motors for its massive downsizing, which directly led to the economic and social deterioration of Flint, Michigan. Asner also is an adviser for the Rosenberg Fund for Children, founded by the two sons of Ethel and Julius Rosenberg who were convicted of conspiracy to commit espionage and executed in 1953. The fund provides aid to U.S. children whose parents are targeted because of their or their parents' progressive activities.

Asner was severely critical of President George W. Bush and his administration and adamantly opposed the Iraq War. After the terrorist attacks on the United States on September 11, 2001, Asner accused the Bush administration of using the attacks to justify endless war. He also has supported the 9-11 Visibility Project, which alleges that the U.S. government knew the terrorist attacks were coming and yet did nothing to stop them. The organization is pressing for a complete investigation of what the U.S. government knew before the attacks. In an open letter in 2004 to peace and justice activists, Asner wrote in part:

> There are many disturbing issues around 9-11 that have yet to be examined in any meaningful way by our media, Congress, and even by the 9-11 Commission. These include accountability for the massive breakdown of air defense and plane intercept procedures.... This breakdown and astounding unpreparedness by U.S. domestic defense agencies is puzzling to say the least, given the detailed reports our government had of the coming attacks, that were bizarrely suppressed by key officials.... I fear that if the underlying issues of 9-11 truth are not demanded, that Iraq may be but a flame on an ocean of gasoline that may be used to ignite war after war after war. We cannot, as a peace & justice movement only address the flames. We must look at the fuel being used to justify the flames of war and repression at home and abroad. We must look deeply at the events leading up to, on and since 9-11. We must demand full 9-11 truth. (Asner 2004)

As Asner continues with his dissident messages, he also carries on with his acting. In 2011, he appeared in various movies and television shows, including the TV comedies *Working Class* and *The Cleveland Show* (as the narrator).

Throughout the years, Asner has received numerous awards for his activities on behalf of social justice. To name a few, along with the Eugene Debs Award, he has received the Worker's Rights Committee Award from the American Civil Liberties Union, the Anne Frank Human Rights Award, the Organized Labor Publications Humanitarian Award, and the National Emergency Civil Liberties Award.

See also Abu-Jamal, Mumia; Debs, Eugene V.; Moore, Michael; Peltier, Leonard; Rosenberg, Ethel, and Rosenberg, Julius

References

Asner, Ed. "A Letter to the Peace and Justice Movement from Ed Asner." *9-11 Visibility Project*, April 26, 2004. http://septembereleventh.org/alerts/asner.php (cited April 8, 2011).

Asner, Ed, and Burt Hall. *Misuse of Power: How the Far Right Gained and Misuses Power.* Mahomet, IL: Mayhaven Publishing, 2005.

Daniel, Douglass K. *Lou Grant: The Making of TV's Top Newspaper Drama.* Syracuse, NY: Syracuse University Press, 1996.

Dowie, Mark, and David Talbot. "Asner: Too Hot for Medium Cool." *Mother Jones*, August 1982.

"Ed Asner." n.d. http://www.discoverthenetworks.org/printindividualProfile.asp?indid=1941 (accessed April 11, 2011).

Hamill, Pete. "What Does Lou Grant Know about El Salvador?" *New York Magazine*, March 15, 1982.

Ayers, William (1944–)

In October 1969, a newly formed group of leftist radicals known as Weatherman (often called the Weathermen) staged its first public spectacle. The organizers dubbed it the Days of Rage, and it was conceived as a provocative demonstration to protest the trial of the Chicago Seven then taking place in Judge Julius Hoffman's court. The trial was the big news of the day in the Chicago of Mayor Richard J. Daley. A police assault against scores of antiwar demonstrators at the Democratic National Convention had taken place the year before near the lakefront. More radicalized elements of the growing national student movement were convinced that a direct confrontation with the city would make a strong point for their cause. And they were willing to cross a line into violent behavior to make their case with great exclamation points. In Chicago, the plan for the 500 Weathermen who convened there was to attack police officers as well as civilians to make the point: no one is safe in a culture that thrives on brutality.

Spawned from leadership elements of the 10-year-old Students for a Democratic Society (SDS), Weatherman (officially the Weather Underground Organization, or WUO) formed for the purpose of bringing more direct action to the causes of antiwar activism and government resistance. The SDS had a roster of almost 80,000 members across the United States, but it began to fade away after much of its leadership left to pursue the tactics of confrontation and lawlessness. This very small subset of white, college-educated intellectuals included William Ayers, Bernardine Dohrn, and Mark Rudd. They, and a few others, had become convinced that the country had fallen into the brutality of a near-fascist state; and that their violent reaction was not only justified, but an absolute necessity if they were to stay authentic and consistent in their beliefs. Like many of their generation, the choices one needed to make in pursuit of a moral personal life seemed wildly inconsistent with the brutal policies and actions of the U.S. government.

Bill Ayers had been moved by the images he had seen emerging from the Vietnam conflict when he was going to college at the University of Michigan. Like many of his peers at the time, he saw the newsreel photos of young people being maimed and killed in the name of democracy. As he notes in his memoir *Fugitive Day* (2001), he could especially remember seeing the disturbing image of "a slim peasant boy, his torso pocked with tiny razor cuts from knees to shoulders, a thousand little rivulets of blood sucking his life out of him." And when the moment came at the teach-in against the Vietnam War in Ann Arbor, Michigan, in 1965 when the SDS president of that time, Paul Potter, asked the question, "How will you live your life so that it doesn't make a mockery of your values?" Ayers knew that he could not choose to stand idly by. "To stand still was to choose indifference. Indifference was the opposite of moral" (Ayers 2001, 61).

The Weatherman's conclusion was to take action, hard and fast. Very soon they had declared "war on Amerikkka." The organization consistently spelled America with the three k's to indicate their contempt for the policies and actions that seemed to be rooted in racist ideology.

William Ayers was born and raised in the middle-class Chicago suburb of Glen Ellyn, Illinois, the middle child of five brothers and sisters. His parents are Mary Andrew and Thomas G. Ayers. His father served as the chairman of the board and CEO of Commonwealth Edison, the regional Illinois power company, from 1973 to 1980. He was also honored and memorialized when Thomas G. Ayers College of Commerce and Industry was named for him. William attended public school until his last two years of high school, when he transferred to the preparatory academy, Lake Forest Academy.

Throughout his childhood and up until the Vietnam era, there is little in Bill Ayers's history to suggest that he would become a radical bomb-maker and provocateur, nor a man who would become a fugitive from prosecution for almost a decade. He has described his early upbringing as "a golden childhood." But by the time he left college in 1968, he possessed a total commitment to an ethical and moral truth that he believed had the power to create change. In an interactive online conference on *The Well* in 2003, Ayers tried to explain the radicalizing pressures that caused such a dramatic shift in his thinking about life:

> I don't think I had or have an obsession with violent change... The real problem with most of the discussion about violence is that the powerful, the rulers, have what appears to be a monopoly on violence and they use it not just occasionally, but daily, constantly. And moreover, violence is built into the structures and the culture that we live in. It is invisible to us and yet if you stop and take a look around you will see that violence is at the heart of so many social relationships including occupier/occupied, police/community, worker/boss, school/children, men/women, or even just the toys we market for our kids, the entertainment we consume and on and on. (Ayers 2003)

In the 1960s and 1970s, the obvious violence in the news was coming from the conflict in Vietnam or in the inner-city ghettos where African Americans were beginning to strike back at an oppressive economic, cultural, and political establishment. The radicalized Weatherman, under the leadership of participants like Ayers, adopted the tactics of Black Power and armed itself against the enemy state. In Ayers's group, bombs became the preferred weapon. And in the late 1960s and during the 1970s, they targeted significant federal institutions and high-profile sites around the United States.

Their first action, Days of Rage, was intended to incite mass demonstrations and a violent uprising among the people of Chicago. They chose their opening target carefully: the statue memorializing the policemen killed in the days of the anarchist Haymarket Labor Riots of 1886. (The City of Chicago restored the statue only to have it blown up once again in 1970 by the Weatherman group.) Two days later, riots broke out in various parts of the city, causing a substantial amount of property damage. Over the period of October 8–11, 1969, the authorities in Chicago arrested almost 300 people associated with the Weatherman. Most would not appear for their arraignments and became long-term fugitives.

By 1973, the Weatherman had changed its name to the Weather Underground Organization (WUO), and in 1974, Ayers along with others in the group wrote and distributed the WUO manifesto known as *Prairie Fire*. The tract is an unapologetic political and social manifesto full of the strident language of revolution. Excerpts from the preface make it clear what Ayers and his coauthors had in mind:

> PRAIRIE FIRE is written to communist-minded people, independent organizers and anti-imperialists; those who carry the traditions and lessons of the struggles of the last decade, those who join in the struggles of today.
>
> PRAIRIE FIRE is written to all sisters and brothers who are engaged in armed struggle against the enemy. It is written as an argument against those who oppose action and hold back the struggle.
>
> PRAIRIE FIRE is based on a belief that the duty of a revolutionary is to make the revolution. This is not an abstraction. It means that revolutionaries must make a profound commitment to the future of humanity, apply our limited knowledge and experience to understand an ever-changing situation, organize the masses of people and build the fight. It means that struggle and risk and hard work and

William Ayers accompanies Bernardine Dohrn to the Criminal Courts Building in Chicago where she surrendered to authorities, ending her 11-year odyssey through the radical underground, December 3, 1980. (AP Photo/Charles Knoblock)

adversity will become a way of life, that the only certainty will be constant change, that the only possibilities are victory or death. (Dohrn 1974, preface)

The book's dedication page featured the names of scores of revolutionaries and radicals including Sirhan Sirhan, the convicted assassin of U.S. senator Robert Kennedy. The "political statement," as it was called, also listed two dozen actions that the WUO had participated in since 1969, such as the bombings of Chicago police cars after the killing of Black Panther Fred Hampton, New York City Police headquarters, and the Long Island City Courthouse, in Queens.

Bombings also took place in New York City, San Francisco and Sacramento, California, the U.S. State Department, the Capitol building, and the Pentagon. All of the bombings were related to specific events, such as the U.S. bombing of Laos.

Ayers has always maintained that the WUO was not a terrorist organization and its actions were perpetrated to educate Americans as to the brutal nature of their government. Despite the revolutionary rhetoric of the leaders, no one was ever killed in any of the WUO attacks. However, an accident in New York City in 1970 did result in the loss of life of three WUO operatives who were very close to Ayers. Diana Oughton (his girlfriend), Ted

Gold, Terry Robbins, Cathy Wilkerson, and Kathy Boudin were living together in a Greenwich Village townhouse. They were planning to take violent action against noncommissioned officers at a dance planned in the coming days at Fort Dix in New Jersey. In this case, the goal did seem to be to kill or maim as many of the military personnel as possible. The group was building a nail bomb (an anti-personnel device) on the night of March 6 and it accidentally ignited. The resulting explosion took the lives of Oughton, Gold, and Robbins.

The incident devastated Ayers, as he relates in his book, *Fugitive Days*. It was the incident in Greenwich Village that led Bill Ayers and Bernardine Dohrn to go underground. The couple soon married, in one of their scores of hideouts throughout the country. Dohrn had been indicted and charged with resisting arrest and assaulting a police officer during the Days of Rage event, and Ayers was wanted for questioning about the explosion in New York City. Federal charges included crossing state lines to incite a riot, among others. Dohrn would end up on the FBI's Ten Most Wanted List and be described as the Most Dangerous Woman in America. That designation ended in 1974 when federal charges had to be dropped because of prosecutorial misconduct (tactics of the FBI's counterintelligence program, or COINTELPRO, that were clearly intended to foster violence had come to light), but Dohrn still had Illinois charges to face, and she was reticent to reveal herself until 1980. That was when their second child was born, and Ayers and Dohrn decided to resurface. Dohrn turned herself in, and she received probation and a fine of $1,500.

The couple made a decision to go back to academia. Ayers earned degrees from the Bank Street College of Education, Bennington College, and Teachers College, Columbia University. He had a substantive career in the Department of Education at the University of Illinois at Chicago, from which he is now retired as a Distinguished Professor of Education and Senior University Scholar. During his tenure, he also founded the Small Schools Workshop and the Center for Youth and Society. Ayers has contributed numerous works on social justice and progressive political issues, such as *Education: An American Problem* (1968), *The Good Preschool Teacher: Six Teachers Reflect on Their Lives* (1989), *A Kind and Just Parent: The Children of Juvenile Court* (1997).

In 1997 Chicago awarded him its Citizen of the Year award for his work on Mayor Richard M. Daley's effort to reform local schools.

Throughout his post-fugitive career, Ayers has not been immune from personal attacks that take him to task for his radical youth. The most famous incident had national implications when U.S. senator John McCain campaigned for president in 2008. McCain began to publicize the fact that Bill Ayers and Democratic candidate Barack Obama were Chicago neighbors who had met and worked on parallel community issues. The accusation that Obama was "palling around with terrorists" became an effective battle cry for the conservative cause that attempted to tar the more liberal Obama with Ayers's more radical political views.

Martin K. Gay

See also Hampton, Fred; Rudd, Mark

References

Ayers, William. *Fugitive Days: A Memoir*. Boston: Beacon Press, 2001.

Ayers, William. *Teaching toward Freedom: Moral Commitment and Ethical Action in the Classroom*. Boston: Beacon Press, 2004.

Ayers, William C., Therese Quinn, and David Stovall, eds. *Handbook of Social Justice in Education*. New York: Routledge, 2009.

Dohrn, Bernardine, Jeff Jones, Billy Ayers, and Celia Sojourn. *Prairie Fire: The Politics of Revolutionary Anti-Imperialism*. Weather Underground Organization, 1974.

Dohrn, Bernardine, Bill Ayers, and Jeff Jones. *Sing a Battle Song: The Revolutionary Poetry, Statements, and Communiqués of the Weather Underground 1970–1974*. New York: Seven Stories Press, 2006.

B

Balch, Emily Greene (1867–1961)

In the American public consciousness, seldom is Emily Greene Balch associated with settlement houses, social reform, women suffrage, and the peace movement. But Balch, from a "proper" Boston, Massachusetts, family, was a social reformer and staunch antiwar campaigner whose activism has been overshadowed by crusaders such as Jane Addams, Anna Louise Strong, and Dorothy Day. Balch's pacifist stand before and during World War I brought her public ridicule and abuse—and the loss of her teaching position as professor of economics at Wellesley College.

Emily was born on January 8, 1867, in Jamaica Plain, then a small village near Boston, Massachusetts. She was the second child in a family of six children of Francis Balch, an attorney, and Ellen Noyes Balch; Francis and Ellen were cousins. The upper middle-class Balch household included servants, nurses, and a hired man. For a time, Francis Balch was a clerk for U.S. senator Charles Sumner, a leading abolitionist, and Francis developed his advocacy for justice through the influence of the senator.

Emily's father had a great influence on her life, particularly in his sense of tolerance, love of reading, and education. Emily's mother was an avid storyteller and helped instill in Emily a love for literature and poetry. According to biographer Kristen Gwinn, Emily's mother also promoted "vigorous outdoor activities" and especially winter "ice-skating on Jamaica Pond. Emily fondly remembered that she and her siblings devoted most of their early years playing outdoors" (Gwinn 2010, 6). When Ellen was a teenager, her mother died during childbirth; the infant also died.

Although Emily was raised as a Unitarian, she and her siblings did not attend Sunday school. However, they did participate in a Bible history class conducted by a neighbor who had studied at Harvard. When Emily was 10 years old, a new minister came to her church and asked the congregation "to enlist in the service of goodness whatever its cost," Emily recalled. She accepted this pledge and was determined to honor it, which set the stage for her life of activism (Massachusetts Foundation for the Humanities).

Emily received her early education at private schools, and when she was 13 years old, she attended Miss Ireland's, a girls' school. Her parents encouraged her to go to college, which was unusual for women at the time. She enrolled at a Quaker school, Bryn Mawr College, in 1886. The school was founded only a year before and "almost from its beginnings it bore the imprint of M. Carey Thomas.... Miss Thomas became, at the astonishingly early age of twenty-six, dean of the college which had not yet opened its doors but whose requirements she insisted be drastically raised.... She succeeded so well that for decades, entrance to, let alone graduation from, Bryn Mawr was a mark of intellectual distinction" (Flexner 1974, 234).

Balch graduated from Bryn Mawr in 1889 with a fellowship to study economics in

Balch, Emily Greene (1867–1961)

France. During her year of study, she lived with a French family in Paris and wrote *Public Assistance of the Poor in France* (1893). When she returned to the United States, she took courses at Harvard and the University of Chicago, and then spent a year in Berlin from 1895 to 1896 studying economics. While in Europe she also attended the 1896 International Social Workers' and Trade Union Congress in London and saw firsthand the deplorable conditions of workers and the degrading poverty of the slums.

While completing her formal education, Emily began an apprenticeship in the fledgling field of social work that was being undertaken by the Boston Children's' Aid Society. She worked in a home for poor and neglected children and delinquents. Then in 1892, she attended the Summer School of Applied Ethics at Plymouth, Massachusetts, where she met a number of stimulating lecturers, among them Jane Addams of Hull House fame, who later became a close associate. The summer gathering focused on the settlement movement and social democracy through humanitarian efforts. Balch and others at the gathering hoped to see a time when class barriers would be eliminated between workers and the upper classes.

Balch, with a group from the summer school, founded Denison House, Boston's first settlement, which was modeled after Hull House in Chicago. At Denison, Emily was exposed to the realities of the labor movement and the struggle for decent wages and working conditions through trade unionism. She organized numerous women from affluent homes to work for labor reforms.

In 1897, Balch began her teaching career in economics at Wellesley, which was among the first colleges to offer study in socialism and the labor movement. Later, at the request of college trustees, she established a course in

Emily Greene Balch, a leader of the pacifist movement, won the Nobel Peace Prize in 1946. (Library of Congress)

sociology, stressing social responsibility and direct action. By 1913, she was professor of economics and sociology at Wellesley and by all accounts was an excellent educator, sharing many of her personal experiences with students.

When war broke out in Europe in 1914, Balch joined several groups working for peace and became part of the Woman's Peace Party cofounded in 1915 by Jane Addams and Carrie Chapman Catt, leader of the American suffrage movement. The congress met at The Hague in the Netherlands. After the United States declared war on Germany in 1917, Balch asked the Wellesley trustees to grant her an extended leave so that the college would not be embarrassed by her activities campaigning for peace. At the time, many well-known pacifists renounced their antiwar stance, but opponents such as Balch joined one of the first religious pacifist groups called the

Fellowship of Reconciliation. She marched, wrote letters, and lectured on behalf of peace. She also spoke out against war profiteering and in favor of workers' rights. All of this was in direct opposition to U.S. mainstream opinion, since the majority of Americans believed that views about social justice were akin to communist ideas in Russia. As a result, the Wellesley trustees decided in 1918 not to renew Balch's contract. So she took an editorial job with the *Nation*, a liberal weekly. She also wrote a book *Approaches to the Great Settlement* (1918) about the aftermath of World War I. Her previous published work included *Public Assistance of the Poor in France* (1893); *Our Slavic Fellow Citizens* (1910); and *The Women at The Hague: The International Congress of Women*, coauthored with Jane Addams and Alice Hamilton (1916).

After the Armistice was signed in 1919, Balch joined the second women's peace congress at Zurich, Switzerland, and was elected to serve as international secretary-treasurer of what then became the Women's International League for Peace and Freedom, or the WILPF. The international office was established at Geneva, and Balch worked for the organization over the next 30 years, traveling frequently to garner support for the league's causes. She joined the Religious Society of Friends (Quakers) in 1920.

Quakers are among the historic peace churches that include the Church of the Brethren and the Mennonite churches. All believe that peace is an essential part of the gospel teachings, and they have rejected the use of force and violence, which of course means they are against war. Balch applied for membership "when she was in Geneva. ... What attracted her to Friends was not only 'their testimony against war, their creedless faith, nor their openness to suggestions for far-reaching social reform,' It was 'the dynamic force of the active love through which their religion was expressing itself in multifarious ways, both during and after the war.' When she returned to live in Wellesley in her last years, she transferred her membership to Cambridge (Massachusetts) Meeting," wrote Irwin Abrams (1996). Balch remained a Quaker for the rest of her life.

In 1930, President Herbert Hoover appointed a commission to investigate conditions in Haiti, which the United States had occupied since 1915 in order to protect U.S. corporations that were threatened by military takeover of the Haitian government. Balch was part of the investigative group, and wrote much of the group's final report for the president.

In 1935, Wellesley College had a change of heart about Balch and asked that she be the guest speaker on Armistice Day (now known as Veterans Day). Originally the day was set aside to remember the sacrifices of men and women during World War I, but it now encompasses remembrance for veterans of all U.S. wars.

During the late 1930s, as World War II began in Europe, Balch publicly urged the United States to welcome refugees from Nazi Germany and personally helped dozens of refugees relocate in the United States. When the United States entered World War II, Balch struggled with her antiwar beliefs. She reluctantly began to change her strict pacifist stance, and came to believe that German dictator and Nazi leader Adolf "Hitler and his ideology presented a great and immediate threat to civilization.... In her view, because the Allied nations had failed to prevent the war, they needed to defeat Hitler." Yet, Balch did not really favor war—she believed that peace could be negotiated. According to biographer Gwinn, "She developed her own mixed position that partially supported the war while protesting it. She refused to buy war bonds, but she did contribute money to 'community war-funds' because they apportioned most of their proceeds to 'wholly peaceful social aid'" (Gwinn 2010, 164–65).

In 1946, Balch along with John R. Mott received the Nobel Peace Prize. In her acceptance speech, which was read for her because she could not attend in person due to illness, she said:

> I am happy in thinking that not I myself but the Women's International League for Peace and Freedom, with which I am identified, is the true recipient. Hoping, as I do, that this internationally organized body of women has ahead of it a great opportunity for usefulness in educating people everywhere toward the world-mindedness on which peace must be based with other people, I am hoping that 1946 will mark a turning point in the age-old effort to rid the world of war, to national disarmament, to renunciation of power politics, and to development of international trusteeship, not only for dependent peoples, but for regions and interests which are essentially supranational in character, such as the Polar regions and the main waterways of the world, including the Mediterranean and all the great strategic canals, among them the Panama. (Balch 1946)

Balch donated most of her share of the peace prize to the WILPF, and even though her health was failing, she maintained her association with the organization. In addition, she was cochair of a committee that arranged a celebration in 1960 to honor Jane Addams's birth date, 100 years earlier.

Though Emily Balch remained a pacifist for the rest of her life, she continued to struggle with the concept of a "righteous" war and to work for the means to create a more rational and peaceful world. She also was committed to internationalism and considered herself a citizen of the world.

In 1961, Balch's health deteriorated, and she became ill with pneumonia. She died at the Mt. Vernon Nursing Home in Cambridge, Massachusetts, on January 9, 1961. During her lifetime, she may have been overshadowed by others, but as her biographer Gwinn noted "Emily Greene Balch...helped to elevate the world in which she lived" (Gwinn 2010, 178).

See also Addams, Jane; Catt, Carrie Chapman; Day, Dorothy; Strong, Anna Louise

References

Abrams, Irwin. "Emily Greene Balch: The First Quaker Nobel Peace Prize Winner." *Friends Journal*, December 1996. http://www.irwinabrams.com/articles/balch.html (accessed April 25, 2011).

Balch, Emily. "Emily Greene Balch—Acceptance Speech." Nobelprize.org, 1946. http://nobelprize.org/nobel_prizes/peace/laureates/1946/balch-acceptance.html (accessed April 25, 2011).

Balch, Emily Greene. *Beyond Nationalism: The Social Thought of Emily Greene Balch*. New York: Twayne Publishers, 1972.

Flexner, Eleanor. *Century of Struggle: The Woman's Rights Movement in the United States*. New York: Atheneum, 1974.

Gwinn, Kristen E. *Emily Greene Balch: The Long Road to Internationalism*. Urbana and Chicago: University of Illinois Press, 2010.

Massachusetts Foundation for the Humanities. "Emily Greene Balch Born January 8, 1867." MassMoments.org. http://www.massmoments.org/moment.cfm?mid=2 (accessed April 25, 2011).

Randall, John Herman. *Emily Greene Balch of New England: Citizen of the World.* Washington, DC: Women's International League for Peace and Freedom, 1946.

Randall, Mercedes M. *Improper Bostonian: Emily Green Balch.* New York: Twayne Publishers, 1964.

Baldwin, James (1924–1987)

"I was thirteen and was crossing Fifth Avenue on my way to the Forty-second street library, and the cop in the middle of the street muttered as I passed him, 'Why don't you niggers stay uptown where you belong?' When I was ten... two policemen amused themselves with me, by frisking me, making comic (and terrifying) speculations concerning my ancestry and probable sexual prowess, and for good measure leaving me flat on my back in one of Harlem's empty lots" (Baldwin 1963, 32). This account of James Baldwin's life growing up in New York City's Harlem appears in *The Fire Next Time*, one of his many acclaimed literary works. Baldwin, a brilliant, complex, and controversial individual, used his talent to write bluntly not only about the racism that he experienced but also about the love he struggled to find. During the 1960s, he became one of the most eloquent spokespeople for African American civil rights.

James Arthur Baldwin was born in Harlem on August 2, 1924, to a single mother, Emma Burdis Jones, who later married David Baldwin, a Pentecostal preacher and factory worker. The couple eventually had eight other children whose care was often James's responsibility, especially when his mother was overwhelmed with household chores. She also did domestic work for affluent whites, since David Baldwin seldom earned enough to support his family.

While growing up, James had little regard for his stepfather, who frequently held "Jimmy" in contempt, calling him ugly and belittling his intelligence. James began to hate the man he thought of as his biological father—he did not learn until his teenage years that he was illegitimate—but he wanted David Baldwin's approval. That would not be forthcoming since the patriarch was a strict disciplinarian and expected obedience to biblical commandments. He had no patience with Jimmy's school studies. He hated white people and berated Jimmy for having white friends. He did not want Jimmy to go to movies and plays or read novels—all sinful activities in David Baldwin's view.

During his school years, James Baldwin was shy. He was physically small and rather

James Baldwin, author of the novel *Go Tell It on the Mountain* (1953), wrote about the effects of race, religion, and sexuality on personal identity. (AP/Wide World Photos)

frail, so was a target for school bullies, unscrupulous neighbors, and anyone who thought he was an easy prey for sex. He often took refuge in a church, and at school, teachers recognized his exceptional intelligence and writing abilities. He was an excellent student and book lover, avidly reading borrowed public library books or the Bible whenever possible.

His Bible reading, his father's sermons, and his faithful attendance at a Pentecostal store-front church led James to an emotional conversion that he believed saved him from the wickedness of the Harlem streets that "were filled with junkies, winos, pimps, pickpockets, girls in shiny dresses.... At the time, he saw the evil surrounding him not as an emanation of injustice, as he did later, but as a warning. Life posed a choice between salvation and damnation" (Campbell 1991, 11).

At 14 years of age, James became an ordained minister and soon was a popular preacher, more in demand than his stepfather. For three years he preached, and when he was not at the pulpit, he was preparing sermons or completing school assignments.

While at Frederick Douglass Junior High School, Baldwin was the editor of the school's newspaper, and in high school he wrote several short stories with religious themes that were published in the DeWitt Clinton High School newspaper, the *Magpie*. By 1941, Baldwin was ready to abandon his ministry, realizing that after service, parishioners shed their Christianity "at the church door. When we were told to love everybody, I thought that meant *everybody*. But no. It applied only to those who believed as we did, and it did not apply to white people at all" (Baldwin 1963, 58). He left the church, disillusioned because of the hypocrisy he saw in the membership and also in himself—a performer who did not believe his own sermons.

After graduation from DeWitt Clinton in 1942, Baldwin hoped to attend college, but because of his family's poverty, that was not possible. His stepfather's mental health had steadily deteriorated, and he had to be institutionalized. The elder Baldwin died in 1943, and shortly after his death, Emma Baldwin gave birth to their ninth child.

James Baldwin at age 19 was now responsible for his family. He held several factory jobs for a time to help support his brothers and sisters. The United States was involved in World War II, and Baldwin found a defense-related job in New Jersey, laying track for a railroad depot. He hated the job and the discrimination against him because of the color of his skin. At the time, most whites would not sell property or rent apartments to blacks or serve them in restaurants. Blacks were barred from bowling alleys and bars. Yet, Baldwin would go into places where he knew he would not be served and force a confrontation. During one such instance at a restaurant, he was so enraged he wanted to strangle the waitress who uttered the familiar words: "We don't serve Negroes here."

He went through periods of rage, ready to react with violence and wondering if he would be overcome with hatred as his stepfather had been. As he wrote years later: "[T]here is, I should think, no Negro living in America who has not felt briefly and for long periods with anguish sharp or dull, in varying degrees or to varying effect, simple, naked and unanswerable hatred; who has not wanted to smash any white face he may encounter in a day, to violate, out of motives of the cruelest vengeance, their women, to break the bodies of all white people and bring them low, as low as that dust into which he himself has been and is being trampled" (Baldwin 1955, 38).

Baldwin quit his defense job, drifted about, and began drinking and brooding. He decided he could no longer help his family and had to save himself. In 1944, he moved to Greenwich Village, where he found odd jobs. He also began writing his first novel that evolved with the encouragement of Richard Wright, author of the award-winning novel *Native Son* (1940). Wright's book was a best seller and made him the wealthiest black writer in the United States at the time. Wright read some of Baldwin's semiautobiographical novel and helped Baldwin obtain a grant so that he could continue working on the book, which went through many name changes.

During his four years in Greenwich Village, Baldwin lived a bohemian lifestyle, gathering with artistic friends for all-night carousing and exploring sexual relationships—both homosexual and heterosexual. He came close to marrying an older woman, but realized that he was mainly attracted to men. Coming to terms with his sexuality was the basis for a few of his writings. He fell in love with one of his artist friends, Eugene Worth, but the man was heterosexual and Baldwin did not approach him for an intimate relationship. His friend committed suicide in 1946, jumping off the Brooklyn Bridge, and Baldwin himself was near that point several times.

In 1948, Baldwin decided to go to Paris, France, where he hoped to find the freedom he needed to write. Once again he met with Richard Wright, who had moved to Paris years earlier. Wright introduced Baldwin to other expatriates, primarily black writers and artists, in bohemia. He also met Lucien Happersberger, a white teenager from Switzerland who left home without his parents' permission to search for an exciting life in Paris. Happersberger and Baldwin became lovers for a time, although Happersberger experimented with female partners as well, and eventually married. Nevertheless, the two remained close friends for the rest of Baldwin's life.

During the 1950s, Baldwin completed his first novel that he finally titled *Go Tell It on the Mountain* (1953), which many literary analysts have called Baldwin's finest work. His first nonfiction book was *Notes of a Native Son* (1955), a collection of essays that had previously been published in such magazines as *Harper's* and *Partisan Review.*

Another novel, *Giovanni's Room* (1956), was rejected when Baldwin first turned it in to his editors because they expected him to deal with the "Negro problem" and the story, which dealt with homosexuality, had no main black characters. His agent and editors told him it was impossible to publish a book by a black homosexual writer. Yet, the book was accepted by a London publisher and later by Dial Press in New York. "Baldwin made it plain that he was profound and tough enough to declare his independence from what others might have called his heritage, his natural subject-matter. For a black man to decide to write a novel with mainly gay white characters, set in France, was a brave political act," declared a reviewer in a London newspaper (Tóibín 2001, books).

In 1957, Baldwin returned to New York and then traveled throughout the South to learn about the exploding civil rights movement—the demonstrations and protests against discrimination that were frequently met with bombings and white mobs. Baldwin interviewed Dr. Martin Luther King Jr. in Atlanta, Georgia, and other black leaders in the South.

During the 1960s, Baldwin traveled frequently between the United States and

France. He also went to Italy, Switzerland, and to the bohemian quarter of Istanbul, Turkey, where he continued his habitual partying. And he continued to write. The increasing violence in the U.S. South outraged Baldwin, and his anger filled the pages of *Nobody Knows My Name* (1961), a collection of essays, and *The Fire Next Time* (1963), a blunt and eloquent look at what it means to be black in the United States. It became a national bestseller. U.S. attorney general Robert Kennedy read the book and wanted to meet with Baldwin to discuss racial problems in the South. Kennedy asked Baldwin to assemble a group who would contribute suggestions for a civil rights bill. Those who gathered were angry black people. They were highly critical of the Kennedy administration for not recommending a strong civil rights bill that protected voting rights and mandated integration of public schools, restaurants, and other accommodations. At first Robert Kennedy reacted with anger, because he knew that if his brother, President John F. Kennedy, supported such a bill, he might not be reelected. But eventually Robert Kennedy told his staff to work on a draft for the bill that would become the landmark Civil Rights Act of 1964, which outlawed segregation in schools, the workplace, and other public facilities and banned unequal voter registration.

Baldwin's work published in the 1960s includes *Another Country* (1962), a novel of sexual and racial passions, love, and hatred; *Blues for Mister Charlie* (1964), a play produced in New York; *Going to Meet the Man* (1965), a collection of short stories; and *Tell Me How Long the Train's Been Gone* (1968), a novel.

While in the United States, Baldwin also went on lecture tours to address college and high school students about the true history of the United States and the inability of whites to see blacks as fellow human beings. He organized protest marches as well, but never saw himself as a black leader, rather as a person who bears witness. He worked with civil rights activists Stokely Carmichael (later known as Kwame Ture), Angela Davis, and Huey Newton, cofounder of the Black Panther Party, on a variety of projects.

Baldwin was devastated when he learned that his friend Medgar Evers, field secretary for the National Association for the Advancement of Colored People, was murdered in Mississippi in 1963. A year later, Black Muslim leader Malcolm X was killed, and in 1968, Martin Luther King Jr. was assassinated. These deaths and the continued racial violence demonstrated to Baldwin that reconciliation between the races was impossible in the United States.

Baldwin returned to France in the early 1970s and produced more essays and two novels, *If Beale Street Could Talk* (1974), a bestseller, and *Just above My Head* (1979). Other works include *A Dialogue* (1973), a collaboration with poet and black activist Nikki Giovanni.

For the most part, he remained in France for the rest of his life, and continued his prolific writing. On November 30, 1987, he died of stomach cancer, in his Saint-Paul-de-Vance home. His body was returned to Harlem for burial.

See also Carmichael, Stokely/Ture, Kwame; Davis, Angela; Giovanni, Nikki; King, Martin Luther, Jr.; Malcolm X

References

Baldwin, James. *The Fire Next Time*. New York: Dial Press, 1963.

Baldwin, James. *Notes of a Native Son*. Boston: Beacon Press, 1955.

Campbell, James. *Talking at the Gates: A Life of James Baldwin*. New York: Viking, 1991.

Leeming, David. *James Baldwin: A Biography.* New York: Alfred A. Knopf, 1994.

Standley, Fred L., and Nancy V. Burt. *Critical Essays on James Baldwin.* Boston: G. K. Hall & Co., 1988.

Tóibín, Colm. "The Henry James of Harlem: James Baldwin's Struggles." *Guardian* (London), September 14, 2001. http://www.guardian.co.uk/books/2001/sep/14/jamesbaldwin (accessed June 16, 2010).

Troupe, Quincy, ed. *James Baldwin: The Legacy.* New York: Simon and Schuster/Touchstone, 1989.

Banks, Dennis (1937–)

When they founded the American Indian Movement (AIM) in the late 1960s, Dennis Banks, an Anishinabe Ojibwa, or Chippewa, Clyde Bellecourt, another Ojibwa, and Russell Means, a Lakota Sioux, became heroes to Native Americans across the United States. But local and federal law enforcement officials had an entirely different view of AIM and considered the founders subversives and instigators of riots. Banks was indeed part of numerous protests against the federal government and its policies toward Native Americans; some of those protests turned violent. One in South Dakota sparked armed conflict between police and protesters; Banks was arrested and convicted of inciting a riot. Before sentencing, he fled the state.

Some sources record the birthdate of Dennis Banks as 1930 or 1932. But in his autobiography, Banks declares he was born on April 12, 1937, on the Leech Lake Chippewa reservation in Minnesota. He was given the Ojibwa name Nowa-Cumig, which means "at the center of the universe." His grandmother helped bring him into the world, and Banks reported that his mother, Bertha, "said that it seemed I was fighting my way out of her womb. I've been fighting ever since" (Banks and Erdoes 2004, 12). Dennis has two older siblings—a brother, Mark, and sister, Audrey.

Bertha often left the family for periods of time, going into town and then returning, but keeping emotionally distant from her children. Dennis had little connection with his father, who joined the military, married, and had another family. In their mother's absence, Dennis and his brother and sister were cared for by his maternal grandparents, Josh and Jenny Drumbeater, and extended family members. Josh and Jenny maintained a traditional Indian life, which Dennis enjoyed. They hunted and trapped wild game, fished, gathered berries and wild rice, tapped maple trees for syrup and sugar cakes, and dried deer skin and beaver hides. "We lived close to nature, in rhythm with the seasons," Banks noted (Banks and Erdoes 2004, 16). They also attended traditional ceremonies at which his grandfather was an admired drummer and singer.

Dennis was five years old in 1942 when his life changed forever. As he explained: "There is one dark day in the lives of all Indian children ... when they are forcibly taken away from those who love and care for them. ... They are dragged, some screaming and weeping, others in silent terror, to a boarding school where they are to be remade into white kids" (Banks and Erdoes 2004, 24).

The U.S. Bureau of Indian Affairs (BIA) managed such schools in accordance with the Indian Reorganization Act of 1934, which was supposed to be a "new deal" for Indians. The schools were meant to be an improvement over previous institutions that tried to "civilize" their students. But the schools still emphasized the predominant white culture and denigrated Native American culture.

Dennis, his older brother, and his sister were put on a bus and taken more than 200 miles away from their home and family to a boarding school in Pipestone, Minnesota. Dennis spent seven miserable years at the boarding school where he was one of 500 Indian children and was required to wear a uniform, live by strict rules and schedules, forbidden to speak his native language, forced to read history books depicting Indians as savages, and subject to beatings for misbehavior. While he was at Pipestone, he ran away nine times but was caught each time and severely punished with beatings.

At the age of 11, Dennis was sent to another boarding school in Wahpeton, North Dakota, and later transferred to still another at Flandreau, South Dakota. When he turned 16 years of age, he "finally decided that enough was enough," and made his "last escape," hopping a freight train, hitchhiking, and walking back to the Leach Lake Reservation. He was reunited with his mother and began to understand that she and none of the family had been responsible for sending him away, "that it was government policy that forced Indian kids away from their families" (Banks and Erdoes 2004, 30–31).

For two years, Banks stayed on the reservation and was able to be part of the traditional life. But for economic reasons, he enlisted in the U.S. Air Force in 1954 and served in Korea (at the end of U.S. involvement in the war there) and also in Japan as an aerial photographer. In Japan, he met and fell in love with a Japanese woman with whom he had a child. They married in a Japanese ceremony, but the military would not recognize the union.

While in Japan, Banks became embittered by the military's bigotry and prejudice against the Japanese. He hoped to stay in Japan with his family and did not want to return to the United States. Several times he was absent from his post without leave to be with his wife and daughter, and when caught, he was jailed. He was flown back to the United States, where he was discharged in the late 1950s.

Through the early 1960s, he drifted around Minnesota looking for work, drinking too much, and ending up in the Stillwater State Penitentiary for robbing a grocery store. While in prison, he met Clyde Bellecourt. When the two were released in 1968, they and Russell Means helped found AIM, using an upside-down American flag as a symbol. The symbol was not meant to show disrespect for the flag, but was and is an official signal of distress that is used to this day to show that someone or an entire nation is in distress.

AIM's purpose was to deal with a variety of Native American issues, such as poverty, housing, and broken treaties between the U.S. government and Indians. The movement appealed to many Native Americans who were disgusted with the Indian Reorganization Act. By the mid-1960s, the movement had spread to all 50 states and to Canada. According to the law and legal reference library law.jrank.org, many Indians "believed that [the Act] opened the way for massive federal land grabs of Indian territory on which valuable minerals were located. Banks and his fellow leaders decided to reclaim former Indian territory, announcing that they would symbolically 'retake the country from west to east' like the 'wagon train in reverse'" (law.jrank.org).

In November 1969, Banks with other AIM leaders joined a group of Native Americans in occupying Alcatraz Island, a former federal prison off the California coast, in an action to claim the property. An 1868 treaty gave the Lakota the right

Native American activist Dennis Banks in 1974. A founder of the American Indian Movement, Banks has been a vocal proponent of safeguarding Indian culture and fighting against discrimination, poverty, and government inequity. (AP/Wide World Photos)

to claim any federal facility when the government ceased providing it with appropriations. The Indian occupation lasted until June 1971, when federal authorities arrested those who still remained.

Another AIM protest action organized by Banks was the Trail of Broken Treaties in November 1972. Caravans of cars traveled from the West, Midwest, and South to Washington, D.C., where a group of Indians was scheduled to meet with BIA and other government officials regarding treaty violations and other mistreatment of Native Americans. When government officials refused to meet with the Indian group, Banks, Means, and Bellecourt led a takeover of the BIA building. The leaders attempted to present their demands for fair treatment of Indians to government officials, but were rebuffed. They then gathered documents that substantiated how Indian affairs had been mishandled. "The evidence filled a good-sized room," Banks reported (Banks and Erdoes 2004, 141). After some violent confrontations, federal officials agreed to set up a task force to investigate conditions on reservations and promised not to prosecute protesters, if they would vacate the BIA building. The federal government never honored any of its agreements.

In February 1973, AIM joined a protest at Wounded Knee on the Pine Ridge Reservation in South Dakota, a place where Sioux were viciously massacred in the 1890s. "On 28 February 1973 several hundred Oglala Lakota people and their backers stormed a church on the Pine Ridge reservation and took hostages to call attention to the fight against [Richard] Wilson and his corrupt tribal government" (Grossman 1996, 431).

At the time, the Oglala people were divided. So-called traditionalists wanted to maintain their cultural ways and independence from the federal government; on the other side, "progressives" advocated government support. "Another severe problem on the Pine Ridge reservation was the strip mining of the land," wrote William Redhawk. "The chemicals used by the mining operations were poisoning the land and the water. People were getting sick, and children were being born with birth defects. The tribal government and its supporters encouraged the strip mining and . . . at that point in time, the tribal government was not much more than puppets of the BIA. . . . Violent confrontations between the traditional people and the GOONS (Guardians of Our Oglala Nation) became an everyday occurrence" (Redhawk 2002). Richard Wilson had formed the GOONS as his private militia, which he employed ruthlessly to maintain his grasp on tribal funds and power.

Responding to a request from the protesters, Banks, Means, and other militant AIM members arrived at Wounded Knee to demand an investigation of the BIA and its support of Wilson. AIM and its supporters had a handful of weapons including shotguns, a few pistols, and some hunting rifles. From February to May when the siege ended, the federal force, including marshals and FBI agents, were well armed and fired their weapons night and day, with Air Force jets roaring overhead. When the confrontation ended, AIM leaders, including Dennis Banks and Russell Means, were arrested. They were tried and defended by the famed civil rights lawyer, William Kunstler. Eventually the judge on the case dropped charges against AIM leaders, citing misconduct by the government.

In 1975, Banks again was on trial, this time for inciting a riot in connection with a violent confrontation at the Custer County Courthouse in 1973 when AIM protested the court decision that freed a white man who murdered an Indian. Banks was convicted and was free on bond until sentencing. He was certain he would be killed once he was sentenced, and he fled. At the time, he was married to Kamook Nichols and they had a daughter, Tashina. They found sanctuary in California, where Democrat Jerry Brown was governor and which refused to extradite Banks to South Dakota because authorities had sworn that Banks would be murdered. While living in California, the couple had two other daughters, Tiopa and Tokala. Later, Dennis and Kamook divorced, and some AIM members believe Kamook became an FBI informant, accepting $42,000 from the FBI and accusing Banks and another AIM leader, Leonard Peltier, of violent crimes.

After Governor Brown completed his term and Republican George Deukmejian took office, Banks fled to Onondaga Reservation in upstate New York, where Indian reservations are not governed by federal law. In the fall of 1984, he surrendered and was sentenced to three years in prison, but was paroled in 1985. He went to Pine Ridge to help provide jobs by convincing companies to locate factories on the reservation. He faced still further charges and another prison term for illegal possession of dynamite, but received probation for five years.

Banks has been active in social justice efforts, speaking at universities about Indian issues, marching for religious freedom (especially as it concerns Muslim Americans currently under attack), protesting the long involvement of the United States in Iraq, attending Native American ceremonies, and teaching native customs. His autobiography, *Ojibwa Warrior: Dennis Banks and the Rise of the American Indian Movement* (2004), tells of his long fight for Native American rights and the oppression of the U.S. government. A documentary about his life, *A Good Day to Die* (2010), won a first-place award at the American Indian Film Festival.

Karen L. Hamilton

See also Kunstler, William; Means, Russell; Peltier, Leonard

References

Banks, Dennis, with Richard Erdoes. *Ojibwa Warrior: Dennis Banks and the Rise of the American Indian Movement*. Norman: University of Oklahoma Press, 2004.

"Dennis J. Banks—Further Reading." law.jrank.org, n.d. http://law.jrank.org/pages/4668/Banks-Dennis-J.html (accessed March 23, 2011).

Grossman, Mark. *The ABC-CLIO Companion to the Native American Rights Movement*. Santa Barbara, CA: ABC-CLIO, 1996.

Redhawk, William. "Siege at Wounded Knee 1973." *Redhawk's Lodge*, 2002. http://siouxme.com/lodge/aim_73.html (accessed March 24, 2011).

Bari, Judi (1949–1997)

"We need a theory of revolutionary ecology that will encompass social and biological issues, class struggle, and a recognition of the role of global corporate capitalism in the oppression of peoples and the destruction of nature." So wrote Judi Bari (1999), who was an activist with the radical environmental group Earth First! She was also a labor organizer for Industrial Workers of the World (IWW) and tried to bring local timber workers together with environmentalists to save ancient trees in the redwood forests of Northern California. Not surprisingly, timber company executives tried to stop her efforts and to discredit Earth First! by sending out news releases declaring that the organization was advocating violent tactics to halt logging.

Judi was born Judith Beatrice Bari in Baltimore, Maryland, on November 7, 1949, to Arthur Bari, a gem cutter, and Ruth Bari, a professor of mathematics. Judi's sister, Gina (now Gina Kolata), is about 18 months older and is currently a well-known science and health writer for the *New York Times*. Another sister, Martha, born 10 years after Judi, became an art historian.

According to Bari biographer Kate Coleman, when Judi was only one year old, the Federal Bureau of Investigation (FBI) raided the Bari home, "badgering" Ruth for information about "a recent houseguest—Morton Sobell, a Soviet spy in flight from the federal government." Sobell was fleeing because he was accused, along with Julius and Ethel Rosenberg, of running an atomic spy ring for the Soviet Union. All were Communist Party members. As good communists, Arthur and Ruth had given Sobell refuge at the party's request. Sobell had then moved to another "safe house" on his escape to Mexico, where he and his family were finally caught and turned over to U.S. agents at the border. He was convicted of espionage and sentenced to 30 years (Coleman 2005, 15).

After a controversial trial, the Rosenbergs were sentenced to death, generating worldwide protests. The Baris were never arrested, but they decided to leave the Communist Party and not discuss their past affiliation with Sobell or the party with their children.

In school, Judi was active in sports, and while in high school, she took pride in her skills as a mechanic and ability to work on cars. Bari attended the University of Maryland, where she was a peace activist, protesting the Vietnam War during the late 1960s and early 1970s. She dropped out after her fifth year of study since she had no plan for a career, although she had taken courses in graphic arts. She took a job as a clerk in a local grocery store where she began organizing a workers' union. At the time, she also studied martial arts and earned a black belt in karate.

During the 1970s, Bari was a bulk-mail handler in Washington, D.C., and organized workers. She led a successful postal workers' strike for better working conditions. In 1979, she met and married Mike Sweeney and moved to Sonoma County, California, where she joined a civil disobedience group associated with the Abalone Alliance—nonviolent activists who rallied to shut down the Diablo Canyon Nuclear Power plant on the coast in central California. The alliance named itself for the abalone killed by waste water from the nuclear plant. She also became involved with Pledge of Resistance, a movement protesting U.S. government military intervention and support for repressive regimes in Nicaragua, El Salvador, and Guatemala.

By the early 1980s, Judi and Mike had two young girls, Lisa and Jessica, and the family had moved to Mendocino County on California's north coast noted for its redwood forests. During this time, Judi confided to friends that her husband was physically abusive. She and the girls sought shelter with friends, and in 1988, Judi and Mike divorced.

Judi Bari joined the environmental movement Earth First! in 1988. Earth First! was based on an ideology known as deep ecology, which advocated preserving Earth regardless of the human consequences. Bari was attracted to the organization because of members' willingness to risk their lives by blocking bulldozers and chainsaws in order to prevent logging old-growth trees—redwood trees that were 1,000 to 2,000 years old.

In its early days, Earth First! used tactics described in Edward Abbey's novel *The Monkey Wrench Gang* (1975). Activities included "monkeywrenching" (vandalizing) machinery and blocking major industries from destroying natural areas. In the Pacific Northwest, Earth First! activists concentrated on logging industries and used obstructive measures such as pouring sand in bulldozers' gas tanks and ramming huge steel spikes into trees, thereby making them unmarketable. The spikes were a hazard to loggers if their saws hit steel.

Bari was against the tree spiking because it endangered loggers and she was dedicated to nonviolent civil disobedience. Under her leadership, some of the Earth First! membership pulled away from the original organization. Her efforts for Earth First! consisted primarily of organizing protests, and she worked out of the Mendocino Environmental Center in Ukiah, the county seat. She played a major role in logging blockades that saved thousands of acres of forest.

In 1988, Bari met Darryl Cherney, a musician and activist who was working at the environmental center. Cherney was planning a campaign to run for the U.S. Congress, and he needed help designing a flyer. Bari, with her graphic skills, offered to prepare the flyer layout and from that time on they soon developed a romantic relationship. Cherney did not win election, but the two worked together in Bari's efforts to unionize timber workers. Bari along with Cherney wrote protest songs and played her violin (or fiddle) in nonviolent demonstrations against old forest logging. In addition, Bari and Cherney took part in a demonstration to counter antiabortion activists who were intimidating women trying to enter a Planned Parenthood clinic in Ukiah.

Bari was so successful at rallies to protest old-growth logging that she gained thousands of followers and supporters who took part in blockades. After blocking one logging truck in 1989, the driver of the truck followed Bari's car and rammed it from behind, sending all six occupants, including four children, to the hospital with relatively minor whiplash injuries. Although photographs showed that the truck was the same one that had been blocked just the day before, police treated it as an accident rather than a deliberate crash. The incident reminded Bari's supporters of Karen Silkwood, whose car was rammed when she was on her way in 1974 to meet a reporter and present evidence of safety violations at the nuclear power plant where she worked. Silkwood was killed in the "accident."

Besides the ramming incident, Bari and Cherney received numerous death threats, which increased when they began the Redwood Summer project in 1990. That year, the California legislature proposed putting Proposition 130, the Forests Forever Initiative, on the fall ballot. It was designed to save old-growth redwood forests from over-cutting. Lumber companies were adamantly against the initiative. To counteract the opposition, Bari and Cherney with Earth First! members recruited college students for their Redwood Summer campaign, modeling it after Freedom Summer, the Mississippi campaign in the 1960s in which college students helped register blacks who had been denied their voting rights. The recruits for the Redwood Summer project held mass demonstrations to prevent loggers from cutting down trees before the proposition could be passed.

In May 1990, Bari and Cherney were on a recruitment tour driving through Oakland, California, when a pipe bomb exploded in the car. Bari was in the driver's seat where the nail bomb had been placed, and the explosion caused nerve and tissue damage and excruciating pain that lasted for the rest of her life. Cherney's injuries were less severe. Both were taken to a hospital, where the Oakland police, backed by the Federal Bureau of Investigation (FBI) arrested them, claiming that the two were carrying the bomb to use in a terrorist attack on loggers. In spite of the fact that there were written death threats in the car and that there were known groups and individuals intent on stopping Earth First! efforts, Cherney was jailed for five days. Bari was hospitalized for eight weeks and in a rehabilitation center for two weeks.

The charges against Bari and Cherney prompted headline stories across the United States while the FBI and Oakland police continued to try to convince the media that Bari and Cherney were guilty of carrying an explosive device. The authorities made claims that the bomb was in the back seat and that the types of nails used were in a bag found in Bari's car. Both charges were false—photographs of the car distinctly showed that the bomb was placed under the driver's seat and that even a noncarpenter could see that the nails on the bomb were not the same as those Bari had in her car. The bomber used nails with round heads and the nails in the bag had flat heads.

After weeks of investigation, the district attorney had no evidence to present in court, and the charges were dropped. But the FBI did not close the case and, for at least one year, did nothing to find the bomber or bombers. That convinced Bari and Cherney that they should file a civil rights lawsuit, *Bari v. Held* (1991), that charged the FBI and Richard Held, the FBI agent in charge, and the Oakland Police Department with false arrest and violation of Bari's and Cherney's free speech and assembly rights. The lawsuit did not go to trial until years later.

Meanwhile, Bari continued with protests, although she was disabled (her right foot was paralyzed) and in constant pain. Bari was diagnosed with breast cancer in 1997, and the disease metastasized quickly to her liver. Knowing she was dying, she began organizing thousands of pages of materials—police reports, death threats, FBI memos, and other pieces of evidence. According to a newspaper report, "Up to a week before her death, though receiving round-the-clock home hospice nursing care, she worked on her case with friends, passing on to them her knowledge and meticulously organized legal notes." She also requested that her obituary say that she was a revolutionary. Bari wanted people to remember what Joe Hill, an IWW labor organizer advised in 1915 before he was executed: "Don't mourn. Organize!" (Wilson 1997). She died on March 2, 1997, at her mountain cabin home near Willits, California.

Bari's death did not stop the lawsuit, which went forward with Cherney and with Bari's friends and supporters. A Redwood

Justice Fund had been set up to help pay for the legal costs. The case finally went to trial in 2002, and jurors watched and listened to Bari's videotaped deposition testimony, which was recorded a month before her death. On the tape, Bari described how terrified she was while in the hospital, petrified that someone would attack her and extremely afraid that she would be framed for the bombing. According to news reports, members of the jury were often in tears listening to the testimony.

In June 2002, the jury in the lawsuit against four FBI agents and three Oakland Police officers decided in favor of Bari and Cherney. The jury found that the defendants had framed Bari and Cherney, who were awarded $4.4 million for violation of their First and Fourth Amendment rights guaranteed in the U.S. Constitution. "Eighty percent of the damages were for violation of free speech rights under the First Amendment, validating Bari and Cherney's longstanding claim that they were targeted for false charges because of their political activism for the redwoods. The balance of the damages were for the Fourth Amendment violations of false arrest and unlawful search," according to a news report (Wilson 2002).

After the trial, the Oakland City Council proclaimed May 24, the date of the bombing, to be Judi Bari Day. In May 2010, a two-day event in the San Francisco Bay area marked the 20th anniversary of the Bari car bombing and commemorated her life with speeches, music, exhibits, and films.

The mystery of who bombed Bari's car has never been solved. Speculation, however, has continued to this day. Some charge that FBI agents and/or lumber company operatives were responsible. Others claim that Bari's ex-husband committed the crime. Still others wonder if a so-called avenger planted the bomb. Not long after the bombing, a news reporter received a letter signed by "The Lord's Avenger," a radical antiabortionist who claimed that he had committed the crime as a revenge for Bari's counter demonstration at the Planned Parenthood clinic in 1988. The avenger's claims have not been substantiated. Bari supporters still hope that the true criminal or criminals will be found. In September 2010, Darryl Cherney went to court to keep the FBI from destroying evidence from the trial, arguing that there might be DNA evidence on bomb fragments, which could eventually identify the person who placed the bomb.

See also Rosenberg, Ethel, and Rosenberg, Julius; Silkwood, Karen Gay

References

Bari, Judi. "Biocentrism and Deep Ecology." February 5, 1999. http://www.judibari.org/revolutionary-ecology.html (accessed July 7, 2010).

Bari, Judi. *Timber Wars*. Monroe, ME: Common Courage Press, 1994.

Coleman, Kate. *The Secret Wars of Judi Bari: A Car Bomb, the Fight for the Redwoods and the End of Earth First!* San Francisco: Encounter Books, 2005.

Harper, Will. "The Unsolved Mysteries of Judi Bari." *East Bay Express*, September 12, 2001. http://www.eastbayexpress.com/eastbay/the-unsolved-mysteries-of-judi-bari/Content?oid=1066036 (accessed July 11, 2010).

Wilson, Nicholas. "Judi Bari Dies but Her Struggle Continues." *Albion Monitor*, March 2, 1997; revised March 6, 1997. http://www.albionmonitor.com/bari/barideath3.html (accessed July 10, 2010).

Wilson, Nicholas. "Jury Awards $4.4 Million Damages to Bari and Cherney." *Albion Monitor*, June 11, 2002; updated June 15, 2002. http://www.albionmonitor.com/0205a/judibaritrial12.html (accessed July 11, 2010).

Beck, Glenn (1964–)

Glenn Beck epitomizes a new breed of twenty-first-century political pundit and celebrity spokesperson for dissidents against liberalism and socialism. He has created a media empire and reaped the rewards of substantial entrepreneurial efforts through his advocacy of American conservative and libertarian issues. An entertainer and a talk show host with a substantial following among right-wing listeners, he became a hero and de facto leader of the burgeoning Tea Party Movement in 2010. Beck skyrocketed to national prominence when he began hosting the *Glenn Beck Show* on Fox News Network the day before President Barack Obama's inauguration in January 2009.

Named Glenn Lee Beck when he was born on February 10, 1964, in Everett, Washington, Beck is the son of William and Mary Beck, who eventually took the family to Mount Vernon, Washington, to open a bakery called the Sweet Tooth. In Mount Vernon, Beck began his path to stardom and influence at the age of 13 when he won a contest to host an hour on KBRC, the local radio station. At age 15, he was sleeping on the floor of Seattle's KUBE 93 FM to be able to perform on-air duties for that newly launched station in his first professional radio position.

Raised a Roman Catholic, Beck attended the parochial elementary school in Mount Vernon until 1977, when he went with his mother and sister to live in Sumner, Washington. Mary Beck's problems with alcoholism were cited as the reason that Beck's father divorced his mother, and the disease eventually led to her death in 1979 as a drowning victim in Puget Sound. Her boyfriend at the time, another heavy drinker, also died in the incident that took place during a boat outing off the city of Tacoma.

Beck and his sister moved to Bellingham, Washington, to live with their father. Beck completed his secondary education in Bellingham, earning a diploma from Sehome High School in 1982. It was around this period of his 18th year that Beck became an alcohol abuser and a confirmed pot smoker. The addictive behavior was to continue for many years. In a *New York Times Magazine* profile on Beck, reporter Mark Leibovich put it this way: "He calls himself a 'recovering dirtbag.' There were many days, he said, when he would avoid the bathroom mirror so he would not have to face himself. He was in therapy with 'Dr. Jack Daniels.' He smoked marijuana every day for about 15 years. He fired an underling for bringing him the wrong pen" (Leibovich 2010, 37).

This destructive behavior occurred during Beck's rise to prominence as a radio personality and occasional stand-up comic. After leaving the state of Washington at the age of 18, he was able to earn a living as well as improve his professional status as a radio show host in several cities across the United States. His first job was in Provo, Utah, where he stayed for just six months in the Mormon-affiliated K-96 FM, a part of the First Media organization of media outlets. He thought the Mormons were "freaks" and made little attempt to fit in. And his off-hours lifestyle of partying, smoking cigarettes, and drinking coffee caused him to stand out as something other than a team player or a Latter-day Saint.

In 1983, First Media had an opening in its highly rated Top 40 station in Washington, D.C., WPGC, and Beck jumped at the chance to get out of Provo. By many accounts, his radio stint in the nation's capital was a seminal experience. He met and married his first wife there, became very good at his job, and added cocaine use to his repertoire of drug-induced experiences. With the partnership/friendship of another of the station's DJs, Bruce Kelly, it looked as if Beck would become one of the stars of the Washington radio scene. But later that same year, he was actually lured to Corpus Christi, Texas, by the Mormon Jim Sumpter, who had befriended and directed him from the time he worked in Provo. Sumpter had left First Media to take charge of a Texas radio company, and he hired Beck as the morning DJ for KZFM, then Corpus Christi's number one Top 40 station.

In his book *Common Nonsense: Glenn Beck and the Triumph of Ignorance* (2009), Alexander Zaitchik describes the scene in south Texas and the national trend in Top 40 radio that had such a profound effect on the young performer:

> Beck's arrival in Corpus Christi coincided with a sea change in morning radio. It was known as the morning zoo revolution, and it is the key to understanding Glenn Beck's career, both in Top 40 radio and beyond. Before the X-rated in-studio antics of the shock jocks, there were the skit-writing shlock jocks of the zoo. In its purest form, the wacky, zany, fast-paced zoo formula consisted of an ensemble cast employing fake voices, loosely scripted skits, adolescent pranks, short topical rants, and spoof songs, backed by a Top 40 soundtrack and peppered with news and traffic reports. Beck was not a pioneer of zoo radio, but he was a member of the founding generation. The influence on his approach to broadcasting endures. (Zaitchik 2010, 23)

Both his detractors and supporters in the days of radio's zoo revolution point to elements of that genre that form the basis for the current Beck talk radio and cable TV enterprises. At the tender age of 19, he was successfully capturing an ever-widening audience while also serving as manager and programmer for the show. He proved to be very talented, and he was not afraid to take the credit for his achievements.

In 1985, he rode his successful tenure in Corpus Christi to a new position as the highest paid disk jockey at WRKA in Louisville, Kentucky. He was now 21 years old with over eight years of experience on radio. Here, he had the show called Captain Beck and the A-Team in the crucial morning slot for the station. The WRKA program that Beck did was replete with nasty attacks on a DJ from rival stations in the local market as well as humorous bits that he continued to hone from his playbook of the zoo radio genre. It was also the scene of Beck's initial foray into the role of right-wing radio patriot. He took a cue from U.S. president Ronald Reagan's order to drop bombs on Muammar al-Gaddafi's palace in Libya in retaliation for Gaddafi's involvement in the explosion at a nightclub in Berlin, Germany, frequented by American military personnel. Beck spent the day after the bombing raids verbally attacking Muslims and the religion of Islam while playing patriotic and anti-Gaddafi songs.

This early evidence notwithstanding, Beck's Top 40 radio trajectory continued unabated for 15 more years. Never able to match the ratings successes he had early on, he set up shop in a series of broadcasting outlets from Phoenix to Houston and from Baltimore to Hamden, Connecticut. In many of these stops in his career he was dogged by controversy because of tasteless jokes, boorish on-air behavior, and the continual use of prescription and illegal drugs and alcohol. He was divorced in 1990 from his first wife Claire, with whom he had two daughters.

By 1994, Beck had reached the low point in his life and was ready to make a change away from suicidal thoughts that had plagued him for years. "There's nothing like being 18 years old in the fifth largest market in America, and then spending the next dozen years dropping 97 spots," is the way Beck encapsulated his career to that point according to biographer Alexander Zaitchik (2010, 46).

His first step in the rehabilitation process that would lead him to the success that he enjoys in the twenty-first century was his visit to an Alcoholics Anonymous (AA) meeting in November 1994. AA support led to his recovery from drug and alcohol use, and by the next year, he was clean and sober for the first time in decades. As he continued to take stock of his life and career with an eye toward changing his personal relationships as well as his radio persona, he started to make choices that would lead him in another direction. With the help of Connecticut's U.S. senator Joe Lieberman, who had befriended him over Beck's on-air ridicule of the state's liberal governor (and Lieberman rival) Lowell Weicker, he became a part-time student at Yale. He was searching for a spiritual identity and was attracted to the class on Early Christology. Beck was never particularly good in an academic setting, suffering from Attention Deficit Hyperactivity Disorder (ADHD) by many accounts, and he never even completed that one class offering.

However, Beck wanted to understand something more about his spirituality, so he started a self-education program that included reading an eclectic array of writers. Beck has talked about this group of thinkers on his programs and in his live shows: Pope John Paul II, Alan Dershowitz, Friedrich Nietzsche, Adolf Hitler, Billy Graham, and Carl Sagan. Friends at the time, including his former partner Pat Gray, suggested that he look into the Church of Jesus Christ of Latter-day Saints (Mormons). While he first ridiculed that suggestion, he would eventually become a Mormon when he and his second wife Tania made a conscious decision to join a religious community in 1999.

At the same time Beck was making the concerted effort to find some personal peace, he began to earnestly pursue a change in his radio career. He had flirted with the idea of migrating to the talk radio format that men like Rush Limbaugh had been using for years, and he had even gotten himself into trouble at a couple of his Top 40 "morning zoo" radio jobs by having long conversations with callers or doing on-air rants about the latest in cultural and political issues. In 1998, then working as a morning DJ for the Clear Channel station in New Haven, Connecticut, his boss told him that his contract would not be renewed after it ended the next year. It was suggested that he pursue his new dream of making it in talk radio.

Even before this, Beck had retained one of the most important talk radio agents of the time, George Hiltzik. Hiltzik got Beck his first job in that genre as a guest host on the biggest talk radio station of the time, WABC in New York City. The next year, Beck got a call from Clear Channel personnel who thought of him for a job in the Tampa, Florida, area on WFLA 970. *The Glenn Beck Program* began on that station on January 3, 2000. Within a year, the new talk radio host had moved the show into first place in the local market ratings from a starting point of number 18. In 2002, the Clear Channel subsidiary, Premiere Radio Networks, moved the program to Philadelphia and began broadcasting *The Glenn Beck Program* nationally on 47 stations. Premiere Radio is the number one syndicated network in the country and it has featured a stable of popular conservative and libertarian-leaning commentators including Rush Limbaugh, Dr. Laura Schlessinger, and Sean Hannity. By 2008, it was reported that Beck was being heard on 280 radio stations, XM Radio, and web streaming interfaces. Glenn Beck became the number three–rated radio personality in America after Limbaugh and Hannity.

Beck has honed his message and his performance on radio to reflect not only the theatrics and shock that were the hallmark of his morning zoo days, but his philosophy of personal redemption, self-reliance, and belief in God. He also discovered that spreading the perception that current government leaders are driving the country into the abyss created a fear-based response in his audience. That fear, driven by an often emotional, weeping Beck, has been considered by some to be used to increase his market share, which in turn would create a demand for services and products promoted on his program and through his Mercury Radio Arts media/entertainment company that began in 2002 in New York City.

His theatricality that drives his messages to the faithful about the threat of liberalism, the importance of protecting the Constitution from socialist tendencies of Democrats in Congress and the White House, and preparing for the worst of times, resonated with the executives at cable television's CNN Headline News when they were looking for a ratings boost. They offered him a slot in their Headline Prime time period in 2006. He was so successful that his show became the second-most popular on the network. By 2009, he had been wooed to Fox News Channel by its president Roger Ailes.

Beck proved to be wildly successful on Fox, where his presence, though not his ratings, eclipsed the mainstay personality Bill O'Reilly in 2010. His fan base continued to grow on radio and television, Because he has embraced the ideals represented by the ultraconservative and libertarian Tea Party and has promoted their events and causes since 2009, Beck is considered by many to be the obvious spokesman for the disparate groups that call themselves tea partiers. Beck has often demurred when asked if he was the de facto head of the Tea Party, but he was able to use the affiliation when he sought to bring people to his Restoring America Rally held on August 28, 2010, on the steps of the Lincoln Memorial. It is likely that at least 100,000 attended the spiritual-themed rally.

However, in 2011, advertisers began objecting to Beck's outrageous antics and statements and dropped their commercials on Fox. Beck left Fox (some say he was fired), but he plans to produce documentaries and work on other projects for Fox. Meanwhile, his followers flock to his web site (one million hits per month), and they also push sales of his books and audio CDs, which include *The Real America: Messages from the Heart and Heartland* (2005), *An Inconvenient Book: Real Solutions to the World's Biggest Problems* (2007), *The Christmas Sweater* (2008), *An Unlikely Mormon: The Conversion Story of Glenn Beck* (2008), *America's March to Socialism: Why We're One Step Closer to Giant Missile Parades* (2009), *Glenn Beck's Common Sense: The Case Against an Out-of-Control Government* (2009), *Arguing with Idiots: How to Stop Small Minds and Big Government* (2009), *Idiots Unplugged* (2010), *The Overton Window* (2010), and *Broke: The Plan to Restore Our Trust, Truth and Treasure* (2010).

Martin K. Gay

See also Limbaugh, Rush

References

Leibovich, Mark. "Being Glenn Beck." *New York Times Magazine*, October 3, 2010.

Zaitchik, Alexander. *Common Nonsense: Glenn Beck and the Triumph of Ignorance.* New York: Wiley, 2010.

Benitez, Lucas (1976–)

For years, Lucas Benitez kept a bloody shirt ready to display. The shirt is now encased in glass and is part of a Florida Modern-Day Slavery Museum—a windowless produce truck that imprisoned tomato pickers. In 1996, the shirt belonged to a Guatemalan boy who picked tomatoes in the fields of southwest Florida near Immokalee, known as "ground zero for modern slavery." The boy fled the fields after being beaten by a crew boss because he stopped working to ask for a drink of water. Seeking help, the boy ran to the community center of the Coalition of Immokalee Workers (CIW), dissident farmworkers who began organizing in 1993. Benitez joined the group later on and became CIW's codirector (Estabrook 2009, 40).

Benitez has helped expose servitude slavery of tomato pickers—men and women, most of whom are undocumented and had come to Florida to work. Unscrupulous employers have offered jobs as field hands to immigrants from Mexico, Guatemala, and Haiti, and the employers have held workers against their will, kept the workers' identification documents, set up debit accounts for food and rent—which the workers could not repay—and held or stole their wages. Benitez and the CIW have helped free some enslaved workers, and federal civil rights officials have successfully prosecuted seven slavery operations involving over 1,000 workers in Florida's fields since 1997.

Benitez and CIW also have campaigned relentlessly for wage increases for tomato pickers. Farmworkers have no right to overtime or to organize because they were excluded from labor reform measures passed in the 1930s. Growers and corporations that control the produce industry have resisted efforts to increase tomato pickers' pay. As Greg Kaufmann reported in the *Nation*, "When the Department of Labor reported 'sub-poverty annual earnings' [for fieldworkers] the growers denied it, claiming tomato harvesters averaged $12–$18 per hour. When the USDA described farmworkers as 'among the most economically disadvantaged groups in the US' with 'poverty more than double that of all wage and salary employees,' the growers maintained that they were performing a service by providing needed entry-level jobs" (Kaufmann 2010).

Lucas Benitez, who was born in 1976, is originally from Guerrero, Mexico. His parents are illiterate, and Lucas came to the United States to work and help support his brothers and sisters. He had received only an elementary-school education in Mexico. In an interview, he reported: "I started working in the fields when I was 17 years old" (Callahan 2004). The fields he referred to are in Immokalee, Florida, an inland area east of Fort Myers.

Ninety percent of the tomatoes grown in the United States during the winter months come from the Immokalee area, where wealthy landowners control tomato production. According to a report by Barry Estabrook in *Gourmet* magazine, "Large packers, which ship nearly $500 million worth of tomatoes annually to major restaurants and grocery retailers nationwide, own or lease the land upon which the workers toil. But the harvesting is often done by independent contractors called crew bosses, who bear

After 10 days on a hunger strike, Lucas Benitez, spokesman for the Florida Coalition of Immokalee Workers, appeals for higher farmworker wages to the governor's aides in Tallahassee, Florida, December 29, 1997. (AP Photo/Mark Foley)

responsibility for hiring and overseeing pickers" (Estabrook 2009, 40). Since 1978, tomato pickers have earned between 40 and 50 cents for each 32-pound bucket of tomatoes harvested. At that rate, to earn a minimum wage, a worker must pick 2.5 tons in a 10-hour day. Since the early 2000s, however, tomato pickers have achieved a small penny-per-pound increase.

Before he became a CIW director, Benitez worked for years picking tomatoes and lived with four other workers in a small trailer in Immokalee. Growers bus workers from the town to the fields. Housing for farmworkers in Immokalee consists of "rusted trailers and dilapidated shacks," according to Tom Philpott, a food-politics writer for *Grist* who visited Immokalee in 2009. Philpott noted that "workers pay $800 per week for the largest two-room trailers and shacks available. That's $3,200 a month.... In order to bring rent to a manageable level, [workers] often live 16 people per structure. That makes rent about $50 per person per week." Philpott also described the interior of a smaller trailer renting for $400 per week. It was shared by seven men who slept on "beat-up mattresses" jammed together on the floor and used milk crates as their only furniture (Philpott 2009). Only when reporters investigate the lives of farm laborers has the public been able to get a glimpse of the poverty and brutal conditions workers encounter.

"The harsh truth is that America's bounty always has been planted, tended and harvested by abused minorities who have remained, and still remain, mostly invisible and powerless," wrote Bill Maxwell in 2010. A columnist for the *St. Petersburg Times* in Florida, Maxwell recalled working in the fields with his father decades ago when most farmworkers were black and they lived in camps south of Immokalee. He reported: "Our living quarters were a tin-roofed, wooden, windowless bull pen where 10 to 15 men and boys slept on pallets. . . . Hard work—stooping, sweating and lifting all day—was at the center of our lives" (Maxwell 2010, opinion page).

In 2001, Benitez and the CIW began a Campaign for Fair Food to raise wages of tomato pickers in a program called penny-per-pound. That penny can boost a worker's pay to at least a living wage, from about $10,000 per year to as much as $17,000 annually. The coalition engaged in protest marches, hunger strikes, and demonstrations to try to persuade growers to increase wages. When those efforts were unsuccessful, CIW turned to major companies that purchase tomatoes from growers. One by one, they won concessions from fast-food chains such as McDonald's, Burger King, Yum! Brands (the parent company of Taco Bell), Pizza Hut, Long John Silver's, Subway, KFC, and Whole Foods Market to pay workers at least one cent more per pound for the tomatoes they purchase. Institutional food service companies also agreed to the increase.

In 2008, Benitez appeared before a U.S. Senate committee hearing that was specifically called because of news reports about the deplorable labor conditions in Florida's fields. The senators also confronted the Florida Tomato Growers Exchange (FTGE), which represents 90 percent of the state's tomato growers. Senators were critical of the exchange's claims that tomato harvesters' wages were $12.46 per hour and its lack of responsibility for the cases of slavery to emerge from the fields. For years the FTGE, based in Maitland, opposed CIW's penny-per-pound program, arguing that the CIW is an unlicensed labor organization and that members of the exchange did not want to be the conduit through which the extra penny would be paid.

In May 2010, U.S. secretary of labor Hilda Solis visited Immokalee and the CIW community center. She toured the Florida Modern-Day Slavery Museum, which includes a replica of the kind of windowless trucks involved in slavery operations of the Navarette family who were prosecuted in *U.S. v. Navarette* (2008). Cesar and Geovanni Navarette enslaved 12 workers from 2005 to 2007 and repeatedly beat the tomato pickers, causing multiple injuries and threatening them with death if they tried to escape. They kept fieldworkers locked inside the truck with no toilet facilities. Workers were forced to urinate and defecate in the back of the truck. Tomato pickers finally managed to escape by punching a hole in the roof and climbing out. The Navarettes were sentenced to 12 years in federal prison. The traveling museum has shocked many visitors, including Solis. She emphasized the department's support for the farmworkers in their fight against such labor abuses.

Even before the Navarette case, CIW assisted in other cases, such as *U.S. v. Flores* (1997). Miguel Flores and Sebastian Gomez had a workforce of over 400 men and women in Florida and South Carolina, harvesting vegetables and citrus. The workers from Mexico and Guatemala were forced to work 10- to 12-hour days for as little as $20 per six-day week. Armed guards constantly watched them. Those who attempted escape were assaulted, pistol-whipped, and even shot. The case was brought to federal authorities after five years of investigation by escaped workers and CIW members. Flores and Gomez were sentenced to 15 years each in federal prison on slavery, extortion, and firearms charges.

In the case of *U.S. v. Tecum* (2001), the CIW helped the Department of Justice with the prosecution of Jose Tecum, who forced a young woman to work against her will both in the tomato fields around Immokalee, and in his home. He was sentenced to nine years in federal prison on slavery and kidnapping charges.

Other cases include *U.S. v. Ramos* (2004). Brothers Ramiro and Juan Ramos had a workforce of over 700 farmworkers in the citrus groves of Florida and in the fields of North Carolina. The men threatened to kill workers if they tried to leave and assaulted anyone who gave workers rides. CIW investigations led to the brothers' arrest and they were sentenced to 15 years each in federal prison on slavery and firearms charges.

During 2010, CIW worked with law enforcement in forced-labor cases that were still under investigation. Yet, the organization points out that most growers do not engage in modern-day slavery to tend their fields where produce is grown and harvested. Rather, it is the conditions that workers endure, including below-poverty wages, no right to overtime pay, and no right to organize as well as health risks such as pesticide poisoning, inadequate sanitary facilities, and crowded and/or substandard housing.

In October 2010, CIW spokesman Benitez announced a landmark agreement between CIW's Campaign for Fair Food and the Pacific Tomato Growers (PTG), one of the largest tomato producers in the United States. The agreement establishes a system for implementing a Code of Conduct, which is the main focus of the Campaign for Fair Food. The code includes a system for resolving complaints and provides for third-party auditors to determine whether the code is being implemented and food companies are paying the increased penny-per-pound wages to workers. Benitez cautioned, however, that the agreement has not brought about the changes in agriculture that are needed, but instead has set up a plan of action to eliminate workplace abuses in Florida agriculture.

After the U.S. Senate hearing and much criticism from labor activists, the FTGE finally reversed its position in November 2010 and announced that growers, shippers, and other participating exchange members would distribute the increased pay, which has been collected from fast food corporations and retailers who buy the tomato crop. In a signed agreement, FTGE also pledged to protect workers and add health and safety provisions.

Benitez and CIW continue their Campaign for Fair Food, focusing especially on supermarkets such as Walmart and Florida-based Publix, which have refused to negotiate regarding the penny-per-pound increase for workers. Publix contends that workplace conditions and pay are the responsibility of tomato pickers' employers, not grocery stores.

CIW, which has more than 4,000 members, also has numerous supporters, including the National Council of Churches, the Presbyterian Church, the Unitarian Universalist Association of Congregations, a variety of foundations, and individuals. In an interview, Peggy Callahan of the Free the Slaves web site asked Benitez when CIW's job would be done. Benitez responded that the organization "could possibly exist forever as things are now, so actually ... I will be dead and the coalition will still be here and so the coalition will have to fight until all the workers have their fair wage until all of the workers have their rights until all the workers can organize until all of the workers [no longer] face these abuses" (Callahan 2004).

References

Callahan, Peggy, interviewer. "Lucas Benitez." *Free the Slaves*, February 14, 2004. http://www.freetheslaves.net/Page.aspx?pid=367 (accessed November 3, 2010).

Estabrook, Barry. "The Price of Tomatoes." *Gourmet*, March 2009.

Kaufmann, Greg. "The Wall Comes Tumbling Down." *Nation*, October 18, 2010. http://www.thenation.com/print/blog/155437/wall-comes-tumbling-down (accessed November 3, 2010).

Maxwell, Bill. "Everyone Benefits When Farmworkers Are Treated Fairly." *St. Petersburg Times*, October 22, 2010.

Pacific Tomato Growers and Coalition of Immokalee Workers. "Pacific Tomato Growers, Coalition of Immokalee Workers Sign Landmark Agreement for Social Responsibility in Florida Tomato Fields." Press release. http://www.ciw-online.org/CIW_Pacific_joint_release.html (accessed November 6, 2010).

Philpott, Tom. "In Industrial-Tomato Country, Workers Suffer Squalid Living Conditions and Even Slavery." *Grist*, March 13, 2009. http://www.grist.org/article/Immokalee-diary-part-II/PALL/ (accessed November 5, 2010).

Benjamin, Medea (1952–)

Medea Benjamin uses a great variety of theatrical tactics to communicate her messages, interrupting political speeches, disrupting conventions, raising banners, and getting arrested. As cofounder of the antiwar group CODEPINK (CP): Women for Peace, and the human rights organization Global Exchange, she has traveled widely in efforts to promote peace and call attention to human rights abuses and sweatshops—workplaces that pay less than minimum wage, use child labor, and jeopardize employee safety and health.

Benjamin has many supporters and also many opponents. The latter argue that she and her group terrorize public officials and support terrorists abroad. Federal Bureau of Investigation (FBI) agents have searched homes of CP members, accusing them of providing "material support" for terrorism. Some opponents call her anti-American, a communist, and even a traitor.

She was born Susan Benjamin on September 10, 1952, in Long Island, New York, to Alvin and Rose Benjamin. Susan is the younger of two daughters in a wealthy family who lived in a quiet, suburban neighborhood. Her father Alvin founded the Benjamin Companies, which develop luxury residential and premier office and professional buildings as well as other major properties. Her sister Karen is deceased, as is her mother.

The Benjamin family went to a reform Jewish synagogue in Baldwin, Long Island, and Susan attended a synagogue school, where she was "taught Jewish values (*tikkun olam*—our responsibility to help heal the planet) and Jewish tradition," she wrote. "I did not continue my studies and have a bat mitzvah, as my sister did, because I started questioning—at any early age—this idea of being the chosen people. When I was 16 I went to live in a Kibbutz (Ein Gedi) on the Dead Sea in Israel. It was just after the '67 war." In the 1967 six-day war between Arab nations and Israel, the Israelis gained control of territories that included the Gaza Strip and the West Bank. Benjamin noted that she "loved the kibbutz life of hard work, fresh air, and all living and working as a community, but I was very concerned by the racism I heard about the Arabs. This made we question some parts of my Jewish identity but I got involved in other issues [the Vietnam War, for example]. I also stayed away from the Israel/Palestine conflict out of respect for my father, who was a great supporter of the Israeli government" (Benjamin 2010).

Interviewers frequently ask Benjamin what motivated her to relinquish the comforts of an affluent life and get involved in demonstrations against war and other protests. She noted in one interview that an incident while she was in high school was one factor. It was during the Vietnam War. "My sister's boyfriend had sent her the ear of a Vietcong, a war souvenir to wear around her neck. That shocked me, and led me to form an anti-war group in my high school," she said (Vesely-Flad 2010). She also was influenced by racial upheavals in the 1960s and she wondered at the age of 15 and 16 what she could do in her life to help people become more tolerant and less inclined to fight each other. Another jolting factor was a trip to Tijuana, Mexico, where she saw starving youngsters begging in the streets.

After high school graduation, Benjamin enrolled at Tufts University in Massachusetts. About this time she changed her name to Medea, a character in a Greek tragedy. Although the Medea of mythology killed her children, Benjamin said she "didn't believe the story.... I think she was a strong woman, and some people just made up the story to discredit her" (Garofoli 2002).

Benjamin attended Tufts for only a year and left to study abroad. But she soon abandoned the classroom for firsthand learning and began hitchhiking across Europe. She also traveled to Africa, eventually returning to the United States and earning a master's degree in public health at Columbia University and another master's in economics at the New School for Social Research in New York.

As a nutritionist and economist, Benjamin worked in Latin America and Africa for the United Nations' Food and Agriculture Organization and other international organizations. In Africa, she was active in a campaign that began in 1977, which eventually forced Nestlé to cease promoting its infant formula as a substitute for breast milk. Poor women could not afford the infant formula. In addition, the formula had to be mixed with water, which often is contaminated in impoverished countries. Even when women boiled water and sanitized bottles, they sometimes diluted the formula to make it last longer but decreased its nutritional value.

Benjamin also spent some time in Cuba accompanying her first husband, who was coaching a national basketball team. At first, Benjamin was impressed with Cuba and in print praised the communist regime of Fidel Castro, which brought harsh criticism from conservatives and liberals alike in the United States. Her views changed somewhat while working for a communist newspaper; she wrote an article against some government policies, and as a result she was deported from Cuba.

Back in the United States, Benjamin took a job in San Francisco with Food First/Institute for Food and Development Policy in 1983. Food First helps low-income people develop sustainable agriculture on a local level in the United States and other countries.

Benjamin and her husband parted ways in 1983. In the mid-1980s, Benjamin traveled to Washington, D.C., where she met Kevin Danaher, an activist and specialist in globalization and advocate for a green or sustainable, environmentally friendly economy. Benjamin and Danaher eventually married, and in 1988, they cofounded with colleagues Global Exchange, an international human rights organization that promotes social, economic, and environmental justice worldwide.

Benjamin and Global Exchange have played key roles in the anti-sweatshop

Code Pink for Peace organizer Medea Benjamin protests the resignation of State Department spokesman P. J. Crowley and the detention of U.S. Army private Bradley Manning in front of the U.S. State Department, March 14, 2011, in Washington, D.C. (Chip Somodevilla/Getty Images)

movement, adding their voices to those of such groups as the National Labor Committee and its executive director Charles Kernaghan to call attention to clothing and sports-shoe companies that exploit workers in the United States and abroad. Anti-sweatshop campaigns have brought about some reforms, such as corporate codes of conduct that prohibit the use of child labor and recognize workers' right to organize and work in a healthy, safe environment. The code also limits the work week to 60 hours and sets a minimum wage. Companies that abide by the code are certified to use a "no-sweat" label or other type of tag stating that their goods are not manufactured in sweatshops.

Through the 1990s and 2000s, Benjamin's activities included diverse struggles and campaigns. In 1999, during the World Trade Organization Conference in Seattle, Benjamin and Global Exchange along with many other groups organized protests against globalization and called attention to corporations that sacrificed labor and environmental concerns over corporate profits. In 2000, with the encouragement of Ralph Nader, once a Green Party presidential candidate, Benjamin ran for the U.S. Senate as a Green Party candidate, but was not included in the debates.

In 2002, before the U.S. invasion of Iraq, Benjamin and several other activists founded CODEPINK, a grassroots peace and justice movement officially known as CODEPINK Women for Peace. The name developed because of the coded system used by the U.S. Department of Homeland Security after the September 11, 2001, terrorist attacks. The color code ranges from green, blue, yellow, and orange to red and was designed to alert the public to the threat level of another attack (low to severe). For the women who founded CODEPINK, the idea was "to turn the color pink on its head from being this nice, feminine, sweet color to one that was very energetic, bold, and determined," according to Benjamin (Birney 2010).

Many CODEPINK activists wear pink during the organization's events, and use the color pink in their signs and web site. CODEPINK has staged numerous antiwar protests since its inception. But Benjamin raised concerns in 2006 that women in large numbers were not demanding the end to U.S. wars. She wrote:

> I remember when we first started CodePink before the invasion of Iraq, and we felt compelled to leave our families, our jobs, our warm homes to camp out in

front of the White House to try to stop the war. "We'll put a call out to women across the country," we said, "and the streets of Washington will be flooded with angry women saying no to an unjustified war." During the four cold, winter months we spent in front of the White House, hundreds of women came to join us, and more than 10,000 marched with us when we ended the vigil. But we kept wondering, "where were the millions of women who, according to the polls, were strongly opposed to the war?" When a grieving Cindy Sheehan [whose son was killed in Iraq] called on people all over the country to join in her vigil at Crawford, Texas [in 2005] a few thousand people—most of them women—responded. But why didn't tens of thousands come? Or 100,000?

Over the years, hundreds of thousands of women—perhaps millions—have marched in antiwar rallies. Why don't they become part of an ongoing movement? Why do they get demoralized so quickly when their efforts don't bear fruit? (Benjamin 2006, 33)

In 2008, Benjamin and retired army colonel Ann Wright, who is an antiwar activist, attempted to cross the U.S. border with Canada, but were denied entrance because their names were in a FBI criminal database. The two were going to appear at an antiwar event in Toronto, and they decried the fact that the FBI listed them because of their arrests for peaceful protests. At a news conference, Wright noted: "I have been arrested for sitting in front of the White House. I've been arrested for standing up and speaking at the U.S. Congress. All of these are misdemeanors," said Wright who gave up her career after the U.S. invasion of Iraq in March 2003. "I've never spent a day in jail as punishment." Benjamin declared: "I travel all over the world on a regular basis. I have never had this kind of problem. Canada is the first country, to our knowledge, that is using this beefed-up database of the FBI as its criteria for judging who enters. It's why we consider this so outrageous and so dangerous" (Canwest News 2007).

After the Israeli attack on Palestinians in the Gaza Strip in the winter of 2008–2009, CODEPINK took delegations to Gaza. The group was especially concerned that humanitarian aid gets to nearly 1.5 million Palestinians who, according to Benjamin, live "in what's equivalent to an open air prison. They aren't allowed the freedom to go in and out of the area, really only surviving thanks to the United Nations and other charitable organizations" (Birney 2010).

In 2010, Benjamin and Ann Wright attended a U.S. Senate hearing on the Pacific Command, which was proposing a military buildup in Okinawa and Guam. The two activists carried signs opposing the expansion of military bases.

In 2010, the Fellowship of Reconciliation honored Benjamin with the Martin Luther King Jr. Peace Prize, which recognizes individuals or groups that work in the tradition of King's nonviolent approach. She is author or coauthor of eight books, including *No Free Lunch: Food and Revolution in Cuba Today* (1986), the award-winning *Don't Be Afraid, Gringo: A Honduran Woman Speaks from the Heart* (1987), *Bridging the Global Gap: A Handbook to Linking Citizens of the First and Third Worlds* (1989), *Greening of the Revolution: Cuba's Experiment with Organic Agriculture* (2002), and *The Peace Corps and More: 175 Ways to Work, Study and Travel at Home and Abroad* (2003), as well as *How to Stop the Next War Now: Effective Responses to Violence and Terrorism* (2005), which she coedited with Jodie Evans.

See also Kernaghan, Charles; King, Martin Luther, Jr.; Nader, Ralph; Sheehan, Cindy; Wright, Ann

References

Benjamin, Medea. Email correspondence with author, November 28, 2010.

Benjamin, Medea. "When Will US Women Demand Peace?" *Conscience*, Summer 2006.

Birney, Angelina Perri. "Waging Peace: Medea Benjamin of CODEPINK." Pure Vision, September 15, 2010. http://perri birney.wordpress.com/ (accessed November 29, 2010).

Canwest News Service. "American Peace Activists Stalled at Canada-U.S. Border." Canada.com, October 4, 2007. http://www.canada.com/topics/news/world/story.html?id=3d25cabf-3bcc-4bea-b607-7d5967c82397&k=66185 (accessed November 29, 2010).

Garofoli, Joe. "S.F. Woman's Relentless March for Peace." SFGate.com, October 26, 2002. http://www.sfgate.com/cgi-bin/article.cgi?file=/chronicle/archive/2002/10/26/MN36571.DTL (accessed November 27, 2010).

Vesely-Flad, Ethan. "Leading Creative Action for Social Change: Medea Benjamin." Forusa.org, September 23, 2010. http://forusa.org/blogs/ethan-vesely-flad/leading-creative-action-social-change-medea-benjamin (accessed November 28, 2010).

Berrigan, Daniel (1921–), and Berrigan, Philip (1923–2002)

Ordained members of the Roman Catholic clergy, brothers Daniel and Philip Berrigan were on the Federal Bureau of Investigation's (FBI) "Ten Most Wanted List" for their Vietnam War protests. Their activism was noteworthy, because "men of the cloth" typically did not engage in such endeavors, which were considered subversive in 1960s America. The Berrigans were some of the first to voice prominent dissent. "When two priests, Daniel and Philip Berrigan, helped found the antiwar movement, they were opposed by their own church, but by holding on to their own convictions, they gave moral authority that helped bring an end to the Vietnam War" (Kisseloff 2007, 4).

Both brothers were born in Minnesota, Daniel on May 9, 1921, in the town of Virginia, and Philip on October 5, 1923, in Two Rivers. The family moved to Syracuse, New York, where Daniel and Philip grew up with four other brothers. Their father ruled with an authoritarian hand while their mother "would feed any hobo who came up the road during the Great Depression, despite her own large, hard-pressed brood" (Jonah House web site).

Daniel was always certain of his calling and joined the Society of Jesus, the Jesuit order, at age 18. Philip's path to the priesthood was less direct. He enlisted and served in Europe during World War II, becoming such a self-described "skilled and remorseless killer" that he was selected for officer candidate school, graduating as a second lieutenant. He returned to civilian status when the United States dropped atomic bombs on Japan in 1945 (Berrigan 2004). Deeply affected by the war, Philip enrolled at Holy Cross College, graduating in 1950 (Bivins 2003, 119). In college, he underwent a religious conversion and decided to become a priest. He entered the seminary at the Society of St. Joseph, whose priests were devoted to the well-being of African Americans in the Deep South. Ordained in 1955, Philip spent seven years in New Orleans teaching at all-boy's St. Augustine high school (Berrigan 2004). With exposure to the South's racism, "Berrigan became politicized. He began to denounce the [Catholic Church's] silence on economic and political injustices" (Bivins 2003, 119). He marched for desegregation, participated in sit-ins and boycotts, and assiduously studied the words of civil rights leader Martin Luther King Jr. (Berrigan 2004).

Daniel's ordination took place in 1952, after 13 years of study. His first assignments were teaching theology. However, his duties did not insulate him from what was going on in the world. His brother Philip also encouraged him to "take a hard look at the world" (Jonah House web site). He began to develop a reputation as a religious radical. Daniel believed he was Christ's representative on earth, with the message: "We are not allowed to be complicit in murder.... Thou shalt not kill. We are not allowed to kill. Everything today comes down to that—everything" (Dear 2007, 1). In 1960, he met social activist and Trappist monk Thomas Merton, with whom the Berrigans would later jointly pen antiwar letters to major newspapers. On sabbatical in 1964, Daniel met Eastern Europeans who enlightened him on the realities of living in immediate range of Cold War weaponry—nuclear armaments (Jonah House web site). He returned to the United States a changed man.

The Berrigan brothers, independently and jointly, spoke out against the Vietnam War. They allied with fellow antiwar activist David Dellinger, drafting a "declaration of conscience" urging draft resistance, and they joined Yale chaplain William Sloane Coffin Jr.'s interfaith coalition, Clergy and Laity Concerned about Vietnam. But, similar to other like-minded protestors, they realized words were inadequate to the task of stopping the war or even swaying the public's almost mindless patriotic support of it.

In 1966, Daniel accepted the post of assistant director of Cornell University United Religious Work, the umbrella for all campus religious groups (Aloi 2006). The following October, he was arrested during a March on the Pentagon. A week before, Philip had been meeting in Baltimore with other "peaceniks." They determined that draft boards were like troughs serving up young American males to meet the demand of the U.S. military and its insatiable appetite. So, Philip and three others, later dubbed the Baltimore Four, entered a Maryland draft office on October 27, 1967, and doused its records with blood (Berrigan 2004). Waiting to be arrested, they distributed *Good News for Modern Man*, an edition of the New Testament, and justified their actions to draft board employees. Philip was convicted and received a six-year sentence (Berrigan 2004).

In February 1968, Daniel, along with activists Howard Zinn and Tom Hayden, flew to Hanoi, invited as representatives of the antiwar movement to receive the first three prisoners of war being released by the North Vietnamese. Shortly after Daniel returned, his brother came to him with a proposal for a large-scale plan, which they carried out on May 17, 1968. Nine Catholic protesters used Daniel's homemade napalm to destroy 378 draft files in the parking lot of the Catonsville, Maryland, draft board (Aloi 2006). They then joined hands in prayer and awaited the police (Berrigan 2004).

With that one action, they finally accomplished what all their previous activities had failed to do. Daniel used the trial to put Vietnam itself on trial. Regardless of the righteous of their cause, the Catonsville Nine, as the protesters were called, were convicted. All received prison terms: six years for Philip, three years for Daniel and the others (Berrigan 2004). Daniel chose to continue his nonviolent resistance to the war, going underground as a "fugitive from injustice." Philip did the same but was captured in 11 days. Daniel led the FBI on a merry chase. He even attended a Cornell music and political festival, "made an appearance and—while federal officers stood by ready to arrest him—escaped by hiding among members of a puppet troupe." He remained in the news until he was caught four months later (Aloi 2006). While on the run, he became the subject of Lee Lockwood's documentary *The Holy Outlaw* (1971). Daniel spent much of his prison time writing, building toward his life's work of more than four dozen volumes of prose and poetry. He was released in 1972 (Aloi 2006).

Philip was indicted again, along with six others, including Sister Elizabeth McAlister. In 1968, Philip and Elizabeth were married secretly, which resulted in Philip's excommunication. During the 1972 trial, the prosecution presented letters that had been illegally smuggled in and out of the Lewisburg federal prison, where Berrigan was serving his six-year sentence. The correspondence referred to kidnapping U.S. secretary of state Henry Kissinger and discussions of plots to damage government property. The case was tried during Easter week, with courthouse demonstrators including notables such as civil right leader Rev. Ralph Abernathy, Pentagon Papers leaker Daniel Ellsberg and Congresswoman Bella Abzug. At trial's end, the "pivotal questioned remained, when does chitchat become conspiracy? . . . after seven days of wearying deliberation, the nine women and three men confessed that they were hopelessly deadlocked on the conspiracy charges, and the case was declared a mistrial" (*Time* 1972).

Philip and Elizabeth were found guilty of the smuggling charge, but the trial brought negative attention to "the conspiracy law . . . [The] charge requires less evidence of actual injurious conduct" and is often used against political groups (*Time* 1972).

After his release in February 1972, Daniel continued his crusade against militarism, nuclear arms, racism, and injustice. He and his brother became "adept at pointing out not only the shortcoming of conventional politics but also the moral compromises they believe are incurred through mainstream political participation" (Bivins 2003, 151). Both would spend many years over the next two decades imprisoned for their ongoing activism. And, although Daniel remained fully committed to the priesthood, he often was "scorned by the hierarchy and their coreligionists." However, he would not back down, perceiving his "actions and resistance as not only consistent with but central to [his] religious tradition" (Bivins 2003, 149).

Philip's separation from the priesthood—and the Catholic Church—occurred in 1973 when he was formally excommunicated for his marriage to McAlister. Soon after, the two founded Jonah House in Baltimore (where he would live out the remainder of his life). To this day, the community is committed to a nonviolent way of life, to speaking about the connection between war making and homelessness, hunger, despair, and poverty. It engages in nonviolent civil resistance against war and for the abolition of all weapons of mass destruction. Peoples of all faiths are welcomed to the community (Jonah House web site).

The Berrigan brothers began their own ministry, focusing on the weapons of war and destruction. In 1980, they began the Plowshares Movement, taking the name from the biblical verse in Isaiah 2:4: "They shall beat swords into plowshares and their spears into pruning hooks; nation shall not lift up sword against nation, nor shall they learn war any more." Plowshares undertook the movement's first action on September 9, 1980, trespassing at the General Electric Nuclear Missile facility in King of Prussia,

Pennsylvania. They hammered Mark 12-A nuclear warhead nose cones and poured blood onto documents (Jonah House web site). The preliminary legal battle for Plowshares was recreated in the film *In the King of Prussia* (1982), starring Martin Sheen.

In subsequent years, Daniel and Philip repeatedly put their freedom on the line, standing up for their beliefs. The second Plowshares action, in which McAlister participated, occurred at Rome Air Force Base in November 1983, earning the seven participants three-year prison terms (Berrigan 2004). The Berrigans' activism continues to inspire ongoing events (Jonah House web site).

Philip's final Plowshares action was in December 1999, when he and others banged on A-10 Warthog warplanes in protest at a National Guard base. Convicted of malicious property destruction, he was sentenced to 30 months and released in December 14, 2001.

Toward his final days, Philip said, "The greatest need of humankind today is peace. Unless peace can become a reality from which all persons inevitably will benefit, humanity itself will flounder, will gasp and will die out" (Berrigan 2004). Philip Berrigan died on December 6, 2002, at age 79 in Baltimore, Maryland. His wife and others maintain Jonah House; its web site details all Plowshares actions and other activist activities. The Berrigans had three children. Kate works with the aged and disabled, Jerome lives in a Catholic Worker community, and Frida is an activist writer.

As of 2011, Daniel had resided more than 30 years in a New York City Jesuit apartment community. He continues years of volunteerism with AIDS victims and writes about terminal illness. Daniel is also poet-in-residence at Fordham University's Lincoln Center (Jonah House web site).

Daniel has spoken out against any and all American endeavors of a non-peaceful nature. He is a pro-life proponent as well as a crusader against capital punishment. He supports LGBT (Lesbian, Gay, Bisexual, and Transgendered) rights, the civil rights issue of the twenty-first century. Daniel received the War Resisters League Peace Prize (1974), the Thomas Merton Award (1988), the Pax Christi USA Pope Paul VI Teacher of Peace Award (1989), the Peace Abbey Courage of Conscience Award (1992) and the Pacem in Terries Award (1993).

The Berrigan brothers were driven by their sense of faith, responsibility, and conscience. They believed that their efforts could effect social change. For Daniel and Philip Berrigan, their protests were not a mere means to a definable endpoint. The Berrigans' tactics "challenge[d] not only particular policies or laws but also our very understanding of what it means to be religious and political" (Bivins 2003, front matter).

Margaret Gay

See also Abzug, Bella; Coffin, William Sloane; Dellinger, David; Ellsberg, Daniel; Hoffman, Abbie; King, Martin Luther, Jr.; Parks, Rosa; Sheen, Martin; Zinn, Howard

References

Aloi, Daniel. "From Vietnam to Redbud Woods: Daniel Berrigan Launches Events Commemorating Five Decades of Activism at Cornell." *Cornell University Online*, April 4, 2006. http://www.news.cornell.edu/stories/April06/berrigan.0406.html (accessed April 27, 2011).

Berrigan, Daniel. *To Dwell in Peace*. Reprint ed. Eugene, OR: Wipf & Stock Publishers, 2007.

Berrigan, Jerome. *Philip Berrigan and the Plowshares Movement: A Presentation by Jerome Berrigan*. December 9, 2004. http://

www.jonahhouse.org/Berrigan,%20Jerome1204.htm (accessed April 27, 2011).

Berrigan, Philip, with Fred A. Wilcox. *Fighting the Lamb's War: Autobiography of Philip Berrigan.* Monroe, MN: Common Courage Press, 2002.

Bivins, Jason C. *The Fracture of Good Order: Christian Antiliberalism and the Challenges to American Politics.* Chapel Hill: University of North Carolina Press, 2003.

Dear, John. *Put Down Your Sword: Answering the Gospel Call to Creative Nonviolence.* Grand Rapids, MI: Wm. B. Eerdmans Publishing Co., 2007.

Jonah House web site. http://www.jonahhouse.org (accessed April 27, 2011).

Kisseloff, Jeff. *Generation on Fire: Voices of Protest from the 1960s, an Oral History.* Lexington: University Press of Kentucky, 2007.

O'Neill, Patrick. "40 Years Dedicated to a Way of Life without Killing." *National Catholic Reporter*, January 20, 2006. 'http://www.jonahhouse.org/McAlister_O'Neill_NCR.htm (accessed April 27, 2011).

"Trials: No Again on the Conspiracy Law." *Time*, April 17, 1972. http://www.time.com/time/magazine/article/0,9171,944463-1,00.html (accessed April 27, 2011).

Bethune, Mary McLeod (1875–1955)

"I could see little white boys and girls going to school every day, learning to read and write; living in comfortable homes with all types of opportunities for growth and service and to be surrounded as I was with no opportunity for school life, no chance to grow—I found myself very often yearning all along for the things that were being provided for the white children with whom I had to chop cotton every day, or pick corn, or whatever my task happened to be." These were the words of Mary Jane McLeod Bethune during an interview in which she recalled events of her early life—when she was about 9 or 10 years old (Johnson interview).

Mary Jane was born on July 10, 1875, in Mayesville, South Carolina, in a log cabin on what was once part of a plantation. Until their emancipation after the Civil War (1861–1865), Mary's parents, Sam and Patsy (McIntosh) McLeod, were slaves, as were most of Mary's older brothers and sisters who were born into slavery and were sold to various masters. When all were free, they gathered at the McLeod plantation (where Sam had been a slave) for a family reunion. After Mary's mother gained her freedom, she took a job cooking for her former master until she had earned enough to buy five acres of land, which the family called the "Homestead." Mary's father and brothers cut the logs to build the cabin that was Mary's birthplace. She was one of only a few members of the family to be born in freedom.

The McLeods farmed their land, growing and selling cotton and corn. Mary Jane along with her brothers and sisters worked in the fields. Mary's mother supplemented the family's meager income by washing clothes or doing other household chores for white people. Sometimes Mary accompanied her mother. On one occasion, she picked up a book that belonged to one of the girls in the home. The girl demanded that Mary put the book down. She knew Mary could not read and told her to look at a picture book instead. That incident helped set Mary on a course that she would follow for the rest of her life. She was determined not only to read, but also to get the best education she could.

Her first opportunity came when a mission teacher from the Presbyterian Church in Maysville arrived at the McLeods' farm and told them the church had set up a school in town and black children could attend. Mary Jane enrolled at the school, which was in the small church building with roughly hewn benches, desks, a pulpit, and a wood stove. The teacher was Miss Emma Wilson, "a very fair Negro—couldn't tell her from white," as Mary noted many years later (Johnson interview). Miss Wilson had received her education from Scotia Seminary, a school for black girls, in Concord, North Carolina.

Under Miss Wilson's tutelage, Mary Jane soon learned to read and write. She attended the school for three years and taught what she learned to members of her family. She read the Bible and magazines for her parents, who were extremely proud of their daughter's education. She often took the neighbors' children to church with her, teaching them how to read and leading them in choral singing. She also gave away some of her personal belongings to people in the community who had less than she did. She demonstrated even as a young girl that people could share with one another for the benefit of all. Her example prompted people to work together to set up small schools close to their rural homes.

Mary Jane earned a scholarship to attend Scotia, which had both black and white teachers. The experience at the North Carolina school convinced her that the races could cooperate. After seven years of study, she graduated from the school in 1894 and had earned a scholarship to Dwight Moody's Institute for Home and Foreign Missions, which later became known as the Moody Bible Institute, in Chicago. She was a deeply religious person and wanted to be a missionary. She trained to serve in Africa, but she was told that African Americans were not placed in such positions, one of her greatest disappointments.

In spite of the setback, Mary McLeod decided to teach black students, almost the only profession open to black women at that time. She taught first at the Haines Institute in Augusta, Georgia, where she met Lucy Craft Laney, principal and founder of the school, who became her role model. Laney inspired Mary to dedicate her life to helping others. Then she accepted a teaching position in Sumter, South Carolina, at the Kendall Institute. There she met her future husband, Albertus Bethune. They married in 1898 and for a time lived in Savannah, where their only child was born in 1899.

Mary Bethune did not adapt well to domesticity and wanted to pursue her goal to educate black children, believing this was the best way to overcome discriminatory practices. In 1900, after the family had moved to Palatka, Florida, she established a community school for girls and worked with prisoners in the jail and with workers at the turpentine camps outside town. Turpentine production was a major industry in Florida where pine trees were a source of the gum stripped from the trees and processed at a still. Many black people lived in camp shanties and worked in for about 10 cents per hour. Years after Bethune ministered to turpentine workers and taught their children, Zora Neale Hurston, the black folklorist and author, visited the camps to investigate and write about the workers in the pine woods.

Albertus Bethune did not share his wife's missionary zeal, and after about eight years, they separated and went their own ways, although they remained married. After five years at Palatka, Mary McLeod Bethune went to Daytona, Florida, in Volusia County, where she hoped to improve educational opportunities for black people there—at the time, the majority of the population in the South opposed education for blacks. She only had a small amount of money that she had earned from selling insurance for the Afro-American Life Insurance Company. Bethune rented a small house for $11 per month near a former landfill to establish the Daytona Literary and Industrial School for Training Negro Girls in 1904. With little cash and few supplies, she had to create desks from crates for her class of five little girls and her own five-year-old son. She poked around the dump and trash containers behind hotels for materials ranging from cleaning supplies to lamps. She begged for dishes and food. The children used charred splinters of wood instead of pencils for writing and elderberry juice for ink. Nevertheless, she had a deep religious faith that the school would survive and grow. Her faith sustained her as it did all her life. And the school thrived, but not without a lot of effort.

At first, to help finance her school, Bethune and her students held bake sales and sold fried fish and homemade ice cream; later, Bethune sought financial aid from industrialists such as James N. Gamble of the Proctor & Gamble Company and Thomas White of the White Sewing Machine Company.

Supported by business people and others in Daytona, the school eventually offered secondary education and a teacher-training program for young women. In addition, the school conducted numerous outreach programs such as summer camps and schools, grew food products for sale, and held worship services. Whatever the support for the school, there was also opposition. According to Volusia County history, Bethune was working in her office one night in 1920 when:

> [S]he noticed that all street lights had gone out...she heard car horns and horse hooves, then she saw a procession of people masked in white sheets following a burning cross. Ku Klux Klan intimidation was never far removed from her life, her struggles, nor her efforts. At the time her school was an all black girl school, many of whom boarded on campus. The terrifying sight dredged up the images of the brutality and violence perpetuated against blacks since the times of slavery. Mary Bethune ordered the lights turned off on campus and all outdoor floodlights turned on. The Klan was left standing in a pool of light, and watched by the terrified students, as Mary rallied her girls to sing spirituals. The Klan soon dispersed and scattered into the night. (Volusia County)

Mary McLeod Bethune fought fiercely to achieve social, economic, and educational opportunities for African Americans, and particularly for African American women. (Library of Congress)

In 1923, Bethune merged the Daytona Institute with the men's school, the Cookman Institute of Jacksonville; it became the coeducational Bethune-Cookman College, which she headed as president until 1942.

During the 1920s, Bethune also worked for the advancement of black women through the Southeastern Association of Colored Women and then the National Association of Colored Women (NACW), serving as president of NACW from 1924 to 1928. Beginning in 1929, Bethune met with prominent black leaders to discuss her idea for a national organization that would unify the diverse women's groups. In her view, the NACW with its emphasis on local issues could not be effective nationally. Many black women opposed her idea, some because of jealousy, others because they did not see how a unified organization could benefit black women. Zora Neale Hurston was one of the opponents, criticizing Bethune for not being an original educator or writer of significance. In spite of opposition, Bethune prevailed, and in 1935, she established the National Council of Negro Women, an organization that helped link black female leaders to federal government officials, an organization she headed for 14 years.

Along with her organizational activities, Bethune worked tirelessly to improve the images of black women, making speeches, writing articles, and publishing the *Aframerican Women's Journal*. She also encouraged black women to maintain their dignity and not answer to people who addressed them with the term "Auntie" or other derogatory name that suggested she was the female version of "Uncle Tom."

In 1936, President Franklin D. Roosevelt, whose wife Eleanor and Bethune were friends, appointed Bethune director of the Division of Negro Affairs of the National Youth Administration, a federal agency assisting young people during the Great Depression and throughout World War II. She was the first African American woman to head a federal office. Because of her many contacts with officials in the Roosevelt administration and Eleanor Roosevelt, who twice was a guest in Bethune's home in Daytona Beach, Florida, Bethune was able to present the needs of black Americans. She made the case for equal rights, recommending federal government responses, such as integrating the military, eliminating the poll tax in the South, and supporting an anti-lynching law.

However, being in government and in the good graces of the president and First Lady Eleanor Roosevelt did not prevent prejudicial acts and statements. But she often used humor to deal with bigotry, as in one instance when she was leaving the White House and a southern politician said "Auntie, what are you doing here?" and she replied, "Which one of my sister's children are you?" (Height and Trescott 1994, 102).

Bethune worked outside government as well. She gave speeches for the National Association for the Advancement of Colored People; participated in protest marches against businesses that would not hire blacks; and encouraged educational opportunities for African Americans. She received numerous honors and awards. Her life of service ended on May 18, 1955, when she died in Daytona Beach of a heart attack. Memorials to Bethune are many and varied, including a statue of her in Lincoln Park, Washington, D.C., and a commemorative postage stamp issued in 1985.

See also Hurston, Zora Neale; Roosevelt, Eleanor

References

Height, Dorothy I., and Jacqueline Trescott. "Remembering Mary McLeod Bethune." *Essence*, February 1994.

Holt, Rackham. *Mary McLeod Bethune: A Biography*. Garden City, NY: Doubleday, 1964.

Johnson, Charles Spurgeon, "Interview with Mary McLeod Bethune." 1939 or 1940. http://www.floridamemory.com/OnlineClassroom/MaryBethune/interview.cfm (accessed May 22, 2010).

Peare, Owen. *Mary McLeod Bethune*. New York: Vanguard Press, 1951.

"Portraits of Leadership: Great African Americans in the Struggle for Freedom." *Black Collegian*, January–February 1994.

Sicherman, Barbara, and Carol Hurd Green, eds. *Notable American Women: The Modern Period*. Cambridge, MA: Belknap Press of Harvard University Press, 1980.

Smith, Jessie Carney, ed. *Notable Black American Women*. Detroit, MI: Gale Research, 1992.

Volusia County Historic Preservation Board and the Volusia County Government. "Volusia County Heritage: Mary McLeod Bethune." n.d. http://volusiahistory.com/mary.htm (accessed May 23, 2010).

Boggs, Grace Lee (1915–)

Just months before her 96th birthday, Grace Lee Boggs saw the publication of her book *The Next American Revolution: Sustainable Activism for the Twenty-First Century* (2011), written with Scott Kurashige. Since the 1940s, Boggs has been an activist for social justice, participating in civil rights, labor, environmental, antiwar, and women's movements as well as Asian American liberation. She declared in an article written in 2003 that her activism began, as it did with others of her generation, "on the revolutionary theories of Marx and Lenin." She pointed out that the German philosopher Karl Marx (1818–1883) and Russian communist Vladimir Lenin (1870–1924) developed their

> ideas and strategies . . . during the industrial era, when the prevailing concern of social-change activists was to extend our material powers. People's lives were determined by economic necessities—hence our strategies for radical change centered on the economic arena. The goal was to help workers understand that they were victims of the economic system, and that the only solution was to get rid of it. We struggled for political power as a way to abolish the unjust economic system. That is still the revolutionary scenario for most radicals. . . . One of the weaknesses of such a revolutionary vision is its failure to recognize the great divide created by the dropping of the atom bombs that ended World War II. The splitting of the atom brought human beings face to face with the reality that we had expanded our material powers to the point where we could destroy our planet. No longer could we afford to act as if everything that happened to us was determined by external or economic circumstances. (Boggs 2003, 24)

Over seven decades, Boggs experienced numerous changes in activist movements and her involvement in them. Her aptly titled autobiography *Living for Change* (1998) reflects that.

On June 27, 1915, Grace Lee was born in Providence, Rhode Island, to immigrant parents from a village in Guangdong Province, China. Grace's Chinese name was Jade Peace. Her father's surname was Chin and his first name was Lee, but he became Mr. Lee and a successful restaurant owner in the United States. Grace's mother Yin Lan was Lee's second wife and was 20 years younger than Chin Lee. The family consisted of George, a son of Chin Lee and his first wife; he was brought to the United States at a young age. A daughter Kay, Grace's older sister, was born aboard the ship that carried Yin Lan from China to the United States.

Grace's older brothers Philip and Robert, and her two younger brothers Harry and Edward, were American-born.

Grace's birth took place in an apartment over her father's Chinese American restaurant in downtown Providence. Previously, he had owned restaurants in Lawrence and Boston, Massachusetts, and dreamed of establishing a restaurant on Broadway in New York City. That became a reality when Grace was eight years old. He opened Chin Lee's on Broadway in 1924 and four years later opened another on Broadway: Chin's.

Grace Lee grew up in a household in which her mother had adapted quickly to American ways, although Yin Lan did not read or write English. Grace's father clung to some of his Chinese ways and hired a tutor to teach his children how to read and write Chinese. "But we were Chinese Americans who were more American than Chinese in our behavior," Grace Lee wrote. "We thought it was a huge joke to lock our tutor in the bathroom" (Boggs 1998, 11). However, Grace did learn Chinese characters during the tutoring sessions. She also was influenced by her father's insistence on getting a good education.

The family lived in the Jackson Heights neighborhood of Queens, a borough of New York City. Grace noted that she "was a tomboy; my brothers boasted that I didn't throw like a girl and that when we played baseball I often hit the ball over the fence" (Boggs 1998, 12). Nevertheless, she was shy when around strangers. She became an avid reader, borrowing numerous books from the local library. She graduated from eighth grade before she was 12 years old, and during her last year in high school, she also took courses in a business school to learn shorthand and typing.

At the age of 16, Grace Lee enrolled at Barnard College for women, affiliated with Columbia University. In the midst of the Great Depression of the 1930s, she graduated with a degree in philosophy, but "had no idea" what she would do to earn a living. She considered looking for an office job, but "most companies in those days would come right out and say 'We don't hire Orientals' " (Boggs 1998, 28). By this time, her mother and father had separated and with the difficult economic times, her father was struggling to keep his restaurants open. Yet, when Grace enrolled at Bryn Mawr in Pennsylvania, her father sent restaurant food by special delivery to help her out.

She was fortunate to obtain a $400 scholarship for graduate work at Bryn Mawr. There she continued her studies in philosophy, with a focus on pragmatism. That is, rather than a metaphysical or abstract approach to finding the truth or meaning of an idea, pragmatism looks at what works, the practical results of an idea or proposition.

Grace Lee graduated with a doctorate from Bryn Mawr in 1940. Once again, however, she was puzzled about what to do next. Teaching at a university was not possible because of discrimination against Asians. She decided that Chicago might be the place to put her philosophical ideas into action.

In Chicago, Grace Lee began her transition from philosophy to politics. She became involved in a tenant's organization that was protesting rat-infested apartment buildings in black communities. For the first time, she had the opportunity to talk with black people and learn about their experiences with discrimination. The organization had been established by the Workers Party, which had broken away from the Socialist Workers Party. She also witnessed the effects of the 1941 March on Washington Movement, designed to call attention to the fact that blacks were turned away from good jobs in defense plants that were begging for workers.

She "discovered the power of a movement to bring about massive changes in the life of a people," she stated in 2008 for the web site *In These Times*, adding: "At the beginning of World War II, thousands of blacks all over the country were mobilizing in response to a call from A. Philip Randolph, Brotherhood of Sleeping Car Porters President, to march on Washington to demand jobs in defense plants. When President [Franklin D.] Roosevelt pleaded with Randolph to call off the march and Randolph refused, FDR was forced to issue Executive Order 8802 banning discrimination at defense plants" (Boggs 2008).

In 1942, Grace Lee returned to New York City and for the rest of the decade was involved with the Johnson-Forest Tendency, a minority faction of the Workers Party named for founders C. L. R. James, a black man from Trinidad who used the pseudonym Johnson, and Russian Raya Dunayevskaya, who was known as Freddie Forest. Along with being active in New York, the faction had comrades in California and Michigan and set up an office in Detroit, where they formed the Correspondence Publishing Committee, taking the name from the American Revolution's Committee of Correspondence. One of the members of the committee was James (Jimmy) Boggs, a black worker in a Detroit automobile manufacturing plant, who wrote articles for the committee's newspaper, *Correspondence*. Grace Lee first met Boggs in 1952, and then a year later when she left New York and went to Detroit to work on *Correspondence*.

In 1953, Grace and James married, and over the next 40 years (until Boggs died in 1993), the couple worked together organizing grassroots groups and advocating for a great variety of projects and issues. During the 1960s, Grace and James paid little attention to Martin Luther King Jr. and his nonviolent approach to civil rights. King's ideas seemed ineffectual. The couple supported Malcolm X and his concept of African American separatism and self-determination. They also championed Black Power—racial pride and self-esteem and political empowerment for African Americans. In Detroit, black people were seeing no changes in the white power structure and the city council included only one African American. Tensions were rising in Detroit as manufacturing jobs were disappearing and black unemployment was double that of whites. African Americans also resented being harassed by white police.

In 1967, a police raid of a local unlicensed bar resulted in an explosion of violence across the city that lasted for four days. More than 7,000 people were arrested and some were brutalized by police. Hundreds were injured, and 43 people died. The Boggs called it a rebellion; the media and city officials called it a riot.

The chaos in the city was a turning point for Grace Boggs. She began to study the work of King and his philosophical and spiritual views regarding social change and justice. She determined that "King was a revolutionary in the best sense of the word. ... He envisioned a nonviolent revolution that would challenge all the values and institutions of our society, and combine the struggle against racism with a struggle against poverty, militarism, and materialism" (Boggs 2003).

In 1969, James and Grace Boggs wrote a 40-page booklet for the National Black Economic Development Conference. Called the *Manifesto for a Black Revolutionary Party* (1969), it was different from the abrasive *Black Manifesto* that James Foreman, former director of the Student Nonviolent Coordinating Committee, presented. Foreman's manifesto demanded $500 million from white churches and synagogues as reparations for exploiting blacks. In contrast, Boggs wrote, "Our *Manifesto* challenged blacks to assume the awesome responsibility of making a revolution to reorganize all the institutions of the country for the benefit of the entire society. The *Black Manifesto* ... put blacks back into the posture of supplicants playing on the guilt of white liberals to extract reparations" (Boggs 1998, 159). About five years later, Monthly Review Press published *Revolution and Evolution in the Twentieth Century* (1974) by James and Grace Lee Boggs.

Throughout the 1970s and 1980s, Grace and her husband lectured nationwide, speaking to university students, community organizations, and radical groups in efforts to gain support for their view of revolution. In 1992, Grace and James helped establish Detroit Summer, a multiracial, intergenerational collective in Detroit. Young people and the adults who work with Detroit Summer are all volunteers who help transform communities. For example, young people plant community gardens and organize community potlucks, clean streets, and create public art and murals.

After James Boggs died in 1993 of cancer, Grace Lee began questioning how she was going to proceed and stay active. She became involved with the Environmental Justice Movement (EJM), first articulated in *Dumping in Dixie: Race, Class and Environmental Quality* (1990), by sociology professor Robert Bullard. He called attention to toxic waste dumps, incinerators, and chemical plants and their poisonous emissions that are located in primarily African American communities in southern states. In Michigan, Grace Boggs and others in the EJM held workshops and other events to bring activists together to help solve local environmental problems.

At the end of 2010, Grace Lee Boggs was writing her *Michigan Citizen* column (as she has for years), looking back at some of the accomplishments in Detroit. She pointed out that 20,000 people traveled to Detroit for the second U.S. Social Forum (USSF) in June 2010. The USSF is designed to find ways to "build a powerful multi-racial, multi-sectoral, inter-generational, diverse, inclusive, internationalist movement that transforms" the United States, according to its web site (USSF 2010). Once in Detroit, participants "were surprised and delighted to discover that Detroiters are in the process of creating a 21st century self-healing, sustainable city from the ground up," Boggs wrote. "Detroiters are growing [their] own food in over 1000 community gardens and turning war zones into peace zones to bring the neighbor back to the 'hood" (Boggs 2010–2011).

Grace Lee Boggs has received numerous awards over the years. Some examples include the Human Rights Day Award, presented in 1993 by the Center of Peace and Conflict Studies, Wayne State University; the Boggs Center to Nurture Community Leadership founded in 1995 to honor Grace Lee and her late husband James as movement activists and theoreticians; Distinguished Alumnae Award from Barnard College in 2000; Chinese American Pioneers Award from the Organization of Chinese Americans in 2000; the Women's Lifetime Achievement award presented by the Anti-Defamation League in 2001; and many others from universities and colleges presented throughout the 2000s.

See also Bullard, Robert; King, Martin Luther, Jr.; Malcolm X; Randolph, A. Philip

References

Boggs, Grace Lee. "From Marx to Malcolm and Martin." *The Other Side*, January–February, 2003.

Boggs, Grace Lee. "Grace Lee Boggs Answers 20 Questions for *In These Times*." *In These Times*, November 22, 2008. http://www.inthesetimes.com/community/20questions/4060/grace_lee_boggs (accessed December 29, 2010).

Boggs, Grace Lee. *Living for Change: An Autobiography*. Minneapolis and London: University of Minnesota Press, 1998.

Boggs, Grace Lee. "Looking Back at 2010." *Michigan Citizen*, December 26, 2010–January 1, 2011. http://www.boggscenter.org/ (accessed December 31, 2010).

USSF. "What Is the US Social Forum?" 2010. http://www.ussf2010.org/about (cited December 31, 2010).

Bowe, Frank G. (1947–2007)

"No minority group in America has such dismal records of participation in the labor force as do persons with disabilities," wrote Professor Frank G. Bowe in 1989 (Bowe 1989, 37). Bowe, who lost his hearing at age three, was a leader in the disability rights movement and worked for years to help disabled Americans obtain jobs, education, rehabilitation, and other services long denied to them. He was a dissident fighting the stigma, misunderstandings, and low expectations regarding the disabled held by the general public.

Frank Bowe was born on March 29, 1947, in Danville, Pennsylvania, to Frank G. and Katherine Windsor Bowe. He and his sister Robin, who was born in 1949, grew up in Lewisburg, Pennsylvania, in the Susquehanna Valley. Lewisburg is the home of Bucknell University and a federal penitentiary. According to Bowe, "A standard joke in town was that Lewisburgers either went to Bucknell or they went to the Pen" (Bowe 1986, 6).

When he was preschool age, Bowe had three bouts of measles. He recovered from the contagious disease, but was left with impaired hearing. Bowe's parents consulted numerous doctors about their son's hearing loss and bought him hearing aids. A major task was helping Bowe develop a vocabulary by teaching him how to read books. Seeing the words in print and associating them with the spoken word helped Bowe learn to lip read, which his parents believed was an essential factor in being able to understand what others were saying. They adamantly opposed using sign language, declaring that their son would depend exclusively on that form of communication rather than lip reading and reading printed words. However, later in his life, when Bowe attended the famous school for the deaf, Gallaudet College in Washington, D.C., he learned American Sign Language (ASL) and subsequently taught it to others.

Bowe went to public schools rather than a special school for hearing impaired. While in elementary grades, Bowe met numerous obstacles trying to fit in with other students. Years later, he noted:

> Deafness means being alone.
> You don't hear the sounds people make as they move about in the house; there is no connection with others unless you can see them.
> Being deaf, too, means that even when others are in the room with you, you don't know what they say to each other.
> There is no incidental learning. None.
> . . .
> There is no idle chitchat, no talking for relaxation.
> You do not pick up the bits and pieces of someone's character, personality, interests, and worries that others get in the course of talking "about nothing." . . . Slowly, surely, your isolation grows. (Bowe 1986, 21)

At school, he was often singled out for teasing and physical abuse because he was an avid reader and wore a hearing aid; thus he was considered "different." Sometimes, he refused to wear his hearing aid in an attempt to be like his classmates. Yet, he played baseball with a Little League team that won a championship. In high school, he played soccer and tennis and excelled at the latter. He also continued his avid reading, noting in his autobiography that "Few books have changed my life. Ayn Rand's towering novel *The Fountainhead* is one that did." Rand's hero "refused merely to exist; rather he exalted and excelled," Bowe wrote, adding that after reading the book, he "could see now that great things were possible" (Bowe 1986, 133). He was 14 years old at the time.

Bowe enrolled at Western Maryland College in Westminster, Maryland, majoring in English and graduating summa cum laude in 1969. He won a fellowship to attend Gallaudet College, which later became Gallaudet University. There he learned that sign language was not a detriment to deaf children, and he earned a master's degree in education of the deaf. He studied for his doctorate at New York University (NYU). During that time he met Phyllis Schwartz. The two dated for six months and married in 1971, living in a Washington Square apartment in Greenwich Village. The couple eventually had two daughters, Doran and Whitney.

While at NYU, Bowe worked as a research scientist in a training center for people specializing in deafness. He attended conferences, conducted surveys, and studied job discrimination against deaf people. He also met Eunice Fiorito, a blind social worker and director of the New York City Mayor's Office for the Handicapped. In 1975, she founded and became president of the volunteer American Coalition of Citizens with Disabilities (ACCD), a coalition of national, state, and local disability organizations. Fiorito hoped to develop a national civil rights movement operated by disabled people. It would tackle such disability problems as lack of access to public transportation, employment, and housing.

Bowe continued to meet with Fiorito and was convinced that ACCD "was the vehicle I needed to change the rules" and achieve equal opportunities for disabled people (Bowe 1986, 180). The two planned to work to get section 504 of the Rehabilitation Act of 1973 implemented. The act itself expanded "special Federal responsibilities and research and training programs with respect to handicapped individuals" and mandated that the U.S. Department of Health, Education, and Welfare (HEW) coordinate all programs with respect to handicapped individuals. Section 504 of the act simply states that "No otherwise qualified handicapped individual in the United States...shall, solely by reason of his handicap, be excluded from the participation in, be denied the benefits of, or be subjected to discrimination under any program or activity receiving Federal financial assistance." But the federal government had issued no regulations for compliance with this portion of the law, and institutions receiving federal funds, such as schools and hospitals, ignored section 504.

In 1976, Fiorito appointed Bowe executive director of the ACCD, and Bowe traveled to Washington, D.C. to advocate for HEW to enforce regulations in section 504, known by then as the "bill of rights for handicapped persons." As Bowe began to pressure federal government officials to implement section 504, support for ACCD grew. "Organizational membership doubled, then tripled, as people with deafness, blindness, cerebral palsy, paraplegia, quadriplegia, mental retardation, and epilepsy, together with their families, counselors, teachers, and friends sensed in ACCD a vehicle for the long-awaited breakthrough that would transform their lives" (Bowe 1986, 184–85). But no regulations were forthcoming, and Bowe helped develop a nationwide protest. For nearly one month, activists for the handicapped conducted sit-ins at HEW offices in 10 major cities, including Washington, D.C. The protest finally led to HEW issuing landmark regulations for Section 504 in 1977, a forerunner of the Americans with Disabilities Act of 1990 that bans discrimination against the handicapped within the private sector.

Soon after federal regulations were implemented in 1977, Bowe's first book, *Handicapping America: Barriers to Disabled People* (1978), was published. He explained in the book that when a child is labeled as having a disability, parents, teachers, and others may see that child differently—not as a child with abilities, but one with primarily a disability. His next book, *Rehabilitating America: Toward Independence for Disabled and Elderly People* (1980), discussed plans for removing the barriers that disabled people face. Because of Bowe's work in that regard, many handicapped individuals currently are able to access public transportation, obtain jobs once denied to them, find adequate housing, and enjoy other services.

During the 1980s, Bowe continued his efforts on behalf of disabled people. He was a U.S. representative at the United Nations' International Year of Disabled Persons in 1980, and was chairman of the U.S. Congress Commission on Education of the Deaf from 1984 to 1986. Bowe also served as a regional commissioner of the U.S. Department of Education's Rehabilitation Services Administration, and he was director of research for the U.S. Architectural and Transportation Compliance Board from 1984 to 1987.

In 1989, Bowe wrote an article for *Worklife*, a publication of the U.S. Department of Labor, in which he noted that at the time, "About one third of all disabled adults receive[d] federal and state benefits because of their disabilities. . . . fully 67 percent of these beneficiaries would rather work, even if it meant giving up governmental aid." Bowe further pointed out that across the United States there are "specialized programs designed to serve physically and emotionally handicapped residents. A variety of services is available and, very often, assistance in finding suitable employment is one of them. Some groups are geared toward serving a single disability group; others are more general in clientele and objectives. Employers can often find a pool of job-ready persons by contacting the director, personnel officer, or placement counselor of any of these specialized programs. The various community programs are listed in the yellow pages of local phone directories under Social Service Organizations and Rehabilitation Services" (Bowe 1989, 37–41).

From 1989 to 2007, Bowe was a professor at Hofstra University on Long Island, New York. He held the Dr. Mervin Livingston Schloss Distinguished Professorship for the Study of Disabilities and trained special education teachers. He urged his students as well as the general public to look beyond individual disabilities to the whole person.

Bowe received numerous honors throughout his years at the university. U.S. president George H. W. Bush honored Bowe for his lifetime achievements with the Distinguished Service Award in 1992. Bowe was inducted into the National Hall of Fame for People with Disabilities in 1994. In 1996, Hofstra honored him with the university's

Distinguished Teaching Award based on the recommendation of graduating seniors.

In 2005, Bowe became acting chair of Hofstra's counseling, research, special education, and rehabilitation department. Along with his full-time work in the department, he was a consultant to the National Association of the Deaf (NAD). In 2006, he released his study showing that Americans with disabilities comprise the third-largest minority in the United States. According to the *Rolling Rains Report*, written by Dr. Scott Rains for the hospitality and travel industries that attempt to accommodate handicapped individuals, the study revealed that "more than a quarter of this demographic live in poverty (75% earn less than $20,000 annually) and fewer than half have private health insurance.... [M]any adults with disabilities subsist on Social Security Disability Insurance (SSDI) and Supplemental Security Income (SSI), and although the monthly funds received from those programs provide barely livable wages, the benefit of Medicare and/or Medicaid is something this population cannot do without" (Rains 2007).

During his career, Bowe wrote numerous books for the general public as well as reports and textbooks for students and professionals, such as *U.S. Census and Disabled Adults: The 50 States and the District of Columbia* (1984), *Black Adults with Disabilities: A Statistical Report Drawn from the Census Bureau Data* (1985), *Equal Rights for Americans with Disabilities* (1992), *Physical, Sensory, and Health Disabilities: An Introduction* (2000), and *Universal Design in Education: Teaching Nontraditional Students* (2000).

Bowe continued to teach even though he became terminally ill with cancer in 2007. He was cared for in a hospice in Melville, New York, where he died on August 21, 2007. An obituary from Gallaudet University included the words of Nancy J. Bloch of the National Association of the Deaf: "A true giant is gone, but he paved the way for many generations to come.... Frank Bowe's commitment to accessibility and 'leveling the playing field,' his wit and humor, and his uncanny ability to encourage others to action are important elements of his legacy. The American deaf community and disabled Americans are the beneficiaries of his passion" (NAD 2007).

See also Rand, Ayn

References

Bowe, Frank. *Changing the Rules*. Silver Spring, MD: T. J. Publishers, 1986.

Bowe, Frank. *Handicapping America: Barriers to Disabled People*. New York: Harper & Row, 1978.

Bowe, Frank. *Rehabilitating America: Toward Independence for Disabled and Elderly People*. New York: Harper & Row, 1980.

Bowe, Frank G. "Recruiting Workers with Disabilities." *Worklife*, Summer 1989.

McMahon, Brian T., and Linda Shaw. *Enabling Lives: Biographies of Six Prominent Americans with Disabilities*. Boca Raton, FL: CRC Press, LLC, 2000.

National Association for the Deaf (NAD). "Frank G. Bowe, Advocate for Hearing Impaired and Deaf." *HearingReview*. http://www.hearingreview.com/insider/2007-11-15_05.asp (accessed October 20, 2010).

Rains, Scott. "Dr. Frank Bowe: Longtime Professor and Renowned Champion of People with Disabilities." *Rolling Rains Report: Precipitating Dialogue on Travel, Disability, and Universal Design*, August 24, 2007. http://www.rollingrains.com/archives/001784.html (accessed October 20, 2010).

Brown, Ruth (1891–1975)

A memorial bronze bust of Ruth Brown sits prominently in the Bartlesville, Oklahoma, public library. Commissioned by the Bartlesville Women's Network and the Friends of Miss Brown, it was presented on March 11, 2007—57 years after Brown was fired in spite of 30 years of excellent service. She was described as an activist who "relentlessly challenged the racial taboos and legal inequities of her time.... [A] Fearless champion of intellectual freedom in a fearful world, she was ahead of her time in her quest for truth and justice. She lost her job because of her courageous struggle" (Bartlesville Public Library).

Born on July 26, 1891, in Hiawatha, Kansas, Ruth Brown was the older of two children of Silas and Jennie Brown. The family lived for a time in California where Ruth attended high school, but she returned to Oklahoma for her college years, graduating in 1910 from Northwestern State Normal School in Alva. She began her career as a teacher. However, eager to live near her parents, she soon accepted a position as the library director of the Bartlesville Carnegie Library in November 1919. In no time, "Miss Brown," as she came to be known, knew all of her patrons—particularly the children—by name. She never married, but she wanted a family. At a time when single women seldom were allowed to adopt, Brown, after considerable effort, adopted Ellen Holliday and became a foster mother to Ellen's older sister, Holly.

Ruth Brown viewed her library work as a calling and felt passionate about the services she provided to the library patrons. Soon after she was hired, she became active in her professional society, the Oklahoma Library Association (OLA) and quickly took on a leadership role within the organization, being elected secretary in 1920. Six years later she held the position of treasurer. Five years after that, Brown was president of OLA.

During the organization's 1931 annual convention, Brown used her presidential pulpit to express her philosophies to her fellow librarians. She urged them to "reduce to a minimum worry about lost books and other red tape." She further pushed them to encourage people to "make use of their right to library service." To Brown, libraries were to be a source of "recreational culture suited to all needs" of the broad and diverse communities that they served (Oklahoma Library Association).

Since the 1920s, Brown had set an example by providing service to African Americans. Historical examination of the Bartlesville library records turns up a small number of borrowers' names identified in the registry in red ink as "colored." Brown took a story hour to Douglass School, the local public school for African American children, eventually bringing the Douglass children into the library, though story hours remained segregated. In time, she braved activities and programming specifically directed at the African American community, such as subscriptions to *Ebony* and *Negro Digest* and display of an educational exhibit titled "The Negro Culture from Africa to Today."

Brown did not believe that enforcement of racial equality should be limited to within the walls of the Bartlesville library. Thus, she increasingly translated her beliefs into her personal activities as well. She joined the Bartlesville chapter of the Committee on the Practice of Democracy (COPD) in 1946. The group strived to foster race relations—among all people—and sought to end any type of discrimination based on race, creed or color. That year, Brown's group affiliated with the Congress of Racial Equality (CORE), making it notable as the sole CORE chapter south of the Mason-Dixon Line. Among its activities, Brown's chapter worked to recruit an African

American doctor to live and work in Bartlesville's black community. It worked with the YWCA to sponsor seminars featuring both black and white speakers, such as a lecture by African American Bayard Rustin, a Quaker of some renown.

Brown truly riled the local community when she audaciously brought Clara Cooke and Mary Ellen Street, two African American teachers, to Hull's Drugstore in downtown Bartlesville. Not surprisingly—in the era of whites-only lunch counters—they were refused service, as Brown certainly knew they would be. But it was February 1950, CORE Brotherhood Month, and to Brown, it seemed an appropriate time for such an action. All of this transpired five years before Rosa Parks refused to give up her bus seat to a white man in 1955 and well before the civil rights movement sit-ins. As a librarian, Brown credited reading books such as Richard Wright's *Black Boy* as being particularly influential in the development of her views about this type of discriminatory practice.

A scant two weeks after the Hull drugstore protest, Senator Joseph McCarthy became a household name with his accusations of communists and communist sympathizers crawling out of every nook and cranny of virtually every corner of the United States. On the national scene, the Cold War was just in its infancy after World War II, and the climate was ripe for a Red Scare and McCarthy's blacklists, witch hunts, and loyalty oaths. Such talk, however, also resonated on the small stage of Bartlesville, Oklahoma, giving opponents of Brown's interracial activities a chance to come at her from another angle—suspicion that she was a communist. As her biographer put it: "This story of a brief episode in a small city in a sparsely populated state . . . does more than recall an interesting local event. It reveals, in addition, much about movement and countermovements during that part of the cold war that we call the McCarthy era and foregrounds the kind of people—mostly females—who labored for racial justice, sometimes at great cost, before the civil rights movement" (Robbins 2000, 3–4).

A tipping point had finally been reached in the conservative community of Bartlesville, and community leaders began their efforts to reign in Brown. A citizens' commission was formed with the unwritten yet expressly understood intent that its aim was Brown's dismissal from her position as Bartlesville's librarian. Acknowledging that the activities with which they took offense were conducted outside of the workplace, the city leaders and commission realized that her political views and civil rights activities could not be used as grounds for termination. At its first meeting, Brown was accused of providing subversive materials at the library, namely the *Nation* magazine; at a later commission meeting, the *New Republic* and *Soviet Russia Today* were added to the list of offensive periodicals that Brown was supplying. At this time, the library board quietly removed the magazines in question to a locked area in the building.

The commission now felt it had grounds to warrant an investigation of Brown's overall operation of the library. It called for the library board to audit its entire book collection, as well as evaluate Brown's performance. The board reported back to the commission that it found no evidence of subversive materials or teachings, nor any failing on the part of Brown's work ethic or character. On March 9, 1950, the front page of Bartlesville's local paper, the *Examiner-Enterprise*, ran an incendiary photo. It depicted a pile of the so-called subversive magazines, topped by two copies of, *The*

Russians, a book whose subtitle, *The Land, the People and Why They Fight*, was conveniently or inconveniently covered up—depending on one's point of view. It should be noted that the book was published in 1943, a time when the United States was allied with Russia in World War II. Additionally, the Bartlesville library had never owned even a single—let alone more than one—copy of this book. Gossip of the day was that the library's custodian had (either willingly or by coercion) given after-hours access to the library, allowing for some underhanded activity to take place and leading to the production of the photo. The *Examiner-Enterprise* never divulged its source.

The hullabaloo over Brown's activities actually stemmed from the fact that Bartlesville simply was not ready for a change in the status quo—that is, integration. Brown's efforts to promote the equality between the races both angered and frightened many people in the community, and they struck back in the only way that they knew how, fighting to preserve their way of life.

In early July 1950, a city ordinance was changed, allowing for dismissal of the entire library board. The current board was let go and a brand new board was seated; not a single new member supported Brown or even necessarily professed support of the library itself. One of the new appointees commented with some astonishment about his selection, citing his poor academic performance while in school and noting that he had never even set foot in the library. The new board took over on July 10 and set immediately to its task of relieving Brown of her duties as town librarian.

On July 25, 1950, she was summoned to an executive session of the commission; no minutes were taken. Brown's attorney had advised her to respond only in writing to questions of a personal nature. Many of the queries directed at her dealt with her interracial activities and her loyalties. When the topic of the subversive periodicals was raised, Brown stated that they were but 3 of 75 total publications to which she had subscribed and, moreover, the subscriptions had been in effect for 15 to 20 years. She went on to explain that she did not view her role as that of a censor, someone whose job it was to determine what the public could or could not read. The die was cast. Regardless of any response Brown might have given during that meeting, the result was a foregone conclusion. By day's end, she was advised that she was no longer the librarian for the town of Bartlesville.

The commission's official position was that Brown had been let go on grounds of insubordination; to the outside world, it appeared more realistic that she had been fired for trying to safeguard the library's and public's right to intellectual freedom, as well as their right to free speech. The Oklahoma Library Association, the American Library Association, and the American Civil Liberties Union joined in the outcry against Brown's firing. The community of Bartlesville was surprised and mortified by the national spotlight the scandal cast upon it—although not enough for the commission to rescind its action with regard to Brown.

While the story of this somewhat obscure Oklahoma librarian may not be familiar to many today, it resonated across the country at the time. To that end, Brown's saga became the catalyst for the film, *Storm Center*. The premise of the film has to do with a librarian's battle against pressure to remove so-called subversive books amidst the background of the Red Scare. Starring Bette Davis, the movie's plot struck a chord with the film industry as well. A few years before Brown's problems began, the U.S. House Committee on Un-American Activities had held its infamous hearings to root out communist influences in the film industry, creating an atmosphere of suspicion and fear throughout Hollywood. Some individuals who were accused of being communist sympathizers or actual card-carrying communists never recovered. Those who refused to inform on their professional colleagues risked imprisonment.

After her dismissal, Brown set up a rental library at her home, but she could not generate enough income to keep it going. Because of her interest in black civil rights, she took a job as librarian with an African American school, Piney Woods Country Life School south of Jackson, Mississippi. She enjoyed working with the students, but did not agree with the administrator of the school, who demanded that young people follow his strict rules, which included a ban on boys and girls holding hands. Brown left the school after three years and eventually found a job in a public library in Sterling, Colorado. She retired from there in 1961 and moved to Cincinnati, Ohio, to live with Holly, her foster daughter, and her family.

When Brown's health began to fail, her daughter Ellen took her to Collinsville, Oklahoma, to live with her family. Brown died on September 10, 1975, in Collinsville, leaving her mark on the world in many ways, some apparent and some less so. During her years as Bartlesville's librarian, she fostered a love of learning in many a young person. She took great pride in mentoring children—of all races—and encouraging their lifelong education. Two of her prodigies followed in her professional footsteps, one going on to work in the stacks at the Library of Congress, another becoming head of the Research Libraries of the New York Public Library. In addition to keeping the spirit of Miss Brown alive via the bronze bust located on site at its library, the Oklahoma Library Association presents an award each year in her honor for programs that address issues of social concern.

Margaret Gay

See also McCarthy, Joseph; Parks, Rosa; Rustin, Bayard

References

Bakken, Gordon Morris, and Brenda Farrington, eds. *Encyclopedia of Women in the American West*. Thousand Oaks, CA, and London: Sage Publications, 2003.

Bartlesville Public Library. "Miss Ruth Brown," n.d. http://www.bartlesville.lib.ok.us/aboutlibrary/missbrown.htm (accessed May 4, 2010).

Horn, Zoia. "Book Review." *Progressive Librarian*, 2001.

Oklahoma Library Association. "Oklahoma Library Legends, An OKL Centennial Project: Ruth Brown," n.d. http://www.library.okstate.edu/dean/jpaust/legends/people/brown.htm (accessed May 4, 2010).

Robbins, Louise S. *The Dismissal of Miss Ruth Brown: Civil Rights, Censorship, and the American Library*. Norman: University of Oklahoma Press, 2000.

Brownmiller, Susan (1935–)

Known as a political dissident and activist in the Women's Liberation movement, Susan Brownmiller cofounded New York Radical Feminists in the 1960s. She is a journalist and author of an influential book *Against Our Will: Men, Women, and Rape* (1975), in which she discusses the long history of rape as a form of male intimidation of women. The best-selling book raised public awareness of violence against females of all ages and races. It also brought her plenty of criticism from those who argued that she

Susan Brownmiller poses with her book *Against Our Will—Men, Women and Rape*, in New York, October 18, 1975. (AP Photo/Suzanne Vlami)

was a lesbian, anti-male, or too simplistic in her views about male dominance. Others contend that at the time Brownmiller's 1975 work was published, society was obsessed with rape and that her book lacks objectivity with its focus on gruesome tales.

One of her critics, professor and political activist Angela Davis, argues that Brownmiller used racist scare tactics in her book. Davis takes issue with a chapter titled "A Question of Race" and passages such as this: "[T]he incidence of actual rape combined with the looming spectre of the rapist in the mind's eye, and in particular the mythified spectre of the black man as rapist to which the black man in the name of his manhood now contributes, must be understood as a control mechanism against the freedom, mobility and aspirations of all women, white and black. The crossroads of racism and sexism had to be a violent meeting place. There is no use pretending it doesn't exist" (Brownmiller 1986, 281–82).

Brownmiller has denied using racist scare tactics. In her book *In Our Time: Memoir of a Revolution* (1999), she argues that such criticism has come from political activists on the left.

Susan was born in Brooklyn, New York, on February 15, 1935, to Mae and Samuel Warhaftig. Her father was a salesperson, and her mother held a secretarial job. Her parents sent her to East Midwood Jewish Center on Ocean Avenue to learn Hebrew and Jewish history. She became intensely involved in her lessons and eagerly shared her learning with her parents and relatives. When Israel became a Jewish state in 1948, she wanted to go there to work the land. She went to the synagogue each Saturday morning for prayers. She reported:

> My parents grew somewhat alarmed by my sudden intensity. My aunts and uncles started calling me "the *Rebbetzin*." "What's a '*rebbetzin*'?" I asked my mother, thinking it must mean a serious, dedicated, intelligent person. "A *rebbetzin* is a rabbi's wife," she laughed.
>
> What a deflating blow to my ego and ambitions! A rabbi was a revered personage; a rabbi's wife served cake and tea. ... My instinctive feminism (no lessons needed) could not be reconciled with this severe limitation on my life's path. The sly mockery had its effect. So much for Judaism, so much for religion—I became an atheist, a secularist, and never looked back. (Jewish Women's Archive)

From 1952 to 1955, Susan attended Cornell University and also the Jefferson School of Social Sciences, but did not earn a degree. She left to study acting, using the stage name Brownmiller. She legally changed her name in 1961. While training for an acting career, she took a variety of jobs, including editorial work at confession (or romance) magazines—publications with anonymous first-person accounts that followed a sin-suffer-repent formula. Her editing experiences led to an interest in journalism, and she held jobs at such publications as *Coronet*, *Newsweek*, and *Village Voice*.

In 1960, Brownmiller joined the Congress of Racial Equality (CORE), a national civil rights organization with chapters throughout the country. She became a political activist by organizing a picket line in front of a Woolworth's store in New York. Such pickets were taking place in a number of cities to support sit-ins by African Americans at a "whites-only" Woolworth's lunch counter in Greensboro, North Carolina. CORE, the Student Nonviolent Coordinating Committee (SNCC), which was founded in 1960 and practiced civil disobedience in their efforts to end segregation in the South, and the National Association for the Advancement of Colored People (NAACP) conducted a campaign called Freedom Summer in 1964. Brownmiller was one of about 1,000 white people who took part in the campaign, which was an attempt to help African Americans in the Deep South register to vote. At the time, southern white officials systematically kept blacks from voting by requiring them to pay poll taxes and pass literacy tests. Officials also intimidated potential black voters with arrests, beatings, and lynchings. During Freedom Summer, famed civil rights activist Fannie Lou Hamer of Mississippi was nearly beaten to death because she tried to register to vote.

By the time Brownmiller became involved in Freedom Summer, she began to sense that "a revolution was brewing" among American women. She had read Betty Friedan's *The Feminine Mystique* (1963), a year after the book was published. Brownmiller said the book "changed my life" (Brownmiller 1999, 3).

After Freedom Summer, Brownmiller returned to New York and became a TV newswriter at the American Broadcasting Company. She worked at the network until 1968, when she "quit the safety net of my TV job for the marginal life of a feminist soldier." She joined a consciousness-raising group known as the New York Radical Women, and learned for the first time that she could say aloud that she had had illegal abortions. She found that she was not alone, and that other women in the group had abortion stories to tell publicly. New York Radical Women existed for only two years—1967 to 1969—and in 1969, another group called New York Radical Feminists formed. It was part of the Women's Liberation Movement (or Women's Lib, or women's movement). Brownmiller points out that there were two different factions of the women's movement—reformers who were members of the National Organization of Women (NOW) cofounded by Betty Friedan, and the radicals. As Brownmiller explains: "NOW was a dues-paying membership organization that welcomed the participation of men. . . . Women's Liberation, in name and spirit, sprang from the radical ferment of the civil rights, antiwar, and counterculture movements" (Brownmiller 1999, 7).

In 1970, Brownmiller helped coordinate a sit-in against *Ladies' Home Journal* magazine. The purpose was to protest the magazine's stereotypical representation of women, lack of female writers, and exclusion of women in top editorial positions. During the protest, the group of 100 women confronted John Mack Carter, editor and publisher, and Lenore Hershey, senior editor.

The women read a list of more than a dozen demands that included hiring a woman as editor-in-chief, using women writers for columns and freelance assignments, opening editorial conferences to all employees, refusing to publish advertisements that degrade and exploit women, and publishing a column by the Women's Liberation Movement. As a result, the magazine commissioned Brownmiller and other protesters to write articles with a feminist slant.

In 1971, Brownmiller with New York Radical Feminists gathered for a speak-out at which women publicly told their stories about rape. At the rally, Brownmiller began to realize how wrong she had been in her views about rape. She had believed that women were at fault because they had lured men on with their behavior. After hearing women's stories, she had to reexamine her views, acknowledging that women she knew had been raped and that females of all ages and backgrounds are raped. She became more objective as she researched and developed ideas for a book. She presented her proposal to Simon and Schuster, and the company published *Against Our Will: Men, Women, and Rape* four years later. The book, which is the result of Brownmiller's extensive research in multiple fields, explores the history of rape and the political use of rape in war from ancient Greece through the Vietnam War. After the book's publication, Brownmiller gained national fame as a leading feminist and was interviewed by numerous magazine reporters and television hosts. In a 1975 interview for *People* magazine, she told Sally Moore: "Most women live in fear of rape. In my research I found there is less provocation on the part of rape victims than any other crime of violence.... Rape is just one form of victimization. We are trained to view our sexuality as submitting to male aggression. There's a lot of cultural conditioning that makes women vulnerable, and 99 percent of men don't understand it. It was only with the women's movement and the book that I began to see women's weakness and terror" (Moore 1975).

Brownmiller's book helped propel changes in social attitudes toward rape and rapists. Rape crisis centers opened across the United States, and women became less reticent about reporting rape. Laws also changed. For example, over the years, all states have overturned laws that included a marital and spousal rape exemption. The exemption was based on the theory that a married woman is legally obligated to have sexual intercourse with her husband. Even though the exemption has been rescinded in all 50 states, spousal rape still takes place and perpetrators often receive lenient penalties.

In 1979, a group known as Women Against Pornography (WAP) formed with Brownmiller's organizational help. For example, she orchestrated WAP demonstrations to illustrate the "hidden life"—pornographic sex shops and theaters—in New York City's Times Square. WAP conducted marches, tours of lurid attractions in Times Square, and educational discussions that brought pornography to national attention. Organizations in various cities held marches through red-light districts carrying banners such as "women unite, take back the night." The WAP campaigns also created a backlash. When WAP lobbied for legislation to ban pornography, some legal experts charged that the radical feminists were condoning censorship like McCarthyites—supporters of U.S. senator Joseph McCarthy (1908–1957) who falsely accused hundreds of Americans in government and business of being communists. Some feminists argued that WAP tactics were infringing on free speech rights; others complained that WAP was attacking sexual freedom and individual choices for sexual pleasure. By the late 1980s, the organization turned its attention to international sex-trafficking—the buying and selling of women and children for sex. WAP disbanded in the mid-1990s.

Brownmiller has continued to lecture and write about feminist issues. Her book *Femininity* (1984) examines how the very term "femininity" has affected women's lives over the centuries and forced conformity in everything from body shape to sexuality. She also has written about other topics such as *Seeing Vietnam: Encounters of the Road and Heart* (1994), in which she describes her tour of Vietnam in 1992 and her impressions of the people.

In 2010, Brownmiller celebrated her 75th birthday. Currently, her books are still being read and discussed.

See also Davis, Angela; Hamer, Fannie Lou; McCarthy, Joseph

References

Brownmiller, Susan. *Against Our Will: Men, Women, and Rape*. New York: Bantam/Simon and Schuster, 1986. First published 1975.

Brownmiller, Susan. *In Our Time: Memoir of a Revolution*. New York: Dial Press, 1999.

Brownmiller, Susan. *Seeing Vietnam: Encounters of the Road and Heart*. New York: HarperCollins, 1994.

Brownmiller, Susan. "Susan Brownmiller Statement." *Jewish Women's Archive*, n.d. http://jwa.org/feminism/_html/JWA008.htm (accessed September 30, 2010).

Davis, Angela. *Women, Race, and Class*. New York: Random House/Vintage Books 1981.

Moore, Sally. " 'Rape Is a Crime Not of Lust, but Power,' Argues Susan Brownmiller." *People*, November 10, 1975. http://www.people.com/people/archive/article/0,,20065841,00.html (accessed August 3, 2011).

Bullard, Robert (1946–)

In a 2006 interview, Robert Bullard recounted his early involvement in the environmental justice movement. "I . . . started connecting the dots in terms of housing, residential patterns, patterns of land use, where highways go, where transportation routes go, and how economic-development decisions are made. It was very clear that people who were making decisions—county commissioners or industrial boards or city councils—were not the same people who were 'hosting' these facilities in their communities." He went on to say, "Without a doubt, it was a form of apartheid where whites were making decisions and black people and brown people and people of color, including Native Americans on reservations, had no seat at the table" (Dicum 2006).

Robert D. Bullard was born on December 21, 1946, to Myrtle and Nehemiah Bullard in Elba, Alabama. They had five children, including Robert. He began his academic career at Alabama Agricultural and Mechanical University, where he majored in history and government with a minor in sociology. He studied sociology at the graduate level, receiving his master's degree from Atlanta University (now Clark Atlanta University) and his PhD from Iowa State University.

In 1979, Bullard's wife, Linda McKeever Bullard, was the lead attorney in a class-action lawsuit, *Bean v. Southwestern Waste Management, Inc.* She represented Margaret Bean and other African American Houston residents of Northwood Manor, a middle-class neighborhood, located in the suburbs of Houston. The lawsuit, filed against the city of Houston, the State of Texas and locally headquartered Browning Ferris Industries (the second-largest waste disposal company in the United States) made novel use of civil rights law to claim environmental discrimination by a waste facility siting. In all other circumstances, Northwood Manor would be a highly unusual spot for a garbage dump—except for the fact that its residents' racial composition was 82 percent black.

At the time, Robert Bullard was employed as an untenured assistant professor at Texas Southern University, having just completing his PhD in sociology at Iowa State University two years earlier. His wife called upon him to act as an expert witness in the trial, and he undertook various methods of research to bolster the case. The study he produced, *Solid Waste Sites and the Black Houston Community* (1983) is considered the first documented case study of ecoracism in the United States.

Bullard discovered that Houston historically would locate its waste facilities in areas that were largely populated by African Americans. He found that, additionally, Houston's black neighborhoods were frequently chosen as the sites for toxic waste dumps. In his study, Bullard reported that the five city-owned garbage dumps, six of eight city-owned incinerators and three of four private landfills were in African American neighborhoods; however, at the time, blacks made up only 25 percent of the city's population (Bullard 1983, 273–88). As his research accumulated, he came to the conclusion that the placement of local waste facilities was not occurring in a haphazard and arbitrary fashion. In every case, the neighborhoods' character (i.e., racial component) had been well established prior to any consideration of siting waste facilities among them. The conclusion was apparent: waste facilities were being deliberately, intentionally located in African American areas.

This initial exposure set Bullard on what would be a lifelong academic and activist campaign; he would devote his career to fighting against environmental racism and for environmental justice. A web site defines two terms most relevant to Bullard's pursuits as follows: "Environmental racism is the disproportionate impact of environmental hazards on people of color; Environmental justice is the movement's response to environmental racism" (Environmental Justice/Environmental Racism web site). The Environmental Protection Agency (EPA) has a somewhat more complex definition of the term environmental justice: "[T]he fair treatment and meaningful involvement of all people regardless of race, class, nationality, origin, or income with respect to the development, implementation, and enforcement of environmental laws, regulations, and policies. Fair treatment means that no group of people, including racial, ethnic, or socio-economic groups, should bear a disproportionate share of the negative consequences resulting from industrial, municipal, and commercial operations or the execution of federal, state, local, and tribal programs and policies" (Bullard 2005, 4).

Bullard began to further his knowledge of these issues when he used what he had learned in Houston to broaden his studies and apply it in a larger context to a greater portion of the American South. He spent the 1980s investigating mostly black areas in Houston and Dallas, Texas, neighborhoods as well as in Alsen, Louisiana; Institute, West Virginia; and Emelle, Alabama. He theorized that these communities would have an abundance of "locally unwanted land uses" (LULUs) amongst them due to their populace's economic and political vulnerabilities. As a result, Bullard believed that the residents living in these areas would manifest more environmental and health risks than the general population overall. Indeed, his research findings bore out a clear

Robert Bullard, founder of the Environmental Justice Center, poses in his office on the Clark Atlanta University campus in Atlanta, between enlarged versions of two of his books, August 24, 2004. (AP Photo/Ric Feld)

overrepresentaion of hazards in African American populated areas versus those inhabited by whites, with marked health risks increased to blacks. Bullard published his findings in his first of many books, *Dumping in Dixie: Race, Class and Environmental Quality* (1990). In recognition of his groundbreaking work, the National Wildlife Federation gave him a Conservation Achievement Award that year. Since then, the book has become a standard text in the environmental justice field.

Using the words "minority" and "environment," Bullard did a literature search in the late 1980s and found 12 articles, six of which were his own. Deciding that more investigation was warranted, he soon joined forces with fellow academics Bunyan Bryant of the University of Michigan and Charles Lee of the United Church of Christ. They started out holding seminars and conferences. Then they wrote to the secretary of the U.S. Department of Health and Human Services and to the head of the EPA, requesting to meet and discuss policy on environmental discrimination. While the former never answered them, the head of the EPA did, meeting with them on multiple occasions. As a result, the EPA's Work Group on Environmental Equity was formed, later becoming the Office of Environmental Equity, then the Office of Environmental Justice under EPA Administrator Carol Browner in 1993 (Cole and Fisher 2001, 24).

In 1991, Bullard was instrumental in bringing about the First National People of Color Environmental Leadership Summit. He began with a small list of 30 groups that were working on environmental issues and expanded it to include more than 300 groups, including ones outside the United States. On the last day of the Summit, held on Capitol Hill in Washington, D.C., from October 24 to 27, 1991, a list of 17 "Principles of Environmental Justice" was adopted (Bullard 2005, 3, 299).

The Environmental Justice Resource Center was Bullard's creation, established in 1994 at Clark Atlanta University in Georgia. Over the years, it has become "a nationally recognized powerhouse for environmental policy, analysis, community-driven research, education, and training." The center is an archival resource for various media—photos, videos, slides, and tapes—all of which offer documentation of the history of the movement. The center's web site provides information and acts as a curriculum resource guide "on environmental justice, environmental racism, healthy communities, transportation equity and suburban sprawl" (Environmental Justice Resource Center web site).

On February 11, 1994, after receiving advice from the National Environmental Justice Advisory Council (NEJAC), President Bill Clinton signed the Environmental Justice Executive Order 12898. Prior to that, Bullard had been part of a national coalition that developed an environmental justice position paper, which was instrumental in the establishment of NEJAC as an advisor to the EPA. At the time the NEJAC gave its advice to President Clinton, Bullard was NEJAC's Health and Research Subcommittee chair. Bullard also had some impact during the Bush administrations. He and some other environmental justice advocates convinced the EPA to create an Office on Environmental Equity.

Bullard has concentrated his career in both study and research. But he has not lived in an "ivory tower." He believes that change must come from the people whom it affects, a belief shared by Lois Gibbs, who directs the grassroots Center for Health, Environment and Justice. In his very first book, Bullard wrote that the environmental justice movement was a grassroots effort, made up of people of color that would spread across the United States in protest of environmental racism. From the start, Bullard believed that the movement signified a convergence of two preexisting movements of the 1960s: the African American civil rights movement and the environmental movement. Bullard continues to work hands-on with grassroots community groups from all parts of the United States and all over the world. He attends public hearings, offers expert testimony, gives speeches, and continues to pioneer research in his field.

In 1992, he once again helped coordinate participation in an environmental summit, this one taking place in Rio de Janeiro. He cosponsored an Environmental Justice Exchange Study Tour, taking a dozen environmental justice leaders to South Africa in 1996. As a member of the Washington Office on Environmental Justice delegation, he attended the United Nations' 1996 Habitat II Summit in Istanbul, Turkey. He also helped prepare environmental racism documents presented in 1999 at the UN's Human Rights Commission in Geneva, Switzerland.

One of his most significant accomplishments came about in 1997, years after the lawsuit began. The case of *Citizens Against Nuclear Trash (CANT) v. Louisiana Energy Services* (1989) was decided in favor of the plaintiff—the first such environmental justice lawsuit declared by a federal court. The decision by the Nuclear Regulatory Commission was upheld in 1988, forever stopping construction of the nation's first privately owned uranium enrichment plant that had been contested for over nine years. Bullard's analysis and expert testimony was largely credited with the positive outcome.

Bullard was asked in 2006 what keeps him going after all his years in his pursuit of environmental justice. He replied, "People who fight . . . People who do not let the garbage trucks and the landfills and the petrochemical plants roll over them. That has kept me in this movement for the last 25 years. And in the last 10 years, we've been winning: lawsuits are being won, reparations are being paid, apologies are being made. These companies have been put on notice that they can't do this anymore, anywhere" (Dicum 2006).

In its April 3, 2008, edition, *Newsweek* named Bullard one of 15 of "The Century's Environmental Leaders," noting his ongoing involvement with the Hurricane Katrina catastrophe in Louisiana. Bullard previously went on the record about this disaster:

> Katrina was not isolated. It was not an aberration, and it was not incompetence on the part of FEMA and Michael Brown and the Bush administration. This has been going on for a long time under Republicans and Democrats, and the central theme that drives all of this is race and class.... From coast to coast, you see this happening. It's not just the landfill, it's not just the incinerator, it's not just the garbage dump, it's not just the crisscrossing freeway and highway, and the bus barns that dump all that stuff in these neighborhoods—it's all that combined. Even if each particular facility is in compliance, there are no regulations that take into account this saturation. It may be legal, but it is immoral. Just like slavery was legal, but slavery has always been immoral. (Dicum 2006)

Margaret Gay

See also Gibbs, Lois

References

Bullard, Robert. *Dumping in Dixie: Race, Class, and Environmental Quality*. Boulder, CO: Westview Press, 1990.

Bullard, Robert. *The Quest for Environmental Justice: Human Rights and the Politics of Pollution*. San Francisco: Sierra Club Books, 2005.

Bullard, Robert. *Race, Place, and Environmental Justice after Hurricane Katrina: Struggles to Reclaim, Rebuild, and Revitalize New Orleans and the Gulf Coast*. Boulder, CO: Westview Press, 2009.

Bullard, Robert. "Solid Waste Sites and the Black Houston Community." *Sociological Inquiry*, April 1983.

Cole, Luke, and Sheila Foster. *From the Ground Up: Environmental Racism and the Rise of the Environmental Justice Movement*. New York: New York University Press, 2001.

Dicum, Gregory. "Justice in Time, Meet Robert Bullard: The Father of Environmental Justice." *Grist*, March 14, 2006. http://www.grist.org/article/dicum (accessed October 25, 2010).

Environmental Justice/Environmental Racism web site. http://www.ejnet.org/ej/ (accessed October 21, 2010).

Environmental Justice Resource Center web site. http://www.ejrc.cau.edu/ (accessed October 20, 2010).

Burroughs, William (1914–1997)

William S. Burroughs was a writer and seminal character at the onset of the Beat Generation. The term was coined by one of its best-known members, Jack Kerouac. This time of experimental expression is also referred to as the Beat Movement, reflecting the effect of its pulse across successive generations of western culture. The original Beat Generation was a set of writers, often members of a Midwest creative diaspora whose lives were informed by the rise of institutionalized power and the co-opting influences of consumerism just after World War II (1939–1945). These men disdained middle-class lifestyles and goals, and their art, especially in written works, was an often highly creative, shocking attack on the modern world they did not want to inhabit.

One of the forefathers of the Beat Generation of the 1950s and 1960s, William S. Burroughs was responsible for radically changing the form of the American novel (undated photo). (AP Photo)

One of the Beat cohorts wrote on the influences attending the group. John Clellon Holmes explained in a 1952 article for *New York Times Magazine* that the Beat practitioners were: "brought up during the collective bad circumstances of a dreary depression, weaned during the collective uprooting of a global war, they distrust collectivity. But they have never been able to keep the world out of their dreams... Their adolescence was spent in a topsy-turvy world of war bonds, swing shifts, and troop movements" (Holmes 1952).

The Beat Generation found its voice on the streets of Manhattan in the years just after World War II. It would later reach its heyday in San Francisco, a few blocks from where the movement would help spawn the hippies of Haight-Ashbury. Though hardly as well known as the hippie culture of the 1960s, it was Burroughs and the Beat writers who laid the foundation for that transcendentally inspired phenomenon. City Lights Books served as the spiritual home of many of the emerging Beat writers. Opened in 1953, the nation's first all-paperback bookstore served as the intellectual locus of antiauthoritarian politics and insurgent thinking that was the hallmark of Beat output.

Burroughs was an instrumental force within the small coterie of City Light's celebrities in the mid-1950s. They included Allen Ginsberg, the poet whose most famous work is "Howl" and a collection titled *Howl and Other Poems* (1956), and Jack Kerouac, author of *On the Road* (1957). Burroughs had met them and a few other like-minded individuals in late 1943. Burroughs was older than either Ginsberg or Kerouac and tended to act as a teacher, doing more encouraging than actual writing. But then, writing had not been his top priority by the time he had reached Manhattan on a path that began soon after his birth in St. Louis, Missouri.

Born on February 5, 1914, William Seward Burroughs II was the son of Laura Lee Burroughs, a direct descendant of Robert E. Lee. His father Mortimer was the son of the first William Seward Burroughs, who invented a mechanical adding machine that launched what would become the Burroughs Corporation. The family was successful in business, and their wealth afforded young William the resources to be educated at various private schools. It was apparent to his parents that their son was not going to be satisfied living a "normal life," at least in any manner that was familiar to them. The young man would spend a lot of time by himself, passing time mostly with books that helped him conjure up fantasies of homo-erotica, guns, violence, criminal pursuits, and a life free from constraint. He was not a poor student, but he was hardly engaged in the academic life. He was not a rule follower.

In high school, Burroughs's first romantic interest was another boy. He would become renowned for his descriptions of gay love, and he is forthright in his defense of that realm of sexuality in many examples of his writing. But it is certainly shortchanging the man to describe him, as many biographers do, as a "homosexual writer." In fact, his sometimes-tortured writings deal with male and female sexuality and the intense drive of all physical desire, which he would liken to an addiction.

After he graduated from Harvard with a degree in English literature in 1936, Burroughs's parents accepted the inevitable and, through a trust, kept him in an allowance of $150 per month for years afterward. This stipend, substantial in its day, allowed the young man to continue his studies, travel, and avoid thinking about employment. As he wrote, "That was in the depression and there were no jobs and I couldn't think of any job I wanted, in any case. I drifted around Europe for a year or so ... U.S. dollars could buy a good percentage of the inhabitants of Austria, male or female. That was in 1936 and the Nazis were closing in fast" (Burroughs 1953, xiii–xiv).

While in Austria studying medicine, Burroughs met and married a Jewish woman who was desperate to get to the United States. This was an obvious marriage of convenience and mercy, and it lasted only a short time after the couple settled in New York City. In the United States, Burroughs recounted how he "fooled around with taking graduate courses in psychology and jiu-jitsu lessons. I decided to undergo psychoanalysis and continued it for three years. Analysis removed inhibitions and anxiety so that I could live the way I wanted to live" (Burroughs 1953, xiv).

He attempted to enter military officer training programs no less than five times. He was rejected consistently. But then when he was drafted to serve as a private in the army during World War II, they found him to be fit for unlimited service. By then, Burroughs had decided that he "was not going to like the Army and copped-out on my nuthouse record." This referred to an incident when he got "a Van Gogh kick," and cut off the last joint of his little finger on his left hand. The Dutch painter Vincent van Gogh cut off his left ear lobe in 1888 because of mental illness or love. Burroughs was trying to impress a man with whom he was infatuated in 1939 (Burroughs 1953, xiv).

Burroughs took on various jobs in the months following the brief military sojourn, working as a private detective, a summons-server, a bartender, a factory worker, and an office denizen. He even started to pull some petty crimes: more as homage to the exploits described in Jack Black's memoir *You Can't Win* (1926, 1988) than from actual need. Burroughs, after all, was still bolstered by the family stipend. It was the Wild West–era safecracker's story that served as precursor to more than the dalliance with crime that Burroughs was living out in New York. He also admired the drug-taking and general debauchery that marked many of Black's exploits. As it happened, a powerful synergy was present in the same year—1927—that Burroughs discovered *You Can't Win*. The teenage Burroughs had badly burned his right hand while playing with his chemistry set. The family physician injected him with a large dosage of morphine, and he was smitten with the feeling generated. As he recalls in later writings, a nurse who told him about a particular benefit of narcotics reinforced this first taste of opiates. "As a boy I was much plagued by nightmares. I remember a nurse telling me that opium gives you sweet dreams, and I resolved that I would smoke opium when I grew up" (Grauerholz and Silverberg 1998, 5). Jack Black was also an opium addict.

By the time Burroughs met Herbert Huncke, the drifter and streetwise heroin junkie who was to serve as inspiration for many of Burroughs's colleagues, he was pretty well hooked on morphine. As he tells it in *Junkie* (also published as *Junky*), he was selling a gun and morphine to a couple of heroin underworld figures that he knew as Roy and Harold when he first saw Huncke: "Waves of hostility and suspicion flowed out from his large brown eyes like some sort of television broadcast. The effect was almost like a physical impact. The man was small and very thin, his neck loose in the collar of his shirt. His complexion faded from brown to a mottled yellow, and pancake make-up had been heavily applied in an attempt to conceal a skin eruption. His mouth was drawn down at the corners in a grimace of petulant annoyance" (Grauerholz and Silverberg 1998, 52).

It was almost an instantaneous recognition of a common purpose for Burroughs. He was seeking this path and soon after began to shoot heroin. He was soon addicted. Starting with his first buys of morphine in 1944 and progressing through the haze of a daily heroin boost, he remained an addict for most of the next 15 years. His experiences and impressions during these years formed the basis of the writings that would eventually flow from his pencil and typewriter. His first literary attempt was at the urging of Kerouac, who was coauthor of a fictionalized retelling of the story of one of the Beat's inner circle, Lucien Carr. Carr was accused of shooting a man who had made sexual advances toward him. The book *And the Hippos Were Boiled in Their Tanks* (2008) was eventually published, but the Burroughs and Kerouac manuscript had been rejected in 1945. For years afterward, Burroughs would not attempt to write anything else.

Burroughs's adventures and his travels would continue, however. One of the central figures among the early Beats in New York City was the young Columbia student Joan Vollmer Adams, who lived in an off-campus apartment with Edie Parker (who would later marry Kerouac for a brief time). Burroughs and the other men of the group used this apartment as a second home, and

Adams and Burroughs became romantically involved. Though he preferred sex with men, Adams would become his common-law wife, and they produced a son, William S. Burroughs Jr.

When the group of friends began experimenting with Benzedrine stimulants, Adams was soon addicted, and her life spiraled out of control. Many in their group began to avoid her. Burroughs himself found it necessary to leave her when problems with his own drug use made life in New York too difficult for him. He decided to move to the southern part of the United States, settling in New Orleans and Texas where he would try his hand at cotton and marijuana farming. He eventually sent for Adams, his son, and a daughter from Adams's first marriage.

On one of their frequent trips to Mexico in 1951, the couple was entertaining a group of friends. An inspired Burroughs, a man who loved his guns, decided to show off his marksmanship by having Adams place a glass on her head. He was going to shoot it off. He fired the shot and it passed through his wife's head, killing her instantly. While there is still controversy surrounding the facts of this story (was it an accident, or actually murder?), it is clear that this event had a profound effect on the trajectory of his life. To avoid arrest, he sent his son to live with his parents, and he set off on a tour of South America, eventually ending up in Tangier, Morocco, where he started to write in snippets of thought and drug-fueled inspiration. At the urging of Ginsberg, he did complete a manuscript for an autobiographical novel of his drug exploits that would be published as *Junkie: Confessions of an Unredeemed Drug Addict* (1953) by the pulp fiction house Ace Books. Burroughs insisted on using the pen name William Lee.

At this same time, Ginsberg, Kerouac, and others were expanding the Beat genre by including more transcendental themes and embracing Buddhist philosophy in their writing. They moved from New York to San Francisco and became celebrities. Often they would travel to see their friend and old mentor Burroughs in Tangier, where they could escape from their newfound fame and perhaps do some writing. On one of these trips, Kerouac and Ginsberg discovered the stories and the odd paragraphs that their host had been writing for years, and they urged Burroughs to compile the snippets into a book form. Kerouac and Ginsberg actually typed up the pieces and helped with the editing. Jack Kerouac suggested the name: *Naked Lunch*.

The Naked Lunch (1959) was published by the Parisian house Olympia Press, and it created a worldwide sensation when it was reprinted as simply *Naked Lunch* (1962) by the American house Grove Press. The narrator of the work is William Lee, a junkie whose adventures are chronicled in a series of barely connected vignettes. Often shocking, sometimes funny, and always intense, the writing is now considered not only Burroughs's best work, but also a landmark American literary publication. However, at the time of its publication, it became a test case in Boston when the courts banned it as obscene. The case was appealed to the Massachusetts Supreme Court in 1966, and Norman Mailer and Allen Ginsberg testified in the work's defense. The court overturned the obscenity charges and declared the book was protected by the First Amendment of the U.S. Constitution.

Other works by Burroughs include *The Soft Machine* (1961), *The Ticket That Exploded* (1962), *Nova Express* (1964), *The Last Words of Dutch Schultz* (1969), *The Wild Boys: A Book of the Dead* (1971), *Port of Saints* (1973), *Cities of the Red Night* (1981), *The Place of Dead Roads* (1983),

The Western Lands (1987), and *My Education: A Book of Dreams* (1995). He also wrote essays and even plays, and dabbled in painting and spoken-word productions.

On August 2, 1997, Burroughs died of a heart attack in Lawrence, Kansas. Burroughs may have been the prototypical Beatnik as the themes of much of Beat writing (and certainly his) included reflections on their own experiences of homosexuality, bisexuality, vagrancy, lawlessness, alcoholism, and drug addiction. Their method of presenting ideas and experiences tended to avoid the norms of artists who had gone before. Streams of consciousness, nonlineal organizing, disturbing details, and taboo subjects were often utilized to help break the hold of conventionality that they so abhorred.

His work has influenced untold writers in their use of subject, punctuation, word usage, and nonlinear thinking in the telling of a story. Burroughs's legacy as an outsider and as an innovator of language and style is difficult to overestimate. He continues to be vilified by those who find his writings offensive. But new generations of artists continue to find inspiration in his life and his work.

Martin K. Gay

References

Burroughs, William S. *And the Hippos Were Boiled in Their Tanks*. New York: Grove/Atlantic, 2008. (Originally written in 1945 with the bylines William Lee and John Kerouak.)

Burroughs, William S. *Junkie: Confessions of an Unredeemed Drug Addict*. New York: Ace Books, 1953.

Grauerholz, James, and Ira Silverberg, eds. *Word Virus: The William S. Burroughs Reader*. New York: Grove/Atlantic, 1998.

Holmes, John Clellon. "This Is the Beat Generation." *New York Times Magazine*, November 16, 1952. http://www.rooknet.net/beatpage/writers/holmes.html (accessed November 15, 2010).

C

Cammermeyer, Grethe (1942–)

While still in the U.S. military, Colonel Margarethe (Grethe) Cammermeyer was the first high-ranking officer to publicly say she is a lesbian, which in 1989 violated the military's rule that prohibited homosexuals from serving in any branch of the service. The U.S. Army began discharge proceedings and by 1992, Col. Cammermeyer was forced from the military despite her exemplary record—she is a Vietnam veteran, Bronze Star recipient, and recipient of the VA Nurse of the Year award in 1985 as well as many other honors. But one of her most notable achievements was her refusal to accept the military ban and to successfully challenge the military in court. She filed a lawsuit charging that her forced discharge was unconstitutional. After more than two years in and out of court, she was reinstated in 1994. As she noted years later in an interview: "Social justice and human rights don't come from those who have the power to deny it. They come from the people who are most affected and from their allies realizing that we need to change policy and that some of these issues are not worthy of a country as great as the United States of America" (Moon 2009).

Margarethe Cammermeyer was born in Oslo, Norway, on March 24, 1942. Her father was a neuropathology scientist and her mother a homemaker. At the time, World War II was underway, and German Nazi troops occupied Norway as well as other European countries. Her parents were involved in the Norwegian resistance, and when Grethe (as Margarethe prefers to be called) was just a few months old, a friend arrived at their apartment with a package of weapons for the Norwegian freedom fighters. Her mother and her friend put the weapons underneath the mattress of a baby carriage with Grethe on top. As Grethe explained in her autobiography *Serving in Silence* (2005), the two women "pushed me up and down the streets of Oslo for hours, casually chatting and window-shopping, a young mother and her friend on an afternoon outing. Suddenly they popped into an alley, stopped at a doorway; two men jumped out. Mother lifted me up; the men pulled all the weapons out from underneath my blanket and vanished. Seconds later we were back out in the street continuing our leisurely wandering" (Cammermeyer 2005, 12).

When Grethe was nine years old, her family, which included two younger brothers at the time, immigrated to the United States and settled in Washington, D.C. Grethe had to learn English, a difficult task at first, but then she became bilingual, speaking Norwegian at home and English at school. While she was still struggling with the English language, she skipped fourth grade and went on to fifth. She thought the advancement was due partly to her height—she was much taller than her classmates. Also, she wrote, "I suspect the teachers moved me ahead because I could 'speak' math well and they assumed the rest of my skills were similarly advanced" (Cammermeyer 2005, 22).

While attending high school, she enjoyed science classes and wanted to become a medical doctor or scientist like her father. Her father did not encourage her to study for the profession—he believed females should have subservient roles and care for the home and children. However, he did advise Grethe on various methods for dissecting animals—from snakes to a cat's head. This was one of Grethe's favorite pastimes, and in her bedroom she kept a shelf full of glass bottles with dissected eyeballs preserved in formaldehyde.

Another passion was sports. When she was 15 years old, Grethe was almost six feet tall and could throw "a mean softball" (Cammermeyer 2005, 24). She was asked to join a fast-pitch softball team, made up of older females. Although she often was relegated to the bench, for three years she practiced and stayed with the team and shared in their camaraderie.

Grethe's goal as a teenager was still to become a medical doctor, but before medical school, she had to complete a college degree. At age 17, she enrolled at the University of Maryland and began "a grueling schedule of pre-med courses: microbiology, chemistry, zoology, calculus, history, and English" (Cammermeyer 2005, 32). Because she received no financial help from her father to further her education, Grethe was forced to alter her plan; she changed her major to nursing. She also made a change in citizenship—she became a U.S. citizen in 1960. The following year, she learned about the Army Student Nurse Program. If she signed up, the military would pay for her college tuition and she would graduate as an army nurse. Then she would be required to serve for a minimum of three years. That was the path she took, beginning her active duty in 1963 at Fort Sam Houston, Texas.

During one of her tours of duty, she was stationed in Nuremberg, Germany, where she served two years and met her future husband, Harvey Hawken. Both were army officers. In 1965, Grethe and Harvey married. When they completed their tour in Germany, they both were transferred back to the United States and stationed at Fort Lee, Virginia. Harvey received orders to deploy to Vietnam, where the military was building up its forces for its long war in that country. Grethe volunteered to go to Vietnam as well and served in an intensive care unit for 14 months. When Grethe and Harvey returned to the United States, they settled in Seattle, Washington.

In 1968, Grethe left the army; she was pregnant and the military did not allow women with dependents to serve, a policy that changed in 1972. That year, she returned to the military but in the U.S. Army Reserves.

Grethe and Harvey eventually had four sons, but their marriage began to falter and Grethe found it difficult to be around her husband. She became depressed about her situation and frequently had thoughts of suicide. She sought the help of a psychiatrist and began to deal with new feelings about sexuality and her struggle to find who she really is. She and Harvey became further estranged and separated; by the end of 1980, they were divorced. Grethe then dropped her married name and retook her maiden name Cammermeyer. She went on to pursue her education and weekend service with the Army Reserves. As an army nurse, she was steadily promoted.

For reasons that were not clear, a judge awarded Harvey Hawken custody of the boys; Cammermeyer was required to pay child support and had visitation rights, but those visits often ended with outbursts of anger from Hawken, who would scream at her "You dyke, faggot, queer!" He yelled it so many times that "the boys joined in"

(Cammermeyer 2005, 222). However, as adults, Cammermeyer's sons have been supportive of their mother.

Obviously, these outbursts were devastating for Cammermeyer. Nevertheless, she persevered in the military; she was promoted to colonel in 1987 and became chief nurse of the Washington State National Guard in 1988. That year she met art professor Diane Divelbess, who became her life partner. At their first meeting, they felt that they were closely connected, and for Cammermeyer, it was a revelation: finally she no longer had to question who she was and was certain about her sexual orientation.

Cammermeyer hoped to apply for the U.S. Army War College and take courses there in order to earn a promotion. Entrance to the War College required top security clearance. While she was being questioned during the investigation procedures, she was asked about homosexuality. At the time the "Don't Ask, Don't Tell" (DADT) policy had not been established. Authorized by President Bill Clinton in 1993, the policy restricts military personnel from asking about sexual orientation and prohibits service members from discussing sexual preferences. At that time an estimated 65,000 to 66,000 homosexuals were serving in the military, with 11,000 discharged because their sexual orientation was revealed.

When Cammermeyer said matter-of-factly that she was a lesbian in 1989, it led to her honorable discharge and a legal battle that resulted in a court decision declaring that her discharge was unconstitutional; she was reinstated in 1994. All the publicity that surrounded the court case prompted her autobiography *Serving in Silence* (1994), written with Chris Fisher. In 1995, a made-for-television movie, *Serving in Silence: The Margarethe Cammermeyer Story*, was released. It starred Glenn Close as Cammermeyer and was produced by Barbra Streisand.

Cammermeyer retired from the military in 1997 and, in 1998, campaigned to represent Washington State in the U.S. Congress. Cammermeyer did not win election, but she went on to become a popular speaker at numerous political events and at universities. In 2000, she became chairperson for the county Democratic Party of Whidbey Island, Washington, which is where she and her partner live. She also was the host for a radio talk show on an Internet channel GAYBC.com that included interviews with people opposed to homosexuals. For example, she interviewed Pastor Fred Phelps, a zealous anti-gay activist who established a godhatesfags.com web site. Cammermeyer hoped the interview would help her understand the mind-set of gay-rights opponents.

Cammermeyer and Divelbess were married in Portland, Oregon, in 2004, when civil marriages were allowed in Multnomah County, where Portland is located. But that marriage was declared invalid in 2005 when the Oregon supreme court ruled that Multnomah County could not violate state laws that ban gay marriages. Nevertheless, Cammermeyer and Divelbess repeated their marriage vows in Washington in a religious ceremony before two Episcopal clergy with Cammermeyer's family members in attendance. And in 2007, they registered as "domestic partners," a legal relationship certified by the state of Washington. Such partnerships vary by states, but in Washington a domestic partnership covers such rights and responsibilities as insurance coverage, ownership of property, inheritance, personal health, finances, and other issues.

Cammermeyer has worked consistently to advocate for the civil rights of lesbian, gay, bisexual, transgender (LGBT) persons and in conjunction with LGBT advocacy efforts, Cammermeyer has marched in the annual Seattle Pride parade, wearing her military uniform. In addition, she has campaigned for the repeal of DADT. Since the DADT went into effect, controversy has swirled around the policy. One of the major outspoken opponents has been U.S. representative Barney Frank, an openly gay member of Congress. Another is U.S. Army first lieutenant Dan Choi, a veteran of the Iraq war and Arabic linguist, who was discharged for violating DADT and was sent a bill for $2,500 to cover "the unearned portion" of his army contract. Many other Americans in and out of government have expressed their disapproval of DADT also and urged that the policy and all bans on LGBT individuals in the military be repealed. In mid-2010 the U.S. House of Representatives voted to overturn DADT, and in December 2010, the U.S. Senate repealed the policy. President Barack Obama signed the bill, and Cammermeyer was invited to witness the ceremony. However, the Pentagon has to implement procedures, and U.S. secretary of defense Robert Gates indicated that training for DADT repeal would be completed in 2011.

In 2010, the U.S. Department of Defense (DOD) announced that Cammermeyer had been appointed to the Defense Advisory Committee on Women in the Services. Secretary of Defense George C. Marshall established the committee in 1951 as an independent advisory committee that provides the DOD with advice and recommendations on matters and policies relating to professional women in the armed forces.

In 2011, Cammermeyer received the Point Courage Award, which recognizes an individual who has advocated for the future of the LGBT community and provides scholarships for LGBT students of merit. A press release announcing the award noted: "As a colonel and nurse, serving our country as an out lesbian, Grethe is living proof of what Point instills in each of its scholars: to be resilient, giving and passionate about what they believe in."

See also Choi, Daniel; Frank, Barney

References

Cammermeyer, Grethe. "Biography." cammermeyer.com, n.d. http://www.cammermeyer.com/bio.htm (accessed February 11, 2011).

Cammermeyer, Grethe, with Chris Fisher. *Serving in Silence.* Bloomington, IN: Author House, 2005. First published 1994.

Knight, Richard. "Silent No More: Interview with Col. Margarethe Cammermeyer." *Windy City Times*, September 20, 2006. http://outlineschicago.com/gay/lesbian/news/ARTICLE.php?AID=12658 (accessed February 14, 2011).

Moon, Margo. "Grethe Cammermeyer Interview." Our Big Gayborhood, September 12, 2009. http://www.ourbiggayborhood.com/2009/09/grethe-cammermeyer-interview/ (accessed February 12, 2011).

Muhlstein, Julie. "Retired Officer, Grethe Cammermeyer Lauds Talk to End 'Don't Ask, Don't Tell.'" HeraldNet, February 5, 2010. http://www.heraldnet.com/article/20100205/news01/702059871 (accessed February 14, 2011).

Carlin, George (1937–2008)

He began his career as a conventional comedian, but during the 1970s, George Carlin became an antiestablishment comic, a dissident with social commentary that many called "brash," "salty," "cynical," "irreverent," "rude," "vulgar," "confrontational," "provocative," and "profane." He was all of that, but he also became a highly acclaimed and respected comedian and artist known for his mastery of the English language. "Carlin was especially fascinated with the ways we blunt our language for the sake of our comfort," wrote Marty Beckerman in *Reason*. Carlin "despised our watered-down sexual descriptions and ethnic categories, and hated the delicate euphemisms we use when speaking about aging and death. Such terms, he believed, were real-life manifestations of George Orwell's Newspeak, words and phrases intended to obscure reality, numb the mind, and discourage criticism. 'By and large,' he once said, 'language is a tool for concealing the truth'" (Beckerman 2008, 59).

Carlin insisted on replacing euphemisms with down-to-earth terms, as for example in his infamous comedy routine "Seven Words You Can Never Say on Television." The words, sometimes called "dirty," were also forbidden on radio. However, currently the "dirty" words are being used on cable television and in movies and videos.

Born on May 12, 1937, in New York City's Morningside Heights section, George was named George Denis Patrick Carlin by his parents Patrick and Mary Beary Carlin. George and his older brother Patrick were raised by their mother who left their alcoholic father when George was an infant. George never again saw his father, who died in 1945 of a heart attack.

Mary Carlin had grand ideas about what her children ought to be. As George Carlin explained in his autobiography, his mother "was a woman with decidedly aristocratic pretensions, indoctrinated with the idea that she was 'lace-curtain Irish,' as opposed to the shanty kind with its stereotypes of drinking, lawlessness, laziness, rowdiness, all the things which—to the degree that ethnic generalities have any meaning—come from that side of their national character that makes the Irish fun" (Carlin 2009, 17).

According to George, his mother was "obsessed with appearances" and controlling her boys' lives. Yet, she had a sense of humor that George appreciated and a "love of words" that was passed on to him (Carlin 2009, 19).

A devout Irish Catholic, Mary Carlin sent her children to Corpus Christi School, a parochial school, in their neighborhood. However, Carlin frequently was in trouble in the school and was expelled several times but allowed to return. He rejected Catholic teachings and early in his life declared himself an atheist.

As a youngster, he liked to entertain with impersonations. He became a class clown in school and loved doing silly and sometimes revolting tricks to get attention. He also was a music lover and played in the school band.

George grew up in an area that included major institutions, such as Columbia University, Barnard College for women, the prestigious divinity school Union Theological Seminary, the huge multiethnic Riverside Church, the Jewish Theological Seminary, and the headquarters of the National Council of Churches. George spent many after-school hours playing on the grounds of these institutions and on the streets and parks nearby.

George and his older brother Patrick (Pat) were good friends while growing up, although Pat went to a boarding school and came home only on holidays. The two of them often were in street fights and engaged in petty thefts. They also experimented with illegal drugs. Pat joined the military when he was 19 years old, and George dropped out of school at age 17 to join the U.S. Air Force.

While in the air force, Carlin never considered being a pilot, and he found ways to avoid hard duty. He just wanted to be a regular guy in the service. He wrote that he "gravitated toward the black airmen, some of whom were from around my neighborhood. . . . Others came from the south Side of Chicago or . . . Cleveland. I had more in common with them—jazz, R&B, stuff I could talk about" (Carlin 2009, 58).

After his basic training, Carlin was stationed in Shreveport, Louisiana, where he often defied authority and received several court-martials, losing his pay and rank. Yet he was reinstated and eventually received a general discharge under honorable conditions in 1957.

While in Shreveport, Carlin worked part time as a disc jockey, and after he was discharged, he found an announcing job on radio in Boston, Massachusetts. There he met Jack Burns, a newsman. Carlin and Burns had the same sense of humor and became good friends, practicing comedy routines together.

When Carlin left Boston, he went to Fort Worth, Texas, taking a disc jockey job at the top radio station in the city. Six months later, Burns also arrived at the station, and as Carlin reported, "Jack resumed his steady radicalization of me that he had begun in Boston" (Carlin 2009, 72). That is, Carlin was beginning to turn away from much of the conservative thinking and attitudes that his Irish Catholic mother and the Catholic Church had instilled. For example, during the 1950s, Carlin supported (as did his mother and her employers) the work of U.S. senator Joseph McCarthy, who held Senate hearings and accused the federal government and the U.S. Army of harboring known communists or communist sympathizers. Under Burns's influence, Carlin became more liberal in his views.

Carlin and Burns continued their comedy routines and played them before an audience at a local coffeehouse. That was the beginning of their two years together entertaining at nightclubs and other venues across the United States as stand-up comedians. While on the entertainment circuit, Carlin met his future wife, Brenda Hosbrook, who worked at a nightclub in Dayton, Ohio, and was a friend of comedian Lenny Bruce. Bruce recommended that Carlin and Burns be booked for the Dayton nightclub. In 1961, Brenda and George were married. The following year, 1962, the Carlin and Burns team broke up, although the two comedians remained

Comedian George Carlin gestures during a news conference in Los Angeles, July 3, 1978. Carlin said the U.S. Supreme Court "just took another little part out of the First Amendment" when it ruled that the Federal Communications Commission may restrict the broadcast of indecent language. One of Carlin's recordings discusses the use of "dirty words" in our society; it was considered in the case. (AP Photo/Robbins)

good friends and each went on to his own successful career.

With Brenda traveling beside him, Carlin went on to do his own stand-up comedy in and around Chicago, Illinois, and later in New York City and then Los Angeles, California. According to Carlin, Brenda was a constant helpmate. "She helped me with the details and logistics, booked travel, kept the books, made suggestions, she was my sounding board, she sat in every club I played every night, whether there was one person or it was packed" (Carlin 2009, 131). Their daughter, Kelly, was born in 1963.

During the latter half of the 1960s, Carlin appeared on numerous TV shows, including *The Merv Griffin Show*, *The Mike Douglas Show*, *The Jimmy Dean Show*, *The Jackie Gleason Show*, *The Perry Como Show*, *The Dean Martin Show*, and many others. By the end of the 1960s, Carlin had decided that he needed to change his mainstream comedy routine (and his conservative suit-and-tie appearance) to appeal to audiences who were likely to be part of the counterculture, protesting the Vietnam War, using illegal drugs, and defying authority and social standards of the day. Those became the subjects for his routines in the 1970s, and he presented his acts with a "hippie" look, wearing jeans, a beard, and long hair tied back in a ponytail. In 1970, Carlin appeared on *The Carol Burnett Show* and impersonated Federal Bureau of Investigation director J. Edgar Hoover. The act infuriated a TV viewer who sent a letter of complaint to Hoover. As a result, the FBI started a file on Carlin (Meyers 2009).

According to Richard Zoglin writing for *Time*:

Carlin saw the stand-up comic as a social commentator, rebel and truth teller. . . . He made fun of society's outrage over drugs, for example, pointing out that the "drug problem" extended to middle-class America as well, from coffee freaks at the office to housewives hooked on diet pills. He talked about the injustice of Muhammad Ali's banishment from boxing for avoiding the draft—a man whose job was beating people up losing his livelihood because he wouldn't kill people: "He said, 'No, that's where I draw the line. I'll beat 'em up, but I don't want to kill 'em.' And the government said, 'Well, if you won't kill people, we won't let you beat 'em up.' " (Zoglin 2008).

Carlin's most contentious routine was the monologue called "Filthy Words" that he performed for a live audience. In 1972, he was arrested in Milwaukee, Wisconsin, for using the words in a show, but a judge dismissed the case, acknowledging the offensiveness of the language and upholding free speech rights. The monologue was recorded and broadcast in the early afternoon on October 30, 1973, by a New York radio station owned by Pacifica Foundation. That led to a complaint to the Federal Communications Commission (FCC) from a man who was driving with his young son and heard the broadcast on radio. The man did not think the monologue was appropriate to air on the radio at a time when children could hear the broadcast. The FCC sent the complaint to Pacifica, but did not sanction the company. Instead, the FCC warned that if further complaints were filed, it would take action. The FCC characterized the language used in the Carlin monologue as "patently offensive," but not necessarily obscene. That decision was challenged as being an infringement of free speech and was eventually heard before the U.S. Supreme Court in *FCC v. Pacifica Foundation* (1978), which determined that the FCC had the right to condemn the daytime broadcast as indecent and could sanction the radio station.

All the publicity surrounding the High Court decision profited Carlin and his routines. During the 1970s, he recorded a number of albums, such as the best-selling *FM & AM* (1972), *Class Clown* (1972), *Occupation: Foole* (1973), *Toledo Window Box* (1974), and *On the Road* (1977). Carlin also appeared as a host for the first *Saturday Night Live* show in 1975, and he made frequent appearances on *The Tonight Show*.

Yet the 1970s were years of substance and alcohol abuse by both Brenda and George Carlin. George slowly decreased his drug use, but he suffered a mild heart attack in 1978 and had two other heart attacks in later years—1982 and 1991. Brenda was institutionalized in order to detoxify and eventually quit her habits. Neither Brenda nor George was prepared to deal with their daughter Kelly, who had been using drugs since she was a young teenager. Her drug abuse "began to spiral out of control." Kelly was skipping school, in a relationship with an abusive boyfriend, and pregnant. But Carlin "didn't want to be an intrusive parent." He wrote "My own parent's fearsome need to control me scared me off any behavior like that. Don't be like Mary," he told himself (Carlin 2009, 204–5). However, he finally faced Kelly's boyfriend. Carlin, with a baseball bat in hand, convinced the boyfriend that he should never see Kelly again.

The 1980s began with Carlin fading in popularity and deeply in debt. He found a new manager who helped revive Carlin's act and career. Carlin also overcame his drug abuse. He appeared at Carnegie Hall and, over the next two decades, continued to record or produce live stand-up comedy specials for Home Box Office (HBO). He appeared on more than a dozen specials over 30 years, the last titled "It's Bad for Ya" released in 2008. He was nominated for five Emmy awards for his specials.

In 1997, Carlin's wife Brenda died. Carlin married Sally Wade, a comedy writer and performer, in 1998. Ten years later, Carlin was admitted to a Santa Monica, California, hospital with chest pains and died of heart failure on June 22, 2008. After Sally Wade returned from the hospital, she found a note from Carlin with the words that became the title for Wade's book *The George Carlin Letters: The Permanent Courtship of Sally Wade* (2011). The book contains notes and letters that George Carlin wrote to Sally on a daily basis.

Throughout Carlin's career he received many honors, including five Grammy awards, a star on the Hollywood Walk of Fame, a Lifetime Achievement Award at the 2001 Annual American Comedy Awards, and the Free Speech Award at the U.S. Comedy Arts Festival in 2002. He was honored posthumously with the Mark Twain Prize for American Humor, which had been announced shortly before he died.

See also Ali, Muhammad; McCarthy, Joseph

References

Associated Press. "Carlin Broke Rules." *Daily Variety*, June 24, 2008.

Beckerman, Marty. "The Cunning Linguist: George Carlin's Literary Genius." *Reason*, October 2008.

Carlin, George, with Tony Hendra. *Last Words*. New York and London: Free Press/Simon and Schuster, 2009.

Myers, Jim. "J. Edgar Hoover Irked by George Carlin." *Newsmax*, January 30, 2009.

Zoglin, Richard. *Comedy at the Edge: How Stand-Up in the 1970s Changed America*. New York: Bloomsbury USA, 2009.

Zoglin, Richard. "How George Carlin Changed Comedy." *Time*, June 23, 2008.

http://www.time.com/time/printout/0,8816,1817192,00.html (accessed January 24, 2011).

Carmichael, Stokely/Ture, Kwame (1941–1998)

Stokely Carmichael was an African American activist who championed the catchphrases "Black Is Beautiful" and "Black Power" in the 1960s. Unlike many other civil rights activists of that era, who preached nonviolence and change through cooperative efforts, Carmichael, over time, espoused more radical, revolutionary goals and methods. In his words:

> Black people must redefine themselves, and only *they* can do that. Throughout this country, vast segments of the black communities are beginning to recognize the need to assert their own definitions, to reclaim their history, their culture; to create their own sense of community and togetherness. There is a growing resentment of the word "Negro," for example, because this term is the invention of our oppressor; it is his image of us that he describes. Many blacks are now calling themselves African-Americans, Afro-Americans or black people because that is *our* image of ourselves. When we begin to define our own image, the stereotypes—that is, lies—that our oppressor has developed will begin in the white community and end there. The black community will have a positive image of itself that *it* has created. This means that we will no longer call ourselves lazy, apathetic, dumb, good-timers, shiftless, etc. Those are words used by white America to define us. If we accept these adjectives, as some of us have done in the past, then we see ourselves only in a negative way precisely the way white America wants us to see ourselves. Our incentive is broken and our will to fight is surrendered. From now on we shall view ourselves. As African-Americans and as black people who are in fact energetic, determined, intelligent, beautiful and peace-loving. (Carmichael 1992, 37–38)

Carmichael was born on June 29, 1941, in Port-of-Spain, Trinidad. When he was just two years old, his parents, Aldolphus and Mabel, immigrated to the United States where they had hopes of bettering their lot in life. He was left behind, in the care of relatives. He attended Trinity Boys School until he turned 11, when he joined his parents in Harlem, where they had found work—his father as a cab driver and his mother as a maid. He initially enjoyed life in the United States. His outgoing demeanor and unique accent made him popular, even among his affluent white classmates. He claimed to have been the only black member of local neighborhood street gang. He became more interested in academics after he was accepted and attended the Bronx High School for Science and simultaneously began to develop an interest in politics and social issues.

In the late 1950s, as Carmichael was nearing his graduation from high school, the U.S. civil rights movement was just coming into its own. He began taking steps to show his support of various causes, participating in sit-ins against segregated public areas. When it came time to select a college, he opted for Howard University—a historic all-black institution in Washington, D.C.—even though he had many other offers. On campus, Carmichael joined the Non-Violent Action Group, which was an affiliate of the Student Non-Violent Coordinating Committee

(SNCC), based in Atlanta, Georgia. Carmichael spent his collegiate summer breaks working with the Congress on Racial Equality (CORE) in the southern states. CORE "Freedom Riders" traveled together along the interstate highways in integrated groups, challenging the federal government's lack of enforcement of desegregation of interstate buses and bus depots. These young people were often harassed and frequently beaten. Many were incarcerated—Carmichael himself spent 49 days in a Mississippi jail in spring 1961.

When he graduated from Howard with his degree in philosophy in 1964, Carmichael was committed to continuing his civil rights activism on a full-time basis. He returned south to again work with the SNCC. Soon, he was head of this group, which did everything from organize voter registration drives to participate in sit-ins, from coordinate boycotts and pickets to found fledgling opposition political parties.

As time passed, Carmichael grew more and more demoralized as he saw good intentions and peaceable efforts met with uncalled for violence. His views gradually began to shift, and he saw defending oneself from unprovoked violence, with violence, as acceptable. And so he began to set himself apart himself from other civil rights activists of the day, such as civil rights leader Martin Luther King Jr., who was a strident proponent of nonviolence.

However, Carmichael did join forces with King, along with other prominent leaders of the civil rights movement, in June 1966, taking part in what had begun as a previously interrupted "March against Fear." On June 6 in Memphis, Tennessee, James Meredith, the first African American student to attend the University of Mississippi, had begun what was initially a solo journey in protest of racism. Soon after starting off, a sniper injured Meredith with a round of birdshot. So, 10 days later, Carmichael, King, and others gathered in Greenwood, Mississippi. They set up a camp, and Carmichael was briefly arrested on trespass charges. King left with plans to return two days later. Carmichael remained and gave a televised speech—referred to later as his "Black Power" speech. King would return to a camp divided between Carmichael's revolutionary SNCC followers and King's own less confrontationally styled Southern Christian Leadership Conference (SCLC).

The march eventually proceeded to Jackson, Mississippi, as planned, concluding on March 26, with Meredith rejoining the group the day prior. Carmichael's concept of "Black Power" held appeal for a zealous core element. However, moderate black Americans found the term unsettling, and white Americans found the phrase outright terrifying. It conjured up a racial uprising in their minds. Carmichael seemed to grow impatient as he was repeatedly queried about what he meant by the phrase, insisting that he merely meant that blacks needed to gain control of the same things that whites had: political power, economic power, legal power. Blacks wanted control of their communities and the institutions that influenced their lives. But to achieve that control, Carmichael asserted, blacks would use any means necessary, aligning himself with the pro-activist Malcolm X.

Carmichael's call for Black Power scandalized American society. For blacks, Black Power was a righteous exhortation. Whites, however, "interpreted the term to be filled with violent foreboding. Newspapers brooded over Carmichael's words, quickly forming a consensus that judged the slogan to be intemperate at best and, at worst, a blatant call for antiwhite violence and reverse racism. It would galvanize blacks, outrage whites, and

Stokely Carmichael, an effective leader of the Student Nonviolent Coordinating Committee (SNCC), brought the concept of black power into the U.S. civil rights struggle. In 1967, Carmichael, an advocate of militancy rather than nonviolent cooperation, broke with SNCC and joined the more radical Black Panthers. (Library of Congress)

inspire a large and varied group of ethnic and racial minorities" (Joseph 2010, 108).

From that day forward, the black SNCC leaders' focus was continually on the topic of "revolution." Their vocabulary was filled with references to themselves as the "oppressed" and white society as the "oppressor." The group withdrew from the White House Conference on Civil Rights; all of the other "old guard" civil rights groups—the SCLC, the National Association for the Advancement of Colored People and the Urban League—condemned the move. Many supporters revolted; older blacks resigned their memberships, and white supporters withdrew their financial contributions. Late in 1966, the organization moved to expel all whites from its membership roster. Added to this, in his book, *Black Power: The Politics of Liberation in America* (1967), Carmichael outlined his beliefs. Contrary to the assurances he was continually giving to the media, passages such as this garnered fresh concern, "Malcolm X had said just before his assassination that the U.S.A. could avoid violent Revolution; perhaps. Revolutionaries do not take to the path of spilling blood easily. But Malcolm's statement is no longer true" (Carmichael 1992, 190).

Carmichael and SNCC had managed to draw the attention of law enforcement. As they became more and more militant in their activities, fights between SNCC's members and police officers took place across the nation. In August 1966, Carmichael himself was arrested for inciting a riot. As far back as 1960, the Federal Bureau of Investigation (FBI) had been keeping SNCC under surveillance. In the summer of 1967, the group was formally added to the FBI's list of revolutionary groups to monitor, infiltrate, and—if possible—discredit. Perhaps seeing the handwriting on the wall as SNCC grew more and more destabilized, Carmichael decided not to run for reelection to lead the organization that year. He broadened his scope of interests to include speaking out against the United States' involvement in Vietnam and overall foreign policy of imperialism. He began to travel extensively, including outside of the country. His new rhetoric further inflamed people back home. "We do not want peace in Vietnam. We want the Vietnamese people to defeat the United States," he claimed in Cuba. "Carmichael added, 'We feel we are not paying too high a price even if we destroy the structures of the United States.'" From February to July 1967, he visited "at least a dozen countries, from Havana to Hanoi—and has not missed an opportunity to attack the U.S. at any stopover ... he has spent his time advocating negritude and nihilism" (*Time* 1967, 28). His passport was confiscated upon his return to the United States.

SNCC, in disagreement with Carmichael's change in politics, expelled Carmichael in August 1968. By this time, he had a new alliance—the Black Panther Party (BPP), which advocated for African American liberation "by any means necessary." Acting in his new role of honorary BPP prime minister, he helped set up more than two dozen chapters across the country. The Panthers' appeal and/or danger—depending on the audience one was addressing—reached its apex at the 1968 Olympics in Mexico City, when Tommie Smith and Juan Carlos, U.S. gold and bronze medal recipients, respectively, stood on the winners' dais and raised their clenched fists in solidarity with the Panther movement. Their action resulted in U.S. Olympic officials being forced by the International Olympic Committee to expel the two from the Games and to suspend the two from the American team.

Carmichael severed ties with the Panthers in 1969, opposing its willingness to work with white groups to achieve its aims. His interests turned to Pan-Africanism, a political movement that favors uniting African countries under a common socialist leadership; he founded a branch of the All-African People's Revolutionary Party (AAPRP) in Washington, D.C. Pan-Africanism, he noted in a speech, "is grounded in the belief that all African peoples, wherever we may be, are one. ... our dispersal was the result of European imperialism and racism. Pan-Africanism is grounded in socialism which has its roots in communalism. Any ideology seeking to solve the problems of the African people must find its roots in Pan-Africanism" (Carmichael 1971, 221).

Carmichael and his then wife, South African singer-activist Miriam Makeba, decided to go into self-imposed "exile." Carmichael's departure essentially signaled the end of the Black Power movement; by the early 1970s, it was basically just a slogan in name only. The couple left the United States and arrived in their new homeland of Conakry in the Republic of Guinea, located in West Africa, where AAPRP had been founded. Carmichael worked with AAPRP and taught at the Conakry University. In 1978, he changed his name to Kwame Ture—both names being tributes to African national leaders, Kwame Nkrumah and Sékou Touré, the latter additionally the former president of Guinea as well as a friend and benefactor to Carmichael.

In 1996, he was diagnosed with prostate cancer. The government of his nation of birth, Trinidad and Tobago, as well as numerous organizations and individuals, stepped up to help him obtain and pay for medical treatment. Until his dying day, Carmichael, a.k.a. Kwame Ture (he answered to both names indiscriminately), advocated passionately for revolution as the answer to the problems of racism and injustice. Those close to him remarked that although his time was nearing an end, he would still answer his telephone enthusiastically, "Ready for the Revolution!" He died on November 15, 1998, in Conakry, Guinea, and his remains are buried there. His ideas presented in books and published speeches are part of his legacy. As activist and political prisoner Mumia Abu-Jamal wrote in a foreword to *Stokely Speaks*: "A steadfast Pan-African revolutionary, Ture worked tirelessly, almost to his last breath. ... Perhaps his words, which reflect his brilliance, his courage, his evergrowing anticapitalist, anti-imperialist ideology, and his will to bring into being a Black revolutionary world, will feed a new generation who will heed his call" (Carmichael 2007, ix).

Margaret Gay

See also Abu-Jamal, Mumia; King, Martin Luther, Jr.; Malcolm X

References

Carmichael, Stokely. *Stokely Speaks: Black Power to Pan-Africanism.* Chicago: Chicago Review Press, 2007. First published 1965.

Carmichael, Stokely, and Charles V. Hamilton. *Black Power: The Politics of Liberation in America.* New York: Random House, 1992.

Joseph, Peniel E. *Dark Days, Bright Nights: From Black Power to Barack Obama.* New York: Civitas Books, 2010.

"Races: The Road to Hell." *Time*, December 15, 1967. http://www.time.com/time/magazine/article/0,9171,837582,00.html (accessed March 28, 2011).

Carson, Rachel (1907–1964)

"With the publication of *Silent Spring* in 1962, Rachel Louise Carson, the essence of gentle scholarship, set off a nationally publicized struggle between the proponents and opponents of the widespread use of poisonous chemicals to kill insects. Miss Carson was an opponent. Some of Miss Carson's critics, admiringly and some not so admiringly, compared her to Carrie Nation, the hatchet-wielding temperance advocate. This comparison was rejected quietly by Miss Carson, who in her very mild but firm manner refused to accept the identification of an emotional crusader" (Leonard 1956).

Born on May 27, 1907, in Springdale, Pennsylvania, Rachel Carson grew up exploring the natural surroundings that were part of the daily life she shared with her brother, sister, and parents. She was raised on her family's 65-acre farm in Springdale, close to the Allegheny River near Pittsburgh. From an early age, Rachel's goal was to become a writer and her first published story appeared in one of her favorite children's periodicals, *St. Nicholas Magazine*, before she reached her teens. Many of Rachel's early writings involved animals. She particularly favored literature that involved nature, especially novels about the ocean.

Rachel's mother Maria would have a deep influence on what would become her daughter's reverential respect for life. Rachel recalled her mother going so far as to carry spiders and other insects out of the house rather than killing them. Said Rachel of Maria, "Her love of life and of all living things was her outstanding quality ... more than anyone else I know, she embodied Albert Schweitzer's 'reverence for life' " (Hynes 1989, 55). It is no small coincidence that among the many honors that were bestowed upon Rachel Carson for her life's work was the Albert Schweitzer Medal of the Animal Welfare League.

After graduating from high school, Carson attended Pennsylvania College for Women (now Chatham College), intending to major in literature (and "not boys," as she told a girlfriend at the time); but a chance course in biology with a passionate teacher who became her mentor and friend, Mary Skinker, led her toward the natural sciences. She did some postgraduate work at the Marine Biology Laboratory in Woods Hole, Massachusetts, at Cape Cod, completing her master of arts degree at Johns Hopkins University in 1932, having become a member of its zoology staff in 1931. She also had taught several summer sessions at Johns Hopkins.

In 1935, Carson's father died. Facing the financial constraints of providing for herself and for her aging mother, Rachel decided that she needed to seek more substantial employment. The next year, she was hired on a temporary basis by the Federal Bureau of Fisheries to write a series of 57 radio scripts entitled "Romance under the Waters." At the same time, she supplemented her income by writing natural science articles for local magazines and newspapers. In short time, her stellar job performance was parlayed into a full-time position as a junior aquatic biologist, due to Rachel having outscored all the other civil service exam applicants. Rachel was only the second woman ever to be hired by the bureau.

In her position, she wrote pamphlets on conservation and natural resources, as well as scientific articles, many of which appeared in the *Baltimore Sun*. Her job allowed her to blend her dual passions for writing and nature. Satisfaction with her career was tempered when she experienced personal upheaval in 1937. Her family duties increased dramatically upon the death of her sister. Rachel took on the responsibility of raising her two nieces with her mother, as always, by her side. In this same year, Carson wrote an article for the July issue of *Atlantic Monthly* entitled "Undersea." An interested publishing house encouraged her to set her sights higher, and a greatly expanded version of the article became her first book, *Under the Sea Wind* (1941).

Carson rose in the ranks with the bureau (which became the Bureau of Fish and Wildlife Service), being appointed editor of publications in 1949. Two years later, she produced *The Sea around Us* (1951). This

Rachel Carson, shown here giving testimony before Congress in 1963, was a noted biologist and ecology writer whose books played a major role in launching the modern environmental movement. Carson's book *Silent Spring*, published in 1962, became a best seller and touched off a controversy that led to a fundamental shift in the public's attitudes toward the use of pesticides. (Library of Congress)

second book skyrocketed to the best-seller list where it remained for 86 weeks, 39 at first place; and by 1962, it had been translated into 30 languages. The fame and financial success of this book allowed Carson to quit working altogether by 1952, so that she could devote herself to a full-time career. Three years later, she released the last in her trilogy, *The Edge of the Sea* (1955).

In 1957, one of her two nieces passed away, and Carson accepted responsibility for a five-year old orphaned nephew. She decided to move her household to Silver Spring, Maryland, taking him along with her aging mother.

After establishing herself and her family in their new home, Carson turned her attention to the project that had, in fact, been on her radar screen for nearly 10 years: synthetic pesticides and their impact on the environment. World War II had resulted in scientific funding that had led to the development of various pesticides, including dichlorodiphenyltrichloroethane (DDT). When the U.S. Department of Agriculture unveiled a fire ant eradication program that involved the aerial spraying of DDT and other pesticides, Carson decided that the time had come for her to concentrate her efforts on pesticides and focus her next book on this topic. She spent about four years researching the issues, gathering data, and speaking with various experts.

In 1962, Carson released her fourth and final book, *Silent Spring*. In doing so, she became one of the first to challenge science, industry, agriculture, and government in demanding the right of individuals to live in a safe environment, positing the argument that nothing exists in nature alone and that science and technology must therefore demonstrate a reverence for life. The book was, in its simplest categorization, a warning that overuse of pesticides could cause a "Silent Spring," resulting in destruction of the earth's ecosystem. Its name came at the suggestion of Carson's literary agent, Marie Rodell. *Silent Spring* is a metaphorical title, predicting a grim outlook for the world if the warnings of nature are not heeded.

Prior to the book's publication in 1962, it was first released in serialized form in the *New Yorker* magazine, appearing on June 16, 23, and 30 of that same year. It was also selected as the October 1962 Book-of-the-Month Club selection. Both of these things helped to deflect the onslaught of criticism that the agricultural, chemical, and technological industries unleashed on Carson and her book. Efforts were made from all sides to attack her credentials, research, and motivations. Corporations such as DuPont, Monsanto, and Velsicol Chemical had vested financial interests in refuting Carson's claims. The National Agricultural Chemicals Association (NACA) took the industry lead by producing and distributing *Fact and Fancy*, a tract that quoted selectively from Carson's book (without citing it as a source) and then providing one-sided rebuttals. The NACA budgeted significant sums for public relations damage control after *Silent Spring* was written.

Not only was Carson attacked by expected sources, such as those within the agricultural and technological industries, but also by the medical and nutrition industries. The American Medical Association's *AMA News* directed its readers, member physicians, away from Carson's book toward NACA for information. The Nutrition Foundation, Inc., created by the food industry, formed an alliance with the Manufacturing Chemicals Association, printing and distributing a collection of negative book reviews.

Carson had her supporters lined up well in advance of the book's release, however, including respected national voices such as Supreme Court justice William O. Douglas, a long-time environmental advocate. The academic community largely backed Carson, and before long, the chemical and industrial companies' characterization of Carson as an emotional extremist proved unsuccessful.

Given her health status at the time, Carson was hard pressed to be as visible of an advocate for her book as she might have been otherwise. Still, she rose to the occasion whenever possible. On April 3, 1963, she appeared on a *CBS Reports* segment entitled "The Silent Spring of Rachel Carson." She also appeared on the *Today* show and spoke at numerous functions at which she was recognized for her groundbreaking efforts. She testified before President John F. Kennedy's Science Advisory Committee as well as before a Senate subcommittee to make policy recommendations.

According to biographer Mark Lyle, "Carson's main argument is that pesticides have detrimental effects on the environment; they are more properly termed 'biocides' ... because their effects are rarely limited to the target pests. DDT is a prime example, but other synthetic pesticides come under scrutiny as well—many of which are subject to bioaccumulation." Not only did Carson take to task the biochemical industry for the impact of its activities, but she also called into question its ethics, making a blatant accusation that the industry knowingly and intentionally spread disinformation. Further, Carson charged public officials with blind acceptance of industry claims, thereby jeopardizing the public safety with whose well-being they had been entrusted (Lyle 2007, 166–72).

The majority of *Silent Spring* deals with pesticide issues and their adverse impact on the environment. But the book does not suggest banning helpful pesticides; rather, it suggests responsible, managed usage. Four chapters of the book discuss the effects of pesticides on human beings, such as poisoning and links to various illness and cancer. But her book said very little about the correlation between the toxic insecticide DDT and cancer in humans. In a somewhat ironic twist of fate, Carson was in the process of working on the book's cancer-related chapters around the time that she received word that the breast cancer she had been diagnosed with in early 1960 was malignant and had metastasized. Undeterred, she resolved to see her project through.

In her book, Carson made some predictions about future consequences, such as what might happen if insects developed resistance to pesticides and the effect that could have. She ended *Silent Spring* with a call for a biotic approach to pest control as an alternative to chemical pesticides.

Silent Spring, despite its opposition, had far-reaching consequences. It led to the formation of the U.S. Environmental Protection Agency and the Environmental Defense Fund. The latter launched the first-ever courtroom battle against the pesticide DDT, resulting in the EPA banning its use in 1972. It is no overstatement to say that much of the momentum of the modern-day environmental movement can be attributed to awareness raised by Carson's book.

Carson developed complications related to her cancer in early 1964, and on April 14 of that year, she passed away in Silver Spring, Maryland. In recognition of her many and far-reaching achievements, several honors were bestowed upon Rachel Carson during her lifetime: Conservationist of the Year from the National Wildlife Foundation, the first female Audubon Medal recipient, the Cullom Medal of the American Geographical Society. One of the ones she was reportedly most proud of was her election to the American Academy of Arts and Letters, whose citation read, "A scientist in the grand literary style of Galileo and Buffton, she had used her scientific knowledge and moral feelings to deepen our conscientiousness of living nature and to alert us to the calamitous possibility that our short-sighted technological conquests might destroy the very sources of our being" (Hynes 1989, 41). Carson was also posthumously awarded the Presidential Medal of Freedom by President Jimmy Carter in 1980. Her work lives on, and her name recognition—and recognition of the importance of her life's work—has grown exponentially since her death.

Margaret Gay

References

Carson, Rachel. *Silent Spring: 40th Anniversary Edition*. New York: First Mariner Books/Houghton Mifflin Company, 2002.

Hynes, H. Patricia. *The Recurring Silent Spring*. New York: Pergamon Press, 1989.

Lear, Linda. *Rachel Carson: Witness for Nature*. New York: Henry Holt and Company, LLC, 1997.

Leonard, Jonathan Norton, "Rachel Carson Dies of Cancer; 'Silent Spring' Author Was 56." *New York Times*, April 15, 1964. http://www.nytimes.com/books/97/10/05/reviews/carson-obit.html (accessed September 8, 2011).

Lyle, Mark Hamilton. *The Gentle Subversive: Rachel Carson, Silent Spring, and the Rise of the Environmental Movement*. New York: Oxford University Press, 2007.

Catt, Carrie Chapman (1859–1947)

"Woman Suffrage is coming—no intelligent person in the United States or in the world will deny that fact. The most an intelligent opponent expects to accomplish is to postpone its establishment as long as possible" (Catt 1917, 69). These words by Carrie Chapman Catt were written while she was leading efforts in 1917 for passage of an amendment to the U.S. Constitution that would grant voting rights to women nationwide. Although some states had already enfranchised women, Catt was a dissident who refused to quietly accept the fact that women in many parts of the nation were not allowed to vote. She was up against opponents who argued, for example, that each state should be free to decide whether women should have the right to vote, or that women should be subservient to men and abide by male political decisions. Opponents frequently heckled, jailed, and sometimes physically abused woman suffrage supporters.

Carrie was born on January 9, 1859, in Ripon, Wisconsin, and named Carrie Linton Lane. Her parents, Lucius and Maria (Clinton) Lane, had graduated from Potsdam Academy, Potsdam, New York, and had moved west to settle in Wisconsin. Carrie was the second of their three children.

In 1866, when Carrie was seven years old, her family moved to a farm near Charles City, Iowa, where she grew up, developing an independent mind and a feminist perspective even at an early age. On one occasion, she questioned her parents about voting, pointedly asking why her mother was not accompanying her father to the polls. The question was humorous to her father, who explained that voting was a function too important to allow women to participate.

Carrie graduated from Charles City High School in 1877, and planned to go to college. Her father opposed the idea of a college education for females, so Carrie Lane worked for a year to earn tuition at Iowa

Agricultural College and Model Farm in Ames (now Iowa State University). She paid her way through school by washing dishes, working in the school library, and teaching. While in college, she developed speaking skills in the debating society, the first female debater at the school. Because she believed females should have the same opportunities as males, she organized a military unit called Company G (G stood for Girls). She graduated in 1880 as valedictorian and set another first by being the only woman in her graduating class.

After college, Carrie Lane took a job in Charles City as a law clerk and also as a teacher. Then in 1881, she accepted a position as principal of the high school in Mason City. In 1883, she became the superintendent of Mason City schools, one of the first women appointed to such a position.

In 1885, Carrie Lane gave up her career to marry Leo Chapman, editor and publisher of the *Mason City Republican*. Tragedy struck a few months later when Leo, who had gone to San Francisco, California, became infected with typhoid fever and died. At the time, typhoid was common because of contaminated water and food supplies. Carrie Chapman was unable to reach San Francisco until after her husband's death, and since she had no financial resources, she decided to stay and found work as a freelance journalist. She also earned some income by lecturing, a popular occupation at the time.

Carrie Chapman returned to Charles City in 1887 and became a member of the Iowa Woman Suffrage Association (IWSA). The IWSA hired her as a writer and speaker, and by 1890, she was the state organizer for the association, serving for two years. During that time, she also married George Catt, whom she had known in college and also had met again while in San Francisco. A wealthy engineer, George encouraged and financially supported his wife's suffrage activities.

Carrie Chapman Catt's work included national and international efforts for women's right to vote. She was an active member of the National American Woman Suffrage Association (NAWSA) and became its president in 1900, succeeding Susan B. Anthony, a prominent voting rights activist who had retired. As head of NAWSA, Catt gave speeches and organized women for suffragist campaigns. She also played a major role in founding the International Woman Suffrage Alliance (IWSA), which was launched in Berlin, Germany, in 1904. Her organizing and speaking activities helped her become a respected and well-known suffragist.

Carrie Chapman Catt was one of the leading fighters for the passage of the Nineteenth Amendment, which gave women in the United States the right to vote in 1920. (Library of Congress)

Catt was forced to resign in 1904 due to her husband's failing health. He died in 1905, and a younger brother and her mother died in 1907. She lost interest in the suffrage movement, and friends urged Catt to go to Europe to ease her grief. She followed their advice and resumed her presidency of the IWSA. In 1911, with companions, she began a world tour advocating for women's suffrage worldwide and establishing suffrage organizations.

After she returned to the United States, Catt once again resumed the leadership of NAWSA, which was faltering because of divisions within its membership. Alice Paul led one faction, which wanted to work primarily at the federal level for a constitutional amendment to assure women's right to vote. Catt, on the other hand, advocated working at the state and federal levels simultaneously, which, in her view, would bolster efforts for an amendment to the U.S. Constitution. Paul and Catt could not agree on how to proceed, and Paul's faction left the NAWSA to form a more militant suffrage and equal rights organization called the National Woman's Party.

After the outbreak of World War I in Europe in 1914, Catt with Jane Addams, founder of the U.S. settlement house movement, called a conference in January 1915 to discuss the request of European women to join them in dissent and protests against the war. About 3,000 American women met in Washington, D.C., and formed the Women's Peace Party (WPP) to advocate for ending war through mediation, education for peace, arms control, and other efforts. One of the many suffragists in the organization was Jeannette Rankin, a lobbyist for NAWSA who was elected to the U.S. House of Representatives in 1916 and became known for her antiwar vote.

While campaigning, Catt continued to make numerous speeches and publish suffrage materials. A 1917 publication was a compilation of articles about suffrage addressed to the members of Congress. In the book, Catt pointed out that southern congressmen generally opposed the federal amendment because it would "confer the vote upon Negro women of their respective states and that would interfere with white supremacy." Catt countered: "White supremacy will be strengthened, not weakened, by women's suffrage," primarily because statistics showed more white women than black women would vote. In another section of the book, she argued that "there are vast groups of totally illiterate, and others of gross ignorance, groups of men of all nations of Europe, uneducated Indians and Negroes" who were enfranchised, while intelligent, well-educated, prosperous women were among the disenfranchised (Catt 1917).

Some critics have labeled Catt's comments as racist and xenophobic. Others have excused such statements as a contrast between male and female voters that would appeal to white legislators, whom she needed for support.

Catt's efforts were bolstered in part by a bequest from a wealthy publisher, Miriam Leslie, who wanted women's suffrage to succeed. Leslie died, leaving $2 million to Catt, but for several years, Leslie's relatives fought the bequest in court. However, Catt prevailed, although after legal fees were paid, less than $1 million was awarded to Catt, who invested all of the funds in suffrage campaigns.

Even as the United States entered World War I in 1917, campaigning went on, albeit in a somewhat subdued manner. Many women were working on war efforts. Yet, during the war, Alice Paul, founder of the National Woman's Party, led suffragists in marches in front of the White House. By

1917, 16 states had enfranchised women, and at the end of World War I in 1918, President Woodrow Wilson announced support for a suffrage amendment, which the U.S. House passed. Some congressmen in opposition did all in their power to delay the vote on the amendment in the Senate. But on June 4, 1919, the U.S. Senate adopted the amendment, which then went to the state legislatures for ratification.

Suffragists immediately began ratification campaigns "so women may vote in the Presidential election in 1920," Catt noted, adding: "This we are confident will be achieved. The friends of woman suffrage in both parties have carried out their word. . . .' Eyes front,' is the watchword as we turn upon the struggle for ratification by the States" (*New York Times* 1919). While campaigns were under way in 1919, Catt anticipated that woman suffrage would be a reality, and she founded the League of Women Voters (LMV) to help women vote intelligently. The LMV eventually was the successor to the national suffrage association. On August 26, 1920, Tennessee became the 36th and last state needed to ratify the Nineteenth Amendment to the U.S. Constitution, which in Article 1 states: "The right of citizens of the United States to vote shall not be denied or abridged by the United States or by any State on account of sex."

After that victory, Catt published with Nettie Rogers Shuler *Woman Suffrage and Politics: The Inner Story of the Suffrage Movement* (1923) and she focused on equal suffrage worldwide. She also campaigned for world peace. She urged U.S. participation in the League of Nations (and later the United Nations), whose purpose was to prevent conflict and promote peace between countries.

Catt's pacifist stance prompted the Federal Bureau of Investigation (FBI) to monitor her activities between 1924 and 1929. At that time, the U.S. government was concerned that the Communist takeover of Russia (in 1917) would spread worldwide, and anyone who believed in disarmament was suspect. The FBI condemned Catt, along with other pacifists like Jane Addams, for spreading what the agency called antiwar propaganda and being associated with peace groups. To the FBI, Catt and other dissidents against war were unpatriotic.

During the 1930s, with the rise of Adolf Hitler and his Nazi Party's persecution of German Jews, Catt helped form the Protest Committee of Non-Jewish Women against the Persecution of Jews in Germany. Thousands joined the cause. Catt also spoke out publicly, urging changes in U.S. immigration laws to help Jews find refuge in the United States. She received the American Hebrew Medal in 1933 for her work.

Other awards included honorary degrees from the University of Wyoming, Iowa State College, Smith College, and Moravian College for Women. In 1941, First Lady Eleanor Roosevelt presented Catt with the Chi Omega award, given to women for their outstanding achievement. In 1940, the National Institute of Social Sciences awarded her with a gold medal; in 1947, the League of Women Voters established the Carrie Chapman Memorial Fund in her honor.

On March 9, 1947, Carrie Chapman Catt died of heart failure at her home in New Rochelle, New York. After her death, Iowa State University received Catt's entire estate, including her peace library. The university also maintains the Carrie Chapman Catt Center for Women and Politics in her honor.

See also Addams, Jane; Paul, Alice; Rankin, Jeannette; Roosevelt, Eleanor

References

Baker, Jean H., ed. *Votes for Women: The Struggle for Suffrage Revisited*. Oxford and New York: Oxford University Press, 2002.

Burnett, Constance (Buel). *Five for Freedom: Lucretia Mott, Elizabeth Cady Stanton, Lucy Stone, Susan B. Anthony, Carrie Chapman Catt*. New York: Abelard Press, 1953.

Catt, Carrie Chapman, and Nettie Rogers Shuler. *Woman Suffrage and Politics: The Inner Story of the Suffrage Movement*. New York: C. Scribner, 1923.

Catt, Carrie Chapman, compiler. *Woman Suffrage by Federal Constitutional Amendment*. New York: National Woman Suffrage Publishing Co., 1917. http://www.gutenberg.org/files/13568/13568.txt (accessed May 31, 2010).

McCartney, David. "FBI Kept a Close Eye on Chapman Catt." *Charles City Press*, July 10, 1999. http://www.catt.org/ccabout4.html (accessed June 3, 2010).

Peck, Mary Gray. *Carrie Chapman Catt: A Biography*. New York: H. W. Wilson Co., 1944.

"Suffrage Wins in Senate; Now Goes to States." *New York Times*, June 5, 1919. http://www.fordham.edu/halsall/mod/1920womensvote.html (accessed June 2, 2010).

Chávez, César (1927–1993)

As an activist battling for the rights of migrant farm workers, César Chávez once received a telegram from civil rights leader Martin Luther King Jr. that read, in part, "Our separate struggles are really one—a struggle for freedom, for dignity, and for humanity. You and your valiant fellow workers have demonstrated your commitment to righting grievous wrongs forced upon exploited people. We are together with you in spirit and in determination that our dreams for a better tomorrow will be realized" (Levy 2007, 246).

César Chávez was born on March 31, 1927, the son of Mexican Americans, Librando and Juana Chávez. They and their six children lived in an adobe home on a ranch near Yuma, Arizona. César's grandfather, Cesario, had homesteaded the land at the turn of the century. Librando made a deal to receive an adjoining 40 acres in exchange for clearing some land, but the landowner reneged. On the advice of an attorney, Librando then borrowed money to buy the land; when he could not pay interest on the loan, the attorney bought the land and sold it back to the original owner. These unjust dealings, coupled with the economic challenges of the Great Depression, caused the Chávez family to lose the ranch. In pursuit of a way to earn a living, in 1939, the Chávez family headed for the fields of California.

César Chávez went to school sporadically as he was growing up and, although he would remain an avid reader until death, he disliked school immensely. It did not help that his family lived an itinerant lifestyle, resulting in his attending close to three dozen grade schools. The family followed the crops, picking peas and lettuce in the winter, cherries and beans in the spring, corn and grapes in the summer, and cotton in the fall (United Farm Workers web site). These early experiences were crucial in shaping Chavez's outlook. He and his coworkers often worked long, grueling days for as little as a dollar—sometimes, even cheated out of those rightful, meager wages. Workers had no recourse; few laws existed for protection. Essentially, migrant workers were powerless.

In 1944, Chávez joined the U.S. Navy. His two years in the military were just as demeaning as working in the fields had been. After his service in World War II, he returned to farm work. He married Helen Favela in 1948, and moved to San Jose, California. In the early 1950s, he met Fred Ross, an organizer with the Community Service Organization (CSO), a Mexican American civil rights group. Ross recruited Chávez initially to help with voter registration drives. Soon, Chávez held a staff position and, by 1958, he was CSO's national director. Chávez believed that migrant workers needed to be mobilized—unionized—an idea not shared by CSO. So, he and the organization parted ways.

Chávez, his wife, and their children set up base in Delano, California. Along with Dolores Huerta, in 1962, Chávez cofounded the fledgling National Farm Workers Association (NFWA), consisting largely of Hispanic farm workers from Arizona and California. Chávez began working to raise public awareness of the conditions in which U.S. migrant workers lived. NFWA came to be the first effective farm workers union in the history of California agriculture.

Chávez firmly believed in nonviolence and followed the philosophies of Mahatma Ghandi and Martin Luther King Jr. He said, "Nonviolence also has one big demand—the need to be creative, to develop strategy. Gandhi described it as moral jiu-jitsu. Always hit the opposition off balance but keep your principles . . . Nonviolence has the power to attract people and to generate power . . . That's what happened to Gandhi. . . . We can respond nonviolently because that's what swings people to our side, and that gives us our strength" (Levy 2007, 270–71). Although he never met Dr. King, he did speak with him on occasion by phone. "I had followed King's actions from the beginning of the bus boycott in Montgomery, when I was organizing the CSO, and he gave me hope and ideas. When the bus boycott was victorious, I thought then of applying boycotts to organizing the Union. Then every time something came out in the newspaper, his civil rights struggle would jump out of the pages at me . . . Martin Luther King definitely influenced me, and much more after his death. The spirit doesn't die, the ideas remain. I read them, and they're alive" (Levy 2007, 289).

César Chávez organized the first effective migrant worker union in the United States. His political skill and his unswerving dedication to one of society's most unprotected sectors made him a popular hero. (Library of Congress)

In September 1965, Filipino workers who were members of the Agricultural Workers Organizing Committee (AWOC) went on strike against the grape growers in Delano, California, demanding wages equal to the federal pay standards for foreign workers. One of the oldest strikers and farmworker leaders was Philip Vera Cruz, who was 60 years old. He and others were soon joined by predominantly Mexican members of the National Farm Workers Association led by Chávez. The two organizations merged in

1966 to become the United Farm Workers (UFW).

Six months later, Chávez organized a California grape pickers strike and led a 250-mile march to the state capitol in Sacramento. Farm workers carried banners adorned with the union's black eagle and the words "*Huelga*" (strike) and "*Viva la Causa*" (Long Live Our Cause). They wanted the ability to unionize and to put in place collective bargaining agreements, as well as basic dignity and respect for all workers, no matter their occupation or race (United Farm Workers web site).

UFW asked Americans to boycott table grapes in support of the farm workers. The strike (which lasted a total of five years) garnered national attention. Chávez drew on iconic civil rights imagery and its language, relying on nonviolent tactics and calling upon support from academic institutions and religious organizations. The first few contracts were signed in 1966, but were followed by years of continued strife. Some of the grape growers banded together, bringing lawsuits, harassing picketers, and even changing wine labels to evade the boycott. As time passed, some strikers lost patience. Although Chávez advocated nonviolence, physical confrontations started to become more commonplace.

The strikers did gain an important ally. While on the U.S. Senate Subcommittee on Migratory Labor, Robert Kennedy met Chávez at a public hearing in 1966. Getting to know Chávez and his commitment to nonviolent protest strengthened Kennedy's resolve to fight for the farm workers. Dolores Huerta recalled Kennedy's support, "He said that we had the right to form a union and that he ... not only endorsed us but joined us." Kennedy's backing was great publicity as well as a morale boost for the strikers. "Robert didn't come to us and tell us what was good for us," Huerta said later. "He came to us and asked us two questions: 'What do you want? And how can I help?' " (Public Broadcasting Service).

Chávez was willing to make the ultimate sacrifice—to give up his own life—for "*la Causa*," and would choose any method to achieve his aims except for violence. In 1968, to avert growing restlessness and increased calls for violence within the union, Chávez went on a water-only, 25-day fast. Chávez explained, "Farm workers everywhere are angry and worried that we cannot win without violence. We have proved it before through persistence, hard work, faith and willingness to sacrifice. We can win and keep our own self-respect and build a great union that will secure the spirit of all people if we do it through a rededication and recommitment to the struggle for justice through nonviolence" (United Farm Workers web site).

Then presidential candidate Robert Kennedy flew to California to help Chávez end his fast. Chávez had lost over 30 pounds and was too weak to speak at the Mass of Thanksgiving in his honor. Chávez had someone else relay his message: "It is how we use our lives that determines what kind of men we are ... I am convinced that the truest act of courage, the strongest act of manliness, is to sacrifice ourselves for others in a totally nonviolent struggle for justice. To be a man is to suffer for others. God help us be men" (Public Broadcasting Service).

In 1970, the growers and the union settled the strike. Chávez was thus the first to organize a union for farm workers in California, and which, by getting contracts from the agricultural industry, showed that the UFW spoke for the workers. This brought an end to the five-year boycott and a measure of peace to the vineyards.

Chávez continued to espouse—and practice—his motto of nonviolence. In 1972, he again fasted, this time for 24 days in objection to legislation passed by Arizona lawmakers that prohibited boycotts and strikes by farm workers during harvest (United Farm Workers web site). In 1976, Chávez led UFW through a major reorganization. In 1984, he led another boycott of grapes, protesting toxic pesticides used in their growth, once again fasting to draw public attention. However, his influence was in decline, as the union continued to lose members and economic and political conditions allowed growers to increasingly return to their former practices of hiring nonunion workers and reduce wages.

In 1988, Chávez was in the national spotlight once more, this time for his most famous and final public fast, his "Fast For Life." Chávez did not eat for 36 days. His aim was to publicize the continuing injustices visited upon grape pickers and the dangers of chemicals sprayed on the fruit. At the Mass ending his debilitating fast, Rev. Jesse Jackson accepted a wooden cross from Chávez, vowing to the thousands present that he would continue Chávez's fast for another three days, before "passing it on." The fast was passed on to actor Martin Sheen; Southern Christian Leadership Conference president Reverend J. Lowery; actor Edward Olmos; actor Emilio Estevez; the daughter of Robert Kennedy, Kerry Kennedy; legislator Peter Chacon; actress Julie Carmen; actor Danny Glover; singer Carly Simon; and actress Whoopi Goldberg, among others (United Farm Workers web site).

Chavez addressed the purpose of his fasts:

> It is ... for the purification of my own body, mind, and soul. ... also a heartfelt prayer for purification and strengthening for all those who work beside me in the farm worker movement ... also an act of penance for those in positions of moral authority and for all men and women activists who know what is right and just, who know that they could and should do more ... finally a declaration of noncooperation with supermarkets who promote and sell and profit from California table grapes ... This solution to this deadly crisis will not be found in the arrogance of the powerful, but in solidarity with the weak and helpless. I pray to God that this fast will be a preparation for a multitude of simple deeds for justice. Carried out by men and women whose hearts are focused on the suffering of the poor and who yearn, with us, for a better world. Together, all things are possible. (United Farm Workers web site)

In April 23, 1993, after a day testifying in a lawsuit brought against UFW, Chávez passed away at home in San Luis, Arizona. His funeral was attended by over 50,000—farm workers, family members, friends, and union staff alike stood vigil over Chávez's plain pine coffin. The service was held at the site of his first (1968) and last (1988) fasts—the United Farm Workers Delano Field Office (United Farm Workers web site).

The year before he died, Chávez was awarded the Pacem in Terris (Peace on Earth) Award. The year after his death, he received the Presidential Medal of Freedom, the highest civilian honor given in the United States. He has received many other awards and honors.

In the introduction to *Cesar Chavez: Autobiography of La Causa*, Fred Ross Jr. (son of his former CSO colleague) wrote in 2007:

> I learned ... that the organizer works quietly behind the scenes, patently asking questions, listening respectfully,

agitating, teaching new leaders, pushing them to take action, and creating hope ... The organizer finds people one at a time, teaches them to develop their own powerful voices, turns their anger about injustice into hope by encouraging them to take action, raises hell, stirs up trouble, and has fun doing it ... The lessons in this story, illustrating the power of nonviolent action and the art of moral jiujitsu, are meant to be practiced. Those who were part of the farm workers movement have passed on their trade to thousands of organizers who are now working in human rights, environmental justice, labor, and electoral politics. The efforts of these young organizers, for me, are the farm workers' most enduring legacy. (Levy 2007, xviii)

Margaret Gay

See also King, Martin Luther, Jr.; Sheen, Martin; Vera Cruz, Philip

References

Levy, Jacques E. *Cesar Chavez: Autobiography of La Causa*. Minneapolis: University of Minnesota Press, 2007.

"RFK American Experience, People and Events: Cesar Chavez (1927–1993)." Public Broadcasting Service, PBS Home Programs web site, July 1, 2004. http://www.pbs.org/wgbh/amex/rfk/peopleevents/p_chavez.html (accessed September 8, 2011).

"The Story of Cesar Chavez." United Farm Workers web site, n.d. http://www.ufw.org/_page.php?inc=history/07.html&menu=research (accessed April 21, 2011).

Chavis, Benjamin Franklin (1948–)

Benjamin Chavis has been an activist—a dissident—most of his life. He grew up at a time when the U.S. civil rights struggle was well under way, and he was part of it at an early age. When he was sentenced in the 1970s to 34 years in prison on a conviction that was later overturned, he noted in an interview with *Ebony* magazine: "All of us have to be revolutionaries ... but we have to be revolutionaries like the chameleon. The chameleon is a little lizard. Whatever thing he lands on, that is what color he becomes. That's his defense mechanism. But a chameleon never forgets that he's a lizard. I'm saying to you, be engineers and doctors but realize you're a Black person. Never forget it! Wake up with it! Sleep it! And, whatever, love it!" (Pointsett 1979, 72).

Born on January 22, 1948, in Oxford, North Carolina, he was given the name Benjamin Franklin Chavis Jr. by his parents Benjamin and Elisabeth Chavis, both of whom were educators. But he adopted a new name much later in his life, after he joined the Nation of Islam and converted to the Muslim faith: Benjamin Chavis Muhammad.

Benjamin Chavis became a member of National Association for the Advancement of Colored People (NAACP) at age 12 (Norment 1993, 76) and was a youth leader for Oxford County's Grandville County branch. Around that time, he decided to take a stand against segregation and walk into an all-white library, which he passed every day on his way to and from school. Although librarians ordered him to leave, he refused to do so. Not long afterward, the library was integrated—a result of his defiant protest.

Benjamin graduated from all-black Mary Potter High School in 1965 and earned an undergraduate degree in chemistry from the University of North Carolina at Charlotte in 1969. While a college freshman, he was state youth coordinator for the Southern Christian Leadership Conference (SCLC), spending time with Martin Luther King Jr., who greatly influenced him. He joined the Congress on Racial Equality, the Student Nonviolent Coordinating Committee and the American Federation of State, Municipal and County Employees, and he volunteered for Robert F. Kennedy's presidential campaign in 1968. He also began working as a field officer for the United Church of Christ's Commission for Racial Justice (UCC-CRJ), a group that coordinated regional and national strategies and campaigns for social justice.

By 1969, Chavis was UCC-CRJ's southern regional program director. In this capacity, two years later, he was called to help in the town of Wilmington, located in New Hanover County, North Carolina. The U.S. Supreme Court had determined that segregation of schools was unconstitutional in *Brown v. Board of Education* (1954). But Wilmington did not implement the ruling until 16 years after the fact, when it closed the local all-black high school. Integration efforts were poorly received by students of both races; additionally, school administrators were neither enthusiastic nor supportive. When black students were integrated, they were not accepted on athletic teams, in student government, or in extracurricular activities. There were physical attacks, suspensions, and a sit-in.

The pastor of the Gregory Congregational Church asked Chavis to lead a march on the Wilmington Board of Education. In counterprotest, angry whites made harassing phone calls to the church's white minister, Eugene Templeton; shots were fired into both the church and his home. Police refused to protect blacks at the church. Following the dictates of self-defense, a barricade was implemented around the area and guns were brought in for protection. Four days into what eventually turned into an armed siege, a fire broke out in a nearby, white-owned grocery store. Since phone and electrical lines to the church had been cut, a black youth emerged to place a call to the fire department; he was fatally shot by police. The following day, an armed white man approached the barricades and was also mortally wounded by an unknown assailant. Hundreds of national guardsmen who had been called out to resolve the situation arrived to discover that the people who had been barricaded in the church had managed to slip away under the cover of night (Poinsett 1979, 66).

Fourteen months later, Chavis and more than a dozen students were indicted on charges of assault and arson; Chavis was charged with conspiracy to commit murder. The death of the young black man was ruled a "justifiable homicide"; no charges were brought against the policeman who shot him. Only seven whites were charged; they received light—and suspended—sentences for "being armed to terrorize people." The black defendants had been jailed for four months awaiting trial. The initial jury of 10 blacks and two whites was dismissed; a mistrial was declared immediately after jury selection when the prosecutor became suddenly and mysteriously ill. A second jury was chosen, with the opposite racial composition—the judge allowed known racist Ku Klux Klan members to be considered. The "Wilmington 10," as they were called, were convicted and Chavis received a 34-year sentence. The prosecution relied heavily on eyewitnesses who placed Chavis at the scene. The North Carolina Court of Appeals found numerous trial errors but said the witnesses' testimony was "overwhelmingly sufficient to support the verdicts of guilty." North Carolina's Supreme Court dismissed the higher appeal for "lack of substantial 'constitutional question' and the U.S. Supreme Court refused a petition for review" (Poinsett 1979, 68).

The Wilmington 10 headed off to prison, where Chavis took on the role of pastoral minister. In August 1976, there was a major turn of events. One of the witnesses came forward to recant his story, saying it was given "because of favors and promises of early release from prison." Also, law officers had convinced him that Chavis had threatened his family. A second witness came forward stating that he had been coached to lie, testifying, "They told me to cooperate or I would face life in prison" (on a first-degree murder charge). The third eyewitness, similarly, told a tale of being promised a minibike at Christmas and a job at a gas station—the prosecutor admitted making good on those promises, but didn't "recall" any pretrial coercion factoring into any of the witnesses' testimony (Poinsett 1979, 65–68).

In May 1977, there was a two-week hearing. Backing up the three witnesses' recantations, Reverend Templeton and his wife testified that Chavis and other defendants had been in the church with them when the firebombing and shooting occurred. Regardless, the Superior Court judge deemed a new trial unwarranted. On television, facing reelection, Jim Hunt, the state's governor, recommended that the Wilmington 10's sentences be reduced, although he denied any wrongdoing by the prosecution. A U.S. Justice Department friend of the court brief soon offered support that the defendants had not received due process. By 1979, all but Chavis had been paroled (Poinsett 1979, 70). Eventually, there was a ruling in 1980 in the Fourth U.S. Circuit Court of Appeals, reversing and overturning all 10 defendants' original convictions. Chavis served four-and-half years wrongfully imprisoned before his release.

According to the teachings of his role model Dr. King, Chavis had tried to make the best of a bad situation. While in prison, he had taken advantage of a study-release program that allowed him to obtain his master's degree in divinity at Duke University. This was the same year he was ordained a UCC minister. He continued his education, pursuing a doctorate in divinity from Howard University in 1981; he did additional graduate work later on at Union Theological Seminary.

In 1983, Chavis went to Cleveland, Ohio, to be the deputy director for UCC-RJC. Within two years, he was the group's executive director and CEO. He was now better known on the national stage. He took an active role in mainstream political issues—not just those pertinent to blacks. And he was visible in the role of clergy coordinator for the 1984 presidential campaign of Reverend Jesse Jackson. From 1985 to 1993, Chavis wrote a nationally syndicated newspaper column called *Civil Rights Journal*; he simultaneously hosted a radio show by the same name.

While working for UCC, Chavis was also leading the charge in "environmental racism," that is, dumping toxic waste materials in communities of color. The environmental movement was in its infancy when, in 1983, he led a protest against dumping contaminated soil in the 75 percent black-populated Warren County, North Carolina. Three years later, Chavis sponsored a landmark study, *Toxic Waste and Race in the United States: A National Report on the Racial and Socioeconomic Characteristics of Communities with Hazardous Waste Sites*. It statistically revealed the direct correlation between race and the location of toxic waste throughout the United States.

Throughout the years, Chavis has been one of the most prominent spokespersons on environmental policy, even serving on the 1992 Clinton-Gore presidential transition team studying the departments of

Energy, the Interior, and Agriculture and the Environmental Protection Agency. In the 2000 foreword to *Confronting Racism: Voices from the Grassroots* by Robert Bullard, Chavis was direct in stating, "People of color bear the brunt of the nation's pollution problems" (Bullard 1993, 3). To Chavis, this is overt racial discrimination, the deliberate targeting of ethnic and minority peoples, knowingly exposing them to toxic and hazardous waste, as well as the systematic exclusion of these same people from environmental policy making, enforcement, and remediation.

Chavis was elected vice president of the National Council of Churches in 1988 and served as chairman of its Prophetic Justice Unit. In 1993, he was the youngest person ever elected as executive director and CEO of the NAACP. "In the succeeding weeks, he hosted a gang summit in Kansas City, met with President Clinton and Vice President Gore, participated in the gay rights rally in Washington, testified at a hearing on environmental waste, spoke at the Detroit NAACP Freedom Fund Dinner and met with the Congressional Black Caucus ... Ben Chavis is a man on the move and a man with a mission, and he appears to have the heart, soul and stamina that will be necessary assets of his new job," wrote Lynn Norment in *Ebony* (Norment 1993, 77–78).

However, in the following year, NAACP's board of directors terminated Chavis after charges of improper use of funds and sexual harassment arose. True to form, he turned what could have been a negative time in his life into a positive one. In 1995, he formed the National African American Leadership Summit (NAALS) and was its executive director and CEO until 2001. In that first year, he participated in the "Million Man March" organized by Louis Farrakhan, leader of the Nation of Islam. Recounting the march in Washington, D.C., Chavis noted: "I know that God was truly at work in getting 2 million black men to come to grips with the theological imperatives of atonement. The Christian-Muslim unity displayed at the Million Man March shook the grave[s] of ... all the ancestors who have yearned and cried out for unity, freedom, justice, and equality" (Othow 2001, 3).

In 1997, Chavis became a Muslim and a member of the Nation of Islam. He was appointed East Coast regional minister and minister of the historic Mosque #7 in Harlem, where Malcolm X once preached.

Dr. Chavis cofounded and is president of the Hip-Hop Summit Action Network (HSAN), an international coalition of artists and recording industry executives that acts as a catalyst for education advocacy and youth empowerment. In April 2009, he also became president of Online Education Services (EOServe), where he aids in the development and implementation of online curriculum infrastructure, student recruitment, enrollment, and retention on behalf of historical black colleges and other diverse institutions of higher learning (EOServe Corp PR Office 1999).

Chavis has written two books, *An American Political Prisoner Appeals for Human Rights* (1979) and *Psalms from Prison* (1983). He has been married twice and is father to eight children.

Margaret Gay

See also Bullard, Robert; Farrakhan, Louis; King, Martin Luther, Jr.; Malcolm X

References

Bullard, Robert D., ed. *Confronting Racism: Voices from the Grassroots*. Cambridge, MA: South End Press, 1993.

EOServe Corp PR Office. "Dr. Benjamin F. Chavis, Jr. Joins Education Online Services EOServe Corp as President." *Education*

Online Services Corporation Press Release, April 1, 2009. http://www.educationonline services.com/Pressrelease_04_02_09.htm (accessed September 8, 2011).

Norment, Lynn. "Ben Chavis: A New Director, a New Direction at the NAACP." *Ebony*, July 1993.

Othow, Helen Chavis. *John Chavis: African American Patriot, Preacher, Teacher, and Mentor (1783–1838)*. Foreword by Benjamin F. (Chavis) Muhammad. Jefferson, NC: McFarland & Co., 2001.

Poinsett, Alex. "Wilmington 10: Rev. Ben Chavis Serves 17-Year Prison Sentence while Earning Duke University Master's Degree." *Ebony*, June 1979.

Sadler, Kim Martin, ed. *Atonement: The Million Man March*. Cleveland, OH: Pilgrim Press, 1996.

Choi, Daniel (1981–)

Daniel Choi is a graduate of the West Point Military Academy and served as an officer during two tours in Iraq. He is also a homosexual who, because he publicly announced his sexual orientation, was in violation of the U.S. military's Don't Ask, Don't Tell (DADT) policy established in 1993 (McMichael 2009). The rationale for the policy was that knowing about the presence of homosexual individuals "would create an unacceptable risk to the high standards of morale, good order and discipline, and unit cohesion that are the essence of military capability." Although people were not supposed to "ask" or investigate the sexual orientation of military personnel, in reality, unauthorized investigations and harassment occurred repeatedly under DADT. Since 1993, more than 13,000 troops had been discharged under the policy. In February 2005, the U.S. Government Accountability Office estimated nearly $100 million in recruiting costs and an equal amount for training replacements for approximately 9,500 discharged under DADT between 1994 and 2003. Others have estimated costs significantly higher, taking into account service members' separation travel, additional officer training, and enlistee costs, not to mention other incalculable, intangible losses accruing from DADT separations.

Increasingly throughout his years of service, Choi felt DADT compelled him to live a lie—a direct violation of the Cadet Code, which student officers in training at West Point are required to honor. The Code is a formalized statement of the minimum ethical standard expected of cadets. It reads, in entirety, "A cadet will not lie, cheat, steal, or tolerate those who do." Anyone accused of violating the Honor Code faces a standardized investigative and hearing process; severe consequences face one whose peers find him in violation, up to and including expulsion. A cadet violates the Code's tenet of "lying" through deliberate deception—that is, "stating an untruth *or* by any direct form of communication, including telling a partial truth and vague or ambiguous use of information or language with intent to deceive or mislead."

Choi eventually took a stand, one that would result in his forced separation from service. He wrote to President Barack Obama and U.S. Congressional members, pleading his case for remaining in the military:

The Cadet Honor Code demanded truthfulness and honesty. It imposed a zero-tolerance policy against deception, or hiding behind comfort. Following the Honor Code never bowed to comfortable timing or popularity. Honor and integrity are 24-hour values. That is why I refuse to lie about my identity. I have personally served for a decade under Don't Ask,

Don't Tell: an immoral law and policy that forces American soldiers to deceive and lie about their sexual orientation. Worse, it forces others to tolerate deception and lying. These values are completely opposed to anything I learned at West Point. Deception and lies poison a unit and cripple a fighting force. (Choi 2009)

Choi, born in 1981, is the son of a Baptist minister. He grew up in Orange County, California, attending high school in Tustin. He not only set his sights on West Point but also on someday becoming the first Korean-American general. Choi graduated with a specialized and highly desirable degree in Arabic.

Choi served in "Operation Iraqi Freedom" in 2003 and served a second Iraq tour, from 2006 to 2007, as an infantry officer with the rank of first lieutenant. In June 2008, Choi transferred from active duty status to service with the New York National Guard, headquartered in Manhattan, where he was platoon leader (James 2010).

During this time period, then Illinois senator Barack Obama was speaking about issues of great significance to Choi and others in the LGBT (lesbian, gay, bisexual, and transgendered) community. As a candidate, Obama promised to repeal Don't Ask, Don't Tell (Obama 2008). However, after his election as president, Obama was distracted from his campaign commitments by the financial crisis and the multitude of related issues facing him after he took office. Some military members took matters into their own hands and on March 16, 2009: "Thirty-eight graduates of the U.S. Military Academy at West Point, N.Y., came out of the closet ... with an offer to help their alma mater educate future Army leaders on the need to accept and honor the sacrifices of lesbian, gay, bisexual and transgender troops. 'Knights Out' wants to serve as a connection between gay troops and Army administrators ... We're publicly announcing our sexuality, our orientation," said 1st Lt. Dan Choi" (McMichael 2009). Knights Out members, like Choi, are committed to the principles learned at the Academy.

In "outing" themselves, Choi and the other men had just risked their military careers under the provisions of DADT. On March 19 and 20, 2009, Choi appeared on MSNBC's highly rated cable television program, *The Rachel Maddow Show*. Choi declared:

By saying three words to you today, I am gay, those three words are a violation of Title 10 of the U.S. Code. It's a code that is polluted by the people who want us to lie and basically they want us to lie about our identity.... [O]ne of [the] harder things was coming back from Iraq. Being an Iraq combat veteran, an Arabic linguist, a West Point graduate, I come back to America as a second-class citizen who's forced to lie because of this rule, because of this law. And because Congress has not yet overturned this, and we're saying once and for all, it needs to be repealed. (*The Rachel Maddow Show* transcript, March 19–20, 2009)

Following his revelations, Choi was sent a letter notifying him of his honorable discharge from the military; it was delivered to his parents' Tustin residence, where he had not visited for over a year. In the interim, his New York National Guard commander advised him of the news. Reached for comment, Choi said, "Now I realize military service is a lot more than just rank or a paycheck or those constructs of honor. Real honor and dignity are doing what the

Lieutenant Daniel Choi is seen in front of the White House in Washington, moments before he handcuffed himself to the fence of the White House during a protest for gay rights, November 15, 2010. Choi was part of a group demanding that President Obama keep his promise to repeal "Don't Ask, Don't Tell." (AP Photo/Pablo Martinez Monsivais)

military uniform stands for, and that's fighting for freedom and justice." He added that he planned to continue his use of civil disobedience to bring attention to DADT (James 2010). This is when Choi wrote to President Obama and Congress; about 150,000 others joined his plea, signing a Courage Campaign Petition (Courage Campaign web site).

Regardless, on June 30, 2009, a panel of New York National Guard officers recommended discharge for Choi. A spokesperson from Knights Out said, "the Guard's Federal Recognition Board heard from members of Choi's unit, his commanding officer and fellow soldiers who served in Iraq, and reviewed more than 150 letters of support for Choi ... At the end of the day, they did not consider any of that material ... It was solely about whether he said he was gay." Choi's reaction was firm: "[M]ore important than the consequences, more important than punishments or those fears that we might have, we take courage and we take those things very seriously of the values that we were taught. And it's more important that we be honest with ourselves, we have integrity, and we have courage" (CNN.com 2009).

President Obama committed in his January 26, 2010, State of the Union Address that he would "work with Congress and our military to finally repeal the law that denies gay Americans the right to serve the country they love because of who they are. It's the right thing to do" (Obama 2010). The defense secretary and Joint Chiefs chairman soon added their support for DADT repeal. Two weeks later, people speculated that DADT was starting to crumble. On February 11, Lt. Choi drilled with his Manhattan Guard unit at, he said, his commanding officer's encouragement. He had been participating in substitute drills, due to his schedule lobbying for DADT repeal. His unit faced possible deployment to Afghanistan in 2012 (Bumiller 2010).

On March 18, Choi and Capt. Jim Pietrangelo cuffed themselves to the White House fence. They asserted they were obeying the president's order to pressure him to change DADT, going so far as to issue a subpoena (unserved) for Obama to testify on their behalf at trial. Ultimately, charges were dropped (James 2010; Osborne 2010).

Not content with the progress being made, Choi and five others again handcuffed themselves to the White House fence in April. At the end of May, Choi and Pietrangelo tried a tactic used by labor leader César Chávez—a hunger strike, lasting seven days. Choi considered it successful in that it brought attention to their demands.

Choi's discharge was finalized, with no further appeals possible, on June 29, 2010. Commenting about the pros and cons of Choi's visibility, Aaron Belkin, director of the Palm Center, the University of California think tank studying DADT, said, "There are a lot of gay servicemembers who are a little concerned that this kind of activity [politicking in uniform] could cast them in a negative light. Others believe that the community has to do what it takes to end discrimination." Belkin knew of some complaints but saw Choi's work as "important and positive. It took a Malcolm X for people to be willing to deal with a Martin Luther King. Dan has kept the temperature up on this issue" (Osborne 2010).

On October 12, 2010, U.S. federal judge Virginia Philips ordered the Department of Defense to stop enforcing DADT. A week later, she denied the federal government's request for a stay of her order pending appeal. That day, former Lt. Dan Choi went to the New York City Times Square recruiting station to attempt to enlist in the U.S. Army; he tried to join the Marines but was too old (Salon.com 2010).

On May 28, 2010, the U.S. House of Representatives took action that would repeal relevant sections of DADT 60 days after completion of a U.S. Department of Defense study and certification given by the U.S. defense secretary, the Joint Chiefs of Staff chairman, and the president that repeal would not harm military effectiveness.

A bill to repeal DADT passed both the U.S. House and Senate on December 15, 2010. President Obama signed the repeal into law on December 22, 2010. Daniel Choi was invited to the signing ceremony. With passage of the law, the 60-day waiting period must expire after certification. Reports as of April 2011 indicated that progress was ahead of schedule, with completion expected by year's end.

Two days before Choi went to the bill signing, the Defense Department was putting yet another letter in the mail to him—along with a $2,500 bill for the "unearned portion of your enlistment or reenlistment bonus." Failure to remit payment within 30 days could result in Choi's debt being reported to credit bureaus and turned over to a collection agency (or deducted from any tax refund that might be due), as well as cause follow up legal action from the U.S. Justice Department (HuffingtonPost.com 2011). Lt. Daniel Choi has most definitely "paid a price" for publicly standing up for his principles.

Margaret Gay

See also Chávez, César; King, Martin Luther, Jr.; Malcolm X

References

Bumiller, Elisabeth. "Gay Guardsman Has Returned to Drills with His Unit." *New York*

Times, February 11, 2010. http://www.nytimes.com/2010/02/12/us/12military.html (accessed April 23, 2011).

Choi, Daniel. "Lt. Daniel Choi Begs to Keep His Job in National Guard: Open Letter to President Obama and Every Member of Congress." ABC News/U.S., May 11, 2009. http://abcnews.go.com/US/story?id=7569476 (accessed April 23, 2011).

CNN. "National Guard: Gay Iraq Veteran Must Leave Service." CNN.com, June 30, 2009. http://www.cnn.com/2009/US/06/30/us.military.gays/index.html?ref=storysearch (accessed April 23, 2011).

Community of LGBT Centers web site. http://www.lgbtcenters.org/ (accessed April 23, 2011).

Courage Campaign web site. http://www.couragecampaign.org/page/s/dontfiredan (accessed April 24, 2011).

Crary, David. "Gay West Point Grads Target Ban on Serving Openly." Washington Examiner.com, April 12, 2009. http://washingtonexaminer.com/news/2009/04/gay-west-point-grads-target-ban-serving-openly (accessed April 23, 2011).

"Dan Choi Told to Repay Military $2,500 after Being Discharged under DADT." Huffington Post.com, January 27, 2011. http://www.huffingtonpost.com/2011/01/27/dan-choi-repay-army-bonus-dadt-discharge_n_815102.html (accessed April 23, 2011).

James, Elysse. "Gay Soldier's Discharge Delivered to Parents' Tustin Home." OC Register.com, July 23, 2010. http://articles.ocregister.com/2010-07-23/cities/24631469_1_civil-disobedience-honorable-discharge-tustin-high-school (accessed September 16, 2011).

Knights Out web site. http://www.knightsout.org (accessed April 23, 2011).

McMichael, William H. "West Point Grads Form Support Group." *Navy Times*, March 16, 2009. http://www.navytimes.com/news/2009/03/military_westpoint_knightsout_031609w/ (accessed April 21, 2011).

Obama, Barack. "Equality Is a Moral Imperative: Open Letter Concerning LGBT Equality in America, Reaffirming His Steadfast Commitment to Equal Rights for ALL Americans." *2012 BarackObama.com*, February, 28, 2008. http://my.barackobama.com/page/community/post/alexokrent/gGggJS (accessed April 23, 2011).

Obama, Barack. "Remarks by the President in State of the Union Address, U.S. Capitol." January 27, 2010. http://www.whitehouse.gov/the-press-office/remarks-president-state-union-address (accessed April 23, 2011).

Osborne, Duncan. "Dan Choi, Now Discharged, Sees DC Protest Charge Dismissed." *Gay City News*, July 20, 2010. http://gaycitynews.com/articles/2010/07/20/gay_city_news/news/doc4c465ff7a178c126438367.txt (cited April 23, 2011).

Pareene, Alex. " 'Don't Ask, Don't Tell' No Longer Enforced, Dan Choi Reenlists." Salon.com, October 20, 2010. http://www.salon.com/news/politics/war_room/2010/10/20/dadt_choi_appeal (accessed April 23, 2011).

"*The Rachel Maddow Show* for Friday, March 20, 2009" (transcript). MSNBC.com, March 20, 2009. http://www.msnbc.msn.com/id/29836340 (accessed April 23, 2011).

Chomsky, Noam (1928–)

Noam Chomsky is best known for his scholarly work in linguistics, but he also is known as a dissident intellectual. He has described himself as a libertarian socialist, and he has expressed anarchist views. He has also been an antiwar activist. Chomsky rarely takes the safe path in regard to politics. He has always been fearlessly unflinching in his critique of power structures both internationally and within the United States, which has prompted critics to call him "un-American" and sometimes "anti-Zionist."

Dr. William Zev Chomsky and Elsie Simonofsky Chomsky named their first son Avram Noam Chomsky when he was born on December 7, 1928, in Philadelphia, Pennsylvania. His father, a Jewish immigrant, had fled Russia in 1913 to avoid military service in the tsar's army. The Chomskys were also the parents of another son, David Eli Chomsky. Both sons were considered gifted and were greatly influenced by their intellectual parents, who taught in the religious school of the Mikveh Israel congregation. Dr. Chomsky, a Hebrew language scholar, eventually took the principal position at this school.

The Chomskys were one of just a few Jewish families living in a working-class Irish and German Catholic neighborhood, where anti-Semitism was rampant. During the 1930s, many of their neighbors supported Adolf Hitler's Nazis until the United States entered World War II in 1941.

At the Chomsky dinner table, the family often held discussions about a variety of social and political issues. Both parents honored education and intellectual pursuits, and in fact were brilliant and in demand as speakers on scholarly topics. They were Zionists—that is, they were part of a movement that supports the existence of the state of Israel and helps to inspire a revival of Jewish national life, culture, and language.

The Chomskys sent Noam to a progressive day school before age two, continuing his education there until he was 12. When he was 10 years old, Noam wrote an essay on the Spanish Civil War for the school's newspaper. The family also was actively involved in Jewish cultural activities and study of the Hebrew language and literature, which Noam would read with his father.

While an adolescent, Chomsky frequently visited his mother's relatives in New York City. His uncle operated a newsstand in New York at Broadway and 72nd Street, which was a gathering place for exiled intellectuals and Jewish anarchists who discussed their political views. Chomsky at times stayed all night at the newsstand, absorbing the discussions and arguments. To increase his knowledge, he also read library materials on radical political thought and philosophy.

Noam attended a public, college-oriented high school in Philadelphia. At first he never understood he was a good student because of the emphasis put on creativity and individual learning, but it soon became obvious that Chomsky was an exceptional scholar. His "first two years of college [at the University of Pennsylvania] were pretty much an extension of high school, except in one respect," he said in an interview. "I entered with a great deal of enthusiasm and expectation that all sorts of fascinating prospects would open up, but these did not survive long." After two years, he was ready to put aside his formal schooling to pursue his own areas of interest. "This was 1947," he noted, "and I had just turned eighteen. I was deeply interested, as I had been for some years, in radical politics with an anarchist or left-wing (anti-Leninist) Marxist flavor, and even more deeply involved in Zionist affairs and activities" (Peck 1987, 6–7).

He considered a trip to a kibbutz in Israel to pursue his interest in politics and the possibilities of Arab-Jewish cooperation, as opposed to the Zionist antidemocratic movement that was very popular at the time. However, before he could leave the university completely, he began dating Carol Schatz, whom he had known since childhood. They attended the same Hebrew school, and Carol's parents and Noam's parents were friends. Noam and Carol married on December 24, 1949, and eventually had three children, two daughters and a son.

Chomsky also stayed on at the university because of Zellig Harris, a leading linguist who founded the first department of linguistics in the United States. Chomsky began taking graduate courses under Professor Harris, a charismatic scholar with broad interests. Harris suggested that Chomsky try to diagram a systematic structure of some language. Chomsky turned his attention to the Hebrew language, and for his master's honors thesis he wrote "Morphophonemics of Modern Hebrew" in 1951; he rewrote this in book form, completing it in 1955, but not published until 20 years later as *Logical Structure of Linguistic Theory* (1975). This most original and controversial work was the basis for the groundbreaking analysis of language that would, in and of itself, assure the scholar a place in history.

Chomsky studied linguistics from both the biological and psychological perspectives. His doctorate was conveyed in 1955, even though he had almost no formal contact with the university after the initial years. His doctoral dissertation "Transformational Analysis" and the seminal work *Syntactic Structures* (1957) defined a new form of linguistic analysis called transformational-generative grammar.

In 1953, Noam and his wife, Carol, spent a brief time in an Israeli kibbutz, but were disappointed with the conformity and anti-Arab bias exhibited by the young kibbutzim. The Chomskys left the communal settlement and returned to the United States and the Boston, Massachusetts, area. By 1955, Chomsky was teaching linguistics at the Massachusetts Institute of Technology (MIT), and by 1961, he was full professor at MIT. Carol Chomsky returned to school and earned a doctorate from Harvard University, where she later taught at the Graduate School of Childhood Education; she died in 2008.

Noam Chomsky's work changed the study of linguistics in the second half of the twentieth century. Many linguistic theorists contend that language is learned, but Chomsky argues that humans have an innate ability to understand the hidden structures of language. However, that theory has had its detractors.

Linguistics is not the only field in which Chomsky has had controversy. His views on politics and the prevailing social structure have created much debate. When the Vietnam War was accelerating, Chomsky became a political activist and dissident. In 1967, he founded RESIST, which organized antiwar demonstrations. His close friend Howard Zinn, author of one of the earliest books calling for the U.S. withdrawal from the Vietnam War, *Vietnam: The Logic of Withdrawal* (1967), strongly supported RESIST and took part in some protests. During one of the protests, Chomsky was arrested and jailed. But after serving his time, he continued to speak out at rallies. His speeches were the basis for his book *American Power and the New Mandarins* (1969).

After Beacon Press published its four-volume *The Pentagon Papers* (1972), the publisher asked Chomsky and Zinn to edit a fifth volume: *The Pentagon Papers: Critical Essays: Volume Five* (1972). The book is a collection of essays commenting on the Pentagon Papers, a study commissioned by the U.S. Department of Defense that analyzed U.S. involvement in Vietnam. When completed, it contained more than 7,000 pages of text and government documents. Chomsky and Zinn defended Daniel Ellsberg, a former Defense Department official who leaked the papers to the *New York Times*, setting off a major legal and political debate. The two editors hoped that the critical essays would alert the public to the human consequences of the Vietnam War.

For years he has argued that the United States has been internationally aggressive because of its industrial system that not only dehumanizes but also prompts military intervention. Some of his ideas are presented in such books as *At War with Asia* (1970); *For Reasons of State* (1973), The *Political Economy of Human Rights* (1979), and *Towards a New Cold War* (1982).

Chomsky calls himself a libertarian socialist, but his views readily live alongside prominent anarchist thinkers. In fact, in a 1996 interview with *Znet*, he noted: "Anarchism, in my view, is an expression of the idea that the burden of proof is always on those who argue that authority and domination are necessary. They have to demonstrate, with powerful argument, that that conclusion is correct. If they cannot, then the institutions they defend should be considered illegitimate. How one should react to illegitimate depends on circumstances and conditions: there are no formulas" (Lane 1996).

His special contribution to anarchist thought in the modern era is his analysis of the comparable evils engendered by dictatorial and democratic governments alike. Always willing to focus the spotlight on hypocrisy, he chastises his and other governments and the institutions that maintain the "necessary illusions" of liberty and individual freedom, the vital elements in the props of modern capitalistic governance. Business, the press, and the intellectual elite are some of Chomsky's favorite targets. He has harshly criticized them for their hypocrisy and lack of elementary principles of logic in order to justify and maintain Western political and economic power. He also has long been an outspoken critic of U.S. foreign policy, presenting his views in such

Massachusetts Institute of Technology professor Noam Chomsky was a leading intellectual critic of U.S. involvement in Vietnam. (AP/Wide World Photos)

works as, *Rent-a-Cops of the World: Noam Chomsky on the Gulf Crisis* (1991); *The New World Order Debate* 1991); *Free Trade and Democracy* (1993); *The ABC's of U.S. Policy Toward Haiti* (1994); *Rogue States: The Rule of Force in World Affairs* (2000); *9-11* (2001); *Hegemony or Survival: America's Quest for Global Dominance* (2003); *Failed States: The Abuse of Power and the Assault on Democracy* (2006); and *Hopes and Prospects* (2010).

In Chomsky's view, the United States has an imperial strategy for worldwide military dominance. He supports this view with many logical examples, such as U.S. interventions abroad, disregard for international agreements, and allowing democracy to be controlled by narrow commercial and financial elites. In addition, Chomsky long has criticized the concept that Israel is a Jewish state, which has prompted his critics to label him anti-Semitic. But he has often pointed out that the idea of a nation being strictly Jewish, Christian, or Islamic is improper, and he has no quarrel with the fact that Israel exists.

In May 2010, Chomsky was involved in a highly publicized encounter in Israel—he was refused entrance to the West Bank to speak at Birzeit, a Palestinian university. The Israeli government declared that the incident was a "mishap" and that some official at the border had "overstepped his authority," the *New York Times* reported. However, Chomsky told a television interviewer that "the government of Israel does not like the kinds of things I say—which puts them into the category of I suppose every other government in the world . . . they seemed upset about the fact that I was just taking an invitation from Birzeit and I had no plans to go on to speak in Israeli universities, as I have done many times in the past, but not this time" (Bronner 2010).

As the author of more than 100 books and hundreds of articles and pamphlets on psychology, politics, cognitive science, philosophy, and linguistics, Chomsky's work has been published in numerous countries. He has been awarded honorary degrees from universities around the world. Some of his many awards include the Kyoto Prize in Basic Sciences (1988); the Benjamin Franklin Medal in Computer and Cognitive Science (1999); the President's Medal from the Literary and Debating Society of the National University of Ireland, Galway (2008); the Erich Fromm Award (2010); the A. E. Havens Center's Award for Lifetime Contribution to Critical Scholarship (2010); and many others.

See also Zinn, Howard

References

Barsky, Robert F. *Noam Chomsky: A Life of Dissent*. Cambridge: MIT Press, 1998.

Bronner, Ethan. "Israel Roiled after Chomsky Barred from West Bank." *New York Times*, May 18, 2010. http://www.nytimes.com/2010/05/18/world/middleeast/18chomsky.html?_r=2&partner=rss&emc=rss (accessed September 10, 2010).

Chomsky, Noam. *Failed States: The Abuse of Power and the Assault on Democracy*. New York: Metropolitan Books/Henry Holt, 2006.

Chomsky, Noam. *Hegemony or Survival: America's Quest for Global Dominance*. New York: Metropolitan Books/Henry Holt, 2003.

Chomsky, Noam. *Hopes and Prospects*. Chicago: Haymarket Books, 2010.

Doyle, Kevin (interviewer). "Noam Chomsky on Anarchism, Marxism and Hope for the Future." First published in *Red and Black Revolution*, no. 2, 1996. http://struggle.ws/rbr/noamrbr2.html (accessed September 8, 2011).

Lane, Tom (interviewer). "On Anarchism." *Znet*, December 23, 1996. http://www.chomsky.info/interviews/19961223.htm (accessed September 9, 2010).

Peck, James. *The Chomsky Reader*. New York: Pantheon Books, 1987.

Clark, Ramsey (1927–)

A *Salon* magazine headline called him "the war criminal's best friend" (Williams 1999), and others have labeled him an American traitor. Ramsey Clark has been for many years an outspoken dissident, critical of U.S. foreign policy. He also is known as a peace and human rights advocate. A former U.S. attorney general in President Lyndon Johnson's administration, Clark has provided legal help for such controversial figures as Slobodan Milošević, the Bosnian Serb leader who was charged with committing genocide in the Balkans and tried by the United Nations war crimes tribunal in The Hague, Netherlands, beginning in 2002 (Milošević died in prison in 2006). Clark was also defense attorney for Iraqi leader Saddam Hussein, who was tried in 2005 and convicted of crimes against humanity and hanged in 2006. Asked by a reporter how he could defend dictators and thugs, Clark responded: "The question contains the assumption of guilt.... Whatever my political views, the main thing I am about is this: are you going to follow the law?" He said he "stands up for the despised, the demonised and the impoverished" (Laughland 2005, 22).

He was named William Ramsey Clark when he was born on December 18, 1927, in Dallas, Texas, to Mary Jane Ramsey Clark and Tom C. Clark. While growing up, he began to notice the differences in the lives of poor black families and his family and the fact that no Negroes (as blacks were called then) attended his school. He was captivated by the story of Abraham Lincoln freeing slaves. And, according to an *Esquire* profile of Ramsey Clark, "sometime around the fourth or fifth grade" the death penalty was discussed at school and [Ramsey] "had a powerful instinctive reaction—the death penalty wasn't just bad, it was horrible. To take a helpless man and kill him and call it justice? Horrible" (Richardson 2007, 91). For the rest of his life, he had repugnance for the death penalty.

The family moved to Washington, D.C., in 1937 when Tom Clark became U.S. attorney general, serving from 1945 to 1949. That year, President Harry Truman appointed Tom Clark to the U.S. Supreme Court.

Ramsey Clark attended Woodrow Wilson High School in Washington, D.C., but he dropped out at age 17 to enlist in the U.S. Marine Corps. For the last few months of World War II, he served in Europe. After returning to the United States in 1946, he enrolled in the University of Texas at Austin, where he met Georgia Welch. They married in 1949 during their senior year, and eventually had two children, Tom, and Ronda, who was born with severe handicaps and lives with her parents.

Clark attended law school at the University of Chicago, where he received his doctor of jurisprudence degree in 1950. He was admitted to the Texas bar in 1950, and over the next decade he was an associate and partner in his father's law firm Clark, Reed and Clark. In 1961, President John F. Kennedy appointed Ramsey Clark assistant attorney general of the lands division. In that role, he was involved from 1961 to 1965 in such issues as how to deal with pollution on federal lands, apportionment of the Colorado River waters between Arizona and California, and settlement of Indian land claims in California. He also worked with

Attorney General Robert Kennedy on a variety of cases and civil rights matters. The attorney general, in 1962, sent Clark to oversee the admission of James Meredith to the University of Mississippi; Meredith was the first African American to enroll at the university. Clark also traveled throughout the South to investigate public school integration mandated by federal law.

After the assassination of President Kennedy in 1963, Vice President Lyndon Johnson became president, and Clark was instrumental in numerous civil rights efforts of the Johnson administration. For example, he went to Alabama to supervise the court-ordered protection of Selma-to-Montgomery civil rights marchers who were demanding their right to vote. Two thousand U.S. soldiers were alongside the demonstrators on the route. Prior to the successful march on March 21, 1965, police with billy clubs and tear gas had attacked a group of 600 demonstrators in Selma, preventing them from reaching Montgomery.

In 1965, Clark also was part of a task force that visited the Watts neighborhood in Los Angeles, California, after riots had erupted over racial tensions, and he exposed abuses by the National Guard and police. In addition, he helped draft the Voting Rights Act of 1965 and the Civil Rights Act of 1968.

Johnson nominated, and Congress confirmed, Clark for attorney general in 1967, and Clark's father resigned from the U.S. Supreme Court to prevent a conflict of interest. Attorney General Ramsey Clark began his tenure by stopping all federal executions and the construction of more prisons. Clark was in charge during the many protests against the mounting deaths in the Vietnam War and the draft based on a lottery system that seemed unfair to many Americans. Antiwar demonstrations occurred in numerous cities and on college campuses.

Some of these protests were acts of civil disobedience, such as turning in draft cards, which were then mailed to the Justice Department. Although Clark opposed the Vietnam War, he was a stickler for the rule of law. In 1968, he prosecuted a group of antidraft leaders, which included the well-known pediatrician and author Dr. Benjamin Spock and Yale chaplain William Sloane Coffin Jr. They were convicted of conspiracy to encourage draft evasion, but the verdicts were appealed and overturned. Clark also took legal action against boxing legend Muhammad Ali, who refused to be inducted in the military on the basis of his Muslim beliefs.

Clark's term as attorney general ended in 1969, and he moved to New York City to practice law, often handling international law and human rights cases. He also was a law professor and followed his true beliefs by being active in anti–Vietnam War activities.

In the 1970s, he ran twice as a candidate for the U.S. Senate from New York, but was unsuccessful. In the early 1970s, Clark and Roy Wilkins, a civil rights leader, led a privately sponsored investigation of the death of Black Panther Fred Hampton, who was shot multiple times when Chicago police raided his apartment in 1969. Police claimed Hampton and his colleagues instigated the shootings. A state grand jury and a federal grand jury issued reports, but neither indicted any of the police officers. After a three-year study, Wilkins and Clark published *Search and Destroy: A Report by the Commission of Inquiry into the Black Panthers and the Police* (1973). That report basically concluded that law enforcement officials endorsed lawlessness, racism, and violence, and later forensic evidence showed that all but one of the 99 bullets shot into Hampton's apartment came from police guns.

By the 1980s, Clark had given up on politics and government and had become one of the most controversial figures in the legal profession. He has made it clear many times that he represents individuals labeled by the public as indefensible. In Clark's view, everyone accused of a crime deserves to be represented in court. To that end, he has been defense lawyer for clients who were arrested while engaging in acts of civil disobedience such as Jesuit priests Daniel and Philip Berrigan; the priests, with other members of a group known as Plowshares, damaged the nose cones of nuclear missiles manufactured at a Pennsylvania plant. Clark also has defended American Indian activist Leonard Peltier, who was convicted (wrongly, his supporters say) of killing an agent of the Federal Bureau of Investigation; Mumia Abu-Jamal, a Black Panther convicted of murder; and extremist political candidate Lyndon LaRouche, once a Marxist. Other notorious persons he has defended include Rwandan pastor Elizaphan Ntakirutimana, convicted of genocide; Sheik Omar Abdel-Rahman, convicted in the 1993 plot to bomb the World Trade Center in New York City; and Karl Linnas, a former Nazi concentration camp guard. When questioned about defending these hated criminals, Clark told a reporter, "If you let fear, hatred and prejudice determine who gets a trial, you don't have a system of law" (Schneidau 2005).

In 1991, after the Gulf War, Clark and his associates took a tour of Iraq to document the results of the U.S. bombings. Clark noted that there were "110,000 aerial sorties in forty-two days, an average of one every thirty seconds, which dropped 88,500 tons of bombs. (These are Pentagon figures.)... We hit reservoirs, dams, pumping stations, pipelines, and purification plants. Some associates and I drove into Iraq at the end of the second week of the war, and there was no running water anywhere. People were drinking water out of the Tigris and Euphrates Rivers" (Jensen 2001).

Returning to the United States, Clark initiated the International War Crimes Tribunal, which gathered information from around the world and resulted in 19 separate charges that President George H. W. Bush, Vice President Dan Quayle, Secretary of Defense Richard Cheney, Generals Colin Powell and Norman Schwarzkopf, and others had violated international law and committed war crimes. Clark's book *The Fire Next Time: U.S. War Crimes in the Gulf* (1992) presents eyewitness reports and evidence that supports the tribunal's charges.

Clark often has been asked why he and the tribunal have concentrated on U.S. violations rather than Iraqi crimes. He argues that Americans need to insist that their government adheres to its principles. "When you see your government violating those principles, you have the highest obligation to correct what your government does, not point the finger at someone else" (Jensen 2001).

In 2003, Clark began a campaign calling for the impeachment of President George W. Bush, Vice President Richard Cheney, Secretary of Defense Donald Rumsfeld, and Attorney General John Ashcroft for at least 18 offenses regarding their plans to invade Iraq and create a police state in the United States. Many of the crimes listed are similar to the charges against the first President Bush and his administration. After Bush left office, the impeachment campaign took a different form and is currently a global effort called "Indict Bush Now" to charge Bush, Cheney, and others for war crimes and crimes against humanity.

Clark has continued his activities to call attention to war crimes. He traveled to Calgary, Alberta, Canada, in June 2009 to be on hand when the Canadian government sentenced Splitting the Sky, a Mohawk activist, for his attempt to make a citizen's arrest of George W. Bush, who was visiting Calgary in March 2009. Splitting the Sky was arrested for his action, but in court he condemned George W. Bush, calling him a war criminal. He also declared that the Canadian parliament had passed the Crimes Against Humanity and War Crimes legislation, and that police had violated that law by aiding an accused war criminal.

In April 2010, a group of 150 lawyers and legal experts from around the world met in Beirut, Lebanon, to initiate an international campaign to investigate Bush administration war crimes. The group chose the 82-year-old Clark to head the movement to conduct independent inquiries in several countries regarding the conduct of Bush and his administration's officials.

See also Abu-Jamal, Mumia; Ali, Muhammad; Berrigan, Daniel, and Berrigan, Philip; Coffin, William Sloane; Hampton, Fred; LaRouche, Lyndon; Peltier, Leonard

References

Clark, Ramsey. *The Fire This Time: U.S. War Crimes in the Gulf*. New York: Thunder's Mouth Press, 1992.

Jensen, Derrick. "Neighborhood Bully: Ramsey Clark on American Militarism." *The Sun*, August 2001. http://www.thesunmagazine.org/issues/308/neighborhood_bully (accessed September 8, 2011).

Laughland, John. "The Devil's Advocate: John Laughland Meets Ramsey Clark, Who Is Campaigning for the Rights of the Two Most Despised Men in the World." *Spectator*, March 19, 2005.

Richardson, John H. "How the Attorney General of the United States Became Saddam Hussein's Lawyer: The Dictator's Time Is Up." *Esquire*, February 2007.

Wilkins, Roy, and Ramsey Clark, chairmen. *Search and Destroy: A Report by the Commission of Inquiry into the Black Panthers and the Police*. New York: Metropolitan Applied Research Center, Inc., 1973.

Williams, Ian. "Ramsey Clark, the War Criminal's Best Friend." *Salon*, June 21, 1999. http://www.salon.com/news/feature/1999/06/21/clark (accessed June 30, 2010).

Coffin, William Sloane (1924–2006)

The title of the book *William Sloane Coffin, Jr.: A Holy Impatience* (2006) by Professor Warren Goldstein aptly pinpoints Rev. Coffin, who called himself a Christian revolutionary. As a Yale chaplain during the 1960s when the Vietnam War was escalating, Coffin had no patience with the war or the military draft system that he along with many others thought was unjust. He was a firm believer in civil disobedience and encouraged rebellious college students to return their draft cards to the U.S. Justice Department, a type of dissent that outraged his colleagues.

William Sloane Coffin Jr. was born on June 1, 1924, in New York City. His wealthy and socially well-connected parents, William and Catherine Butterfield Coffin, lived in Manhattan and raised William and his brother and sister in a two-level penthouse. William Sr. was president of the Metropolitan Museum of Art and an executive in his family's real estate and investment company. William Jr. and his siblings attended private schools in New York and were cared for by a nanny who taught them French.

In 1929 at the beginning of the Great Depression, the Coffins suffered significant financial losses. When William Sr. died of a heart attack in 1933, Catherine Coffin had to find a more affordable lifestyle. With the help of her brother-in-law Henry Coffin, she moved her family to Carmel, California, where the children attended public schools.

Henry Coffin came to the family's aid again in 1938, arranging for William to enroll at the Deerfield Academy, a college preparatory school in Massachusetts. William was a talented musician and hoped to be a classical pianist. In 1939, his mother took him to Paris, France, to study piano. But when World War II engulfed France in 1940, the family moved to Switzerland, then back to the United States. William continued his music studies at Phillips Academy at Andover, Massachusetts, where he met and developed a friendship with George H. W. Bush who would become the nation's 41st president. Coffin graduated in 1942 and enrolled at Yale University's School of Music in New Haven, Connecticut, for piano studies.

With the United States at war, Coffin left school for the army, enlisting in 1943. Processed at Fort Dix, New Jersey, he received basic training at Camp Wheeler, Georgia, where like the other trainees he marched, fired weapons, and drilled in the excessive heat of summer. As he wrote years later, "All the physical energy bottled up during four years of four hours a day at the piano now came pouring out. It was healthy exercise, almost good clean fun" (Coffin 1977, 35).

Coffin was selected for officer training and, in 1945, was sent to Europe to work as a liaison officer with the French and Russian forces for two years. During that time, he became fluent in the Russian language, adding to his previous French language skills. As a liaison officer, he took part in sending 2,000 Russian prisoners of war (POWs) back to the Soviet Union. The operation was required because of an agreement signed by British prime minister Winston Churchill, U.S. president Franklin Delano Roosevelt, and Soviet premier Joseph Stalin that at the end of the war, all prisoners should be repatriated to their countries of origin. Many of the prisoners were Russian citizens who did not want to return to their homeland, where they were likely to be seen as traitors. From some of the Russians, Coffin learned about Stalin's brutalities. Most repatriated Russians would face execution or a slow death in labor camps. American soldiers stood by to be sure that the POWs were forcibly repatriated. Coffin was conflicted over his role—whether to follow orders or warn some Russians that they needed to escape. He reported seeing several men commit suicide rather than be repatriated. The experience, he wrote, left him with "a burden of guilt" that he carried for the rest of his life. It influenced his decision later on "to spend three years in the CIA opposing Stalin's regime" (Coffin 1977, 77–78).

After returning to the United States in 1947, Coffin returned to Yale University to complete his degree. He joined the Yale Glee Club, which toured the United States and Europe. While at Yale, he was invited to attend a conference at the Union Theological Seminary, where his uncle Henry had been president but had recently retired. The gathering was for seniors who might have an interest in the ministry. Coffin decided to take part primarily because Reinhold Niebuhr was a speaker. Neibuhr was a theologian and social activist who helped shape liberal Protestant theology in the United States. Coffin credited Niebuhr with influencing his decision to enroll at the seminary.

During his first year at the seminary, Coffin worked at a storefront church in East Harlem, where, he "learned that the wisdom of the uneducated could be as stunning as the folly of college students" (Coffin 1977, 89). In 1950, Coffin decided he should leave the seminary and heed the call of the U.S. Central Intelligence Agency, which recruited him for a tour of duty in Europe. He spent three years with the CIA, which was attempting to help anti-Soviet Russians establish an underground mission to topple the Stalin regime. The mission was "dreadfully unsuccessful," Coffin told interviewer Ira Schorr during a video broadcast (Center for Defense Information 1995).

In 1953, Coffin returned to the United States and enrolled in the Yale Divinity School. During his second year there, he met Eva Rubinstein, the eldest daughter of the famous pianist Arthur Rubinstein. Eva was a ballet dancer and actress who performed on and off Broadway. The two dated on occasion over the next few years and married in December 1956. That same year, Coffin earned his bachelor of divinity degree and was ordained a Presbyterian minister.

After his marriage, Coffin accepted a position to serve as chaplain at Phillips Academy, Andover, Massachusetts, for one year. The following year, he became chaplain at Williams College. In 1958, the president of Yale asked Coffin to be the university's chaplain. He agreed immediately and remained in that position until 1975.

During the years Coffin was at Yale, the civil rights movement gained momentum in the 1960s, and Coffin became a highly vocal critic of the segregation laws of the American South. He was appalled when reading about the violence against students who staged sit-ins to integrate all-white lunch counters in Alabama and Mississippi. Brutal encounters were even worse for Freedom Riders who rode buses to the South to draw public attention to state and local Jim Crow laws. Coffin and other ministers organized a bus ride that ended with their arrest for "disturbing the peace" and time in jail. News of the ministers' jail time made headlines across the United States and outraged some of the Yale alumni who declared that Coffin had disgraced the university. Public criticism came in the form of hate letters and phone calls, some threatening to kill him. Yet Yale's president noted that Coffin "acted out of Christian convictions" and did not censor him let alone fire him as his critics demanded (Coffin 1977, 163). Coffin continued his protests and was arrested several more times, once with his wife when a large group staged a desegregation action at an amusement park outside Baltimore, Maryland.

In 1961, he took a temporary leave from his Yale position to work for the Peace Corps. At the request of Sargent Shriver, first director of the Corps, Coffin set up training programs for Peace Corps volunteers.

The 1960s was a time when many Americans were traumatized by the assassination of President John F. Kennedy in 1963 and the increasing involvement of the United States in the Vietnam War with its mounting casualties. As the war escalated under President Lyndon Johnson, students on some U.S. college campuses began protests, especially against the draft that many thought was unfair. Coffin had questioned U.S. policy in regard to the war, but he carefully considered what actions to take in protest. He became known across the United States when he decided to apply civil disobedience actions as he had done in the South. In the fall of 1967, Coffin and Dr. Benjamin Spock, a famous pediatrician and activist, led a rally in Boston hailed as a "Call to Resist Illegitimate Authority." Nearly 1,000 men handed over draft cards, and Coffin and four other men (dubbed the Boston Five) presented the draft cards to the U.S. attorney general, Ramsey Clark. In 1968, Clark prosecuted this group of antidraft leaders. They were convicted of conspiracy to encourage draft evasion, but the verdicts were appealed and overturned.

Even as Coffin's trial was under way, he and his wife Eva were discussing divorce.

They had grown apart with Coffin's attention to so many causes and Eva's need to be someone other than the wife of a very public person. The couple's major concern was their three children, and the two agreed that the children should stay with Coffin. He hired a housekeeper to help with their care. In 1969, Coffin married again, bringing his family and that of his wife Harriet Gibney together. However, that marriage also ended in divorce in 1983.

Coffin left his Yale position in 1976 and the following year became senior minister at the interdenominational Riverside Church in New York City. The congregation was (and still is) interracial and international, and many famous people have been guest speakers, among them Rev. Martin Luther King Jr. and Archbishop Desmond Tutu of South Africa. At Riverside, known for its social programs, Coffin also worked with Clergy and Laity Concerned, a peace group that he helped found during the Vietnam War. Other founders included Rev. King and Father Philip Berrigan, a Jesuit priest known along with his brother Father Daniel Berrigan for civil disobedience to protest nuclear weapons. In the late 1970s and in the 1980s, the group focused on nuclear disarmament.

Disarmament was such an important issue to Coffin that he resigned from Riverside Church in 1987 to become president of SANE/FREEZE, a merger of the Committee for a SANE Nuclear Policy and the Nuclear Weapons Freeze Campaign. Now called Peace Action, the organization works for nuclear disarmament and supports nonviolent conflict resolution. It is the nation's largest peace and justice organization.

By the time Coffin became head of the peace organization, he had married Virginia Randolph "Randy" Wilson (1984). They lived in Strafford, Vermont, where in 1999, he had a stroke and lost his speech, but with the help of his wife and hospital therapists he regained most of his vocal abilities. When the United States invaded Iraq in 2003, Coffin was just as adamantly opposed to the injustice of the war (except for World War II) as he had been during previous conflicts involving the United States.

In spite of his poor health, Coffin continued to write and to give interviews. In one interview with consumer and peace activist Ralph Nader, he explained why it was important to protest the Iraq invasion. In Coffin's words, "dissent in a democracy is not unpatriotic, what is unpatriotic is subservience to a bad policy" (Nader 2006).

Coffin's books include *Letters to a Young Doubter* (2005), *The Heart Is a Little to the Left: Essays on Public Morality* (1999), and collections of sermons. His book *Credo* (2003) was a national best seller and is packed with reflections on his faith and musings such as "We don't have to be 'successful,' only valuable. We don't have to make money, only a difference, and particularly in the lives society counts least and puts last" (Coffin 2004, 7).

Coffin died of heart failure on April 12, 2006, at his home in Strafford. An obituary in the *New York Times* offered one summary of his life: "Dr. Coffin had a distinctive view of his own role as a dissenter. His argument with American social practices and political policies, he said, was that of a partner engaged in a 'lovers' quarrel' " (Charney 2006).

See also Berrigan, Daniel, and Berrigan, Philip; Clark, Ramsey; King, Martin Luther, Jr.; Nader, Ralph

References

Center for Defense Information. "Modern American Patriot: William Sloane Coffin, Jr." (video transcript). Washington, DC:

America's Defense Monitor, February 6, 1995.

Charney, Mark D. "Rev. William Sloane Coffin Dies at 81; Fought for Civil Rights and against a War." *New York Times*, April 13, 2006. http://www.nytimes.com/2006/04/13/us/13coffin.html (accessed July 15, 2010).

Coffin, William Sloane, Jr. *Credo*. Louisville, KY: Westminster John Knox Press, 2004.

Coffin, William Sloane, Jr. *Once to Every Man: A Memoir*. New York: Atheneum, 1977.

Ferguson, Bruce. "Different Agendas, Styles Shape SANE/Freeze." *Bulletin of the Atomic Scientists*, April 1988.

Goldstein, Warren. *William Sloane Coffin, Jr.: A Holy Impatience*. New Haven, CT: Yale University Press, 2006.

Nader, Ralph. "Carry On, Finish the Job: William Sloane Coffin." CommonDreams.org, April 15, 2006. http://www.commondreams.org/views06/0415-29.htm (accessed July 14, 2010).

Collier, John (1884–1968)

"There is no reason why [the U.S. government] should go on disgracing itself in Indian matters," declared Commissioner of Indian Affairs John Collier while speaking to tribal leaders at a 1930s pow-wow in the Black Hills of South Dakota. He noted that U.S. president Franklin D. Roosevelt, U.S. interior secretary Ickes and the Indian Bureau "have determined that the time has come to stop wronging the Indians and to rewrite the cruel and stupid laws that rob them and crush their family lives" (History Matters). Collier, who was appointed commissioner in 1933 by Roosevelt, brought about dramatic reforms in federal policy affecting Native people. He was responsible for developing and successfully pressuring passage of the Indian Reorganization Act of 1934, which restored tribal sovereignty, allowing tribes to govern themselves and their lands. While he won respect from many Indian groups, various white individuals and organizations, such as Protestant reformers, opposed Collier and supported the view that Indians should be assimilated into the dominant Anglo-Saxon society and disavow their Native culture.

Collier was born in Atlanta, Georgia, on May 4, 1884, to Charles A. Collier, mayor of Atlanta, and Susie (Rawson) Collier. Raised as a Methodist, Collier converted to Roman Catholicism during his teenage years. Between 1902 and 1905, he was a student at Columbia University in New York City and the Marine Biological Laboratory in Woods Hole, Massachusetts. While at Columbia, Collier, with guidance from instructor Lucy Crozier, studied the adverse effects of industrialism. He developed a philosophy that U.S. culture should be more community-oriented and responsible to one another. Those ideas carried over to his social work with immigrants on Manhattan's Lower East Side beginning in 1905.

On October 20, 1906, Collier married Lucy Wood of Philadelphia. The couple had three sons: Charles, Donald, and John Jr. In later years, Collier had two other wives: Laura Thompson, whom he married in 1943, and Grace E. Volk, whom he married in 1957.

From 1906 to 1907, Collier studied psychology at the College de France in Paris. Returning to the United States, he became civic secretary of New York City's People's Institute, which, through its religious, recreational, and educational activities, attempted to create a sense of community in immigrant neighborhoods. The institute established a National Training Center for Community Workers, and Collier served as its director from 1915 to 1919.

In 1919, the Collier family moved to Mill Valley, California, where Collier directed an adult education program. While in Mill Valley, the Colliers' youngest son, John Jr. was in a motor vehicle accident that resulted in the loss of his hearing and other disabilities. His mother Lucy invented a program of home schooling for the 10-year-old. Since John Sr. was studying the Indians of the southwestern United States, especially the Pueblo in Taos, New Mexico, John Jr. stayed in or near Pueblo villages and received guidance and help with his education from the Pueblo elders. He later became a well-known anthropologist and photographer of Indian life.

In the view of John Collier Sr., the Pueblo way of life was a "Utopia," and he spent the two years between 1920 and 1922 observing and investigating Native culture. Much later, he wrote:

> These Southwestern Indians have much that we know we need. And they have one possession, the most distinguishing of all, which we have forgotten that we need. . . . That possession is a *time sense* different from ours, and happier. Once our white race had it too, and then the mechanized world took it away from us. . . . We think, now, that any other time than linear, chronological time is an escapist dream. The Indians tell us otherwise, and their message and demonstration addresses itself to one of our deepest distresses and most forlorn yearnings.
>
> We bow to clockwork time. We think we must yield to it our all—body, conduct and soul. . . . [W]e think it is our master. . . . And we abide so briefly, within that rush of linear time which subconsciously we experience as a kind of panic rout; and we are old, so soon, and we are done, and we hardly had time to live at all. (Collier 1962, 15)

In 1923, he became executive secretary of the American Indian Defense Association (AIDA), a post he held for 10 years, and conducted a campaign to return land to the Pueblo. While at AIDA, he also edited *American Indian Life*, the organization's magazine. Numerous articles in the publication criticized the federal Bureau of Indian Affairs (BIA) for their repressive policies, failure to protect Indian rights, and lack of social services.

When Franklin D. Roosevelt took office as U.S. president in 1933, Secretary of Interior Harold Ickes, who knew about Collier's activism, encouraged the president to nominate Collier commissioner of the BIA. Collier served at that post for 12 years, longer than any commissioner before him. During that time he was able to enact numerous reforms, the most significant of which was the Indian Reorganization Act of 1934, officially titled the Wheeler-Howard Act. It was named for Senator Burton K. Wheeler of Minnesota, who had at first opposed the bill until it was modified to his liking, and Representative Edgar Howard of Nebraska. The act abolished the Dawes Allotment Act of 1887 named for its author, Senator Henry Dawes of Massachusetts.

The intent of the Dawes Act was to accelerate the assimilation of Indians into the dominant white society and capitalist system. Senator Dawes believed that if Indians owned their own property and became farmers, they would become more "civilized." The act allowed the president to break up reservation land, which was held in common by the members of a tribe, into small allotments to be parceled out to individuals in this manner: "To each head of a family, one-quarter of a section; To each single person over eighteen years of age, one-eighth of a section; To each orphan child under

Commissioner of Indian Affairs from 1933 to 1945, John Collier devoted his life to securing the rights of Native Americans. (Library of Congress)

eighteen years of age, one-eighth of a section; and To each other single person under eighteen years now living, or who may be born prior to the date of the order of the President directing an allotment of the lands embraced in any reservation, one-sixteenth of a section." The remaining tribal lands were to be declared "surplus" and opened up for whites. Supporters of the act expected tribal ownership and tribes themselves to disappear, but it did little to bring Indians into the larger society. In fact, after all individual allocations were made, the "surplus" that remained was sold to whites, and Indians lost millions of acres.

The 1934 Indian Reorganization Act states that it was intended "to conserve and develop Indian lands and resources; to extend to Indians the right to form business and other organizations; to establish a credit system for Indians; to grant certain rights of home rule to Indians; to provide for vocational education for Indians; and for other purposes." Because of passage of the act, Indian lands once again were held in common by tribal members. Bans on using traditional languages and observing religious customs were overturned, and tribal ownership was restored. Collier also used other Roosevelt programs to set up an Indian Civilian Conservation Corps. He also made sure that schools and hospitals were established for Indians.

Yet, some Indian tribes opposed the Reorganization Act. Although 174 tribes approved the act, 73 rejected it. Some had assimilated into the dominant culture and did not want to revive tribal government. One of the largest tribes, the Navajo of southeast Utah, turned against the act because they blamed Collier's BIA for the livestock reduction program of the 1930s. That program was designed to prevent Navajo sheep, goats, and horses from overgrazing reservation lands, which left dry topsoil that was eroding and allowing silt to build up in the Hoover Dam. The federal government set a quota for the number of livestock that could be raised. Some were systematically shot and killed or confiscated; others were sold for small sums or voluntarily turned over to the government. To the Navajo, the stock reductions were devastating, financially and culturally. The number of livestock determined their wealth (for example, sheep wool was used to make blankets that sold well) and the animals themselves were considered sacred. "To this day, older Navajos tell stories of being hounded and even jailed by grazing officials for not cooperating with the reduction. Some remember thousands of goats or sheep being shot and thrown in ditches to rot because prices were too low to warrant shipping the animals to market. A few say it caused so much distress that their husbands or wives died along with their sheep," wrote Elizabeth Manning in *High Country News* (1996).

In 1941, Collier initiated a research program on Indian life, and author and anthropologist Laura Thompson directed five areas of study: Hopi, Navajo, Zuni, Papago, and Sioux. Two years later, Collier and Thompson were married. In 1945, Collier resigned from the BIA, which had restored some tribal life. "But in the decades that followed, no fundamental change took place," wrote historian and social activist Howard Zinn. "Many Indians stayed on the impoverished reservations. The younger ones often left" (Zinn 2003, 524).

After Collier left the BIA, he and Thompson established the nonprofit Institute for Ethnic Affairs in Washington, D.C. Its "purpose was to search for solutions to problems within and between white and colored races, cultural minority groups, and dependent peoples at home and abroad. The Institute's goal was to recommend administrative changes requiring governmental action" (Institute of Ethnic Affairs). The couple "campaigned for self-government and economic self-sufficiency for Native Americans and native peoples of the South Pacific" (Grossman 1996, 76).

In 1947, Collier became professor of sociology and anthropology at City College, New York City. His book *The Indians of the Americas: American Colonial Record* (1947) was published. Two years later, another of his books, *Patterns and Ceremonials of the Indians of the Southwest* (1949), was in print. It was later renamed and published as *On the Gleaming Way* (1962).

Collier retired from City College in 1954 and taught for one year at Knox College in Galesburg, Illinois. In 1956, he moved to Taos, New Mexico, where he lived with his third wife, Grace E. Volk, and wrote articles about Indian life and his memoir *Every Zenith: A Memoir and Some Essays on Life and Thought* (1963). He died in Taos on May 8, 1968.

See also Zinn, Howard

References

Brodoff, Maureen, and Andrew M. Patterson, compilers. *Guide to the John Collier Papers*, April 1973; revised April 2009. http://drs.library.yale.edu:8083/fedora/get/mssa:ms.0146/PDF (accessed November 2, 2010).

Collier, John. *From Every Zenith*: *A Memoir and Some Essays on Life and Thought*. Denver, CO: Sage Books, 1963.

Collier, John. *On the Gleaming Way: Navajos, Eastern Pueblos, Zunis, Hopis, Apaches, and Their Land; and Their Meanings to the World.* Chicago: Sage Books/Swallow Press, 1962. First published 1949.

Daily, David. *Battle for the BIA: G. E. E. Lindquist and the Missionary Crusade against John Collier.* Tucson: University of Arizona Press, 2004.

Grossman, Mark. *The ABC-CLIO Companion to the Native American Rights Movement.* Santa Barbara, CA: ABC-CLIO, 1996.

"Indian Fighter." *Time*, February 19, 1945. http://www.time.com/time/printout/0,8816,778328,00.html (accessed November 1, 2010).

History Matters. " 'A Bill of Rights for the Indians': John Collier Envisions an Indian New Deal" (from "A New Deal for the American Indian," *Literary Digest*, April 7, 1938, 21). http://historymatters.gmu.edu/d/5059 (accessed October 31, 2010).

"Institute of Ethnic Affairs." Guampedia, n.d. http://guampedia.com/institute-of-ethnic-affairs/ (accessed November 2, 2010).

Manning, Elizabeth. "Drought Has Navajos Discussing a Taboo Subject—Range Reform." *High Country News*, August 5, 1996. http://www.hcn.org/issues/87/2696 (accessed November 2, 2010).

Zinn, Howard. *A People's History of the United States: 1492–Present.* New York: HarperCollins, 2003.

Commoner, Barry (1917–)

Barry Commoner, a biologist whom *Time* magazine called the "Paul Revere of Ecology" in 1970, helped initiate the modern environmental movement. He is best known for publicizing the radiation fallout from nuclear bomb testing. Controversy surrounds him because of his dissident views. He believes that science and technology can be a threat to the environment even though at the same time their applications help to prevent and cure diseases. He argues that the public needs to be educated about the destructive potential of technological advances. In the early 1960s, he wrote in *Science and Survival* (1963): "The environment is a complex, subtly balanced system, and it is this integrated whole which receives the impact of all the separate insults inflicted by pollutants. Never before in the history of this planet has its thin life-supporting surface been subjected to such diverse, novel, and potent agents. I believe that the cumulative effects of these pollutants, their interactions and amplification, can be fatal to the complex fabric of the biosphere" (Commoner 1967, 122).

Critics accuse Commoner of being more an activist than a scientist. He came under attack during the 1950s when he proposed a ban on nuclear bomb testing, an idea U.S. senator Joseph McCarthy and his supporters adamantly opposed. Scientists who dissented were considered communist sympathizers. In more recent times, the industrial agriculture industry and the biotechnology (or biotech) industry, which have developed genetically engineered (GE) plants and animals, are especially critical of Commoner. They call him irresponsible for suggesting that GE organisms could have dangerous consequences.

Born in Brooklyn, New York, on May 28, 1917, Barry Commoner is the son of Isidore Commoner and Goldie Yarmolinsky Commoner, who were Russian immigrants. Isidore worked as a tailor in the Flatbush neighborhood of Brooklyn. While growing up, Barry belonged to a street gang, but he also exhibited an interest in nature. When not in school, he spent his free time in the local park hunting for specimens to study under his microscope, a gift from his parents. Later in his life, he attributed his pursuit of

Commoner, Barry (1917–)

Ecologist Barry Commoner, in 1970. He helped initiate the modern environmental movement, and is best known for publicizing the radiation fallout from nuclear bomb testing. (Michael Mauney/Time Life Pictures/Getty Images)

science to that gift. During the Great Depression of the 1930s, Barry's parents, like many others, suffered economic hardships; and his father lost his sight and thus was unable to work.

After graduating from James Madison High School, where he took biology courses, he enrolled at Columbia University, paying his way by working at odd jobs. He graduated in 1937 with a fellowship to Harvard, where he earned his PhD in biology in 1941. That year, the United States entered World War II (1939–1945), and Commoner joined the U.S. Navy, attaining the rank of lieutenant. He served in the Pacific and took part in spraying the highly toxic insecticide dichlorodiphenyltrichloroethane (DDT) on the islands to eradicate insects that carried disease. Later, he campaigned against the use of DDT and credits Rachel Carson, who had studied the devastating effects of DDT, for halting the spread of this deadly chemical. Carson, like Commoner, posited the argument that nothing exists in nature alone and, hence, science and technology must therefore demonstrate a reverence for life.

After his military service, Commoner married psychologist Gloria Gordon and took a position at Washington University in St. Louis, Missouri, teaching and eventually chairing the botany department. At the university, Commoner conducted an experiment combining ribonucleic acid (RNA), a component that is present in the cells of all life, with proteins, complex molecules in cells, to create an active virus—a life form. The success of the experiment prompted him to "study the relationships between viruses and genetics that earned him an award from the A.A.A.S [American Association for the Advancement of Science]" (*Time* 1970, 62). In his analysis, he concluded that RNA and its various forms transmit genetic information from deoxyribonucleic acid (DNA) to protein. He found that DNA is not wholly responsible for genetic differences.

By the 1950s, Commoner had become an environmental activist. Like many other scientists, he was deeply concerned about the radioactive fallout from nuclear bomb tests. The federal government in 1946 had created the Atomic Energy Commission (AEC), which was responsible for overseeing the development of nuclear weapons and energy. When atomic bombs were tested, the AEC revealed only that a test had taken place. The Cold War between the Soviet Union and the United States was underway, and both sides were engaged in a nuclear arms race. Many officials were convinced that the more nuclear weapons a country had, the more powerful it was. There was little public discussion about nuclear buildups.

However, after a bomb test in 1953 in Nevada, high levels of radiation were discovered in upstate New York. The mushroom cloud from the bomb had traveled more than 2,000 miles high in the atmosphere until a heavy and violent rain storm brought debris to the ground in New York and parts of Vermont and Massachusetts. Scientists communicated information about the discovery among themselves. Commoner learned that the fallout from the nuclear bomb contained radioactive strontium-90 (Sr90), which is a byproduct produced from nuclear bomb testing, nuclear reactor operations, and nuclear accidents. Sr90 is chemically similar to calcium, and it is readily taken up in the tissues of plants and animals. It can enter the food supply, mainly in milk, and is especially dangerous for growing children, since it is easily deposited in the bones and is believed to induce bone cancer and leukemia.

In 1958, Commoner and colleagues formed the St. Louis Committee for Nuclear Information, publicizing the origin of Sr90 and its movement through the environment. The committee members spoke before civic and church groups and "discussed the potential human cost of the supposed benefits of new nuclear weapons," Commoner wrote. "We emphasized that the balancing of social judgment against cost should be made by every citizen and not left to the experts" (Commoner 1971, 56).

The committee's first major project was the Baby Tooth Survey in the metropolitan St. Louis area. They collected 300,000 primary teeth that children had lost, and scientists tested the teeth for Sr90, which, investigators surmised, had been absorbed from St. Louis milk. Radioactive material fell on grass that cows ate, and their milk contained high levels of Sr90. The survey continued for 10 years, and scientists found that the teeth collected during the nuclear-bomb testing period contained high levels of the radioactive material, but levels dropped when testing stopped after the United States and the Union of Soviet Socialist Republics signed the Nuclear Test Ban Treaty in 1963.

During the 1960s, Commoner was among numerous scientists who studied the effects of pesticide residue in soil and water. In 1966, he founded the Center for the Biology of Natural Systems, a research organization to analyze environmental and energy problems, at Washington University in St. Louis. Commoner's first book *Science and Survival* (1966) warned that people could not depend on science and technology to solve environmental crises such as water, air, and land pollution. Scientists, he declared, should alert the public to problems and citizens should insist on preventive action.

Commoner's next book, *The Closing Circle: Nature, Man and Technology* (1971), continues with the theme of an environmental crisis created by science, technology, nuclear and petrochemical industries. In this, his best-known book, he includes case histories of air, earth, and water poisoning and shows how technology developed since World War II has disrupted ecological systems and contributed to an imbalance in nature that threatens to destroy humanity. Commoner presents four basic laws of ecology: (1) everything is connected to everything else—what affects one part of the environment affects all; (2) everything must go somewhere—there is no such thing as waste disappearing; (3) nature knows best—technological changes in nature are more likely to damage the ecosystem than improve it; and (4) there is no such thing as a free lunch—nothing in nature is free since everything comes from something (Commoner 1971, 33–46).

Over the next four decades, Commoner was active in many aspects of the environmental movement, writing, lecturing, and teaching. He wrote *The Politics of Energy* (1979), which called for renewable energy such as solar power and more use of public transportation rather than gasoline-powered vehicles. In 1980, hoping to press environmental issues, he was the Citizens Party candidate for U.S. president, but received less than 1 percent of the vote. In 1981, he returned to teaching. He was professor of environmental science at Queens College. The Center for the Biology of Natural Systems also was moved to Queens College, City University of New York (CUNY) in 1981.

During the 1990s, Commoner turned his attention to the damaging effects on human health of dioxin compounds from trash and medical waste incinerators, and proposed intensive recycling efforts as alternatives to burning waste. There are more than 200 dioxin and dioxin-like substances that are formed from industrial manufacturing and burning activities. Dioxin contamination has been widely publicized since the late 1970s and through the 1980s by such activists as Lois Gibbs, who alerted the public to the toxic wastes, including dioxin, dumped in Love Canal in Niagara Falls, New York. Families living near Love Canal were eventually evacuated. Dioxin contamination also led to the evacuation of Times Beach, Missouri, where waste oil with dioxin components was spread on roadways to control dust. It was blamed for ailments of Vietnam War veterans who had been exposed to Agent Orange, a herbicide with a highly dangerous dioxin compound. Commoner has discussed these cases and others in numerous speeches, specifically in a keynote address to a Citizens Conference on Dioxin in 1994.

By the 2000s, Commoner was embroiled in a controversy regarding his views on DNA and heredity. He argued his position in an article for *Harper's*, in which he stated that "Genetic information derives not from DNA alone but through its essential collaboration with protein enzymes." He contradicts the decades-old established theory called the "central dogma" that DNA is the "exclusive agent of inheritance in all living things," which he writes, "assumes that an organism's genome—its total complement of DNA genes—should fully account for its characteristic assemblage of inherited traits. The premise, unhappily, is false."

Commoner's article reviews scientific literature that reveals the errors in the central dogma, and he points out that not enough genes have been identified to account for the many complex human characteristics. In addition, he argues that the biotech industry bases its development of genetically engineered organisms on a false premise—that is, "moving a gene from one species to another is ... specific, precise, and predictable," thus safe. "The genetically engineered crops now being grown represent a massive uncontrolled experiment whose outcome is inherently unpredictable. The results could be catastrophic" (Commoner 2002, 39–47).

The biotech industry and supporters of genetic engineering object to Commoner's view, calling it and him unreliable and unscientific, and aligning him with activist environmental groups such as Greenpeace, Friends of the Earth, and organic farming groups.

In spite of critics, Commoner has continued his call for transforming industrial production and developing ecologically sound technologies. He presents his ideas in his books that include *The Poverty of Power: Energy and the Economic Crisis* (1976), *The Politics of Energy* (1979), and *Making Peace with the Planet* (1990), plus his two earlier books, many lectures, and scientific papers. At age 90 in 2007, he was still going to the Center for the Biology of Natural Systems, although in 2000, he relinquished his position as director. He has been writing another book on DNA and heredity.

See also Carson, Rachel; Gibbs, Lois; McCarthy, Joseph

References

Commoner, Barry. *The Closing Circle: Nature, Man, and Technology*. New York: Alfred A. Knopf, 1971.

Commoner, Barry. *Making Peace with the Planet*. Paperback ed. New York: New Press, 1992.

Commoner, Barry. *Science and Survival*. New York: Viking Press, 1967. Reprint ed., 1963.

Commoner, Barry. "Unraveling the DNA Myth: the Spurious Foundation of Genetic Engineering (Report)." *Harper's Magazine*, February 2002.

Egan, Michael. *Barry Commoner and the Science of Survival*. Cambridge, MA: MIT Press, 2007.

"Environment: Paul Revere of Ecology." *Time*, February 2, 1970.

Kriebel, David, ed. *Barry Commoner's Contribution to the Environmental Movement*. Amityville, NY: Baywood Publishing Company, 2002.

Corbett, Jim (1933–2001)

"To the Central Americans whose lives he saved, Jim Corbett was a saint. To the U.S. government, he was a dangerous subversive. To those who knew him, he was a thoughtful, quiet, unassuming man. And to a world still struggling with the issues he confronted, his legacy is only beginning to be known" (Davidson 2001, 16). Jim Corbett helped initiate and establish sanctuary for Central American refugees seeking asylum in the United States during the 1980s.

Jim Corbett was born on October 8, 1933, in Casper, Wyoming, to Gladys and Raymond Corbett. His parents were teachers who believed in self-reliance. During the summer, they took Jim and his older sister to the nearby Shoshone Indian Reservation or the Teton Mountains, where they lived in a tent and caught trout and gathered wild plants for food. Jim was greatly influenced by his father, who often championed civil rights. His mother once said that Jim was taught "to be honest and stand up for what he thought was right" (Davidson 1988, 54).

Corbett earned a degree in philosophy at Colgate University in Hamilton, New York, and then went to Harvard on a fellowship, completing a master's degree in one year. But he decided not to teach philosophy, pointing out "the main thing I learned from studying philosophy was that I knew nothing to teach. Mulling it over, I saw that I was really concerned with doing something notable with my life" (Corbett n.d.). He eventually developed a set of values based on the nonviolent works of people like the Society of Friends, Martin Luther King Jr., and Gandhi and the 1948 Universal Declaration of Human Rights, which was drafted by the United Nations Commission on Human Rights chaired by Eleanor Roosevelt.

After earning his degree, he married, and the couple eventually had three children, Laurie, Megan, and Geoffrey. The family lived on a ranch in Casper, Wyoming, which Corbett's wife disliked. The marriage ended in divorce, and Corbett moved to Tombstone, Arizona, to live on his parents' ranch.

While he was in his late twenties, Corbett became a member of the Religious Society of Friends, the Quakers, who believe in living their moral convictions and bringing about political change through acts of conscience. He also continued his education in the field of library science at the University of Southern California, where he met Pat Collins, whom he married in 1963. Corbett held several teaching jobs in California and also was active in protests against the Vietnam War. The Corbetts eventually moved to Arizona, where they lived on a ranch and he was a cowboy and goat herder. Corbett also worked for the Forest Service and National Park Service and was a guide for student groups in the Tucson area. He became involved in efforts to help El Salvadoran refugees somewhat by accident. As he wrote in an essay for *Weber Studies*, a Weber College (now Weber State University) journal:

> On 4 May 1981, I heard about a Salvadoran refugee who had been caught by the Border Patrol. The following day I went looking for him. The day after that, having learned that refugees were pouring across the border but were being caught and returned by federal officials, my wife Pat and I set up an apartment for them in our home. It was soon jammed full. Assuming that life-and-death crises of this kind are always short-term emergencies, we held nothing in reserve, but in the course of the next few months we began to realize, as our energy and resources dwindled, that the emergency was chronic and the crisis in Central America may be no more than the beginning. (Corbett 1988)

Because he could speak Spanish, Corbett helped refugees who had been arrested and imprisoned file necessary papers for political asylum. He and his wife visited imprisoned Salvadorans on a regular basis and learned about the violence they had witnessed or endured in their homeland. In fact, Corbett discovered later from court evidence that the U.S. Immigration and Naturalization Service (INS) deliberately prevented Salvadorans from getting legal aid, and between mid-1980 and mid-1981, more than 10,000 of the 13,000 Salvadorans caught in the United States by the INS were sent back to their homeland.

In 1981, Corbett mailed letters to Quakers across the United States, alerting them to the plight of Central American refugees. According to Corbett, "A refugee support network began to appear even where no refugees had yet arrived, and relays formed to help them reach any part of the United States or Canada. John Fife, the pastor of Southside Presbyterian Church [in Tucson, Arizona] had a good deal to do with informing and mobilizing Presbyterians nationwide to provide most of the initial communications and material support" (Corbett 1988). Fife, in fact, placed two banners on his church, one announcing "This is a sanctuary for the oppressed of Central America," and the other addressing the INS "Immigration: do not profane the sanctuary of God."

The Sanctuary Movement in Arizona was based on ancient traditions—efforts that have existed for thousands of years, such as Moses creating safe havens for persecuted Jews. The United States also has a history of providing refugees for the oppressed, especially runaway slaves.

During the 1980s sanctuary movement, most of the refugees seeking political asylum in the United States had fled their countries because they feared death squads, who tortured and killed activists protesting their repressive governments. Statistics show that during the 1970s and 1980s, more than 200,000 Central Americans were killed in civil wars while countless others tried to escape to nearby countries or to the United States.

Many believed they would be able to find safety in the United States because the U.S

Congress had passed the 1980 Refugee Act, whose intent was to broaden eligibility requirements for political asylum. The act allowed asylum for refugees who faced persecution in their countries but banned so-called economic migrants—those seeking jobs—from safe haven. Since at the time the United States supported the Central American governments' war efforts, U.S. immigration officials declared that Salvadorans, Guatemalans, and Nicaraguans were not escaping maltreatment but instead wanted to take advantage of a rich country's economic opportunities. Thus, thousands of people who tried to cross into the United States from Mexico were turned away, which usually meant certain death.

In mid-1981, Corbett took part in a two-week effort by about two dozen people to bail out 150 refugees from a deplorable detention center in El Centro, California, which was surrounded by electrified fences. Guards kept prisoners outdoors where there was little or no shade and temperatures reached 110 to 120 degrees. Corbett's group had to obtain a federal court order and raise almost $200,000 so that Salvadorans could go free on bond. That experience spurred Corbett's resolve to help refugees avoid capture and imprisonment and remain in the United States.

Over the next few years, Corbett and Rev. Fife, whose church was declared a sanctuary in March 1982, sheltered hundreds of refugees. The sanctuary movement spread, and by the end of 1984, large numbers of Americans endorsed the movement, and hundreds of Protestant, Jewish, and Catholic congregations supported sanctuaries. They provided bail money and legal aid for refugees plus food, medical care, and jobs. Some workers went to Mexico and illegally transported Central American refugees across the border into the United States.

However, there were also arrests of sanctuary members in 1984, and the federal government sent spies to infiltrate the sanctuary movement. In late 1985, Corbett, Fife, and 14 others were indicted in an Arizona federal court on charges of conspiracy and transporting and harboring illegal aliens, a felony. Eleven of the 16, including Corbett, went to trial in 1986 and special assistant U.S. attorney Donald Reno Jr. charged that four of the defendants—Corbett, Fife, a church employee, and a Catholic nun—were operating a so-called underground railroad that smuggled aliens from Mexico into Arizona and on to other states. All of the defendants countered that they were acting out of humanitarian and religious concern and that the federal government was actually breaking its own laws and international agreements by refusing to grant refugee status to people who were fleeing political repression and, in some cases, torture or certain death in El Salvador and other Central American countries.

The trial lasted for six months, and the outcome appeared to be a defeat for the sanctuary movement. Eight defendants were convicted of conspiracy to smuggle and transport illegal aliens from Central America into the United States. Corbett and two others were acquitted of all charges. The judge, however, placed the convicted members of the sanctuary movement on probation, which they appealed. In 1989, a U.S. federal court in San Francisco upheld the convictions. But Corbett insisted that the sanctuary work would go on as long as necessary no matter what the consequences.

In spite of all the legal battles, the sanctuary movement continued to operate and was strongly supported by churches throughout the United States through 1992. Corbett tried to find his own sanctuary out of the limelight on his Arizona ranch. He stayed active in peace and justice movements, but concentrated on environmental protection, which had been his concern for years but was not as well known as his sanctuary work. He was an advocate for what he called "earth rights" and conservation projects in the Sonoran/Chihuahuan Desert region. He also wrote *Goatwalking: A Guide to Wildland Living* (1992) and was working on another book, *Sanctuary for All Life* (published posthumously in 2005, when he fell ill with a rare brain disease called paraneopalpic cerebellar syndrome in mid-2001. He died on August 2, 2001, at his home near Benson, Arizona. Obituaries emphasized "his philosophy of living simply and humbly in harmony with nature ... based on his Quaker beliefs in nonviolence and respect for life" (Davidson 2001, 16).

Part of Corbett's legacy and the 1980s sanctuary effort is the New Sanctuary Movement that began in 2007. Church congregations in New York City, Chicago, Los Angeles, San Diego, Seattle, and other cities have united to call for humane immigration policies. They are helping undocumented immigrant families and workers fight arrests and deportation.

See also King, Martin Luther, Jr.; Roosevelt, Eleanor

References

Collins, Sheila D. "The New Underground Railroad." *Monthly Review*, May 1986.

Corbett, James. *Goatwalking: A Guide to Wildland Living*. New York: Viking Penguin Press, 1991.

Corbett, James. "Sanctuary, Basic Rights, and Humanity's Fault Lines: A Personal Essay." *Weber Studies*, Spring–Summer 1988. http://weberstudies.weber.edu/archive/archive%20A%20%20Vol.%201-10.3/Vol.%205.1/5.1Corbet.htm (accessed May 14, 2010).

Crittenden, Ann. *Sanctuary: A Story of American Conscience and the Law in Collision*. New York: Weidenfeld & Nicolson, 1988.

Davidson, Miriam. "Appreciation: Corbett Offered Sanctuary to Refugees." *National Catholic Reporter*, September 14, 2001.

Davidson, Miriam. *Convictions of the Heart: Jim Corbett and the Sanctuary Movement*. Tucson: University of Arizona Press, 1988.

Gzesh, Susan. "Central Americans and Asylum Policy in the Reagan Era." Migration Policy Institute, 2006. http://www.migrationinformation.org/USfocus/display.cfm?id=384 (accessed August 7, 2011).

"Jim Corbett and Saguaro Juniper," n.d. http://www.saguaro-juniper.com/corbett/jim-corbett.html (accessed September 8, 2011).

Randall, Margaret. "Deporting Dissent." *Nation*, April 19, 1986.

Spilken, Aron. *Escape*. New York: New American Library, 1983.

Warner, John. "The Goatwalker" (sermon). Unitarian Universalist Church of Concord, NH, November 19, 2009. http://www.concorduu.org/sermons/sermon%2011-15-2009%20The%20Goatwalker.pdf (accessed May 14, 2010).

Corrie, Rachel (1979–2003)

Rachel Corrie died at a young age—23 years old. Some say Corrie, an American member of the International Solidarity Movement (ISM), was a martyr and was killed while trying to prevent destruction of a Palestinian home by an Israeli bulldozer in the Gaza Strip. She was considered by many Palestinians to be a victim of their intifada—an Arabic word meaning "to shake" and a term used to describe a Palestinian uprising.

Others say Corrie was a naïve ISM participant, that her death was an accident, and that pro-Palestinian activists have been using the incident as propaganda against Israel. Some Americans accused her of being a traitor because she criticized U.S. support of Israel and lack of U.S. support for Palestine.

The two points of view reflect the Israeli-Palestinian conflict that has a long history, dating back to ancient times. But the current arguments have been ongoing since the United Nations divided Palestine into Arab and Jewish states in 1947. The nation of Israel was created in 1948. Since then, wars between Arabs and Jews have been fought over the rights to the land. After a 1967 war, Israel occupied the Gaza Strip, a narrow piece of land on the Mediterranean Sea between Egypt and Israel. The West Bank is in the midst of Israel, except for a portion on the west bank of the Jordan River and another portion adjacent to the Dead Sea. Palestinians have demanded that Israel stop building settlements in Gaza and the West Bank, and want the area to become a Palestinian state. Israel has resisted a Palestinian state, claiming that it would be a base for terrorists. Fighting between the two sides has gone on for decades, and the conflict has been especially fierce in Rafah, which is on the border with Egypt in the Gaza Strip. Rafah is where Rachel Corrie died.

Born on April 10, 1979, in Olympia, Washington, Rachel Aliene Corrie was the youngest child of Craig Corrie, an insurance executive, and Cindy Corrie, an accomplished flutist. Rachel's brother Chris was seven years older, and sister Sarah was five years older. "She grew up in a small house wedged between Puget Sound and the Black Hills of Washington State," wrote Craig Corrie in an introduction to Rachel's journal *Let Me Stand Alone: The Journals of Rachel Corrie* (2008). Writing for the family, Craig Corrie points out that "Rachel was the observer in the family, the child on the floor in the evening—sometimes with toys, but as often with paper and crayons—always joining in the family conversation, but also chronicling it in a drawing or poem. Her more formal education began at Westside Cooperative Preschool, a cottage on the beach where Cooper Point juts north into Puget Sound. It was an idyllic place to be a child, with swings and climbers among the rhododendrons, a short trail to the beach and the Olympic Mountains in the distance to the north" (Corrie 2008, x).

When Rachel was seven years old, an exchange student from Japan lived with the Corries, and later when she was in Capital High School, exchange students from other countries shared their home. By living with students from abroad, Rachel was introduced to other cultures and languages besides her own—a significant factor in her education. After a visit from a Russian student, Rachel went to Russia as an exchange student herself in 1995.

Rachel graduated from high school in 1997, and attended the Evergreen State College in Olympia. During this time, she met Colin Reese, the young man she loved, although the two had an on-again, off-again relationship. In part of her journal, Rachel focuses on Colin, his eccentricities, and his leaving and returning. He committed suicide in 2004.

Rachel left her studies for a year to be a volunteer in the Washington State Conservation Corps. She also volunteered for a crisis center and a mental health program. In 2001, she joined the Olympia Movement for Justice and Peace (OMJP), which formed after terrorists in planes crashed into the World Trade Center in New York City and the Pentagon, and another attack plane crashed in a Pennsylvania field, on September 11, 2001. OMJP hoped to avoid violent U.S. retaliation and to seek peace and justice. However, being part of any peace effort was difficult after the terrorist attacks, and, as Rachel penned in quick notes in her journal: "Difficulty integrating 'peace' message into social justice, human rights, economic justice movement.... Lack of media coverage/support" (Corrie 2008, 173).

Along with joining OMJP, Rachel was active in other peace groups and was known as a behind-the-scenes organizer. She organized a march for peace, creating art objects, costumes, and other materials for the procession. But she had "misgivings" about spending time in these activities when, as she put it, "People were offering themselves as human shields in Palestine" (Corrie 2008, 200).

As a member of various peace groups in Olympia, Rachel began to focus on the conflict between Israel and Palestine in the Middle East. She learned about the ISM, which says on its web site that it "is a Palestinian-led movement committed to resisting the Israeli apartheid in Palestine by using nonviolent, direct-action methods and principles. Founded by a small group of primarily Palestinian and Israeli activists in August 2001, ISM aims to support and strengthen the Palestinian popular resistance by providing the Palestinian people with two resources, international solidarity and an international voice with which to nonviolently resist an overwhelming military occupation force" (International Solidarity Movement).

Rachel Corrie left the United States to join ISM volunteers in January 2003. She arrived in the divided city of Jerusalem, claimed as a capital by both Israel and Palestine, where she took a training course to learn how to be a nonviolent protester in Gaza. She left Jerusalem for Rafah, the only border crossing from the Gaza Strip to Egypt and the outside world. Rafah comprises families who have lived there for generations and also refugees, many of them from what was once Palestine but is now part of Israel.

One of Corrie's early experiences was helping to carry a 19-year-old dead man on a stretcher from the Egyptian side of the border to the Gaza side. Corrie described the scene: "We started into the field: five internationals plus Jehan [a Palestinian]." One of the group called "over the bullhorn, saying 'Do not shoot,' 'We are unarmed civilians,' 'We are internationals,' naming the countries we came from and letting the IOF [Israeli Occupation Forces—or Defense Forces] know our intention to retrieve this man's body." Yet the Israeli Defense Forces (IDF) shot at the group as they walked toward the body, ordered them to leave, and told them they could recover the body later (Corrie 2008, 238–39).

Corrie wrote: "I have been in Palestine for two weeks and one hour now, and I still have very few words to describe what I see.... no amount of reading, attendance at conferences, documentary viewing, and word of mouth could have prepared me for the reality of the situation here.... In addition to the constant presence of tanks... there are more IDF towers here than I can count. Along the horizon—at the end of streets" (Corrie 2008, 243, 245). Evidence of the devastation created by the Israeli military was everywhere. She saw homes riddled with bullets, buildings shattered and left in rubble, injured children and adults, homeless people, damaged wells that had produced much needed water, and homes demolished by bulldozers.

Human Rights Watch, Amnesty International, and an Israeli human rights group have noted that from 2000 to 2004, the Israeli military destroyed 2,500 homes in the Gaza Strip; nearly two-thirds of the demolished homes were in Rafah. The rights organizations have denounced such destruction as violations of international law. Government officials from Israel have argued that it is defending itself against terrorist attacks and weapon smugglings that have originated in Rafah. Israeli officials say they are clearing the area along the border with Egypt in order to build a steel wall and create a "buffer zone" to prevent terrorist attacks.

On March 16, 2003, Rachel Corrie was standing as a human shield in front of the home of her friends, pharmacist Samir Nasrallah, his brother Khaled Nasrallah, and their wives and children. Rachel, like other ISM members, was using nonviolent means to try to prevent bulldozers from destroying the Nasrallah home, which was occupied by the family. A bulldozer with two soldiers in the cab came toward the home in the late afternoon. Corrie was wearing an orange fluorescent jacket as she tried to ward off the bulldozer. But it kept moving forward, pushing dirt ahead. Other ISM members nearby yelled and waved frantically trying to get the driver to stop the bulldozer. According to multiple reports, Corrie tried to climb up on the pile of dirt to get the soldiers' attention, but she fell and the bulldozer drove over her and then backed up. Her friends ran to help her, but by the time an ambulance arrived, Corrie was dead.

The Israeli military claimed that Rachel's death was an accident and that she fell and hit her head. The bulldozer operators insist they did not see her. Eyewitnesses to the incident said otherwise.

Reaction to Rachel's death was widespread and diverse. Rachel's parents knew that their daughter wanted Americans to "be aware of what she was witnessing," so they "made her e-mail letters from Gaza available within hours after her death." Some of the e-mails were published in the *Olympian* and other U.S. newspapers. A British newspaper, the *Guardian*, ran nearly all of the e-mails, which prompted actor Alan Rickman to take the published feature to the Royal Court Theatre in London. The theatre used the e-mails as a basis for a one-person play titled *My Name Is Rachel Corrie* (2005). Edited by Rickman and Katharine Viner, the play was first performed in London with Megan Dodds in the title role (Corrie 2008, xviii). Later it was scheduled for the New York Theater Workshop, but was canceled due to fear that Jewish groups would be offended. It was, however, performed off-Broadway in 2006. In addition, the drama was staged in other U.S. cities; in Edmonton, Vancouver, Montreal, and Toronto, Canada; and in other countries. Rachel's e-mails and journal entries also appeared in book form *Let Me Stand Alone* (2008).

The play and book have been criticized by numerous members of the Jewish community as well as by the organization StandWithUs, which advocates for Israel. For example, Roberta Seid, education director of StandWithUs, was highly critical of Rachel Corrie's journal in an article she wrote for *Commentary*:

> There is not a word in the journals about the terrorist campaign unleashed on Israel in September 2000, not a word that reveals that Gaza, especially Rafah (where Corrie stayed) was a hotbed of terrorism and arms smuggling. She apparently never watched the videos of suicide bombers' last statements, or questioned the increasing radicalization of Palestinian society. Rachel never mentions the Palestinian Authority or Yasser Arafat, and gives no inkling of Gaza as a clan-based society with competing clans vying for power. There is no sense that she tried to understand or was even aware of the society in which she now lived. (Seid n.d.)

Other critics have called Rachel an accomplice of terrorists and charge that her published journal and the play based on the journal entries are anti-Israeli propaganda that promotes hatred for Israel. Even more outrage greeted the showing of a documentary about Corrie that was produced by Israeli filmmaker Simone Bitton. Titled *Rachel* (2009), it presents the conflicting reports about Corrie without drawing any conclusions. When it was shown, some in the Jewish community boycotted the film, calling it anti-Semitic. But in an interview for *Sojourners Magazine*, Bitton noted that it was important for people to be made aware of human rights violations in Gaza. "The biggest human rights violation is depriving the Palestinian people of their independence," she said. "You cannot continue to keep accepting all that Israel is doing to the Palestinians. It's bad for America and it's bad for Israel. I'm saying this as an Israeli" (Garrison 2009, 44).

Even as Corrie's critics and supporters debate, Rachel's parents and activists have established the Rachel Corrie Foundation for Peace and Justice in Olympia, Washington. The foundation supports the kind of work that Rachel began—grassroots efforts for peace and justice. Craig and Cindy Corrie also have filed a civil lawsuit in Israel against the Israel Ministry of Defense. The Corries charge that the State of Israel violated "constitutional rights (right to life, dignity), anchored in international humanitarian and human rights law, as well as in Israel's Basic Law: Human Dignity and Liberty, for the intentional and unlawful killing of Rachel Corrie." The trial in Haifa began in Spring 2010 and was delayed numerous times. By early 2011, it had not been concluded.

References

"About ISM." International Solidarity Movement. n.d. http://palsolidarity.org/about-ism/ (accessed January 17, 2011).

Corrie, Craig, and Cindy Corrie, eds. *Let Me Stand Alone: The Journals of Rachel Corrie*. New York and London: W. W. Norton, 2008.

Garrison, Becky (interviewer). "Death of an Activist: An Interview with Israeli Filmmaker Simone Bitton." *Sojourners Magazine*, August 2009.

Seid, Roberta E. "Rachel Corrie's Dreams: The (Self) Deceit of Rachel Corrie." *Commentary Online*, n.d. http://www.commentarymagazine.com/viewarticle.cfm/the—self—deceit-of-rachel-corrie-11453?page=all (accessed January 18, 2011).

Coughlin, Charles E. (1891–1979)

"Charles Coughlin's emergence as a national media celebrity defined a critical turning point in American public life and popular culture. He was the first public figure to obliterate the distinction between politics, religion, and mass-media entertainment.... The radio priest stood at the dawn of an age in which radio and later television could create media celebrities who could rival in their power those public figures who held elective office or who claimed a media following" (Warren 1996, 6–7).

Father Charles Coughlin never ran for election. He never held political office. Yet at the height of his career in the 1930s, Father Coughlin was one of the most influential men in the United States. His influence continues to the present day. Father Coughlin created political talk radio.

Charles Edward Coughlin appears to have been destined for the priesthood since the day he was born on October 25, 1891, in Hamilton, Ontario, Canada. His parents, Thomas and Amelia Coughlin, had risen from the working class to achieve a comfortable, middle-class existence. The Coughlin home was across the street from St. Mary's Cathedral. The family could hear the cathedral's organ while sitting at the dinner table.

Amelia Coughlin's greatest hope was that her son might become a priest. Coughlin entered St. Basil's Seminary in Toronto, from which he graduated as an ordained priest in 1916.

Coughlin's seminary training shaped his future political and economic views. The Basilian Order required priests to take an active role in modern industrial society, speaking out against the injustices of the capitalist system. According to the Basilians, lending money at interest—modern systems of banking and finance—led to social inequality and a widening gap between rich and poor. The solution was a return to the "organic" practices and values of preindustrial communities.

Coughlin began teaching at a Assumption College in Windsor, Ontario. He taught several subjects, from Greek to English literature. He soon revealed a flair for the stage. Coughlin's Shakespearean productions earned high praise. However, the dean of students warned Coughlin that student actors needed to devote more time to their other subjects. In a pattern to be repeated throughout his public career, Coughlin ignored him.

Coughlin also served as assistant pastor in two small churches across the border in the United States. His dramatic sermons attracted attention, and he soon became a sought-after speaker for local service organizations. These luncheon speeches added to his reputation in business circles as well as in the non-Catholic community. Coughlin's friends and supporters included Protestants as well as Jews.

In 1924, Coughlin left Assumption and moved to Detroit, Michigan, where he enjoyed the support of Michael Gallagher, Detroit's bishop. Bishop Gallagher sent Coughlin to Royal Oak, a growing suburb, to establish a new church in honor of Saint Thérése of Lisieux, the Little Flower, who had just been canonized.

Although the parish only had two dozen families, Coughlin built the Shrine of the Little Flower as a church that could seat 600. The seats themselves were theater seats, not pews. His immediate challenge was to pay off a $100,000 loan from the diocese.

Coughlin set about promoting the church as well as himself. His sermons attracted a growing following that included some of Detroit's wealthiest figures. One was George A. "Dick" Richards, owner of radio station WJR. Richards gave Coughlin access to the airwaves, and Coughlin made his first broadcast on October 17, 1926. What began as a program to teach catechism to children soon expanded to address contemporary social and political issues.

Coughlin became a media success. He spoke the language of ordinary people, and his warm, rich baritone made listeners believe that they were hearing someone who understood and cared. Author Wallace Stegner described it as "a voice made for promises" (Stegner 1949, 234). Radio pioneer Frank Stanton referred to Coughlin as "the greatest voice of the twentieth century" (Warren 1996, 26).

The Columbia Broadcasting System—today's media giant CBS—began syndicating *The Hour of the Little Flower* in 1930. Coughlin's radio audience, already strong in the Midwest and New England, now spanned the nation with an estimated total of 40 million listeners. Although only two of five American families in 1930 actually owned a radio, friends, neighbors, and relatives gathered to listen to the broadcasts. They, in turn, would discuss with others what they had heard.

In this way, Coughlin built a network of individuals with close personal ties to each other, who in turn believed they had a personal relationship with him. It might be said that he created a "digital community" long before the Internet existed. Modern social networking sites, such as Facebook and Twitter, may have their roots in Coughlin's Radio League of the Little Flower.

Listeners became contributors. Thousands joined Coughlin's Radio League. One daily deposit amounted to more than $21,000, most of it in one- and five-dollar bills—the equivalent of $672,000 today.

Coughlin was obsessed with communism, which he regarded as a threat to religion, the family, and western civilization. At the same time, his broadcasts expressed deep concern for workers, small businessmen, and their families. As the worldwide economic Depression deepened, he saw ordinary Americans losing their homes and livelihoods.

The United States' only hope, as he saw it, was for the government to enact needed reforms. These included increasing the money supply by going off the gold standard, providing pensions for the elderly, protecting workers' right to organize, and limiting the ability of banks and brokerages to engage in irresponsible financial manipulation. He denounced corporate greed and concentrations of extreme personal wealth. Invited to testify before Congress about the "Communist Menace," he ended by attacking auto manufacturer Henry Ford.

Coughlin reserved his most vehement attacks for the Hoover administration, which he felt had done little to ease the ravages of the Depression. He supported Franklin Delano Roosevelt in the 1932 presidential election. Coughlin's broadcasts definitely played a part in winning Michigan and contributing to Roosevelt's landslide victory. Many of Coughlin's proposed reforms became part of the New Deal. Social Security, the Security and Exchange Commission, income tax reform, and abandoning the gold standard were all part of Coughlin's program for social justice.

Coughlin expected to play an influential role in the new administration. Roosevelt, however, had no intention of giving the "Radio Priest" any influence. Disillusioned, Coughlin's broadcasts and political activity became increasingly extreme. He founded the National Union for Social Justice, an organization with disturbing similarities to fascist movements in Europe. He began publishing *Social Justice*, a weekly newspaper distributed through the mails. He supported Louisiana's populist governor Huey Long as a potential third-party candidate in the 1936 presidential election. After Long's assassination, Coughlin switched his support to the new Union Party and its candidate, William Lemke, a colorless North Dakota congressman.

Despite Coughlin's efforts, the Union Party failed to elect a single candidate. The humiliating defeat led Coughlin to temporarily abandon his radio broadcasts. They did not resume until January 1937.

The Coughlin who emerged began showing signs of pro-fascism and anti-Semitism. In broadcasts and articles published in *Social Justice*, Coughlin expressed the worldview common to modern anti-Semites, who declared that since individuals of Jewish background had at times been among the leaders of various Communist parties, Jews controlled the International Communist Movement. Similarly, the existence of prominent Jewish bankers such as Bernard Baruch and the Rothschilds "proved" that Jews controlled the banking and finance industries. The illogic of Jews being communists and capitalists at the same time was explained away as a vast Jewish conspiracy. This was the position of Germany's Nazi Party, which took power in 1933. Coughlin's broadcasts began to sound disturbingly like Nazi propaganda.

While Coughlin never advocated mass murder, neither did he oppose it. On November 9, 1938, the Nazis unleashed an orgy of

Coughlin, Charles E. (1891–1979) | 159

Perhaps the most widely heard anti-Semite of the pre-war period was Father Charles E. Coughlin, a Michigan-based Roman Catholic cleric, whose extremely popular 1930s radio program routinely attracted up to 40 million listeners. After 1938, Coughlin added increasingly vicious anti-Semitic comments to his already strident programs. (Library of Congress)

violence against Germany's Jews. Coughlin was urged to speak out, if for no other reason than to prove that he was no anti-Semite. Instead, he attributed the Nazi persecutions to the Jews themselves. "Nazism, the effect of Communism, cannot be liquidated in its persecution complex until the religious Jews in high places—in synagogue, finance, in radio and the press—attack the cause, attack forthright the errors and spread of Communism, [for] Jewish persecution only followed after Christians were first persecuted" (Warren 1996, 157).

A month later, Coughlin gave American Jews this warning: "Were my advice of any value, I should counsel the Jews to refrain from joining with others in adopting a program—even though constitutional—which breeds resentment to their race ... Intolerance towards men is always reprehensible. But often times intolerance is provoked by injudicious and erroneous policies" (Warren 1996, 164–65).

Catholics, as well as Jews, found Coughlin's views unsettling. Letters written at the time reflect both unease and outrage. "I am an ordinary Catholic girl with a thorough Catholic education ... I am ashamed that Father Coughlin has not been rebuked. I could repeat all of the reasons why we, as Catholics, should be ashamed of intolerance of any sort voiced by a minister of Christ" (Warren 1996, 216–17). Donald Warren summarizes the Catholic community's concern: "As Coughlin moved from populist protest to ever more direct sympathy for, or at the least benign tolerance of, totalitarian fascism and Nazism, he besmirched not only his own career but the Catholic church, for which he claimed to speak. In equating his own political ideas with Catholic doctrine, he challenged the church to respond. It did only slowly, but a response finally did come" (Warren 1996, 198).

The Church had been aware of the problem since 1932. Bishop Michael Gallagher of Detroit had been repeatedly urged by his fellow bishops to bring Coughlin to heel. The Vatican itself became involved. Gallagher politely, but firmly, ignored them. As one of Coughlin's oldest friends and supporters, he would not allow anyone to interfere.

The situation changed with Gallagher's death in 1937. Gallagher was replaced by Archbishop Edward Mooney, who understood that disciplining Coughlin would be his first challenge. Mooney realized that Coughlin had tapped into a well of popular resentment against the elitism of the Catholic hierarchy, exploiting social class tensions within the community itself. Given his enormous popularity and influence, Coughlin had to be handled carefully.

Over the next two years, Coughlin and Mooney played a cat-and-mouse game. Coughlin attacked the Jewish community in nearly every broadcast. Mooney expressed disapproval, but not condemnation. A message from the Vatican offered far less support than Mooney expected: "As an American citizen, Father Coughlin has the right to express his personal views on current events, but he is not authorized to speak for the Catholic Church nor does he represent doctrines or sentiments of the Church" (Coppa 2006, 172). When Mooney declined to approve certain articles in *Social Justice*, Coughlin reestablished the journal as an independent weekly no longer subject to the Church.

By 1940, Coughlin's anti-Semitic attacks became even more extreme. *Social Justice* reprinted excerpts from the notorious anti-Semitic forgery, *The Protocols of the Elders of Zion*. The FBI raided a Brooklyn chapter of the Christian Front, a Coughlin-inspired militia, and uncovered weapons, ammunition, and bombs, along with plans to assassinate prominent Jewish figures and overthrow the government.

Coughlin denied any connection. However, the U.S. State Department, Treasury, and Federal Bureau of Investigation probes began discovering evidence of Coughlin's connections with fascist organizations in Latin America, as well as possible evidence that he was receiving support and financial aid from Nazi Germany. As the United States drew closer to war, it appeared that Coughlin might be indicted for treason.

In April 1940, the Post Office revoked *Social Justice*'s mailing privileges. In May 1940, the National Association of Broadcasters declined to carry Coughlin's broadcasts. Archbishop Mooney forced Coughlin to refrain from all political activity. If he violated his agreement this time, he would be removed from the priesthood.

Coughlin, for the most part, kept his word. He returned to the Shrine of the Little Flower where he died, unrepentant, on October 27, 1979. Coughlin's career remains a puzzle. A man of genuine compassion, insight, and charisma, he chose to ally himself with America's most extreme elements. He established a link between right-wing politics and the media that continues to the present. For example, on August 1, 1988, less than 10 years after Coughlin's death, Rush Limbaugh made his first broadcast on New York's radio station WABC. Limbaugh has continued the kind of ultraconservative dissent that creates fierce loyalty or outright disdain.

Eric A. Kimmel

See also Limbaugh, Rush

References

Brinkley, Alan. *Voices of Protest: Huey Long, Father Coughlin, and the Great Depression.* New York: Vintage Books, 1983.

Coppa, Frank J. *The Papacy, the Jews, and the Holocaust.* Washington, DC: Catholic University of America Press, 2006.

Coughlin, Charles Edward. *A Series of Lectures on Social Justice.* Royal Oak, MI: Radio League of the Little Flower, 1935.

Stegner, Wallace. *The Radio Priest and His Flock in the Aspirin Age: 1919–1941.* Edited by Isabel Leighton. New York: Simon and Schuster, 1949.

United States Holocaust Memorial Museum. "Charles E. Coughlin." *Holocaust Encyclopedia*, last updated April 1, 2010. http://www.ushmm.org/wlc/en/article.php?ModuleId=10005516 (accessed July 23, 2010).

Warren, Donald. *Radio Priest: Charles Coughlin, the Father of Hate Radio.* New York: Free Press, 1966.

Darrow, Clarence (1857–1938)

"I am tried here because I have given a large part of my life and my service to the cause of the poor and the weak, and because I am in the way of the interests. These interests would stop my voice . . . which from the time I was a prattling baby my father and mother taught me to raise for justice and freedom, and in the cause of the weak and the poor" (Cowan 1993, 418). In 1912, Clarence Darrow, a long-time dissident, issued this statement as part of a long trial summation in which he was defending himself against charges that he had bribed a jury. That trial almost convicted one of the most famous lawyers in American history, a man remembered for defending a young physics teacher, John T. Scopes, who had defied Tennessee law that banned the teaching of evolution. Darrow also defended such dissident labor leaders as Eugene V. Debs and William D. "Big Bill" Haywood. When he was the defense attorney for Nathan Leopold and Richard Loeb, who murdered a 14-year-old boy, he became known as an "attorney for the damned" (Cowan 1993, 5).

Born on April 18, 1857, near Kinsman, Ohio, Clarence Seward Darrow was the fifth child of Amirus and Emily Darrow. Although Clarence hated his first name, he was proud of his middle name, which honored William Henry Seward, an avid abolitionist. His parents were intelligent individuals who were avid readers and taught their seven children to be critical thinkers. His father had studied at a seminary but rejected religious teachings upon graduation and became an agnostic. Emily also was an agnostic. Yet both Amirus and Emily insisted that their children attend Sunday school and church. In their view, their children should be exposed to religious teachings and make up their own minds about their beliefs.

Since Amirus had not prepared for any career except preaching, he turned to cabinetmaking and eventually coffin making to help support his large family. He was a Democrat in a predominantly Republican farming community, a religious free thinker, and an abolitionist. In short, he was the opposite of his conservative neighbors. Yet he turned this into strength, courageously living his beliefs and standing firm despite their unpopularity. This was the kind of character strength Darrow adopted and would need to practice law in a way consistent with his own beliefs.

Darrow's mother was an advocate of women's rights and kept up her knowledge of current events. Neither Emily nor Amirus were demonstrative; they cared for their children but showed little affection. When Clarence was 14, his mother died after a long illness.

From the time he was a small child, Darrow's older siblings, Edward and Mary, took him on Friday nights to a literary society. Darrow thrilled to the lectures and debates. At home, he loved to listen to traveling philosophers who came to take part in stirring discussions with his father. Their home was also a stop on the Underground Railroad and a place where abolitionists were welcome guests.

Darrow, Clarence (1857–1938)

One of the most brilliant trial lawyers in U.S. history, Clarence Darrow used his remarkable abilities in the courtroom to defend the common person in a number of celebrated cases. (Library of Congress)

While Darrow was growing up, his family members frequently attended Saturday night debates held in their farm town. He joined in as he got older and in that forum "found that he could win the minds of his listeners with a homespun blend of warmth, humor, and simple phrasing—and a well-placed and biting attack on his opponent's inevitable intellectual inconsistencies. It was that skill—his brilliant gift of oratory, orneriness, and originality—that prepared Darrow to become America's greatest lawyer" (Cowan 1993, 16).

Darrow's higher education began at his father's alma mater, Allegheny College, a Methodist institution where he stayed only one year. He taught for three years, until his family convinced him to enroll at the University of Michigan. Amirus, Edward, and Mary believed he would make a good lawyer, and they offered to pay for his education. Darrow completed one year there before becoming a lawyer's apprentice.

In 1880, during his early 20s, Darrow married Jessie Ohl, a young woman he had known since his teenage years. They made their home in the farming community of Andover, Ohio, for three years. The couple had one child, a son Paul born in 1883. Darrow made a paltry income from farmers who needed legal assistance with lawsuits. After 17 years of marriage, Clarence and Jessie divorced in 1897.

His legal career, which began in small Ohio towns, did not really take off until he moved to Chicago, where he practiced law for the city's legal department and with the Chicago and North Western Railway Company. He became involved in trying to free eight anarchists who had been charged with killing seven police officers in a bombing at an 1886 worker's rally at Haymarket Square in Chicago. Three of the men's sentences were commuted to life, while four were hanged and one committed suicide in prison. Darrow successfully petitioned Illinois governor John Peter Altgeld to grant the three imprisoned men clemency. Darrow had read Altgeld's book *Our Penal Machinery and Its Victims* (1886) and had been impressed with Altgeld's views on criminal justice. Darrow was deeply opposed to capital punishment and became active in the Amnesty Association, an organization that worked to obtain pardons for convicted criminals who were sentenced to die.

During the 1890s, Darrow defended labor organizer Eugene V. Debs, who was leading a strike against the Pullman Sleeping Car Company (first called the Pullman Palace Car Company) manufactured in a company town south of Chicago, a town that eventually became part of the city. Workers were striking because of wage cuts, layoffs, and poor working conditions, but federal courts brought an injunction to stop the strike. Debs ignored it, was arrested and indicted for conspiracy to interfere with interstate commerce, and President Grover Cleveland sent federal troops to Illinois to smash the strike. Darrow was unsuccessful in his attempt to defend Debs, who spent six months in jail for contempt of court.

While involved in labor issues, Darrow met a newspaper journalist, Ruby Hamerstrom, whom he married in 1903. The marriage lasted through the rest of his life; the couple had no children.

In a major labor case, Darrow successfully defended William D. "Big Bill" Haywood in a 1907 trial. Haywood was the leader of the newly formed Industrial Workers of the World. In an attempt to destroy the union, the federal government accused Haywood of a murder plot and brought him to trial, but a jury acquitted Haywood.

For 17 years, Darrow took cases defending unions and workers' rights to strike. The last case Darrow fought for labor law was in 1911, in defense of Joseph and James McNamara, socialists and brothers accused of dynamiting the *Los Angeles Times* building. Twenty-one people had died in the explosion. Darrow agreed to defend the McNamaras in California and persuaded them to plead guilty and accept a pretrial sentencing agreement. With this maneuver, Darrow hoped to avoid a jury trial that he was sure would end in conviction and the death penalty for his clients. The deal outraged labor leaders, who felt it ruined the socialist candidate's chances in an upcoming Los Angeles election. On the eve of that election, there were accusations that Darrow, through an intermediary on his staff, had attempted to bribe a juror into voting for the McNamaras' acquittal. After two long trials, Darrow was set free, but many reporters, friends, and other observers of the time believed he was guilty. Evidence gathered since then supports that conclusion.

Darrow returned to Chicago and never again argued another labor case. He rebuilt his private practice, and until the end of World War I, he defended people who refused to serve in the military or who were communists or socialists. He was an impassioned defender, seldom raising his voice but presenting his case for hours on end. The passion Darrow displayed in the courtroom was part of his nature. "Not only did he not believe in dispassionate advocacy; he was incapable of it. Once possessed by an emotion, he could not rid himself of it; there was an obsessive aspect to his make-up that would not let him rest after his feelings had been engaged" (Tierney 1979, 30).

Two of Darrow's most famous trials occurred in the 1920s. In 1924, he defended Nathan Leopold and Richard Loeb, who kidnapped 14-year-old Bobby Franks and confessed to killing the young teenager just for thrills. Darrow took the case but avoided a jury trial by pleading his clients guilty. He persuaded the presiding judge that Leopold and Loeb were mentally ill; the judge sentenced them to life in prison. During their term, a fellow prisoner stabled Loeb, who died of his wounds at age 30. Leopold was released on parole in 1958 and moved to Puerto Rico, where he died in 1971 of a heart attack.

In 1925, Darrow defended John T. Scopes, who was arrested for teaching evolution in violation of Tennessee law. The American Civil Liberties Union planned to defend Scopes, but Darrow waived a fee to act as counsel. Like the Leopold and Loeb case, the Scopes trial generated worldwide attention. Darrow, an agnostic, was pitted against William Jennings Bryan, a former presidential candidate who was devoutly religious and believed in the biblical story of creation. The trial became a passionate confrontation between two men who had had years to develop their dislike of each other. In the first place, their arguments stemmed from totally different points of view. During the trial, they went well beyond creationism versus evolution to debate in eloquent and dramatic fashion whether there was a God and whether the Bible contained literal truths.

While Darrow was believed to have won Scopes' argument, he changed his client's plea to guilty near the end of the trial to protect Scopes from a retrial. The case then went to the Supreme Court of Tennessee, where it was dismissed. The court later repealed the law against teaching evolution.

In another famous case, Darrow in 1925 successfully defended members of an African American family accused of murdering a member of the Ku Klux Klan (KKK). The Klan had attacked the home of Dr. Ossian Sweet, whose family had bought a house in Detroit, Michigan, during the time when blacks were escaping the Jim Crow South for the North but were still being persecuted. A mob tried to drive the family from their home but family members fired back, killing one man. Dr. Sweet and his family were arrested and charged with murder. The National Association for the Advancement of Colored People (NAACP) asked Darrow to assist on defense. Darrow asked Dr. Sweet to take the stand and tell what he felt when the mob attacked.

> Sweet told of the race riots he had seen in Washington, when colored men had been hunted through the streets by mobs; of the violence of the Chicago race riots; of the five Negroes who were shot to death in Rosewood [Florida] when eighteen Negro homes and a Negro church were burned; of the four Johnson brothers of Arkansas, one a physician and another a dentist, who had been taken from a train and lynched; of Dr. A. C. Jackson of Tulsa ... who was murdered by the police ... after trying to protect his home from a mob; of the three thousand Negroes who had been lynched within one generation; of the mobs that had burned, hung, shot and beaten his fellow Negroes to death. (Stone 1989, 481–82)

While this was not the only defense tactic Darrow used, it was one of the deciding factors. The trial ended in a hung jury, but a second trial, almost a replica of the first, ended with an eloquent plea from Darrow and resulted in a not guilty verdict.

Darrow retired in 1929, lectured, and wrote numerous articles for national magazines as well as his autobiography that was published in 1932. He had also written *Crime: Its Cause and Treatment* (1922) and was coeditor with Wallace Rice for *Infidels and Heretics* (1929). During the 1930s, Darrow's health steadily declined because of heart disease. He died on March 12, 1938, in Chicago.

See also Debs, Eugene V.

References

Baatz, Simon. "Criminal Minds: In 1924, Nathan Leopold and Richard Loeb Kidnapped and Murdered a 14-Year-Old Boy." *Smithsonian*, August 2008.

Cowan, Geoffrey. *The People v. Clarence Darrow: The Bribery Trial of America's Greatest Lawyer.* New York: Random House, 1993.

Darrow, Clarence. *The Story of My Life.* New York: Charles Scribner's Sons, 1932.

Johnson, Anne Janette. *The Scopes "Monkey Trial."* Detroit, MI: Omnigraphics, 2004.

Stone, Irving. *Clarence Darrow for the Defense: A Biography.* New York: Doubleday, 1941, 1989.

Tierney, Kevin. *Darrow: A Biography.* New York: Thomas Y. Crowell, Publishers, 1979.

Vine, Phyllis. *One Man's Castle: Clarence Darrow in Defense of the American Dream.* New York: HarperCollins/Amistad, 2004.

Dart, Justin, Jr. (1930–2002)

His signature outfit was a cowboy hat and boots that hardly seemed to fit with the pale figure, who depended on a wheelchair rather than a horse for mobility. But Justin Dart Jr. spent most of his adult life on the move, advocating for people with disabilities. He is known as a revolutionary in his long-time efforts for the economic and social empowerment of disabled individuals. He dedicated his life to human and disability rights, and frequently was called the "Father of the Americans with Disability Act." He also was compared with Martin Luther King Jr. as a leader of the disability civil rights movement.

Justin Dart Jr. was born into a prominent, wealthy family on August 29, 1930, in Chicago, Illinois. His parents held views quite different from each other's. Justin Dart Sr. had been an All-American football player, and competition was a major factor in his life. He established multinational Dart Industries and was a conservative Republican. Justin's mother, Ruth Walgreen Dart, the daughter of Charles Walgreen, founder of the Walgreen Company chain, was a feminist writer and publisher of an innovative magazine. The couple had two children, Justin Jr. and Peter Dart before the two divorced in 1939. Justin Sr. married again in 1940 to actress Jane O'Brien, and they had three children: Guy, Jane, and Stephen.

Justin's childhood was one of privilege. In a compilation of biographies about disabled persons, the author of Dart's sketch noted: "Most people who knew Justin Dart, Jr. when he was a child would never have expected him to become a beloved and respected leader of anything." In Dart's own words, he was "an obnoxious child" (McMahon and Shaw 2000, 66). He and his brother Peter were raised primarily by maids and other household help. During his childhood, Justin and Peter were bitter enemies, and Justin once threw a dart that hit his brother in the nose. Not only was Justin obnoxious, as he described himself, but he also was rude, unruly, and thoroughly disliked. He attended the prestigious prep school Phillips Academy Andover and had so many demerits that he broke a record. He entered and left seven different high schools.

In 1948, when he was 18 years old, Dart contracted poliomyelitis (polio). Although President Franklin D. Roosevelt, who was a polio victim, had helped establish the March of Dimes in the 1930s to raise funds for research to eradicate polio, Jonas Salk and other researchers in the 1940s were just beginning to develop a vaccine for this contagious viral illness. Dart developed one of the most severe forms, and doctors said he would not live. But he was admitted to the Seventh Day Adventist Medical University in Los Angeles, California, and as Dart explained, "For the first time in my life I was surrounded by people who were openly expressing love for each other, and for me, even though I was hostile to them. And so I started smiling at people, and saying nice things to them. And they responded, treating me even better. It felt so good! . . . I count the good days in my life from the time I got polio. These beautiful people not only saved my life, they made it worth saving" (Fay and Pelka 2002).

Dart's life changed thereafter. He was confined to a wheelchair, but he never forgot the transforming experiences in the medical facility. He continued his education in Texas at the University of Houston, earning a bachelor's degree in political science in 1953 and a master's degree in history in 1954. He hoped to be a teacher, but could not get a teaching certificate because he was in a wheelchair, a discriminatory factor that was abolished years later.

While he was at the university, Dart initiated the first-ever integration club. But with only five members, the club did little to integrate the school, although it gave Dart the opportunity to demonstrate his stand on human rights. In addition, he helped establish a political party—the Harris County Democrats.

Dart then turned to business ventures. He managed two bowling alleys in Mexico, which he sold at a profit. He then went to work in Japan, setting up a Tupperware factory in 1963. The company expanded rapidly and, within a few years, employed more than 25,000 people. "Dart hired and promoted women as salespeople and managers in his corporation, an unusual practice in Japan at that time," according to his biographer. He also hired young men with paraplegia to work in his factory and helped them create a wheelchair basketball team, a first for Japan. In addition, he supported campaigns to help the handicapped (McMahon and Shaw 2000, 69).

Shortly after arriving in Japan, Dart met Fusako Michishita, and they married. The couple had two children, but the marriage did not last because, as Dart explained, he was "being flamboyant and doing photo ops, making money by any means, drinking, and chasing women" (McMahon and Shaw 2000, 70).

While he was married, Dart was attracted to Yoshiko Saji, who worked for his company and was instrumental in training the workers with disabilities for their jobs. She also helped them gain self-confidence. Dart eventually hired Yoshiko as his administrative assistant. They fell in love, and their affair created a great scandal. But they became partners and comrades in the fight for a more humane world.

In 1966, Justin and Yoshiko traveled to Vietnam and visited a Saigon (Ho Chi Minh City) facility for children with polio. The visit was part of a media event and included a photographer. Dart described for reporter Jean Dobbs with *New Mobility* what he observed:

> The floor of the whole place was covered with children ages 4 to 10, with bloated stomachs and matchstick limbs.... They were starving to death and lying in their own urine and feces, covered with flies. A little girl reached up to me and looked into my eyes. I automatically took her hand and my photographer took pictures. She had the most serene look I have ever seen—and it penetrated to the deepest part of my consciousness.... I was engulfed by the devastating perception.... The way I'm living and dealing with disability is killing this little girl. I'm going to go to my hotel, drink Johnnie Walker, eat a steak, and this picture is going to be in some magazine. I told Yoshiko, "We cannot go on as we have been. Our lives have got to mean something. We have got to get into this fight and stop this evil." (Dobbs 1989)

Two years after the Saigon visit, Dart and Yoshiko married. They decided to devote their lives to gaining human and disability rights. For six years they studied the best ways to achieve their goals. They left Japan and moved back to the United States in

1974 when his mother died, and lived in Seattle for the next four years. In 1978, they moved to Texas, where Dart helped found an independent living center for people with disabilities.

During the 1980s, Dart was appointed to various government posts. He worked for the National Council on the Handicapped in Washington, D.C., and after a few months, President Ronald Reagan appointed him commissioner of rehabilitation services for the U.S. Department of Education in 1986; but the following year, he was fired because he publicly criticized the department in testimony at a congressional hearing. At the hearing, he announced that he would "depart from politics as usual protocol to make a statement of conscience." He declared that in spite of some accomplishments the rehabilitation agency was

> confronted by a vast, inflexible federal system which, like the society it represents, still contains a significant proportion of individuals who have not yet overcome obsolete, paternalistic attitudes about disability and, indeed, about government itself. There is a resistance to any sharing of their centralized authority with people with disabilities, their families, advocates and professional service providers, in or out of the federal service. Good management is too often subordinated to the protection of power. And, magically, a small but all too effective minority in the federal service and in the community seem dedicated to divide and conquer strategy and promoting hostility among government, advocates and professional service providers. (Dart 1987)

After Dart was fired for his comments, support for him came from across the United States with letters urging President Reagan to keep Dart as commissioner. Many supporters expressed their anger and concern about the effects on people with disabilities. But Dart himself was unruffled and had no desire to return to a government job. His firing helped focus public attention on discrimination against handicapped people.

Over the remaining years of the 1980s, Dart traveled to every state, organized grassroots groups on behalf of disabled people, spoke at dozens of forums, and compiled lists of people in the disability community that he could mobilize to contact members of Congress for passage of the Americans with Disabilities Act (ADA). Its purpose was "to provide a clear and comprehensive national mandate for the elimination of discrimination against individuals with disabilities; to provide clear, strong, consistent, enforceable standards addressing discrimination against individuals with disabilities; to ensure that the Federal Government plays a central role in enforcing the standards established ... on behalf of individuals with disabilities; and to invoke the sweep of congressional authority ... in order to address the major areas of discrimination faced day-to-day by people with disabilities."

The bill was first introduced in 1988, and coalitions of civil and disability rights groups and individuals wrote letters and lobbied members of the U.S. Congress to enact the bill. People with disabilities created diaries of their experiences with discrimination, and Dart, with his wife helping to organize forums, collected more than 5,000 documents and tape recordings detailing discrimination and supporting the ADA. "Between 1988 and 1990 Justin Dart chaired a total of 63 forums in all fifty states, Guam, and Puerto Rico, with over 7,000 people in attendance overall," according to the National Council on Disability, a federal agency. Justin and Yoshiko used their own funds to pay for most of their activities. And those activities along with efforts of many others brought success. The ADA became law in 1990.

For the next decade, the Darts continued their advocacy to empower people with disabilities. In 1995, Justin Dart cofounded Justice for All, which in 2001 became part of the American Association of People with Disabilities as an e-mail network called the Justice for All E-mail Network. It provides action alerts regarding legislation and other information to the disability community.

In 1998, Dart received the presidential medal of freedom from President William J. Clinton. The medal is the highest honor for a civilian, but Dart believed the medal belonged to all the activists and colleagues who helped empower people with disabilities. Clinton presented the medal with these words:

> Justin Dart literally opened the doors of opportunities to millions of our citizens by securing passage of one of the nation's landmark civil rights laws: The Americans with Disabilities Act. . . . At the University of Houston, he led bold efforts to promote integration. He went on to become, in his own words, "a full-time soldier in the trenches of justice," turning every state in the nation to elevate disability rights to the mainstream of political discourse. He once said, "Life is not a game that requires losers." He has given millions a chance to win. He has also been my guide in understanding the needs of disabled Americans. And every time I see him, he reminds me of the power of heart and will. I don't know that I've ever known a braver person.

After he received the medal, he presented it to Yoshiko to show his appreciation for her partnership in the struggle. He declared that the medal belonged to everyone in the disability rights movement; he made copies of the medal and sent them to activists in the cause.

Dart died in Washington, D.C., on June 21, 2002, from pneumonia and congestive heart failure. In the obituaries that followed, former U.S. presidents George H. W. Bush and William Clinton praised Dart's work as did several U.S. senators. His honors include induction into the U.S. Department of Labor's hall of fame in 2010.

See also King, Martin Luther, Jr.

References

Dart, Justin, Jr. "Statement by Justin Dart, Jr., Commissioner, Rehabilitation Services Administration, to the Oversight Hearing on the Rehabilitation Services Administration held by the Select Education Subcommittee of the House Committee on Education and Labor, November 18, 1987." http://www.bcm.edu/ilru/html/about/Dart/statement_of_conscience.htm (accessed December 14, 2010).

Dart, Mari Carlin. "The Resurrection of Justin Dart, Jr.: A Quest for Truth and Love." *Ability Magazine.* http://www.abilitymagazine.com/carroll_dart.html (accessed December 12, 2010).

Dobbs, Jean. "And Justin for All." *New Mobility*, March 1998. http://www.newmobility.com/articleView.cfm?id=84 (accessed December 13, 2010).

Fay, Fred, and Fred Pelka. "Justin Dart—an Obituary" (written at Justin Dart's request). *Disability Social History Project*, June 22, 2002. http://www.disabilityhistory.org/people_dart.html (accessed December 13, 2010).

May, Lee. "Dart's Defiance." *Los Angeles Times*, December 10, 1987. http://articles.latimes.com/print/1987-12-10/news/vw-27981_1_justin-dart-jr (accessed December 13, 2010).

McMahon, Brian T., and Linda Shaw, eds. *Enabling Lives: Biographies of Six Prominent Americans with Disabilities*. Boca Raton, FL: CRC Press, 2000.

National Council on Disability. "Publicizing the ADA: Advocacy and the Government Response." *Equality of Opportunity: The Making of the Americans with Disabilities Act*, 2010. http://www.ncd.gov/publications/2010/equality_of_Opportunity_The_Making_of_the_Americans_with_Disabilities_Act (accessed September 8, 2011).

Davis, Angela (1944–)

"Revolution is a serious thing, the most serious thing about a revolutionary's life. When one commits oneself to the struggle, it must be for a lifetime" (Stone 2008). These words by Angela Yvonne Davis have appeared in countless publications and Internet sites, and represent the underlying principle of her life as philosopher, college professor, communist, and fierce activist in the fight for human rights.

Davis was born on January 26, 1944, in Birmingham, Alabama, to Sallye and B. Frank Davis. The oldest of four children, Angela had two brothers, Benjamin Frank Jr. and Reginald (Reggie) and a sister, Elizabeth (Fania). Both parents were educators, but Frank Davis left teaching to run a service station where he prospered.

Compared to the average black families of the 1940s and 1950s, the family was well off and enjoyed the "black bourgeoisie" lifestyle. They were quite comfortable living in a large house on a hill, and the parents made sure that the children received a good education. Angela's parents—especially her mother—were very involved in every aspect of their children's lives. At an early age, she encouraged vocabulary building by inventing and playing word games with the children. They all developed a love of books, and Angela became an avid reader. Angela did well in school and got good grades. People who knew her then spoke of her as being friendly but shy and quiet.

At home, Angela's parents also taught their children about African American struggles in the segregated South. Frank and Sallye Davis joined the National Association for the Advancement of Colored People (NAACP) to underscore their belief in social justice and also were interested in the views of their communist friends.

Birmingham was a factory town with coal, iron ore, and bauxite industries that welcomed white employees. But the black community was extremely poor and lacked good housing and jobs. Blacks were banned from most movie theaters, the county fairgrounds, public libraries, and downtown restaurants. But all these things paled in comparison to the terror under which blacks had to live. Racism was rampant at that time throughout most of the South. The human rights of African Americans were trampled on at every turn. The community was run by Eugene "Bull" Connor, who was commissioner of public safety (1936–1963). He believed firmly in segregation and was fierce in his treatment of blacks. When the federal government passed legislation such as the School Desegregation Act of 1954 and the Civil Rights Act of 1964, angry whites in retaliation committed even more brutal acts against blacks. Bombs went off in Birmingham nightly and drive-by cars tossed bombs at and into black homes. No one was prosecuted for the bombings or the fatalities that occurred.

In the Davis neighborhood, the black men formed a watch group that would notify households when perpetrators were spotted so the families could be ready to flee if necessary. Many families left the area permanently, and the Davis family discussed moving. But Angela's father had the final say, and he refused to be driven from his home and business. So the family remained despite the constant harassment from whites.

During some summers, Angela's mother went to New York University in New York City to work on her master's degree. She brought the children with her, and they stayed with relatives. Here they experienced freedoms that were denied to them in Birmingham. They were introduced to parks, museums, and theaters. They were even able to go swimming in an integrated pool. All this made the children anxious to move north.

As a teenager, Angela began to rebel against the way most blacks were forced to live in Birmingham, and she wanted to get away. She applied for an experimental program developed by the American Friends Southern Negro Student Committee (the American Friends Service Committee) to go to an integrated school in the North. She was accepted, and in 1959, at the age of 15, she enrolled in Elizabeth Irwin High School in Greenwich Village, New York.

She was amazed by Elizabeth Irwin, as the teachers were unconventional and students were allowed to call them by their first names. The school was very liberal in its outlook and teachings, and Angela was exposed to socialist and communist philosophies, which interested her. Part of her education was community service, and she worked at the Brooklyn Heights Youth Center. She enjoyed working with the troubled youths she met there. She also participated in picketing Woolworth's retail store. The school picketed Woolworth's every Saturday morning to protest the store's support of segregated lunch counters in the South.

While in New York, Davis lived with the Rev. and Mrs. William Howard Melish. He

Civil rights activist and communist Angela Davis addresses the press at the University of California, Berkeley, where she received a standing ovation following her first class, October 6, 1969. University regents had banned her employment, but she had support from the school's chancellor and faculty. (AP Photo/David F. Smith)

was minister of the Trinity Episcopal Church in Brooklyn and believed that the United States and Communist Russia should continue the friendly relationship they had formed during World War II. But this was a time when many Americans feared communist infiltration, and Melish was labeled a communist and lost his pulpit. He fought to regain his position, and his struggle taught Angela about the power of taking a stand. Everywhere around her, people were involved with politics and the fight for human rights.

After graduating from high school in 1961, Davis attended Brandeis University in Waltham, Massachusetts. She majored in

French and, during her junior year, went to France to continue her studies. There she met people from Algeria who were fighting for independence from France and sympathized with their cause, sometimes joining protest marches. In France she happened to read a newspaper article about the four girls in Birmingham who were killed in September 1963 when members of the Ku Klux Klan (KKK) bombed the Sixteenth Street Baptist Church. Angela knew the family and was deeply affected by these racist acts, prompting her to search for a philosophy that would bring justice to oppressed blacks.

Returning to Brandeis, she heard a lecture by Herbert Marcuse, a Marxist professor of philosophy. She read his books and decided that she would study philosophy. She graduated with high honors and received a scholarship to continue her studies in Frankfurt, Germany, at the Institute for Social Research at Goethe University. She studied the works of Georg Wilhelm Friedrich Hegel (1770–1831), Immanuel Kant (1724–1804), and Karl Marx (1818–1883) and delved deeper into the philosophy of social change and communism. In 1967, when attending a Congress on the Dialectics of Liberation in London, she met Stokely Carmichael, a black activist and one of the leaders of the Student Nonviolent Coordinating Committee. She admired his stance on black pride and ideas on separatism.

When she returned to the United States, she was energized by the black movement for liberty and for the first time determined to become completely involved in the cause. She continued to work on her doctorate degree at the University of California at San Diego, studying under Marcuse, who was then teaching there. She finished her master's courses in one year and by this time was a Marxist, although she had done little to apply or spread her views about communism.

Davis was not always readily accepted by African Americans. She had made many white friends while studying in mostly white colleges and living abroad, and some blacks were bothered by this and by the fact that she had lived an upper middle-class existence far removed from the very poor. Also, she was light skinned and had a white grandfather, which caused some African Americans to be skeptical of her.

In 1965, Davis was hired as an acting assistant professor at UCLA. To gain understanding about communism, she visited Cuba and toiled alongside sugarcane workers, coming away convinced that the workers were not being exploited. Soon an article appeared in the university's *Daily Bruin* written by an FBI informant stating that Davis was a communist. This story spread and soon appeared in the *San Francisco Examiner*. The Board of Regents of the university at first did nothing, but in 1969, under pressure and the direction of then governor Ronald Reagan, she was fired. The firing did not take effect immediately, so she had time to appeal the decision. She was questioned about her communist affiliations. She won in court and was rehired as political connections had historically not been a cause for dismissal. She continued to teach, but to legally get rid of her, the university did not rehire her for the 1970–1971 year. The university cited breach of professional ethics and her support of three African American inmates of California's Soledad Prison, who had been convicted of killing a prison guard even though the three were unarmed.

Davis had become a leader in the defense of the three men who were known as the Soledad Brothers: John Clutchette, Fleeta Drumgo, and George Jackson. She held rallies and made speeches on their behalf. The activism took place as part of the

Che-Lumumba Club, an all-black militant collective of the Communist Party in California, which was formed to fight for black justice. Angela met George Jackson on a visit to the prison, and they immediately formed a strong bond. She became friends with his 17-year-old younger brother Jonathan, who acted as her bodyguard. Threats had been made on Angela's life as well as on members of Che-Lumumba, so she had purchased guns, which she kept at the club's headquarters.

Jonathan Jackson was intent on freeing his brother and planned to take hostages and hold them until the Soledad Brothers were released. In August 1970, Jonathan smuggled weapons registered to Angela Davis into the Marin County Courthouse and gave guns to three prisoners in the courtroom: James McClain, William Christmas, and Ruchell Magee. They attempted to kidnap and hold hostage Judge Harold Haley and Gary Thomas and three women jurors. A shootout followed, and the judge was killed. Jonathan Jackson, James McClain, and William Christmas also died.

Davis was sought for questioning, as she had been deeply involved in the cause to help the Soledad Brothers and her guns had been used. She also was in love with George Jackson. The FBI placed her on the list of Ten Most Wanted fugitives, which meant she could be shot on sight, so she fled and went in to hiding. She feared for her life at the hands of law enforcement, as it was assumed that officers often killed blacks who were wanted, both the innocent and the guilty. She was finally tracked down in New York City staying with a friend, John Poindexter. He was also arrested, but acquitted in April 1971. The FBI turned her over to the New York City Police Department. She was charged with kidnapping, murder, and conspiracy, and was taken to the Women's House of Detention in Greenwich Village. She was locked into a cell in the psychiatric ward. Here she saw firsthand how the legal system mistreated women who had not been convicted of any crimes, but were housed in deplorable conditions without access to competent counsel.

Her attorneys—John Apt, who had defended communists, and Margaret Burnham, a close friend—fought against her extradition to California, where the death penalty was on the books. Eventually, they lost the battle and she was returned to California to stand trial. Both the federal and state governments spent millions on security as they feared violent attempts to free her.

Davis was incarcerated for 16 months. The outpouring of support for her was worldwide, but anyone related to her, and all her friends, were harassed by police. Many were arrested and abused. Her prison stay depressed her, as it illustrated so clearly all that was wrong with a prison system that allowed harsher treatment for blacks than for whites. She feared for her life and was afraid to sleep as she knew that many African Americans were murdered in prisons and no one was ever held responsible. In fact, George Jackson was killed in prison in 1971 by a guard who claimed Jackson was trying to escape.

In early 1972, Davis was released on bail, and her lawyers immediately planned to go to trial. The trial lasted for several months, and on June 4, 1972, the jury acquitted Davis on all counts.

After her release, Davis continued her numerous and dissident activities, writing, lecturing, and teaching. She ran as a Communist Party candidate for U.S. vice president in 1980 and 1984. She left the Communist Party in 1991. In 1997, Davis addressed an event sponsored by the Diverse Sexuality and Gender Alliance at Johns Hopkins University, where she verified that she is a lesbian, viewing her sexuality and statement regarding it as a political issue. In her view, "every facet of life is weighted with political significance" (DiscoverTheNetworks.org).

In 2008, Davis retired from the University of California, where she was professor emeritus of the History of Consciousness, but she continues to advocate for racial, gender, and gay rights, and reforming the U.S. penal system, which, she charges, incarcerates an inordinate number of African Americans and Hispanics for profits. Her numerous books include *If They Come in the Morning: Voices of Resistance* (1971), *Angela Davis: An Autobiography* (1974), *Women, Race and Class* (1981), and *Women, Culture, and Politics* (1989).

Anni Margrethe Callaghan

See also Carmichael, Stokely/Ture, Kwame

References

"Angela Davis." DiscoverTheNetworks.org: A Guide to the Political Left, n.d. http://www.discoverthenetworks.org/individualProfile.asp?indid=1303 (accessed May 29, 2010).

Aptheker, Bettina. *The Morning Breaks: The Trial of Angela Davis*. New York: International Publishers, 1975.

Davis, Angela Y. *Angela Davis: An Autobiography*. New York: Bernard Geis Associates Book/Random House, 1974.

Jackson, James E. *Revolutionary Tracings*. New York: International Publishers, 1974.

James, Joy, ed. *The Angela Y. Davis Reader*. Oxford, UK, and Malden, MA: Blackwell Publishers, 1998.

Major, Reginald. *Justice in the Round: The Trial of Angela Davis*. New York: Third Press, 1973.

Nadelson, Regina. *Who Is Angela Davis?* New York: Peter H. Wyden, 1972.

Stone, Nick. "Angela Davis: Black Liberation and Socialism." *Permanent Revolution*, November 2, 2008. http://www.permanentrevolution.net/entry/2392 (accessed May 29, 2010).

Day, Dorothy (1897–1980)

"Dorothy Day remains . . . the radical conscience of American Catholicism," noted Stephen J. Krupa in *America Magazine* (2001, 7). Dorothy Day was an activist who tried to bring about social justice through nonviolent actions. She was a political radical but also a religious conservative, a combination that confused many casual observers. Some praised her pacifism and her civil disobedience, calling her a saint. Others referred to her as a subversive seeking to undermine the American capitalist system through her advocacy for Christian communism.

Born on November 8, 1897, in Brooklyn, New York, Dorothy was the third of five children of John and Grace (Satterlee) Day. The Days moved to Oakland, California, across the Bay from San Francisco, where her father was a sportswriter for a local newspaper and the family enjoyed a comfortable lifestyle with household servants. After the 1906 San Francisco earthquake that left their house in shambles, the family moved to Chicago, but John Day struggled to find another newspaper job. The family lived in what Dorothy called a "dingy six-room flat." The apartment was over a tavern on Chicago's South Side, and Dorothy confessed that she felt ashamed of her home with its make-do furniture of crates and kegs and curtains hanging from fishing poles. However, during this period, she began to understand what it was like to be on the lower rungs of the social ladder and to empathize with people dealing every day with economic hardships.

Fortunately for the Day family, they soon overcame their poverty. John Day found a job as a sports editor, and they were able to move to Chicago's North Side, a more prosperous area of the city near Lake Michigan. She attended Chicago's public schools and also studied on her own. She read religious works and numerous biblical passages, and also such works as Dostoyevsky's *The Brothers Karamazov* (1880) and Russian anarchist Peter Kropotkin's *Memoirs of a Revolutionist* (1899).

Day was especially impressed with Upton Sinclair's novel *The Jungle* (1906), an exposé of the filthy and dangerous meat-packing industry in Chicago. Against the slaughterhouse background, Sinclair wove his tale of an impoverished immigrant family that experiences the hard, dangerous life in their slum neighborhood. Jurgis, one of its members, tries to escape the miserable working conditions and his family life and in the process eventually joins the Socialist Party. The story prompted Dorothy to take long walks to the city's stockyard district. Walking the streets, she felt connected to the people in the area. "Their interests were to be mine," she wrote. "I had received a call, a vocation, a direction to my life" (Day 1980, 38). That "call" had spiritual undertones, but for much of her young adult years, she was conflicted about religion, rejecting it for a time as a "prop" that she felt "I must ruthlessly cut out of my life" (Day 1980, 43).

In 1914 at the age of 16, Day received a scholarship to the University of Illinois in Urbana, where she studied history, science, Latin, and English. She joined the Socialist Party, although she seldom went to meetings. She was greatly influenced by writers who raised her awareness of the poor and stressed the need for social reforms. She noted that while she "was free to go to college," she also "was mindful of girls working in stores and factories through their youth and afterward married to men who were slaves in those same factories. The Marxist slogan 'Workers of the world, unite, you have nothing to lose but your chains' seemed a most stirring battle cry, a clarion call that made me feel one with the masses, apart from the bourgeoisie, the smug, the satisfied" (Ellsberg 1988, 14).

In 1916, Day's father took a job with the *Morning Telegraph*, a New York newspaper, and the entire family moved East again. Day realized she missed her family a great deal and decided to go to New York with them. Since she intended to be a writer, she had no regrets about leaving school to pursue her career. In New York, her first job was as a reporter for the *Call*, a socialist newspaper. There she learned about the work of various labor unions, among them the Industrial Workers of the World (IWW), organized by such activists as William "Big Bill" Haywood, Eugene Debs, Mother Jones, and Lucy Parsons. The IWW, frequently called the "Wobblies," hoped to form one large labor organization that would help replace the capitalist system with socialism. In her stories for the newspaper, Day often covered union meetings and their protests. She later worked for the *Masses*, a socialist/communist publication.

When the United States entered World War I in 1917, Day along with many of her friends, who were anarchists, socialists, or communists, opposed the war. Day wrote protest pieces for the *Masses*, which resulted in the arrest of her editor for obstructing the war effort. Numerous pacifists, conscientious objectors, and other antiwar protesters faced beatings, arrests, jail time, and sometimes torture and death during the war.

Authorities suppressed publication of the *Masses*, and Day decided to accept an invitation from a friend to accompany her to a suffragist rally in Washington, D.C., where protesters planned to picket the White House. Women wore suffragist banners and marched in groups. Boys threw stones and soldiers and sailors attacked the women, attempting to tear off their banners. Police arrived to arrest the pickets and jail them in an abandoned workhouse in Occoquan, Virginia. Guards brutally beat, kicked, choked, and nearly killed some of the inmates. Day's group was sentenced to 30 days. "I would be utterly crushed by misery before I was released," she wrote (Day 1988, 79). The inhumanity, cruelty, and terrible injustices devastated her.

After her release from prison, Day believed she ought to do something to help people in need, and took a job as a nurse trainee at King's County Hospital in Brooklyn. She stayed for a year, nursing throughout the influenza epidemic of 1918. About this time, she met newspaperman Lionel Moise, with whom she had a love affair, became pregnant, and, in 1919, had an abortion.

After the war, she decided to travel to Europe and explore places described in the stories of Dickens, Balzac, Hugo, and other literary figures. Returning to the United States, she appeared unable to settle on any specific goal and held a series of different jobs from cashier to an editorial assistant at the *Liberator*, successor to the *Masses*. Meantime, she wrote a semiautobiographical novel, *The Eleventh Virgin*, in which she described her bohemian lifestyle in Greenwich Village, New York City, her various lovers, and her abortion. She later regretted the publication, but movie rights sold for $5,000, a large sum at the time that allowed her to buy a small home on Staten Island, New York.

In 1925, Day and anarchist Forster Batterham, the man she loved, began a life together in a common-law marriage. He was a biologist whose "enthusiasms were such that I could not help but be fascinated by the new world of nature he opened up to me," Day wrote (Day 1988, 115). She longed to have a child, but because of her abortion, she feared that would be impossible. She was delighted when she became pregnant. The couple's daughter, Tamar Theresa, was born in 1927.

The relationship between Day and Batterham faltered, however, primarily because he was an anarchist and atheist and she had been developing strong Christian convictions, in spite of years of questioning and doubt about religious beliefs. She began going to Mass on a regular basis. As she became more absorbed in the supernatural, Batterham rebelled. He believed religion was escapism; reason was the only thing that ruled. He had no use for the Church or any state institution, and Day found it impossible to talk about religion with him.

When Day decided she would join the Roman Catholic Church, the breakup with Batterham became ever more certain. "He would not talk about the faith and relapsed into a complete silence if I tried to bring up the subject," Day wrote. "The point of my bringing it up was that I could not become a Catholic and continue living with him" (Day 1980, 147). Her bohemian associates and her partner's atheism were unacceptable to a practicing Catholic. She knew she had to give up her bohemian lifestyle if she was to be true to her faith.

Day converted to Catholicism and had her daughter baptized in the Catholic Church. However, she was critical of the Church's alignment with the wealthy and powerful. Her conversion to Catholicism stemmed from a belief that the "Church was Christ made visible."

After her breakup with Batterham in 1927, Day worked as a screen writer, library researcher, and freelance journalist for Catholic publications such as *Commonweal* and *Catholic Reporter*. In 1932, she met Peter Maurin, a French priest and Catholic reformer who had developed a philosophy that combined the ideals of communism and Catholicism. Maurin was a visionary who believed in changing the social order through an action program that included hospitality houses for needy people.

Maurin and Day shared common concerns about social justice and serving victims of poverty. Together they launched the Catholic Worker movement, and in 1933, at the beginning of the Great Depression, they established a newspaper by the same name to spread information about their purpose: to establish communal farming and hospitality houses for the urban poor. The paper sold for one cent per copy, and it is still being published at the same price. Circulation of the *Catholic Worker* in 1933 was 100,000 and by 1936 reached 150,000. The paper publicized the movement and prompted people to donate food, clothing, and money to help the homeless and unemployed.

In 1934, the cofounders of the movement established the St. Joseph's House of Hospitality in New York City. Within 10 years, there were at least 30 more hospitality houses across the United States, and farm communes also developed. Day herself vowed to live a life of poverty and continually spoke out against materialism in whatever form it took. She spent many of her days in the New York hospitality house, and worked to restore dignity and self-respect to the poor, homeless, and unwanted.

Because of her outspoken opposition to the capitalist system and her pacifism, the FBI often investigated her activities. But she continued her work undaunted and was even somewhat scornful of the federal authorities. For more than 50 years, she continued to write, publishing numerous articles and books including *From Union Square to Rome* (1938), *House of Hospitality* (1939), her autobiography *The Long Loneliness* (1952), and *The Duty of Delight: The Diaries of Dorothy Day* (edited by Robert Ellsberg, 2008).

Day's last years were spent at Maryhouse, which had become a shelter for homeless women. She continued to write for the *Catholic Worker* whenever she could, and near the end of her life received a great deal of media attention. She died on November 29, 1980, in New York City. She was remembered as a kind of saint. An editorial in the *Progressive*, for example, noted that "Dorothy Day deserved to be called a saint," but it was not a "sentiment she would have appreciated." Nevertheless, Day "devoted her life to achieving a peaceful and just world. She didn't embrace peace and justice as a goal or a cause or a vocation: she lived peace and justice, and she brooked no compromise" (Knoll 1994, 4).

A call for Day's canonization as a saint began in 1983, and in 2000, Vatican officials approved the start of the lengthy investigation of Day's life that could lead to sainthood.

See also Debs, Eugene V.; Jones, Mary Harris; Parsons, Lucy

References

The Catholic Worker Movement. http://www.catholicworker.org/ (accessed May 5, 2011).

Day, Dorothy. *The Long Loneliness: The Autobiography of Dorothy Day*. San Francisco: HarperCollins, 1980. Reprint of 1952 edition.

Ellsberg, Robert, ed. *By Little and By Little: The Selected Writings of Dorothy Day*. New York: Knopf, 1988.

Knoll, Erwin. " 'Put Away Your Flags.' " *Progressive*, April 1994.

Krupa, Stephen J., S.J. "Celebrating Dorothy Day." *America Magazine—the National Catholic Weekly*, August 27, 2001.

Lynch, Dan. "Dorothy Day's Pro-Life Memories." *Catholic Exchange*, September 24, 2002. http://www.catholiceducation.org/articles/abortion/ab0063.html (accessed March 8, 2010).

McCarthy, Tim. "Light of Day Shines Yet at Catholic Worker." *National Catholic Reporter*, May 21, 1993.

Nies, Judith. *Nine Women: Portraits from the American Radical Tradition*. Berkeley, Los Angeles, and London: University of California Press, 2002.

Debs, Eugene V. (1855–1926)

"Well, I've heard so damned much about you, Mr. Debs, that I am now glad to meet you personally" (Dean 2004, 128). Those were the words with which President Warren Harding greeted Eugene Victor Debs, who was a notorious labor union rabble rouser and avowed socialist, jailed for being a subversive. He had stopped by for an impromptu "social call" at the White House. After being sentenced to 10 years' confinement under the country's Espionage Act, Debs was en route to his own home upon his early release from prison, made possible by Harding.

On December 24, 1921, the headlines of the front page of the *New York Times* blared: "Harding Frees Debs and 23 Others Held for War Violations; Socialist Leader's Sentence of Ten Years Is Commuted, Effective Christmas." The ensuing article went on to explain that "There is no question of his [Debs's] guilt. . . . He was by no means as rabid and outspoken in his expressions as many others, and but for his prominence and the resulting far-reaching effect of his words, very probably might not have received the sentence he did. He is an old man, not strong physically. He is a man of much personal charm and impressive personality, which qualifications make him a dangerous man calculated to mislead the unthinking and affording excuse for those with criminal intent" (*New York Times* 1921, 1).

When Debs was born on November 5, 1855, in Terre Haute, Indiana, his parents named him after famous French writers Victor Hugo and Eugene Sue. His parents, Marguerite and Jean Daniel Debs, immigrated from their more than comfortable life in the Alsace region of France to the United States.

The Debs eventually settled in Terre Haute and made a life for themselves and their family. However, it was not an easy one, and young Eugene was forced to drop out of school at age 14 to help out financially. He began his career in town working at various positions with the local railway, joining the Brotherhood of Locomotive Firemen (BLF), maintaining his affiliation even when he changed careers, and accepting work as a clerk for a wholesale grocery store. Debs was the first secretary of the Terre Haute BLF chapter and before long was appointed editor of the *Locomotive Fireman's Magazine*. He also served as BLF grand secretary-treasurer from 1980 to 1981, remaining as the editor for some time and helping to grow the membership with his written "oratorical" style. He was often described as something akin to an evangelical, although he was never overly fond of organized religion. After a sole visit to a cathedral where a priest delivered a sermon on hell and threatened eternal damnation, he left "with a rich and royal hatred of the priest as a person, and a loathing for the church as an institution" (Bromell 1978, 15).

Concurrent to his union involvement, Debs began developing his political interests. In 1879, he ran for and was elected to the first of two terms as Terre Haute city clerk. In 1884, he successfully ran on the Democratic ticket for a single term to represent Terre Haute in the Indiana General Assembly. The

Eugene V. Debs, about 1909. He founded one of the first industrial unions, was an avowed socialist, and was jailed for being a subversive. (Library of Congress)

following year, he married Kate Metzel. They remained childless and, from all accounts, it appears that Debs devoted most of his efforts to his dissident and political causes at the expense of his personal life.

Despite his active involvement and local leadership roles in the BLF, Debs eventually concluded that craft unions—those that were segmented (broken into separate groups such as firemen, brakemen, switchmen, and so forth)—were less effectual than industry unions—those that consolidated and encompassed all factions of a particular industry. The former were typically more conservative in their approach and tended to focus their agendas on providing benefits and services to their members. The latter tended to be much more assertive on their members' behalf in pursuit of collective bargaining. So, in 1893, Debs founded one of the first industrial unions: the American Railroad Union (ARU) with headquarters in Chicago, Illinois. The negative national economic climate, coupled with the charismatic Debs at its helm as president, caused membership to grow rapidly during ARU's first year. That year was also notable with ARU's successful labor strike against the Great Northern Railroad. The conflict settled after a mere 18 days, with almost every demand the union made being conceded by management.

The subsequent year proved more tumultuous for the fledgling union. At ARU's May 1894 annual convention, a delegation of members employed by the Pullman Palace Car Company appealed to their colleagues for support in their struggles against management. Pullman had laid off workers and reduced wages with no commensurate reduction in prices at company-owned stores where employees were required to shop, or in rents set by their Pullman landlord; working conditions were also substandard. Debs was in favor of negotiating with Pullman, but agreed to go along with the membership's decision to impose a boycott on the company, effectively stopping rail traffic between Chicago and all points west, an act that included interference with delivery of the U.S. mail. A federal injunction was ordered to halt the obstruction of interstate commerce and, against the wishes of Illinois governor John P. Altgeld, President Grover Cleveland sent in troops to smash the strike. As a result, Debs was sentenced to a six-month prison term, which he served out in Woodstock, Illinois, in 1895. Debs's lawyer, Clarence Darrow, unsuccessfully appealed his client's case all the way to the U.S. Supreme Court.

It was during his incarceration that Debs's political philosophies shifted strongly to the left. He had time to absorb the readings of Karl Marx and came to appreciate the tenets of socialism. Once released from prison, Debs still was concerned with labor issues; now, however, he felt politics offered the most powerful arena from which to effect change. Convinced that capitalism caused competition and bred disharmony between the classes, Debs was a convert for a socialistic society. He was a radical in his thinking—considered a dangerous revolutionary by many—but he rejected violence at all costs. He helped to found the Social Democracy of America and then, about a year later in 1898, broke off to form the Social Democratic Party of the United States, which was renamed the Socialist Party of America in 1901 and finally became the Social Democratic Party in 1972. Debs was elected chair of the executive board of the national council of the group in 1898 and, thus, was a natural choice when the party put forward its first U.S. presidential candidate in 1900.

Debs was the face of the Socialist Party in the United States. In those days, there were limited media sources that later generations would take for granted. If Debs wanted to publicize and advocate for socialism, it usually meant doing so face to face—literally. He traveled extensively to give speeches across the country. And, once again, his journalistic skills were put to use, this time writing guest editorials for *Appeal to Reason*, a progressive voice that rallied many to the causes of the Socialist Party. And while there was frequent disunity among party members. Debs typically stayed above the fray, sticking to championing the core party beliefs, including: protecting workers' rights to form and join unions and, when necessary, to strike; passing child labor laws; improving workplace safety, particularly in industries such as mining and railways; and achieving women's suffrage. With regard to the latter, Debs and the Socialist Party can claim a large part of the credit for women gaining the right to vote. Debs had been a vocal advocate on this issue since 1900.

Debs was once again the Socialist Party's presidential candidate in 1904 and would be so also in 1908, 1912, and 1920; the only time he did not run was in 1916, when he declined the party's nomination. In 1905, Debs joined together with Bill Hayward to form the Industrial Workers of the World (IWW), but there was a fair amount of dissension among the leadership, not the least of which was Debs's commitment to nonviolence. After a short time, he parted ways with the group, as it grew more and more militant in its views and actions.

Debs continued to maintain his high profile as the recognized voice of socialism. When the United States entered World War I, he embarked on a speaking tour, railing against the overall evils of war. He expressed his thoughts in one such speech that took place in Canton, Ohio, on June 16, 1918. With agents for J. Edgar Hoover's Protective Services sitting in the crowd taking notes, Debs expounded, "The master class has had all to gain and nothing to lose, while the subject class had nothing to gain and all to lose—including their lives ... [T]he working class who fight all the battles, the working class who make the supreme sacrifices, the working class who freely shed their blood and furnish the corpses, have never yet had a voice in either declaring war or making peace. It is the ruling class that invariably does both" (Debs 1948, 425).

This speech was part of the evidence on which a case was built to charge Debs with sedition under the U.S. Espionage Act of 1917. In his defense, Debs called no witnesses; rather, he was granted the unusual courtesy of addressing those present in the courtroom, uninterrupted, for two hours. That strategy proved unsuccessful and, on September 12, 1918, he was found guilty.

Debs was first sent to Moundsville, Pennsylvania, and then moved on to the federal penitentiary in Atlanta. While imprisoned, he found a new cause to rally behind: penal reform, writing columns about the subject during his incarceration. After he regained his freedom, he expanded them into his one and only book, *Walls and Bars* (published posthumously in 1927). He also conducted his fifth and final run for the U.S. presidency from prison, complete with campaign buttons showing Debs outside the penitentiary in his prison garb, captioned: "For President Convict No. 9653." Nearly a million votes were cast for convict Debs.

President Woodrow Wilson refused to consider pardoning Debs, having been at the receiving end of many of the crusader's critiques. However, President Harding was somewhat more receptive to the idea. Thus, on Christmas Day, 1921, Debs found himself a free man, although not fully pardoned and without having his right to vote restored.

His health greatly diminished, Debs's scope of physical activity was similarly restricted during his final years. He worked on his book and did all he could to continue support of his lifelong beliefs. Debs succumbed to heart failure on October 20, 1926, in a sanitarium in Elmhurst, Illinois. On his passing, he was mourned not only by those he championed, but also by some opponents who developed a grudging respect of him as a fair foe.

See also Darrow, Clarence

References

Brommel, Bernard J. *Eugene V. Debs: Spokesman For Labor and Socialism*. Chicago: Charles H. Kerr, 1978.

Dean, John Wesley. *Warren G. Harding*. New York: Henry Holt, 2004.

Debs, Eugene V. *Writings and Speeches of Eugene V. Debs*. New York: Hermitage Press, 1948.

Eugene V. Debs Foundation. http://www.eugenevdebs.com/ (accessed April 22, 2010).

Ginger, Ray. *The Bending Cross: A Biography of Eugene Victor Debs*. New Brunswick, NJ: Rutgers University Press, 1949. Reprint ed., Kirkville, MO: Thomas Jefferson University Press at Northeast Missouri State University, 1992.

"Harding Frees Debs and 23 Others Held for War Violations; Socialist Leader's Sentence of Ten Years Is Commuted, Effective Christmas." *New York Times*, December 24, 1921. http://query.nytimes.com/gst/abstract.html?res=9B0DE2D71539E133A25757C2A9649D946095D6CF (accessed May 5, 2010).

Pietrusza, David. *1920: The Year of Six Presidents*. New York: Carroll & Graf, 2007.

Salvatore, Nick. *Eugene V. Debs: Citizen and Socialist*. Urbana: University of Illinois Press, 1982.

Dees, Morris (1936–)

He has had many enemies who call him a liar, pervert, womanizer, or more despicable terms. They have spread their messages on hundreds of Internet sites and through rallies and publications. But supporters of Morris Dees, a prominent civil rights lawyer, refer to him as a hero who has won widely publicized court cases against such hate groups as the Aryan Nations, White Aryan Resistance, neo-Nazi skinheads, and the White Patriot Party, a paramilitary group that targets people of color, Jews, homosexuals, and others who do not subscribe to their white supremacist beliefs. These groups have harassed and threatened to kill Dees and have set fire to his home and office. Nevertheless, he has chosen to pursue a career to make the haters pay for their crimes.

Morris Seligman Dees Jr. was born in Shorter, Alabama, on December 16, 1936, the first of five children in the family. His parents, Morris Seligman Dees Sr. and Annie Ruth (Frazer) Dees were tenant farmers, working on cotton plantations and eventually buying 125 acres near Mount Meigs, Alabama, to grow cotton. The elder Dees also owned a cotton gin operation that separated the cotton fibers from the seeds.

During his early childhood, Morris worked in the fields with black farmhands and played with their children. From his parents, Morris learned to respect people whatever their racial or economic background. He often tells the story of his first lesson in that regard. When he was five years old, he was out in the cotton field and called a black worker an insulting name. Morris Sr. pulled off his belt and whipped his son's behind. As Dees recalled the incident, he explained to a reporter that his father was not a liberal or a saint. "He just gave black people what they didn't get most anywhere else, a modicum of respect. Just sitting with black friends of my daddy's, I began to feel their hurt, and I took it personal. I'm not a crusader. I don't represent causes. I represent people who have been hurt" (Shaw 1991, 50).

Dees did not plan to be a civil rights lawyer. He aspired to be a farmer and vowed he would own his own land and earn a good living from it. He did not want to struggle financially like his father had. He began earning money as a child, buying and raising pigs and selling them for a profit. While a teenager, he created a business selling the refuse from his father's cotton gin; people purchased the material to use for mulch. He bought hogs and cattle to raise for market, and constantly looked for ways to make money. By the time he graduated in 1955, he had saved $5,000. His father urged him to go to college and become a lawyer, but Morris eloped during his senior year, marrying Beverly Crum, a teenager whose parents were in the military; she longed for a stable life on a farm that Morris Dees still hoped to buy one day.

The elder Dees continued to encourage Morris to go to law school, and in 1955, Morris and Beverly Dees went to Tuscaloosa, where he enrolled at the University of Alabama. It was during that year that he heard about the kidnapping, beating, and murder of a young black teenager—14-year-old Emmett Till—by two white men. The story enraged much of the nation, and Dees said it "touched me so deeply that for the first time I seriously examined the Southern way of life" (Dees and Fiffer 1991, 76). The

Southern Poverty Law Center director Morris Dees stands in front of Montgomery, Alabama's Civil Rights Memorial. Dees has been a staunch supporter of the civil rights movement since its earliest days. (AP/Wide World Photos)

following year, the effects of white supremacy beliefs were on display when under a federal court order, Autherine Lucy, a black student, entered the University of Alabama, and Dees watched from the Student Union building as a mob of angry white people, including Ku Klux Klan (KKK) members, assailed Lucy with insults and tried to smash her car. "I felt sick to my stomach. In Autherine Lucy's face, I saw the faces of many of the black people I had known in [Mount Meigs]. . . . all my sympathy for the underdog came out at that moment," Dees wrote (Dees and Fiffer 1991, 77).

Another life-changing experience happened in 1963 when white supremacists bombed a black Baptist church in Birmingham, Alabama, killing four little girls in Sunday school. Dees tried to get members of his all-white church to pray for the girls and their families, but the congregation walked out on him. Years later, he realized this was the beginning of a great change in his life—he would commit himself to civil rights and justice.

While in law school, Dees and his friend Millard Fuller developed a direct-mail business. Like Dees, Fuller came from a sharecropper family and as a child created a business selling farm animals. After graduating from law school in 1960, Dees and Fuller set up a law practice in Montgomery and expanded their business, which was called Fuller and Dees Marketing, with offices in Montgomery, Alabama, and Chicago, Illinois. Their enterprise included a publishing company that produced cookbooks and brought in millions of dollars in profits for the two lawyers. In 1965, Dees bought Fuller's share of the marketing company and

Fuller went on to become a multimillionaire lawyer who eventually founded Habitat for Humanity, which provides housing for low-income people.

After Dees established his law firm in Montgomery, he became involved in various civil rights activities, although he was not connected with the efforts of Martin Luther King Jr. or other activists. He supported the Voting Rights Act of 1965 and became president of the Alabama chapter of the American Civil Liberties Union (ACLU), which did not sit well with many whites in Montgomery; they ostracized his family. Yet Dees persevered. According to numerous reports, he was inspired to continue his civil rights efforts after reading a book about Clarence Darrow, who gave up a lucrative legal practice to represent labor organizers. "It was the mentorship that I needed to get the courage to completely get out of the business world and go full-force as a civil rights lawyer," Dees told an interviewer (Groth 2009).

During the late 1960s, Morris and Beverly divorced, and he later married Maureene Buck who had worked for his company, blending a family of Morris's two sons and Maureene's son and daughter. Two years after their marriage, another daughter was born. At the time Dees remarried, he also sold his business to the *Times Mirror*, owner of the *Los Angeles Times* and other newspapers. Dees and a partner from New York City, Joe Levine Jr., established a law firm. On some occasions, Dees worked for the ACLU. In one case, he argued for the free speech rights of Yale chaplain William Sloane Coffin, a Vietnam War protester. Because of his protest activities, Coffin was not allowed to speak at Auburn University in Montgomery. Dees won the case but suffered the wrath of the KKK, who vandalized his office.

In 1971, Dees and Levine formed the nonprofit Southern Poverty Law Center (SPLC), a legal and educational foundation. "Our primary goal was to fight the effects of poverty with innovative lawsuits and education programs . . . [targeting] customs, practices, and laws that were used to keep low-income blacks and whites powerless," Dees wrote (Dees and Fiffer 1991, 132).

In 1972, Dees worked on Senator George McGovern's campaign for U.S. president. Dees was the chief fundraiser, bringing in an estimated $20 million. McGovern lost the election to Richard Nixon, but Dees gained a valuable asset—McGovern's mailing list, which Dees used to solicit funds for his SPLC.

Since the early 1970s, Dees and the SPLC have won numerous cases that have helped protect the rights of minorities and the powerless. As chief counsel for SPLC, Dees has obtained multimillion-dollar verdicts against violent hate groups. One widely publicized case in 1981 was on behalf of Vietnamese fishermen in Galveston Bay, Texas. The Vietnamese were refugees who had come to the United States from their war-torn country. They owned shrimp boats in Galveston Bay, and between 1979 and 1981, arsonists set fire to several of their boats. Snipers shot at them, and armed men harassed the fishermen. Investigations and Klan rallies that were covered by news reporters showed that Louis Beam, grand dragon of the Texas Knights of the KKK, and a military group of Klan members had threatened the Vietnamese. Dees and his partner filed a lawsuit against Beam and the KKK, and won the case for the Vietnamese—U.S. marshals were assigned to protect the fishermen.

Another successful case, *Donald v. United Klans of America* in 1987, was against members of the United Klans of America (UKA) who beat and strangled 19-year-old Michael Donald and hung his body from a tree in

Mobile, Alabama. Three Klan members were found guilty of murder; two received life sentences and a third, Henry Francis Hays, received a death sentence and was executed in 1997. In addition, the court awarded Michael's mother $7 million, which bankrupt the UKA.

In 1990, Dees and the SPLC brought a civil suit against Tom Metzger and his White Aryan Resistance group for inciting three skinheads in Portland, Oregon, to beat to death a young Ethiopian college student, Mulegeta Seraw. A jury found them guilty and awarded the Mulegeta family $10 million in punitive damages.

The successful lawsuits resulted in numerous threats on Dees's life by white supremacist and racist groups. Some have attempted to assassinate him. When he was out on his 2,000-acre ranch in Mathews, Alabama, he carried a gun and was accompanied by armed bodyguards. In 2001, he and his fifth wife, Susan Star Dees, moved to Montgomery, where he had installed a sophisticated security system for his home and the law center.

Although Dees "is vastly admired by many people, he is also fiercely disliked and is seldom out of the spotlight," write biographers Diana Klebanow and Franklin L. Jonas. Some say he "craves attention." Critics also fault him for his failure to mention in his autobiography his "third wife, Mary Farmer—who ran an abortion clinic that he partially financed.... The same fate later befell his fourth wife, Elizabeth Breen Dees, who was omitted from the reprint of his autobiography" (Klebanow and Jonas 2003, 468).

Along with fighting for civil rights, Dees and the SPLC have established a Teaching Tolerance program that produces and distributes free films, magazines, books, and other materials that promote tolerance and respect for diversity in American schools. The Center also publishes the *Intelligence Report*, a quarterly magazine that provides information on extremist hate groups in the United States.

Dees has received numerous awards. In 1987, the Trial Lawyers for Public Justice named him the Trial Lawyer of the Year. The American Bar Association honored him with the Young Lawyers' Distinguished Service Award, and he also has received the ACLU's Roger Baldwin Award. The National Education Association awarded him the Martin Luther King Jr. Memorial Award in 1990. He received the Humanitarian Award from the University of Alabama in 1993 and the National Education Association's Friend of Education Award in 2001. In 2006, the University of Alabama School of Law established the Morris Dees Justice Award to honor a lawyer noted for addressing social justice issues. In 2010, the John Marshall Law School Alumni Association presented Dees with the Freedom Award. As Dees noted, "I certainly have had my share of victories and pats on the back and awards. But the greatest reward is to look into the face of somebody you've helped who would otherwise be powerless and have few champions, and to be able to go up against the powerful and the rich and violent people and gain a sense of justice" (Groth 2009).

In 1991, a television movie entitled *Line of Fire: The Morris Dees Story* depicted Dees's battle against hate groups. His books include an autobiography, *A Season for Justice* (1991), *Hate on Trial: The Case against America's Most Dangerous Neo-Nazi* (1993), and *Gathering Storm: America's Militia Threat* (1996).

See also Coffin, William Sloane; Darrow, Clarence; King, Martin Luther, Jr.

References

Dees, Morris, and Steve Fiffer. *A Season for Justice: The Life and Times of Civil Rights Lawyer Morris Dees*. New York: Macmillan, 1991.

Dees, Morris, and Steve Fiffer. *Hate on Trial: The Case against America's Most Dangerous Neo-Nazi*. New York: Villard Books/Random House, 1993.

Groth, Aimée. "Q&A: Morris Dees." *Alabama Super Lawyers 2009*. May 2009. http://www.superlawyers.com/alabama/article/QandA-Morris-Dees/21f62c22-a996-4e33-87c9-10a6646468f6.html (accessed May 26, 2010).

Klebanow, Diana, and Franklin L. Jonas. *People's Lawyers: Crusaders for Justice in American History*. Armonk, NY: M. E. Sharpe, 2003.

Roane, Kit R. "He's Hated by the Haters." *U.S. News and World Report*. October 30, 2000, 16.

Shaw, Bill. "Morris Dees: A Wily Alabamian Uses the Courts to Wipe Out Hate Groups and Racial Violence." *People Weekly*, July 22, 1991.

Dellinger, David (1915–2004)

"When Dellinger's Yale class of 1936 held its fiftieth reunion, the reunion book carried the thoughts of the class's leading rebel. 'Lest my way of life sounds puritanical or austere,' he [Dellinger] wrote, 'I always emphasize that in the long run one can't satisfactorily say no to war, violence, and injustice unless one is simultaneously saying yes to life, love, and laughter' " (McCarthy 2004, 20).

Family, friends, and fans of David Dellinger endorse this quote as one that truly encapsulates his dissent and philosophy of life. Foes take quite another perspective. For many whose path Dellinger crossed during his lifetime, he did little to bring levity into their existence—his passionate causes were always ones deeply committed to nonviolence and pacifism. Dellinger made his mark as one of the preeminent antiwar and social activist crusaders of the twentieth century, taking a vow to foment change, from the bottom up, in a peaceable yet powerful fashion. How he came to set upon this course was counterintuitive to his privileged upbringing.

David was born on August 22, 1915, in Wakefield, Massachusetts, with the proverbial "silver spoon in his mouth." His grandmother was a prominent member of the Daughters of the American Revolution, claiming Benjamin Franklin in the family lineage. His father was a staunch Republican, a Yale and divinity school graduate; he was a "player" in the local political scene, a lawyer who counted among his friends notables such as then-governor Calvin Coolidge who went on to become president.

In high school, David was both an excellent student and an outstanding athlete, competing as a long-distance runner and tournament-level golfer. From his upbringing, it seemed likely that he would pursue a career in law or government, but even before entering college, he had begun to get other ideas about what direction his life might take. He entered Yale at age 17 "without a lot of questions about its class composition even though that concern had led me to refuse to spend a year at an exclusive prep school between high school and college" (Dellinger 1993, 17). Once there, however, his views about the differences experienced by the classes began to solidify. Greg Guma, former editor of *Toward Freedom*, a world affairs magazine whose board of directors Dellinger cochaired for more than a decade, worked closely with him for the last 20 years of his life. In an article, Guma includes an excerpt from Dellinger's autobiography, noting a particular event at Yale that shaped David's outlook:

It happened after a football game between Yale and Georgia. Tensions between the Yale students and "townies" were high ... In the ensuing fight, Dave decked one of them—and then experienced revulsion at what he'd done ... "The lesson I learned was as simple, direct and unarguable as the lesson a child learns the first time it puts its hand on a red-hot stove: Don't ever do it again! But the pain I felt was a spiritual pain, as if I had suddenly emerged from a fit of anger and realized that I had pressed a child's hand onto the stove. I knew that I would never be able to strike another human being again." ... He stayed with the young man he had hit, apologized, and walked him home. As they parted, Dave felt what he called "the power of our unexpected and unusual bonding." The impact of the encounter stayed with him. (Guma 2004)

Dellinger's political activism increased throughout his college days. He joined the cause of nonacademic university employees to form a union, against the advice of the dean who warned that the "communists" would try to harness him to aid in their organizational efforts. After becoming involved, Dellinger discovered that in fact, Christian radicals were spearheading the movement. Their love ethic made a huge impression on him, as did their commitment to nonviolent action—the spirit of which was in keeping with the teachings of Mohandas Gandhi.

He graduated in 1936 from Yale as a Phi Beta Kappa economics major and set sail for England where he had been awarded a year's study at Oxford. En route, he visited Spain, which was embroiled in its civil war. Although sympathetic to the cause of the Loyalist Communist troops, Dellinger's belief in nonviolence kept him from joining their ranks. So, he went on to Oxford as originally planned and also traveled to Nazi Germany and made other efforts to broaden his knowledge of the world's people.

Back in the United States, he returned to Yale for what was to be another year of postgraduate work. But, while in the middle of his studies, he took off, living the life of a vagabond hobo and intermingling with the common man for three years. He compared his experience to that of Saint Francis of Assisi, who had similarly rejected his privileged heritage. Dellinger's eyes were opened as he met not the drunkards and slackers that he had grown up hearing about, but "ordinary people" caught up in the havoc of the Depression, many who befriended and extended a helping hand to him, even when down on their own luck.

Dellinger decided to enroll in Union Theological Seminary (where his father had also attended) not to become a minister, but to deepen his perspectives. Because of his status as a seminary student, when the conscription law was passed in 1940, all he needed to do was register, not serve. However, his moral precepts would not allow him to do so, resulting in his being sentenced to a year at Danbury federal prison. Early on in his prison term, he was placed in solitary confinement for sitting in the Black section during the Saturday movie. Later, various protests resulted in his being thrown into "the hole," where there was no light or bed and it was damp and cold. The experience, while physically debilitating, was spiritually uplifting. Dellinger felt invigorated and developed an even stronger love for his fellow human beings and, indeed, all creatures.

Not long after his release from prison, Pearl Harbor was attacked and the United States was fully enmeshed in World War II. Dellinger jumped right into antiwar activities. It was at an antiwar speaking engagement at the National Conference of the Student Christian Movement in Ohio that a coed from Pacific College in Newburgh, Oregon, interviewed him. Betty Peterson shared his political activist leanings and, a month later, on February 4, 1942, David's father performed their marriage ceremony.

The two eventually had five children, but their family was never considered "typical." Betty largely held the family together while Dellinger charged off to advocate for his causes. From the early days of their marriage, they had little chance to settle into any sort of normalcy. Almost immediately after they exchanged their vows, as part of his work with the People's Peace Now Committee, Dellinger coordinated a Washington, D.C, protest of the continued bombings in Germany. Soon he found himself serving a two-year sentence at the prison farm outside the Lewisburg penitentiary. He again took on an activist role while in prison. He and others protested racial segregation in the dining halls, censorship of mail, and inhumane use of "the hole" for punishment.

After World War II, Dellinger joined forces with kindred spirits such as Dorothy Day to launch *Direct Action*, an antiwar magazine based on the precepts of nonviolence. This periodical took on several incarnations, in succession: *Alternative, Individual Action*, and, finally, *Liberation*—widely read and respected for two decades. Contributing writers included Noam Chomsky, Dorothy Day, and Howard Zinn. Dellinger's activities brought him a diverse circle of acquaintances and friends, spanning Ho Chi Minh, Eleanor Roosevelt, and members of the Black Panthers.

From the 1950s through the 1970s, he was involved in everything, from protests against the hydrogen bomb, to marches and freedom rides for racial equality, to antinuclear demonstrations. He was an active participant in groups such as the Peacemakers, the Committee for Nonviolent Revolution, the Fellowship of International Communities, the National Coordinating Committee to End the War in Vietnam, and the War Resisters League.

He worked with various antiwar groups as chair of the Fifth Avenue Vietnam Peace Parade Committee and helped bring Dr. Martin Luther King Jr. and James Bevel into leadership positions in the 1960s. In 1964, along with A. J. Muste and two radical Catholic priests, brothers Daniel and Philip Berrigan, he helped to produce a "declaration of conscience" encouraging resistance to the draft. He made his way to China and North Vietnam in 1967, still finding time to help coordinate that year's October march on the Pentagon about which Norman Mailer would later base his prize-winning book *Armies of the Night* (1968).

While his activities were varied, his causes had a central theme of seeking justice for the repressed and un- or underrepresented and, above all, doing so in a peaceful and nonviolent manner. His lifelong demonstrable commitment to the latter principle was called into question by the U.S. government in a very public way at the time of the 1968 Democratic Convention, held at the height of the Vietnam War protests in Chicago, Illinois. On August 18, Dellinger addressed 50,000 protesters gathered outside the Convention Hall. As the police swarmed in with clubs raised, Dellinger exhorted the peaceful crowd, "The whole world is watching!" And indeed it was, as millions watched horrific scenes of police brutality occur—live and unedited, with commentary provided by viewers' familiar dinnertime television commentators. The most prominent radical leaders of the antiwar movement, dubbed the "Chicago Eight," were arrested: Bobby Seale, Tom Hayden, Rennie Davis, Abbie Hoffman,

Jerry Rubin, Lee Weiner, John Froines, and David Dellinger. Charges of conspiracy and crossing over state lines to incite a riot were brought against the men, and the trial of the "Chicago Seven" (Seale's case was separated from the other defendants) commanded national attention. While awaiting trial, Dellinger and codefendant Davis were among a delegation of five who flew to Hanoi at the request of the Vietnamese, who released a group of U.S. prisoners of war into their care.

The trial, *U.S. v. David Dellinger et al.*, ran from September 1968 through February 1969. At its conclusion, Dellinger and four of the others were found guilty of conspiracy; sentences were also issued for defendants' "contemptuous conduct" during the trial. A mere year later, an appeals court acquitted Dellinger and the others of the conspiracy charge, citing Judge Julius Hoffman's handling of the case, as well as the FBI's case-related actions (bugging the defense counsel). Although the contempt citations were upheld, the appeals court declined to impose any sentences.

Unrest concerning the Vietnam War began to cool as President Nixon announced his plans in 1971 for the withdrawal of U.S. troops. That spring, Dellinger helped coordinate one of the last major Vietnam protests, the Mayday March, in Washington, D.C. When the country's focus shifted to the Watergate scandal the next year, Dellinger's own attentions began to reorient as well. He stopped publishing *Liberation* in 1975, but he took on a new periodical, *Seven Days*, which he edited for five years. In the 1980s, he accepted a position at Vermont College and set about writing his memoirs, *From Yale to Jail: The Life Story of a Moral Dissenter* (1993). He authored more books prior to his passing, such as *More Power than We Know* (1975) and *Vietnam Revisited: From Covert Action to Invasion to Reconstruction* (1986).

The 1996 Democratic National Convention was the first to be held in Chicago since the infamous one of 1968. A crowd of about 500 demonstrators gathered to protest a variety of issues. David Dellinger was front and center and, not surprisingly, was among the nine who were arrested—also including his grandson and Abbie Hoffman's son, Andrew—during a sit-in at the Dirksen Federal Building.

Even as he aged and he faced the challenges of Alzheimer's disease (a diagnosis he disputed), Dellinger continued to champion the causes to which he had devoted his life. He was awarded the Peace Abbey Courage of Conscience on September 26, 1992. His idealism served as an inspiration to many as witnessed by the gathering of activists and artists in Burlington, Vermont, in October 2001. As the United States went to war once again, this community of kindred souls joined together to pay tribute to Dellinger—a man whose actions and values set an exemplary path for them to follow.

Dellinger died in Montpelier, Vermont, on May 25, 2004, survived by his wife Betty.

Margaret Gay

See also Berrigan, Daniel, and Berrigan, Philip; Chomsky, Noam; Day, Dorothy; Hayden, Tom; Hoffman, Abbie; Roosevelt, Eleanor; Seale, Bobby; Zinn, Howard

References

Dellinger, David. *From Yale to Jail: The Life of a Moral Dissenter.* New York: Pantheon Books, 1993.

Farber, David. *Chicago '68.* Chicago: University of Chicago Press, 1988.

Guma, Greg. "Dave Dellinger: The Life of a Nonviolent Warrior." ZNet, May 26, 2004. http://www.zcommunications.org/dave-dellinger-the-life-of-a-nonviolent-warrior-by-greg-guma (accessed April 21, 2010).

Hunt, Andrew E. *David Dellinger: The Life and Times of a Nonviolent Revolutionary.* New York: New York University Press. 2006.

McCarthy, Colman. "In Memoriam: A Man Who Didn't Obey." *Progressive*, August 2004, 20.

Winthrop, Nat. "Life on the Edge: The Turbulent Public and Private Lives of David Dellinger and Elizabeth Peterson." *Rutland Herald/Times Argus Sunday Magazine* (Rutland, VT), May 29, 2006. http://www.towardfreedom.com/dellinger/index.php?option=com_content&view=article&id=34:life-on-the-edge-the-turbulent-public-and-private-lives-of-david-dellinger-a-elizabeth-peterson&catid=20:dave-dellinger (accessed September 8, 2011).

Deloria, Vine, Jr. (1933–2005)

The vital difference between Indians in their individualism and the traditional individualism of Anglo-Saxon America is that the two understandings of man are built on entirely different premises. White America speaks of individualism on an economic basis. Indians speak of individualism on a social basis. While the rest of America is devoted to private property, Indians prefer to hold their lands in tribal estate, sharing the resources in common with each other.

Vine Deloria Jr. expressed this dissent with Anglo-Saxon America in his books and with his activism (Deloria 1970, 170). He was a legal advocate for and leader of Indian nations. Deloria believed strongly that the Indian way of life was superior to that of the dominant white culture.

Deloria was born on March 26, 1933, in Martin, South Dakota, to Vine Sr. and Barbara (Eastburn) Deloria. Later, the family included two younger siblings, another son and a daughter. They lived near the Oglala Lakota (Sioux) Pine Ridge reservation, one of the poorest regions in the United States. By World War I, after many years of deprivation on the reservations with little resources, many Sioux families had raised themselves out of abject poverty and had developed prosperous farms. "Then the government stepped in, sold the Indians' cattle for wartime needs, and after the war leased the grazing lands to whites, creating wealthy white ranchers and destitute Indian landlords" (Josephy 1971, 249).

Deloria's father was an Episcopal archdeacon and missionary of Lakota ancestry, serving 18 chapels. His grandfather, Philip Joseph Deloria, was a tribal chief of the Yankton Sioux nation whose reservation is along the banks of the Missouri River. Philip Deloria converted to Christianity in the 1800s and became an Episcopal priest.

Because Indians were considered wards of the state, Philip Deloria asked U.S. government officials to grant $8,000 for new tools to refurbish the tribal factory, which would help provide jobs to the Santee Sioux. The Santee sought part-time work so they could pursue their other interests, such as hunting and fishing. With the factory retooled, the Santee could cross the Missouri River when it was frozen over to get to work; otherwise they would not make the long trip by road. The federal government instead offered to build a $115,000 electronics plant. Steiner quotes an old Sioux as saying "The white man works like a slave all his life in order to retire, to be able to loaf and hunt and fish. We already have this for which the white man is working. So why should we adopt his ways and work all our life for what we already have?" The Yankton Sioux turned down the government's offer and instead received the $8,000 from the Episcopal church.

Vine Deloria Sr. moved his family from Pine Ridge to the Standing Rock Lakota reservation when Vine Jr. was very young. Of his Lakota (Sioux) ancestors, Deloria Jr. says: "The Sioux were fierce and successful warriors, whose worst losses (at least until they met the United States Cavalry) were meted out by the Chippewa (Ojibway), who drove them out of Minnesota." According to Deloria Jr., the bitterness between the two tribes still exists, though the battles occurred long ago. In fact, the name "Sioux" is derived from a name given by the Chippewa nation describing their enemy to the French—"Nadewisou" or "cutthroats," which the French shortened to the final syllable, Sioux. Deloria states that when the Sioux were not fighting the cavalry, they made war on 18 other tribes (Velie 1979, 6).

Deloria also noted that "The most memorable event of my early childhood was visiting Wounded Knee where 200 Sioux, including women and children, were slaughtered in 1890 by troopers of the Seventh Cavalry in what is believed to have been a delayed act of vengeance for Custer's defeat" (Josephy 1971, 250).

Vine Jr. attended elementary school in Martin, and high school at St. James Academy in Faribault, Minnesota. After graduating, he spent two years in the U.S. Marine Corps, and then enrolled at Iowa State University, earning a bachelor's degree in 1958. He also married about this time, and eventually he and his wife Barbara became parents of three children: Philip, Daniel, and Jeanne.

Even though Deloria earned a theology degree in 1963 from the Lutheran School of Theology in Rock Island, Illinois, he chose not to be the third of his line to become a minister. Between 1964 and 1967, he was the young executive director of the National Congress of American Indians (NCAI), which was founded in 1944 by World War II veterans. NCAI is known as the United Nations of tribes that under Deloria's leadership went from an enrollment of 19 tribes to 156 tribes in just three years. According to author Stan Steiner, Deloria "spoke not merely for the young but for tribes that represented four hundred thousand Indians. He was the Rousseau of the new Indians. He talked of a turning point in tribal history" (Steiner 1968, 26).

Organizing Indian nations would be a huge challenge, Deloria found. In early 1970, he stated "there are some 315 Indian tribal groups in 26 states still functioning as quasi-sovereign nations under treaty status; they range from the mammoth Navajo tribe of some 132,000 with 16 million acres of land to the tiny Mission Creeks of California with fifteen people and a tiny parcel of property. There are over half a million Indians in the cities alone, with the largest concentrations in San Francisco, Los Angeles, Minneapolis and Chicago" (Deloria 1970, 248). One of the initial difficulties was determining who accurately recorded the number of American Indians in the United States. The 1960 U.S. Census Bureau listed 552,220 Indians, changing that figure to an estimated 792,000 in the 1970 census (Vogel 1972, 255). As of 2011, there are 564 federally recognized Indian tribes and Alaska Native entities in the United States, according to the U.S. Bureau of Indian Affairs.

During his time with NCAI, Deloria learned that tribes had no legal counsel, so he decided to study law in order to help tribes obtain their rights. He earned a law degree from the University of Colorado in 1970. Twenty years later, he joined the university's faculty and taught history.

A pivotal event for Deloria, as a young man a year away from becoming an attorney, was the American Indian occupation of Alcatraz Island off the coast of San Francisco on November 20, 1969. A former

Deloria, Vine, Jr. (1933–2005) | 191

Vine Deloria Jr., a Native American scholar, author, and activist, influenced two generations of Native and non-Indian leaders promoting Indian sovereignty. He died in 2005. (AP Photo)

federal prison, the island had been abandoned, but under an 1868 Sioux treaty, Indians could claim any such federal property if it was no longer in use. Thus, 89 Indians from various tribes landed on the island much like white Europeans coming to foreign shores through the fifteenth and seventeenth centuries under a so-called Christian Doctrine of Discovery that gave Christians the right to invade, conquer, occupy and enslave non-Christian peoples. Among the Indians in the original landing party at Alcatraz was the father of American Indian Movement (AIM), activist Russell Means. "Indians wanted to create five centers on Alcatraz: a North American studies program, a spiritual and medical center where Indian religion and medicines would be used, an ecological studies program based on the Indian view of nature, and a job training center and museum" (Josephy 1971, 255).

They occupied Alcatraz for 19 months, with the number of people on site varying from as high as 1,000 to as little as 19 before U.S. marshals removed all Indians and supporters on June 11, 1971.

Other important events were the "fish-ins" in the Pacific Northwest where American Indian nations exercised their treaty rights to fish and hunt in their traditional locations and ways. Indians "were forced to adopt the vocabulary and techniques of Blacks in order to get their grievances serious consideration by the media" (Nagel 1997, 161). These "fish-ins" provided a training ground for future Red Power activists. The term "Red Power" was first uttered by Deloria during a 1966 convention of the National Congress of American Indians (NCAI).

Deloria was more than an activist and a legal advocate for American Indian nations; he was also a theologian and philosopher for twentieth- and twenty-first-century Red Power. Rather than begging for a bigger share of the federal government's aid to indigenous people who were considered wards of the state and tenants on lands they had occupied for thousands of years, Deloria argued that the American Indian way of life is far superior to that of the predominant white European culture that invaded, conquered, and occupied the North American continent. And he envisioned a future where the American Indian culture and spirituality will once again become predominant if this continent and planet Earth are to survive with human beings in it.

One of Deloria's greatest efforts on behalf of modern American Indians was promoting Indian sovereignty. In his many books and public appearances, Deloria advocated thinking of tribes as nations, and realizing the commonality of these nations to create a pan-American Indian movement, while maintaining each nation's language, customs, and unique spirituality. Since 2000, a movement has grown among indigenous peoples worldwide to seek recognition of their unique but shared roles in modern society. The UN Declaration of the Rights of Indigenous Peoples has been signed by every nation with the exceptions of Australia, New Zealand, and the United States, which have refused to give such recognition and status respectively to its Aboriginal peoples, Maoris, and American Indians. While both Australia and New Zealand are reconsidering their earlier refusals to sign on, the United States remains obstinate in this regard.

"It isn't important that there are only 500,000 of us Indians," Deloria once wrote, "What is important is that we have a superior way of life. We Indians have a more human philosophy of life. We Indians will show this country how to act human. Someday this country will revise its constitution, its laws, in terms of human beings, instead of property. If Red Power is to be a power in this country, it is because it is ideological" (Steiner 1968, x).

Deloria is the author of more than 20 books. In one of them, *God Is Red: A Native View of Religion* (1972), he contrasts the concept of sacredness espoused by Native American religions, noting how native spirituality is closely tied to the environment and thus to ecological concerns. Deloria also analyzes the way in which each culture perceives reality—Europeans seeing time as linear and history as a progressive sequence of events while native cultures do not. Further, he notes that "Christianity usually portrays God as a humanlike being often meddlesome and vengeful, whereas many native religions place supreme authority in a great spirit or great mystery symbolizing the life-forces of nature" (Grinde and Johansen 1994, 16).

Deloria retired from his faculty position at the University of Colorado in 2000, but he continued to write and lecture until his sudden death. He suffered an aortic aneurysm and died on November 13, 2005, in Golden, Colorado. In a tribute to him, Holly Boomer of Oglala Lakota College wrote: "Part of Deloria's legacy is his verbal challenge to Indians to educate themselves in both tradition and in mainstream; his challenge to the establishment is to hear what Indians have to say as authentic and valid in the context of history" (Boomer 2006, 114). Other tributes include an Annual Vine Deloria Jr. Indigenous Studies Symposium held in Bellingham, Washington. The symposium which began in 2006, brings together Native and nonnative scholars and tribal elders who are interested in honoring Deloria's life and work.

Daniel Callaghan

See also Means, Russell

References

Boomer, Holly. "Writing Red: A Tribute to Vine Deloria Jr." *Great Plains Quarterly* 26, no. 2 (Spring 2006): 113–15. http://digitalcommons.unl.edu/cgi/viewcontent.cgi?article=1118&context=greatplainsquarterly (accessed October 22, 2010).

Deloria, Vine, Jr. *Custer Died for Your Sins: An Indian Manifesto*. Norman: University of Oklahoma Press, 1988.

Deloria, Vine, Jr. *God Is Red: A Native View of Religion*. Golden, CO: Fulcrum Publishing, 2003. First published 1972.

Deloria, Vine, Jr. *The Red Man in the New World Drama*. New York: Macmillan, 1974.

Deloria, Vine, Jr. *We Talk, You Listen: New Tribes, New Turf*. New York: Macmillan, 1970.

Grinde, Donald A., and Bruce Elliott Johansen. *Ecocide of Native America: Environmental Destruction of Indian Lands and Peoples*. Santa Fe, NM: Clear Light Books, 1994.

Josephy, Alvin M., Jr. *Now That the Buffalo's Gone: A Study of Today's American Indians*. New York: Alfred Knopf, 1982.

Josephy, Alvin M., Jr. *Red Power: The American Indians' Fight for Freedom*. New York: McGraw-Hill, 1971.

Nagel, Joane. *American Indian Ethnic Renewal: Red Power and the Resurgence of Identity and Culture*. New York: Oxford University Press, 1997.

Steiner, Stan. *The New Indians*. New York: Harper and Row, 1968.

Velie, Alan R., ed. *American Indian Literature: An Anthology*. Norman: University of Oklahoma Press, 1979.

Vogel, Virgil J. *This Country Was Ours: A Documentary History of the American Indian*. New York: Harper and Row, 1972.

Wundler, John R. *Retained by the People: A History of American Indians and the Bill of Rights*. New York: Oxford University Press, 1994.

Dennett, Mary Ware (1872–1947)

In 1929, a 53-year-old dissident (some would call her subversive), Mary Ware Dennett, appeared in federal court in Brooklyn, New York, accused of sending obscene materials through the mail. She had distributed a sex education booklet, using medical terminology, which she titled *The Sex Side of Life—An Explanation for Young People*. She had written it for her two young sons.

Sex education and birth control information were banned under the Comstock Law passed in 1873. Mary Dennett was indicted on obscenity charges and found guilty. She faced a hefty fine and jail time. But she was defiant: "If a few federal officials want to use their power to penalize me for my work for the young people of this country, they must bear the shame of a jail sentence. It is the government which is disgraced, not I" (Craig 1995, 145).

Ware was born on April 4, 1872, in Worcester, Massachusetts. Her parents George and Livonia (known as Vonie) Ware had four children—the eldest was William (Willie) and Mary was the second born. A third child died in infancy and the youngest, Clara, was born two years later. During the nation's economic downfall from 1873 to 1879, the family moved to Texas where George Ware, a traveling merchant, could be closer to his customers. But after three years in Texas, Vonie Ware, dissatisfied with the Southwest, returned to Massachusetts to raise the children alone.

As Mary was growing up, she "showed signs of precocious intellect," and at the age of five, she "wrote her first letter to her father in Texas—less than two months after she formed her first writing character." She was a bold child, not intimidated by older children or boys who competed with her in spelling bees (Chen 1996, 16).

When Mary was 10 years old, her father died of cancer, and Vonie took in borders to earn a living. Later, the Wares moved to Boston to be near relatives and Vonie began a successful business taking young women on European tours. While their mother was away, Mary, her brother, and her younger sister stayed with their two aunts. One of their aunts, Lucia, was a social reformer and teacher who was Mary's mentor. With Aunt Lucia as a role model, Mary developed a sense of social consciousness and an understanding that women could lead as productive a life as men.

All of the Ware children attended Boston's public schools. Mary was a top student and thought of herself as a dissident advocating for radical social reform. But she did not reject traditional customs and instead hoped to effect change through existing institutions. She spent her last two years in high school at a school for girls in Northampton, Massachusetts, graduating in 1891. She then studied at the School of Art and Design at the Boston Museum of Fine Arts and became part of the arts and crafts movement that flourished during the late 1800s and early 1900s. The movement was an effort to counteract mass production and industrialization through architecture and decorative arts that were simple in design and with an emphasis on craftsmanship. Mary went on to a teaching position at the Drexel Institute of Art in Philadelphia, where she was appointed head of the department of design and decoration. Her sister Clara, also an arts devotee, joined Mary in Philadelphia, and the two shared an apartment. They also shared in the mission to create beauty through art in all its forms.

While in Philadelphia, Mary began corresponding with William Hartley Dennett, a fellow arts and crafts enthusiast and budding architect in Boston. Their relationship became more serious when Mary took a summer job at Boston's Museum of Fine Arts and worked with Hartley, as he was called. The two married in January 1900 and by the end of 1903 had two children, Carleton (born 1900), and another son who died shortly after birth. Devon, a third child, was born in 1905.

A few years later, Hartley became involved in a romantic relationship with one of his married clients, Margaret Chase, while his wife was recovering from serious surgery. His affair created a scandal in the community but Hartley continued his relationship, insisting that it was his right to love another woman—his soul mate—and often included his sons in outings with Margaret. Hartley also tried to sway his sons' opinions against their mother, and refused to pay family bills. Mary Dennett filed for divorce in 1913 and sued for legal custody of the two boys. She won her case, which was an unusual decision in a time when women had few rights or the financial means to raise a family.

While her marriage was falling apart, Mary Dennett took a job in 1908 with the Massachusetts Suffrage Association. She had been interested in women's suffrage early on, and her Aunt Lucia and some of Mary's friends were involved in women's voting rights campaigns. So the idea of working for the cause was somewhat familiar territory. Also, devoting herself to the movement was a way to "alleviate her anguish" over her failed marriage (Chen 1996, 129). Mary's organizing, campaigning, and speaking skills helped convince many reticent individuals to support women's suffrage.

In 1910, the National American Woman Suffrage Association (NAWSA) begged Dennett to come to work at their headquarters in New York City. She agreed to move, enrolled her sons in a boarding school, and lived in a small apartment near Greenwich Village. However, when she joined NAWSA's staff as corresponding secretary, she faced rivalries between factions in the organization. She had a talent, though, for remaining neutral in disputes while tending to her many tasks—writing, advising campaigns, sending out news releases, and managing the office. "Although unrecognized today, Mary Ware Dennett was the turning point for the NAWSA. After her arrival, the reach at headquarters grew massively. She saw to it that an enormous amount of information was compiled and distributed," wrote her biographer Constance Chen (1996, 137).

Over the next few years, Dennett became part of a bohemian lifestyle in Greenwich Village where artists, social workers, writers, students, and others gathered to discuss radical ideas of the day, including feminism, free love, sexual experimentation, birth control, and anarchist views. She also was an activist in the Intercollegiate Socialist Society and the American peace movement, especially after the beginning of World War I, and was a member of the Woman's Peace Party.

During this time, she met Margaret Sanger and was impressed with the birth-control information that Sanger shared, which prompted Mary to become involved with the birth-control movement. Those who distributed birth-control information were subject to arrest for violating the 1873 Comstock Law, named for Anthony Comstock, a special agent for the U.S. Post Office Department and zealous Christian who crusaded against birth-control advocates. He considered himself the moral guardian of the U.S. mails, and successfully lobbied for passage of the law that banned "Every obscene, lewd, or lascivious, and every filthy book, pamphlet, picture, paper, letter, writing, print, or other publication of an indecent character" and declared these materials "to be nonmailable matter and shall not be conveyed in the mails or delivered from any post office or by any letter carrier" (Chen 1996, 306).

Contraceptive information was not the only issue that Dennett met head on. As her boys grew older, they began to ask questions about sex, and Mary searched for information in public libraries and books stores, hoping to find the "right sort of little book" to teach her sons about sex (Dennett 1930, 4). She was dissatisfied with what she found—the books were based on fear of sexuality and not on fact. In 1915, Dennett decided to write a straightforward essay using scientific terminology for the sex organs and illustrating her text with her own drawings. She titled the essay "The Sex Side of Life: An Explanation for Young People," and sent a copy of it to her sons. She also loaned a copy of the essay to friends for their children and later published it as a pamphlet that was widely distributed by a variety of groups championing women's health and women's rights.

Dennett was convinced that, along with sex education, information about birth control should be legalized. She helped found the National Birth Control League (NBCL) and took a position as its executive secretary. Dennett believed that the league should emphasize public education about birth control and lobby for removal of contraceptive information from the federal obscenity law. Margaret Sanger, who in 1921 founded the American Birth Control League, had a different view; she was convinced that the Comstock Law should be amended to allow only doctors to distribute contraceptive information. The rift between the two women increased, especially as Sanger insisted in her public pronouncement that she was in charge of the birth control movement. Because of all the friction and stressful working conditions, Dennett left the league in 1919 and formed the Voluntary Parenthood League (VPL), which she directed until 1925. She resigned that year because the VPL membership decided to support Sanger's "doctors only" position.

Dennett continued to lobby congressional leaders, hoping to convince one of them to introduce a bill to allow open dissemination of birth-control information. But she had no success. Nevertheless, because of her many speaking engagements and writings, the U.S. public became more aware of birth-control issues. Her enemies were on the alert as well, and in 1928, a woman complained to the Post Office inspector that her daughter had received a copy of Dennett's pamphlet in the mail. The inspector ordered a copy for himself, without revealing his name, and after reading it began legal proceedings against Dennett.

After many postponements, Dennett's case went to trial in 1929, and she was convicted on the obscenity charges. But there was a major public outcry across the United States. A defense fund was formed to pay for an appeal in *United States v. Dennett* (1930), and with the aid of the American Civil Liberties Union, her conviction was overturned. Circuit Court Judge Augustus N. Hand wrote:

> The defendant's discussion of the phenomena of sex is written with sincerity of feeling and with an idealization of the marriage relation and sex emotions. We think it tends to rationalize and dignify such emotions rather than to arouse lust. While it may be thought by some that portions of the tract go into unnecessary details that would better have been omitted, it may be fairly answered that the curiosity of many adolescents would not be satisfied without full explanation, and that no more than that is really given. It also may reasonably be thought that accurate information, rather than mystery and curiosity, is better in the long run and is less likely to occasion lascivious thoughts than ignorance and anxiety. Perhaps instruction other than that which the defendant suggests would be better. That is a matter as to which there is bound to be a wide difference of opinion, but, irrespective of this, we hold that an accurate exposition of the relevant facts of the sex side of life in decent language and in manifestly serious and disinterested spirit cannot ordinarily be regarded as obscene. Any incidental tendency to arouse sex impulses which such a pamphlet may perhaps have is apart from and subordinate to its main effect. The tendency can only exist in so far as it is inherent in any sex instruction, and it would seem to be outweighed by the elimination of ignorance, curiosity, and morbid fear. The direct aim and the net result is to promote understanding and self-control.
>
> No case was made for submission to the jury, and the judgment must therefore be reversed.

Dennett wrote an account of her case, which was titled *Who's Obscene?* (1930). She also published *The Sex Education of Children* (1931).

After her trial, Dennett withdrew somewhat from the birth-control movement, allowing Margaret Sanger to be the public spokesperson. However, she continued to conduct letter-writing campaigns to overturn the Comstock Law, and was involved in peace activities during World War II. In 1945, she moved to a home for seniors in Valatie, New York, where she died on July 25, 1947. Although her efforts did not result in the repeal of the Comstock Law, Dennett and her nonconformist activities set the stage for women to gain better access to birth-control information and contraceptive devices.

See also Sanger, Margaret

References

"Books: Facts of Life" (review of *Who's Obscene?*). *Time*, April 7, 1930. http://www.time.com/time/magazine/article/0,9171,787606,00.html (accessed August 10, 2011).

Chen, Constance M. *"The Sex Side of Life": Mary Ware Dennett's Pioneering Battle for Birth Control and Sex Education*. New York: New Press, 1996.

Craig, John M. " 'The Sex Side of Life': The Obscenity Case of Mary Ware Dennett." *Frontiers: A Journal of Women Studies*, September 1995, 145–66.

Dennett, Mary Ware. *Who's Obscene?* New York: Vanguard Press, 1930.

Heins, Marjorie. " 'The Sex Side of Life': Mary Ware Dennett's Pioneering Battle for Birth Control and Sex Education." *Atlantic*, October 1996.

Maurice, Lori Klatt. "Stamping Out Indecency the Postal Way." March 8, 2004. http://academic.evergreen.edu/k/klalor09/post%20office%20censorship%20home.htm (accessed June 22, 2010).

Douglas, Marjory Stoneman (1890–1998)

"There are no other Everglades in the world" (Douglas 1997, 5). So wrote Marjory Stoneman Douglas when introducing her groundbreaking book, *The Everglades: River of Grass* (1947). The book is often compared to Rachel Carson's *Silent Spring* (1962) that helped launch the environmental movement. However, John Rothchild notes in the introduction for Douglas's autobiographical *Voice of the River* (1987) that Douglas was the pioneer in the field, "an environmentalist long before the word existed" (Douglas 1987, 23). Douglas became known as the patron saint of the Florida wetlands (Severe 1998).

Marjory Stoneman was born on April 7, 1890, in Minneapolis, Minnesota. Her parents were musician Florence Lillian Trefethen, and Frank Bryant Stoneman, future founder and editor in chief of the *Miami Herald*. In 1984, when she was four, Marjory visited Florida for the first time and fell in love with the wetlands. As she reflects in her autobiography, "I never forgot the quality of the tropic light as if I had ... loved and missed and longed for all my life" (Douglas 1987, 31).

In 1896, when Marjory turned six, her parents divorced. Frank Stoneman moved to Miami, Florida, and Marjory would not meet him again for 19 years. She and her mother moved in with her maternal grandparents in Taunton, Massachusetts. Florence was prone to nervous breakdowns, and was committed to a mental sanitarium several times over the next few years. Meanwhile, her grandparents and aunt, who also lived with the family, were often critical of the divorce, considering it disgraceful (Douglas 1987, 56). Because of the contentious environment in her upbringing, Marjory was herself prone to night terrors. But, she credits the volatile childhood as making her "a skeptic and a dissenter" all her life (Douglas 1987, 50).

In high school, Marjory was an avid reader and researcher, describing herself as having "a writer's temperament" (Douglas 1987, 67). After her graduation from high school in 1908, she enrolled at Wellesley College, where she majored in English and excelled in writing. During her senior year, she was editor of *Legende*, the college annual, and was elected class orator. It was during this time that she made her first venture in political activism, serving on the executive board of the Equal Suffrage League. She graduated in 1912. That year her mother was diagnosed with cancer, and Marjory returned home right after graduation to take care of her. Within months, her mother died, and Marjory decided to move to Newark, New Jersey, where she met Kenneth Douglas, 30 years her senior and purported to be an editor of the *Newark Evening News*. They were married in 1913. The marriage quickly turned sour and ended in 1915.

With the encouragement of her uncle, and upon invitation from her father, Marjory Douglas moved to Miami, Florida, where she reconciled with her estranged father. The move proved to be a pivotal turning point in her life. She moved in with Frank Stoneman and his new wife. At this point, Stoneman was editor in chief of the *Miami Herald*, and he hired Douglas as the newspaper's society columnist. Within a year, she became responsible for an editorial page. As she notes in her autobiography, she did not care what she was writing as long as it was writing: "It was a great leap forward in my individuality" (Douglas 1987, 102).

Continuing her suffrage work that she had begun in college, Douglas joined a group of women to argue for the women's suffrage amendment before the Florida state legislature. They wore their best hats, she wrote of the experience, but "[t]alking to them was like talking to graven images" (Byers 1999).

In 1917, Douglas became the first Florida woman to enlist in the naval reserves. She served a year before requesting a discharge. Soon thereafter, she volunteered for the American Red Cross. Stationed in Paris, France, she cared for the war refugees. The

Marjory Stoneman Douglas was an environmentalist who wrote many books and helped to preserve the Florida Everglades for future generations. When she was 79, she founded the Friends of the Everglades to fight on behalf of the wilderness. (AP/Wide World Photos)

experience helped her to understand the plight of the refugees in Miami 60 years later (Douglas 1987, 116). She was also assigned to write articles about the Red Cross in Europe. In 1920, she returned to Miami, where she began work as assistant editor at the *Herald*. She began writing a daily column, "The Galley," where she explored topical issues including women's suffrage and civil rights. She also began to explore environmental issues, noting that "it was in the column that I started to talk about Florida as landscape and as geography, to investigate it and to explore it" (Douglas 1987, 127). Thus began her career as an environmentalist, and her fervent devotion to the Florida wetlands.

The pressures of the newspaper deadlines took their toll on her health, and Douglas suffered a nervous breakdown (Garfield 1989). In 1923, Douglas left her position on the *Miami Herald* in pursuit of a full-time career as a freelance writer. From 1920 to 1990, she sold to the *Saturday Evening Post, Woman's Home Journal*, and other markets. She often explored environmental themes in her writings, and also wrote several books about state and regional history, including *Road to the Sun* (1951); *Hurricane* (1958), in which she traveled to North Carolina, Jamaica, Martinique, and Cuba for research; and *Florida: The Long Frontier* (1964).

In 1924, Douglas moved to Coconut Grove, Miami's oldest neighborhood and the first black settlement on the South Florida mainland. She built her home and stayed for the rest of her life. Known for its architecture, the house was designated an historic site, and in 2007 was placed in the care of the Florida Park Service. Also in 1924, Douglas became one of the original faculty at the University of Miami a year after its founding. She eventually organized the Friends of the University of Miami Library, and became the editor of the University of Miami Press, where she focused on books on regional and topical issues.

In 1941, Douglas's father Frank Stoneman died. In her grief, she suffered another emotional breakdown.

During the 1940s, Douglas was asked by Hervey Allen, her friend and editor at Rinehart, to write a book about the Miami River. Allen was creating a series of books on the rivers of the United States. Douglas suggested the focus be expanded to include the Everglades. For five years, she researched the unique ecosystem of the wetlands. Eventually she would write 40 papers on the subject. Ironically, she found the wetlands "too buggy, too wet, too generally inhospitable," and yet understood their significance to the environment (Davis 2003).

The Everglades: River of Grass was published in 1947, the same year in which the Everglades National Park was established. The Everglades was the first park to protect primarily biological resources. The book captured the public's imagination with the analogy, river of grass. Novelist John Henry called the book "a remarkable almost poem" (Severo 1998). The book became a best seller and transformed the public perception of the Everglades as useless swamps to an environmental treasure, a unique ecosystem that cannot be replaced. Eugene Garfield points out in *Current Comments* that "the achievement of the book is all the more impressive considering that Douglas had little formal scientific training beyond one college course." As she told Garfield, "I'm just a writer. Writing implies research... If you want to write about something, you have to know it thoroughly. And I was so fortunate, you see, in that the Everglades had not been written about... So I did a lot of research nobody else did... I discovered the Everglades, you might say" (Garfield 1989, 224).

In 1948, Douglas served on the Coconut Grove Slum Clearance Committee, an organization founded to fight social injustice. The committee worked to pass ordinances requiring running water, flushing toilets, septic tanks, and the creation of many community services.

Douglas became a charter member of the first American Civil Liberties Union chapter (Davis 2003). In the 1960s, she entered the political fight to help preserve the Everglades. Despite the creation of the park, the wetland environment was constantly threatened by exploitation. Under the supervision of the U.S. Army Corps of Engineers, canals had been dug; levees, dikes, and pumping stations had been built; and canals and roads had been expanded. Water was diverted to farmlands and coast cities. Agricultural runoff from farm and sugar industries further polluted the environment. As the wetlands were drained, the natural resources and wildlife suffered. Half of the existing alligator population was lost. Wading birds, once endangered for their plumage, faced extinction because of their vanishing environment. In response to the devastation, Douglas formed the grassroots organization, Friends of the Everglades. She was 79 at the time, but age did not slow her down. Despite her failing eyesight and hearing, she traveled the region to educate and promote communities on the importance of the Everglades (Garfield 1989). She was often critical and impatient with her audience, at one point describing the people of the South as selfish, distrustful, and refusing to consider the truth of the whole situation (Severo 1998). Her sharp tongue garnered much criticism from her audience. At one point, when jeered by the audience, she chided them with humor, "Can't you boo any louder than that?" (Davis 2009). As she said, "I'm a tough old woman ... They can't be rude to me. I have all this white hair. I take advantage of everything I can—age, hair, disability—because my cause is just" (Slaight 2000).

Over her lifetime, Douglas received many awards for her writing as well as her activism. She received two O. Henry Awards for fiction published in the *Saturday Evening Post*. In 1952, the National Council of State Garden Clubs awarded her for her work in wetland preservation. She was the recipient of the Wellesley College Alumnae Achievement Award (1977) and the *Miami Herald* Spirit of Excellence Lifetime Achievement Award (1985). She was inducted into the National Wildlife Federation Hall of Fame (1999) and the National Women's Hall of Fame (2000). Perhaps her greatest tribute occurred in 1997, when 1.3 million acres of the Everglades National Park was designated as the Marjory Stoneman Douglas Wilderness.

Douglas never deterred from her work. On her 100th birthday, she was asked if she had hope for the Everglades survival. She replied, "I am neither an optimist nor a pessimist. I say it's got to be done" (Severo 1998).

In 1993, President Bill Clinton awarded Douglas with the Medal of Freedom, the highest honor given to a civilian. The citation read, in part, "Marjory Stoneman Douglas personifies passionate commitment. Her crusade to preserve and restore the Everglades has enhanced our Nation's respect for our precious environment, reminding all of us of nature's delicate balance. Grateful Americans honor the 'Grandmother of the Glades' by following her splendid example in safeguarding America's beauty and splendor for generations to come" (Slaight 2000).

Douglas died on May 14, 1998, at her Coconut Grove home. As Paul Sutter offers in the introduction of *An Everglades Providence* (2009), "other environmental figures defined certain eras in American environmental movement, such as John Muir (Progressive), Aldo Leopold (interwar) and Rachel Carson (post war); Douglas' long life embodied the full American environmental century, and that makes her significant and unique" (Davis 2009, xiv).

Bobbi Miller

See also Carson, Rachel; Leopold, Aldo

References

Burns, Ken, dir. "The National Parks: America's Best Idea." Florentine Films. PBS.org, 2009. http://www.pbs.org/nationalparks/people/behindtheparks/douglas/ (accessed March 31, 2011).

Byers, Stephen. "The Lives They Lived: Marjory Stoneman Douglas; Don't Mess With Her Wetlands." *New York Times*, January 3, 1999. http://query.nytimes.com/gst/fullpage.html?res=9E07EEDA143FF930A35752C0A96F958260 (accessed March 31, 2011).

"Conservation in Florida's Everglades." Florida's Everglades National Park. http://www.design42.com/everglades/conservation.html (accessed April 1, 2011).

Davis, Jack. *An Everglades Providence: Marjory Stoneman Douglas and the American Environmental Century*. Athens: University of Georgia Press, 2009.

Davis, Jack. " 'Conservation Is Now a Dead Word': Marjory Stoneman Douglas and the Transformation of American Environmentalism." *Environmental History*, January 2003.

Douglas, Marjory Stoneman. *The Everglades: River of Grass*. 50th anniversary ed. Sarasota, FL: Pineapple Press, 1997.

Douglas, Marjory Stoneman. *Voice of the River*. 1st revised ed. Sarasota Springs, FL: Pineapple Press, 1987.

"Early Years: Marjory Stoneman Douglas, Writer and Conservationist." Special Collections, University of Miami, 2006. http://scholar.library.miami.edu/msdouglas/early_years.html (accessed March 30, 2011).

Garfield, Eugene. "In Honor of Marjory Stoneman Douglas, Guardian of the Everglades." *Current Comments*, August 14, 1989. http://www.garfield.library.upenn.edu/essays/v12p223y1989.pdf (accessed March 31, 2011).

Grunwald, Michael. *The Swamp: The Everglades, Florida, and the Politics of Paradise*. New York: Simon and Schuster, 2006.

"Miami: Marjory Stoneman Douglas, Writer and Conservationist." Special Collections, University of Miami, 2006. http://scholar.library.miami.edu/msdouglas/miami.html (accessed March 30, 2011).

Severo, Richard. "Marjory Douglas, Champion of Everglades, Dies at 108." *New York Times*, May 15, 1998. http://query.nytimes.com/gst/fullpage.html?res=9500E0D91330F936A25756C0A96E958260&pagewanted=1 (accessed March 29, 2011).

Slaight, Wilma. "Person of the Week: Marjory Stoneman Douglas." Wellesley College, December 11, 2000. http://www.wellesley.edu/Anniversary/douglas.html (accessed April 1, 2011).

Dowie, John Alexander (1847–1907)

Major segments of American society—doctors, pharmaceutical makers, political leaders, the press, and established religious denominations—publicly and loudly criticized John Alexander Dowie, a Congregational minister in Scotland who left the church, emigrated to the United States, and became a dissident evangelist known throughout the world. As for Dowie, he presented himself in the late 1800s and early 1900s alternately as a "Divine Healer," "Dr. Dowie," "Elijah the Restorer" (complete with priestly robes and crown), and the "First Apostle."

Dowie was born on May 25, 1847, in Edinburgh, Scotland, to John Murray and Ann Dowie. John Alexander reportedly was a "precocious child" who "read the Bible through at the age of six." In 1860, when Dowie was 13 years old, the family moved to Australia where the young Dowie's uncle hired him to work in his business. Dowie "received extensive business training," but he wanted to be a minister and returned to Scotland to attend the University of Edinburgh (Cook 1996, 6).

Dowie became an ordained minister in the Congregational Church and served pastorates in Australia during the 1870s. At the time, many of his parishioners suffered serious illness and death from such diseases as diphtheria and scarlet fever, and Dowie began his healing practice, calling on God to destroy the devil's work. His parishioners were healed, according to Dowie, and by the late 1870s, he decided to leave the Congregational Church and start his own independent ministry based on literal interpretations of the Bible. Not only did he establish a church in Melbourne, but he also founded the International Divine Healing Association and later published *Leaves of Healing* that included testimonies of people he had healed and some of his sermons.

In 1888, Dowie planned to go to London for healing missions, but decided instead to visit the United States, where he traveled the West Coast and delivered sermons and practiced divine healing, sometimes called divine intervention, spiritual healing, or faith healing. People who practice faith healing believe that a specific person or place has a connection to a higher power and can eliminate disease or cure injuries. It was a time when numerous faith healers were gaining followers in the United States. For example, Mary Baker Eddy was preaching her philosophy of Christian Science and had founded the Church of Christ, Scientist in 1879. She claimed to be a miracle worker and healer through prayer.

According to Dowie's own reports, his healing ministry was so well received that he believed he should stay in the United States. He went to Chicago in 1890 to attend a healing convention and reported that his prayers healed a woman with a tumor. Thus he was convinced that Chicago was the place for his ministry. A big opportunity presented itself during Chicago's World Columbian Exposition (a world's fair) in 1893. He set up a small tabernacle called the "little wooden hut" outside the fair grounds near Buffalo Bill Cody's Wild West Show. Dowie declared his power of healing and conducted a "Holy War" against all elements of society that he considered evil. He received a boost in popularity when Cody's niece testified to a healing through Dowie.

After the fair, Dr. Dowie, as he was by then popularly known, continued as a hell-fire warrior against the evil power of Satan. He hoped to establish a community of saints—a Zion movement that would destroy evildoers. His plan was to build an "ideal state" for an "ideal people," beginning with a communal Zion Home. This seven-story building at 12th Street and Michigan Avenue in Chicago was the church headquarters and a Christian temperance hotel housing numerous families. In the same area, a Zion school, bank, and investment association were established. The Zion enclave was quite different from the settlement work of Jane Addams and Hull House that she established in 1889 in Chicago. Hull House offered services from artistic programs to medical help for people in need, regardless of their religious beliefs.

In his sermons, Dowie often denounced doctors, drugs, and devils, condemning hospitals, pharmacies, liquor and tobacco industries, and the secular press. Because he attacked so much of the establishment and medical "quacks," who indeed were common at the time, authorities found ways to retaliate. He was frequently accused of libel or practicing medicine without a license and was jailed hundreds of times. Controversies surrounding him created the kind of stories that newspaper reporters loved, and Dowie was one of the most widely publicized evangelists of the time.

In late 1899, Dowie waged a three-month "Holy War against the Hosts of Hell in Chicago," which became the title for a compilation of his sermons published in 1900 in book form. One of his long sermons blasted what he called "apostate Protestant churches" and masons, some of his favorite targets. He called for the Lord to "have mercy on you miserable Baptists ... on you miserable Congregationalists.... And as for you Presbyterians, the Lord have mercy upon you, for, if there is a hard, miserable people on God's Almighty Earth, it is you.... As for the Methodist Church, it has gone to the Devil ... Today, the Methodist Church is ruled by Worldly Policy and by Secret Societies. ... [it] has gone to the Devil, because it has gone into the Masonic Order" (Dowie 1899, 31–32). He also attacked the Christian and Missionary Alliance that ministered to urban populations, the Salvation Army, and Dwight Moody and his Moody Bible Institute in Chicago.

Dowie made plans for a theocracy—a place ruled by God rather than governed by elected officials. His views were quite different from others who set up their versions of nongovernment communities much earlier. His Zion City for Christians was to be built on the shores of Lake Michigan. Dowie and some of his followers, through the investment association they had formed, sold shares for $100 apiece. The association, under the full control of Dowie, bought up 6,600 acres of prime land 42 miles north of Chicago. By 1901, Dowie had formed the basis for a theocratic city to be ruled by God with orders delivered through an Overseer—Dowie—and his elders. Dowie urged his followers to sell all their possessions and invest in the "holy city" of Zion, where everyone would be educated in Christian beliefs and business of all kinds would be conducted on the cooperative plan with each employee sharing in the "fruits of his industry."

Thousands heeded the call. There was no need for residents of the town to own their land, businesses, or factories, so said the leader. Rather, they should lease their land for 1,100 years and work for the businesses and factories owned by the Christian Catholic Apostolic Church. The church name, Dowie frequently reminded people, had nothing to do with the Roman Catholic Church, but instead referred to its all-inclusive nature. Apostolic meant the church was patterned somewhat after the biblical New Testament, in which people gave up their land and houses and the apostles of Jesus distributed these possessions among people in need.

In short order, the investment association built several industries in Zion City, including: an entire lace factory imported from England; a lumber company; candy, handkerchief, and canning factories; a commercial baking industry; and a radio station and publishing company that produced two weeklies: the *Theocrat*, and *Leaves of Healing*.

Private ownership of business was considered unnecessary because at the end of the lease period, Jehovah was supposed to appear to claim the faithful. But while they were waiting for the Second Coming, those who flocked to the new theocratic Zion City were expected to live by numerous thou-shalt-not rules. Certain foods, such as shellfish and meat of swine, as described in Deuteronomy's biblical injunctions, were forbidden.

There were dozens of restrictions on land use. Tobacco factories and retail tobacco sales were banned. No saloons or beer gardens, theaters, opera houses, or dance halls were allowed. Pork could not be sold. On and on the rules and regulations went. But no matter what the restrictions, new church members—many of them seeking "divine healing"—appeared regularly in Zion City, traveling from Australia, Scotland, and many parts of Europe and from across the United States and Canada. Families had to live in tents or rooms in a blocklong three-story Elijah Hospice (later known as the

Zion Home) until they could build homes or find rental housing.

All through the first year of development, from sunrise to sunset, a familiar chorus rang out. Hammers, sometimes in unison, sometimes echoing each other, pounded nails into rafters, into siding, into roofs, all over Zion City. Meantime, more and more people arrived by horse-drawn wagon or by Chicago and North Western Railroad cars.

A wooden tabernacle was built. It was planned as a temporary structure to be replaced by a great temple patterned after the Mosque of Omar in Jerusalem. The three-story wooden building seated nearly 7,000 people and contained a gallery for a 300-member choir. Its walls were covered with hundreds of "trophies"—crutches, braces, high-heeled boots, casts, pill bottles, guns, and numerous other items said to have been surrendered by those "saved, healed, cleansed, and blessed in Zion."

Jutting out from the tabernacle plot called the Temple Site and its circular drive were four boulevards, laid out like spokes of a wheel, with all other streets crossing them in a perfect grid. It was a well-designed city, planners from around the world declared, and it would accommodate a population of up to 50,000, which never materialized. The plan included business, industrial, and residential zones, wooded parks and tree-lined avenues and boulevards with biblical names such as Bethel, Ezekiel, Galilee, and Horeb. Just across a park from the Temple Site was a four-story church school built of Indiana limestone. Called Zion Preparatory College, it included all the grades and a two-year college. Nearby was a separate gymnasium.

Within a year, Zion was well established as "A Clean City for a Clean People," according to one advertisement. By 1903, it boasted a population of more than 10,000, and Dowie had realized part of his dream for a theocracy. However, he also created great controversy throughout the state of Illinois and across the United States with his demands that church members reject any medical treatment and drugs, including vaccinations, for whatever ailment or illness they might suffer. Elders prayed to bring about healings.

Yet, in spite of hundreds of testimonies attesting to divine intervention, Dowie's own daughter, Esther, did not survive terrible burns she suffered when her nightgown accidentally caught fire from a burning alcohol lamp. She was burned over three-fourths of her body and was in a semi-coma for days. Because of his belief in faith healing, Dowie refused to allow any treatment for Esther's burns except Vaseline applications and saltwater washes. His critically burned daughter suffered for weeks before succumbing at the age of 21 to infection caused by the burns.

The death of Dowie's daughter in 1902 tested the faith of some of his followers. His ideas of communal property and grandiose plans to establish other church communities across the United States and particularly a Paradise Plantation in Mexico also caused conflicts. He staged expensive revivals, once ordering nine trainloads of church people to follow him to New York City where in 1903 he held a series of meetings in Madison Square Garden, laying hands on thousands who came to be healed of ailments ranging from broken bones to cancer. But New York City was not impressed with Dowie and his cause, and the church lost hundreds of thousands of dollars in the venture.

Dowie's exploits eventually led the church and its many business holdings toward bankruptcy. However, Dowie suffered a stroke in 1905, leaving him paralyzed and requiring others to restore solvency and save the church.

The newly elected general overseer—Wilbur Glen Voliva—quickly created more conflict when he took charge in 1906. The church leadership split between those who were faithful to Dowie and those who were ready to follow a new overseer. Then there was the major question of who owned Zion City and its industries, which a Chicago court placed in receivership until the issue could be decided. Voliva began raising funds to buy back some of the Zion properties from the receivers and soon regained control over most of the industries.

Meanwhile, Dowie remained in his home, a mansion called Shiloh House, which he and his wife shared with a grown son, Gladstone. It was a 25-room brick building with a colorful tiled roof, porticos, etched glass windows, and ornate woodwork, and it was filled with expensive furniture. Compared to the average Zion residence, Shiloh House was a veritable palace. Only a few faithful actually visited Dowie at his home and remained loyal to the "prophet" during his last days, although followers and believers honored him after his death on March 9, 1907, in Zion, Illinois.

Dowie's legacy includes his home in Zion, which has been turned into a museum. The city itself is no longer a theocratic community. Instead, it is the home of numerous denominations, independent businesses, public schools, and a civic government.

See also Addams, Jane

References

Cook, Philip L. *Zion City, Illinois: Twentieth-Century Utopia*. Syracuse, NY: Syracuse University Press, 1996.

Dowie, John Alexander. *Zion's Holy War against the Hosts of Hell in Chicago*. Chicago: Zion Publishing House, 1899.

Gay, Kathlyn. *Communes and Cults*. New York: Twenty-First Century Books/Henry Holt, 1997.

Leaves of Healing. Zion, IL, and Chicago: Zion Publishing Company, various issues and dates. In author's collection.

Du Bois, W. E. B (1868–1963)

"History cannot ignore W. E. B. Du Bois because history has to reflect truth and Dr. Du Bois was a tireless explorer and a gifted discoverer of social truths." So said Dr. Martin Luther King Jr. in 1968 when he was addressing a Carnegie Hall audience celebrating the centennial of Du Bois's birth. Yet during his lifetime, Du Bois had numerous critics who strongly disagreed with his support for the Socialist Party and the Soviet Union, considering this subversive advocacy. He was also criticized for promoting black separatism.

On February 23, 1868, in Great Barrington, Massachusetts, William Edward Burghardt Du Bois was born to Mary Sylvina Burghardt and Alfred Du Bois. William's name reflects his African, French, and Dutch lineage. Because Alfred Du Bois left the family soon after William's birth, Mary and her son—she called him "Willie"—went to live with her father for a short time and then moved to a "cozy cottage, with a living-room, a tiny sitting-room, a pantry, and two attic bedrooms," Du Bois wrote. "Here mother and I lived until she died, in 1884, for father early began his restless wanderings. I last remember urgent letters for us to come to New Milford, where he had started a barber shop. Later he became a preacher. But mother no longer trusted his dreams, and he soon faded out of our lives into silence" (Du Bois 1920).

Du Bois grew up in a mill town of about 5,000 people with only 25 to 50 black individuals among them. He noted that he "very gradually" realized he "was different from other children." He wrote:

W. E. B. Du Bois was called the father of Pan-Africanism for his work on behalf of emerging African nations. He devoted his life to the fight for equality for African Americans, insisting that blacks struggle for civil rights, political power, and higher education. (Library of Congress)

> At first I think I connected the difference with a manifest ability to get my lessons rather better than most and to recite with a certain happy, almost taunting, glibness, which brought frowns here and there. Then, slowly, I realized that some folks, a few, even several, actually considered my brown skin a misfortune; once or twice I became painfully aware that some human beings even thought it a crime. I was not for a moment daunted,—although, of course, there were some days of secret tears—rather I was spurred to tireless effort. If they beat me at anything, I was grimly determined to make them sweat for it! (Du Bois 1920)

In high school Du Bois excelled in his studies and literary talent, becoming a correspondent for the *Springfield Republican*, a major newspaper in western Massachusetts. He was valedictorian of his class when he graduated from Great Barrington High School at the age of 16. His mother died just months after his graduation.

Du Bois wanted to go to Harvard University in Cambridge, Massachusetts, but did not have the funds needed to enroll. Instead, he was able to get a scholarship to attend the historically black Fisk University in Nashville, Tennessee. While at Fisk he spent summers teaching in rural African American schools in the Nashville area. Although his three years at Fisk were "miraculous," from his teenage standpoint, he faced the kind of southern racism and discrimination that he had never confronted before, which made him determined to do what he could to free his people from white domination.

After graduating from Fisk in 1888, he received scholarships to Harvard and enrolled as a junior. He graduated cum laude from Harvard University in 1890 with a bachelor of arts degree. He learned that there was a fund to help qualified blacks study abroad, and Du Bois applied for a grant, received it, and "crossed the ocean in a trance" to study what was then the new science of sociology at the University of Berlin, Germany. His studies convinced him that scientific principles could be applied to solve social problems.

While in Germany, he traveled about the country and also visited France, Italy, and England, gaining a "broader sense of humanity and world-fellowship." In 1894, he returned to the United States where, in his words, he "dropped suddenly back into 'nigger'-hating America!" (Du Bois 2005). However, he also returned to Harvard and, in 1895, earned his PhD in history, the first black person to receive a doctorate from Harvard. His doctoral thesis became the first volume in Harvard's Historical Series, published as *The Suppression of the African Slave Trade to the United States of America 1638–1870* (1896).

In spite of a doctorate degree and additional advanced education, he was turned down by several universities and other schools for teaching jobs—there were no openings. He finally received an offer from Wilberforce, an African Methodist school in Ohio. He taught Latin, Greek, German, and English and began to write scholarly books. While at Wilberforce he met Nina Gomer, whom he married in 1896. By then he was dissatisfied with his work at Wilberforce and embarked on a research project for the University of Pennsylvania—a study of blacks in Philadelphia, which was published as *The Philadelphia Negro: A Social Study* (1899).

In 1897, Du Bois accepted a position at Atlanta (Georgia) University, where he stayed until 1910, teaching economics, history, and sociology. While in Atlanta, Nina and William Du Bois lost their first child Burghardt, a young son, to a typhoid epidemic. Their daughter Yolande was born 16 months later.

Du Bois turned away from scholarly writings to publish *The Souls of Black Folk* (1903), a collection of essays on the black experience since emancipation. In the book he also blasted Booker T. Washington, a black leader and founder of Tuskegee Institute, for his conciliatory approach to racist white America. Washington urged African Americans to be patient, cooperate with whites, adjust, and even accept segregation in order to gradually gain economically through industrial education and work. But Du Bois would have none of this, declaring that Washington was in effect apologizing for injustice. He wrote that Washington's doctrine "tended to make the whites, North and South, shift the burden of the Negro problem to the Negro's shoulders and stand aside as critical and rather pessimistic spectators; when in fact the burden belongs to the nation, and the hands of none of us are clean if we bend not our energies to righting these great wrongs" (Du Bois 1903). Du Bois insisted on blacks struggling for civil rights, political power, and higher education. His opposition to Washington thrust him into a conflict between blacks who supported Washington's view and those who were aligned with the dissenting and more radical approach that Du Bois expressed.

Because of his opposition to conciliation and accommodation with white America, Du Bois with other leaders founded a black civil rights organization of scholars and professionals in 1905. Called the Niagara Movement, it was named for the Niagara Falls location where the group first met. The organization eventually merged with the National Association for the Advancement of Colored People (NAACP), which was founded by a multiracial group in 1909.

By 1910, Du Bois was disenchanted with academia. He along with some of his friends joined the Socialist Party led by Eugene V. Debs. He remained in the party for only two years, but throughout his life, he was influenced by the ideas of Karl Marx, a German philosopher who with Friedrich Engels wrote the *Communist Manifesto* (1848), which presented the principles of communism. He also left his professorship for a position with the NAACP at its headquarters in New York City. He was the director of research and editor of the organization's magazine, the *Crisis*, which he insisted had to be a forthright publication. In the first editorial, Du Bois presented the purpose of the publication:

[T]o set forth those facts and arguments which show the danger of race prejudice, particularly as manifested today toward colored people. It takes its name from the fact that the editors believe that this is a critical time in the history of the advancement of men. Catholicity and tolerance, reason and forbearance can today make the world-old dream of human brotherhood approach realization; while bigotry and prejudice, emphasized race consciousness and force can repeat the awful history of the contact of nations and groups in the past. We strive for this higher and broader vision of Peace and Good Will. (Du Bois 1910, Editorial)

The magazine became a foremost journal for the civil rights of blacks and all people of color. Du Bois editorialized against lynching, segregation laws, and for black and woman suffrage. *Crisis* also published black writers of literature and drama and artists' works, and it presented not only the terror of racism, but also the joys and hopes of African American culture. While with the NAACP, he also published a novel, *The Quest of the Silver Fleece* (1911), which addressed the fact that even though African Americans were emancipated, their oppression was still widely practiced, particularly in the cotton industry, the "silver fleece," that depended on black labor. His book *The Negro* (1915) discusses Africa, its ancient kingdoms, varied races, and the "Distribution of Negro Blood, Ancient and Modern." The book represents his growing advocacy for Pan-Africanism, a belief that people of African descent share a common history and culture and should unite.

During and after World War I (1914–1918), Du Bois used *Crisis* to harshly criticize the United States for its treatment of African Americans who attempted to join the U.S. military but were rejected at first and then drafted for menial tasks. At the same time, blacks were taking part in the "Great Migration" north to find jobs vacated by whites in the armed forces. That created a white backlash and violent attacks, including lynching, against blacks. When the war ended, African American veterans who had fought for their country faced as much hatred and prejudice as they had before. In a blistering *Crisis* article, Du Bois decried the lynching, disenfranchisement, and insults to America's black citizens: "This is the country to which we Soldiers of Democracy return. This is the fatherland for which we fought! But it is our fatherland. It was right for us to fight. . . . Under similar circumstances, we would fight again. But by the God of Heaven, we are cowards and jackasses if now that that war is over, we do not marshal every ounce of our brain and brawn to fight a sterner, longer, more unbending battle against the forces of hell in our own land" (Du Bois 1919, 13).

During the 1920s, Du Bois organized numerous Pan-African conferences in such cities as Paris, London, Lisbon, and New York. He also made an extensive visit to the Soviet Union.

In 1934, Du Bois left the NAACP because of his disagreement with the organization's advocacy for racial integration. Du Bois argued that blacks should establish separate businesses, industries, schools, and other institutions to improve their economic condition. He returned to Atlanta University to teach and was chairman of the sociology department. His writings during those years included *Black Reconstruction in America, 1860–1880* (1935) and articles for a social science quarterly, *Phylon*, which he founded in 1940. It was dedicated to academic and social issues concerning African Americans.

During the 1940s, Du Bois again returned to the NAACP as director of research, but once more resigned because of disagreements with the leadership. His accomplishments during the decade included a presentation to the United Nations to appeal for banishment of segregation laws, organizing a peace conference in New York City, and attending peace congresses in Paris and Moscow.

The decade of the 1950s was a time of upheaval. Nina Du Bois died in 1950. That year Du Bois was the Progressive Party's candidate in New York for the U.S. Senate and also was chairman of the Peace Information Center that called for banishing atomic weapons. The center refused to comply with the Foreign Agents Registration Act of 1938, which requires persons acting as agents of foreign principals to publicly disclose their relationship. Because the center had distributed the Stockholm Appeal, which called for a ban on nuclear weapons, Du Bois and other center officers were accused of disseminating Soviet propaganda and were indicted for failing to register as a "foreign agent." All were acquitted of the charges, but the nation was in the midst of a "Red Scare," with U.S. senator Joseph McCarthy accusing hundreds of citizens and government officials of being communists. Because of the communist charges, Du Bois was unwelcome among many of his former friends and associates.

Amidst the turmoil, Du Bois at age 83 married a longtime friend, Shirley Graham, an author and activist in the Communist Party. Du Bois had become increasingly disheartened over the U.S. government policies and socialized with others who shared his views, such as Paul Robeson, black concert singer and actor who was publicly accused of being a communist, nearly ending his career. Just as Robeson and others were denigrated, Du Bois and his wife were prime targets of the U.S. State Department, which revoked the couple's travel visas until 1958. After their passports were renewed, the couple traveled to Russia and China.

Du Bois joined the Communist Party in 1961, and he and his wife moved to Ghana, Africa, where they were warmly welcomed by Kwame Nkrumah, Ghana's first president and advocate of Pan-Africanism. Du Bois became a citizen of Ghana and, for the next two years, directed the *Encyclopedia Africana* project until his death on August 27, 1963, in Accra, Ghana.

The dissident views of W. E. B. Du Bois are recorded in his more than 20 books and hundreds of articles, essays, and pamphlets. An extensive bibliography of his works, added by the editor, appears in his autobiography, published posthumously in 1968.

See also Debs, Eugene V.; McCarthy, Joseph; Robeson, Paul

References

Balaji, Murali. *The Professor and the Pupil: The Politics and Friendship of W. E. B. Du Bois and Paul Robeson*. New York: Nation Books, 2007.

Du Bois, W. E. B. *The Autobiography of W. E. B. Du Bois: A Soliloquy on Viewing My Life from the Last Decade of Its First Century*. New York: International Publishers, 1968 (published posthumously).

Du Bois, W. E. B. *Darkwater: Voices from Within the Veil*. New York: Harcourt Brace, 1920. Project Gutenberg e-book, released February 28, 2005.

Du Bois, W. E. B. "Editorial." *Crisis*, 1910. http://www.thecrisismagazine.com/TheCrisis1910.html (accessed July 23, 2010).

Du Bois, W. E. B. *The Negro*. 1915. Project Gutenberg e-book, released March 14, 2005.

Du Bois, W. E. B. "Returning Soldiers." *Crisis* 18 (May 1919).

Du Bois, W. E. B. *The Souls of Black Folk*. 1903. Project Gutenberg e-book, released January 29, 2008.

Horne, Gerald. *W. E. B. Du Bois: A Biography*. Santa Barbara, CA: Greenwood Press/ABC-CLIO, 2010.

Lewis, David Levering. *W. E. B. Du Bois, 1868–1919: Biography of a Race 1868–1919*. New York: Henry Holt and Company, 1994.

Lewis, David Levering. *W. E. B. Du Bois, 1919–1963: The Fight for Equality and the American Century*. New York: Henry Holt and Company, 2001.

E

Ellsberg, Daniel (1931–)

"The fact is, presidents rarely say the whole truth, essentially never say the whole truth of what they expect and what they're doing and what they believe, why they're doing it. And rarely refrain from lying, actually, about these matters. It's simply more convenient and more politically effective, they feel, for them to present matters to the public in a way that happens not to correspond to reality" (Ellsberg 1998). This was the opinion of Daniel Ellsberg, a longtime analyst and adviser to the U.S. military and presidents. He became widely known when he released documents about the U.S. government's maneuvering in Vietnam from 1945 to 1968.

Nothing in Ellsberg's upbringing, education, and initial career endeavors would have ever suggested that he would be indicted by the U.S. government—a country whose uniform he had once proudly worn—in the spring of 1973 for the possession and release of classified documents.

Daniel Ellsberg was born in Chicago, Illinois, on April 7, 1931. His father, a structural engineer, moved the family—consisting of Dan, one sister and their parents—to Detroit, Michigan, several years later. There, in the neighboring suburb of Bloomfield Hills, Dan attended the prestigious Cranbrook Kingswood School on scholarship. He excelled both academically as well as in his role as captain of the basketball team. Tragedy entered his life in 1946 when his sister and mother were killed in an automobile accident. A few years later, he earned another academic scholarship, this time to Harvard University, where he studied economics. He earned his bachelor of arts degree, graduating summa cum laude in 1952. He was selected as a Woodrow Wilson Fellow at King's College at Cambridge University and spent the year following college in Oxford, England. In 1953, Ellsberg then returned to the United States and to Harvard, this time to pursue a doctorate degree.

However, in April 1954, he decided to take time off from his studies and enlisted in the U.S. Marine Corps. He was accepted for officer's candidate school, which he completed, earning the rank of second lieutenant. He served until 1957, initially at Quantico and then at Camp Lejeune, both as platoon leader and company commander in the Marine Second Infantry Division. He held the rank of first lieutenant upon his discharge from the Corps.

Once again, Ellsberg returned to Harvard to resume his academic pursuits, broadening his interests to include coursework in political science and psychology. He eventually earned his PhD in 1962. His dissertation, entitled "Risk, Ambiguity and Decision," has been noted for its impact in the field of decision and behavioral economics.

In 1959, Ellsberg accepted a position as a strategic analyst with the Rand Corporation based in Santa Monica, California. He concurrently worked as a consultant to the White House, the secretary of defense, and the Department of State. Those dual roles enabled him to develop an expertise in the areas of crisis decision making, strategic war planning, and nuclear command and control. He decided to work for the government full time in August 1964 and resigned from his job at Rand. He took a job as a special assistant working at the Pentagon for the U.S. Department of Defense, under Assistant Secretary of Defense for International Security Affairs John McNaughton. Most of Ellsberg's efforts focused on the country's growing involvement in Vietnam.

In 1965, Ellsberg transferred to the State Department, where he spent two years as a senior liaison officer attached to the U.S. embassy in Saigon. After two years, he resigned that position and returned to Rand. As part of his new job, he participated in compiling a study commissioned at the behest of Secretary of Defense Robert McNamara—a comprehensive analysis of U.S. policy and decision making concerning Vietnam, spanning the years 1945 through 1968. It was to be a secret and highly classified internal report, and ultimately comprised approximately 7,000 pages of documentation.

From the first time he visited Vietnam until he resigned his position with the State Department in July 1967, Ellsberg had viewed U.S. involvement in Vietnam as futile. His increased and firsthand exposure had only served to multiply his frustration with the country's deepening commitments. After returning to the United States, he grew more and more dissatisfied with his country's policies and became increasingly predisposed to those actively opposing them.

It was in August 1969 that he finally reached a major turning point, going from acting one way in his professional life and feeling another way personally. He was somewhat "covertly" attending a War Resisters League (WRL) conference, when he decided to join antiwar activists distributing leaflets in support of Bob Eaton, a protester awaiting

Daniel Ellsberg at a press conference on December 30, 1971. He became widely known when he released classified documents about the U.S. government's maneuvering in Vietnam from 1945 to 1968. (AP Photo)

sentencing for refusing to register for the draft. He recounted the thoughts that went through his mind that day: "This was hardly the place, or the way, to announce to Rand, the Pentagon, and the White House that I was joining the public opposition to the war. Their war." But in hindsight, he later recalled, "I felt liberated . . . my first public action, had freed me from a near universal fear . . . I had become free of the fear of stepping out of line. One other thing happened . . . I had stepped across another line, an invisible one . . . I had joined a movement" (Ellsberg 2003, 268–70).

On August 28, the last day of this conference, Ellsberg was truly inspired. He listened to the words of fellow Harvard alumnus Randy Kehler, who now headed up the San Francisco office of the WRL. Randy was committed to serving time in jail for his beliefs. Ellsberg was strongly moved by Kehler's words. "What I had just heard from Randy put the question in my mind, What could I do, what should I be doing, to end the war now that I was ready to go to prison for it? ... I knew myself from Vietnam. I had risked my life, or worse, my body, my legs, a thousand times driving the roads there or walking in combat. If I could do that when I believed in the war, and even after I didn't, it followed self-evidently that I was capable of going to prison to help end it" (Ellsberg 2003, 272). If he had not heard Kehler's words that day, Ellsberg says he never would have thought about taking the actions that would make him famous and alter the course of U.S. and world history.

Thus, with the assistance of fellow Rand colleague Anthony Russo, Ellsberg began a stealth campaign to photocopy the documents related to McNamara's study. They plainly showed that the Kennedy, Johnson, and Nixon administrations had systematically lied—to the American people and to Congress—about the odds against the war being waged successfully and about the number of casualties expected. He resigned his job with Rand and began trying to make the information contained in the documents public knowledge. He attempted to get them into the hands of various congressional leaders, made offers to testify before Congress about his knowledge, and worked in conjunction with others from Rand to conduct a letter-writing campaign before turning the documents over to the press.

The first of nine excerpts of what would come to be known as the "Pentagon Papers" appeared in the *New York Times* on June 13, 1971. Ellsberg also provided the documentation to the *Washington Post* and 17 other periodicals for distribution. At President Richard Nixon's direction, U.S. attorney general John Mitchell ordered the *Times* to cease and desist its publication of the materials. The administration then obtained an appellate court order to issue an injunction against the newspaper—the federal government's first successful attempt to restrict publication by a major newspaper since Abraham Lincoln sat in the White House during the days of the Civil War. The victory was short-lived, however, and on June 30, the U.S. Supreme Court issued its ruling that the *Times* could resume its publication practices unfettered. Ellsberg's identity as the source for the documentation was not immediately known, but Ellsberg chose to turn himself in to the U.S. Attorney's Office in Boston on June 28. "I felt that as an American citizen, as a responsible citizen, I could no longer cooperate in concealing this information from the public. I did this clearly at my own jeopardy and I am prepared to answer to all the consequences of this decision" (United Press International 1971). He and Anthony Russo were then federally indicted under the Espionage Act of 1917 for the possession and unauthorized release of classified documents, along with charges of theft and conspiracy.

In the meantime, the Nixon administration began a campaign to discredit Ellsberg personally, as well as to discourage any future "leakers." Thus was born what would become the infamous "White House Plumbers," a group that would go on to take part in the 1972 break-in of the Democratic National Headquarters in the Washington, D.C, Watergate Hotel; revelation of their tactics led to President Nixon's resignation two years later.

Nixon's presidential assistant John Ehrlichman approved of and supervised a break-in of Dr. Lewis Fielding's Los Angeles–based psychiatrist's office on September 3, 1971; it was an attempt to locate Ellsberg's medical files but was unsuccessful. Another planned break-in, this time of Ellsberg's residence, failed to get a green light from Ehrlichman. However, in his 1980 biography, G. Gordon Liddy, a top-level Nixon aide, described yet another plot—this one involving Cuban waiters and LSD—indicating that people were becoming increasingly desperate in their vindictiveness against Ellsberg.

Ellsberg's trial took place in Los Angeles, beginning in January 1973 with U.S. district judge William Matthew Byrne Jr. presiding. It was not until April that the defense learned of the attempted burglary at Dr. Fielding's office. The next month, it was disclosed that the FBI had illegally wiretapped Ellsberg's conversations. Furthermore, during proceedings, the judge announced that he had met twice with Ehrlichman and been offered the FBI directorship (he stated he would not consider the offer with the case pending). On May 11, 1973, the case was dismissed due to gross government misconduct, tampering, and illegal evidence gathering.

The leak of the Pentagon Papers in 1971 was instrumental in turning the tide of public opinion against the Vietnam War. It also began to prepare mainstream Americans to consider the possibility that their leaders—indeed, even their president—might be capable of failure and falsehood, thus paving the way for the eventual resignation of President Richard M. Nixon in 1974.

Ellsberg has remained an ardent and proactive activist. His causes have been many and varied. Antiwar and antinuclear issues remain core passions. He was very vocal prior to the run-up of the United States' invasion of Iraq in 2003 and was arrested two years later while protesting against the war. More recently, he spoke out about U.S. Army private first class Bradley Manning, whom he classifies as a hero. Manning was arrested after allegedly providing the WikiLeaks web site with a classified video showing U.S. military helicopter gunships deliberately targeting and killing Iraqis who were alleged to be civilians and journalists. Manning reportedly has given WikiLeaks other damaging evidence, including over a quarter million classified State Department cables.

Several organizations have recognized Ellsberg for his willingness to take a stand for what he believes in, among them the Gandhi Peace Award in 1976; the inaugural Ron Ridenhour Courage Prize in 2004—and since shared with the likes of Seymour Hersch, Gloria Steinem, President Jimmy Carter, Bob Herbert, and Howard Zinn. He received the 2006 Right Livelihood Award, referred to as "the alternate Nobel Prize."

Margaret Gay

See also Zinn, Howard; Manning, Bradley

References

Ellsberg, Daniel. *Secrets: A Memoir of Vietnam and the Pentagon Papers*. New York: Penguin Books, 2003.

Ellsberg, Daniel, and Harry Kreister. "Presidential Decisions and Public Dissent." *The Institute of International Studies*, July 29, 1998. http://globetrotter.berkeley.edu/people/Ellsberg/ellsberg98-2.html (accessed March 12, 2011).

Liddy, G. Gordon. *Will: The Autobiography of G. Gordon Liddy*. New York: St. Martin's Press, 1980.

United Press International. "1971 Year in Review: The Pentagon Papers." UPI.com, 1971. http://www.upi.com/Audio/Year_in_Review/Events-of-1971/The-Pentagon-Papers/12295509436546-7/ (accessed March 12, 2011).

F

Farrakhan, Louis (1933–)

Take this pledge with me. Say with me please, I, say your name, pledge that from this day forward I will strive to love my brother as I love myself. I . . . from this day forward will strive to improve myself spiritually, morally, mentally, socially, politically, and economically for the benefit of myself, my family, and my people. I . . . pledge that I will strive to build business, build houses, build hospitals, build factories, and then to enter international trade for the good of myself, my family, and my people.

On October 16, 1995, Minister Louis Farrakhan shouted these words to a gathering estimated between 400,000 and 837,000 in an event called the Million Man March. Farrakhan structured his speech, as did other speakers in the event, around themes of atonement, reconciliation, and responsibility as he addressed urban and minority issues experienced by the black community. Charles Bierbauer points out, however, the controversy surrounding the leader of the Nation of Islam often overshadowed the message of the march. As Bierbauer notes, "The dilemma for many black men was whether to march for a message they can believe in—unity—without marching to a drummer they may not follow—Farrakhan" (Bierbauer 1995).

Louis Eugene Walcott was born May 11, 1933, in Bronx, New York, the younger of two sons whose mother was Sarah Mae Manning Clark, an immigrant from the Caribbean islands St. Kitts and Nevis. She was employed as a domestic worker. His father Percival Clark had emigrated from Jamaica and worked as a taxi driver. After her husband died in 1936, Sarah married Louis Walcott, and the children took his surname. The family lived in the West Indies neighborhood of Roxbury, Massachusetts, where Louis and Alvan were raised. Sarah introduced Louis to playing the violin when he was six years old. He became an accomplished violinist, eventually becoming one of the first black performers to appear on the Ted Mack Original Amateur Hour in 1946.

A strict disciplinarian and religiously devote, Sarah often discussed with her children the struggle for freedom and equality. At an early age, Louis began reading the *Crisis*, the premier crusading voice for civil rights, founded by W. E. B. Du Bois, and the official publication of the National Association for the Advancement of Colored People (NAACP). The family was very active in the St. Cyprian's Episcopal Church, where Louis sang in the church choir.

Louis attended the Boston Latin School and later the English High School, both established public schools for gifted children. During the summer, he worked as a camp counselor. When he was 16, Louis began performing in Boston nightclubs as a calypso musician, dancer, and violinist, calling himself "The Charmer." After graduating from high school, Louis accepted a track scholarship and enrolled at Winston-Salem Teachers College in North Carolina.

Louis Farrakhan addresses his followers at the Nation of Islam's Saviour's Day Convention at the University of Illinois–Chicago Pavilion, February 23, 1997. The convention included a live speech via satellite from Libya's Muammar al-Qaddafi and taped messages from the leaders of Ghana and Nigeria. In his speech, Farrakhan condemned American values and said that African Americans should form a nation of their own. (AP Photo/ Michael Conroy)

While in college, he met and married Betsy Ross of Boston, who later changed her name to Khadijah. The couple eventually had nine children. To support his family, Louis pursued a professional music career.

In 1955, Louis was introduced to Elijah Muhammad and the Nation of Islam (NOI). The NOI is an African American religious movement founded in 1931 by itinerant silk merchant Wallace D. Fard, whose teachings differed from orthodox Islam to include elements of the black nationalist movement, a contradictory blend of Islam, Jehovah's Witness doctrine, Gnosticism, and heretical Christian teachings. Fard also taught that the black man was not African, nor Arabic, but "Asiatic" in origin (Pement 1997).

Fard's doctrines were transmitted orally in the Secret Ritual of the Nation of Islam, which members had to memorize verbatim. The doctrine was available also in book form distributed only to registered, loyal followers. Members were required to give up their surname, considered a slave name, and take a new Arabic name (Pement 1997). After the disappearance of Fard in 1934, Elijah Muhammad became the leader, his teachings loosely based on Fard's instructions (Pipes 1984). The movement focused on the social and cultural improvement of the black community. With the rising civil rights movement, membership in the NOI surged. Muhammad and the NOI differed from other civil rights movements because it discouraged followers from participating in civil rights demonstrations or participating in the voting process (Stanford University News Service 1995). Rather, Muhammad and fellow leaders such as Malcolm X practiced militant rhetoric.

In a 1997 interview, Dr. Jerry Buckner offers several reasons why young black men were attracted to the NOI. It offered community programs, supported black-owned and operated businesses, dissuaded members against a heavy reliance on government welfare, and often recruited men behind bars and led them away from a life of crime. However, as Pement details, "While the NOI undoubtedly draws a higher percentage of people on the margins of society, an underclass who has felt anger toward the legal system, it is also true that its rhetoric tends to inflame that anger. Farrakhan's speeches often paint American society in terms of oppressed and oppressor, of slaves and slavemasters. While it is understandable that blacks can relate to a movement [that] 'addresses' racial problems, sometimes leaders of that same movement call for bloodshed" (Pement 1997).

Louis Walcott fulfilled the requirements for membership into the NOI, and he became Louis X, also known as Louis Farrakhan Muhammad. Farrakhan accepted his "X," used by members to acknowledge that their historic African family names were lost in the slave trade. As NOI leader Malcolm X, born Malcolm Little, had said, "The Muslim's 'X' symbolized the true African family name that he never could know. For me, my 'X' replaced the white slavemaster name of 'Little' which some blue-eyed devil named Little had imposed upon my paternal forebears" (Haley 1987, 229). Farrakhan became a protégé of Malcolm X.

As a function of his membership, Farrakhan had to give up his music. He became a member of the Muhammad's Temple in Boston, where Malcolm X was minister. He soon became assistant minister to Malcolm X. He also worked as a contributing writer to the NOI's national newspaper, *Muhammad Speaks*.

In the early 1960s, Malcolm X discovered, and made public, Muhammad's numerous infidelities with his teenage secretaries. Having these affairs, Muhammad violated his own teachings about the importance of fidelity in marriage. Muhammad justified his actions by comparing himself ironically to the Jewish biblical prophet of David (Pement 1997). On March 8, 1964, Malcolm X, disillusioned with the movement, announced that he was leaving NOI. He would eventually convert to Sunni Islam, moving away from militant rhetoric to militant politics. Farrakhan replaced him as minister of the Boston temple.

Farrakhan considered Malcolm X a traitor for his disloyalty, and condemned Malcolm for his efforts to establish ties with civil rights groups, writing that "the die is set, and Malcolm shall not escape, especially after such evil foolish talk about his benefactor, Elijah Muhammad. Such a man as Malcolm is worthy of death" (Stanford University News Service 1995). More death threats were made against Malcolm X, as Muhammad told his followers Malcolm's days were numbered. The NOI newspaper carried a cartoon of Malcolm's severed head bouncing down a street (Pement 1997).

On February 21, 1965, 10 weeks after Farrakhan's fateful words, Malcolm X was assassinated. In 1993, Farrakhan seemed to justify the assassination by stating, "Was Malcolm your traitor or ours? As if we deal with [Malcolm] like a nation deals with a traitor, what the hell business is it of yours? A nation has to be able to deal with traitors and cutthroats and turncoats" (Perazzo). In 2000, Farrakhan admitted in an interview with Mike Wallace on CBS News' *60 Minutes* that his incendiary rhetoric played a role in the assassination. Three members of the NOI were eventually convicted of the crime.

In 1967, Farrakhan became the national speaker for the NOI. Farrakhan, like his predecessors, continued the anti-Semitic rhetoric, calling whites "blue eyed devils" and Jews "bloodsuckers" who controlled the slave trade, the media, Hollywood, and various black individuals and organizations. As documented by the Anti-Defamation League (ADL), he has in various speeches and writings accused Jews of controlling the U.S. government and banking industries, and of world domination. He has referred to Judaism as a "gutter religion" and called Adolf Hitler "a great man," although he later claimed to mean that Hitler was "wickedly great." In 2004, Farrakhan addressed his anti-Semitic statements by offering, "I don't hate Jews. I honor and respect those who try to live according to the teachings of the Torah, but you can't criticize Jewish people.

If you criticize them you are anti-Semitic. If you don't agree with what they are doing, you are anti-Semitic" (ADL 2011).

In October 1995, Farrakhan helped to organize, and was keynote speaker, for the Million Man March. Included in the march were many local (but not national) groups of NAACP and other civil rights organizations. The march sought political attention to urban and minority issues. Although the march was regarded as a positive event, Farrakhan's presence often overshadowed the positive. "The Ku Klux Klan hates blacks, Jews and Catholics. The Nation of Islam hates whites, Jews and Catholics," said Congressman Gary Franks of Connecticut. "Both should be despised for these warped beliefs" (Bierbauer 1995). The Jewish Anti-Defamation League took out newspaper ads critical of Farrakhan's involvement in the march. Another controversial point was the exclusion of women. "I encourage black men to stand up and take care of their families," said Myrlie Evers-Williams, president of the NAACP. "But in all honesty, to eliminate women completely from this march does bother me a great deal" (Bierbauer 1995). In 1997, black nationalist Phile Chionesu organized the Million Woman March.

In 1996, Farrakhan went on several World Friendship Tours, traveling to Iran, Iraq, Libya, Syria, and Sudan. During these tours, Farrakhan publicly denounced the United States as "the Great Satan" (Perazzo). In the wake of the September 11, 2001, attacks, Farrakhan stated that the United States had insufficient proof on Osama bin Laden and Al-Qaeda's culpability, and portrayed the attack on Iraq as an unprovoked act of aggression, adding that "Sanctions are a weapon of mass destruction (against the Iraqi people). America is angry with Saddam Hussein because his people love him" (Perazzo).

Although Farrakhan initially supported Barack Obama as a presidential candidate, he rejected President Obama's backing for the 2011 military intervention in Libya. Instead, Farrakhan supported his longtime friend the late Moammar El-Gadhafi, whom he called brother. The Libyan leader had at one time loaned Farrakhan $3 million to purchase Chicago's Mosque Marryam, headquarters for the NOI. Farrakhan blamed demons for altering Obama's moral conscience and driving the assault on Libya (Brachear 2011). Gadhafi was killed in October 2011.

In 2007, Farrakhan stepped down as leader of the NOI because of an extended illness stemming from previous bouts with colon and prostate cancer. Some have said the illness may have mellowed the NOI leader, reflecting on Farrakhan's words in a 2007 speech, "Christians and Muslims, we have to break down these artificial divisions that divide us and come together as a family." However, as Farrakhan also noted, he remains steadfast in his stance on controversial issues: "I said to some of the groups that have quote-unquote been offended by my words, 'Come, let's sit down and reason together.' ... Show me where what I said was wrong. I can correct the manner of my delivery, that I can regret. But the words, if they're true, I would be a hypocrite to back down on the truth that I spoke" (Bashir 2007).

Bobbi Miller

See also Du Bois, W. E. B.; Malcolm X

References

Bashir, Martin, and Eileen Murphy. "Nightline Exclusive: Farrakhan Lauds Obama's Fresh Approach to Politics." *Nightline*, ABC News, March 8, 2007. http://abcnews.go.com/Nightline/story?id=2937953&page=1 (accessed April 9, 2011).

Bierbauer, Charles. "Its Goal More Widely Accepted Than Its Leader." CNN Interactive,

October 17, 1995. http://www.cnn.com/US/9510/megamarch/10-17/notebook/index.html (accessed April 8, 2011).

Brachear, Manya. "Farrakhan Defends 'My Brother' Gadhafi." *Chicago Tribune*, March 31, 2011. http://www.chicagotribune.com/news/local/ct-met-farrakhan-gadhafi-0401-20110331,0,1163420.story (accessed April 11, 2011).

CBS and Associated Press. "Farrakhan Admission on Malcolm X." *60 Minutes*, CBS News, May 10, 2000. http://www.cbsnews.com/stories/2000/05/10/60minutes/main194051.shtml (accessed April 11, 2011).

"Farrakhan in His Own Words." Anti-Defamation League (ADL), Updated April 7, 2011. http://www.adl.org/special_reports/farrakhan_own_words2/farrakhan_own_words.asp (accessed April 11, 2011).

Funk, Ray. "Farrakhan the Mighty Charmer." *Sunday Express*, January 16, 2000. http://www.nalis.gov.tt/Biography/calypsomusic_LouisFarrakhan.htm (accessed April 8, 2011).

Haley, Alex, and Malcolm X. *The Autobiography of Malcolm X*. New York: Ballantine Books, 1987.

Holland, Bernard. "Sending a Message, Louis Farrakhan Plays Mendelssohn." *New York Times*, April 19, 1993. http://www.nytimes.com/1993/04/19/arts/sending-a-message-louis-farrakhan-plays-mendelssohn.html?pagewanted=all (accessed April 8, 2011).

Judis, John B. "Maximum Leader." *New York Times*, August 18, 1996. http://query.nytimes.com/gst/fullpage.html?res=9900E4DC1531F93BA2575BC0A960958260 (accessed April 8, 2011).

MacFarquhar, Neil. "Nation of Islam at a Crossroad as Leader Exits." *New York Times*, February 26, 2007. http://www.nytimes.com/2007/02/26/us/26farrakhan.html?_r=1 (accessed April 8, 2011).

"Minister Farrakhan Challenges Black Men: Transcripts from Minister Louis Farrakhan's Remarks at the Million Man March." CNN Interactive, October 17, 1995. http://www-cgi.cnn.com/US/9510/megamarch/10-16/transcript/index.html (accessed April 8, 2011).

"Nation of Islam." Southern Poverty Law Center. http://www.splcenter.org/get-informed/intelligence-files/groups/nation-of-islam (accessed April 9, 2011).

Parsons, Monique. "The Most Important Muslim You've Never Heard Of." Beliefnet.com. http://www.beliefnet.com/Faiths/Islam/2003/09/The-Most-Important-Muslim-Youve-Never-Heard-Of.aspx?p=1 (accessed April 11, 2011).

Pement, Eric. "Louis Farrakhan and the Nation of Islam." *Cornerstone* 26, no. 111 (1997). http://www.cornerstonemag.com/features/iss111/islam1.htm (accessed April 9, 2011).

Perazzo, John. "Louis Farrakhan." Discover TheNetworks.org: A Guide to the Political Left. 2003–2010. http://www.discoverthenetworks.org/individualProfile.asp?indid=1325 (accessed April 6, 2011).

Pipes, Daniel. "Louis Farrakhan Is Not a Muslim." *Washington Post*, July 2, 1984. http://www.danielpipes.org/167/louis-farrakhan-is-not-a-muslim (accessed April 8, 2011).

Russert, Tim. "Farrakhan Meets the Press (Interview with Tim Russert)." *Final Call*, online edition, April 13, 1997. http://www.finalcall.com/national/mlf-mtp5-13-97.html (accessed April 11, 2011).

"Religion: White Muslims?" *Time*, June 30, 1975. http://www.time.com/time/magazine/article/0,9171,917589,00.html (accessed April 11, 2011).

Stanford University News Service. "Farrakhan Helped Build Climate for Malcolm X's Death, Historian Says." News release, January 1, 1995. http://news.stanford.edu/pr/95/950117Arc5411.html (accessed April 11, 2011).

Flynn, Elizabeth Gurley (1890–1964)

In 1964, a crowd of 25,000 gathered in Moscow's Red Square—this plaza held in such high regard by the Russian people—to pay tribute to an American citizen. A unique and rare honor was being bestowed on a noncitizen who had passed away while visiting on Russian soil: a state funeral was held for Elizabeth Gurley Flynn. Many mistakenly believe that Red Square, "*Krásnaya plóshchad*," is named either for the Kremlin's adjacent red walls or in symbolic honor of communism. Neither is correct. The significance of the term "red" derives from the old Russian meaning of the word—"beautiful."

After the ceremony for Flynn in Red Square, her remains were returned to the United States and Chicago's Waldheim Cemetery, where, per Flynn's request, she was buried near the graves of Eugene V. Debs and other labor activists. What did this woman do during her 74 years on earth to merit such an honor as was awarded her in Red Square?

Flynn's beginnings were modest enough. She was born in Concord, New Hampshire, on August 7, 1890, to Thomas and Annie Gurley Flynn. The family lived in impoverished circumstances, moving frequently during Elizabeth's first 10 years before settling in the South Bronx of New York in 1900. Her parents were first-generation Irish immigrants. Their beliefs instilled in her what was, for the times, considered to be a radical way of thinking—that is, socialist and feminist principles. The family often had guests stay with them—Irish Freedom Fighters visiting from overseas—and Elizabeth became schooled in the tales they told about standing up for one's rights and beliefs. Her views were also shaped by her relationship with her high school beau, Fred Robinson. His father, Dr. William Robinson, was a strident anarchist and also a proponent of birth control (Flynn 1977, 11).

All of Flynn's education was by virtue of the public school system. People responded to her oratory and written skills with high praise. Conflicting reports exist as to whether or not she willingly quit high school or was expelled; regardless of which version is correct, Flynn began to participate in workplace organizing activities and was drawing the attention of many for her persuasive skills at an early age. In 1906, she joined Local No. 179 of the International Workers of the World (IWW), a mixed local (which meant that it allowed both men and women as members). That same year, Flynn gave a speech at the Harlem Socialist Club entitled, "What Socialism Will Do for Women." From the very start, she was on a path to pursue rights for all, regardless of gender. By 1907, Flynn was organizing for IWW on a full-time basis.

IWW was founded in Chicago in June 1905 at a convention of 200 socialists, anarchists, and radical trade unionists from all over the country. Its aim was to promote worker solidarity in the revolutionary struggle to overthrow the employing class. IWW contended that all workers should be united as one class against their oppressors.

One year after joining IWW's membership, at the age of 17, Flynn was elected as a delegate to the organization's third convention and also asked to make her first speaking tour on behalf of IWW on her way back from the meeting in Chicago. She possessed a natural ability to captivate and motivate a crowd. Friend, feminist, and pioneer labor journalist Mary Heaton Morse recounted: "The excitement of the crowd became a visible thing. She stood there, young, with her Irish blue eyes, her face magnolia white, and her cloud of black hair, the picture of a revolutionary girl leader. She stirred them, lifted them up in her appeal for solidarity. Then at the end of the meeting they sang. It was as though a spurt of flame had gone through the audience, something stirring and powerful, a feeling which had made the

Elizabeth Gurley Flynn, known as the "Rebel Girl," was a 20th-century activist whose causes included the labor movement, woman suffrage, civil liberties, socialism, and peace. (Library of Congress)

liberation of the people possible, something beautiful and strong had swept through the people and bonded them together, singing" (Baxandall 1989, 17).

Within another year, she met and married Jack Archibald, a fellow organizer who was a miner by trade. They were often separated due to their respective work obligations but managed to have two children in rapid succession: one in 1909, who died shortly after a premature birth, and the second in 1910, a son named Fred. Shortly thereafter, Flynn and Archibald ended their marriage.

Flynn returned with her son to the Bronx, where she entrusted her mother and sister with her son's day-to-day welfare whenever she traveled for her work—which was frequently. She never remarried but did have a long-term affair with well-known anarchist Carlo Tresca. John Updike's novel *In the Beauty of the Lilies* (1996) includes a fictionalized version of the Flynn-Tresca romance.

Working for IWW, Flynn traveled all over the United States. Her activities ranged from organizing workers to participating in strikes and giving rousing speeches. She was arrested many times but never convicted until the end of her career. She took part in free-speech fights in Missoula, Montana, and Spokane, Washington, in 1908 and 1910. She took part in the Lawrence Textile Workers' Strike of 1912, the Patterson Silk Weavers' Strike of 1913, the Minnesota Mesabi Iron Range Strike of 1916, and the Passaic Textile Strike of 1926, to name but a few. Although Flynn's activities were varied and she was quick to champion anyone who was downtrodden, she always returned to what she saw as the special causes of women and children. She also loudly opposed the chauvinism she saw in IWW itself, and tried to change how the group dealt with its female members and their concerns.

Flynn was also a founding member of the American Civil Liberties Union (ACLU). This group formed in 1920 for two main purposes: (1) to protect aliens who were being threatened with deportation; and (2) to defend U.S. nationals who were being threatened with criminal charges by U.S. attorney general Alexander Mitchell Palmer for their so-called communist or socialist activities and agendas. The ACLU also defended the rights of IWW and other labor union members to meet and organize and helped organize protests against the racist Ku Klux Klan.

Never one to sit idle, Flynn also chaired the Workers' Defense Union and its successor, the International Labor Defense (ILD). ILD was formed in 1925 by the Central Committee of the Communist Party of the

United States to support those it saw as "victims" in an ongoing class war. It defended strikers and other workers facing unjust labor environments, foreigners who were discriminated against or faced deportation, and African Americans who, particularly in the southern states, faced hostility and racism. ILD believed that militant strikes and direct action against oppressors would lead to equality among the classes, and ultimately, the workers would seize the methods of production from their oppressors. On the whole, ILD was aggressive, assertive, and combative—which contrasted sharply with the methods employed by other civil rights groups that typically preached peace and pacifism.

Over time, Flynn's involvement in these groups expanded beyond organizing and speechmaking. She reached out to those imprisoned as "radicals," fund-raising for their defense, helping to hire lawyers for them, and working to sway public opinion. One case of national prominence that she was involved in was that of Nicola Sacco and Bartolomeo Vanzetti, which held the nation's attention for more than seven years. These two Italian immigrant anarchists were convicted of murdering two men during a 1920 robbery. Following a controversial trial and a series of appeals, the two men were executed. On the 50th anniversary of their execution, Massachusetts governor Michael Dukakis, on the recommendation of the State Office of Legal Counsel, declared August 23, 1977, Nicola Sacco and Bartolomeo Vanzetti Day, proclaiming that they had been unfairly tried and convicted and that "any disgrace should be forever removed from their names" (Sinclair 1978, 797–99; Young 1985, 3–4).

Ill health, burnout, and emotional stress from her romance with Tresca prompted Flynn to relocate to Portland, Oregon, from 1926 until 1936. She lived with IWW activist and birth-control advocate Dr. Marie Equi and lent her support to labor issues from time to time.

Flynn returned to New York in 1936, whereupon she joined the Communist Party of the United States of America (CPUSA). Although the ACLU was aware of her intent to join and her subsequent membership in the CPUSA when they unanimously elected her to a three-year term on its executive board, the group eventually expelled her from its ranks for her communist ties. In late 1940, when Germany and the Soviet Union joined forces so that the former could evade the British blockade, anti-Soviet sentiment escalated in the United States, and that likely was the impetus behind Flynn's expulsion.

The CPUSA had been in existence in the United States since 1919. It had a major part in the labor movement from the 1920s into the 1940s. It played a major role in the founding of many of the first industrial unions (which would, in turn, show their "appreciation" by expelling communist or communist-sympathizing members via adoption of the Smith Act). CPUSA also fought for integration, both in the workplace and in communities during the height of U.S. racial oppression.

Flynn was undeterred by ACLU's ostracism and continued to work zealously for the Communist Party throughout World War II. In fact, the war heightened her zeal to push for equal economic opportunities and pay for women, as more and more women entered the workforce; she also lobbied for the establishment of day care centers. She and others used the war as an opportunity to publicize the many contributions that women were making to the military effort. Going further than most, Flynn advocated for women's participation in the draft. She did other, more conventional things, such as urge purchase of savings bonds and campaign for President Roosevelt's reelection.

Flynn's hard work caused her to rise rapidly in CPUSA's ranks; she was rewarded with a seat on its national board early on. She was not only one of the organization's most popular speakers, but she also wrote a column for the CPUSA's *Daily Worker* for more than two decades, appearing two to four times weekly.

As the decades progressed, various events steadily weakened CPUSA's structure and confidence. Anticommunist critics painted the party as a threatening, subversive, "un-American" entity. Those members who were not imprisoned for their role in CPUSA activities either began to quietly drop their affiliation or go on to adopt more mainstream political beliefs.

After World War II ended, when fear of communism rose to perhaps its greatest heights, Flynn fell prey to the "red frenzy" along with many of her colleagues. In 1952, under the Smith Act, she was arrested, tried, and convicted of conspiring to teach and advocate the overthrow of the U.S. government. As a result, from January 1955 until May 1957, she was imprisoned at the women's federal penitentiary at Alderson, West Virginia. She wrote two books about her life—the first while awaiting jail, *The Rebel Girl: An Autobiography, My First Life* (reprint), originally published as *I Speak My Own Piece: Autobiography of "The Rebel Girl"* (1955); and the second written after her release from prison, *The Alderson Story: My Life as a Political Prisoner* (1963).

When freed, Flynn again took up her work in the Communist Party. She became national chairman in 1961—the first female in that role, which is what occasioned her to take several trips to the Soviet Union. And, thus, during one such visit, when she fell ill and died on September 5, 1964, her personage was regarded in such high esteem that her passing was honored with a state funeral in Red Square.

The ACLU reinstated Elizabeth Gurley Flynn as a member posthumously in 1976.

Margaret Gay

See also Debs, Eugene V.; Sacco, Ferdinando Nicola, and Vanzetti, Bartolomeo; Sinclair, Upton

References

Baxandall, Rosalyn Fraad. *Words on Fire: The Life and Writings of Elizabeth Gurley Flynn*. New Brunswick, NJ: Rutgers University Press, 1989.

Flynn, Elizabeth Gurley, *The Rebel Girl: An Autobiography, My First Life (1906–1926)*. Rev. ed. Lincolnwood, IL: Publications International, 1976.

Flynn, Elizabeth Gurley, Walker C. Smith, William E. Trautman, and Salvatore Salverno. *Direct Action and Sabotage: Three Classic IWW Pamphlets From the 1910s*. Chicago: Charles H. Kerr Publishing Co., 1977.

Sinclair, Upton. *Boston: A Documentary Novel*. Cambridge, MA: Robert Bentley, Inc., 1978.

Updike, John. *In the Beauty of the Lilies*. New York: Random House Publishing Group, 1996.

Young, William, and David E. Kaiser. *Postmortem: New Evidence in the Case of Sacco and Vanzetti*. Amherst: University of Massachusetts Press, 1985.

Frank, Barney (1940–)

"Barney's stage is the floor of the House of Representatives chamber. When he approaches the microphone to speak, members conversing in the rear of the chamber tend to stop their chatter to hear what he has to say," wrote Stuart Weisenberg in a biography about Barney Frank. The author explained that U.S. representative Frank "is a master of thinking on his feet and speaking extemporaneously. Many consider him to be without peer in Congress as a debater, whether engaging in ideological combat or in skirmishes on narrowly defined issues" (Weisenberg 2009, 2). An admitted cranky congressman and also a compassionate one, Frank has consistently worked for the common good and equality for the powerless. He is outspoken in his dissent against those who would deny lesbian, gay, bisexual, and transsexual (LGBT) individuals their civil rights. As an openly gay congressman, he won his 16th term in office in 2010.

Barney was named Barnett Frank on his birth, March 31, 1940, to Samuel and Elsie Frank, Jewish immigrants from Eastern Europe. Samuel Frank was co-owner of a truck stop and Elsie was a secretary for a law firm. Barney, as he has always been called, is the second of four children. He has an older sister, Ann, and a younger sister Doris and younger brother David, all of whom have been politically involved in some way as adults.

The family lived in a middle-class, multiethnic neighborhood in Bayonne, New Jersey, "where Catholics and Jews, Italians, Poles, Irish, and other ethnic groups lived together in relative harmony" (Weisenberg 2009, 23). The Franks were members of a nearby orthodox synagogue primarily because there was not a reform temple in their area. Barney's father helped raise funds to build a reform synagogue near their home.

When Barney was in first grade, his father was arrested in connection with a bribery case. According to biographer Weisenberg, "Bribery and kickbacks were time-honored traditions and mob influence and corruption were part of the fabric of life in Bayonne." Sam Frank's older brother "Harry Frank and a partner owned an auto dealership and got the contract to sell cars to the city." They gave "a kickback for the contract to two Bayonne Democratic commissioners.... Sam was subsequently arrested as a material witness. When he refused to testify before a grand jury, he was found in criminal contempt." Sam Frank was sentenced to a year in prison. Although Sam Frank was sure his family would be ashamed of him, just the opposite was true. Barney admired his father "for not breaking down and testifying." The rest of the family expressed similar reactions (Weisenberg 2009, 28–29).

Barney and his siblings attended Washington Elementary School in Bayonne and also the public high school. While in high school, Barney worked on Saturdays at his father's truck stop, pumping gas. He was involved in sports—softball, football, and tennis, on the staff of the school newspaper, and member of the debating club and National Honor Society. Barney followed major league baseball as a devoted fan of the Yankees, attending games whenever he could as did his younger sister Doris.

Politics and civic affairs were topics of conversation at the Frank dinner table, and the children were taught that government had the power to do good for society. The Franks entertained numerous politicians as well as their children's friends in the finished basement—which was more like a fancy lounge—of their home.

At an early age, Barney's goal was to become a member of the U.S. Congress. He was especially interested in the political actions revealed on television during the 1954 congressional hearings, when Senator Joseph McCarthy of Wisconsin accused the U.S. Army of allowing communists to infiltrate the service. The U.S. Senate eventually censured McCarthy for his fraudulent charges. In 1956, Barney campaigned for Adlai Stevenson in his second bid for U.S. president. Although Stevenson lost, Frank's love of politics never diminished. After graduating from high school in 1957, he and his family traveled to Washington, D.C., and Barney spent most of the time observing congressional sessions.

As a teenager, Barney dated many girls, but he had known from the time he was about 12 years old that he had a sexual preference for boys. He hid his homosexuality from his family and friends for years. At the time, there was widespread discrimination against and harassment of homosexuals in the United States—a condition that still exists in some parts of the nation. Frank struggled for years trying to deal with his sexual preferences. During his university years, he had female friends, but broke off any relationship when it began to get serious.

In 1957, Frank enrolled at Harvard University in Cambridge, Massachusetts. He took courses in government and was involved in student political activities. While he was at Harvard, his father died of a heart attack, and Frank left his studies for a year to take care of the family's business affairs. He graduated in 1962, and went on to study for a doctorate degree, but left Harvard in 1968 to work as chief assistant for Mayor Kevin White of Boston.

In 1972, Frank ran for a seat in the Massachusetts state legislature and won, serving for eight years. While in office, he taught part time at Harvard and other universities and earned a law degree. He was admitted to the Massachusetts bar in 1979. The following year, he was a successful candidate for the U.S. House of Representatives and began representing the fourth district of Massachusetts in 1981.

Representative Frank became well known nationwide in 1987 when he publicly announced that he was gay. He was the first member of Congress to voluntarily reveal his homosexuality, although other congressional members have been forced to do so. "At the time, the disclosure provoked more curiosity than controversy," wrote Jeffrey Toobin in the *New Yorker*. He pointed out that "two years later, Stephen Gobie, a prostitute whom Frank had patronized and then befriended, made a series of lurid allegations about him—claiming that they had had sex in the House gym and that Frank had permitted Gobie to run a prostitution ring out of his home. An investigation by the House Ethics Committee failed to substantiate those charges, though it determined that Frank had written a misleading letter of recommendation for Gobie and had Gobie's parking tickets waived" (Toobin 2009, 37).

The House investigation was not a hindrance to Frank's reelection and during the 1990s, he became a strong, vocal critic of Republicans. He was especially adamant in his criticism of those on the Judiciary Committee who wanted to impeach President William Jefferson Clinton for lying about his affair with Monica Lewinsky, a White House intern. As Frank noted: "Bill Clinton is . . . not a purely innocent person having suddenly been mugged. The guy's done something he shouldn't have done and he should have known better," Frank told Sally Quinn of the *Washington Post*. Clinton, Frank argued, deserved "[s]trong censure," not impeachment. "In defense of the president at the House Judiciary Committee hearings," Quinn wrote, "Frank put on a tour de force—interjecting procedural questions, leaping on points of order, deftly zinging an opponent, cracking jokes when the atmosphere became particularly poisonous" (Quinn 1998, D01). In spite of Frank's arguments, Clinton was impeached but eventually acquitted at a Senate trial.

Currently, in Congress, at town meetings, on talk shows, and elsewhere "Frank never speaks from a prepared text, and he talks so quickly that transcription is nearly impossible. His staff in Washington sometimes posts videos of his remarks on the Web instead," wrote Jeffrey Toobin in a *New Yorker* profile of Frank (2009).

There is no question that Barney Frank is an ardent Democrat, but he has often helped to pass bipartisan legislation. In fact, congressional members named Frank as "one of the most partisan *and* one of the most bipartisan Members," according to Frank's congressional web site.

Frank has sponsored, cosponsored, or introduced legislation on a variety of issues, and he has been outspoken regarding LGBT issues. In 1995, for example, Republican Dick Armey, the majority leader in the House at the time, held a press interview in which he referred to Frank as "Barney Fag" (a shortened version of the homophobic slur "faggot" to describe LGBT people). Although Armey apologized and insisted he had made an innocent mistake, he created an uproar. Frank was quick to point out that his mother, who had been married for decades at the time, had never ever been introduced as Elsie Fag. In Frank's view, Armey had heard the disparaging term so often that he uttered it without a thought.

During the 2000s, Frank became chairman of the House Financial Services Committee, which has oversight of the financial and insurance industries. In the view of his older sister Ann Frank Lewis, who was President Clinton's director of communications, Barney Frank had been aiming for such a leadership role for most of his life.

Among Frank's many concerns as a congressman, he has consistently supported the Employment Non-Discrimination Act, which he and others have introduced repeatedly in the House. The Act would extend existing legal protections prohibiting discrimination on the basis of race, religion, gender, national origin, age, and disability to include prohibiting discrimination based on sexual orientation and gender identity—that is, incorporate transgender protection. In support of the 2009 version, Frank testified before the House Education and Labor Committee, and said in part: "It just seems to me so self-evident, that an American who would like to work, and support himself or herself, ought to be allowed to do that judged solely on his or her work ethic and talents." Several times Frank addressed the fears of those who opposed adding transgender protection. In one instance, he said: "there's nothing to be afraid of. These are our fellow human beings. They aren't asking you for anything other, in this bill, for the right to earn a living" (Frank 2009).

Frank has also been a staunch advocate for repealing the so-called Don't Ask, Don't Tell (DADT) policy of the U.S. military. The policy banned gays and lesbians from serving openly in the armed forces. If they revealed their sexual orientation, gay and lesbian personnel were discharged. Although President Obama signed a law repealing DADT in December 2010, the Pentagon did not officially repeal DADT until September 2011.

Whatever issues Frank champions, some of the most contentious have been related to his support for federal funds to prevent financial institutions from failing. Critics also condemn him for not strongly regulating the Federal National Mortgage Association (Fannie Mae) and the Federal Home Mortgage Corporation (Freddie Mac) that were seized by the federal government in 2008. He especially angered Bill O'Reilly of the Fox News show *The O' Reilly Factor*. When Frank was on the show in 2008, O'Reilly called on Congressman Frank to resign as chairman of the House Financial Services Committee, because, according to O'Reilly, Frank had encouraged people to invest in the failing mortgage companies. Frank denied the charge and O'Reilly yelled: "Come on, you coward, say the truth," and continued to berate his guest. Frank retorted: "You start ranting, and the only way to respond is to almost talk as boorish as you." The show deteriorated further into more shouting and insults.

Although Frank can be grumpy, cantankerous, and impatient, he is also witty (but never smiles) and empathetic. According to biographer Weisenberg, Frank is also "open-minded, astute, and [a] practical deal maker who works across party lines to craft compromises and build bridges" (Weisenberg, 2009, 8). Speaker of the House Nancy Pelosi called Frank "an enormously valuable intellectual resource for the Congress" (Toobin 2009). Few expect Frank to change his persona, whether appearing in or out of Congress.

Karen L. Hamilton

See also McCarthy, Joseph

References

Bollen, Peter D. *Frank Talk: The Wit and Wisdom of Barney Frank*. Lincoln, NE: iUniverse, 2006.

Frank, Barney (testimony). "Frank Testifies in Support of the Employment Non-Discrimination Act." Press release, September 23, 2009. http://www.house.gov/frank/pressreleases/2009/09-23-09-enda-testimony.html (accessed November 15, 2010).

Quinn, Sally. "Clinton Accused Special Report." *Washington Post*, December 18, 1998.

Toobin, Jeffrey. "Barney's Great Adventure." *New Yorker*, June 12, 2009. http://www.newyorker.com/reporting/2009/01/12/090112fa_fact_toobin (accessed November 11, 2010).

Weisenberg, Stuart. *Barney Frank: The Story of America's Only Left-Handed, Gay, Jewish Congressman*. Amherst: University of Massachusetts Press, 2009.

Franken, Al (1951–)

Al Franken has been a political dissident for most of his adult life, presenting his opinions as a satirist, comedian, author, and in his role as U.S. senator from Minnesota. Most of his early dissent as an entertainer was aimed at public figures on the far right of the political spectrum, such as Rush Limbaugh, Bill O'Reilly, and Glenn Beck. His outspoken comments and published ridicule have angered many Republicans who call Franken a public enemy and many other denigrating names.

Franken was born on May 21, 1951, in New York City. His parents, Phoebe G. Kunst and Joseph P. Franken, the latter a printing salesman, named him Alan Stuart Franken. Al was four years old when he and his older brother Owen moved with their parents to St. Louis Park, Minnesota, a suburb of Minneapolis. The boys grew up in a Jewish household, which Franken noted in a *Beliefnet* interview was "Not particularly devout. We were reform Jews and I didn't even get bar mitzvahed. I was confirmed. . . . [The] confirmation process was about history of Judaism, learning about the Bible the spiritual aspects of all that. It wasn't incredibly rigorous. I'd have to go in on Saturday. It wasn't that long. It was like 2 years, and I hated it" (Waldman 2003).

In the interview, Franken also commented about the religious right, claiming:

> They sometimes forget we don't live in a theocracy. They can be in the public

square and express their opinion but to expect other people to alter their behavior to say that, for example, that homosexuality is immoral because it says so in the Bible... I mean there's stuff in the Bible about how to sell your daughter. They kind of are pretty selective about what is important and what isn't. I think slavery is ok in the Bible. It's stupid! It's like the dumbest thing that they want to proscribe other people's behavior based on their belief. (Waldman 2003)

Comedy was very much a part of the Franken household. Al liked to watch Jewish comedians on television with his father. When he was growing up, he also liked Dick Gregory and his political comedy. Those times helped establish Franken's love for comedy and his own comic routine, which later was mixed with a large dose of politics.

Politics was a favorite topic in the Franken home. Al's parents were loyal Republicans until Barry Goldwater (1909–1998), the Republican candidate for U.S. president in 1964, opposed the Civil Rights Act, declaring it an infringement of states' rights and people's right to do business with anyone they pleased. The Frankens switched political parties and were Democrats for the rest of their lives.

Al attended the Blake School, a Protestant private school for preschool through 12th grade, in Minneapolis, Minnesota. Franken once joked that in the 1950s, the school admitted Jews in order to raise their Scholastic Aptitude Test (SAT) scores. A writer for the Jewish newspaper *Forward* noted that "In high school, Franken did experience anti-Semitism.... The senior lounge was sprayed with anti-Jewish graffiti, but rather than get angry or upset, Franken wrote an amusing retort and appeared in the school chapel to read it to his classmates while sporting a Nazi armband. This shocking but clever tactic ... showed him how humor could be used to defuse and challenge unfunny situations" (Lazarus 2005). During his teenage years, Franken was on the varsity wrestling team and also began to write and perform comedy with his friend Tom Davis. The two went to local comedy clubs to develop their skills and worked together during and after their college years. Franken graduated cum laude from Harvard University in 1973, earning a master's degree in political science.

At the university, Franken met his future wife, Franni Bryson, at a college dance. They dated throughout their college years and married on October 2, 1975, making their home in New York City. They eventually had two children—a daughter, Thomasin, born in 1981; and a son, Joe, born in 1984.

Franken and his friend Davis continued their comedy acts and in 1975, they were hired to write scripts for and occasionally perform in the *Saturday Night Live* (*SNL*) television show. They left the show in 1980 but again were employed by *SNL* between 1985 and 1995. Franken won five Emmy awards and seven nominations for his work on the show.

The two friends, who were "close as brothers," split up in 1989, because according to *New York Times* writer Russell Shorto, Franken believed "that Davis had a drug and alcohol problem and urged him to go into a 12-step program. Davis didn't agree, and Franken tried to take on the problem himself by attending Al-Anon meetings for partners of abusers. It didn't work" (Shorto 2004). Franken actually joined Al-Anon in 1987 because of his wife's alcoholism. Franni Franken has discussed publicly her alcohol dependency and credits Al with helping her during her struggle for recovery.

Al Franken (right) campaigning for U.S. Senate at the Minnesota State Fair in 2008. Franken has had a long career as a comedian, actor, writer, and radio talk show host. (Shutterstock)

As a political satirist, Franken was widely praised for his commentary on cable channel CNN during the 1988 Democratic National Convention in Atlanta. In 1992, he covered both the Republican and Democratic conventions for Comedy Central's eight-day programming called "Indecision '92."

Franken continued writing and acting, and between 1995 and 2005, four of his books of political satire were published: *The Truth: With Jokes* (2005), *Lies and the Lying Liars Who Tell Them: A Fair and Balanced Look at the Right* (2003), *Why Not Me? The Inside Story of the Making and Unmaking of the Franken Presidency* (1999), and *Rush Limbaugh Is a Big Fat Idiot: And Other Observations* (1996). The latter was on the *New York Times* bestseller list for eight months. As background for the Limbaugh book, Franken actually listened to the talk show host daily for five days. Franken recorded the book, and the tape won the 1997 Grammy for Best Comedy Album.

After he wrote *Lies and Lying Liars*, which attacked U.S. president George W. Bush and his policies as well as conservative talk-show hosts like Bill O'Reilly, Franken found himself in a highly publicized dispute with O'Reilly and Fox News, the cable channel where O'Reilly appears. In August 2003, Fox hoped to block publication of Franken's book and sued (*Fox News Network, LLC v. Penguin Group USA, Inc. and Alan S. Franken*), claiming the phrase "fair and balanced" in the title of Franken's book was an infringement of Fox's registered trademark. The lawsuit also charged that the cover of the book gives the impression that it originated at Fox News. However, the lawsuit was dismissed as being "wholly without merit."

In 2004, Franken launched an Air America Radio show designed to counteract conservative radio talk shows. At its peak, the show had 1.5 million listeners per week. A year later, Franken moved with his wife (their children were grown and leading their own lives) from New York to Minnesota, continuing his show from there. In 2007, he announced on his last show that he would be a candidate for the U.S. Senate seat from Minnesota.

Franken had been considering a run for political office for some time, especially after his good friend, Minnesota senator Paul Wellstone, and his wife and daughter were killed in a plane crash in 2002. Wellstone's death affected Franken deeply, and he wanted to continue Wellstone's progressive approach to politics. He debated with himself and with others whether to run for office. But in 2007, he made it official—he would make the transition from comedian to serious Democratic-Farmer-Labor Party candidate. The party is a merger of Minnesota's Democratic Party and the Farmer-Labor Party and is associated with the national Democratic Party. Franken's opposition was Republican senator Norm Coleman, who was running for a second term.

In 2008, while the campaign was under way, the state of New York claimed that Franken's corporation did not carry workers' compensation for its employees. As a result, the corporation had to pay a $25,000 fine to the state. The corporation also was assessed fines and penalties for failure to pay income taxes to the state of California and other states where Franken had appeared as an entertainer. Nevertheless, the tax issues had little effect on the election, which was covered by news media nationwide.

After the election, Coleman held a lead, but both Coleman and Franken received 42 percent of the vote, which by Minnesota law required a recount. Franken won initially. But Coleman objected, eventually taking his case to the Minnesota Supreme Court. On June 30, 2009, more than eight months after the election, the court ruled that Franken had won the most votes—by a margin of 312 votes out of 2.9 million cast. Coleman conceded, and on July 7, 2009, Franken was sworn in as Minnesota's junior senator. In 2010, he was on the Health, Education, Labor, and Pension Committee; the Judiciary Committee; the Committee on Indian Affairs; and the Special Committee on Aging.

His first year in office was nonconfrontational and he stayed out of the spotlight for the most part. Franken wanted to convince his constituents that he was in Congress to work. "He turned down requests from national TV shows, choosing to focus on the arcane details of issues like health care and banks. He held meetings in Minnesota to hear experts and advocates outline views on everything from Wall Street to the Afghanistan war," according to a report in *U.S. News and World Report* (2010). Although many believe Franken will continue to be a serious politician, his opponents are eager to challenge him in 2014. Opponents contend that Franken's liberal views make him vulnerable in a relatively conservative state.

Over the years, Franken was a volunteer with the United Service Organizations (USO), visiting Germany, Bosnia, Kosovo, Uzbekistan, Iraq, Afghanistan, and Kuwait, plus Bethesda Naval Hospital and the Walter Reed Army Medical Center. In 2009, the USO presented him with a Merit Award for his decade of service to the organization.

See also Beck, Glenn; Gregory, Dick; Limbaugh, Rush

References

Franken, Al. *Lies and the Lying Liars Who Tell Them: A Fair and Balanced Look at the Right.* New York: Penguin, 2003.

Franken, Al. *Rush Limbaugh Is a Big, Fat Idiot and Other Observations.* New York: Delacorte Press, 1996.

Hirsh, Michael. "Al Franken Gets Serious." *Newsweek*, July 5, 2010. http://www.newsweek.com/2010/07/05/al-franken-gets-serious.html (accessed August 29, 2010).

Lazarus, Catie. "A Fair and Balanced Look at Al Franken." *Forward*, February 4, 2005. http://www.forward.com/articles/2877/ (accessed August 31, 2010).

"Minnesota's Al Franken Turns in Understated First Year." *U.S. News and World Report*, July 2, 2010. http://politics.usnews.com/news/articles/2010/07/02/minnesotas-al-franken-turns-in-understated-first-year.html (accessed September 1, 2010).

Shapiro, Mark. "The Salon Interview: Al Franken." *Salon.com*, n.d. http://www.salon.com/07/features/franken.html (accessed August 29, 2010).

Shorto, Russell. "Al Franken, Seriously." *New York Times Magazine*, March 21, 2004. http://www.nytimes.com/2004/03/21/magazine/21FRANKEN.html (accessed August 27, 2010).

Waldman, Steven (interviewer). "Why Would the Anti-Christ Write Chorus Line?" September 2003. http://www.beliefnet.com/News/Politics/2003/09/Why-Would-The-Anti-Christ-Write-Chorus-Line.aspx?p=1 (accessed August 27, 2010).

Friedan, Betty (1921–2006)

"I never set out to start a women's revolution. I never planned it. It just *happened*, I would say, by some miracle of convergence of my life and history, serendipity, one thing leading to another" (Friedan 2000, 13). Betty Friedan penned those words in her memoir, in which she describes not only her life but also how her best-selling book *The Feminine Mystique* (1963) initiated the modern women's movement and encouraged women to go beyond their traditional roles of tending to husbands and caring for children. Her dissident writings, lectures, protests, and organizational efforts were catalysts for social changes that liberated many women, although there have been setbacks since and full equal rights for women in the United States and worldwide still have not been attained.

She was named Bettye Naomi when she was born on February 4, 1921, in Peoria, Illinois, to Harry and Miriam Goldstein. Bettye Goldstein was the oldest of three children; her sister Amy was 18 months younger, and her brother Harry Jr. was five years younger. Their father was a Russian Jewish immigrant and owned a thriving jewelry store in downtown Peoria. He earned a comfortable living and could afford a maid and chauffeur for his family. But as a Jew, he was not accepted among elite groups and was barred from the local country club. He sometimes complained about the discrimination and prejudice, but was a proud American.

Miriam Horowitz Goldstein had once been a newspaper editor but left the job when she married, as was the custom at the time. As Friedan explained, her mother "had to quit her job when she married my father. Wives of businessmen did not work in towns like Peoria then, not even in the Depression, which clouded my childhood" (Friedan 2000, 17).

Friedan's childhood indeed was "clouded." The Depression of the 1930s affected the Goldsteins as it did millions of other families. Harry Goldstein's business suffered and he and his wife often argued about finances. Bettye hated the shouting and decided not to allow herself to feel sadness and dismay over her parents' conflicts. She would just toughen herself and not cry.

While she was growing up, Bettye had a poor relationship with her mother, who was a perfectionist and often criticized her daughter—as well as her husband. She did not want to be identified with Judaism and tried to discourage her daughter from thinking of herself as being Jewish. Her mother insisted that Bettye "take swimming lessons, tennis, golf, piano lessons, dancing lessons. I wasn't good at any of it" (Friedan 2000, 19).

Early in her life, Bettye realized that her mother was unhappy and resentful because she had given up her job and had no work outside the home. When Bettye's father became ill with heart disease, her mother had to take over the jewelry business, which changed her dramatically. Miriam was happier and less judgmental. That observation helped set Bettye on her path toward developing the concept that many women wanted to go beyond their traditional roles, although not until later years did she find evidence of this.

Although her family life was dysfunctional, Bettye found refuge in school and in books. She loved to read and often borrowed numerous books from the local library. She also spent a lot of time writing—essays, poetry, and plays. When she was in junior high school, at her mother's urging, she joined the staff of the school newspaper.

After graduating from high school as the valedictorian, Bettye went on to Smith College in Northampton, Massachusetts, majoring in psychology. During her years at Smith, she developed a severe asthma problem that resulted in a burst lung while she was a sophomore. She was editor of the college newspaper, which took a stance against European fascism and for union organizing and black civil rights in the United States. She graduated summa cum laude in 1942. About this time, she dropped the final "e" from her first name, considering it pretentious.

Betty continued her education at the University of California, Berkeley, for a year as a psychology research fellow, and began attending radical meetings. In 1943, she moved to Greenwich Village in New York City, where she worked as a reporter for Federated Press, a news service for radical and labor newspapers. She had become a follower of Karl Marx (1818–1883), a German philosopher who along with his long-time collaborator Friedrich Engels established the communist ideal, which appealed to those championing the working class. During this time, she also was having affairs with various men and was unable to concentrate on writing. She decided to get help with psychoanalysis.

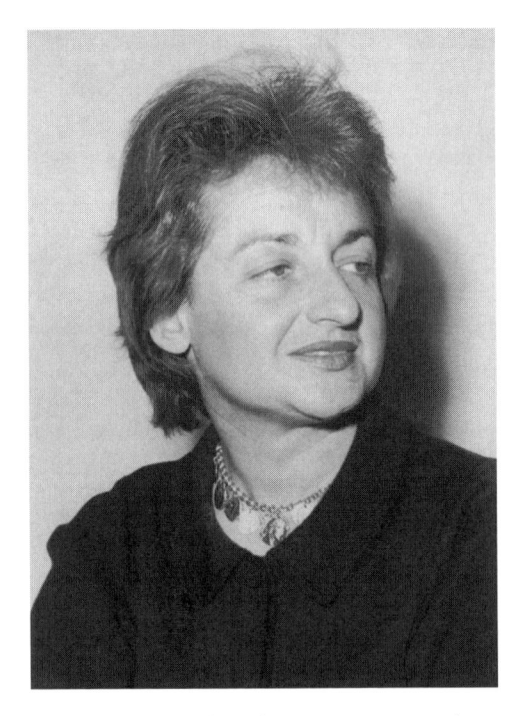

Few individuals played as important a role in the rise of the feminist movement as did Betty Friedan, author of *The Feminine Mystique*, published in 1963, and cofounder of the National Organization for Women. (Library of Congress)

When World War II ended and soldiers returned to the United States, they took the jobs that women temporarily had filled while they were in the military. Thus, Betty Goldstein lost her job. She found another with the *U.E. News*, the union newspaper of the United Electrical, Radio and Machine Workers of America. She held the job for six years, and during that time met Carl Friedman, a producer of summer theater shows. He changed his name by dropping the "m" to become Friedan.

Betty and Carl married in 1947 and eventually had three children. Their first child was born in 1949. When Betty was pregnant for the second time in 1953, she was fired, and she began writing freelance articles for women's magazines in order to supplement the family income. They were living in a garden apartment community in Queens, but with a third child on the way, the two-bedroom apartment was not large enough. The family moved to suburban Rockland County, northwest of New York City.

As a suburban housewife and caregiver for three children—Daniel, Jonathan, and Emily—and her husband, Friedan was contented for a few years. She was living a life typical for women of the 1950s. But, like her mother, she soon began to resent her home-bound roles and that Carl was less educated than she and earned little from his theater work. During the 20 years of the couple's marriage, many arguments developed, some of them resulting in physical fights. The two divorced in 1969.

On the 15th anniversary of her Smith College reunion in 1957, Friedan completed an alumni questionnaire about her experiences following graduation. "I felt so guilty, somehow, that I hadn't done the big things everybody expected me to do with my brilliant Smith education," Friedan wrote much later (2000, 97). Because of the alumni questionnaire, she created her own queries to Smith alumni to learn about their lives. Many were unhappy, depressed, and anxious. She also queried psychologists, sociologists, and marriage counselors. The responses she received were the basis for a magazine article contending that highly educated women were frustrated because of the roles society expected them to play. The article was rejected numerous times, and Friedan withdrew it from her agent. She decided to use her findings in a book that, after five years of additional research, became *The Feminine Mystique* (1963).

That book's opening chapter is titled "The Problem That Has No Name" and describes the frustrations of women who manage the household, care for the family's needs, try to be more attractive for a husband, and wonder if that is all she could expect. It was a problem that Friedan called the "feminine mystique." And women across the nation could relate to the issue. The book sold more than three million copies and catapulted Friedan into the national spotlight.

Her national prominence was underscored when she helped found the National Organization for Women (NOW). In 1966, Friedan attended a national conference on the status of women in Washington, D.C., and met with activists who hoped to pressure the Equal Employment Opportunity Commission (EEOC) to enforce the Civil Rights Act of 1964; Title VII of the act required EEOC to end gender discrimination in employment. The delegates to the conference were unsuccessful in their attempts, but a group of participants met in Friedan's hotel room and together organized NOW, with Friedan as its first president. Friedan wrote the organization's statement of purpose that said in part: "We organize to initiate or support action, nationally, or in any part of this nation, by individuals or organizations, to break through the silken curtain of prejudice and discrimination against women in government, industry, the professions, the churches, the political parties, the judiciary, the labor unions, in education, science, medicine, law, religion and every other field of importance in American society" (NOW 1996).

In 1967, Friedan encouraged NOW to support legalized abortion and the Equal Rights Amendment (ERA), which Alice Paul had introduced in 1923 but the U.S. Congress had not passed. The amendment simply stated: "Men and women shall have equal rights throughout the United States and every place subject to its jurisdiction." The amendment was introduced in every congressional session until 1972, when it finally passed and was sent to the states for ratification. It was ratified by 35 states within the seven-year time limit allowed (extended to 1982), but 38 states must ratify before an amendment can become part of the Constitution. Thus the amendment has to be passed again by Congress, and it has been reintroduced in every Congress since 1982, but to date has not passed.

Friedan served as NOW's president through 1969, the year she also obtained a divorce, and was cofounder of the National Abortion Rights Action League (NARAL), now called NARAL–Pro Choice America. The following year, she organized a march called the Women's Strike for Equality, which took place in New York City on the 50th anniversary of the ratification of the Nineteenth Amendment to the U.S. Constitution that gave women the right to vote. Thousands of U.S. women demonstrated, carrying signs that indicated their displeasure with being confined to caretaker roles: "Don't Iron While the Strike Is Hot," or to being a sex object: "I Am Not a Barbie Doll" (*Time* 1970).

In 1971, Friedan with congresswomen and civil rights activists Bella Abzug (1920–1998) and Shirley Chisholm (1924–2005) convened the National Women's Political Caucus (NWPC). The NWPC encouraged women to run and get elected to political office.

Through the 1970s and 1980s, Friedan continued her fast-paced activities, writing, lecturing, teaching, and organizing. Her articles appeared in numerous magazines ranging from *Cosmopolitan* to *The New Republic*. She wrote *It Changed My Life: Writings on the Women's Movement* (1976), in which she explained her concerns about the women's movement focusing on sexual relationships and men as the enemy. In her view, such a focus diverts women "from serious political action. Women fighting for the basic changes necessary in society will at once affirm themselves and produce much more positive relationships with men. ... But if the main enemy is seen as the man, women will wallow around in self-pity and man-hatred and never really be moved to action" (Friedan 1998, 203–4).

During the late 1970s and early 1980s, Friedan was a visiting professor of sociology at several universities, and along with teaching wrote *The Second Stage* (1981). As she wrote: "In the second stage, women, with men, have to take back the *day*—take a stand on regaining human control over what was once called women's sphere (family, children, home), and join men in jobs, unions, companies, professions, asserting new human control over work. Focusing our new political mode on what once were ignored as women's issues and are now being exploited by male demagogues, we could perhaps transcend some either/or dilemmas that currently seem intractable, and take back from the Right the offensive 'for family' and 'for life' " (Friedan 1986, 257).

Friedan's *Fountain of Age* (1993) attacked what she called the "age mystique," which stereotypes aging people as ailing, infantile, and helpless. She criticizes society's focus on the illusion of youth. Rather, she emphasizes the reality of aging and the fact that people can and do see "Age as Adventure," as a chapter of the book is titled.

From the 1990s into the 2000s, Friedan did not let up on her advocacy for older Americans, attending national and international conferences on aging. Her many awards through the years include Humanist of the Year in 1975, Outstanding Magazine Journalism award in 1979, and the Eleanor Roosevelt Leadership Award in 1989. She also received numerous honorary doctorates.

Friedan died of congestive heart failure on her 85th birthday, February 4, 2006, in her Washington, D.C., home. A *Washington Post* obituary noted that Friedan "alienated many who worked with her by insisting on holding the floor, claiming credit and running roughshod over her assistants" (Sullivan 2006). However, she left a huge legacy, changing the way American society views women and the way many women view themselves.

See also Abzug, Bella; Paul, Alice

References

Friedan, Betty. *The Feminine Mystique*. 20th Anniversary ed. New York: W. W. Norton, 1983. First published 1963.

Friedan, Betty. *The Fountain of Age*. New York: Simon and Schuster, 1993.

Friedan, Betty. *It Changed My Life: Writings on the Women's Movement*. Cambridge, MA: Harvard University Press (paperback edition), 1998. Originally published, New York: Random House, 1976.

Friedan, Betty. *Life So Far: A Memoir*. New York: Simon and Schuster, 2000.

Friedan, Betty. *The Second Stage*. Rev. ed. New York: Summit Books, 1986.

Hennessee, Judith Adler. *Betty Friedan: Her Life*. New York: Random House, 1999.

Horowitz, Daniel. *Betty Friedan and the Making of the Feminine Mystique: The American Left, the Cold and Modern Feminism*. Amherst: University of Massachusetts Press, 1998.

"Nation: Women on the March." *Time*, September 7, 1970. http://www.time.com/time/magazine/article/0,9171,902696,00.html (accessed September 5, 2010).

NOW. "The National Organization for Women's 1966 Statement of Purpose." 1996. http://www.now.org/history/purpos66.html (accessed September 5, 2010).

Sullivan, Patricia. "Voice of Feminism's 'Second Wave.'" *Washington Post*, Obituary section, February 5, 2006. http://www.washingtonpost.com/wp-dyn/content/article/2006/02/04/AR2006020401385.html (accessed September 5, 2010).

G

Gaskin, Stephen (1935–)

Stephen Gaskin, a counterculture icon and self-described "hippie," is best known for leading busloads of people from San Francisco, California, to southwest Tennessee, where in 1971 they founded a commune, although members did not use that term. They referred to themselves as a collective or as an intentional community called "The Farm," which still exists. From colonial days and throughout U.S. history, communes or collectives have been established by diverse groups for religious, economic, utopian, or social reasons. Most of them have shared similar characteristics such as stressing cooperative production and consumption of goods and services, living by group rules, and creating a society based on justice.

During the 1960s and 1970s, many Americans were disillusioned by the Vietnam War and civil rights injustices. Rejecting traditional ways, they sought alternative religions and lifestyles. They established communes and demanded freedom of expression and religion. The general public frequently stereotyped communes as nests of anarchists or revolutionaries intent on erotic pleasures. Numerous firsthand reports during the 1960s and 1970s indicated that "doing drugs," nudity, group marriage, sexual experimentation, and other radical practices were part of hippie communes. But the main purpose of many counterculture communes was to escape mainstream society and embrace a simple tribal way of life. Back-to-nature communes were common, and The Farm fit that description, although the group also stressed spirituality, pacifism, and reverence for life.

Since its beginning, The Farm and its founder have had critics. Some have called Gaskin a "brainwashing cult leader," "manipulator," or "user." The Federal Bureau of Investigation (FBI), following orders of its director J. Edgar Hoover, harassed this communal group and its members from the time of its founding. "That The Farm persevered in the face of this harassment and overcame the obstacles the government imposed is a testament to the courage and integrity of the core group of founders, most notably Stephen Gaskin," wrote Albert Bates, author, lawyer, and spokesperson for The Farm (Bates 1993).

Stephen Gaskin was born February 16, 1935, in Denver, Colorado, to Enzell Floyd, a construction worker, and Carolyn Ruth (Carter) Gaskin. But not much is known about his childhood, although in a 2010 interview, he had this to say:

> My father was from a very square Indiana family, and he had bad asthma. He went at 91 pounds to Idaho to get over his asthma, and he stayed in Idaho until he became a cowboy, among other things. He used to do mail work, the kind of mail clerk that has a badge and a gun. He raised me through the Southwest. I got raised in Santa Fe and Denver, Phoenix, San Bernardino, and like that. And then a couple of other places I was raised—we were commercial fishermen fishing out of Newport Harbor in California for

a while. My father taught me to read when I was four, sitting on his lap, and by the time I was in first grade, I always got in trouble for reading ahead in the book. (Versluis 2010, 141)

During the Korean War, Gaskin served in the Marine Corps from 1952 to 1955. He saw combat near the end of the war and took care of the wounded. The injuries and loss of life convinced him that violence solved nothing. Between 1957 and 1964, he was married and divorced twice. According to some published sources he has married at least four times during his life.

Gaskin earned a master's degree from San Francisco State College in 1964 and taught creative writing and general semantics at the college from 1964 to 1966. He was not rehired after two years of teaching because, as he put it, "I'd gotten too weird." By this time, he was using drugs and wearing "hippy garb with beads and long hair." Since he was no longer teaching, Gaskin "took off and drove across Mexico and the Yucatan Peninsula to British Honduras (now Belize) in a 1952 Volkswagen bus.... Even then, the black people of Belize were charming and reggae-like. It was obvious that the people there smoked a lot of grass, and nice as it was getting stoned under the palm trees, I began to miss the revolution that was going on back home" (Gaskin 2005, 8–9). He then returned to San Francisco and began "Monday Night Class," an experimental college course that met weekly and discussed topics ranging from drugs to religion to politics.

As the course evolved, more than 1,500 people attended—college and high school students, people from the military and police academies, and from communes along the California coast. The sessions became religious/spiritual gatherings, which was of interest to the American Academy of Religion, an organization "dedicated to furthering knowledge of religion and religious institutions in all their forms and manifestations" (American Academy of Religion). Gaskin frequently was asked to speak to students at other campuses and to church congregations. Gaskin and many of his supporters left San Francisco in October 1970 and toured the country in about two dozen live-in old school buses, Volkswagen vans, and trucks for four months, stopping in towns where Gaskin was scheduled to speak. The caravan of vehicles returned to San Francisco in January 1971, and Gaskin with all of his loyal followers from the caravan decided to go to southern Tennessee, an area they particularly liked while on tour, and look for land where they could all settle. In late 1971, they pooled their money and bought more than 1,000 acres south of Nashville for a farm. Eventually, The Farm, as the community became known, expanded to 1,750 acres.

The Farm membership included people from diverse religious backgrounds and was established as a spiritual community of families and friends who considered themselves free thinkers. The cooperative included rules for all members: For example, no animal products were allowed, and members were expected to be vegetarians. No tobacco, alcohol, or chemically produced psychedelics were permitted, although organics like marijuana and peyote were acceptable because they were thought to "expand the mind." Members had to accept that Gaskin was their teacher and spiritual guide.

During the first few years, members of The Farm established a construction company and built schools, commercial buildings, and welding and machine shops. Also in the early days of The Farm, members grew marijuana, which was discovered by law enforcement authorities. As a result,

Gaskin was arrested and spent a year in jail, and the Farm members established a rule that no cannabis plants would be grown on their land.

In 1977, the editors of *Mother Earth News* conducted a long interview with Gaskin, who in part explained what his community was about:

> The first thing we do is we are a church and we live a spiritual life of "right vocation."
>
> If you really want to be spiritual, you don't want to have to sell your soul for eight hours a day in order to have 16 hours in which to eat and sleep and get yourself back together again. You'd like for your work to be seamless with your life and that what you do for a living doesn't deny everything else you believe in.
>
> We're complete vegetarians and we grow most of the food we eat. We've also delivered 600 babies at home. We have our own school, bank, motor pool, construction company, public utilities, medical clinic, and ambulance service . . . all of which are incorporated as a nonprofit, religious foundation. We hold all property in common and share what we have according to need. There ain't nothing devious about it: Right out front, we're trying to build an alternative culture. (*Mother Earth News* Editors 1977)

Since its inception, The Farm has gone through many changes. During the 1970s, its population grew to about 1,500, and other similar intentional communities were formed in nine states from Florida to Michigan and also in Canada and Ireland. In addition, The Farm established an international relief operation called Plenty, which has provided aid for victims of natural disasters and the poor in many parts of the world.

In the early 1980s, The Farm faced economic problems through no fault of its own. Across the United States, thousands of farm families, who had once been prosperous and borrowed money to grow more and more crops, faced an economic recession, low farm prices, and overwhelming debt. The Farm was no exception, and the community was in danger of losing its land. But "in 1983, the Farm abruptly changed from a collective to a privatized economy," reported Michael Niman in *High Times*, a New York–based magazine devoted to cannabis culture. He added:

> In order to raise money to pay off the debt, collective businesses were sold and residents were charged fixed membership fees, a sort of regressive tax, to remain on their land. Many who worked on collective Farm projects such as road maintenance, suddenly found themselves facing expenses but not having an income. The Farm motorpool was privatized, leaving many residents without transportation to go out and find work. . . . most people were unprepared to cope with the rapid changes. In 1983 alone, approximately 700 people left the Farm. By the late 1980's, less then [*sic*] 300 people remained on the land. The Farm's debt, however, was paid off in three years. (Niman 1995)

By the mid-1980s, The Farm was privatized—that is, it was no longer a total collective, where all things were held in common, but became a cooperative with only the land held in common. Many members found "outside" jobs in Nashville, which helped them pay monthly dues to keep their community going. Members maintain their own roads, municipal buildings, and public water system. Some members have started their own businesses or work in The Farm's cottage industries, such as a mail-order company, soy dairy, and book publishing company. Members also farm their land, growing organic foods, composting, rotating crops, using "natural" pesticides (insects and other organisms that control pests), and other sustainable farming methods.

"The Farm has morphed into something like a hands-on environmental think tank," according to Jim Windolf of *Vanity Fair*, who visited the Farm in 2007. "Its self-reliant residents are comfortable with the long-lost country skills of natural home building and midwifery but they're also adept at the newer arts of biodiesel mechanics and nuclear-radiation detection."

The Farm has continued to survive. Gaskin is no longer the leader and spiritual "guru" of The Farm. He has founded a not-for-profit development and intelligence corporation called Rocinante, for example, and in 1999, he ran for U.S. president on the Green Party ticket, advocating campaign finance reform, universal health care, and decriminalization of marijuana. He and his wife, Ina May, whom he married in 1976, live on The Farm. Ina May is a midwife and well-known author of *Spiritual Midwifery* (1975), *Ina May's Guide to Childbirth* (2003) and *Ina May's Guide to Breastfeeding* (2009).

Gaskin has managed a midwife quarterly magazine called *The Birth Gazette* and he has written numerous books, among them *Monday Night Class* (2005); *Caravan* (1972, 2007); *Rendered Infamous* (1981); *Cannabis Spirituality* (1996); *Amazing Dope Tales* (1980, 1999); and *An Outlaw in My Heart: A Political Activist's User's Manual* (2000). In 2011, Gaskin was working on his autobiography.

References

Bates, Albert. "J. Edgar Hoover and The Farm." *International Communal Studies Conference on Culture, Thought and Living in Community New Harmony, Indiana,* October 16, 1993. http://www.thefarm.org/lifestyle/albertbates/akbp3.html (accessed January 31, 2011).

Fike, Rupert, ed. *Voices from the Farm: Adventures in Community Living*. Summertown, TN: Book Publishing Co., 1998.

Gaskin, Stephen. *The Caravan*. Rev. ed. Summertown, TN: Book Publishing Co., 2000. First published 1972.

Gaskin, Stephen. *Monday Night Class*. Rev. ed. Summertown, TN: Book Publishing Co., 2005.

Gaskin, Stephen. *An Outlaw in My Heart: A Political Activist's User's Manual*. Philadelphia: Camino Books, 2000.

"Mission Statement." *American Academy of Religion*, n.d. http://www.aarweb.org/About_AAR/Mission_Statement/default.asp (accessed February 3, 2011).

Mother Earth News Editors. "An Interview with Stephen Gaskin the Founder of The Farm Commune in Tennessee." *Mother Earth News*, May–June 1977. http://www.motherearthnews.com/Nature-Community/1977-05-01/Stephen-Gaskin-Interview.aspx#ixzz1CdcyT6fn (accessed February 3, 2011).

Niman, Michael I. "Out to Save the World: Life at The Farm." Originally published by *High Times*, 1995. http://www.mediastudy.com/articles/farm.html (accessed February 2, 2011).

Sachs, Dana. "Mac on the Farm." *MacWEEK*, August 16, 1988.

Sirius, R. U. "Gore's Hay Day." *Salon.com*, February 15, 2000. http://www.salon.com/politics2000/feature/2000/02/15/farm (accessed February 2, 2011).

Versluis, Arthur. "Stephen Gaskin Interview." *Journal for the Study of Radicalism*, January 1, 2010.

Gibbs, Lois (1951–)

In the late nineteenth century, a builder named Joseph Love left behind a legacy that would bear his name in infamy—an unfinished canal. Located in the upper northwest corner of New York State, Love Canal ultimately became a toxic landfill extraordinaire. From 1947 to 1952, the Hooker Chemical Corporation (a subsidiary of Occidental Petroleum) used the canal as a repository for 82 different chemical compounds, including a variety of pesticides and dioxin, a chemical found in DDT and Agent Orange. Additionally, it later came to light that the local and U.S. governments likely had been complicit in using the canal as a landfill over the course of the past half-century. All told, more than 20,000 tons of toxic waste had been disposed, with complete disregard to its potential impact (Kaplan 1997, 18).

In 1956, for the grand sum of $1, the city of Niagara purchased land encompassing Love Canal with a stipulation written into the contract terms: the chemical company would be held harmless for any subsequent health damages or deaths that might arise. Niagara wasted little time in granting permission to begin construction of both a school and a housing development over the landfill. It was not long—just shy of the end of the decade—before local residents began to take note of things being "not quite right." The initial signs were reports by some residents of black sludge seeping into their basements. Throughout the 1960s, additional occurrences heightened residents' concerns. They noticed strange growth patterns in their yards and gardens—things that would not grow or that would grow abnormally. One resident's pool rose up from the ground, showing barrels underneath that were rising to the surface (Gibbs 1998, 21).

Harry and Lois Gibbs were unaware of these strange happenings when they moved to Love Canal in 1973. This was their shot at the American dream. Harry worked for Goodyear Chemical, while Lois was a stay-at-home mom of two children, Michael and Melissa.

Shortly after previously healthy Michael started school, he began getting ill. His doctors offered diagnoses running the gamut from epilepsy to asthma. Michael suffered from frequent and mysterious infections and rashes. Melissa also developed a rare blood disease. Then, in the spring of 1978, a series of articles written by reporter Michael Brown ran in the *Niagara Falls Gazette*. For the first time, Gibbs learned of the trash dump near her home and began to wonder if there was a correlation with her son's health problems. Gibbs obtained written documentation from her son's physician stating that his illness since starting school seemed to indicate an irritant. Her goal was to get Michael transferred to another school. However, her request was denied because it might set a precedent, ceding that a problem existed and spur similar requests.

In 1978, Gibbs was a young, suburban housewife. She had no education beyond high school and was, by nature, a shy and unassuming person. But she forced herself to go door to door, soliciting her neighbors' experiences living in Love Canal. She soon learned that her son's odd illnesses were not so odd after all, but rather more or less the norm for a child living in the community. She also learned that that there was an alarmingly high rate of miscarriages among the women living in Love Canal, as well as infants facing significant health issues at birth. Spurred on by these facts, Gibbs organized her neighbors into the Love Canal Homeowners Association (LCHA). She transformed herself from an uninformed person into someone who had the facts on toxic waste issues at her fingertips. She became the spokesperson for the LCHA and the nearly 1,000 families it represented.

She soon went from her timid knocking on a neighbor's door to addressing college classes, giving press conferences and, eventually, testifying before Congress. "Part of what outraged Gibbs... Instead of protecting them, authorities put a price on the heads of their children... Lois Gibbs compares her awakening to what happens 'when you find out your government really does not work for you, and your heart's broken for a long time before you get angry'" (Kaplan 1997, 75–76). Motivated by this view of what they saw as an attack on their families and community, Gibbs and LCHA were unrelenting in pursuit of reparation. Their goals were to get the government to relocate them and to clean up the poisonous site.

Lois Gibbs in 1978 organized her community to fight the hazardous contamination of the Love Canal neighborhood in Niagara Falls, New York. (Getty Images)

Gibbs and the members of the LCHA had an uphill fight, but they did not allow that to deter them. They diligently collected data and medical records and submitted them to the Department of Health, time and time again, only to be told that they were at no risk. Over and over again, Gibbs and others were told that the data they collected was useless because they were "housewives." But, by year's end, the New York Department of Health had issued a warning to residents not to eat or sell anything grown in their yards, had begun blood testing, and also had announced finding dioxin in the soil. Yet the department still claimed the area was safe for habitation.

In August 1978, the Department of Health recommended the temporary relocation of all pregnant women and children under the age of two because of a high incidence of miscarriages in families living closest to the canal. A week later, the governor permanently relocated these families. Six months later, in February 1979, another order was issued, evacuating pregnant women and children under the age of two from outlying neighborhoods. But the state still refused to concede that there was any direct or immediate danger due to the presence of chemicals in the neighborhood. Some additional families were temporarily housed in motels, but that was just a stopgap measure, as the situation in Love Canal grew more dire with each passing day. Things finally came to a head on May 19 when members of the LCHA took two representatives of the U.S. Environmental Protection Agency (EPA) hostage. Seeking a peaceful resolution to the situation, as well as satisfaction of residents' demands, Gibbs placed a phone call to President Jimmy Carter. While Gibbs waited for the president's reply, the hostages were rescued by the Federal Bureau of Investigation (FBI); no arrests were made as the hostages claimed to be unable to remember the identities of their captors. President Carter then issued an emergency declaration, and the Federal Disaster Assistance Administration took steps to house 700 families at a nearby air force base at government expense.

In October 1980, Carter signed a bill permanently evacuating all families from Love Canal (Gibbs 1998, 22–23). He recognized the critical role that Gibbs had played, stating, "Most important, my thanks to the grassroots leader of the Love Canal residents, Lois Gibbs. Without her impassioned advocacy and dedication there might never have been a Love Canal emergency declaration and the agreement may never have come to pass" (Gibbs 1998, xii).

As a direct result of what Gibbs and the LCHA accomplished in New York, on December 11, 1980, Congress passed the Comprehensive Environmental Response, Compensation and Liability Act (what is more commonly referred to as the "Superfund Legislation"). An allocation of $1.6 billion was made to search out and clean up toxic waste sites, including Love Canal. Love Canal was not just a grassroots success for Gibbs and the LCHA; it also made the U.S. public aware of the dangerous chemicals lurking around every corner of their daily environments. She also set an example for every citizen—even those presumed to be without much power, such as "the lowly housewife"—as to how to go about demanding and achieving a safe and healthy space in which to live.

Gibbs was forever changed by her experience at Love Canal. As she noted: "The world is a very different place for families who lived through the crisis... Eyes were opened at Love Canal to the way our democracy works—and doesn't work. For the first time in this blue-collar community, people understood that corporate power and influence dictated the actions at Love Canal, not the health and welfare of citizens... It was not conceivable to families that their government would turn its back on their suffering... It was difficult to grasp the reality, the obvious conclusion, that corporations had more influence and rights than taxpaying citizens. This realization left people feeling alone, abandoned, and empty inside" (Gibbs 1998, 222).

Gibbs went on to form the Citizen's Clearinghouse for Hazardous Waste. In 1981, it was renamed the Center for Health, Environment and Justice (CHEJ). She continued to serve as executive director at this grassroots environmental crisis center as of 2011. CHEJ is a resource for at-risk communities, providing information, resources, technical assistance, and training to groups throughout the country. A large part of the organization's mission is to empower individuals to protect themselves, their families, and their neighborhoods from unnecessary chemical hazards.

Gibbs has been instrumental in broadening CHEJ's mission beyond the issue of toxic waste to encompass a wide variety of environmental health issues. Some examples of the organization's accomplishments include: assistance in passage of the 1986 Federal Right-to-Know Law, which provides citizens with access to information about the toxins stored and disposed of in their neighborhoods; the 1990 capitulation of McDonald's to CHEJ's McToxic's campaign to end the use of Styrofoam packaging; the 1995 Stop Dioxin campaign, resulting in a 90 percent reduction in dioxin emissions; the 2005 collaborative PVC (polyvinyl chloride or the so-called "poison plastic") campaign, that persuaded Crabtree & Evelyn, Target, Sears/Kmart, Microsoft, J. C. Penney, Best Buy, and others to phase out PVC in products and/or packaging; and assistance in passage of the 2009 Federal Toxic Toys Law that phases out toxic materials in products and packaging.

In 1999, Gibbs received the Annual Heinz Environmental Award with these words in commendation:

> Love Canal was not the first toxic waste dump in America, but it did change the way society thinks about the disposal of such material. Likewise, much of the history of American environmentalism in the past 20 years reflects the leadership and genius of Lois Gibbs. The community participation and local empowerment she pioneered became part of later statues and regulatory policy. Her early writings on community involvement in environmental issues were the blueprint for a form of participation that is now commonplace. At a time when local action is of increasing importance in the work to preserve public health and the natural world, Lois Gibbs continues to inspire and empower a growing number of Americans to help themselves, their communities, and the planet. (Heinz Awards web site)

Although Gibbs is not linked to the environmental justice movement founded by sociologist Robert Bullard in the 1990s to call attention to toxic dumping on communities of color, Gibbs's activism has helped countless citizens fight for a safe and clean environment. She has been recognized by many institutions. Along with the Heinz award, she also received the 1990 Goldman Environmental Prize, was named to *Outside* magazine's "Top Ten Who Made a Difference Honor Roll" in 1991, received the 1999 John Gardner Leadership Award, and was nominated for the Nobel Peace Prize in 2003. Her distinctions also include honorary degrees awarded from the State University of New York, Cortland College, Haverford College, and Green Mountain College.

She is a frequently requested speaker on the lecture circuit and has authored countless articles and books. She has also appeared on many television and radio shows, including *60 Minutes*, *20/20*, *Oprah Winfrey*, *Good Morning America*, *The Morning Show* and the *Today Show*. A two-hour prime-time movie, *Lois Gibbs: The Love Canal Story*, starring Marsha Mason, appeared on CBS in 1982.

Margaret Gay

See also Bullard, Robert

References

Gibbs, Lois. *Love Canal: The Story Continues*. Gabriola Island, BC, Canada: New Society Publishers, 1998.

"The Heinz Awards, Fifth Annual: Lois Gibbs." Heinz Awards web site, 1999. http://www.heinzawards.net/recipients/lois-gibbs (accessed March 2, 2010).

Kaplan, Temma. *Crazy for Democracy: Women in Grassroots Movements*. New York: Routledge, 1997.

"Timeline—CHEJ Highlights: 1980–2010." *Center for Health, Environment and Justice* http://chej.org/about/our-story/timeline/ (accessed March 5, 2010).

Gilman, Charlotte Perkins (1860–1935)

"To develop human life in its true powers we need fully equal citizenship for women," wrote Charlotte Perkins Gilman in 1911 (Gilman 1911). Gilman was one of the most widely known activist women of the late nineteenth and early twentieth centuries. She refused to quietly accept the dominant status of men in society. She fought for women's right to vote and for social reforms. Her dissident opinions were expressed in numerous written works—poems, stories, journals, and books, many of which are in the public domain and have been reprinted.

Charlotte Anna Perkins was born on July 3, 1860, in Hartford, Connecticut. She was the third child of Mary Fitch Westcott and Frederick Beecher Perkins, a librarian and writer. Their first child died within a month of his birth in 1858; Charlotte's brother Thomas was born a year later. Relatives on the Beecher side included great aunt Harriet Beecher Stowe (1811–1896), author of *Uncle Tom's Cabin* (1852); great uncle Henry Ward Beecher (1813–1887), a prominent minister and abolitionist; great aunt Catharine Beecher (1800–1878), author and proponent of education for women; and great aunt Isabella Beecher Hooker (1822–1907), an ardent suffragist. Her great aunts, with their independence and advocacy for social reforms, served as role models for Charlotte later in life.

Charlotte and her brother Thomas grew up in a loveless home. Their father left the family when they were in their early childhood; Frederick returned only for occasional visits. Their mother withheld affection from her children and was a strict disciplinarian—in attempts to make the children strong and able to withstand hurtful relationships. In Charlotte's words, their mother was "absolutely loyal as a spaniel" to her estranged husband, but would not allow herself to show love for her and Thomas (Gilman 1991). Yet Charlotte and Thomas had some good times and were mischievous children, often playing tricks on adults when they could get away with it. One of their reported antics was rolling a hoop through mud puddles, then letting it "accidentally" roll into a woman's long billowing skirt; they pretended innocence and immediately apologized, thus saving themselves from punishment.

The family struggled with poverty and had to depend on various Beecher relatives, some of whom grudgingly provided help. On occasion, Frederick rented places for the family to live. According to biographer Anna J. Lane, by 1873, when Charlotte was a young teenager, "the family had been forced to move nineteen times in eighteen years" (Lane 1990, 29). Because of the frequent moves, Charlotte and her brother received sporadic educations, sometimes being taught at home by their mother and occasionally attending a public school. Reading was a favorite part of Charlotte's studies, and stories that she read or her mother read to her sparked her imagination. Charlotte was writing fantasy tales at the age of 10 or 11. But the most enjoyable part of school was physical fitness. For much of her life, she reveled in physical exercise and wanted to perfect herself as a strong, vibrant woman, quite the opposite of the feminine ideal of the 1800s that expected women to be dependent and frail.

During her teenage years, Mary Perkins was often ill and Charlotte became the caregiver for her mother. In spite of ailments, her mother was controlling, requiring Charlotte to report on almost everything she did and refusing to let her accept invitations from college students and even adult family members to dances, concerts, plays, and other events. Nevertheless, Charlotte's life was not all bleak. She especially liked visiting an uncle in Boston, Massachusetts, where she was entertained with teas, parties, and sleigh rides.

With the aid of an inheritance, Charlotte was able to attend a private school for two years. When she was 16 years old, she began developing artistic skills, and by the time she was 19, she had enrolled in the Rhode Island School of Design in Providence. Although she did not plan to pursue a career in the field, she designed advertising cards to earn an income, and she also taught art classes.

As an advocate of economic independence for women, Charlotte Perkins Gilman made a major intellectual contribution to the American feminist movement of the early 1900s. (Library of Congress)

In January 1882, Charlotte met a local artist, Walter Stetson, who was beginning a promising art career. The two quickly became friends and in less than three weeks Walter proposed marriage. But Charlotte was not ready yet for such a commitment. In the first place, she was rebounding from a relationship with her very close friend, Martha Luther, whom she loved deeply but not in a sexual way, she proclaimed. Martha had married, leaving Charlotte bereft over her loss of friendship. In later years, Charlotte developed close friendships with other women; biographers as well as Charlotte herself wondered whether she had transgender tendencies.

Over a two-year period, she vacillated between accepting Walter's proposal and wanting to remain independent. She wrote long letters and poems to Walter, expressing her ambivalence and her reasons for wanting to stay single. She also wrote love poems for Walter. At the same time, she was being pressured by her mother, aunts, friends, and Walter to get married, which she did on May 2, 1884.

Marriage for Charlotte Stetson, however, was not satisfying, and she was often depressed. When she became pregnant, she was ill much of the time, and even after her daughter Katharine was born in March 1885, she was miserable. For months she complained of one ailment after another; there were quarrels with Walter and periods of hysteria. In the fall of 1885, her good friend Grace Channing, a writer, invited Charlotte to Pasadena, California, for the winter months; she accepted the offer, leaving Katharine with her mother and a maid in Providence. After she returned to Providence in the spring of 1886, her marriage and home life did not improve. In 1888, with the help of Grace Channing, Charlotte Stetson moved to Pasadena with her daughter and mother, who had no means of support. She began writing poetry and short stories to earn an income.

By 1890, Charlotte had separated from her husband, and Walter and Grace Channing had developed an intimate relationship, which Charlotte did not condemn. She was busy writing and lecturing, producing, as biographer Mary A. Hill writes, "a rather impressive array of subversive writings on the fraudulence of love and marriage myths" (Hill 1980, 185). Her short story about a woman's mental deterioration, titled "The Yellow Wallpaper," was published in 1892, and at first, most readers thought it was only a haunting, frightening tale. However, later analysis concluded that the story was autobiographical and about the repression of women in marriage and their second-class citizenship. It has become a feminist classic.

Speaking tours took Charlotte to the Los Angeles and San Francisco areas, where she presented her lectures to women's organizations, tax clubs, suffrage groups, and social reformers. At these meetings, "she met other women who were questioning their 'feminine' responsibilities, women who had fallen into wife and mother roles without clearly choosing them, women who were alone, without an income, or without a means of satisfying work" (Hill 1980, 185).

In 1894, Charlotte sent her daughter Katharine to live with Grace and Walter, which created a scandal among friends and relatives at the time; and she moved to San Francisco, where she found a job editing feminist publications. In San Francisco, she took a great interest in women's suffrage and social reform efforts. She helped plan the California Women's Congresses of 1894 and 1895. At the latter Congress, she met social reformer Jane Addams, who invited Charlotte to visit the settlement house Addams had established in Chicago, Illinois. Charlotte left California and made Hull House her home for a time, joining suffragists and reformers such as Florence Kelley, who fought against child labor and later founded the National Consumers League.

After her Hull House stay, Charlotte embarked on another lecture tour in England and the United States. In her many lectures and well as journal articles, she developed ideas that eventually took book form in *Women and Economics—A Study of the Economic Relation between Men and Women as a Factor in Social Evolution* (1898), using the byline Charlotte Perkins Stetson. It is her most influential and famous nonfiction work, frequently called the "feminist manifesto." Some of her statements have current relevance for many women who still struggle for equality. For example, she wrote:

[W]hatever the economic value of the domestic industry of women is, they do not get it. The women who do the most work get the least money, and the women who have the most money do the least work. Their labor is neither given nor taken as a factor in economic exchange. It is held to be their duty as women to do this work; and their economic status bears no relation to their domestic labors, unless an inverse one. Moreover, if they were thus fairly paid,—given what they earned, and no more,—all women working in this way would be reduced to the economic status of the house servant. (Stetson 1900, 14–15)

By 1900, Charlotte was ready to marry again—this time to her cousin, George Houghton Gilman, a lawyer who was seven years younger than she. Since childhood, she had been corresponding with "Ho," as she called him, on occasion, and as an adult in 1897, she contacted him for legal advice at his New York office. Over the next three years they conducted a courtship primarily by mail, since Charlotte was traveling on her lecture tours. They married on June 12, 1900, and made their home in New York.

After her marriage to Ho, Charlotte Gilman continued her work for social reforms and her writing and lecturing, which her husband supported. She wrote books of fiction and nonfiction, articles, short stories, and verse. From 1909 to 1916, she published a monthly journal called *The Forerunner*. Gilman wrote nearly all of the content, which included stories, poems, essays, editorials, serial fiction, and nonfiction. Some of the serialized work was published in book form, such as *Our Androcentric Culture or the Man-Made World* (1911). Her works of fiction include *Moving and Mountain* (1911), *Herland* (1915), and *With Her in*

Ourland (1916). A major nonfiction book, *His Religion and Hers: A Study of the Faith of Our Fathers and the Work of Our Mothers* (1923), was one of her most significant works.

When Houghton, his brother Francis, and Francis's wife Emily inherited a house in Norwich, Connecticut, in 1922, Charlotte and Ho moved to Norwich. They shared their home with Francis and Emily, but it was a tense relationship. In addition, Houghton's law practice in Connecticut was not as profitable as his practice in New York, and Charlotte's income from lectures had dropped. However, Ho and Charlotte were content and happy with each other during their marriage, which lasted until 1934 when Houghton died suddenly of a cerebral hemorrhage.

Before her husband's death, Charlotte had assumed she would die first. In 1932, she learned that she had inoperable cancer and decided that she would end her own life if living became unbearable. She reached that point while she was living with her daughter in Pasadena. On August 17, 1935, she used chloroform to commit suicide; she died quickly and without pain. After her death, *The Living of Charlotte Perkins Gilman: An Autobiography* (1935) appeared in print. The book was reprinted in the 1970s and the 1990s, testifying to the importance of her life and work in modern times.

See also Addams, Jane; Kelley, Florence

References

Davis, Cynthia J. *Charlotte Perkins Gilman: A Biography.* Stanford, CA: Stanford University Press, 2010.

Gilman, Charlotte Perkins. *The Living of Charlotte Perkins Gilman: An Autobiography.* Madison: University of Wisconsin Press, 1991. Originally published 1935.

Gilman, Charlotte Perkins. *Our Androcentric Culture, or the Man Made World.* 1911. Project Gutenberg e-book released January 15, 2009.

Hill, Mary A. *Charlotte Perkins Gilman: The Making of a Radical Feminist 1860–1896.* Philadelphia: Temple University Press, 1980.

Lane, Ann J. *To Herland and Beyond: The Life and Work of Charlotte Perkins Gilman.* New York: Pantheon Books, 1990.

Stetson, Charlotte Perkins. *Women and Economics—a Study of the Economic Relation between Men and Women as a Factor in Social Evolution.* Boston: Small, Maynard, & Company, 1990. First published 1898. (A Google digital copy of a book in the public domain.)

Giovanni, Nikki (1943–)

"I was just a woman looking at the world, trying to find a way to be happy and to be safe and to make a contribution. And, in order to do that, a lot of bush had to be cut down . . . there were a lot of weeds out there. . . . racism, poverty, just basic prejudice against women. Prejudice against any number of things. And so you go through . . . that field. And you say to yourself, 'I have got to knock some of those weeds down.' " So said Nikki Giovanni in a 2009 interview with Bill Moyers as she described her life as poet, civil rights activist, and social critic (Moyers 2009).

Yolande Cornelia Giovanni Jr. was born on June 7, 1943, the second daughter to Yolande Cornelia and Jones "Gus" Giovanni. Nikki's birthplace was Knoxville, Tennessee, the home of her maternal grandparents, John Brown and Emma Louvenia Watson. While Yolande was still a baby, her older sister Gary Ann gave her the nickname "Nikki."

During the first years of her life, Nikki's family moved several times as her parents sought work. At one point, her parents worked as houseparents at the Glenview School, a home for African American boys, in Cincinnati, Ohio. The family moved to Woodlawn, a suburb of Cincinnati, in order for Gus Giovanni to take a teaching position at South Woodlawn School and work nights and weekends at the YMCA. During this time, when many of the schools were still segregated, there was no elementary school for African American children. So Nikki's older sister Gary was sent to live with relatives in Columbus, Ohio, where she could attend school. Eventually the family settled in Lincoln Heights, Ohio, an all-black suburb of Cincinnati, where both of Giovanni's parents found jobs as teachers.

The relationship between Giovanni's parents became increasingly explosive because of issues with alcoholism. In 1958, Giovanni moved in with her grandparents in Knoxville, and Giovanni credits her grandmother Louvenia Watson for teaching her the importance of helping others and fighting injustice, and for speaking her mind. As Giovanni would later say, "Grandmother was very outspoken, which meant she said what was on her mind. One of her messages to me was 'Just tell the truth and let it fall'" (Giovanni 2009, 133).

Louvenia Watson was involved with many charitable and political endeavors, including the controversial Highlander Folk School. Founded by Myles Horton and Don West, the school's program focused on self-respect and self-empowerment, based upon the conviction that education should be used to help people work collectively toward a more democratic and humane society. In 1953, the school began holding workshops on public school desegregation, nearly a year before the U.S. Supreme Court's decision in *Brown v. Board of Education* (1954). Civil rights activists Rosa Parks, Martin Luther King Jr., and Andrew Young learned the ways of non-violent protest at Highlander.

In 1958, Giovanni enrolled at Austin High School, where her grandfather had taught Latin for many years. Giovanni credits him with instilling in her the love of words and story that would define her literary career as well as her activism. It was during this time that Giovanni also participated in one of her first demonstrations as an activist, protesting the segregation at a local diner. Another important influence for Giovanni was her English high school teacher, Alfredda Delaney, who required the young Giovanni to read African American writers and then write about what she read.

By 1970, poet Nikki Giovanni had become a nationally recognized figure on the black literary scene. She is shown here with her son Thomas on her shoulder at a soul picnic in New York City in 1972. (AP Photo/Jim Wells)

In 1960, Giovanni entered the all-black Fisk University, her grandfather's alma mater, in Nashville, Tennessee. After only one semester at the school, she was expelled because she visited her grandparents without receiving formal permission from the university authorities. Giovanni also believed it was because of her increasing involvement in the civil rights movement. She returned to Lincoln Heights to help her parents and also to help support her nephew Christopher. In 1962, her grandfather John Brown Watson died.

In 1964, the new dean of the Fisk University, Blanche McConnell Cowen, encouraged Giovanni to return to her studies, promising to purge the student files collected by the previous dean that led to her expulsion. Giovanni returned to Fisk, and with the support of Dean Cowen, she flourished academically and became a student leader. She edited a student literary journal, *Elan*. She also established the Student Nonviolent Coordinating Committee (SNCC), a national campus-based organization engaged in the civil rights movement.

Giovanni became actively involved in the Black Arts movement, a branch of the early Black Power movement, in 1966. Started by writer and activist Amiri Baraka (born Everett LeRoi Jones), the movement was rooted in the civil rights movement, Malcolm X and the Nation of Islam, and is often regarded as the single most controversial movement in the history of African American literature. The movement called for African Americans to break away from the white-dominated publishing industry to start their own publishing houses, magazines, and journals dedicated to the African American experience. It was often criticized as misogynist, homophobic, anti-Semitic, and racially exclusive. Other writers involved in the movement included Robert Hayden, Maya Angelou, Sonia Sanchez, and Rosa Grey.

Giovanni graduated with honors from Fisk with a bachelor of arts in history in 1967, and moved to Cincinnati, where she continued her work in the civil rights movement. She organized Cincinnati's first Black Arts Festival and became an editor for *Conversation*, a revolutionary art journal. On March 8, 1967, Giovanni's beloved grandmother died. Giovanni described this moment as the most significant loss of her life. She took refuge in her writing, creating many of the poems that would later be included in her first work.

In 1967, Giovanni received a fellowship from the Ford Foundation and enrolled in the University of Pennsylvania's School of Social Work. As part of her graduate studies, she worked at the People's Settlement House. However, she soon dropped out of the school as her life took a more creative direction. In 1968, Giovanni attended the funeral of Martin Luther King Jr. She considered King one of the most important public men of the 1960s, proving that words speak as loudly as action in the civil rights movement. In the years to follow, Giovanni's life would reflect this same sentiment.

Shortly after King's funeral, Giovanni borrowed money to self-publish her first book of civil rights poetry, *Black Feeling Black Talk* (1968). Reflecting her grandmother's message, in which she spoke her truth, many of the poems were her response to the assassination of King as well as those of Malcolm X, Medgar Evers, and Robert Kennedy. The book sold 2,000 copies its first year. Its success and a grant from the National Endowment for the Arts prompted Giovanni to move to New York City, enrolling at Columbia University's School of Fine Arts. Using money she received from the sale of her first book and a grant from the Harlem Council of Arts, she privately published her second volume of poetry, *Black Judgement* (1968). This book proved to be more successful, selling over 6,000 copies in the three months following publication. Later, *Black Feeling, Black Talk, Black Judgement* (1970) included work from both her earlier books. Giovanni was quickly becoming an icon of the Black Arts movement. The *Amsterdam News* called her one of the 10 most admired black women. But her straightforward, passionate approach to racial and feminist issues also earned her the label "The Princess of Black Poetry" and "revolutionary poet" by the media. In 1969, author Thomas A Johnson called her work a "basically angry anthology."

After receiving her degree in 1969, Giovanni began teaching at Rutgers University. On August 31, 1969, she gave birth to her only child, Thomas Watson Giovanni. Having a child out of wedlock was a deliberate choice for Giovanni, who wanted a child but denounced the conventional politics of marriage.

Between 1969 and 1971, Giovanni traveled extensively to Africa and throughout the Caribbean. Her travels not only broadened her artistic scope, but softened her political rhetoric. She was criticized by some for abandoning the black revolutionary issues in order to pursue more personal writing, but as biographer Effy Bergstein offered, Giovanni was now a mother, and becoming more settled.

By 1970, Giovanni had become a nationally recognized figure on the black literary scene. A popular speaker and reader, she began making regular appearances on such television show as *Soul!* Giovanni collaborated with the New York Community Choir to create her Grammy-nominated spoken-word album, *Truth Is On Its Way*. In promoting the album, she made over 200 public appearances. Literary critic Margaret McDowell praised Giovanni, calling her a poet of the people. The album proved a phenomenal success, selling more than 100,000 copies in its first six months.

In 1972, Giovanni received an honorary doctorate from Wilberforce University, the nation's oldest African American college, located in Ohio. She was the youngest person to be so honored. Throughout the 1970s, Giovanni published several literary successes, including her autobiography, *Gemini: An Extended Autobiographical Statement on My First Twenty-Five Years of Being a Black Poet* (1971), and her poetry collection, *My House* (1972). With the poetry collection, according to Bergstein, Giovanni brings together those personal elements that reflect Giovanni's domestic feminine side and internal growth with the social, political, and cultural elements of Giovanni's ancestry. In so doing, Giovanni became the first author to emphasize the importance of subjectivity in writing and to promote the power of individuality. In November 1972, she collaborated with Paula Giddings, an editor at Howard University Press, to write a book composed of several discussions between Giovanni and activist and political poet Margaret Walker. Walker's first book, *For My People* (1942), firmly established her career as a political poet. Walker advocated a more equitable system for disadvantaged people. Her poetry often showcased African Americans as emblems of the working class. Giovanni's books feature several interviews with Walker, in which they discuss political and literary issues. A joint effort was published as *A Poetic Equation: Conversations Between Nikki Giovanni and Margaret Walker* (1974).

Giovanni continued to write and lecture on social and political issues. She wrote essays for the magazine *Encore: American and World-Wide News*, founded by political writer Ida Lewis.

In 1978, Giovanni's father suffered a debilitating stroke, and was subsequently diagnosed with cancer. She returned home to Lincoln Heights to take care of her parents. Now faced with the financial challenge of growing medical bills, and a growing son, Giovanni began in earnest her lecturing and speaking tour, spending less time on her writing. Her father died in 1982.

In 1989, Giovanni accepted a permanent position as tenured professor of English at Virginia Polytechnic Institute and State University (Virginia Tech) in Blacksburg. In 2007, she delivered the closing remarks at the memorial for the victims of the April 2007 shooting spree, in which student Seung-Hui Cho killed 32 people before killing himself. Bill Moyers describes the reading, "We Are Virginia Tech," as a moment of profound healing, in which her words "brought thousands to their feet in a tearful standing ovation" (Moyers 2009).

In January 1995, Giovanni, a lifelong smoker, was diagnosed with lung cancer. To stop the spread of the disease, she had numerous ribs and part of her lung removed. As she recovered from the disease and surgery, she rediscovered her love of, and found new purpose in, her poetry. In 1996, she published her first children's books, *The Genie in the Jar* and *The Sun Is So Quiet*. The following year, her first volume of poetry in 14 years was published, *Love Poems* (1997). In June 2005, her mother died of lung cancer, and in August of the same year, her sister died of the same disease.

Giovanni is the recipient of numerous awards and honors, including 25 honorary degrees as well as Woman of the Year honors by *Mademoiselle*, *Ladies Home Journal* and *Ebony* magazine. She was included in the Ohio Women's Hall of Fame and named Outstanding Woman of Tennessee. She is the first recipient of the Rosa L. Parks Woman of Courage Award, and she has received the National Book Award and the NAACP Woman of the Year award.

Bobbi Miller

See also Horton, Myles; King, Martin Luther, Jr.; Malcolm X; Parks, Rosa

References

Bergstein, Effy. "Giovanni, Yolande Cornelia (Nikki)." *Pennsylvania Center for the Book*, Pennsylvania State University, Summer 2008. http://pabook.libraries.psu.edu/palitmap/bios/Giovanni__Nikki.html (accessed November 6, 2010).

Academy of American Poets. "A Brief Guide to the Black Arts Movement." Poets.org, 1997. http://www.poets.org/viewmedia.php/prmMID/5647 (accessed November 6, 2010).

Fowler, Virginia C., and Nikki Giovanni. *Conversations with Nikki Giovanni*. Jackson: University Press of Mississippi, 1992.

Giovanni, Nikki. *Gemini: An Extended Autobiographical Statement on My First Twenty-Five Years of Being a Black Poet*. New York: Penguin, 1976.

Giovanni, Nikki, "Reading the Rainbow." In *Audacious Aging*, edited by Stephanie Marohn. Fulton, CA: Elite Books, 2009.

McDowell, Margaret B. "Groundwork for a More Comprehensive Criticism of Nikki Giovanni." *Studies in Black American Literature*, 1986.

Meyer, Susan. "Nikki Giovanni and Martin Luther King, Jr." *Ohioana Authors*. WOSU Stations, in partnership with the Ohioana Library, n.d. http://www.ohioana-authors.org/giovanni/mlk.php (accessed November 6, 2010).

Moyers, Bill. *Bill Moyers Journal*. Public Affairs Television (transcript), February 13, 2009. http://www.pbs.org/moyers/journal/02132009/transcript2.html (accessed October 28, 2010).

Romano, Lisa. "Nikki Giovanni (1943–)." *Encyclopedia Virginia*, edited by Brendan

Wolfe. Virginia Foundation for the Humanities. June 16, 2009. http://www.EncyclopediaVirginia.org/Giovanni_Nikki_1943 - (accessed November 6, 2010).

Goldman, Emma (1869–1940)

"Emma Goldman is one of the few who, while thoroughly preserving their individuality, have become an important factor in the social and intellectual atmosphere of America. The life she leads is rich in color, full of change and variety. She has risen to the topmost heights, and she has also tasted the bitter dregs of life." So wrote anarchist Hippolyte Havel in a biographical sketch of Goldman for a 1910 publication (Goldman 1969, 7). The U.S. press and law enforcement were not so kind; they portrayed Emma Goldman as the most dangerous woman in the country, a charge that was never proven. What was true, however, was that Emma Goldman was a spellbinding speaker and a passionate and prolific writer for the supremacy of individual rights and against repressive governments.

Emma Goldman was born June 27, 1869, in a rural province of Czarist Russia to Jewish parents, Abraham and Taube, whose marriage of convenience was arranged, as was the custom, by Taube's parents. Taube was a widow with two daughters, Helena and Lena. Emma was Abraham's first child, and she was born at a time when Abraham had lost his business. He resented having another family member to feed and also that the child was a girl.

Like many Jews, the Goldmans suffered devastating anti-Semitism. Laws prevented them from earning a decent living—they were banned from farming and most public service jobs. Laws also required that Jews pay special taxes to the czar and restricted where Jews could live, travel, and build synagogues. Before Emma was one year old, Abraham received permission from the government to manage a stagecoach system, caring for the horses and operating an inn for travelers in the village of Popelan.

The family lived in the village for seven years, and during that time two other children, Herman and Morris, were born. Emma often was left to her own devices, as her mother cared for her younger brothers, and her older sisters worked in the busy inn. She became independent and often expressed her own opinions, which irritated her father, who expected strict obedience to his commands. She suffered violent outbursts, beatings, and taunts from her father about being an unwanted child. In a word, Emma called her childhood "ghastly." Yet, she experienced some pleasant times, babysitting on occasion for her young brother Herman, playing with her half-sister Helena and a village boy, Petrushka, who cared for the Goldmans' cows and sheep.

Emma's formal education was interrupted frequently by moves. In 1876, her father sent her to Koenigsberg, Germany, to live with her maternal grandmother and family members and attend school. Her aunts and uncles mistreated her, and Emma's father came to rescue her, for the first time showing real concern about her welfare. They returned to Popelan, but within a few months, Abraham lost his job. Since the Goldmans had no place to live, they went back to Koenigsberg to stay with Taub's family. After Emma completed her elementary schooling, the Goldmans moved in 1881 to St. Petersburg, Russia, where Abraham was able to get work managing his cousin's store. Emma was able to attend school again—but only for six months. She had to drop out at age 13 because her father once more lost his job. Emma went to work in a corset factory, a mind-numbing job that she hated. She found refuge in reading, particularly books about Russian Nihilists who fought repressive authority.

When Abraham arranged for his 15-year-old daughter to marry, Emma balked. She begged to accompany her half-sister Helena, who planned to go to the United States. Her other half-sister Lena had already made the trip, had married, and was living in Rochester, New York. Abraham finally relented and allowed Emma and Helena to immigrate to the United States in December 1885, reaching Rochester in January 1886. That same year, the rest of the Goldman family left Russia because of the growing anti-Semitism; they settled in Rochester's Jewish community.

In Rochester, Emma took several factory jobs and met another worker from Russia, Jacob Kershner. The two became friends, and after several months, Jacob asked Emma to marry him. She refused at first, but she wanted companionship, and the two married in 1887. Emma soon discovered she had little in common with her husband, and they divorced.

During her time in Rochester, Goldman read about the execution of the anarchist men convicted of inciting the riot that ensued while workers were rallying in Haymarket Square in Chicago. Goldman and many others believed the men were tried and convicted to deter the efforts of other labor organizers protesting for better pay and working conditions. When she heard of their execution, Goldman vowed to dedicate herself to the martyrs' anarchist cause. She read the works of anarchists who saw the industrial-based economy and the modern state as the successor to the czars, kings, and despots who kept the common people in Europe in a perpetual condition of slavery. For Goldman, the ancient communities of individuals and families who gathered together to meet their own needs were the appropriate social and economic structure.

As an anarchist writer, lecturer, and agitator during the late 1800s and early 1900s, Emma Goldman was one of the most outstanding, and notorious, rebels in American history. (Library of Congress)

In 1889, Emma Goldman moved to New York City, where the anarchist movement had many supporters, especially among recently arrived immigrants from Germany, Poland, and Russia. She met anarchist leader Johann Most, who became her mentor. She also met Alexander Berkman, a young anarchist agitator, with whom she fell in love.

Goldman soon became an activist, believing it was her mission to help her fellow humans throw off the yoke of oppressive government: any form of government or oppression. She had a gift for oratory and gave speeches at many anarchist events and before striking workers whom she supported. Her controversial statements attacking social institutions were reported by newspapers in every city where she appeared, and the popular media vilified and demonized her for her outspoken attacks against injustice.

On September 6, 1901, President William McKinley was shot by Leon Czolgosz, who said he had been inspired to act after hearing a speech by Goldman days before. Although Goldman had been introduced to Czolgosz by an associate, there was no evidence that she had collaborated with him. When McKinley died from gunshot wounds, Goldman was arrested in Chicago and held in jail for 15 days. The chief of police was convinced of her innocence, and he ordered her released. The publicity, however, linked McKinley's assassination to anarchism and Emma Goldman.

Wherever she appeared on her speaking tours throughout the nation, Goldman was in danger from individuals or crowds of vigilantes who blamed her for the death of the president. In one instance a crowd captured her manager, Ben Reitman, tarred and feathered him, and drove him out of town. The police did little to protect her. Quite often they would attempt to ban her appearances on the pretense that she was out to provoke violence, lawlessness, and revolution. Goldman was arrested numerous times for defying police orders, which she knew violated the right to free speech guaranteed by the U.S. Constitution. However, she found many ways to circumvent the obstacles and to speak out for workers' rights, birth control, and women's rights. In 1903, she organized a branch of the Free Speech League, a society of liberal activists who opposed the Anarchist Exclusion Act designed to "regulate the immigration of aliens into the United States."

Between 1906 and 1915, Goldman cofounded and edited *Mother Earth*, a magazine that contained essays by anarchists and libertarians. She also wrote articles for the magazine and a book *Anarchism and Other Essays* (1910). Throughout this period, she spoke to numerous audiences from New York to California. When the United States entered World War I in 1917, Goldman and Berkman helped organize the No-Conscription League, which opposed the draft as well as U.S. involvement in World War I in Europe.

Goldman's and Berkman's antidraft activities brought on increased government surveillance. In June 1917, the U.S. government seized an opportunity to finally silence Emma Goldman, arresting her and her friend Alexander Berkman for conspiring to oppose the draft. In short order, Goldman was convicted without evidence and sentenced to prison.

The federal government went one giant step further. Goldman's U.S. citizenship was based on her marriage to a naturalized citizen, Jacob Kershner in Rochester. The immigration department found that part of Kirshner's application for citizenship was false, and they voided her ex-husband's legal status. That made Goldman an illegal alien too, so federal officials could charge her under the Anarchist Exclusion Act, which barred known alien anarchists from entry into the United States and sanctioned deportation of those already in the country. The U.S. government deported Goldman, Berkman, and 247 aliens that they labeled anarchists.

Goldman and Berkman went to Russia, where at first they championed the 1917 revolution in their homeland, but soon became disillusioned with the Bolsheviks and their brutal treatment of workers. In fact, Goldman became highly critical of Vladimir Lenin, called the "father" of the revolution. In her view, Lenin had sacrificed both the country and the revolution to the centralized state.

Goldman had understood during her deportation trial that the state controlled her destiny, and she decided to use the opportunity to make a final point to the United States.

Acting as her own lawyer, she told the jury, "whatever your decision, the struggle must go on. We are but the atoms in the incessant human struggle towards the light that shines in the darkness—the Ideal of economic, political and spiritual liberation of mankind!" (Shulman 1972, 327).

For the next 21 years, Goldman lived in Russia, England, France, and Spain, never ceasing to write and speak out for the anarchist ideals that were her *raison d'être*. Although the United States got rid of Goldman, the major issue she raised during her lifetime of activism—the role of government in the individual's life—is still being debated. Although she could not return to the United States, she was able to travel to Canada, where she lived for a time and raised funds for the Spanish Revolution. While traveling in Canada, she suffered a massive stroke from which she never recovered. She died in Toronto, Canada, on May 14, 1940. Her body was buried in Chicago, Illinois, near the Haymarket martyrs. In an essay written toward the end of her life, she puts her efforts into perspective: "I think my life and my work have been successful. What is generally regarded as success—acquisition of wealth, the capture of power or social prestige—I consider the most dismal failures. I hold when it is said of a man that he has arrived, it means that he is finished—his development has stopped at that point. I have always striven to remain in a state of flux and continued growth, and not to petrify in a niche of self-satisfaction" (Shulman 1972, 397).

References

Chalberg, John. *Emma Goldman: American Individualist*. New York: HarperCollins, 1991.

Drinnon, Richard. *Rebel in Paradise: A Biography of Emma Goldman*. Chicago: University of Chicago Press, 1961.

Falk, Candace. *Love, Anarchy, and Emma Goldman*. New Brunswick, NJ: Rutgers University Press, 1990.

Goldman, Emma. *Anarchism and Other Essays*. New York: Dover, 1969. Reprint of 1910 ed.

Goldman, Emma. *Living My Life*. New York: Knopf, 1970. Reprint of 1931 ed.

Goldman, Emma. *The Traffic in Women and Other Essays on Feminism*. Albion, CA: Times Change Press, 1970. Reprint of 1917 ed.

Shulman, Alix. *Red Emma Speaks: Selected Writings and Speeches by Emma Goldman*. New York: Random House, 1972.

Solomon, Martha. *Emma Goldman*. Boston: Twayne, Macmillan, 1987.

Goodman, Paul (1911–1972)

Paul Goodman inspired dissidents of the 1960s, and as a teacher and an author of poems, plays, books, and articles, he championed numerous causes, including anarchism, personal and sexual freedom, nonviolence, draft resistance, alternative schooling, psychotherapy, and city planning. Goodman was an influential social critic in the United States, known for his best-selling book *Growing Up Absurd: Problems of Youth in the Organized Culture* (1960). Much of his written work condemned conformity in education, government, and other institutions. In short, Goodman opposed centralized authority and hated the status quo.

Goodman was born on September 9, 1911, in New York City. He was the fourth child of Jewish parents. His father Barnett failed in business and left the family when Paul was an infant. Relatives cared for Paul while his mother Augusta worked and led a bohemian lifestyle. While he was growing up, Paul was allowed to roam New York

City streets. Although he attended public school as well as Hebrew school, his curiosity led him to derive much of his education from museums and libraries. When he graduated from Townsend Harris High School, he was first in his class.

Between 1927 and 1931, Goodman was a student at City College of New York. In 1936, he audited graduate philosophy courses at Columbia University, and then went on to study for his doctorate at the University of Chicago, where he also taught. He was fired from his teaching position when he openly pursued homosexual relationships with his students, believing he had the right to do so. He considered himself bisexual and was sexually active with women as well as men. In fact, he lived with Virginia Miller for five years and the couple had a daughter, Susan, born in 1939.

In 1940, Goodman left Chicago and returned to New York City, where he lived for the rest of his life. He began a relationship with Sally Duchsten in 1945; they had a daughter, Daisy, and a son Matthew Ready. Matthew was killed while mountaineering in 1967, an accident that affected Goodman for the rest of his life.

Paul and Sally "got by on little jobs including a $5 per story contract with the MGM story department in New York for plot synopses of French novels," according to John Fitzgerald writing for an online research center on anarchism. Goodman "considered himself an artist and produced mostly poems, plays and short stories. He promoted himself vigorously but met with little acceptance of his mostly avant-garde style. He was involved with little literary magazines, theater groups and political activities centered around the Spanish Anarchist Hall" (Fitzgerald n.d.).

In the 1940s, Goodman proclaimed that he was a conservative anarchist in the tradition of Thomas Jefferson who famously said that "the best government is that which governs least." According to Richard Wall, Goodman explained much later: "The idea of Jeffersonian democracy is to educate its people to govern by giving them initiative to run things, by multiplying sources of responsibility, by encouraging dissent. This has the beautiful moral advantage that a man can be excellent in his own way without feeling special, can rule without ambition and follow without inferiority. Through the decades, it should have been the effort of our institutions to adapt this idea to ever-changing technical and social conditions. Instead, as if by dark design, our present institutions conspire to make people inexpert, mystified, and slavish" (Wall n.d.).

In Goodman's view "only anarchism or, better, anarcho-pacifism—the philosophy of institutions without the State and centrally organized violence—has consistently foreseen the big shapes and gross dangers of present advanced societies, their police, bureaucracy, excessive centralization of decision-making, social-engineering, and inevitable militarization" (Goodman 1971, 143).

According to biographer Kingsley Widmer, "in several ways it is odd that Goodman became an avowed anarchist in the mid-1940s.... He was not in most usual senses a rebellious character," except for his bisexuality. Widmer noted that "Goodman arrived at anarchism during World War II. His rejection of the draft, which he avoided, and his revulsion at the cultural and social conditions of wartime, which he saw as ugly, may have provided some of the specific occasion for his first anarchist essays in 1945" (Widmer 1980, 37–38).

Because of Goodman's antiwar stance, he "was ostracised from New York literary circles of influence," according to British sociologist Carissa Honeywell at Sheffield

Hallam University. As a result, Goodman associated "with the smaller, more marginal bohemian New York scene, including radical sub-communities, small cooperatives, anarchist publications, avant-garde theatres, and bohemian clusters. Goodman also began to write for the anarchist magazine *Why?* published by the new generation of young radicals meeting in the Spanish Anarchists Hall on Lower Broadway" (Honeywell 2010).

However, Goodman's writings dealt with much more than anarchism. He also wrote about politics, psychotherapy, and urban living. He and his brother Percival, a prominent architect, coauthored *Communitas: Means of Livelihood and Ways of Life* (1947), which criticizes city planning and suggests ways to improve housing, transportation, and other aspects of urban life. *Gestalt Therapy: Excitement and Growth in the Human Personality* (1951) was a collaborative effort with psychoanalyst Fritz Perls and psychology professor Robert Heferline. Goodman also wrote a novel, *The Empire City* (1959), that depicts characters struggling for emotional good health in a New York City environment.

"By the mid-1950s Goodman's hour had come round at last. The prevailing 'squeaky-clean' image of American youth was under attack and was being relinquished by a film industry increasingly dependent on the patronage of youth," wrote Edgar Friedenberg for UNESCO's journal *Prospect*, adding: "In 1955 the young actor, James Dean, whose image might have been designed to win Goodman's heart, was killed in an automobile accident at the age of 24. This was the same year the two films that made Dean an icon as well as a falling star, *East of Eden* and *Rebel Without A Cause*, were released. The immortal Elvis Presley's first hit-movie *Love Me Tender* appeared in 1956. Clearly, the time was ripe for movies and books that celebrated the sexuality of adolescent males" (Friedenberg 1999).

By the time Goodman's *Growing Up Absurd* was published in 1960, the stage had been set for his book to be highly successful. He became a guru of sorts for youth who were rebelling against the excessive conformity of the 1950s. He frequently made comments that could be applied to current issues, such as this from his book's Preface:

> The school system has been subjected to criticism. And there is a lot of official talk about the need to conserve our human resources lest Russia get ahead of us... many people are quite clear about the connection that the structure of society that has become increasingly dominant in our country is disastrous to the growth of excellence.... people are so bemused by the way that business and politics are carried on at present, with all their intricate relationships, that they have ceased to be able to imagine alternatives. (Goodman 1960, x)

One young admirer of Goodman's work was Susan Sontag (1933–2004), who became well known as a literary essayist. She read almost everything Goodman wrote, which Sontag called

> a nervy mixture of syntactical stiffness and verbal felicity; he was capable of writing sentences of a wonderful purity of style and vivacity of language, and also capable of writing so sloppily and clumsily that one imagined he must be doing it on purpose. But it never mattered. It was his voice, that is to say, his intelligence and the poetry of his intelligence incarnated, which kept me a loyal and passionate addict. Though he was not often graceful

as a writer, his writing and his mind were touched with grace. (Sontag 1972, 6–7)

Throughout the 1960s, Goodman wrote numerous essays for the literary journal *New York Review of Books*. Some were on topics such as improving New York City, the rights of children, and politics. Other writings were letters to the editor. For example, one submission was a copy of a letter he had written to U.S. attorney general Robert Kennedy (1925–1968). Goodman described an incident with customs when he and his son were returning from Montreal, Canada. His son had purchased a book titled *Nuevos Cuentos Cubanos* or *New Cuban Tales* (1964), which the customs officer confiscated and planned to burn. The U.S. government prohibited financial and commercial transactions with Cuba. The Cuban book was considered a commercial transaction, and the customs officer asked Goodman to sign an assent form allowing disposal of the book. "Naturally, as an intellectual man and a writer I could not assent to the burning of a book and I refused to sign until the superior officer at the station scratched out the word 'assent.'" Goodman asked in his letter to the attorney general for help in rectifying the situation and reimbursing the price of the book (Goodman 1967). Robert Kennedy was gunned down in 1968, the same year that civil rights icon Martin Luther King, Jr. was killed and five years after his brother President John F. Kennedy was assassinated in 1963.

During the 1960s and 1970s, Goodman was a strong supporter of young men who resisted the Vietnam War draft. He helped initiate a Stop the Draft Week in 1967, an event that also included Reverend William Sloane Coffin, who had collected draft cards from resisters and delivered them to the U.S. government. Coffin later was charged with criminal conspiracy. Goodman addressed the National Security Industrial Association (NSIA) meeting at the U.S. State Department. He called the men the most dangerous in the world for their part in the military-industrial complex that profited from war. In part, he said:

> The survival of the human species, at least in a civilized state, demands radical disarmament, and there are several feasible political means to achieve this if we willed it. By the same token, we must drastically de-energize the archaic system of nation-states.... Instead, you—and your counterparts in Europe, Russia, and China—have rigidified and aggrandized the states with a ... policy called Deterrence, which has continually escalated rather than stabilized ... Past a certain point your operations have increased insecurity rather than diminished it. But this has been to your interest. (Goodman 1967)

When Goodman publicly stated that he was helping draft resisters, the U.S. Federal Bureau of Investigation classified him as a "subversive homosexual."

A prolific writer, Goodman's numerous books include *The Community of Scholars* (1962); *Utopian Essays and Practical Proposals* (1962); *The Society I Live In Is Mine* (1963); *Seeds of Liberation* (1964); *Compulsory Miseducation* (1964); *People or Personnel: Decentralizing and the Mixed System* (1965); *Five Years: Thoughts during a Useless Time* (1966); *Like a Conquered Province: The Moral Ambiguity of America* (1967); *New Reformation: Notes of Neolithic Conservative* (1969); and his final book, *Little Prayers and Finite Experience* (1972).

Goodman died of a heart attack on August 2, 1972, at his farm in North Stratford, New Hampshire. But his essays, poems, and other written materials did not die with him. Professor Taylor Stoehr, University of Massachusetts, Boston, edited and published posthumously Goodman's works such as *Collected Poems* (1973), *Drawing the Line: The Political Essays of Paul Goodman* (1977), and *Crazy Hope and Finite Experience: Final Essays of Paul Goodman* (1994).

Paul Goodman Changed My Life (2011) is the first documentary about Goodman. Produced by Jonathan Lee, the film includes interviews with Goodman's family members and a variety of celebrities such as well-known linguist, dissident intellectual, and antiwar activist Noam Chomsky. The main purpose of the movie is to introduce young people who are unaware of Goodman to this man who inspired dissidents in the 1960s and 1970s.

See also Chomsky, Noam; Coffin, William Sloane; King, Martin Luther, Jr.; Sontag, Susan

References

Fitzgerald, John. "Paul Goodman Biography." Anarchy Archives, n.d. http://dwardmac.pitzer.edu/Anarchist_Archives/bright/goodman/goodman-bio.html (accessed January 9, 2011).

Friedenberg, Edgar Z. "Paul Goodman." *Prospects: The Quarterly Review of Comparative Education*. Paris: UNESCO, 1999.

Goodman, Paul. "Book Burning." *New York Review of Books*, September 28, 1967.

Goodman, Paul. "A Causerie at the Military-Industrial." Speech before National Security Industrial Association, November 23, 1967.

Goodman, Paul. *Compulsory Mis-Education and the Community of Scholars*. New York: Vintage, 1962.

Goodman, Paul. *Growing Up Absurd: Problems of Youth in Organized Society*. New York: Vintage, 1960.

Goodman, Paul. *New Reformation: Notes of Neolithic Conservative*. New York: Vintage Books, 1971. First published 1969.

Honeywell, Carissa. "Paul Goodman: Finding an Audience for Anarchism in 20th Century America." *Political Studies Association*, May 2010. http://www.psa.ac.uk/journals/pdf/5/2010/397_543.pdf (accessed January 9, 2011).

Sontag, Susan. "On Paul Goodman." *New York Review of Books*, September 21, 1972. http://www.nybooks.com/articles/archives/1972/sep/21/on-paul-goodman/ (accessed January 12, 2011).

Sontag, Susan. *Under the Sign of Saturn: Essays*. New York: Picador USA/Farrar, Straus, and Giroux, 2002 (first published 1972).

Stoehr, Taylor. *Decentralizing Power: Paul Goodman's Social Criticism*. New York: Black Rose Books, 1994.

Wall, Richard. "The Radical Individualism of Paul Goodman." LewRockwell.com, n.d. http://www.lewrockwell.com/orig3/wall10.html (accessed January 9, 2011).

Widmer, Kingsley. *Paul Goodman*. Boston: Twayne Publishers, 1980.

Gregory, Dick (1932–)

"We thought I was going to be a great athlete, and we were wrong, and I thought I was going to be a great entertainer, and that wasn't it either. I'm going to be an American Citizen. First class" (Gregory 1969, 207). These were the words that Dick Gregory used to describe himself early on in life when writing his first memoir, *Nigger: An Autobiography*. More than half a century later, they remain an apt description of a man who has remained committed to activism and championing a multitude of causes. Gregory's web site catalogs his varied professions as "activist, philosopher, anti-drug crusader, comedian, author, actor, recording artist, nutritionist"—quite an impressive resume for an individual of his modest origins (Biography Dick Gregory n.d.).

Born in St. Louis, Missouri, on October 12, 1932, Gregory was the second in a poor family of six children. He was named Richard "Dick" Claxton Gregory. As the second oldest, he found odd jobs to help out his mother Lucille, who had been abandoned by Gregory's father. Lucille taught her children to maintain a sense of personal pride and accountability for their own accomplishments, regardless of their limited financial circumstances, and instilled in them an ability to see humor in everyday events. The latter would especially take root with Dick Gregory.

While still in his teens, Gregory began to develop two passions: advocacy for social justice, and athletics. He led his first demonstration, protesting segregated schools, while attending Sumner High School. It was during his high school years that his prowess at track drew the attention of college recruiters. From multiple scholarship offers, he chose to attend Southern Illinois University (SIU) in Carbondale, Illinois, where he studied business administration from 1951 to 1956. In 1953, he was named outstanding athlete for his track record, excelling in both the half-mile and mile. His education was interrupted in 1954 when drafted by the U.S. Army. During his two-year stint in the service, Gregory began performing routines for the troops—his first foray into comedy. After his discharge from the army, he returned to SIU briefly but left before earning his degree. He is often quoted as saying that the university did not want him to study; they wanted him to be a track star.

Gregory moved to Chicago in the hopes of making it big as a comedian. He was joining a new generation of black entertainers—the likes of Bill Cosby, Nipsey Russell, and Sammy Davis Jr. These men did not give the minstrel show performances that had been expected of black men and accepted by both black and white audiences alike. They had broken away from the stereotypical portrayal of black performers and, instead, came out on stage and performed simply as themselves, unique individuals who could and would not be categorized by their skin color.

Most of the stand-up work Gregory could get was in clubs drawing largely black crowds. The pay was typically about $5 per night, so he supported himself with odd jobs, from working for the U.S. Postal Service, to washing cars, to an attempt at owning his own club. His "big break" came about in 1961, when he was given a chance to perform at the Playboy Club in Chicago. At first, he was almost turned away because the room had been booked to a group of southern conventioneers, but he insisted on going on stage despite the more than frosty initial reception that he received. He turned the catcalls and insults around faster and funnier than they came; soon, he had the audience of hecklers in the palm of his hands. His scheduled 50-minute act ran more than twice as long.

On the heels of that night's success, Playboy offered him a two-month contract. And within a month, *Time* magazine ran a feature article on him, noting: "The audience always laughs and usually applauds the performer, who is just getting started on what may be one of the more significant careers in American show business. With intelligence, sophistication, and none of the blackvoice buffoonery of Amos 'n' Andy, Dick Gregory, 28, has become the first Negro comedian to make his way into the nightclub big time" (*Time* 1961). Soon Gregory was appearing on national television shows, such as *The Tonight Show* with Jack Paar and *The*

Comedian Dick Gregory, who spoke to about 2,000 students at the University of South Florida in Tampa on April 14, 1971, said the fate of the United States depends on its youth. Gregory made pointed jabs at racism, the CIA, President Nixon, and the economic recession at that time. (AP Photo)

Mike Douglas Show. Not only was he fast becoming known as one of the hottest comedians around, but he was also becoming one of the best-known black men in the United States.

Gregory's style was detached, ironic, and satirical. He was sometimes called the "Black Mort Sahl" after the popular white comedian of the day, known for his sharp social commentary. Gregory's friends, on the other hand, referred to Mort Sahl as the "White Dick Gregory." Gregory's routines often focused on current events, and he never shied away from the issue of race: "Segregation is not all bad ... Have you ever heard of a wreck where the people on the back of the bus got hurt?" he joked (*Time* 1961).

In his autobiography, Gregory described his approach to the subject of race with this joke he used while performing: "These three cousins come in [to the restaurant], you know the ones I mean, Klu, Kluck, and Klan, and they say: "Boy, we're givin' you fair warnin'. Anything you do to that chicken, we're gonna do to you." About then the waitress brought me my chicken. . . . So I put down my knife and fork, and I picked up that chicken, and I *kissed* it" (Gregory 1969, 144). Then, after introducing race in a nonthreatening way, he would be a bit more confrontational, pointing to his face and saying, "Wouldn't it be a hell of a thing if all this was burnt cork and all you folks were being tolerant for nothing?" (Gregory 1969, photo caption).

As time went on, Gregory began to vocalize his feelings about politics and social justice more stridently—both on stage and off. His prominence drew media coverage whenever he joined a protest or sit-in, participated in a march, or fasted for a cause. His social stature guaranteed that public attention would be drawn to an issue.

Iconic civil rights leader Dr. Martin Luther King Jr. was a great source of inspiration to him, as was the Student Nonviolent Coordinating Committee (SNCC). Gregory became very active in the civil rights movement. He participated in SNCC's voter registration drives and in segregation sit-ins (one of the latter was held at an Atlanta, Georgia, restaurant franchise, one in which only later on did Gregory disclose that he held stock). Gregory worked with SNCC again when local Mississippi governments stopped distributing federal food surpluses to poor blacks in retaliation for SNCC voter registration efforts. Gregory organized food drives and then chartered a plane to deliver supplies.

Gregory was front and center during the infamous 1965 Watts Riot in Los Angeles. What began as a routine traffic stop—a highway patrolman pulled over a black man who was driving a motorcycle unsteadily—escalated into a six-day riot culminating in the deaths of nearly three dozen, the injury of more than 1,000, and the arrest of almost 3,500. The riot was seen as reaction to Los Angeles police brutality, and injustices perpetrated on blacks in the community. Gregory attempted to bring peace to the situation and, in doing so, was shot by one of the rioters, although that did not deter his efforts. Some fellow blacks were angered by his actions, but at least one white policeman was thankful for his intervention. The officer had a wife and children at home, and he was glad that the gunfire had stopped.

In 1967, Gregory ran unsuccessfully for mayor of Chicago. In 1968, he ran for U.S. president, receiving 1.5 million votes as a write-in candidate. Democratic candidate Hubert Humphrey lost the election to Republican Richard Nixon by 510,000 votes; many believe Humphrey would have won had Gregory not been on the ballot.

Race was not Gregory's only focus. He fought injustice on a varied and wide scale, including the investigation into President John F. Kennedy's assassination; the U.S. involvement in the Vietnam War; Native American rights; anti-Semitism; discriminatory housing practices; feminism; and the issues of poverty and hunger. His celebrity status did nothing to shield him, either. He was arrested on numerous occasions but always maintained his strict adherence to nonviolent protest.

Gregory coauthored *Code Name Zorro: The Murder of Martin Luther King Jr.* (1971) with Mark Lane. The book was released in paperback under the title *Murder in Memphis* (1993). Gregory was also a vocal critic of the investigation into President Kennedy's assassination, disagreeing with the Warren Commission's finding that Lee Harvey Oswald was the responsible party. Gregory credited Lane's *Rush to Judgment* (1966), which included information Gregory widely promoted for years, with raising questions throughout the nation as to who assassinated the president and bringing to light contradictions contained in the Warren report. In 1975, Gregory and assassination researcher Robert Groden appeared on ABC's *Goodnight America*, hosted by Geraldo Rivera. That night, the famous Zapruder film of Kennedy's assassination was shown publicly for the first time, resulting in a public outcry that led to the formation of the Hart-Schweiker investigation, which contributed to the Church Committee

Investigation on Intelligence Activities by the United States. That investigation in turn resulted in the House Select Committee on Assassinations investigation.

In 1978, Gregory stepped out as an ardent feminist activist marching down Pennsylvania Avenue in Washington, D.C., to the U.S. Capitol in support of the National ERA March for Ratification and Extension. Bella Abzug and Betty Friedan, famous for their women's rights advocacy, were among his fellow marchers that day. The following year, Gregory spoke at the Amandla Festival in Boston, Massachusetts, prior to Bob Marley, cult reggae star, taking the stage. The music festival performers supported the antiapartheid movement in South Africa.

During the 1970s, Gregory had moved to the East Coast and, there, began to develop an interest in vegetarianism (partly due to his abhorrence of violence and murder of any living creature) that soon became a full-blown interest in the pursuit of a healthier lifestyle. By his own reports, at one point, Gregory had weighed 350 pounds, smoked four packs of cigarettes, and drank a fifth of scotch a day. By 1981, he had radically changed his ways and had lost a tremendous amount of weight. He decided to conduct what he called "the longest medically supervised scientific fast in the history of the planet," the "Dick Gregory's Zero Nutrition Fasting Experiment," during which he said he would live on a gallon of water and prayer for 70 days at Dillard University's Flint-Goodridge Hospital. When his experiment was over, he demonstrated his claim of good health by walking and jogging the 100-mile distance between New Orleans and Baton Rouge, Louisiana. Out of this experience, Gregory created his "4-X Fasting Formula," inclusive of a "Life-Centric Monitor," with an emphasis on colonetics.

Also in 1981, Gregory announced a commitment to celibacy—this despite no plans to leave his wife Lillian, with whom he had fathered 10 children—Michele, Lynne, Pamela, Paula, Stephanie (Xenobia), Gregory, Christian, Miss, Ayanna, and Yohance—as well as another child who had died at birth. Given his reputation as a somewhat risqué performer, this news came as a surprise to many but was consistent with his ongoing pursuit of a more spiritual life. While spiritual in nature, Gregory was not committed to any one particular dogma. He promoted attaining oneness with a "God-self," or a complete state of being through a holistic approach to living, including diet, fitness, and overall spiritual awareness.

A few years later, Gregory founded Health Enterprises, Inc., which distributed weight-loss products. In 1987, the company released a highly profitable powdered, seaweed-based diet mix, the Slim-Safe Bahamian Diet. He then sold the rights to Cernitin America for $100 million. He gave $1 million each to 15 different charitable and civil rights organizations via the Dick Gregory Health Enterprise located in Chicago.

Gregory continued to expand his business enterprises, acquiring a major interest in the Frankie Jennings Cosmetics Company as a means of marketing diverse products like vitamins, shampoo, juices, and cookies. He grew into a fierce advocate for diet and health awareness among blacks, lamenting the lack of health food stores in black communities. He started proclaiming the importance of natural foods, as well as the dangers of a traditional soul food diet. Gregory came to believe that there was a direct correlation between the shorter life expectancy of blacks and their diets, which included higher-than-average amounts of salt, sugar, cholesterol, alcohol, caffeine, and drugs.

To some observers, Dick Gregory evolved into a wild-eyed conspiracy theorist and a health-food zealot. But to others, spanning multiple generations, he remains an inspiration, both for his comedic prowess—Comedy Central has named him number 81 of the 100 Stand-Ups of All Time—and for his commitment to social justice.

Margaret Gay

See also Abzug, Bella; Friedan, Betty; King, Martin Luther, Jr.

References

"Comedian: Humor, Integrated." *Time*, February 17, 1961. http://www.time.com/time/magazine/article/0,9171,826883,00.html (accessed October 14, 2010).

Dick Gregory Biography, n.d. http://www.dickgregory.com/about_dick_gregory.html (accessed October 14, 2010).

Gregory, Dick. *Up from Nigger*. New York: Stein and Day, 1976.

Gregory, Dick, with Robert Lipsyte. *Nigger: An Autobiography*. New York: Pocket Books, 1969. Originally published, New York: E. P. Dutton, 1964.

Lutz, Phillip. "A Bit Slower, but Still Throwing Lethal Punches." *New York Times*, February 19, 2010.

H

Hall, Gus (1910–2000)

Gus Hall, leader of the Communist Party USA (CPUSA) for 40 years, was a revolutionist who believed strongly that socialism would and should supplant capitalism. J. Edgar Hoover, director of the Federal Bureau of Investigation (FBI), called Hall "a powerful, deceitful, dangerous foe of Americanism" (Tanenhaus 2000). Hall's beliefs and actions landed him in prison, where he served an eight-year sentence. After his release, Hall continued his activism for the Communist Party and never relinquished his contention that a uniquely American socialist society would develop.

Born on October 8, 1910, Gus Hall was named Arvo Kusta Halberg by his parents Matt and Susannah Halberg, who were Finnish immigrants. Arvo Kusta (Gustav) Halberg, who used various assumed names while he was young, legally became Gus Hall in the 1930s.

The Halberg family lived in the Mesabi Iron Range, Minnesota, where Matt Halberg was a miner. He struggled to support his family that included 10 children. He and his wife were members of the Industrial Workers of the World (IWW), commonly known as the Wobblies. The IWW formed in Chicago in 1905 to create one big union of both skilled and unskilled workers. The preamble to its constitution begins with these words: "The working class and the employing class have nothing in common. There can be no peace so long as hunger and want are found among millions of the working people and the few, who make up the employing class, have all the good things of life."

Certainly, the Halbergs were among the millions who knew hunger. Matt Halberg was barred from the mines when he took part in an IWW strike, and the family nearly starved. As a young teenager, Gus went to work in a lumber camp where he endured long hours of hard labor, poor food, and little pay. His experiences were proof to him that workers needed the IWW and the strikes it sponsored. During the 1920s, IWW members struck in numerous industries—coal mining, construction, lumbering, railroads, and textile mills.

Gus Hall also became convinced that communism was the answer to many of the problems that working-class people faced. His parents joined the CPUSA when it was organized in 1919 and they encouraged their teenage son to become a member of the Young Communist League (YCL). The YCL sent Gus Hall to mining towns in Michigan, Wisconsin, and Minnesota to recruit members. As Fred Mazelis explained: "In the upper Midwest and throughout the United States, this was a period of bitter class struggles. The Wall Street boom of the 1920s did nothing to alleviate the hardships facing tens of millions of workers, and small but significant sections turned to the ideas of socialism" (Mazelis 2000).

In 1931, the CPUSA sent Hall to Moscow, Russia, to study for two years at the V. I. Lenin Institute, named for Vladimir Ilyich Lenin (1870–1924), who founded the

General Secretary of the Communist Party Gus Hall speaks at a press conference in New York City in the 1960s. The Communist Party, officially known as the Communist Party United States of America, was founded in 1919 in the aftermath of Russia's Bolshevik Revolution. (Hulton Archive/Getty Images)

communist movement in Russia. While at the communist training institute, Hall studied Marxism, the beliefs and political theories of German philosopher Karl Marx (1818–1883). Marx predicted that the proletariat would rise up against the ruling class in a revolution, which would bring about a classless society and an economic system now known as communism. Marx and his fellow philosopher Friedrich Engels presented many of their ideas in *The Communist Manifesto* (1848).

When Hall returned to the United States, he became an active union organizer and took part in the 1934 Minneapolis Teamsters strike, which according to the Minnesota Historical Society, "was one of the most violent in the state's history." In Minneapolis, business leaders had prevented unions from organizing, but by 1934, the Teamsters union had organized 3,000 truckers and called a strike, and "35,000 building trades workers went on strike" to support the truckers. Police and strikers battled for two days, and when the strike ended, truckers were granted better wages and the right to organize unions. "The strike marked a turning point in state and national labor history and legislation ... [And] opened the way for enactment of laws acknowledging and protecting workers' rights" (Minnesota Historical Society n.d.).

Hall's participation in the Minneapolis strike resulted in his arrest for inciting a riot. He was sentenced to six months in jail. Several years later, in 1937, he went to Youngstown, Ohio, to take a job in the steel industry and organize workers. He helped found the Steel Workers Organizing Committee (SWOC) and led steelworkers in a strike against several independent steel companies in Youngstown. These companies were known as "Little Steel," differentiating them from major steel corporations such as United States Steel. The Little Steel Strike of 1937 resulted in violence that caused two deaths and more than 40 injuries.

While working in Youngstown, Hall met Elizabeth Mary Turner, a CPUSA activist who helped sign up members for the SWOC and the Communist Party. She also worked as a tool-and-die maker for the steel industry. Gus and Elizabeth were married in 1935 and had two children—Barbara, born in 1938, and Arvo, born in 1947.

In 1941, when the United States entered World War II (1939–1945), Hall enlisted in the U.S. Navy as a machinist mate, serving in Guam. After his discharge, he continued his work with the Communist Party. At the time, the United States was engaged in a Red Scare—a fear that communists (called "Reds") were trying to take over the country. In 1948, Hall and other party organizers were indicted on charges that they violated the 1940 Alien Registration Act, or Smith Act, which made it illegal to advocate or support the overthrow of the U.S. government. With no evidence supporting the charges, Hall and 10 of his comrades were convicted and sentenced to five years in federal prison. While awaiting an appeal of their conviction, Hall and several others fled to Mexico, but they soon were apprehended, and three years were added to Hall's sentence. He was imprisoned for eight years at the federal penitentiary in Leavenworth, Kansas.

Prison did not change Hall's advocacy for communism. After his release in 1957, he traveled the United States to recruit CPUSA members. In 1959, he was elected general secretary of the CPUSA, which made him more likely to be target of anticommunists. During the 1950s, fear of communism by Americans had reached a fever pitch, bordering on paranoia. U.S. senator Joseph McCarthy began accusing U.S. State Department employees of being known communists or having affiliations with known communists. He claimed these persons as well as many others in government and the movie industry were a serious security risk for the United States. Most of McCarthy's claims were proven false, and the senator lost credibility.

While fear of communism began to wane, that did little to increase membership in the CPUSA. The party, however, did try to gain support through some of the anti–Vietnam War groups and civil rights organizations that were emerging in the 1960s. One prominent civil rights leader, W. E. B. Du Bois, applied for party membership in 1961. In a letter of application to Hall, Du Bois noted that he was a member of the Socialist Party for a while and had studied Karl Marx, traveled to communist countries, and eventually had become convinced that "Capitalism cannot reform itself; it is doomed to self-destruction. No universal selfishness can bring social good to all.... In the end communism will triumph. I want to help bring that day" (Du Bois 1961). Hall and the CPUSA enthusiastically welcomed Du Bois into the party.

Hall led the CPUSA for four decades from the 1960s until his death. He also ran as the party's candidate for U.S. president in 1972, 1976, 1980, and 1984. For the last two campaigns, Hall ran with California philosophy professor Angela Davis as the vice presidential candidate. Davis had been imprisoned in the 1970s on charges of kidnapping, murder and conspiracy in connection with her support of three African American inmates of California's Soledad Prison who had been convicted of killing a prison guard even though the three were unarmed. After a 13-week trial, a jury acquitted Angela Davis of all counts.

As head of the CPUSA, Hall strongly supported the Soviet Union and received millions of dollars in Soviet funds for the CPUSA. As *New York Times* reporter Sam Tanenhaus explained: "in the Communist world, Mr. Hall remained an important figure. He enjoyed the patronage of every Soviet head of state, from Nikita S. Khrushchev to Mikhail S. Gorbachev, and was received as a dignitary on his yearly pilgrimages to Moscow. A high point came in 1981 when he addressed the 26th Party Congress, at the invitation of Mr. Brezhnev, the Soviet leader Mr. Hall most esteemed. He was less admiring of Mr. Gorbachev, whose reforms a few years later, Mr. Hall said, 'literally destroyed the basis for socialism' " (Tanenhaus 2000).

Hall's views on socialism were published by the CPUSA in 1996. He wrote, "We Communists believe that socialism is the very best replacement for a capitalist system that has served its purpose, but no longer meets the needs and requirements of the great majority of our people. We believe that socialism USA will be built according to the traditions, history, culture and conditions of the United States. Thus, it will be different from any other socialist society in the world. It will be uniquely American." He outlined the goals of socialism:

1. A life free of exploitation, insecurity, poverty; an end to unemployment, hunger and homelessness.
2. An end to racism, national oppression, anti-Semitism, and all forms of discrimination, prejudice and bigotry. An end to the unequal status of women.
3. Renewal and extension of democracy; an end to the rule of corporate America and private ownership of the wealth of our nation. Creation of a truly humane and rationally planned society that will stimulate the fullest flowering of the human personality, creativity and talent.

Hall continued: "The advocates and ideologues of capitalism hold that such goals are utopian; that human beings are inherently selfish and evil. Others argue that these goals can be fully realized under capitalism. We are confident, however, that such goals can be realized, but only through a socialist society" (Hall 1996).

Along with his political activities, Hall was a prolific writer, producing articles, reports, and books. His books include *The Energy Rip-Off: Cause and Cure* (1974); *Basics for Peace, Democracy and Social Progress* (1980); *Karl Marx: Beacon of Our Times* (1983); *Fighting Racism* (1985); and *Working Class USA: The Power and the Movement* (1987). Hall was working on another book before he died of diabetes complications on October 13, 2000, in a Manhattan hospital. His remains were interred in the Forest Home Cemetery (previously called the Waldheim Cemetery) in Chicago, Illinois, where other revolutionaries are buried.

See also Davis, Angela; Du Bois, W. E. B.; McCarthy, Joseph

References

Du Bois, W. E. B. "Application for Membership in the Communist Party by W. E. B. Du Bois." Communist Party USA, October 1, 1961. http://www.cpusa.org/application-to-join-the-cpusa-by-w-e-b-du-bois-1961/ (accessed January 29, 2011).

Hall, Gus. *Fighting Racism: Selected Writings.* New York: International Publishers, 1985.

Hall, Gus. "Socialism USA." Communist Party USA, January 1, 1996. http://www.pointofresistance.com/?p=1093 (accessed January 30, 2011).

Mazelis, Fred. "Gus Hall (1910–2000): Stalinist Operative and Decades-Long Leader of Communist Party USA." World Socialist Web Site, November 6, 2000. http://www.wsws.org/articles/2000/nov2000/hall-n06.shtml (accessed January 27, 2011).

"1934 Truckers' Strike (Minneapolis)." Minnesota Historical Society, n.d. http://www.mnhs.org/library/tips/history_topics/81truckersstrike.html (accessed January 29, 2011).

Oliver, Myrna. "Gus Hall; Communist Party Leader in the U.S. for 40 Years." *Los Angeles Times*, October 17, 2000.

Shellock, Marie. "Defining Moment in Local Labor History Occurred 70 Years Ago."

Metro Monthly (Youngstown, OH), 2007. http://www.metromonthly.net/webarchive/feature0607.html (accessed January 29, 2011).

Tanenhaus, Sam. "Gus Hall, Unreconstructed American Communist of 7 Decades, Dies at 90." *New York Times*, October 17, 2000. http://www.nytimes.com/2000/10/17/us/gus-hall-unreconstructed-american-communist-of-7-decades-dies-at-90.html (accessed January 27, 2011).

Hamer, Fannie Lou (1917–1977)

Fannie Lou Hamer was known for her oft-repeated saying, "I'm sick and tired of being sick and tired." Her words are the epitaph etched on her gravestone (Barrett 2001). Being "sick and tired" referred to her long struggle for black civil rights and dissent against whites-only laws in Mississippi. Because of her actions, police arrested her in 1963 and ordered vicious beatings that left her barely recognizable and with permanent disabilities. Yet, when she was released from jail, she forgave her tormentors; she was deeply religious and lived by the biblical verse in Galatians 7, "whatever a man sows, this he will also reap." She believed that hate destroys a person.

Fannie Lou was the last of James Lee and Ella Townsend's 20 children—six girls and 14 boys. She was born on October 6, 1917, in Montgomery County, Mississippi. The family moved to Sunflower County in the Delta region when Fannie Lou was two years old. Fannie's parents, who were sharecroppers on a plantation, and her older siblings picked cotton and took various part-time jobs to eke out a living. Sharecroppers, or tenant farmers, used the plantation owner's land and paid rent with a percentage of the crops they grew. Farmers like James "Jim" Townsend had no say in determining the worth of their crops—the landlord controlled everything from production to marketing. Often landlords cheated farmers and forced them to borrow against their earnings to buy seed and supplies as well as food or clothing, leaving them in constant debt.

The impoverished family had a very difficult life. They seldom had enough food, living on gravy and greens. Clothing and shoes were sparse, and newspapers wrapped around their feet served as substitute footwear. The children went to school when they were not needed in the fields, usually only four months of the year, which was common for most black families in the South at the time. If there was work to do, parents kept their children out of school.

Fannie Lou's father was a preacher as well as a respected bootlegger. According to one biographer, Fannie never spoke about her father's bootlegging "in a critical way." Rather, it was "almost a source of pride. James Lee was simply doing what needed to be done to help the family to survive, and, after his death, Hamer took over the bootlegging operation for a brief time" (Lee 2000, 2).

Jim Townsend was able to save a little money from his bootlegging and preaching, enough to rent new land away from the plantation and to buy his own equipment. He hoped to escape the sharecropping system. But his dreams were dashed when a white neighbor, who resented ambitious blacks, poisoned the family's mules, which they needed to plow and plant the land. The family had to give up the farm and equipment and return to a plantation.

Because of the family's loss, Fannie had to quit school when she was in the sixth grade to work in the fields. But she was an avid reader and read whatever printed materials she could find. She also attended a

Fannie Lou Hamer, a Mississippi field hand for most of her life, became a prominent advocate of civil rights. As Mississippi's Democratic Party refused African American members, Hamer helped form the Mississippi Freedom Democratic Party (MFDP), whose members attempted to unseat the regular party delegation at the Democratic National Convention in 1964. (Library of Congress)

Baptist church and read the Bible regularly. A member of the choir, she frequently received requests to sing gospel songs, which she had been performing since she was a small child. One of her favorites was "This Little Light of Mine." Most of her time, though, was spent working from dawn to dark, picking cotton—between 200 and 300 pounds each day—and cutting dead cornstalks.

Jim Townsend died in 1939, and Fannie's mother had to carry on alone. She worked in the fields and at menial jobs such as washing and cleaning for white people along with caring and providing food for her children.

In the 1940s, Fannie Lou met Perry "Pap" Hamer, a sharecropper on the nearby W. D. Marlow plantation. The two married in 1944 and worked as sharecroppers on the Marlow land, which was near Ruleville, Mississippi. When Marlow learned that Fannie could read and write, he made her a timekeeper for the plantation workers. With that job, Hamer discovered how landlords manipulated the books to cheat sharecroppers.

Fannie and Pap wanted a large family, but Fannie's two pregnancies ended in stillbirths. The couple raised two girls, Dorothy and Vergie, whom they had taken in as their own. By 1953, they also were caring for Ella Townsend, who was ill and an invalid. Nevertheless, Fannie wanted to conceive. During the 1960s, she sought medical help to learn why she could not have children. She was told that when she had had a uterine tumor removed in 1961, the white doctor also had performed a hysterectomy without her knowledge. She discovered that she was among many black women who had been deceived in this way by whites who wanted to prevent an increase in the black population. Involuntary sterilization of black women was so common that "the procedure was called a 'Mississippi Appendectomy'" (Washington 2008, 204). Hamer was furious; to her, this was one more example of how she and other black people, especially those in Mississippi, had no control over their lives.

Mississippi in the 1960s, when the civil rights movement was gaining momentum, was one of the most racist states in the nation, with groups like the White Citizens Council, the Ku Klux Klan, the Christian White Knights, and segregationist government leaders adamantly opposed to equality for African Americans. People—white or black—who worked for the National Association for the Advancement of Colored People (NAACP), the Southern Christian Leadership Conference, and other civil rights groups were constantly at risk of violent attacks—beatings, lynchings, shootings, and bombings.

In 1962, Hamer attended a Student Nonviolent Coordinating Committee (SNCC) meeting in Ruleville. Founded in 1960, the SNCC was a group of students who practiced civil disobedience in their efforts to end segregation in the South. At the meeting, Hamer learned about a voter registration program that the SNCC was conducting. Not long after the Ruleville meeting, Hamer went with a group to Indianola to register at the county courthouse. There, clerks required blacks to take a literacy test, fill out a questionnaire, and explain the meaning of a section of the state constitution before they could become registered voters.

Fannie was not able to register, but after she returned to the Marlow plantation, the owner told her she would have to leave if she persisted in her effort to vote. She left that night, going to the home of her friends, the Robert Tuckers, for safety. She knew someone would try to kill her. Indeed, the Tucker home was riddled with bullets and Fannie fled the county with her two girls. They hid for several months and returned to Ruleville at harvest time. That was when Marlow fired Pap and took all the Hamers' belongings, including animals, crops, farm equipment, and furniture—Marlow claimed the Hamers owed him money, so their possessions were his. Friends, family, and the SNCC workers donated food and clothing and helped the family find a place to live.

Fannie tried once more to register, and in January 1963, she learned that she had succeeded. Through the first part of 1963, she attended voter registration workshops and took a citizenship training course. In June, on a trip home from a workshop, the bus that was transporting Fannie and others made a rest stop at Winona in Montgomery County. When several blacks got off to use the restroom and get lunch, state police officers chased them out and arrested them for violating segregation laws. Fannie, who got off the bus to see what was happening, also was arrested. She was taken to the county jail where police told her they would "make you wish you was dead." In a testimony the following year that was broadcast and also published in numerous books and articles, Fannie told of her savage treatment in a cell where the state highway patrolmen ordered two black prisoners to beat her with a blackjack while she was lying on a bunk.

> I was beat by the first Negro until he was exhausted. I was holding my hands behind me at that time on my left side, because I suffered from polio when I was six years old.
>
> After the first Negro had beat until he was exhausted, the State Highway Patrolman ordered the second Negro to take the blackjack.
>
> The second Negro began to beat and I began to work my feet, and the State Highway Patrolman ordered the first Negro who had beat me to sit on my feet—to keep me from working my feet. I began to scream and one white man got up and began to beat me in my head and tell me to hush. (Ellis and Smith n.d.)

Fannie was in jail for three days, so severely injured that her sister did not recognize her. The SNCC finally was able to bail her out and get her to a hospital. Even though the U.S. Justice Department brought criminal charges against all who took part in the beating, an all-white jury acquitted the police officers.

By 1964, Hamer was again involved in voter registration drives and making plans with SNCC to organize a Mississippi Freedom Democratic Party (MFDP). Hamer was cofounder of the MFDP, which was established in April 1964 because segregationists in Mississippi excluded black representation in the state's regular party. When the Democratic National Convention of 1964 convened, Hamer was there as a delegate to speak to the credentials committee, challenging them to seat members of the MFDP. As part of her speech, Hamer described her beating in the Winona jail and told of the intimidation and risks of death that blacks encountered when attempting to register to vote. MFDP members were not seated, but Hamer's speech was broadcast on national television and published in newspapers. Her testimony, some pundits say, played a role in passage of the Voting Rights Act of 1965.

Throughout 1964 and 1965, Hamer was involved in numerous political arenas and with civil rights groups. With the SNCC, she traveled to Senegal and Guinea, where she saw that African blacks held powerful positions in government and business. That experience encouraged her to keep fighting for black empowerment in the United States. She went to Harlem to appear with Malcolm X at civil rights rallies. She helped bring white northerners into Mississippi to take part in voter registration. She ran for Congress, although she did not win election. She joined the now-famous march led by Martin Luther King Jr. from Selma, Alabama, to Montgomery, Alabama, in 1965.

In 1967, the Hamer family experienced a terrible loss when their daughter Dorothy died from a hemorrhage while on the way to a distant hospital—the nearby hospital would not accept her. The Hamers adopted their daughter's two children, Jacqueline and Lenora.

Still, the fight on behalf of African Americans went on, and Hamer was a part of it, attending rallies, speaking to student groups, organizing antipoverty programs, and working on education issues. Her grueling activities led to nervous exhaustion and hospitalization in 1972. She also was hospitalized in 1974 because of a nervous breakdown, a popular term for depression. Breast cancer and diabetes led to heart failure; she died on March 14, 1977, in a Mound Bayou, Mississippi, hospital. Hundreds of people mourned her passing and dozens of public figures attended her funeral, many extolling her virtues and everyone singing "This Little Light of Mine."

See also King, Martin Luther, Jr.; Malcolm X

References

Barrett, Warick L. "Fannie Lou Hamer." Find a Grave web site, January 28, 2001. http://www.findagrave.com/cgi-bin/fg.cgi?page=gr&GRid=19859 (accessed September 7, 2011).

Ellis, Kate, and Stephen Smith, eds. "Fannie Lou Hamer Testimony before the Credentials Committee, Democratic National Convention Atlantic City, New Jersey—August 22, 1964." *Say It Plain*: *A Century of Great American Speeches*. American Public Media, n.d. http://americanradioworks.publicradio.org/features/sayitplain/flhamer.html (accessed May 9, 2010)

Kinnon, Joy Bennett. "Shine Your Light (Sister Speak)." *Ebony*, July 2004.

Lee, Chana Kai. *For Freedom's Sake: The Life of Fannie Lou Hamer*. Urbana: University of Illinois Press, 2000.

Mills, Kay. "Fannie Lou Hammer: Civil Rights Activist." *Mississippi History Now*, n.d. http://mshistory.k12.ms.us/articles/51/fannie-lou-hamer-civil-rights-activist (accessed September 7, 2011).

Washington, Harriet A. *Medical Apartheid: The Dark History of Medical Experimentation on Black Americans from Colonial Times to the Present.* New York: Anchor, 2008.

Hampton, Fred (1948–1969)

To members of Chicago's African American community in the late 1960s, no leader was more inspiring, more articulate, or more effective than Fred Hampton.... To civic leaders in Chicago, the FBI, and many others, however, he was a dangerous revolutionary leader, committed to the violent overthrow of the white-dominated system. (*Black Commentator* 2003)

Born in Chicago on August 30, 1948, Fred Hampton was the son of Francis and Iberia Hampton, who had two other children, William and Deloris. Hampton's parents had lived originally in Louisiana but left the South, as many African Americans did during the 1930s, to escape racist terror and to find a better life. The middle-class family settled in Maywood, a Chicago suburb. Their home was in an integrated half-black, half-white neighborhood. Both parents worked for a starch manufacturing company.

Hampton was influenced early in his life by the brutal murder of Emmett Till in 1955. Till was a young teenager who had gone to Mississippi to visit relatives, and because he allegedly whistled at a white woman, he was kidnapped, beaten, and killed by two white men. The Tills were friends and neighbors of the Hamptons, and like many Chicago-area blacks, the Hamptons were horrified that a 14-year-old could come to such a vicious and savage end.

Books were another major influence on Hampton. He read a lot about black history and the writings of Marcus Garvey, W. E. B. Du Bois, Malcolm X, Mao, and Martin Luther King Jr. Hampton attended Maywood's Proviso East High School, where he earned three varsity letters and a junior achievement award. He also organized a protest against the school's practice of nominating only white girls for the homecoming queen contest. As a result, black girls were included in the contest the next year.

After graduating from Proviso with academic honors, Hampton attended Triton Junior College, a two-year community college in nearby River Grove, Illinois. He took pre-law courses, hoping someday to be a lawyer. In 1966, he became president of the youth council of the National Association for the Advancement of Colored People. He was an excellent organizer and speaker, and because of his leadership, the NAACP youth council increased its membership from 40 to more than 500. One of his projects was to get more and better recreational facilities established in the black neighborhood. William Hampton, Fred's older brother, gave this account of his sibling: "Fred always wanted to help people out, but he had no real political ideas back in early high school.... I'd say it was in 1966 when he was seventeen years old that Fred developed a true black identity. That was when he began to notice all the oppression and bigotry around him. Fred with his natural outspokenness began to get involved. He began to rankle his teachers and school administrators. They said he was inciting things. Their idea of a good black student was the guy who plays football and keeps his mouth shut" (Travis 1987, 419).

In 1967, Fred Hampton began his attempt to fight against oppression. He led a peaceful march on Maywood's village hall to attend a village board meeting with demands that a swimming pool and recreation center be built in the black community. Blacks were not allowed to use Maywood's pool, which was reserved for whites only. Police officials saw the demonstration as a threat and used tear gas to disperse the crowd that gathered outside. While Hampton and several other leaders were inside the building before the board, angry protesters raced down the main street, damaging stores. Police arrested the leaders, charging mob action. Hampton served three days in jail and was released after raising $500 bail.

The injustice of the police repression was just one factor in Hampton's evolution as a radical dissident. Local police constantly harassed him, stopping and arresting him for traffic violations; he finally quit driving. The FBI also went after him, categorizing him as a "key agitator" and monitoring his actions.

A year after the "mob action" charges, Hampton was arrested and accused of beating and robbing a Good Humor Ice Cream man of ice cream bars worth $71, a crime perpetrated by a black gang. The gang leader identified Hampton as the culprit, but Hampton testified that he was not in the area where the robbery took place. Nevertheless, he was sentenced to two to five years in jail. Many believed he was framed, and his lawyer was able to appeal and get him freed on bond. The charges were eventually dropped, but the experience increased Hampton's radicalization.

In 1968, the Black Panther Party, whose national office was in Oakland, California, was opening chapters in various parts of the nation. Hampton was attracted to the party and its 10-point program for black liberation. He joined the Black Panther Party and, with Bobby Rush (now a U.S. congressman), Jewell Cook, and Billy Brook, cofounded the Illinois branch of the party, which was located in downtown Chicago. The Illinois chapter adopted the national Black Panther's 1966 10-point platform, which among other issues called for freedom, full employment, decent housing, health care, and justice for black people.

Hampton was chairman of the Illinois group and increased its membership from 33 in 1968 to over 1,000 by 1969. Under Hampton's leadership, the Panthers set up a free breakfast program that served children in depressed areas across Chicago. Although some clergy praised the program, Chicago's political leaders were displeased because serving free breakfasts clearly illustrated that elected officials were doing nothing to fulfill obvious needs. Urged on by politicians, the Chicago police began intimidating children and volunteers taking part in the program. The police photographed children and questioned volunteers as if they were criminal suspects. Even the FBI got involved by trying to persuade a prominent black leader, Robert Lucas, to criticize the program. Lucas refused and held a press conference to praise the efforts to feed impoverished children with no government funds involved.

The FBI and other law enforcement officers used more insidious tactics in attempts to break up the Black Panthers. J. Edgar Hoover, FBI chief, believed the Panthers were a black gang like others in the city and were a revolutionary force ready to overthrow the government. One ongoing FBI effort was to pit street gangs against the Panthers, hoping to provoke violence and a reason to destroy the Panthers. But Hampton persuaded street gangs to quit fighting each other, and he negotiated an alliance of black, Puerto Rican, and white gangs that he and Bobby Lee, another Black Panther, called a "rainbow coalition." (The term was later used by Rev. Jesse Jackson after he formed Operation P.U.S.H. in 1971 and launched the National Rainbow Coalition in 1984.) In addition, the FBI sent "forged notes and documents" to

Jewish supporters, claiming that the Panthers were "anti-Semitic and pro-Nazi" (Katz 1995, 523).

Throughout 1969, the FBI continued its surveillance through COINTELPRO, an acronym for a domestic counterintelligence program. They raided the Panther headquarters on West Monroe Street in downtown Chicago several times. Once, the entire office was destroyed along with free breakfasts that were trampled on the floor.

The FBI planted an informant named William O'Neal within the Black Panther Party. A convicted felon released from jail, O'Neal supplied authorities with a detailed map of Hampton's apartment, complete with locations of furniture, including Hampton's bed. O'Neal also gave police a list of legally owned guns in the apartment. Later, the FBI awarded him $300 for the information.

Early on December 4, 1969, before 5:00 a.m., the Chicago police, under the direction of the Cook County state's attorney and the FBI, arrived at the building on West Monroe Street where Hampton's apartment (and Panther headquarters) was located. Ostensibly, the police were there to issue a search warrant, but 14 officers "besieged the apartment and fired about a hundred rounds." Fred Hampton, who was asleep or had been drugged, "died with two bullets in his head fired at close range" (Katz 1995, 523). Another Panther member, Mark Clark, also was killed. Four others in the apartment were wounded.

After this deadly siege, the police issued reports exonerating themselves, but family members and survivors of the raid began to publicize their versions of what happened and demanded to know the truth. Because the apartment was not sealed immediately, Black Panther members conducted tours of the rooms where the killings had taken place. Over a period of 13 days, thousands viewed the damaged doors, walls, and windows, the many bullet holes and blood stains. Prominent black leaders in the city and in the U.S. Congress called for investigations.

A state grand jury and a federal grand jury issued reports, but neither indicted any of the police officers. Roy Wilkins and Ramsey Clark, who had been U.S. attorney general (1967–1969), led one privately sponsored investigation conducted over three years that resulted in *Search and Destroy: A Report by the Commission of Inquiry into the Black Panthers and the Police* (1973). That report generally concluded that law enforcement officials endorsed lawlessness, racism, and violence.

Three years later, in 1976, the FBI's sinister role regarding the Black Panthers was spelled out in a report by the U.S. Senate Select Committee to Study Governmental Operations with Respect to Intelligence Activities. Their findings were included in a publication, which in part notes:

> [T]he chief investigative branch of the Federal Government, which was charged by law with investigating crimes and preventing criminal conduct, itself engaged in lawless tactics and responded to deep-seated social problems by fomenting violence and unrest. . . .
>
> The Select Committee's staff investigation has disclosed a number of instances in which the FBI sought to turn violence-prone organizations against the Panthers in an effort to aggravate "gang warfare." Because of the milieu of violence in which members of the Panthers often moved we have been unable to establish a direct link between any of the FBI's specific efforts to promote violence, and particular acts of violence that occurred. We have been able to establish beyond doubt, however, that high officials of the FBI desired to

promote violent confrontations between BPP members and members of other groups, and that those officials condoned tactics calculated to achieve that end. (U.S. Congress 1976)

Meantime, the Hampton and Clark families sued the city, state, and federal governments. After more than a decade, the court awarded $1.85 million to the nine plaintiffs.

Those who memorialize Hampton frequently repeat his mantra "You can kill the revolutionary, but you can't kill the revolution" (Millies 2008). Part of his legacy is the Fred Hampton Memorial Pool, a swimming pool that Hampton was instrumental in getting the Maywood, Illinois, village council to build as an alternative to the segregated whites-only pool. A scholarship fund also has been established in his name.

See also Clark, Ramsey; Du Bois, W. E. B.; King, Martin Luther, Jr.; Malcolm X

References

Azikiwe, Abayomi. "Remembering Fred Hampton and Mark Clark." *Workers World*, December 11, 2009.

Cockburn, Alexander. "The Fate of the Panthers." *Nation*, July 2, 1990.

"Fred Hampton." *Black Commentator*, December 4, 2003. http://www.blackcommentator.com/67/67_hampton.html (accessed April 28, 2010).

Haas, Jeffrey. *The Assassination of Fred Hampton: How the FBI and the Chicago Police Murdered a Black Panther*. Chicago: Lawrence Hill Books, 2009.

Haas, Jeffrey. "Fred Hampton's Legacy." *Nation*, December 14, 2009.

Katz, William Loren. *Eyewitness: A Living Documentary of the African American Contribution to American History*. Rev. and updated ed. New York: Touchstone/Simon & Schuster, 1995.

Millies, Stephen. "Never Forget Fred Hampton and Mark Clark." *Workers World*, December 11, 2008, http://www.workers.org/2008/us/fred_hampton_1218/ (accessed September 7, 2011).

Travis, Dempsey J. *An Autobiography of Black Politics*. Chicago: Urban Research Press, 1987.

U.S. Congress. Senate. Select Committee to Study Governmental Operations with Respect to Intelligence Activities. *Final Report of the Select Committee to Study Governmental Operations with Respect to Intelligence Activities. The FBI's Covert Action Program to Destroy the Black Panther Party*. April 23, 1976. http://www.archive.org/details/finalreportofse-l06unit (accessed April 26, 2010)

Wilkins, Roy, and Ramsey Clark, chairmen. *Search and Destroy: A Report by the Commission of Inquiry into the Black Panthers and the Police*. New York: Metropolitan Applied Research Center, Inc., 1973.

Hayden, Tom (1939–)

From the 1960s to the present, Tom Hayden has been an outspoken dissident—in speeches, books, articles, and actions that target the U.S. political elite and government oppression; U.S. wars in Vietnam, Iraq, and Afghanistan; economic inequality; environmental pollution; and animal cruelty. In short, Hayden has been a rebel, sometimes taking part in radical protests and other times working through the judicial and political systems.

He was named Thomas Emmett Hayden when he was born on December 11, 1939, in Royal Oak, Michigan, a Detroit suburb. His parents, John Hayden and Genevieve Garity Hayden, were of Irish descent and "lived in a world of big families, small communities, and permanent circles of friends," Hayden wrote in his memoir. "They took the American dream as their goal and their working lifetimes as the means to achieve it. Their ambition centered not on themselves or on public service, but mainly on their children." His father worked for Chrysler Corporation and was a Republican. His mother was a Democrat and supported Adlai Stevenson when he ran for U.S. president in the 1950s (Hayden 1988, 6).

When Tom was four years old, his father was drafted into the U.S. Marines and was stationed in San Diego, California. Tom and his mother went to San Diego to live until the end of World War II in 1945. After returning to Royal Oak, Tom's father was a changed man and often spent time drinking at the American Legion post, which created problems at home. Tom's mother and father divorced, and Tom's mother cared for him, supporting the two of them by working for the local school as a film librarian. "Despite their divorce, my parents cooperated in raising me," Tom wrote. "implicitly teaching me that deep personal divisions could be submerged for a larger purpose" (Hayden 1988, 8).

Tom was educated at a parochial school and attended the Catholic Church whose pastor was Charles Coughlin (1891–1979), known as the "Radio Priest" with a deep baritone voice. Coughlin's radio broadcasts on social issues were popular nationwide, but when he began accusing Jews of controlling banking and finance industries, his anti-Semitic diatribes prompted reprisals. The National Association of Broadcasters refused to carry Coughlin's broadcasts, and his superior, Archbishop Mooney, issued an ultimatum: Coughlin must refrain from all political activity, or be removed from the priesthood. While Tom was growing up, he knew little about the priest's behavior—his attention

Tom Hayden, antiwar radical and founder of the Students for a Democratic Society, talks to reporters about President Nixon's Vietnamization program at a news conference in Berkeley, California, June 14, 1972. (AP Photo)

was more focused on sports, especially baseball. He also was an avid reader and known as "brainy."

After graduating from high school in 1957, Hayden enrolled at the University of Michigan in Ann Arbor. Before long, he was writing for and editing the Michigan *Daily*, one of the most respected college newspapers in the United States. He hoped to be a professional journalist, but in 1960, he attended a Texas meeting of the Student Nonviolent Coordinating Committee (SNCC), which included members who had taken part in sit-ins to integrate lunch counters in the segregated South. Listening to speakers at the conference, Hayden became convinced that he should be more politically active, and he spent his last year at the university studying political science and philosophy. He also corresponded and met with one SNCC member from Texas, Sandra Cason, called Casey. The two became romantically involved, and by 1961, they were married, although they separated after a few years.

Tom and Casey Hayden went to the South in 1961 to work with SNCC in its efforts to test a new order from the Interstate Commerce Commission to integrate segregated interstate buses and trains. The Haydens joined other white and black Freedom Riders, as they were called, on a train trip from Atlanta to Albany, Georgia. Tom Hayden was beaten and jailed for his efforts.

The Haydens also were in an Albany, Georgia, court in 1962 when black and white Freedom Riders attempted to integrate segregated bus stations. Charles Sherrod, a black SNCC member who was attending the trial, "tried to take a seat in the front of the courtroom. Before he could do so, a court judge knocked him down and dragged him to the back of the room—where blacks were supposed to sit," according to Juan Williams, author of a companion volume for the Public Broadcasting System's television series *Eyes on the Prize*. White SNCC members, including Tom and Casey Hayden, tried to sit with Sherrod, but "guards dragged them all out of the courtroom. The judge, looking on, simply commented, 'The officers are enforcing the rules of the court'" (Williams 1987, 171).

In 1962, Hayden began to realize that he should go beyond the SNCC and help Students for a Democratic Society (SDS) become more than a small group of activists at the University of Michigan and create a national organization. Hayden began writing a manifesto for SDS that became the Port Huron Statement. It was named for Port Huron on the shores of Lake Huron, north of Detroit, where Hayden presented the draft for the document at a conference of activists in June 1962. The manifesto was adopted and became the founding document for the national SDS. It spelled out an agenda for the young generation to encourage the United States to live up to its ideals, including social justice for people of color, ending nuclear arms proliferation, making universities the "seat of social influence," supporting labor, and slowing the growth of the military-industrial complex.

By 1964, the Haydens had divorced—Casey went to Atlanta to work with the SNCC, and Tom headed for Newark, New Jersey, where he worked in impoverished black neighborhoods, organizing campaigns for jobs and improvements in city services such as garbage collection and street lights. In the summer of 1967, a riot occurred when a black cab driver was stopped by police, arrested for a traffic violation, and beaten. The riot, which lasted five days, left 26 people dead, "a thousand injured, fourteen hundred arrested and sixteen million dollars' worth of damage done to property, as nearly six thousand police, state troopers, and national guardsmen tried to restore order," Hayden wrote. Police tried to blame Hayden for inciting the riot, but he was playing football at the time, which a policeman's wife confirmed (Hayden 1988, 151–53).

While Hayden was in Newark, the Vietnam War was accelerating. Americans were fighting on the side of the South Vietnamese who were battling communist North Vietnamese. An American antiwar movement had begun, and some young men who were protesting the war burned their draft cards. Hayden supported the antiwar protests with published articles, demonstrations, and teach-ins, seminars that educated large segments of college students about both the moral and political foundations of U.S. involvement in Vietnam. Hayden's activities created a breach with his parents, who believed the government statements that communism had to be contained in Vietnam or all of Southeast Asia would be taken over by communists. John Hayden, always a Marine, eventually cut off any contact with his son.

In 1965, Hayden was invited to accompany pacifist Quaker Staughton Lynd and American communist Herbert Aptheker to attend a meeting of a peace committee in Hanoi. The purpose was to create a "negotiating bridge between [the U.S.] government and Hanoi" (Hayden 1988, 176). The three Americans met with one top North Vietnamese government official, but nothing new developed, except that Hanoi for the first time allowed an American correspondent to report on the war. The Hanoi visit is chronicled in a book *The Other Side* (1966), coauthored by Hayden and Lynd.

After his Hanoi trip and observations of the North Vietnamese, Hayden was convinced that he should continue his antiwar activities, which included attending antiwar protests outside the 1968 Democratic National Convention in Chicago, Illinois. During that protest, thousands demonstrated and the Chicago police attacked with batons, tear gas, and physical assaults. Eight activists, Hayden among them, were arrested and charged with conspiracy to foment a riot. The 1969 trial of the "Chicago Eight," as they were dubbed, was publicized widely, and the defendants became well known. Along with Hayden, the Chicago Eight included Black Panther cofounder Bobby Seale, long-time antiwar activist David Dellinger, and leader of the Youth International Party (known as the Yippies) Abbie Hoffman. Seale became so disruptive at the trial that the judge ordered him bound and gagged, which prompted a seething protest from the defense lawyer William Kunstler.

The judge declared a mistrial and severed Seale's case from that of the other defendants. Seale spent four years in jail. All the other defendants, now called the "Chicago Seven," and Kunstler were charged with contempt of court, but an appeals court later reversed all contempt convictions.

The latter years of the 1960s were times of intense turmoil in the United States. In 1968, Robert Kennedy, brother of assassinated president John F. Kennedy, was shot and killed. Civil rights leader Martin Luther King Jr. was assassinated. Increasingly, in 1969, students on college campuses were rising up against the Vietnam War. The violence continued in 1970 when Kent State (Ohio) students were protesting the U.S. invasion of Cambodia bordering on Vietnam, even though President Richard Nixon had promised to bring the Vietnam War to a close. The Ohio National Guard met the Kent State students with gunfire, killing four and wounding nine.

In 1971, Hayden met actress Jane Fonda when they were at the University of Michigan and spoke against the Vietnam War. They met again a year later, and found that they shared not only antiwar sentiments but also other interests. They fell in love, married, and produced a son, Troy, in 1973. During the latter part of 1973 and early 1974, Tom and Jane traveled with their son from their home in Santa Monica, California, to cities across the United States for antiwar-speaking engagements.

When the war finally ended in 1974, Tom Hayden was ready to take on other challenges: running for political office. He felt he had some background in how government worked—he had been a frequent lobbyist, and he had worked on George McGovern's unsuccessful presidential campaign and also for Jerry Brown's campaign for governor of

California, which Brown won. Hayden organized a grassroots campaign and ran as a Democratic candidate for the U.S. Senate, but lost. However, he was not discouraged.

During the next decade, Hayden ran and won a seat in the California State Assembly in 1982, serving for 10 years. While he was in office, he and Jane Fonda divorced in 1990 and pursued their separate interests—she in film, and he in politics. In 1992, Hayden was elected to the state senate, serving for eight more years in the state legislature.

Throughout his years of activism and dissent, Hayden has written numerous books, including *Rebellion in Newark* (1967); *Trial* (1970); *The Love of Possession Is a Disease with Them* (1972); *The American Future* (1980); *Reunion: A Memoir* (1988), reissued as *Rebel* (2002); *The Lost Gospel of the Earth* (1996, reissued 2006); *Writings for a Democratic Society: The Tom Hayden Reader* (2008); and *The Long Sixties: From 1960 to Barack Obama* (2009).

Hayden also has written extensively for the *Nation* magazine with some of his articles posted on the Peace Exchange Bulletin of the Peace and Justice Resource Center, which Hayden founded and directs. The nonprofit center analyzes the wars in Afghanistan, Pakistan, and Iraq, as well as the failed U.S. wars on drugs and gangs. In addition, he has been speaking and holding seminars on college campuses and other venues regarding the long wars and their effects on U.S. domestic programs and civil liberties. He worked to ensure that the wars would be part of presidential debates in 2011–2012.

See also Coughlin, Charles; Dellinger, David; Kunstler, William; Seale, Bobby

References

Hayden, Tom. *Ending the War in Iraq.* New York: Akashik Books, 2007.

Hayden, Tom. *Peace Exchange Bulletin*, various dates. http://tomhayden.com/ (accessed February 28, 2011).

Hayden, Tom. "Port Huron Statement of the Students for a Democratic Society, 1962." Document courtesy of the office of Sen. Tom Hayden. http://coursesa.matrix.msu.edu/~hst306/documents/huron.html (accessed February 26, 2011).

Hayden, Tom. *Reunion: A Memoir.* New York: Collier Books/Macmillan, 1988.

Williams, Juan, with the Eyes on the Prize Production Team. *Eyes on the Prize: A Companion Volume to the PBS Television Series.* New York: Viking Penguin, 1987.

Height, Dorothy (1912–2010)

I was only twelve years old and had never heard of 'social activism,' nor seen anyone engaged in it, but I barely took a breath before saying I would like to see the executive director . . . I let her know that we were Girl Reserves, that women from this YWCA had come out to Rankin [Pennsylvania] to organize us, and that I was even going to be on the Girl Reserves poster . . . nothing I said made any difference. Young women of color were not welcome in the Chatham Street YWCA pool. We were crushed—and bewildered. In Rankin we were used to playing and working together interracially, and it was inconceivable to us that the YWCA could be so backward. . . . it struck a painful chord that reverberated in each of us long afterwards. (Height 2003, 18–19)

Although Dorothy never learned to swim, she went on to found the Center for Racial Justice of the Young Women's Christian Association (YWCA), "charged with leading a massive campaign to eradicate discrimination in the YWCA and society" (Height 2003, 126).

Dorothy Irene Height was born into a blended family on March 24, 1912. Her parents were widowed when they met; each had children from their prior unions, in addition to the two children they had together. When she was four, the family moved from the South to Rankin, Pennsylvania. The move was hard on her mother, a nurse; many northern hospitals would admit black patients but would not hire black nurses. She eventually was hired as a private duty nurse after establishing credentials as a domestic servant. Height's father did well as a contractor (Height 2003, 2–3). He was self-employed and also provided work for many others during the Great Depression.

In spite of the YWCA pool incident, Dorothy's childhood was largely free from discrimination and racism. "I have many happy memories of being together with people who were so different from one another. My date from the high school junior prom, for instance, was a Croatian boy who was the president of our class when I was class secretary." She did sense the tensions between groups "searching for a better standard of living" and recounted an unequivocal pecking order: "First in line and always on top economically were American-born whites, though they were a minority. Then came the foreign-born ... Negroes from South were the last in line" (Height 2003, 3–4). However, her race did not have a major negative impact in her grade and high school years. She became involved with the American Baptist Home Mission Society in Rankin. It sponsored a kindergarten, which Height passed by daily. Hearing unruly children inside, she offered to teach Bible classes. The director accepted and later admitted that, caught off guard, she did not know how to refuse. Height wrote, "at that moment—the last time I ever had to formally apply for a job—my life's work began" (Height 2003, 16–17).

Height excelled academically in high school and also played on the basketball team. An accomplished speaker, she advanced to the national finals in a contest sponsored by the Elks, where she was the sole black competitor. Her topic was the Thirteenth, Fourteenth, and Fifteenth Amendments—those extending constitutional protection to former slaves and their descendants. An all-white panel awarded her first prize of a four-year college scholarship. Height applied and was accepted to Barnard College. Just prior to starting, the dean advised her that the school had reached its quota of black students. Undeterred, Height applied and was admitted to New York University. In 1933, she earned a bachelor's degree in education and a master's in psychology in 1935 (Fox 2010).

In 1933, Height's civil rights work began in earnest; her causes included antilynching campaigns, military desegregation, and minority access to public accommodations. She was a New York Welfare caseworker for two years, while taking postgraduate courses at the New York School of Social Work. That same year, she helped organize and served as vice president of the United Christian Youth Movement of North America. As a result, she was chosen as one of 10 American youth delegates to the World Conference on Life and Work of the Churches in Oxford, England, in 1937. Two years later, she was a YWCA representative to the World Conference of Christian Youth in Amsterdam, Holland. For Height, the conference, "confirmed that people are born equal, but that society shapes opportunity and determines whether and how equality is realized for each of us" (Height 2003, 73–74).

Dorothy Height, who died in 2010, devoted her life to the cause of civil rights for African Americans. She served as the chair of the Executive Committee of the Leadership Conference on Civil Rights. (Library of Congress)

In 1937, she became assistant director of the Harlem YWCA. On November 7 of that year, First Lady Eleanor Roosevelt was guest speaker at a National Council of Negro Women (NCNW) meeting hosted by Mary McLeod Bethune, the organization's founder. Height, assigned to escort Mrs. Roosevelt, recalled, "As Mrs. Roosevelt gathered her things, Mrs. Bethune turned to me. 'We need you' ... By the time I returned, Mrs. Bethune had already appointed me to the resolutions committee ... She drew me into her dazzling orbit of people in power and people in poverty. I remember how she made her fingers into a fist to illustrate for the women the significance of working together to eliminate injustice. 'The freedom gates are half ajar,' she said. 'We must pry them fully open.' I have committed to the calling ever since" (Height 2003, 82, 84–85). So significant did Height credit the impact Bethune made on her life, she would entitle her memoir *Open Wide the Freedom Gates* (2003).

Height was involved in coordinating the YWCA's 1946 convention, which chartered a policy of integrating YWCA facilities nationwide. There she was elected national interracial education secretary. She was front and center in the civil rights movement, starting in the 1950s and continuing for decades. All the while, Height still managed to conduct her "paid-job" duties with NCNW, proactively assisting black women and families in numerous tangible ways. Height was neither "radical" nor "militant," so that partially explains why she did not receive much attention in the civil rights movement over the years. Mostly, she has been lost in the shadows of the men with whom she worked side by side. In 1960, Height was the lone female leader in the United Civil Rights leadership, consisting of Martin Luther King Jr., Whitney H. Young, A. Philip Randolph, James Farmer, Roy Wilkins, and John Lewis. An article written at the time of her death noted, "Over the years, historians have made much of the so-called 'Big Six' who led the civil rights movement ... Ms. Height, the only woman to work regularly alongside them on projects of national significance, was very much the unheralded seventh, the leader who was cropped out, figuratively and often literally, of images of the era." The article quoted Height in an earlier feature: "I didn't feel I should elbow myself to the front when the press focused on the male leaders." To her, the thing to focus on was not personal recognition, but on the "collective struggle." Of note, she was not only next to Dr. King when he delivered his 1963 "I Have a Dream" speech, but Height—a prize-winning orator herself, and chief organizer of the march at which King's speech was given—was not even asked to say a single word (Fox 2010).

In December 1961, Height was appointed to serve alongside Eleanor Roosevelt on President John F. Kennedy's Commission on the Status of Women. "The commission's brief was to assess the position of women in the home, in the economy, and in society . . . It explored the portrayal of women by the mass media and considered the special problems of Negro women . . . *American Women*, the report of the commission, was presented to President Kennedy on October 11, 1963, the first anniversary of Mrs. Roosevelt's death." Height was chosen to represent the commission that day at the family's graveside commemoration (Height 2003, 92).

Height began an innovative NCNW program in 1964, Wednesdays in Mississippi, flying northern women to small towns to create dialogues of understanding. She also served on the American Red Cross Board of Governors from 1964 to 1970 and on the Board of Directors of CARE, a group fighting poverty and social injustice with specific emphasis on empowering women and girls. It was during this time period, 1965, that she founded the YWCA's Office for Racial Justice. "I decided to encourage a new direction—to move from solving problems to changing systems, from liberalism to liberation, from simply 'giving equal opportunity' to creating an equitable society. We wanted women from different racial groups to talk and listen to each other—to hear how people felt, what and whom they feared, and what obstacles were in the way of their acting together to resolve issues that were tearing their communities apart" (Height 2003, 126).

In 1966, President Lyndon B. Johnson named Height to the advisory committee for his "To Fulfill These Rights" conference on the status of minorities in education, employment, housing, and the justice system. Height took pride in the election of YWCA's first black president in 1967 and its subsequent "constitutional amendment that any association not fully integrated in policy and practice and thereby living up to the Statement of Purpose would be disaffiliated." Under Height, the next year, YWCAs examined the subtleties of racism in the United States; the board adopted Project Equality, pledging to purchase goods and services from equal opportunity employers, to review its own employment practices, and to recruit women leaders from minority groups; groups across the country worked on Operation Breadbasket, supported the Farmworkers' Union grape boycott and supported black businesses and universities from South Africa; racial justice institutes and black economic development seminars were held. "It was gratifying to see women grappling with real issues" (Height 2003, 127).

Along with Gloria Steinem, Shirley Chisholm, Betty Friedan and others, Height helped found the National Women's Political Caucus in the early 1970s. In 1974, Height was a United Nations Educational, Scientific, and Cultural Organization Conference on Woman and Her Rights delegate. She also received a U.S. Agency for International Development grant for an international women's conference. In 1975, Height started the only African American private voluntary organization working in Africa, building on NCNW's programs in other parts of the world. In the 1980s and 1990s, NCNW was in the forefront taking on AIDS education. It also created a program celebrating traditional African American values, promoting the idea of "self-help" and extended family as a means of in combating issues likes drugs, family disintegration, poverty and economic disparity. In 1986, the first of an ongoing series of "Black Family Reunions" was scheduled. These NCNW sponsored gatherings are devoted to the history, culture and traditions of African Americans and reinforce the strengths and values of the Black family. Hundreds of thousands of people attended the first, in Washington, D.C. A quarter million attended the last, held in 2011 at the same local (Fox 2010).

In 1993, Height was inducted into the National Women's Hall of Fame and received the National Association for the Advanced of Colored People Springarm Medal and the Franklin Delano Roosevelt Freedom From Want Award. The nation's highest civilian honor was given to her in 1994, the Presidential Medal of Freedom. She became NCNW president emerita 1998. In April 2000, the YWCA established a Dorothy L. Height Racial Justice Award, the first presented to President William Jefferson Clinton. In 2002, a Who's Who of black celebrities anted up five million dollars to pay off NCNW's mortgage in honor of Height's 90th birthday. During her lifetime, she received approximately three dozen honorary degrees, including ones from Harvard, Princeton, and Tuskegee. Of special significance, in 2004, Barnard College, 75 years after wait-listing her because its quota of blacks had been filled and on the 50th anniversary of *Brown v. Board of Education* (the landmark U.S. Supreme Court case declaring the unconstitutionality of "separate but equal" education), designated Height an honorary alumna (Fox 2010). That year, she also received the Congressional Gold Medal.

Height was an honored guest when President Barack Obama took the oath of office in 2009, with whom she would interact and advise. On the occasion of her passing on April 20, 2010, he called her, "the godmother of the civil rights movement and a hero to so many Americans" and ordered flags flown at half-mast on the date of her funeral (Fox 2010).

Margaret Gay

See also Bethune, Mary McLeod; Chávez, César; Friedan, Betty; King, Martin Luther, Jr.; Randolph, A. Philip; Roosevelt, Eleanor

References

Fox, Margalit. "Dorothy Height, Largely Unsung Giant of the Civil Rights Era, Dies at 98." *New York Times*, April 20, 2010. http://www.nytimes.com/2010/04/21/us/21height.html (accessed April 23, 2011).

Height, Dorothy. *Open Wide the Freedom Gates: A Memoir*. New York: Public Affairs, Perseus Book Group, 2003.

National Council of Negro Women web site. http://www.ncnw.org/about/height.htm (accessed April 23, 2011).

"University of Maryland Honors Civil Rights Activist for Seven-Decade Struggle—Dorothy Height—Brief Article." *Black Issues in Higher Education*, August 16, 2001. http://findarticles.com/p/articles/mi_m0DXK/is_13_18/ai_77807214/?tag=content;col1 (accessed April 25, 2011).

Herrick, William (1915–2004)

"Young Communist. Worker on a communal farm. Hobo riding the rails. Spanish Civil War enlistee. Union organizer for black sharecroppers in Georgia. Outspoken critic of the Communist Party. Court reporter. Novelist beginning in middle age." That is Paul Grondahl's description of William Herrick written for the *Electric Times Union* in Albany, New York (Grondahl 1998). Indeed, Herrick fit all those seemingly contradictory images and more. As Herrick himself concludes wryly in his memoir, "I have not lived the life of a vegetable" (Herrick 2001, 279).

At his birth on January 10, 1915, in Trenton, New Jersey, he was named William Horvitz. His father Nathan Gurevich emigrated in 1909 from Byelorussia, now Belarus, to the United States, but immigration officials called him Horvitz. Years later, William's older brother Harry legally changed the family name to Herrick.

In Trenton, William's father "owned a wallpaper store and himself was a wallpaper hanger" (Herrick 2001, 4). William's mother Mary immigrated in 1910. She had not traveled with her husband Nathan when he left Europe because she was pregnant. She stayed behind until after their first child was born. The family lived in an apartment over the wallpaper store. His mother went to work as a seamstress, "one of the finest in New York." She also "was considered the gayest, among the most beautiful and vivacious women of the Yiddish art world. She was sought after by the leading Yiddish poets and actors of the time to read their poems, to sing their songs" (Herrick 2001, 9).

When William was four years old, his father died, leaving a wife who was pregnant. William's younger sister Natalie was born six months later. Not long afterward, his mother was hospitalized with cancer. His only close relatives were his father's sister Golda and her husband Dave. They already had six children, so an Orthodox Jewish couple, Rosie and Jake Ross, took over the guardianship of William and Natalie until their mother recovered and was able to care for them. They left Trenton to live in the Bronx, New York City, where their mother worked in a dress shop.

William's mother practiced no religion. She declared she was an atheist and a member of the Communist Party USA (CPUSA), which was founded in 1919. William grew up in a milieu of communists, anarchists, and socialists, most of whom (his widowed mother included) believed in free love—that is, they rejected marriage and argued that sexual relationships between adults should be free of government control.

Herrick attended Saturday meetings of the Young Pioneers as well as its summer camp. The Young Pioneers was a program to instill communist beliefs and practices in youth. Through young people, the CPUSA hoped to bring "about a socialist revolution in the United States," according to historian Paul Mishler (1999, 2). Herrick was steeped in communist rhetoric, and images of Russian revolutionaries Vladimir Lenin (1870–1924), Leon Trotsky (1879–1924), and communist leader Joseph Stalin (1879–1953) were on the walls of Herrick's home. Yet as a young adolescent, he was more interested in playing baseball, football, or street games in his neighborhood. He also was an avid reader, devouring books ranging from works by Fyodor Dostoyevsky and John Reed's book *Ten Days That Shook the World* (1919), about the 1917 Bolshevik or worker revolution in Russia, to popular detective stories.

During his teenage years, Herrick lived in an apartment, which his mother had purchased, in the Communist Coops (rhymes with hoops) on Bronx Park East. The coops were housing cooperatives and included other complexes in the same area: buildings constructed by the Amalgamated Clothing and Textile Workers Union and those erected by the Labor Zionists. Residents primarily were Jewish, but they wanted to address segregation issues and encouraged African American families to move in.

At the time, Herrick was "a fundamentalist in [his] belief that the Soviet Union and the Party were the answer to every single problem faced by the human race" (Herrick 2001, 50). He thought he had found utopia when he joined his aunt Golda and uncle Dave at a cooperative farm in Saginaw, Michigan, in 1933. The Sunrise Cooperative Farm, as it was called, "was in fact a commune, a collective," according to Herrick. "In a collective, as an individual, you own nothing. . . . It is a kibbutz. You own everything that is to be owned as a group, and everything owned is owned equally" (Herrick 2001, 55). The families who joined the collective included communists, socialists, anarchists, and Labor Zionists. They worked the farm, with some hired help, growing peppermint (highly valued for its oil), sugar beets, corn, wheat, and other field crops, and raising chickens and meat animals. Herrick liked his work on the farm, but left several times to "jump the line," a hobo term for hopping freight trains or hitchhiking, from the Midwest to the East Coast and back again. While he was on the road, he joined striking workers in picket lines in one city, stayed in hobo camps, wandered into towns to beg or steal food, or forage from restaurant throwaways. He also engaged in violent protests against Trotskyites—groups who believed in permanent revolution as detailed by Leon Trotsky. Herrick was dedicated to revolution, but he along with other communists railed against Trotskyites because Trotsky had been Stalin's rival. And Herrick "adored Stalin" (Herrick 2001, 80).

After Herrick left the collective for the last time, he traveled to the South to work. He also became involved with a communist group secretly trying to unionize black sharecroppers, a project that white police and farm owners murderously opposed. They broke up the organizing meeting, and Herrick and others fled for their lives.

Herrick returned to New York in 1935, and when he earned enough to pay for tuition, he intended to enroll in college—in fact, he was accepted at the University of Wisconsin in 1936. Instead, he surreptitiously joined young communists eager to fight in the Spanish Civil War. The war began with a military revolt in July 1936 against the elected government of the Spanish Republic. The insurrection was led by General Francisco Franco, and included rebels known as nationalists. Opposition to the nationalists came from trade unionists, anarchists, communists, and socialists, a coalition known as loyalists. Less than a year after the civil war began, it became an international conflict. Nazi Germany and Fascist Italy sent aid to the Spanish nationalists. Volunteers from Europe and the United States organized to fight fascism in Spain; many of them were ideological Jews like Herrick. "Between 1936 and 1939, over 7,000 Jews from 45 countries went to join the International Brigades to defend the democratically-elected Republic," according to Sarah Sackman writing for the *Jewish Quarterly* (Sackman 2008).

Before heading for Spain, Herrick explained that he "followed every battle, every political maneuver. The Anarchist and the Workers Party of Marxist Unification (POUM), which my Party called Trotskyite . . . called for socialist revolution as the only way to defeat Franco. . . . We really were for the revolution, but not yet; only when *we*, the vanguard of the proletariat, were prepared to take power ourselves" (Herrick 2001, 121).

By early 1937, Herrick was in Spain to fight the military rebellion and help stem the spread of fascism worldwide. His unit, which was part of the Abraham Lincoln Brigade, was called the Abraham Lincoln Battalion, and joined with units from other countries to form an international brigade. According to Sam Sills of the University of

Pennsylvania, the Lincoln Battalion was "Self-motivated and ideological ... [and] attempted to create an egalitarian 'people's army'; officers were distinguished only by small bars on their berets and in some cases rank-and-file soldiers elected their own officers. Traditional military protocol was shunned, although not always successfully. A political commissar explained the politics of the war to the volunteers and tended to their needs and morale" (Sills 2007).

While involved in the fight, Herrick began to question the capabilities of some of the officers appointed by the communists—some were so incompetent that they caused many of their men to be killed. Herrick also learned that he could not ask about the whereabouts of a friend and comrade who had been demoted. He was told bluntly: "In Party matters ... friendship doesn't count. The Party comes first" (Herrick 2001, 174). In late February 1937, Herrick was on the front line and was hit with a machine gun bullet in the back of his neck. Doctors were unable to extract the bullet but moved it away from his spinal cord so that he would not be paralyzed.

Before leaving Spain to return to the United States, Herrick was tested several times regarding his loyalty to the party. In one case, he was forced by a party official to watch the execution of Spanish revolutionaries, two of them young teenagers, who were noncommunist but still comrades in Herrick's eyes. For years afterward, he struggled with guilt, knowing that he likely would not have had the courage to stop the executions or to refuse to kill the victims if commanded to do so. This and previous incidents were the beginning of Herrick's disillusionment with communism, which he finally rejected outright when the Hitler-Stalin pact was signed in 1939.

Also called the Nazi-Soviet pact, it was an agreement between Nazi dictator Adolf Hitler and communist leader of the Soviet Union Joseph Stalin. The pact stated in part that "The Government of the German Reich and The Government of the Union of Soviet Socialist Republics desirous of strengthening the cause of peace between Germany and the U.S.S.R. . . . obligate themselves to desist from any act of violence, any aggressive action, and any attack on each other, either individually or jointly with other Powers." Germany and the USSR further agreed that they would remain neutral if either country became "the object of belligerent action by a third Power."

By the time this agreement was in force, it was clear that Jews were being persecuted by fascists in Germany and other European countries. Herrick was back in the United States and was shocked (to put it mildly) when the Communist Party, which had been against fascism, supported the Soviet agreement with fascist Germany. The party had become "anti-anti-fascist," as Herrick put it (Herrick 2001, 245). When he protested against the pact in the streets, he lost his job with the communist-supported Furriers Union.

In 1939, Herrick married a young woman he had known when he lived at the Communist Coops. They had a son who died at a young age, and probably because they had little in common, the marriage lasted only three years.

During the 1940s and 1950s, Herrick earned a living as a freelance court reporter and became an official court reporter for the U.S. District Court in New York's Southern District. Always the organizer, he formed the Federation of Shorthand Reporters and became its president. It was a time when U.S. senator Joseph McCarthy was making charges about communists in the U.S. government and the army. Because Herrick had once been a communist and had fought in the Spanish Civil War, his Federation was placed on a subversive list. He was subpoenaed to appear before a government committee, asked to name political affiliations of his union members and people who had been in the Lincoln Battalion. He gave the names of dead men. In the end, the Federation was taken off the subversive list.

While working as a court reporter, Herrick met Jeannette Wellin, a widow, who would become his second wife. They eventually had three children: Jonathan, Michael, and Lisa.

When Herrick was a freelance reporter, his office received a call from theater director Orson Welles, who wanted a stenographer. Jeannette took the job, but the next time Welles called, Herrick responded. During the mid-1940s, he worked off and on for Welles, taking dictation for revisions of play scripts.

Herrick began writing his own works in the 1956, and over the next 40 years, he published 10 novels and an autobiography. Some of his books mirror his own experiences, such as his first novel *The Itinerant* (1967) that took 10 years to find a publisher. His book *¡Hermanos!* (1969) is a war novel based on Herrick's Spanish Civil War experiences and considered his best work. Three other novels are concerned with the Spanish Civil War and Nazi terrorism: *Shadows and Wolves* (1980), *Love and Terror* (1981), and *Kill Memory* (1983). His autobiography *Jumping the Line: the Adventures and Misadventures of an American Radical* (1998) was published by the University of Wisconsin Press and later reissued. He was at work on another book when he became ill with heart disease. Herrick died January 31, 2004, of congestive heart failure at his home in Old Chatham, New York.

See also McCarthy, Joseph

References

Grondahl, Paul. "When the Party Was Over." *Electric Times Union*, April 19, 1998. http://www.albany.edu/writers-inst/webpages4/archives/tuherrik.html (accessed December 21, 2010).

Herrick, William. *Jumping the Line: The Adventures and Misadventures of an American Radical*. Edinburgh; London; and Oakland, CA: AK Press, 2001. First published, Madison: University of Wisconsin Press, 1998.

Mishler, Paul C. Raising Reds: The Young Pioneers, Radical Summer Camps, and Communist Political Culture in the United States. New York: Columbia University Press, 1999.

Sackman, Sarah. "On the Frontlines of Identity." *Jewish Quarterly*, Spring 2008. http://www.jewishquarterly.org/issuearchive/article39ef.html?articleid=366 (accessed September 7, 2011).

Sills, Sam. "Abraham Lincoln Brigade of the Spanish Civil War." July 18, 2007. http://writing.upenn.edu/~afilreis/88/abe-brigade.html (accessed December 24, 2010).

Hill, Joe (1879–1915)

Since 1915, when Joe Hill, Swedish immigrant, laborer, and nonconformist songwriter for the Industrial Workers of the World (IWW), was convicted of murder and executed in Utah, arguments over Hill's guilt or innocence have continued to the present time. To labor organizers and especially to members of the IWW, commonly known as the Wobblies, Hill was a martyr and folk hero to labor's cause. To the many opponents of IWW (who far outnumbered its supporters), Hill was guilty as charged and his execution was justified.

Hill was born in Gävle, Sweden on October 7, 1879, and was named Joel Emmanuel Hägglund. He was one of nine children of

Olof, a conductor for the Gävle-Dala Railroad, and Margareta Hägglund. Three of their children died in childhood. The Hägglunds taught their children to enjoy music, leading family singing and teaching them to play the organ that Olof had built.

When Joel was eight years old, his father died, and Joel along with his siblings went to work to help support the family. Music helped Joel endure some of the hardships in his life. He taught himself to play the accordion, piano, guitar, banjo, and violin. As a teenager, he composed music and played the piano for a local inn. He also liked to paint and draw cartoons. He used his artistic abilities later in his life to show in his cartoons the value of humor and to "spark the laughter of revolt and freedom" (Rosemont 2002, 6).

In 1902, his mother died, and Joel and his older brother Paul immigrated to the United States, while the other surviving siblings stayed in Sweden. The eldest brother Olof went to work for the railroad, and his brother Ruben was a longshoreman. His two sisters "were sent to live with a family far to the north of Gävle, in the mountains" (Rosemont 2002, 45).

Joel and Paul, like millions of other immigrants landing at Ellis Island, New York, in the early 1900s, expected the proverbial streets paved with gold. But they quickly learned otherwise and were forced to work for pennies per day at menial jobs in New York's slums. Joel and Paul soon left New York, each going his own way. Joel made his way to Chicago, where he worked in a machine shop and tried to organize workers to demand their right to a living wage. He was soon fired for his efforts, and began wandering west.

"Very little is known, and virtually nothing is verifiable, about the next eight years of Joel's life," according to a documentary by Ken Verdoia for the Public Broadcasting Service (PBS). Joel took jobs wherever he could find work—in mines, shipyards, construction and logging, and on farms. He was in California during the San Francisco earthquake of 1906, and in 1913, he was in San Pedro taking part in a dockworkers strike. As he drifted from place to place in the West, he "apparently ran into trouble and decided he had to vanish—at least in name," Verdoia states, adding: "Years later, friends in the labor movement would say he had to disappear because of his determined advocacy of worker rights in different locations, and the angry response of powerful companies. Still others maintain that Joel turned frequently to petty crime during these years to support his vagrant lifestyle, and he had to assume a different identity to keep one step ahead of the law. In either case, at

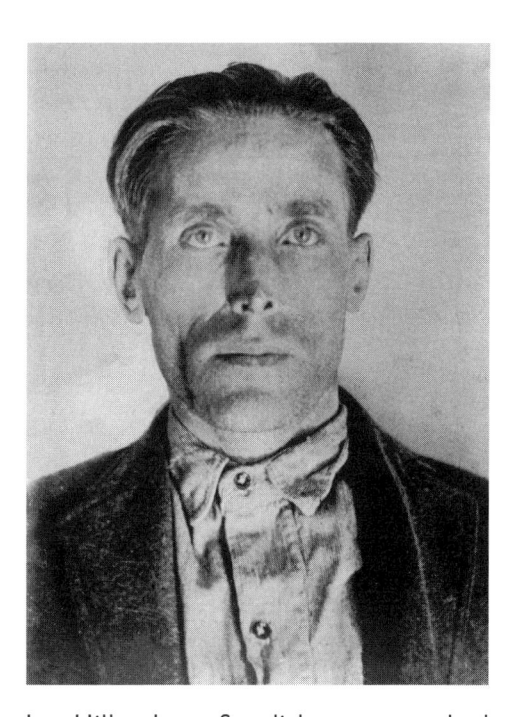

Joe Hill, whose Swedish name was Joel Emmanuel Hagglund, was a labor activist in the early 1900s and songwriter for the Industrial Workers of the World, or Wobblies. (Library of Congress)

a point between 1906 and 1910 the name Joel Emmanuel Haggland disappeared, to be replaced by the moniker Joseph Hillstrom" (Verdoia 2000).

Joseph Hillstrom soon shortened his name to Joe Hill. As he took one job after another while wandering across the United States, he began to write poems and his own lyrics for popular tunes and hymns. The songs frequently were indictments—some of them bitter—of the American social and economic systems that exploited workers. His songs especially appealed to members of the IWW, which Joe Hill joined in 1910. Songs were one form of recruiting for the IWW; the music and lyrics were easier to remember than political pamphlets or other written materials that workers had no time or inclination to read.

The IWW formed in Chicago in 1905 to create one big union of both skilled and unskilled workers, women as well as men, and workers from all racial backgrounds. The preamble to its constitution begins with these words:

> The working class and the employing class have nothing in common. There can be no peace so long as hunger and want are found among millions of the working people and the few, who make up the employing class, have all the good things of life.
>
> Between these two classes a struggle must go on until the workers of the world organize as a class, take possession of the means of production, abolish the wage system, and live in harmony with the Earth.

The preamble concluded: "It is the historic mission of the working class to do away with capitalism. The army of production must be organized, not only for everyday struggle with capitalists, but also to carry on production when capitalism shall have been overthrown. By organizing industrially we are forming the structure of the new society within the shell of the old."

IWW's early organizers included such labor activists as Eugene V. Debs, Mary Harris "Mother" Jones, and Lucy Parsons. After joining IWW, Hill continued to write songs that were picked up by the union and included in various editions of *The Little Red Songbook*, first published in 1909. One of Hill's most well-known songs was "Rebel Girl," named for labor organizer and IWW leader Elizabeth Gurley Flynn, whom Hill greatly admired.

Between 1909 and 1913, the IWW organized major strikes such as the 10-week strike of 25,000 textile workers in Lawrence, Massachusetts. The massive strike frightened many company owners and public officials. As a result, IWW members—Joe Hill included—were targets for attacks by police and company guards. Corporation executives hated unions because they did not want to share profits with workers; the general public had no use for unions because most believed themselves superior to laborers, primarily immigrants, who did society's dirty and dangerous jobs.

Where strikes were held, Joe Hill was likely to be involved, if not physically present at least in spirit through his songs, such as "There Is Power in a Union." That song is still being performed by some folk singers and labor organizations, although it is sometimes updated to apply to modern times and the strength of solidarity.

In 1913, Hill left the West Coast and headed for Chicago ostensibly to meet with IWW leaders. On his way, he stopped in Salt Lake City, Utah, to work at a mine, but he became ill with pneumonia, was hospitalized, and lost his job. Because he was unemployed, Swedish friends who lived near the mines provided him with a place to stay free of charge. While Hill was with friends, a Salt Lake City grocery store owner John G. Morrison, a former policeman, and his son, Arling, were murdered by two masked gunman on January 10, 1914. At first there was a suspect named Frank Z. Wilson who had just been released from prison and wanted revenge; Morrison had arrested him. However, Wilson was no longer a suspect after police accused Hill of the crime even though there was no evidence linking him to the murders. However, Hill had a gunshot wound, which he said occurred when he got into a fight trying to defend a woman, an explanation that did not convince either the doctor who treated Hill's wound or the arresting police in his case. In short, the court, public, and press were hostile. The state of Utah and the general public were eager to find Hill guilty primarily because he was an IWW member and agitator. "Even before his case came to trial, Joe Hill had been convicted in the court of public hysteria," wrote historian Melvyn Dubofsky, adding that there were "minimal prospects for a fair trial. . . . the trial judge reportedly favored the prosecution and hampered the defense. No witness ever absolutely identified Hill as the murderer; no motive was ever introduced to account for the crime; no bullet could be found to link Hill to the killer allegedly wounded in the grocery; and no gun could be located to connect Hill with the murder of either the grocer or his son. Yet on June 26, 1914, a jury found Joe Hill guilty, and on July 8 a judge sentenced him to death" (Dubofsky 1969, 310).

The IWW and their sympathizers around the world launched a protest campaign on Hill's behalf. Thousands of labor leaders, including Eugene Debs, wrote to Utah's governor William Spry, declaring that Hill was innocent and that his trial was unfair. They believed Hill was framed for murder because of his socialist views. Since Hill was still a Swedish citizen, a member of the Swedish government appealed to Governor Spry on behalf of Hill. Even President Woodrow Wilson asked Spry to reconsider the case, which many Utah citizens resented, believing the federal government should not interfere in state business. Still others wrote to commend Spry for supporting the conviction and upholding law and order.

Hill's lawyers appealed, and IWW members protested in marches in major cities. In New York, a "Joe Hill Protest Meeting" was held on November 8, 1915, and IWW activist Elizabeth Gurley Flynn was one of the speakers. Still, after appeals Hill was resentenced, and on November 19, 1915, he was executed by a firing squad. The night before, Hill had written to IWW leader Big Bill Haywood, telling him "Don't waste any time in mourning. Organize!" Those words became the motto and rallying cry for the IWW. And Joe Hill became a martyr for labor's cause.

Thousands attended the two funerals for Hill—one in Salt Lake City and the other in Chicago. His body was cremated at Graceland Cemetery in Chicago, and the ashes were mailed in small envelopes to IWW locals in every state except Utah because Hill had said in no uncertain terms that he did not want to be found dead in Utah. Other Hill supporters worldwide received Hill's ashes as well. On International Workers' Day (or May Day), May 1, 1916, people around the globe opened their envelopes and scattered Hill's ashes in the breeze as he had requested. However, in Sweden, his ashes were placed in a commemorative urn, and his family home became a museum.

Hill's legend has lived on for decades. He has been commemorated in books, plays, and songs, and in a PBS documentary presented in 2000. In his play *Singing Jailbirds* (1924), Upton Sinclair, known for his muckraking novel *The Jungle* (1926), used songs by Joe Hill. Folk singer Pete Seeger performed Hill's songs, and protest singer Phil Ochs wrote songs about Hill. Two decades after Hill's execution, songwriters Earl Robinson and Alfred Hayes wrote "The Ballad of Joe Hill" also known as "I Dreamed I Saw Joe Hill Last Night." The song has been part of the repertoire of artists such as Paul Robeson and Joan Baez. To the present day, Hill is best known by the songs he wrote, but his conviction and execution for murder are still matters of controversy.

See also Debs, Eugene V.; Flynn, Elizabeth Gurley; Jones, Mary Harris; Ochs, Phil; Parsons, Lucy; Robeson, Paul; Seeger, Pete; Sinclair, Upton

References

Dubofsky, Melvyn. *We Shall Be All: A History of the Industrial Workers of the World*. New York: Quadrangle Books, 1969. An abridged edition edited by Joseph A. McCartin was published in 2000 by the University of Illinois Press.

Industrial Workers of the World. "Preamble to the IWW Constitution." http://www.iww.org/culture/official/preamble.shtml (accessed January 8, 2011).

"Joe Hill's Ashes Divided; I.W.W. to Send 600 Shares to All Parts of World." *New York Times*, November 20, 1916. http://query.nytimes.com/mem/archive-free/pdf?res=F4081FFD3B5916738DDDA90A94D9415B868DF1D3 (accessed January 8, 2011).

Rosemont, Franklin. *Joe Hill: The IWW and the Making of a Revolutionary Workingclass Counter Culture*. Chicago: Charles H. Kerr Publishing Company, 2002.

Smith, Gibbs M. *Joe Hill*. Layton, UT: Gibbs M. Smith, Inc. Peregrine Smith Books, 1969.

Verdoia, Ken, producer/director. " 'We'll Scrape Gold Off the Streets!' " Public Broadcasting Service, 2000. http://www.kued.org/productions/joehill/story/biography/scrape_gold.html (accessed January 6, 2011).

Hill, Julia "Butterfly" (1974–)

Julia "Butterfly" Hill is best known for her 738-day stay that began in 1997 in the canopy of a giant redwood tree in her struggle to save the ancient redwoods in Northern California. Pacific Lumber Company had been clear-cutting large areas of ancient forests, leaving barren slopes that quickly turned to mudslides during rain storms. When Hill with other environmentalists attempted to stop the destruction, loggers, company guards, and some employees of the lumber company attacked verbally and intimidated her by felling giant trees close by and flying a helicopter overhead. At one time, Hill thought she would be killed by angry loggers who hated her dissident assault on their livelihood. But Hill sees herself as part of a "resolutionary movement" do-it-yourself activism in which "every moment of every day we are looking for ways to be living examples of all that is beautiful and humble and just and incredible about our world," she told a *Washington Post* reporter (Oldenburg 2004, C01).

Julia Lorraine Hill was born February 18, 1974, to Dale Edward Hill, an itinerant minister, and Kathleen Anne DelGallo Hill of Mt. Vernon, Missouri. During their early childhood, Julia and her brothers Michael and Daniel lived with their parents in Harrisburg, Pennsylvania, where Dale and Kathleen established a church called Freedom Chapel. Julia attended school for first and second grades, but thereafter was home schooled through eighth grade as the family traveled

Environmental activist Julia "Butterfly" Hill during her 738-day "tree-sit" in California. On December 10, 1997, she began her vigil in the 1,000-year-old redwood in an effort to protect it from being cut down by property owner Pacific Lumber Co., and to call for an end to all ancient forest logging. (AP Photo/Shaun Walker)

from place to place—wherever Dale Hill preached. Their home was a camping trailer. According to Julia, her family was "very poor, and my parents taught us how to save money and be thrifty. Growing up this way also taught us to appreciate the simple things in life. We paid our own way as much as possible; I got my first job when I was about five years old, helping my brothers with lawn work. We'd make only a buck or so, but to us that was a lot. I had my share of fun, but I definitely grew up knowing what responsible meant" (Hill 2000, 3).

Julia went to high school in Jonesboro, Arkansas, where the family settled for a time. She graduated from high school in 1991 and worked at various jobs until she enrolled at Arkansas State University at Jonesboro. She left Jonesboro in 1994, moving to Fayetteville, the Washington County

seat, and taking jobs in restaurants and bars. Her life changed drastically in the summer of 1996 when her car was struck from the rear, causing extensive damage to the vehicle and severely injuring her. She underwent nearly a year of intensive physical rehabilitation and mental therapy (she had to retrain her short-term memory and motor skills). "Having survived such a horrible accident, I resolved to change my life," she wrote, "and I wanted to follow a more spiritual path" (Hill 2000, 5).

Hill began seeking that path in 1997 when friends asked her to accompany them on a summer trip to the West Coast. On that trip, the group visited California's Grizzly Creek Redwoods State Park, a remote forest area in Humboldt County. When Hill explored the redwood forest, she found it to be "the holiest of temples, housing more spirituality than any church" (Hill 2000, 9). After her visit, she learned that Pacific Lumber Company/Maxxam Corporation was clearcutting the ancient redwoods near the park, and her mission was born. She wanted to do whatever she could to save the redwoods.

In the fall of 1997, Hill learned that activists in Humboldt County were "tree sitting" to prevent loggers from cutting down ancient trees. The activists were on a platform in the canopy of a giant redwood standing 200 feet high on a cliff. They had named the tree Luna (*moon* in Spanish) because they had built the platform in moonlight, hoping to avoid detection by Pacific Lumber/Maxxam, which owned the land where the tree stood. Earth First! environmental volunteers, practicing nonviolent civil disobedience, had been taking turns sitting on the platform, rotating every few days. Like other Earth First! activists, Hill gave herself another name to protect her identity—she became known as "Butterfly." Before Butterfly Hill could begin her shift, she had to learn how to knot ropes used for tree climbing as well as how to scale the tree and also rappel down to the ground.

When she first became a tree sitter in early December 1997, Hill expected to be there only a short time. But day after day, month after month, she stayed. Support crews hoisted food, drinking water, and other supplies. She had a hand-cranked radio, a cell phone, an old video camera, and writing and reading materials that included a lot of environmental articles and books. She was especially interested in the work of her heroine Judi Bari, an environmentalist with Earth First! who, along with supporters, blocked lumber companies from logging old-growth forests in northern California during the late 1980s. Butterfly Hill was impressed with "the courage Judi Bari showed in the face of threats, a car bombing and finally cancer. I know the same fire that burned in her burns in me. But I can only hope to be a voice like her" (Wilson 1998).

Six months after Hill began her vigil, Nicholas Wilson, a reporter from the *Albion Monitor*, an alternative bimonthly newspaper in Albion, California, along with Earth First! volunteers with supplies, made the two-hour climb up the mountain to the base of Luna. Drummers were part of the entourage, and when they reached Luna, they circled the 14-foot diameter of the tree, and began drumming. Wilson reported: "As the drummers drum, Julia Butterfly climbs from her platform to the very tip of the tallest branch of the ancient tree. Holding on only with her legs and bare feet, she sways her torso, head, and arms, dancing to the rhythm, the cheers, the exuberant wolf-howls of the throng. A brisk and chilly wind blows her long dark hair straight out, giving the impression that she's part of the tree and its foliage" (Wilson 1998).

However, there was little to cheer about in the months ahead. Throughout 1998 and most of 1999, she endured periodic attacks by Pacific Lumber to force her out of Luna. She was bombarded with air horns, floodlights, and loud music. Helicopters endangered her with updrafts as they flew illegally nearby. Guards prevented volunteers from sending up food supplies, trying to starve her out. A professional climber tried to force her to abandon her platform. The weather also battered her at times with freezing rains, sleet, and high winds, and she suffered from frostbite.

Whatever the difficulties and near tragedies, she survived and, after months of negotiating, finally reached a legally binding agreement with Pacific Lumber/Maxxam to protect Luna and create a buffer zone around the tree. Butterfly Hill descended from her platform on December 18, 1999. Her book about her experiences *The Legacy of Luna* (2000) was published soon afterward and became a best seller.

Unfortunately, in November 2000, Hill received devastating news. After her two-year vigil, Luna had been slashed with a chainsaw, in a cut that was 19 feet long and 30 to 36 inches deep, encircling half the circumference of the tree's trunk. No one knew who perpetrated the act, but Butterfly Hill had enemies, many of whom wanted Luna cut down and wished Hill harm. Yet, there were plenty of people who wanted to save Luna. According to California's nonprofit land trust Sanctuary Forest, "Working side by side into the night, leading arborists, engineers, biologists, and employees of Pacific Lumber Company and the California Department of Forestry volunteered to help. These experts designed, manufactured and installed steel brackets and cables to bolster the tree through winter storms. There were predictions that Luna would show signs of dieback, but four years later [in 2004] her canopy still looks green and strong. Supported by the trees around her, Luna's roots are nourished and stabilized and the 1000-year-old tree endures" (Sanctuary Forest n.d.).

Since the giant redwood was vandalized, Hill has been writing, speaking at various venues, and answering questions from interviewers, plus working with Engage Network, a social networking program cofounded by Hill. She coauthored a second book, *One Makes the Difference: Inspiring Actions That Change Our World* (2002). In addition, she has addressed the United Nations, lobbied Congress about environmental concerns, and worked for social justice issues worldwide.

In mid-2002, she went to Ecuador and took part in a protest against the U.S. Occidental Petroleum company, one of the partners building a 300-mile pipeline from oil fields in the Amazon Basin to the Pacific Coast. Environmentalists and some Ecuadorians say the pipeline has and will cause harm to the Amazon region, but government and company officials have argued that the pipeline provides jobs and billions of dollars in foreign investment. The protesters were arrested, and Hill was deported from the country.

Hill has taken part in campaigns to save the South Central Community Garden in Los Angeles. The organic garden is on a 14-acre plot loaned to the Watts community by the city in 1992. It is in one of the city's poorest neighborhoods and the food grown is sorely needed. But a developer wanted to take over the land and won a court order to buy it. Hill joined celebrities and community activists to try to save the garden. Some protested by blocking bulldozers with their bodies. Eventually the farm had to be relocated to Bakersfield, 130 miles away. Yet farmers drive there to work the land and to take crops to Watts, selling their produce in a marketplace near the site of the old community garden.

When she is interviewed or speaking to groups, Hill often decries society's wastefulness. Like biologist Barry Commoner (1917–), who declares that everything thrown away must go somewhere, Hill points out that when people say they are going to throw something away, there is no away. Discarded objects, especially plastics, often pollute the environment. Asked in an interview about corporate "green programs," Hill responded:

I am not a fan of huge corporations (i.e.: Shell, McDonald's and Wal-Mart) who have "green" campaigns. Ultimately these are corporations that are designed to make a huge profit from exploitation of the planet and all its life, including humans. I also challenge the idea that we can somehow buy our way to sustainability. The path to planetary health is in walking away from consumption and towards reducing our ecological footprint. This does include being mindful of what we buy, but first and foremost REDUCING what we are taking from the Earth. The average American consumes approximately 14 generations worth of resources in one single generation. We are a society of addicts, and we are going to have to heal our addiction to consumption if we are to heal the wounds we have and continue to inflict on our planetary home. (Belli 2007)

Hill is the subject of two documentaries, *Butterfly* (2000) and *Tree Sit: The Art of Resistance* (2005), and has been honored in a fictional film, *Greendale* (2004).

See also Bari, Judi; Commoner, Barry

References

Belli, Brita. "Commentary: Behind the Greens: 10 Questions for Activist Julia Butterfly Hill." *E Magazine.com*, 2007. http://www.emagazine.com/view/?3914 (accessed August 24, 2010).

Berton, Justin. "Catching Up with Julia Butterfly Hill." *San Francisco Chronicle*, April 16, 2009.

Hill, Julia Butterfly. *The Legacy of Luna: The Story of a Tree, a Woman, and the Struggle to Save the Redwoods*. San Francisco: HarperSanFrancisco, 2000.

Hill, Julia Butterfly, and Jessica Hurley. *One Makes the Difference: Inspiring Actions that Change Our World*. San Francisco: HarperSanFrancisco, 2002.

Oldenburg, Don. "Julia Butterfly Hill, from Treetop to Grass Roots." *Washington Post*, September 22, 2004.

Sanctuary Forest. "Sanctuary Forest Goes Out on a Limb for Julia Butterfly and Luna." n.d. http://www.sanctuaryforest.org/luna/ (accessed August 24, 2010).

Wilson, Nicholas. "Dancing in the Treetop." *Albion Monitor*, July 1, 1998. http://www.albionmonitor.com/9807a/butterflyprofile.html (accessed August 23, 2010).

Hoffman, Abbie (1936–1989)

Abbie Hoffman called himself "an American dissident." He was a master manipulator of the media. He used them to publicize his outrageous antics in a shrewdly calculated means to deliver his message and get others on board with his causes. He was so front-and-center, unapologetically antiestablishment, in the 1960s that he came to symbolize the composite face of youth activists across the United States.

Florence and John Hoffman welcomed their firstborn, Abbot "Abbie" on November 30, 1936. They had two more children, whom they raised in Worcester, Massachusetts. Abbie got into minor trouble as a youth, transferring high schools because of a disagreement he had with a teacher and for getting arrested for driving without a license. After graduation in 1955, he earned a psychology degree at Brandeis University four years later. Hoffman then headed to the West Coast, enrolling in the University of California, Berkeley, but he soon dropped out to marry his then pregnant girlfriend, Sue Karklin. They would have a second child, staying together until divorcing in 1966.

Hoffman's first after-college involvement in activism came when he traveled to Mississippi to register black voters and was "radicalized" by the civil rights movement. The struggles he witnessed in the South were his initiation into politics. He explained how:

> Liberty House was set up in New York's West Village to serve as a retail outlet for crafts made in cooperatives in Mississippi ... some of us ... formed the Poor People's Corporation and quickly trained poor blacks in craft skills and business management. We were told by all sort of fancy economic experts that it was impossible to train these people, never mind giving them control of the businesses. The experts might be interested in knowing that the program not only has survived three years but has expanded quite successfully without help from the government and in an extremely hostile environment (Mississippi). (Hoffman 2005, 29)

With the Black Power groups becoming less receptive to having whites in their memberships or even to working with white groups, Hoffman turned his focus to Vietnam. In 1968, he cofounded the Youth International Party, whose followers were called "Yippies." In addition to protesting U.S. involvement in Vietnam, they generally found fault with most aspects of American culture, economics, and politics. Unlike other groups, Yippies were not card-carrying, dues-paying folks. They did not attend meetings or elect officers. Instead, at sporadic intervals, they held "Festivals of Life," featuring rock bands, theater, poetry, drugs, and alcohol—all appealing to the young guard and appalling to the old. These events were carefully planned, yet not scripted. In this way, Hoffman attracted young people and appealed to their sense of rebellion—against parents, the establishment, and society—and prompted young people to get involved in activities with which they might not otherwise have bothered. Hoffman made political activism "cool" to the youthful counterculture.

Hoffman was the ringleader in what many dismissed as mere "stunts," but he believed that by ridiculing symbols of authority, he was weakening their power and lessening their legitimacy. In his first book, he describes some of the antics such as throwing soot on Consolidated Edison executives and smoke bombs in their lobby; dumping gallons of blood on another company's leaders and their limos; and interrupting a talk given by Senator Joseph McCarthy at the House Un-American Activities Committee (Hoffman 2005, 53).

In one instance in 1967, Hoffman and others went to the New York Stock Exchange. From the observation area, they began throwing dollar bills over the railing to the delight of some and the disgust of other traders below. Writing of the event four decades later, on the web site CNNMoney, deputy money manager James Ledbetter opined, "If the prank accomplished nothing else, it helped cement Hoffman's reputation as one of America's most outlandish and creative protestors." Ledbetter recalls Hoffman boasting, "In the minds of millions of teenagers the stock market had just crashed." While he does not attribute as much significance to the event himself, Ledbetter concedes it "did appear to have one direct effect: officials moved to insure that nothing like it could occur again. Some three months later, the NYSE installed bulletproof glass panels, 1-3/16 inches thick, around the visitors' gallery, as well as a metal grillwork ceiling. An exchange spokesman told the *New York Times* at the time that it was for 'reasons of security' " (Ledbetter 2007).

Another notable event involved the U.S. Pentagon. In October 1967, David Dellinger of the National Mobilization Committee

During the 1960s, Abbie Hoffman led the Youth International Party (known as Yippies). He became a standard-bearer for the radical youth of the counterculture, often resorting to outrageous behavior to dramatize causes to which he was committed. (AP/Wide World Photos)

to End the War in Vietnam asked Jerry Rubin, another Yippie cofounder, to coordinate a march from the Lincoln Memorial to the Pentagon. As protesters neared their target, they were stopped by about 3,000 soldiers—mostly military police and National Guardsmen—surrounding the Pentagon. Undeterred, Hoffman announced he would use psychic powers to levitate the building, make it vibrate, turn orange, and end the Vietnam conflict (Freeman, UIC web site). Many remember the iconic photo that day of a protester placing a flower in the barrel of a soldier's rifle. While most other demonstrators were peaceful, the day did not end well. About 680 were jailed; nearly 50 others required hospitalization, plus another two dozen law officers needed care. As Hoffman intended, "A weekend of both dead seriousness and utter silliness left an entire nation surprised, disturbed, and debating" (Burns 2005).

Hoffman's greatest notoriety came about during the Chicago Democratic Convention in August 1968. It started out with relatively benign aspirations. In a February 16 letter to friend and Black Power leader Stokely Carmichael, Hoffman offhandedly wrote, "We are working on a huge Youth Festival in Chicago at the time of the Democratic Convention. I hope I get to participate" (Hoffman 2005, 53). The Yippies were joined in Chicago by other groups, such as Students for a Democratic Society and Dellinger's National Mobilization Committee to End the War in Vietnam. More than 10,000 protesters filled the streets, much to the ire of Mayor Richard J. Daley, who dispatched more than twice that number of police and National Guardsmen to deal with the troublemakers. Things started out in the spirit of typical Yippie festival fun. They danced, sang, smoked marijuana, and campaigned for their "Pigasus" (a pig) presidential candidate. Over time, things got out of hand; police began using tear gas, mace, and billy clubs on protesters. Some of the brutality was captured live on television: "a great deal of blood flowed for the networks' conveniently positioned cameras and 'the whole world' (America anyway) proverbially watched" (Gitlin 1987, 332).

Conspiracy and incitement to riot charges were filed against eight men: Hoffman, Rennie Davis, David Dellinger, Tom Hayden, John Froines, Jerry Rubin, Bobby Seale, and Lee Weiner. The trial of the "Chicago Eight" was assigned to the courtroom of Judge Julius J. Hoffman (no relation) but the eight became the "Chicago Seven" when Black Panther Party cofounder

Seale's trial was removed. The year-plus trial was a media sensation, with the defendants making a mockery of the court and judge, who issued over 100 contempt citations. In February 1970, all defendants were cleared on the conspiracy charges, but Hoffman, Davis, Dellinger, Hayden, and Rubin were found guilty of crossing state lines with the intent to start a riot. Subsequently, however, the Seventh Court of Appeals overturned the convictions.

Hoffman released *Woodstock Nation: A Talk Rock Album* in 1969 and later, *Steal This Book* (1971). The latter title led retailers to boycott the book because fans took the author's advice and stole the book. *Vote!* (1972) was cowritten with Jerry Rubin and Ed Sanders. But things ground to a halt in August 1973, when Hoffman was arrested for possession and intent to sell cocaine (he claimed being set up). Hoffman went underground, leaving behind his second wife, Anita Kushner, whom he had married in 1967 and with whom he had a third child (they formally divorced in 1980). He underwent plastic surgery and cut and dyed his trademark unruly curls. He spent the next seven years as "Barry Freed" in Thousand Islands Park, New York. He cofounded the organization Save the River! with Johanna Lawrenson, whom he married. The couple opposed the Army Corps of Engineers' plan to make the St. Lawrence River navigable in the winter, endangering the bald eagle, disrupting the aquatic life chain, and creating other devastation to the environment. Johanna stayed with Abbie until he died. She runs the Abbie Hoffman Activist Foundation (Hoffman 2005, 257–59).

While underground, Hoffman was travel editor for *Crawdaddy!* magazine and released *To America with Love: Letters from the Underground* (1976), cowritten with Anita Robbie Conal. As Barry Freed, Hoffman testified at a hearing held by the Army Corps of Engineers, and gave such an eloquent presentation that U.S. senator Daniel Patrick Moynihan praised his efforts. Congress denied the project's funding (Hoffman 2000, 307).

On September 4, 1980, Hoffman resurfaced, simultaneously surrendering to authorities and—ever the master of the media—appearing on a prerecorded edition of *20/20*, in an interview with Barbara Walters. Hoffman served a one-year sentence, then resumed his environmental activism, interspersed with speaking engagements and other forms of political activism, such as speaking and writing about the country's drug policies. In November 1986, Hoffman was arrested along with 14 others (including President Carter's daughter Amy) who were protesting the CIA's recruitment at the University of Massachusetts at Amherst. At his trial, Hoffman called witnesses such as former attorney general and CIA agent Ramsey Clark, and the man who released the Pentagon Papers hastening the end of the Vietnam War, Daniel Ellsberg. He made the case that the CIA did not meet the university's policy limiting on-campus recruitment to "law-abiding organizations." Hoffman convinced the jury of his own and his codefendants justification for civil disobedience and they were acquitted on April 15, 1987. In his closing argument, Hoffman said, "I grew up with the idea that democracy is not something you believe in, or a place you hang your hat, but it's something you do. You participate. If you stop doing it, democracy crumbles and falls apart ... Young people, if you participate, the future is yours" (Hoffman 2005, 258).

On April 12, 1989, at age 52, Hoffman was found dead in New Hope, Pennsylvania. "On Tuesday a coroner ruled that Mr. Hoffman ... died of a massive overdose of phenobarbital, about 150 tablets, taken in combination with alcohol. It was, said the coroner, Thomas J. Rosko, clearly a suicide" (King 1989). The *New York Times* reported that at Hoffman's funeral, a friend proclaimed, "Abbie was not a fugitive from justice. Justice was a fugitive from him." The *Times* added, "On a more traditional note, Rabbi Norman Mendell said in his eulogy that Mr. Hoffman's long history of protest, antic though much of it had been, was 'in the Jewish prophetic tradition, which is to comfort the afflicted and afflict the comfortable.' But the Rabbi also quoted one of Mr. Hoffman's favorite sayings: 'Sacred cows make the tastiest hamburger' " (King 1989).

In January 2000, Howard Zinn—an accomplished activist in his own right—declared that:

> There was no one quite like him, no one who so combined brilliant, zany wit with serious political purpose. There was also no one who so brought together—with a clash of symbols—the cultural revolution of the sixties with the tumultuous protest for racial justice and the war in Vietnam, and very few who carried over the energy and commitment of those years into the seventies and eighties, without a pause and without any twinge of uncertainty . . . Abbie's comic adventures were educational in the best sense of the word . . . A political movement needs more than astute analysis, efficient organization, and inspiring speeches. It needs heart and soul, which Abbie had in abundance. It needs passion and excitement, which flowed out of Abbie and enveloped the people he touched. . . . what was most striking about his contribution to the movement of the sixties: he helped turn the antiauthoritarian instincts of the younger generation into political resistance to racism and war. (Hoffman 2000, 305–6)

Margaret Gay

See also Carmichael, Stokely/Ture, Kwame; Clark, Ramsey; Dellinger, David; Ellsberg, Daniel; Hayden, Tom; McCarthy, Joseph; Seale, Bobby; Zinn, Howard

References

Burns, Alexander. "The Day the Pentagon Was Supposed to Lift Off into Space." *American Heritage*, October 21, 2005. http://course.cas.sc.edu/germanyk/post1945/materials/AmericanHeritage_com%20-%20The%20Day%20The%20Pentagon%20Was%20Supposed%20to%20Lift%20Off%20Into%20Space.htm (accessed April 2, 2011).

Freeman, Jo. "Levitate the Pentagon (1967)." Jo Freeman.com, http://www.jofreeman.com/photos/Pentagon67.html (accessed April 2, 2011).

Gitlin, Todd. *The Sixties: Years of Hope, Days of Rage*. New York: Bantam, 1993.

Hoffman, Abbie. *Revolution for the Hell of It*. New York: Thunder's Mouth Press, 2005. First published 1968.

Hoffman, Abbie, and Norman Mailer. *The Autobiography of Abbie Hoffman*. New York: Four Walls Eight Windows, 1980; revised 2000.

King, Wayne. "Mourning, and Celebrating a Radical." *New York Times*, April 20, 1989.

Ledbetter, James. "The Day the NYSE Went Yippie." CNNMoney.com, August 23, 2007. http://money.cnn.com/2007/07/17/news/funny/abbie_hoffman/index.htm (accessed March 27, 2011).

Horowitz, David (1939–)

Many progressives, social liberals, socialists, communists, and others on the political left in the United States contend that David Horowitz makes unsubstantiated claims about the American left. Although Horowitz was once far left in his political views, currently he is considered an outspoken proponent of those on the political right, who include conservatives, capitalists, and nationalists. Whatever his political position, he has been a dissident who has vociferously criticized and debated those who disagree and even those who agree with his views.

David Joel Horowitz was born on January 10, 1939, in Forest Hills, New York, to Phil and Blanche Horowitz. His parents were teachers in Queens, New York City, and were members of the Communist Party USA, which was founded in 1919. The party states on its web site that since its beginning, it "has championed the struggles for democracy, labor rights, women's equality, racial justice and peace." At the time, David's parents, who were Jewish, referred to themselves as progressives rather than communists, as did many others in the party. But as Horowitz explained in 2007 on the *Glenn Beck Program*, his parents "wanted [a] Soviet America. They wanted to lose the Cold War and they had views which are... similar to the left today. When I was a kid, I used to be taken by my parents to... a theater called the Stanley Theater and we used to go see Soviet films about Stalin." Because David grew up during the 1950s when U.S. senator Joseph McCarthy was conducting investigations of individuals and groups who were communists or were suspected of being communists, "it was... a hard time for me," he said. "My father... was a teacher who lost his job. New York had a law which said they couldn't be a member of the communist party and teach, and they knew he was a communist.... So they fired him. And his name appeared in the *New York Times* and I got some hate mail, which is not that easy to, you know, handle when you're 14 years old, you get it from people that you know as schoolmates" (Beck 2007).

While in high school in 1952, Horowitz joined a radical club that "was connected loosely to the larger network of Communist Party organizations." At the time, "the big political cause" for the club "was the campaign to save the Rosenbergs," Horowitz wrote (1997, 77). Ethel and Julius Rosenberg, members of the Communist Party, had been arrested in 1950 on charges of conspiring to commit espionage. They were found guilty and sentenced to death. Horowitz recalled "It was the familiarity of the Rosenbergs that made their fate so terrible to me. They were a little Jewish couple that looked like everyone else we knew and made the same progressive gestures, like standing up for Negroes." On the evening that the Rosenbergs were to be executed, Horowitz along with thousands of others attended a vigil in Manhattan. When the throng learned that the Rosenbergs had been taken to the execution chamber, "an unearthly wail went up from the crowd, a terrible keening, trapped and amplified between the darkened skyscrapers, creating the most awful memory of my youth" (Horowitz 1997, 78–79). When the announcement came that the couple had been electrocuted, there was utter silence.

After graduating from high school, Horowitz attended Columbia University, earning a bachelor's degree in 1959. He continued his education at the University of California, Berkeley, where he received a master's degree in English literature. While in California, Horowitz became editor of *Ramparts* in 1969. The magazine, which had originated in 1962, had become a major new-left publication—appealing to readers who championed revolutionary changes in U.S. society. It included articles against the

Vietnam War and features by such civil rights activists as Angela Davis, Noam Chomsky, Abbie Hoffman, Tom Hayden, and César Chávez. Horowitz and the magazine also supported the Black Panthers. In the 1970s, Horowitz met Huey P. Newton, leader of the militant party, who had declared that the Black Panthers would put their guns away and serve the people in Oakland's inner city. As Horowitz explained in a 1997 radio interview:

> I raised about a $100,000 and bought a Baptist church in Oakland's inner city and called it the Oakland Community Learning Center and turned it over to the Panthers. And I encouraged a woman named Betty [Van Patter], who was 42 years old at the time and the mother of three children and who was my bookkeeper at *Ramparts* to do the bookkeeping for this school. And in December, 1974 Betty disappeared. Six weeks later the police fished her body out of San Francisco Bay. Her head had been bashed in by a blunt instrument and I knew at that moment that the Black Panthers had murdered her. And that was really the end of my career in the "left." I was devastated. I felt responsible for encouraging her to take the position. (Baldwin 1997)

Although no one was convicted of murdering Van Patter, the tragedy profoundly affected Horowitz. He rejected political activism and began writing biographies of influential American families. He coauthored with Peter Collier *The Rockefellers* (1976), *The Kennedys: An American Drama* (1984), *The Fords: An American Epic* (1987), and *The Roosevelts: An American Saga* (1994).

During the 1980s, Horowitz returned to politics, but his views had changed dramatically. He repudiated his leftist ideas and espoused ultraconservative policies through the Center for the Study of Popular Culture, which he and Collier founded in 1988. It is currently called the David Horowitz Freedom Center (DHFC). According to its web site, "The DHFC is dedicated to the defense of free societies whose moral, cultural and economic foundations are under attack by leftist and Islamist enemies at home and abroad." The center publishes *Front Page Magazine*, an online journal, and focuses on fighting progressives, liberals, and others who Horowitz believes are destroying democracy. The center's NewsReal Blog challenges "the Left throughout the media." DiscoverTheNetworks is a database of left-leaning individuals and organizations; Jihad Watch "tracks the attempts of radical Islam to subvert Western culture;" and TerrorismAwareness.org "helps educate students to the threat posed against America and the West by international terrorism and its apologists in higher education" (David Horowitz Freedom Center, 2010).

A book by Horowitz and Collier, *Destructive Generation: Second Thoughts about the Sixties* (1989), is an insider's look at the radicalism of the new left and its influence on U.S. culture. Horowitz explained his political transformation in *Radical Son: A Generational Odyssey* (1997). His other books with a conservative focus and attacks on the left include *The Politics of Bad Faith: The Radical Assault on America's Future* (1998), *Hating Whitey and Other Progressive Causes* (1999), *Uncivil Wars: The Controversy over Reparations for Slavery* (2001), *Left Illusions: An Intellectual Odyssey* (2003), *Unholy Alliance: Radical Islam and the American Left* (2004), *The End of Time* (2005), *The Professors: The 101 Most Dangerous Academics in America* (2006), *Indoctrination U:The Left's War Against Academic Freedom* (2007), and *One Party Classroom: How Radical Professors at America's*

Conservative activist David Horowitz, founder of Students for Academic Freedom, addresses a public hearing for a select committee on Academic Freedom in Higher Education at Temple University in Philadelphia, January 10, 2006. (AP Photo/H. Rumph Jr.)

Top Colleges Indoctrinate Students and Undermine Our Democracy (2009).

The 2007 and 2009 books contain information similar to *The Professors*, which includes short profiles about academics whom Horowitz considers a danger to American society. The book stimulated the ire of many individuals in academe and organizations like the American Association of University Professors, who pointed out that Horowitz used materials taken out of context and that were provided by paid assistants to falsely show that many professors are subversives. Some of those profiled in the book have posted their rebuttals on the Internet and in print. And "a coalition of student, faculty and civil liberties groups called Free Exchange on Campus... released a report aimed at discrediting claims made in Horowitz's book," according to Mary Beth Marklein in *USA Today*. "The report cites errors, fabrications and misleading statements, and concludes that Horowitz's research is 'manipulated to fit his arguments'" (Marklein 2006).

Horowitz "mostly dismisses the criticisms as inconsequential. 'I will stake my life that there are professors all over this country in classrooms who are ... venting their prejudices in classes where it has no place,'" he said (Marklein 2006). He has continued his attacks on professors in articles for *Front Page Magazine*, in interviews on talk radio and television shows, and in speeches at college campuses. His views also are repeated by Students for Academic Freedom, which Horowitz began in 2003 as a campaign to convince the U.S. Congress to pass the Academic Bill of Rights. The bill declares that colleges should be intellectually diverse, hire conservative faculty, and prohibit discrimination against students who have conservative political views. Academics argue that those principles already are in place on most campuses and that Horowitz is undermining academic freedom.

Along with his charges regarding liberal bias on campus, Horowitz has campaigned against reparation payments for slavery. The idea of paying blacks for damages caused by slavery has been supported by some politicians, authors, and activists, and angrily denounced by opponents of the idea; it also has been argued in the media. In 2001, during Black History Month, Horowitz attempted to place an advertisement titled "Ten Reasons Why Reparations for Slavery Is a Bad Idea—and Racist Too" in college newspapers. That created even more controversy, and some universities refused to print the ad.

The ad was actually a summary of an article on the topic that Horowitz had written for *Salon* in 2000. He pointed out that the idea of reparations "began as a fringe proposition favored by the politically extreme. But the idea that taxpayers should pay reparations to black Americans for the damages of slavery and segregation is no longer a fixation of the political margin. It is fast becoming the next big 'civil rights' thing." In his article, Horowitz noted that there are numerous questions about who should pay reparations. "It was not whites but black Africans who first enslaved their brothers and sisters. They were abetted by dark-skinned Arabs ... who organized the slave trade. Are reparations going to be assessed against the descendants of Africans and Arabs for their role in slavery? There were also 3,000 black slave owners in the antebellum United States. Are reparations to be paid by their descendants too?" In addition, he asks, "Is there an argument worth considering that would, for example, make Jews (who were cowering in the ghettos of Europe at the time) or Mexicans and Cubans (who were suffering under the heel of Spain) responsible for this crime [of slavery]? What reason could there be that Vietnamese boat people, Russian refuseniks, Iranian refugees, Armenian victims of the Turks or Greek, Polish, Hungarian and Korean victims of communism should pay reparations to American blacks? There is no reason, and no proponent of reparations has even bothered to come up with one" (Horowitz 2000).

In his book *Reforming Our Universities: The Campaign for An Academic Bill of Rights* (2010), Horowitz returned again to his crusade against liberals in universities. He also has published a student guide for his Adopt a Dissenting Book Campaign. The guide assumes that many, if not most, courses in anthropology, history, political science, and sociology are taught by faculty who "indoctrinate students in politically correct orthodoxies." Based on that assumption, which his critics say is not supported by facts but rather by anecdotal material from Horowitz, students are advised to check out syllabi and reading lists to determine if these materials endorse only one side of a particular issue. Then, the guide advises students to ask their professor to add a "dissenting" book to the required reading. "If your professor refuses to grant your request, appeal to the next higher authority, which would be the Department Chair, and after that the Dean of Students," says the guide. "If you are unsuccessful with this appeal, then take the request to the university administration beginning with the Provost or President, then the Chancellor and finally to your university's Board of Trustees" (David Horowitz Freedom Center, *Adopt a Dissenting Book Campaign*, 10).

Few observers expect Horowitz to renounce any of his campaigns or to tone down his rhetoric. In fact, at a Tea Party rally in Santa Barbara, California, in 2010, Horowitz "frequently referred to the Left as a religious cult... and going so far as to say that the Left was 'the fount of global evil,' on par with jihad," according to reporter Seth Miller for the *Santa Barbara Independent*. Miller also noted that Horowitz called U.S. vice president Joe Biden "a bumbling idiot" and declared that "liberals learn politics from 'Commie Camp, trade unions, and apocalyptic crusades to save the environment' " (Miller 2010). With his charges, Horowitz garners media attention and continued publicity for his causes, publications, programs, and his point of view.

See also Beck, Glenn; Chávez, César; Chomsky, Noam; Davis, Angela; Hayden, Tom; Hoffman, Abbie; McCarthy, Joseph; Rosenberg, Ethel, and Rosenberg, Julius

References

"About Us." Communist Party USA, n.d. http://www.cpusa.org/about-us/ (accessed December 7, 2010).

Baldwin, Chuck. "Interview with David Horowitz" (transcript). *Chuck Baldwin Live*, June 6, 1997. http://www.chuckbaldwinlive.com/horowitz.html (accessed December 8, 2010).

Beck, Glenn. "David Horowitz" (interview transcript). *Glenn Beck Program*, November 13, 2007. http://www.glennbeck.com/content/articles/article/196/2071/ (accessed December 7, 2010).

David Horowitz Freedom Center. "Our Mission." Horowitz Freedom Center, 2010. http://www.horowitzfreedomcenter.org/ (accessed December 9, 2010).

David Horowitz Freedom Center. *Adopt a Dissenting Book Campaign: A Student Guide*. 2010.

Horowitz, David. "The Latest Civil Rights Disaster." *Salon*, May 30, 2000. http://www.salon.com/news/col/horo/2000/05/30/reparations/index.html (accessed December 10, 2010).

Horowitz, David. *Radical Son: A Generational Odyssey*. New York: Touchstone, 1997.

Marklein, Mary Beth. "Ex-Liberal Navigates Right." *USA Today*, May 31, 2006. http://www.usatoday.com/news/education/2006-05-31-horowitz-cover_x.htm (accessed December 9, 2010).

Miller, Seth. "David Horowitz Speaks at Tea Party Event." *Santa Barbara Independent*, April 16, 2010. http://www.independent.com/news/2010/apr/16/david-horowitz-speaks-tea-party-event/ (accessed December 10, 2010).

Horton, Myles (1905–1990)

He was a foremost educator, but that meant trouble in the view of racists, unionists, government officials, and segregationists. They attacked Myles Horton and his Highlander Folk School in Monteagle, Tennessee, where in the 1930s Horton developed and led a new kind of social activism. He was a champion of the oppressed in the southern United States and also other parts of the world for more than five decades. Because he was active in the labor and civil rights movements, he was labeled a subversive, a rabble-rouser, and a threat to American values.

Horton was born on July 9, 1905, in Savannah, Tennessee, to Elsie Falls Horton and Perry Horton. He was the first child in the family, which eventually included brothers Delmas and Daniel and sister Elsie Pearl. The family home was a log cabin in an Appalachian region dominated by powerful coal mining companies, not much different from the impoverished region in West Virginia where Mary "Mother" Jones, a famous union organizer for the United Mine Workers (UMW), worked in the 1890s.

Before Myles's birth, both his parents had been schoolteachers at a time when a person with an elementary education could teach. They lost their jobs when the state required teachers to have at least a year of high school. The Hortons did not qualify, so they worked at a variety of jobs from insurance sales to sharecropping. Growing up in Appalachia, Horton recalled: "We didn't think of ourselves as working-class, or poor, we just thought of ourselves as being conventional people who didn't have any money" (Horton and Kohl 1990, 1). Though they had few resources, Elsie Horton often shared with others and taught her neighbors to read and write.

Myles Horton learned from his family the value of education—the kind of education that transforms rather than maintains the status quo—and a straightforward philosophy of what is right and wrong. Although his parents were members of the Cumberland Presbyterian Church, which was fairly conservative, his mother taught him that religion was very basic and simply put: "God is love, and therefore you love your neighbors." Later in life, Horton acted on this belief "on another level... trying to serve people and building a loving world. If you believe that people are of worth, you can't treat anybody inhumanely, and that means you not only have to love and respect people, but you have to think in terms of building a society that people can profit most from, and that kind of society has to work on the principle of equality" (Horton 1990, 7).

Horton wanted a high school education, but there was no secondary school where he lived. He left home to attend high school in Forkadeer River Valley, and worked at odd jobs in factories and sawmills to earn a living. There he learned about the need for workers to organize to protect their jobs and livelihood from factory and mill owners who mistreated their employees. His family eventually moved to the area so they could find work, and Horton was able to live at home again.

After graduation from high school, Horton went to Cumberland University in Lebanon, Tennessee, where he educated himself primarily because he was not satisfied with what he was learning from his teachers. He spent a lot of time in the college library reading and forming his own opinions. While at the university, he had a job with the Presbyterian church, serving as a student field representative in four counties. During summer vacations, the church sent Horton out to Ozone, a rural community in the Cumberland Mountains, to organize vacation Bible schools. While an aide taught the children, Horton held meetings with parents about sanitation projects, cooperatives, and unions. He discovered that the adults thought he had solutions for whatever issues came up, but he told them frankly that he did not. That was the beginning of discussions between the participants about how to solve problems. And Horton brought in people to help—for example someone to explain how to build privies or how to start a co-op.

The year Horton graduated from Cumberland, he had an experience that greatly impacted his life. He visited a local woolen mill to talk to workers about their low wages and unhealthy working conditions. Although he did not urge workers to organize, the president of the mill, John Edgerton, complained to the university that Horton was agitating. In a speech at Cumberland, Edgerton accused outsiders of coming into his plant to disrupt business. Edgerton said: "When we, the manufacturers, in our judgment, see fit to pay people more, or change conditions, we will. But we won't tolerate interference from the workers, because we give them their livelihood, they owe everything they have to us." Horton wrote: "That one statement, that contemptuous attitude, did as much as anything I'd read, or ever heard, to get me thinking.... [It] was one of my most radicalizing experiences. It changed my life...started me thinking about classes of people and economic problems" (Horton and Kohl 1990, 25).

In 1929, Horton enrolled at the Union Theological Seminary in New York not to become a minister, but instead to discover how to influence change through education. The seminary's president, William Sloane Coffin, whom Horton admired, later became a well-known peace and civil rights activist. Reinhold Niebuhr, a Christian socialist, was on the faculty and greatly influenced Horton. While at Union, he had the opportunity to learn about various religious groups by visiting Catholic churches, synagogues, and mosques, then reading books on their beliefs. He also took part in labor organizing activities and demonstrations, once being called a Bolshevik and hit on the head by a club-wielding policeman.

After a year at Union, Horton attended the University of Chicago, studying sociology and often visiting nearby Hull House and its founder Jane Addams, who influenced his ideas on how organizations contribute to social movements. While in Chicago, Horton went to a Danish church that was hosting a folk dance. He talked with two ministers who told him about Danish folk schools. Afterward, he read books on the subject and decided he would go to Denmark and see for himself how folk schools operate. During the year he was in Denmark, he learned among numerous concepts that education takes place in informal settings, the state does not regulate the schools, students and teachers board at the schools, and there is an emphasis on lifelong learning.

Horton returned to Tennessee in 1932 and, along with supporters from Union Seminary including Niebuhr, set up the Southern Mountains School in Monteagle, Tennessee, a coal-mining town near Chattanooga. Shortly thereafter, Horton and codirector Don West renamed the school Highlander Folk School. It was located in an old house and was designed to help impoverished people learn how to make changes that would improve their lives. He was convinced that people should come together to discuss and solve problems by sharing their experiences, conducting research, testing their ideas and becoming their own experts.

The school was integrated in spite of state laws requiring separate facilities for whites and people of color—blacks, Native Americans, and Hispanics. Included in the curriculum were classes on cultural geography, local economic and social problems, and seminars on social justice. Throughout the 1930s, the school was also a meeting place and educational facility for the Congress of Industrial Organizations. Horton conducted workshops to help black and white workers organize in an integrated manner rather than fighting one another for jobs and better working conditions. Throughout the years of the Great Depression and decades thereafter, Horton and the school were active in numerous strikes against mines, mills, and factories, which often resulted in physical attacks and jail sentences.

In 1935, Horton married Zilphia Johnson, who worked at Highlander and developed a music program with plays and songs representing folk culture and the struggles of mountain people. Zilphia revised an old religious song titled "We Will Overcome" to use as a union song. Later, folk singer Pete Seeger changed the song title to "We Shall Overcome," the mantra of the civil rights movement. Many other folk musicians visited Highlander as did numerous civil rights activists and First Lady Eleanor Roosevelt. When the First Lady visited Highlander, she exhibited "empathy with poor people and working people," Horton wrote. "Very few nonworking-class guests had this ability. Most would talk at the people or around them, but not directly to them, because they didn't know how. Mrs. Roosevelt, however, could just sit down and talk to people ... get them to feel comfortable around her" (Horton and Kohl 1990, 190).

Months before Rosa Parks protested segregated buses, the National Association for the Advancement of Colored People (NAACP) asked her to attend a Highlander workshop on desegregation. Parks recalled, "At Highlander I found out for the first time in my adult life that this could be a unified society ... I gained there the strength to persevere in my work for freedom not just for blacks, but for all oppressed people" (Library of Congress 2007). She took part in integrated activities and was impressed that everyone was treated equally.

During the 1950s, Horton initiated a citizenship school that focused on teaching blacks to read and write so they could register to vote. At the time, blacks were required to take a difficult literacy test before they could register. Segregationists were opposed to Horton's efforts and accused him and the school of being communist conspirators. The Federal Bureau of Investigation (FBI) investigated the school, and segregationists, particularly U.S. senator James O. Eastland from Mississippi, kept up their attack. After Martin Luther King Jr. attended the 25th anniversary celebration of the school in 1957, he was immediately accused of being involved in training at a communist school. Southern states pressured Tennessee to close down Highlander, which the state eventually confiscated, auctioning off all the private property, including Horton's belongings, without ever compensating the owners.

Horton and his coworkers were able to open the school again in Knoxville during the 1960s, renaming it the Highlander Research and Education Center, and later moved it to a hilltop farm on 100 acres near New Market, Tennessee. After its reopening, the school focused on its original purpose—regional economic and social problems—concentrating on empowering those in Appalachia demoralized by poverty and also on trying to prevent environmental degradation brought on by strip mining and toxic waste dumps. In 1973, Horton resigned from the school staff, but continued to live on the property and conduct workshops. The school has influenced people from around the world who came to Tennessee or were involved in workshops that Horton conducted in South America, Asia, Africa, and Australia.

During the 1980s, Horton and Highlander received national and worldwide recognition. A PBS documentary in 1981 titled "Adventures of a Radical Hillbilly" featured an interview with Horton by Bill Moyers. In 1982, Horton and Highlander were nominated for the Nobel Peace Prize for its historic role in providing education on behalf of human rights.

One person who gained much from his experiences at Highlander was Brazilian educator Paulo Freire, whose poverty-stricken family life and ideas for a democratic education and advocacy of national literacy programs were similar to Horton's. Freire eventually left Brazil and went to Harvard, where his lectures and writings gained widespread attention. In 1987, Horton and Freire met, became fast friends, and began the process of collaborating on a book about education and social change. Horton was anxious to share his ideas, since he suffered from cancer and was concerned about the time he had left to write. Freire was with Horton in his mountain home for a final meeting in 1990 when it was obvious that Horton was dying. Freire reflected on the sadness of death being part of life, but noted that "It is wonderful that Myles may die here. Dying here is dying in the midst of life" (Horton and Freire 1990, xxxiii). Horton died at Highlander on January 19, 1990. That same year, his autobiography won the Robert F. Kennedy Book Award posthumously.

See also Addams, Jane; Coffin, William Sloane; Jones, Mary Harris; King, Martin Luther, Jr.; Parks, Rosa; Roosevelt, Eleanor; Seeger, Pete

References

Adams, Frank, with Myles Horton. *Unearthing Seeds of Fire: The Idea of Highlander*. Winston-Salem, NC: John F. Blair, 1975.

Berson, Robin Kadison. *Marching to a Different Drummer*. Westport, CT: Greenwood Press, 1994.

Biggers, Jeff. "We Shall Still Overcome: Highlander Folk School Celebrates 75th Anniversary." *National Catholic Reporter*, October 19, 2007.

Horton, Myles, and Paulo Freire. *We Make the Road by Walking: Conversations on Education and Social Change*. Philadelphia: Temple University Press, 1990.

Horton, Myles, with Judith Kohl and Herbert Kohl. *The Long Haul*. New York: Doubleday, 1990.

Library of Congress. "American Memory." Last updated December 5, 2007. http://memory.loc.gov/ammem/today/dec01.html (accessed May 13, 2010).

Thayer-Bacon, Barbara J. "An Exploration of Myles Horton's Democratic Praxis: Highlander Folk School." *Educational Foundations*, Spring 2004.

Wigginton, Eliot, ed. *Refuse to Stand Silently By: An Oral History of Grass Roots Social Activism in America, 1921–1964*. New York: Doubleday, 1991.

Hubbard, Walter, Jr. (1924–2007)

"National borders couldn't stop Walter Hubbard from seeking social justice. He met with leaders and pushed for peace in Northern Ireland and Panama, while being an advocate for civil rights and church reform in Seattle [Washington]," wrote Ashley Bach in an obituary for Hubbard in the *Seattle Times* (Bach 2007). Walter Hubbard Jr. had a vision: a world without racism. He was a long-time civil rights activist and labor leader in the Seattle area.

Born in New Orleans, Louisiana, Hubbard was the son of Walter T. Hubbard and Augustine Medina Hubbard. On his birth certificate, his parents are listed as "colored persons." His father worked as the locksmith for the Whitney National Bank branches in New Orleans (Yockey 2007, 31). Walter's family members were practicing Roman Catholics, and he made his first communion at a church more than 100 years old, although he attended public schools. "This was a family that enjoyed good food, family, and was always pleasant," Walter remembered. "We always seemed to have enough food. We never were on welfare, but we never accumulated any money, never owned a home or a car" (Yockey 2007, 35).

With the outbreak of World War II and despite the segregation policies of the U.S. military, Walter was drafted into the army in 1943. While in a training camp in northern Louisiana, he witnessed a degree of segregation he had not experienced in the city of New Orleans—African Americans were expected to step off the sidewalk when a white person approached them. Stationed at Fort Lewis in Washington in 1943, he lived in a tent city, serving in the 899th Laundry Company with all-black soldiers and all-white officers. Though the blacks were housed in tents, German prisoners of war were housed in wooden barracks just like white American soldiers (Yockey 2007, 36).

Hubbard was sent overseas, participating in the famous Red Ball Express, manned mainly by African American drivers delivering supplies to General George S. Patton's Third Army as it moved across Europe toward Germany. In December 1944, Hubbard and his fellow soldiers were engaged at the Battle of the Bulge, one of the most costly battles of the war. After receiving four battle stars, Hubbard was sent to Marseilles, France, in 1945, where they made preparations to finish the war against Japan in the Pacific theater. When that war ended suddenly, Hubbard returned to the United States aboard a troop ship and went to join his family in New Orleans.

Only three or four months out of his army uniform, Hubbard was told to get out of a public park when he took his future wife, Frances Washington, to a movie on Canal Street. Walter and Frances married in 1947, then purchased a home that allowed many family members to share the house with the newlyweds. In 1948, Walter Hubbard III was born (Yockey 2007, 44). Hubbard could not visit his wife and new son at the hospital because "colored" fathers were not allowed.

In 1951, Hubbard and his family moved to Seattle, Washington, where his wife's father had his own clothes cleaning store (Yockey 2007, 46). He found employment as a skilled cloth cutter at a company that made "bomber jackets" for Sears. According to the King County Library, "Walter gained intimate knowledge of the garment industry, because his two older brothers worked at a shirt factory there. He learned how to spread, cut, and mark the cloth." He soon became active in the labor union as a member of the United Garment Workers Union Local 17, serving eventually as its president and later as a business representative. He also served as an officer in the Seattle union for liquor store clerks (Seattle Civil Rights and Labor History Project n.d.). After being elected president of Local 17, Hubbard was denied a key to his office even though previous presidents all received a key. The building management clearly discriminated against him because of his race. Hubbard had to contact an attorney and was grudgingly given the key a president was entitled to receive and needed to conduct union business. As president, Hubbard helped establish the first pension for members, and conditions significantly improved in wages and benefits (Yockey 2007, 52).

For the Hubbards, trying to purchase a home in Seattle during the 1950s and 1960s was no easy task. Banks and other lending institutions would not loan money to black people who wanted to buy homes in white neighborhoods. As Hubbard reported: "I tried to purchase a home in West Seattle because I wanted to live in Holy Rosary parish. I was informed by the real estate agent when I arrived at his office that he could not sell to a Negro." According to his biographer, Roger Yockey, "Walter got involved in a lot of the civil rights activity after he had been denied the purchase of a home twice in Seattle" (Yockey 2007, 48). "He finally moved his family of four into a duplex with one bedroom. This experience prompted him to begin working for open housing and actively supporting the civil rights movement" (Seattle Civil Rights and Labor History Project n.d.).

The Seattle Civil Rights and Labor History Project declares that: "For most of its history Seattle was a segregated city, as committed to white supremacy as any location in America. People of color were excluded from most jobs, most neighborhoods and schools, and many stores, restaurants, hotels, and other commercial establishments, even hospitals. As in other western states, the system of severe racial discrimination in Seattle targeted not just African Americans but also Native Americans, Asian Americans, Pacific Islanders, people of Mexican ancestry, and also, at times, Jews" (Gregory n.d.).

Not only did Hubbard press for an end to housing discrimination, but he also worked hard to expand opportunities for African Americans in both public and Catholic schools. "Hubbard also was a devoted father," wrote Gregory Roberts. "The family often camped on the Olympic Peninsula, and Walter Hubbard III remembers once worrying how other campers, all white, would regard a black family in their midst. But he said his mother, Frances, reassured him that his father would immediately make friends with everyone else in the campground—and he did" (Roberts 2007).

In the 1960s, Hubbard became a member of the Central Area Civil Rights Committee, an organization of civil rights leaders, who determined the local civil rights agenda in Seattle. "All leaders met every Saturday at the First AME Church. This was a powerful organization because it joined minority consciousness and promoted community involvement regardless of race" (Clark 2005).

In 1964, Hubbard cofounded the Seattle branch of the Catholic Interracial Council (CIC). "The CIC emblem of black and white lines, same size, going in the same direction, was a familiar sight on clothing and cars." In 1969, the Interfaith Rights Banquet sponsored by CIC had 2,500 attendees (Yockey 2007, 88–89).

Hubbard was also president of the Seattle Black Lay Catholic Caucus. From 1966 to 1970, he was executive director of Community Action Remedial Instruction, Tutoring, Assistance and Service (CARITAS), which became a lead organization in the Catholic Church's attempts to deal with poverty. CARITAS served residents of Seattle's Central District, a primarily black area. CARITAS also provided opportunities for whites and blacks to work together. "The vast majority of our students are Negro, and the vast majority of the tutors are white high school and college students," Hubbard said in 1968. During his time as executive director, an estimated 3,000 youths were tutored by 400 to 500 tutors (Yockey 2007, 57).

In 1970, the National Office for Black Catholics (NOBC) was established to serve the needs of black Catholics both within the church and in the wider community (Yockey 2007, 110). Assembled in Washington, D.C., the board of directors consisted of 50 percent lay persons, 25 percent clergy, and 25 percent nuns (Yockey 2007, 111). The NOBC pushed for more black bishops within the church, a larger voice for the laity, and the hiring of more African Americans within the church structure. The NOBC also "supported the development of more innovative and more African-rooted liturgy and ministries and made the Catholic Church more visible in racial justice movements," wrote Mary T. Henry (2007).

Hubbard served as NOBC president for much of its 37 years of existence (Yockey 2007, 112). In 1986, the NOBC conducted the first Black Catholic Life survey in 65 cities, and listed among the people's priorities were a good education in Catholic schools, and leadership training for both young and older people (Yockey 2007, 115). At a presentation at Seattle University in 2006, Hubbard spoke of the great and lasting successes of the NOBC, estimating that its publication *Impact* reached over

200,000 people, inspiring all Catholics and non-Catholics as well (Yockey 2007, 125).

The Seattle Black Catholic Lay Caucus (SBLCC) was founded in 1971, and Hubbard became its first president. Its purpose was to develop leadership among Black Catholics, and to fight racism within and outside the church (Yockey 2007, 96). Hubbard said "Our work . . . created a strong and decisive force in the creating of notable achievement in the areas of open housing, freedom schools, and equality of opportunity plus the passage of civil rights legislation and other critical issues for Black Catholics" (Yockey 2007, 99). The SBLCC sponsored workshops, conferences, seminars, and trained lay people and religious members alike, young and old, to take responsibility for improving Seattle for everyone (Yockey 2007, 104).

As a parishioner of St. Therese Catholic Church, Hubbard mobilized the congregation to participate in civil rights marches and boycotts. Hubbard volunteered to assist the Central Area Motivation Project (CAMP), which was the first totally new community action program in the country to receive funding from the federal Office of Economic Opportunity. CAMP assisted in the planning of Model Cities, a program that Hubbard headed as chair of its advisory committee from 1972 to 1974. Hubbard, who strongly believed in integrated education, worked successfully for the Freedom School boycott of Seattle schools in the spring of 1966. The boycott was a protest against segregated schools in the Central District, an area of primarily black residents. According to Chris Ott, writing for BlackPast.org, "The students and their leaders felt that most of the educational deficiencies among the bulk of Seattle's 9,300 African American students stemmed from their attending thirteen substandard schools that were overwhelmingly and in some cases exclusively African American. All of these schools were under funded, staffed with less experienced teachers, and had lower test scores and graduation rates" (Ott n.d.). The boycott led to a dialogue between the community and school leaders, both public and parochial.

Hubbard's civil and human rights interests were directed beyond Seattle when he went to Northern Ireland in 1972 with a task force from the National Catholic Conference for Interracial Justice, which Hubbard chaired. The task force spent two weeks investigating the civil rights strife and peace efforts in Ireland.

Through public service positions, Hubbard contributed much to civil rights efforts in Seattle and the state of Washington. During the 1970s, he was a compliance specialist for the Washington State Human Rights Commission; it was his responsibility to enforce a federal court order to allow blacks and women to work in the building trades. From 1977 to 1986, he was a State Parole Board appointee, and was on the State Board of Personnel Appeals from 1990 to 2006. Hubbard died on May 5, 2007, in Seattle.

Daniel Callaghan

References

Bach, Ashley. "Walter Hubbard Jr., a Fighter for Justice at Home and Abroad, Dies at 82." *Seattle Times*, May 11, 2007.

Clark, Brooke (interview summary). "Walter Hubbard Interview Conducted by Trevor Griffey and Brooke Clark," February 17, 2005. http://depts.washington.edu/civilr/Hubbard%20interview%20summary.htm (accessed April 11, 2011).

Gregory, James. "Seattle Civil Rights and History Project." University of Washington, n.d. http://depts.washington.edu/civilr/segregated.htm (accessed April 9, 2011).

Henry, Mary T. "Hubbard, Walter Jr. (1924–2007)." HistoryLink.org essay, June 18, 2007. http://www.historylink.org/index.cfm?DisplayPage=output.cfm&file_id=8184 (accessed April 11, 2011).

"Hubbard, Walter, Jr." Seattle Civil Rights and Labor History Project, n.d. http://www.historylink.org/_content/printer_friendly/pf_output.cfm?file_id=8184 (accessed April 9, 2011).

Ott, Chris. "Seattle School Boycott (1966)." BlackPast.org, n.d. http://www.blackpast.org/?q=aaw/seattle-school-boycott-1966 (accessed April 11, 2011).

Roberts, Gregory. "Walter Hubbard, Jr., 1924–2007: A Driving Force for Racial Equality." *Seattle Post Intelligencer*, May 9, 2007. http://www.seattlepi.com/default/article/Walter-Hubbard-Jr-1924-2007-A-driving-force-1236934.php (accessed April 9, 2011).

Yockey, Roger. *I Never Stopped Believing*. Bloomington, IN: Xlibris Corporation, 2007.

Humphry, Derek (1930–)

"The right to choose to die when in advanced terminal or hopeless illness is the ultimate civil liberty," Derek Humphry proclaims on his web site for the Euthanasia Research and Guidance Organization (ERGO), located in Oregon. Humphry and his organization support euthanasia, sometimes called mercy killing or assisted suicide. It is a highly controversial topic and a practice that is often condemned. But Humphry and his supporters long have been dissidents who have campaigned against the established belief that euthanasia is immoral or even murder. In short, "Humphry ranks as one of the preeminent pioneers of the American euthanasia movement" (Dowbiggin 2003, 149).

The word euthanasia is Greek for "good death." Euthanasia is differentiated from an individual act of suicide by the involvement of a doctor, relative, or friend who helps a person die. Although considered an illegal act (namely murder) in a majority of societies throughout the world, caregivers may skirt these legalities by purposefully withholding treatments that would prolong a patient's life or choose to give pain medications that relieve suffering and, in doing so, may even hasten death. The past decades' technological advancements in medicine, allowing for the development of ever-increasing life-sustaining practices, have fueled growing disputes over the legality and morality of euthanasia. The issue is both complex and emotional. How does a society approach active euthanasia versus passive euthanasia? Voluntary versus involuntary? Should there be guidelines defining what exactly constitutes a terminal illness? Should there be a certain level of pain that might be deemed an acceptable level to "qualify" for consideration—and, if so, how should or could such pain be measured?

Born on April 29, 1930, in Bath, England, Humphry grew up in a fractured home. His Irish mother and English father divorced, and ultimately an aunt raised Humphry. He had a spotty educational history, attending numerous different schools. With the onset of World War II, he dropped out of school for good. At that time, he took his first job in the field of journalism, as a messenger boy with the *Yorkshire Post*. Humphry continued in journalism, working for the *Yorkshire Post*, the *Evening World*, the *Manchester Evening News*, the *Daily Mail*, the *Luton News*, the *Havering Recorder*, the *Sunday Times*, the *Los Angeles Times*, then again for the *Sunday Times*, the *Euthanasia Review*, and finally for the *Hemlock Quarterly*. To this day, he hosts an Internet blog that he began in 2006, the *Assisted-Suicide Blog*.

In the early days of his writing career in London, Humphry was involved in investigative and advocacy journalism. He primarily wrote about race relations, immigration, prison conditions, police brutality, and corruption. Much of what he learned in his reporting on these topics became the genesis of his first book, *Because They're Black* (1971). His next book, called *Police Power and Black People* (1972), was an indictment of the racist behavior of the British police. Humphry then followed up with *Passports and Politics* (1974), a book about Idi Amin (a ruthless Ugandan dictator who came to power in Africa in the 1970s), who forced the emigration of thousands of Asians from his country to Britain, resulting in increased racism in Britain. Humphry then joined forces with BBC reporter David Tindall, coauthoring *False Messiah: The Story of Michael X* (1977). This book was a biography of a black British Muslim leader, Michael X, who modeled himself on the American Malcolm X. However, the former was totally corrupt and was ultimately executed for committing murder.

It was when Humphry reached his mid-40s that he first dealt, one on one, with the issue of "self-directed death." His wife, Jean, was diagnosed with terminal cancer. Intentionally overdosing on her medications, she chose to end her life on March 29, 1975. Although they had three children, Humphry was at her deathbed, unwavering and steadfast in support of her choice. Collaborating with his second wife, Ann Wickett, Humphry chronicled the event in a book, *Jean's Way* (1978). Even though he was both an established journalist and author, it took some time for him to find a publisher for the book. But after publication, *Jean's Way* became a best seller. Because Britain classified assisted suicide a crime, an investigation was initiated into Humphry's role in Jean's death. He admitted his guilt but would not name the doctor who provided the fatal medications. Eventually, the matter was dropped. Shortly thereafter, Humphry and Ann Wickett moved to the United States. There, in 1980, along with Gerald Larue and Richard Scott, they founded the Hemlock Society. The name symbolized Socrates, the ancient Greek who was imprisoned and drank poisonous hemlock, which he considered a rational form of suicide. The organization's purpose was to lobby for changes in euthanasia legislation, as well as to provide assistance and information about assisted suicide to those seeking an end to their suffering.

Humphry provided members of the Society with a "how-to book" for patients interested in ending their lives, *Let Me Die before I Wake* (1981). Because of the public demand for information about assisted suicide, the Hemlock Society published Humphry's book for the general public in 1982 and numerous editions since then. A book by Humphry and Wickett, *The Right to Die: An Historical and Legal Perspective of Euthanasia* (1986), is a historical perspective on euthanasia. That same year, Wickett's parents died, and she wrote about their death in a book entitled *Double Exit* (1986). In it, she admitted to actively assisting in her mother's death (some classified it as outright murder) and to passively standing by as her father committed suicide.

Three years later, Wickett filed for divorce. Two years after that, she committed suicide. Although Wickett had been battling breast cancer, it was in remission at the time and, technically, she was not considered terminal. She left a suicide note and, in a handwritten postscript to a friend, claimed that Humphry was a killer and had suffocated his first spouse. On a self-recorded videotape made one day prior to her suicide, Wickett accused Humphry of pressuring her when she became ill: "I remember saying,

'If anything were to happen, if the cancer were to metastasize, I'm getting out of here.' And I remember how relieved he was. I said, 'No hospital beds for me in the middle of the living room, no puking my guts out...' And I remember feeling really chilled to the bone because now it was my life and my dying and it was kind of like 'Good, get out of the way as quickly as possible.' ... I knew I was being pushed out of the picture" (Gabriel 1991). Humphry denied these claims, attributing them to Wickett's ongoing battle with depression and bitterness over their divorce.

Final Exit: The Practicalities of Self-Deliverance and Assisted Suicide for the Dying (1991) is perhaps Humphry's best-known work. Initially the book was not very successful, but an article in the *Wall Street Journal*, as well as a coordinated public relations campaign by the author, soon catapulted the book to top status where it remained on the best-seller list for 18 consecutive weeks. Steven Schragis, who handled publicity for the book, explained that its acceptance by mainstream bookstores signified just how well the voluntary euthanasia movement was growing (Cohen 1991).

As the title states, the book covers practical aspects of "self-deliverance," when a person has decided that he or she is ready to die, and also deals with the various legal concerns that are involved with such a decision. The book also assesses the basic pros and cons of different methods, as well as provides procedural information with regard to the methods. Humphry is blunt in addressing those of religious conviction. "Before we go any further, let me say this: If you consider the God whom you worship to be the absolute master of your fate, then read no more. Seek the best pain management available and arrange for hospice care." He continues, "If you want personal control and choice over your final exit, it will require forethought, planning, documentation, good friends, and decisive, courageous action by you. This book will help in many ways, but in the last analysis, whether you bring your life to a quick end, and how you achieve this, is entirely your responsibility, ethically and legally" (Humphry 1991, 21).

In the year following the publication of *Final Exit*, Humphry founded and became president of the Euthanasia Research and Guidance Organization (ERGO). ERGO "holds that voluntary euthanasia, physician-assisted suicide, and self-deliverance, are all appropriate life endings depending on the individual medical and ethical circumstances" (ERGO web site). The organization conducts polls; provides general information, guidelines, and literature for doctors, patients, journalists and the public; does research; and counsels end-stage terminally ill patients and their families.

Of note, when Humphry started the Hemlock Society, he and the organization worked for the rights of assisted dying for the terminally and hopelessly ill, such as patients with advanced amyotrophic lateral sclerosis (ALS), a neurological disease; or multiple sclerosis (MS), a disease of the central nervous system; or for the very elderly with severe health issues. Over time, however, the Society narrowed its focus to making physician-assisted suicide legal, dropping other illnesses from its agenda, in an effort to be more politically expedient in attaining its primary goal. While personally, Humphry remains committed to the idea that a wider scope of individuals deserve assisted death, he asserts that his beliefs have never—and will never—extend to include the advancement of assisted death for the mentally disturbed, inclusive of the depressed, the disabled, and the handicapped.

After writing *Final Exit*, Humphrey gave up his leadership duties at the Hemlock Society and published *Dying with Dignity: Understanding Euthanasia* (1993) and *Lawful Exit: The Limits of Freedom for Help in Dying* (1994). In 2003, the Hemlock Society changed its name to End of Life Choices and then joined with Compassion in Dying, assuming that name. By 2005, the organization had become Compassion and Choices. A few organizations continue to operate under the Hemlock Society name, although they are unaffiliated.

In the ensuing years, Humphrey has been a prolific advocate for the right-to-die movement. He advises the World Federation of Right to Die Societies, of which he was once president. Founded in 1980, this organization consists of 44 right-to-die organizations in 25 countries and provides a link between groups working to secure or protect the rights of individuals seeking self-determination at the end of their lives.

Humphrey also joined the advisory board of the Final Exit Network in 2004. This organization offers suicide counseling, support, and guidance, believing that those with intolerable illnesses deserve death with dignity, should they so choose such a fate over a prolonged painful "natural death." The Network is a proponent of advanced directives, do-not-resuscitate orders, durable powers of attorney for health care, and living wills.

Humphrey's book *Final Exit* has been published in paperback in over a dozen languages and has sold more than a million copies. In April 2007, *USA Today*'s editors and book critics placed it on its list of the 25 most memorable books of the last quarter century. In 2000, a *Supplement to Final Exit* was published, with a new chapter on a method using helium gas as an alternative means of suicide that did not require the use of controlled prescription drugs. The following year, to mark the 10th anniversary of the book's release, this information was added to a revised, third edition. In 2005, refinements to the helium bag technique were provided in an electronic addendum to the third edition, which was subsequently updated in 2009. Humphrey's autobiography, *Good Life, Good Death: Memoir of an Investigative Reporter and Pro-Choice Advocate* (2008), covers 78 years of his life.

Humphrey has been recognized for his activism many times over the course of his life. In 1972, he received the Martin Luther King Memorial Prize for the contribution to racial harmony in the United Kingdom with his book *Because They're Black*. Two decades later, he was the recipient of the fifth annual Robert Green Memorial Award for distinguished contribution to the movement for death with dignity. In 1997, he was awarded the Socrates Award for right-to-die activism and, in 2000, he earned the Saba Medal for services to the world right-to-die movement.

In 1997, Oregon—Humphrey's state of residence—became the first U.S. state to decriminalize physician-assisted suicide. Euthanasia was legalized in the Netherlands in 2001 and in Belgium in 2002. As medical technology makes more and more strides in its ability to prolong life, it is likely that the euthanasia movement will continue to gain reciprocal ground.

Margaret Gay

See also King, Martin Luther, Jr.; Malcolm X

References

Cohen, Roger. "The Big Sell of 'Final Exit.' " *San Francisco Chronicle*, August 27, 1991.

Dowbiggin, Ian. *Merciful End: The Euthanasia Movement in Modern America*. New York: Oxford University Press, Inc., 2003.

ERGO (Euthanasia Research and Guidance Organization) web site. http://www.finalexit.org/ (accessed October 15, 2010).

Gabriel, Trip. "A Fight to the Death." *New York Times Magazine*, December 8, 1991. http://www.nytimes.com/1991/12/08/magazine/a-fight-to-the-death.html (accessed October 15, 2010).

Humphry, Derek. *Final Exit: The Practicalities of Self-Deliverance and Assisted Suicide for the Dying*. Eugene, OR: Hemlock Society, 1991.

Humphry, Derek, and Ann Wickett. *Jean's Way, 2003 Edition*. Junction City, OR: ERGO/Norris Lane Press, 2003.

"25 Books That Leave a Legacy." *USA Today*, April 9, 2007.

Hurston, Zora Neale (1891–1960)

Sassy. Smart. Brazen. Persistent. Impudent. Dramatic. Imaginary. A powerful presence. Those are some of the descriptions of Zora Neale Hurston, an anthropologist, novelist, poet, and African American folklorist, who frequently defied convention and went her own way in search of reality during the first half of the twentieth century. When the civil rights era began, she refused to portray blacks as victims of white racism. In that regard, she was a dissenter who angered radical black writers.

Although Hurston claimed Eatonville, Florida, located north of Orlando, as her birthplace, she was born in Notasulga, Alabama, on January 15, 1891, the date inscribed in the family Bible, according to Hurston scholar Carla Kaplan. The Hurston web site and encyclopedias say Hurston's birth date is January 7, 1891. Yet, "throughout her life," she gave herself other birth dates "1898, 1899, 1900, 1901, 1902, 1903, and 1910." All were inaccurate, states Kaplan (2002, 37).

When Zora was about two years old, her parents, John and Lucy Potts Hurston, moved their family to Eatonville, the first all-black incorporated town established in 1887. In her autobiography, Zora wrote: "I was born in a Negro town. I do not mean by that the black back-side of an average town. Eatonville, Florida, is, and was at the time of my birth, a pure Negro town—charter, mayor, council, town marshal and all. It was not the first Negro community in America, but it was the first to be incorporated, the first attempt at organized self-government on the part of Negroes in America" (Hurston 1942, 3).

John Hurston was a preacher as well as mayor of Eatonville for several terms. He earned a living as a carpenter and built his own home, a large house that eventually held eight children—two girls and six boys. The family planted a five-acre garden with vegetables, raised chickens, fished in nearby lakes, and gathered tangerines, grapefruit, guava, and oranges from the fruit trees on their land. Zora's sister Sarah, the first girl in the family, was her father's favorite, which did not make Zora jealous since she considered herself her mother's daughter. Lucy Hurston frequently indulged Zora's high spirits, restless nature, and fanciful tales. From a young age, Zora liked to make up implausible stories, some of them about trees, birds, and lakes that talked to her (voices that only she could hear) and tell them to her mother. Her mother also encouraged her children to read and insisted that they complete their school lessons. Zora attended Hungerford School in Eatonville.

Lucy Horton died when Zora was 13 years old; although in her autobiography, she states she was nine years old at the time (Kaplan 2002, 38). Her father sent her to a boarding school in Jacksonville, the Florida Baptist Academy, where her sister Sarah and an older brother were enrolled. She did well in her studies, but did not show the

Zora Neale Hurston, anthropologist and author, was a prominent figure of the Harlem Renaissance. She often emphasized her uniqueness and celebrated her "colored" self. (Library of Congress)

respect that school authorities thought they should have. Zora was at the school less than five months when she received the news that her father had remarried a much younger woman, which upset all the children. She also learned that her father had not paid the tuition for her stay at the boarding school. She was sent home but was not welcome there. Her stepmother made life miserable for Zora, and the two had a brutal fight that Zora claimed she won with only a few scratches to show for it.

Little is known about Hurston's teenage years except that she traveled around a lot, living with friends and relatives and working at menial jobs. Hurston scholars and researchers call the period from 1904 to 1912 the lost years. "What is known about these years comes from *Dust Tracks* [her autobiography], a notoriously unreliable, guardedly written, heavily censored book," writes Kaplan (2002, 39).

According to a variety of accounts, Zora as a teenager took a job as a maid for the star of a traveling theater troupe. She left the group in Baltimore, Maryland, and found odd jobs, hoping to earn enough to pay tuition for school. When that did not work out, she enrolled in a free public night school. Because the school accepted only teenagers, she presented herself as a 16-year-old—she looked the part, but was actually in her 20s. When not in classes, she worked as a waitress.

In 1917, she enrolled in Morgan Academy, connected with Morgan College (now Morgan State University). She did not have the funds for tuition, so the dean of the academy helped her find a job as a maid for the family of a trustee. After graduating from Morgan, she moved to Washington, D.C., and attended Howard University's preparatory school part time, working as a waitress and manicurist in a barber shop to support herself.

Between 1920 and 1924, while at Howard, Hurston began her writing career, publishing her first short story in the university's literary magazine *Stylus*. At the university, she met numerous individuals who became well known in their fields, such as W. E. B. Du Bois, the first African American to graduate from Howard and a civil rights activist, historian, and author.

Hurston moved to New York in 1925 and was associated with the Harlem Renaissance, a cultural movement in the predominantly black community of New York City that flourished during the 1920s and 1930s. Among the luminaries were poets Langston Hughes (1902–1967), who became Hurston's close friend, and Countee Cullen (1903–1946), another friend. Other notables joining in the zeal of the renaissance were labor leader A. Philip Randolph (1889–1979) and singer and actor Paul Robeson (1898–1976), as well as dozens of writers, artists, and musicians.

Granted a scholarship to Barnard College, a liberal arts college for women in New York City, Hurston majored in English and also studied anthropology with the eminent anthropologist Franz Boas at Barnard and also at Columbia University. She earned her bachelor of arts degree from Barnard in 1928, becoming the first African American to graduate from the college. That year one of her essays "How It Feels to Be Colored Me" was published in *The World Tomorrow* (May 1928) and since then has been reprinted many times in other publications. She noted:

> I AM NOT tragically colored. There is no great sorrow dammed up in my soul, nor lurking behind my eyes. I do not mind at all. I do not belong to the sobbing school of Negrohood who hold that nature somehow has given them a lowdown dirty deal and whose feelings are all hurt about it. Even in the helter-skelter skirmish that is my life, I have seen that the world is to the strong regardless of a little pigmentation more or less.... Someone is always at my elbow reminding me that I am the grand daughter of slaves. It fails to register depression with me.... Sometimes, I feel discriminated against, but it does not make me angry. It merely astonishes me. How can any deny themselves the pleasure of my company? It's beyond me. (Walker 1979, 152)

The essay was not well accepted by radical black writers who criticized Hurston for not protesting white racism. Rather, in her essay, she chose to emphasize her uniqueness and celebrate her "colored" self. In addition, as she pointed out years later, she did not approve of African American writers with a political agenda and whose literary characters were primarily angry blacks. As biographer Valerie Boyd noted, Hurston believed that "Black writers should have the same freedom as white writers... They should not feel obligated to write about 'the race problem' or other social ills, but should claim the same liberty that white writers enjoyed. Namely, the right—and the responsibility—to write about anything at all" (Boyd 2003, 311).

Encouraged by Boas, Hurston over the next two years conducted field work in black folklore in the South—Alabama, Florida, and Louisiana—collecting stories, songs, legends, sermons, children's games, and conjure (or folk) medicine. She traveled in her Chevrolet, carrying a pistol for protection, stopping to visit sharecroppers, and driving deep into the pine woods to talk to turpentine workers. The material she collected, much of it in black dialect, was published by Lippincott as *Mules and Men* (1935), although it was not her first book. *Jonah's Gourd Vine* (1934) is an autobiographical novel whose main characters resemble her parents.

In 1936, Hurston received a Guggenheim Fellowship that allowed her to live in Jamaica, where she studied the culture of slave descendants, and in Haiti, where she researched hoodoo (voodoo) practices. She also wrote *Their Eyes Were Watching God* (1937), which is her most celebrated novel. Over the next two years, two more of her books were published: *Tell My Horse* (1938), based on Haitian folklore; and *Moses, Man of the Mountain* (1939), a blend of the Old Testament Moses and black folklore. During the 1930s, she also wrote plays, poetry, and magazine articles, and joined the Works Progress Association (WPA) and its Federal Writers' Project (FWP), which was designed to support writers during the Great Depression. Hurston collected Florida folklore and songs for the FWP. In 1939, Hurston married a fellow WPA worker, Albert Price, who was half her age. This was her second marriage—a decade earlier, she had married a former Howard classmate, but they broke up in less than a year. Hurston and Price also separated within a year.

During the 1940s, Hurston completed her autobiography *Dust Tracks on a Road* (1942), which was well received, but her writing and income were sporadic over the decade. In 1944, she married once again, and that marriage lasted only nine months. At the end of the 1940s, she was falsely charged of child molestation—she was in Honduras at the time of the alleged crime. An indictment against her was dismissed, but the charges and publicity surrounding her arrest were so devastating to her that she considered suicide. But the scandalous stories did not hinder sales of her book *Seraph on the Suwanee* (1948), and as she recovered from depression, she began work on another novel.

By the 1950s, Hurston was searching for ways to earn an income, sometimes living on speaking fees and payments for brief writing assignments and substitute teaching. She was in poor health as well, suffering from a variety of ailments. In addition, she became embroiled in controversy because she did not support civil rights efforts. Her detractors condemned her for writing articles for conservative magazines and criticized her political views. The *Saturday Evening Post* published one of her articles—a complimentary profile of conservative senator Robert Taft, who was a candidate for the Republican presidential nomination. She also wrote a letter to the *Orlando Sentinel* taking issue with the U.S. Supreme Court decision in *Brown v. Board of Education* (1954), which outlawed separate public educational facilities for blacks and whites. Hurston regarded the ruling "as insulting rather than honoring my race" (Kaplan 2002, 739). In her view, there was no tragedy in being separated from whites and that blacks did not need to be associated with whites to succeed. Her position infuriated civil rights groups across the country.

In late 1959, Hurston suffered a stroke, and since she was penniless, she moved into the St. Lucie County Welfare Home in Fort Pierce, Florida, where she had another severe stroke and died on January 28, 1960. Her friends and publishers donated money for her funeral, and she was buried in an unmarked grave.

For years afterward, Hurston and her work were nearly forgotten. But in 1973,

Alice Walker, who became a well-known literary figure, and fellow Hurston scholar Charlotte D. Hunt visited the cemetery where Hurston was buried and placed a marker on her grave. In 1975, Walker wrote an article for *Ms* magazine, "In Search of Zora Neale Hurston," which described her efforts to find Hurston's grave and helped launch a Hurston revival. Robert D. Hemenway's *Zora Neale Hurston: A Literary Biography* (1977) also rekindled interest in Hurston. Since the 1970s, numerous writers, storytellers, and filmmakers have called attention to this prolific author and conscientious collector of folklore who insisted on depicting black life as she saw it. Hurston's legacy is also celebrated in Eatonville when the weeklong Zora Neale Hurston Festival of the Arts and Humanities is held each year in January.

See also Du Bois, W. E. B.; Walker, Alice; Randolph, A. Philip; Robeson, Paul

References

Boyd, Valerie. *Wrapped in Rainbows: The Life of Zora Neale Hurston.* New York: Scribner, 2003.

Hemenway, Robert E. *Zora Neale Hurston: A Literary Biography.* Urbana: University of Illinois Press, 1977.

Hurston, Zora Neale. *Dust Tracks on a Road.* New York: HarperPerennial, 2006 (reprint of 1942 publication).

Hurston, Zora Neale. *Moses, Man of the Mountain.* New York: HarperPerennial, 1991 (reprint of 1938 publication).

Hurston, Zora Neale. *Their Eyes Were Watching God.* New York: HarperPerennial, 1990 (reprint of 1939 publication).

Kaplan, Carla. *Zora Neale Hurston: A Life in Letters.* New York: Doubleday, 2002.

Walker, Alice, ed. *I Love Myself When I Am Laughing and Then Again When I Am Looking Mean and Impressive: A Zora Neale Hurston Reader.* New York: Feminist Press at the City University of New York, 1979.

Johnson, Harriet McBryde (1957–2008)

In self-deprecating fashion and sly humor, Harriet Johnson called herself "gimpy" and part of the "Crip World," as some people with disabilities label their environment. In an article for the *New York Times* in 2003, Johnson wrote: "It's not that I'm ugly. It's more that most people don't know how to look at me. The sight of me is routinely discombobulating. The power wheelchair is enough to inspire gawking, but that's the least of it. Much more impressive is the impact on my body of more than four decades of a muscle-wasting disease.... At this stage of my life, I'm ... a jumble of bones in a floppy bag of skin." Although Johnson was describing her physical appearance, her article was primarily about her encounter with a bioethics philosopher at Princeton University, Professor Peter Singer, who has advocated disability-based infanticide and "wants to legalize the killing of certain babies who might come to be like me if allowed to live." For most of her life, Harriet Johnson fought not only the views of those like Singer, but also many in the general public who believe that people with severe disabilities are "worse off" than able-bodied individuals. "Are we 'worse off'? I don't think so," Johnson wrote. "Not in any meaningful sense. There are too many variables. For those of us with congenital conditions, disability shapes all we are" (Johnson, *New York Times Magazine*, February 2003).

Harriet Johnson was born in Laurinburg, North Carolina, on July 8, 1957, although she lived most of her life in Charleston, South Carolina. Her parents, David and Ada Johnson, were professors: her mother a comparative literature expert; her father a Spanish teacher at the Citadel, a military college in South Carolina. The family included four other children: Elizabeth, David, Eric, and Ross.

Born with a degenerative neuromuscular disease, Harriet's early schooling was segregated—that is, separate from regular classrooms. "It was really a good, happy situation for me but I wouldn't recommend it to anyone else," she reported. "It was very much unstructured. They left me alone so I read books and wrote book reports. I was a big dog in that environment, I guess" (Ervin 2004). However, Harriet had little respect for the education she received, which lacked discipline and challenge. While in her early teens, she led a student campaign to have an abusive teacher fired, which prompted the school to oust her. Her parents found a private high school that accepted her, and she embarked on a challenging mainstream education for the first time.

Johnson earned a bachelor's degree in history from Charleston Southern University in 1978. After graduating from Charleston, she worked for a local disability rights organization, helping to implement regulations of Section 504 of the Rehabilitation Act of 1973, which protects students with disabilities from discrimination. She continued her advanced education, earning a master's degree in public administration from the College of Charleston in 1981 and a law degree from the University of South Carolina in 1985. In an article for the *New York Times*, Johnson briefly described her experience while in law school in 1984:

> I'm living in Columbia, S.C., 100 miles from my family, taking advantage of new possibilities. Until the Section 504 regulations, disability discrimination by universities was routine and unapologetic. Now, at the University of South Carolina law school, I am one of six wheelchair users. Five of us use power chairs; without someone's help, we can't get out of bed. As schoolmates strut in power suits, we whir around with book bags hanging from our push handles and make bottlenecks at the elevators. I think of us as a counterculture that challenges the get-ahead Me Decade. Most people, when they think about us, operate under the delusion that we're inspirations. (Johnson, "The Disability Gulag," 2003)

After she opened her law practice, Johnson took many cases involving discriminatory practices against people with disabilities, invoking the 1990 Americans with Disabilities Act (ADA), whose purpose was "to provide a clear and comprehensive national mandate for the elimination of discrimination against individuals with disabilities." The act came about because of the advocacy of people like Justin Dart, who was confined to a wheelchair most of his life, and who, along with his wife, collected more than 5,000 documents and tape recordings detailing discrimination against people with disabilities between 1988 and 1990. A major portion of Johnson's work was to secure Social Security payments for disabled people and to file civil rights claims for poor and working people with disabilities.

Johnson also began what would be a long-standing dissent against exploitation of young people with disabilities as poster children for fund raisers. Every Labor Day until her death she publicly demonstrated in the streets of Charleston her opposition to the muscular dystrophy telethon hosted by Jerry Lewis. Johnson called the telethon an effort based on a "charity mentality." As she noted in her book *Too Late to Die Young* (2005), she never wanted people to associate her with one type or another of muscular dystrophy (which includes many kinds of neurological diseases) because "they'll make me a pity object, one of Jerry's Kids—someone to make them grateful they are not like me" (Johnson, *Too Late to Die Young*, 11).

Johnson was especially critical of an article Lewis wrote in 1990 for *Parade* magazine in which he imagined having muscular dystrophy and declared that the disease made him "half a person," a statement derided countless times by Johnson and others who did not want to be portrayed as helpless and less than a full human being. "Didn't Hitler's Germany prove the danger of denying full personhood based on genetic characteristics?" Johnson asked. "I'm astounded that anyone, even the likes of Jerry Lewis, could put his name on such a thing. I'm astounded that any magazine, let alone a 'non-controversial' commercial outlet like *Parade*, could run it. Don't they hear the bigotry?" (Johnson, *Too Late to Die Young*, 53–54).

Nevertheless, since 1966, Lewis and his telethon have raised more than $1.6 billion (as of 2011) to aid the Muscular Dystrophy Association (MDA), and Lewis has had many supporters. The future of such a telethon is questionable, however, due to the host's advanced age and the fact that lengthy television variety shows are not as popular as they once were.

In addition to her annual protest of the MDA telethon, Johnson was active politically in the Democratic Party at the county and city levels and as a delegate to the national convention in 1996. She described herself as an atheist Democrat. In 1997, she attended the Second International Conference on the Rights of People with Disablities held in Communist Cuba. Her sister Beth accompanied her as her assistant. Although Cuba had changed drastically since the Johnson family visited the island nation on a vacation in 1959, the sisters were admitted easily into the country. There they met with some of the 200 people from 18 countries in attendance and visited special schools for disabled young people. Harriet came away with varied conclusions, but was impressed with the helpfulness of the Cuban people—they did not look away or avoid her as had happened elsewhere abroad and in the United States, but instead treated her as a person.

After the story about Johnson appeared in the *New York Times Magazine* in February 2003, she received national attention. "Others with disabilities have been celebrated for their brilliance in a particular field (Stephen Hawking) or for their high-profile struggle to overcome disability (Christopher Reeve)," wrote Mike Ervin in *New Mobility* magazine. "Johnson's achievement, however, was more remarkable because she is a woman in a society dominated by the male viewpoint, because she was relatively unknown except in disability circles, and because—by force of will, intellect, personality and skillful writing—she has persuasively challenged the myth that people with disabilities are of inherently less value than nondisabled people. For this considerable accomplishment, *New Mobility* has chosen Harriet Johnson as our Person of the Year for 2003" (Ervin 2004).

Johnson's activism included numerous efforts to educate the general public about the barriers that people in wheelchairs had to face when trying to access public buildings. In a 2004 article for the *New York Times*, she wrote:

> As a lawyer in a power wheelchair, I cannot take access for granted. I cannot even assume others have a basic comprehension of how I move around in the world. Because I cannot walk, crawl or safely be carried, even one step keeps me out as surely as would a sign saying "No cripples allowed." People often offer to carry me, as if the offer itself discharges any duty to remove the unnecessary barriers in my way. When I decline to be carried, I am made to feel ungracious. Beyond that, I am rendered unable to do for myself and my community. (Johnson 2004)

Writing as a way to inform was part of Johnson's life. She wrote to influence attitudes about and behavior toward people with disabilities. Her articles appeared in commercial publications as well as law and disability journals. In the *Oregon Law Review*, Alicia Ouellette praised Johnson's communication skills as "wicked, sharp, insightful, and funny. Her oral presentations are equally compelling. She uses personal stories and insights strengthened by her physical weakness to advocate her positions on issues involving life and death. Specifically, she uses the strongest sort of identity politics, legal acumen, and powerful straight talk to argue against choice in medical decision-making. Her message resonates" (Ouellette 2006, 140).

One of her articles in *Slate* magazine presented arguments regarding end-of-life decisions for disabled people, specifically Terri Schiavo, who was in a vegetative state from 1990 to 2005. Schiavo was being nourished through feeding and hydration tubes that her husband Michael wanted removed. Schiavo's parents objected and took their case to court. Politicians also intervened, with the U.S. Congress passing a law allowing federal district court jurisdiction in the Schiavo case. Eventually, the Florida Supreme Court found the law unconstitutional and, in effect, allowed the removal of Terri's feeding tube.

Johnson in her *Slate* article argued that the Congress was right to step in. Among her 10 arguments, Johnson noted that Schiavo was not terminally ill; she was not suffering, so her death "can't be justified as relieving suffering"; no one knew what her preferences were for discontinuing treatment; Schiavo had "a federal constitutional right not to be deprived of her life without due process of law;" removing Schiavo's feeding tube was a violation of the ADA (Johnson, *Slate*, 2005).

Besides major magazine features, Johnson wrote two books: *Too Late to Die Young* (2005), a memoir; and *Accidents of Nature* (2006). The latter is a young adult novel with a heroine who has cerebral palsy and attends a summer retreat called "Camp Courage," labeled "Crip Camp" by her cabinmate, who also proclaims "I'm crippled and proud!"

Johnson died in her sleep on June 4, 2008, at her home in Charleston. Her memoir carries a statement that underscores her view about her own life and the lives of people with disabilities: "Living our lives openly and without shame is a revolutionary act" (Johnson, *Too Late to Die Young*, 256).

See also Dart, Justin, Jr.

References

Ervin, Mike. "Person of the Year. Harriet McBryde Johnson: A Life Well Lived." *New Mobility*, January 2004. http://newmobility.com/articleView.cfm?id=811&srch=harriet%20mcbryde (accessed March 7, 2011).

Johnson, Harriet McBryde. "Alas for Tiny Tim, He Became a Christmas Cliché." *New York Times*, December 25, 2006. http://www.nytimes.com/2006/12/25/opinion/25johnson.html?_r=3&scp=2&sq=harriet+mcbryde+johnson&st=nyt&oref=login (accessed March 7, 2011).

Johnson, Harriet McBryde. "The Disability Gulag." *New York Times*, November 23, 2003. http://query.nytimes.com/gst/fullpage.html?sec=health&res=9E06E1D71138F930A15752C1A9659C8B63 (accessed March 7, 2011).

Johnson, Harriet McBryde. "Not Dead at All: Why Congress Was Right to Stick Up for Terri Schiavo." *Slate*, March 23, 2005. http://www.slate.com/id/2115208 (accessed September 11, 2011).

Johnson, Harriet McBryde. *Too Late to Die Young: Nearly True Tales from a Life*. New York: Henry Holt, 2005.

Johnson, Harriet McBryde. "Unspeakable Conversations." *New York Times Magazine*, February 16, 2003. http://query.nytimes.com/gst/fullpage.html?sec=health&res=9401EFDC113BF935A25751C0A9659C8B63 (accessed March 7, 2011).

Johnson, Harriet McBryde. "The Way We Live Now: 5-30-04; Stairway to Justice." *New York Times*, May 30, 2004. http://query.nytimes.com/gst/fullpage.html?res=9D02E3DA143EF933A05756C0A9629C8B63&scp=5&sq=harriet+mcbryde+johnson&st=nyt (accessed March 8, 2011).

Ouellette, Alicia. "Disability and the End of Life." *Oregon Law Review*, November 30, 2006.

Rosen, Christine. "A Life Worth Living." *Wall Street Journal*, June 27, 2008.

Jones, Mary Harris (1830–1930)

"In all her career, Mother Jones never quailed or ran away. Her deep convictions and fearless soul always drew her to seek the spot where the fight was hottest and the danger greatest," wrote the famous civil rights lawyer Clarence Darrow (Jones 1980, vi).

Mary Harris, who became known as Mother Jones, could have been typecast as the nurturing grandmother in a period drama. She was barely five feet tall, wore wire-rimmed glasses, was soft spoken, and often appeared in a long black dress with fashionable lace at the neck. She hardly fit the common perception of a tough, radical labor agitator of the early 1900s, demanding a living wage and safe working conditions for miners and other workers. She liked to tell people she was a "hell-raiser."

Although her parents named her Mary Harris when she was born in County Cork, Ireland, she took on the role of Mother Jones during her adult life, most of which was spent in the United States. Mary Harris declared in her autobiography that she was born in 1830, but conflicting records place her birth in 1836 or 1837—she was baptized on August 1, 1837, according to St. Mary's Cathedral in Cork. As an adult, she declared her date of birth was May 1, but she chose that day—the International Workers' Day —after she became deeply committed to the labor movement of the late nineteenth and early twentieth centuries.

When Mary Harris was two years old, her grandfather was hanged because of protest activities in Ireland, and three years later, her father, Richard Harris, left for North America to avoid the same brutal end. Her father was a tenant farmer, living and working on small plots of land owned by British gentry. Ireland was part of the British Empire at the time, and under British rule, no Irish Catholics were allowed to own land. Like other poor farmers, Richard Harris paid his rent with crops he grew and sold, earning barely enough for his family to survive. When landowners began to demand exorbitant rents, bands of tenant farmers rebelled, burning landowners' homes, barns, and crops and ruining pastures. Landowners retaliated by evicting peasants en masse, which led to even more disturbances. The British army cracked down on the violence, arresting known troublemakers.

Mary was 11 years old when her father sent for the family and they relocated to Toronto, Canada, where her father was working with a railroad crew. She was an excellent student and graduated from high school, furthering her education at a teacher's college, Toronto Normal School. However, after completing her studies, she was unable to get a teaching position because she was Roman Catholic. Canada was predominately Protestant and decidedly British; discriminatory practices barred Catholic teachers from local schools. As a result, Mary Harris moved to the United States and found a secular teaching job at a convent in Michigan. But she was dissatisfied with the position, and after six months left Michigan for Chicago, Illinois, where, according to her autobiography, she "opened a dress-making establishment. I preferred sewing to bossing little children," she wrote (Jones 1980, 1).

Around 1860, Mary Harris left Chicago for Memphis, Tennessee. In spite of her apparent aversion to teaching, she once again took a job as an educator. In Memphis, she met George Jones, an iron molder who was active in organizing workers. Jones helped establish a local chapter of the Iron Molders Union to demand improvements in the dangerous conditions of the foundry.

Mary Harris and George Jones married in 1861 and eventually had four children,

Catherine, Elizabeth, Terence, and Mary. Jones put his labor organizing on hold through the Civil War years, but soon thereafter, he became a paid leader in the movement, providing a relatively comfortable living for his family. When a yellow fever epidemic swept through the city in 1867, the neighborhood was hit hard—it was near a swamp that bred disease. In Mary Jones's words: "Across the street from me, ten persons lay dead from the plague. The dead surrounded us. . . . All about my house I could hear weeping and the cries of delirium" (Jones 1980, 1). An estimated 2,500 people in Memphis lost their lives. Each of the Jones children fell ill and died one by one. George succumbed also, and his wife was left to go on alone. She remained in Memphis during the epidemic and helped care for the sick. Her motto at the time was "pray for the dead and fight like hell for the living." That became her slogan later on in her life while working for labor causes.

When the epidemic ended, the Iron Molders Local provided funds so Jones could return to Chicago. There she opened a seamstress shop that catered to the needs of the wealthy in the city. It was the beginning of the industrial age and the rise of robber barons. Major industrialists in oil, railroads, steel, and banking amassed great wealth by profiting from the long, hard labor of their underpaid workers. When Jones went to her clients' lavish homes, she angrily noted the vast gulf between the rich and the hungry and shivering "wretches" whose miserable living conditions for the most part were ignored.

In 1871, a massive fire raged for three days through one-sixth of the city of Chicago, including the central business district. The Great Chicago Fire added to the misery of the poor. Jones lost her home, her shop, and all of her possessions, but her life was spared. Like hundreds of other Chicagoans, she rushed to the shores of Lake Michigan to escape the flames.

The fire left 100,000 people homeless. City officials began to provide help for some of the refugees. Jones found a place to stay in a church and received a gift of a sewing machine, which she used once more to earn a living. Jones began to reconstruct her life as Chicago began to rebuild. Chicago not only rebuilt its businesses and homes, but in the late nineteenth century, it also was "a hotbed of ideological ferment," the "most radical city in America," as Elliott Gorn noted. "There, a constant upsurge of ideas —foreign and domestic versions of trade and industrial unionism, anarchism, socialism, populism—was part of daily working

Mother Jones was a tough, radical labor agitator of the early 1900s, demanding a living wage and safe working conditions for miners and other workers. (Library of Congress)

life" (Gorn 2001, 54). For Jones, Chicago was the place where she began to develop her own political ideas, some of which were sparked by the Knights of Labor.

The Knights' mission was to unite all workers in an effort to change society through education and protective laws for workers. Employers fired any workers who were known to attend meetings or join this secret order. Nevertheless, the movement appealed to Jones, and she asked to join. She quickly became an organizer, speaker, and recruiter for the Knights and was a familiar face to the workers and poor of Chicago as she went throughout the neighborhoods spreading the word about working for the labor cause.

Jones's ideas changed in the 1880s. Anarchist groups in Chicago were advocating strikes and direct confrontation with employers to obtain better pay and an eight-hour workday. Chicago in the mid-1880s was at the center of the eight-hour labor movement, and militant trade unionists frequently marched and agitated for strikes against industries. Jones was not an anarchist herself, but she began to argue that strike action was justified to attain working-class goals. Employers, meantime, tried to kill the movement by accusing those who demanded an eight-hour work day of traitorous acts. "Feeling was bitter," Jones wrote. "The city was divided into two angry camps. The working people on one side—hungry, cold, jobless, fighting gunmen and police clubs with bare hands. On the other side, the employers, knowing neither hunger nor cold, supported by newspapers, by the police, by all the power of the great state itself" (Jones 1980, 6).

Unrest in the city led to the so-called riot that took place in Chicago's Haymarket Square in 1886. Workers at the McCormick Harvester Machine Company had walked out, and McCormick hired nonunion laborers. When the strikebreakers left the plant, union workers outside protested. Police arrived and brutally attacked the strikers. During the hysteria that followed, a bomb exploded, killing some police officers. City officials demanded the arrest of a group of anarchists called the Haymarket Eight, falsely accusing them of instigating the violence. They were tried and sentenced to death. When four of the men were executed, Jones broke from the Knights and their nonconfrontational methods. She could not abide the fact that the leaders distanced themselves from the men who were hanged, simply to protect the organization. She left Chicago determined to act on behalf of labor.

In the 1890s, Jones went to West Virginia to work with coal miners and their families who lived in extreme poverty. In her 60s (according to her stated date of birth), she became a full-time paid union organizer for the United Mine Workers (UMW). It was a dangerous job because mine owners constantly threatened organizers or fired miners who joined a union. Company guards and agents from the Pinkerton Detective Agency, hired by companies to break strikes, often brutally beat strikers and organizers. But Jones continued with her work. She also gave away whatever money, food, and clothing she could spare to poor mining families, who soon began calling her Mother Jones.

Jones was a tireless organizer and speaker. She would exhort miners for hours. Interspersed with humorous stories about her experiences, she cajoled, argued, and pleaded with them to unionize and become fighters for the labor movement. And she organized miners' wives and daughters, leading them in marches to beseech their men to strike. She also faced arrest and jail time on numerous occasions. In one instance in a Parkersburg, West Virginia, court, she faced a judge who told her she should not let herself be used by "designing and reckless agitators." The judge did not sentence her but advised her to engage in charities and other pursuits to help mankind. He admonished her to "follow the paths which the Allwise Being intended her sex to pursue ... and what experience has shown to be the true sphere of womanhood" (Foner 1983, 103). Jones responded with characteristic bluntness and humor, thanking the judge and telling him she would pursue her work in West Virginia even if she was arrested again and had to die in jail. In her parting shot to the judge, she pointed out that they were both old and would die soon, but hoped before that time they would become good friends.

Jones organized workers in industries across the nation. In one instance, she encouraged striking mine workers to join striking American Railway Union (ARU) members in Birmingham, Alabama. The ARU leader, Eugene V. Debs, was in jail, but with the joined unions, Jones helped keep the strike going. Together, the strikers blocked trains hauling coal to markets until the militia forced them back to work.

One of the issues that especially raised her ire was child labor. After a months-long investigation of textile mills in the South, she wrote an article for the *International Socialist Review* that described girls 9 and 10 years old working 12-hour days for 10 cents each per shift. She watched them arrive at the factory each morning trudging from flimsy housing, clothed only in rags, and barely fed. In 1903, she led a Crusade of the Mill Children, a march of child laborers that called attention to the deformities and injuries young children suffered because of inhumane factory work.

Threats from company guards, Pinkerton men, and government agents had little effect on Mother Jones. She gave speeches to workers; addressed U.S. presidents, state officials, law enforcement, legislators, and powerful industrialists; and wrote articles for newspapers and magazines. She constantly encouraged others to stand up for freedom, equality, and the rights of workers. She was still speaking out on behalf of workers on her 100th birthday and, months later, died on November 30, 1930, in Silver Spring, Maryland. Thousands of miners and others attended her funeral.

See also Darrow, Clarence; Debs, Eugene V.

References

Fetherling, Dale. *Mother Jones: The Miners' Angel.* Carbondale, IL: Southern Illinois University Press, 1974.

Foner, Philip S., ed. *Mother Jones Speaks: Collected Writings and Speeches.* New York: Monad Press, 1983.

Gorn, Elliott J. *Mother Jones: The Most Dangerous Woman in America.* New York: Hill and Wang/Farrar, Straus and Giroux, 2001.

Hawxhurst, Joan C. *Mother Jones: Labor Crusader.* Austin, TX: Steck-Vaughn Company, 1994.

Jones, Mother. *The Autobiography of Mother Jones.* Edited by Mary Field Parton. Mineola, NY: Dover Publications, 1980. Republication of the work originally published in 1925 by Charles H. Kerr & Company, Chicago.

Long, Priscilla. *Mother Jones: Woman Organizer.* Boston: South End Press, 1976.

Neis, Judith. *Nine Women: Portraits from the American Radical Tradition.* Berkeley, Los Angeles, and London: University of California Press, 2002.

VERMONT STATE COLLEGES

0 0003 0880076 2

Hartness Library
Vermont Technical College
One Main St.
Randolph Center, VT 05061

DISCARD